"A ROAD TO PEACE AND FREEDOM"

Robert M. Zecker

"A ROAD TO PEACE AND FREEDOM"

The International Workers Order and the Struggle for Economic Justice and Civil Rights, 1930–1954

TEMPLE UNIVERSITY PRESS
Philadelphia • Rome • Tokyo

TEMPLE UNIVERSITY PRESS
Philadelphia, Pennsylvania 19122
www.temple.edu/tempress

Copyright © 2018 by Temple University—Of The Commonwealth System
  of Higher Education
All rights reserved
Published 2018

All reasonable attempts were made to locate the copyright holders for the materials published in this book. If you believe you may be one of them, please contact Temple University Press, and the publisher will include appropriate acknowledgment in subsequent editions of the book.

Library of Congress Cataloging-in-Publication Data

Names: Zecker, Robert, 1962- author.
Title: A road to peace and freedom : the International Workers Order and the
  struggle for economic justice and civil rights, 1930-1954 / Robert M. Zecker.
Description: Philadelphia : Temple University Press, 2018. | Includes index.
Identifiers: LCCN 2017035619| ISBN 9781439915158 (cloth) | ISBN
  9781439915165 (paper)
Subjects: LCSH: International Workers Order. | International labor
  activities—History—20th century. | Labor unions—United
  States—History—20th century. | Working class—Societies,
  etc.—History—20th century. | Working class—United States—Societies,
  etc.—History—20th century. | Labor movement—United
  States—History—20th century. | Civil rights and socialism—United
  States—History—20th century.
Classification: LCC HD6475.A2 I867 2018 | DDC 331.88/6097309041—dc23 LC record
available at https://lccn.loc.gov/2017035619

*This book is dedicated to the former
members of the International Workers Order,
men and women who were confident
that interracial working-class solidarity was indeed
the "road to peace and freedom."
May our current generation take inspiration
from them in these "interesting" times.*

Contents

Acknowledgments		ix
Abbreviations		xiii
	Introduction	1
1	"A Practical Demonstration in Democracy": The IWO	19
2	A "Plan for Plenty": The IWO Tames Capitalism	55
3	"We Dare Entertain Thoughts Not to the Liking of Present-Day Bigots": Race, Civil Rights, and the IWO	97
4	"A Mandolin Orchestra . . . Could Attract a Lot of Attention": Interracial Fun	136
5	Foreign Policy and the IWO	166
6	"A Fraternal Order Sentenced to Death!" Government Suppression	213
	Conclusion	261
	Notes	265
	Index	349

Acknowledgments

During the four years or so that I've followed the International Workers Order (IWO) through various archives and newspaper files, I have benefited from the gracious assistance of many kind librarians, colleagues, and scholars. Research grants and conference funding from my home institution, Saint Francis Xavier University, enabled me to travel to chase the paper trail of the IWO. At. St. FX, my colleagues in the Department of History have offered guidance and support as I bounced ideas and drafts of this project off their (mostly willing) ears. Our department administrative assistants, Margo Boyd and Joanne Bouchard, have been invaluable in helping me move this project along. Sheldon MacDonald, digital archivist at the Saint Francis Xavier University library, graciously provided digitized images for this book's illustrations.

My thinking on race, social movements, and the American working class has benefited from the graduate training I received at the University of Pennsylvania's Program in American Civilization. Although those graduate seminars are fading into the mists of time, I still gratefully acknowledge the scholars there who pushed my thinking on race and immigration, especially Ewa Morawska, Thomas J. Sugrue, Murray Murphey, and the late Michael B. Katz. It was in Dr. Katz's Urban Studies pro-seminar, particularly, that questions of the salience of race to white ethnic Americans' acculturation to the United States first began to gel for me. I am grateful to the intellectual rigor of my UPenn colleagues, particularly Russell A. Kazal and Rachel Batch. Russ and Rachel, as well as other colleagues, have helped me over the years to think rigorously about race, immigration, and much, much more.

The old joke has it that academia is the place where the battles are so fierce because the stakes are so low. But for whatever reason, I've been lucky to have found many truly generous people and avoided (mostly) academic steel-cage matches. Many thanks are due to David Roediger for his insights on race, the American left, and immigrant America. His commentary on an early draft of this manuscript helped me to sharpen and refine my arguments; his encouragement and friendship over the years has proved invaluable. Likewise, the comments and critiques offered by numerous colleagues on various stages of this project have pointed me toward sources, offered astute critiques, and in general strengthened my understanding of the American left and its civil-rights activism. In this respect, special thanks are extended to Rebecca Hill, Rachel Buff, John Enyeart, Barry Goldberg, Jennifer Young, Daniel Chard, Anthony DeStefanis, and Ian Rocksborough-Smith.

I am grateful, too, to the very kind e-mail correspondence I received from MaryLouise Patterson, who clarified some questions I had regarding the activism and career of her mother, Louise Thompson Patterson, particularly with regard to her role as vice president of the IWO, and her work in founding the Harlem Suitcase Theatre.

The assistance I received at many archives not only made this project possible, but made it a joyous odyssey, too. The archivists at Cornell University's Kheel Center for Labor Management Documentation and Archives, especially Patrizia Sione and Melissa Holland, have my gratitude and admiration. The staff at New York University's Tamiment Library/Robert F. Wagner Labor Archives are expert custodians of one of the preeminent collections of material on working-class and radical America. Wayne State University's Walter P. Reuther Library contained a wealth of material on the IWO, and Erik Nordberg, Kristen Chinery, and the rest of the Reuther staff provided invaluable assistance to me. The archival collections at New York Public Library, particularly the Vito Marcantonio Papers, provided much useful material regarding the IWO, and the library's periodicals included foreign-language newspapers that allowed me to retrace coverage of the IWO and other left-wing organizations. I am grateful, too, to the library's Andrea Felder and Tal Nadan for help with providing a digitized illustration from the Marcantonio Papers. The staff at Columbia University's Butler Library, the Wisconsin State Historical Society, and the University of Minnesota's Immigration History Research Center are consummate professionals and assisted me in my research trips to these institutions. Emory University's Stuart A. Rose Manuscript, Archives, and Rare Book Library is the repository of the papers of Louise Thompson Patterson, and I am most grateful for the expertise and courtesy of the staff there in helping me. Special thanks are extended to Courtney Chartier and Kathleen Shoemaker at Emory. Likewise, I am grateful to the expert assistance of the staff at the Library of Congress' manuscript division, especially Jeff Flannery. I also take this opportunity to apologize to any other researchers at the Library of Congress who may have been distracted by Jeff and me debating the relative merits of the Philadelphia Phillies and New York Mets.

The comments of fellow panelists, chairs, and audience members at several conferences where I presented portions of this research helped me hone and refine my arguments, and pointed me toward both primary and secondary sources. The Working Class Studies Association conferences at Stony Brook, NY, and Washington, DC (2016, 2015); Organization of American Historians and Popular Culture Association conferences (2016); the North American Labor History Conference at Wayne State University (2015); and the American Studies Association and Canadian History Association conferences (2014) provided me opportunities to test some of my findings in collegial and intellectually rigorous settings. I was fortunate, too, to present papers on early findings regarding the IWO and American Slav Congress at Oxford University's Mansfield College, where I attended a conference in critical issues of whiteness in July 2014, and at the University of Turku in Finland in October 2013 at a conference, "Travelling Whiteness."

Scholars and colleagues who have offered particularly astute commentary at these conferences and beyond have my continuing gratitude and friendship. Samantha Schulz, Paula De Angelis, Simone Puff, Jarmila Rajas, Carolyn Podruchny, Todd Michney, Joe Varga, Tim Sheard, John Beck, Jack Metzgar, and Michael Zweig are especially acknowledged in this regard.

Many thanks to my editor at Temple University Press, Aaron Javsicas, for his thoughtful guidance of this project, as well as his patience when deadlines were (narrowly) missed. The expertise and professionalism of the Temple University Press team made this project a pleasurable one. Special thanks go out to Ann-Marie Anderson, Jamie Armstrong, Karen Baker, Gary Kramer, Nikki Miller, and Kate Nichols at Temple University Press. Many thanks, too, to the friends who responded to an informal, nonbinding online poll to help me decide between four potential covers designed by the Temple University Press art department, each cover more beautiful and striking than the last. I think we made the right choice.

Abbreviations

ACLU	American Civil Liberties Union
ACPFB	American Committee for Protection of Foreign Born
ACWA	Amalgamated Clothing Workers of America
AFL	American Federation of Labor
AMA	American Medical Association
ANC	African National Congress
ANLC	American Negro Labor Congress
ARFS	American Russian Fraternal Society
ASC	American Slav Congress
CAA	Council on African Affairs
CFU	Croatian Fraternal Union
CIO	Congress of Industrial Organizations
CP	Communist Party
CPUSA	Communist Party of the United States
CRC	Civil Rights Congress
DPs	Displaced persons
FBI	Federal Bureau of Investigation
FEPC	Fair Employment Practices Committee
FLFF	Front Line Fighters Fund
FNB	Foreign Nationalities Branch
GEB	General Executive Board
HUAC	House Un-American Activities Committee
ILD	International Labor Defense
INS	Immigration and Naturalization Service
IRS	Internal Revenue Service

IWO	International Workers Order
IWW	Industrial Workers of the World
JPFO	Jewish Peoples Fraternal Order
JRB	Joseph R. Brodsky Welfare Fund
KKK	Ku Klux Klan
LSNR	League of Struggle for Negro Rights
NAACP	National Association for the Advancement of Colored People
NIRA	National Industrial Recovery Act
NMU	National Miners Union
NNC	National Negro Congress
NRA	National Recovery Administration
NSS	National Slovak Society
OSS	Office of Strategic Services
OWI	Office of War Information
POUM	Partido Obrero de Unificación Marxista
SACB	Subversive Activities Control Board
SWOC	Steel Workers Organizing Committee
SWS	Slovak Workers Society
UAW	United Auto Workers
UE	United Electrical Workers
UMW	United Mine Workers
UNIA	Universal Negro Improvement Association
WPA	Works Progress Administration
YCL	Young Communist League

"A ROAD TO PEACE AND FREEDOM"

Introduction

This book examines the International Workers Order (IWO), a consortium of ethnic mutual self-insurance societies that conceived of its mission as far broader than writing disability checks. Members were mainly attracted to this left-wing society because of the accident and death policies, and the IWO offered dental and medical clinics and sanitariums, too. But from its birth in 1930, the IWO advocated for unemployment insurance, Social Security, and vibrant industrial unions as the only true means of guaranteeing the health of its working-class members. While many early leaders of the IWO were indeed Communists, the Order drew its members from a broad ethnic, racial—and *political*—spectrum. The IWO was an insurance fraternal like no other in the nation. It must have been doing something right, for by 1948 it enrolled more than 180,000 white, black, Hispanic, and Arabic members across the country.[1] What accounted for the popularity, then notoriety, of this left-wing insurance consortium?

Imagine a mutual benefit society that offers low-cost life insurance as well as accident and sickness benefits to help tide its members over in times of need. This fraternal society offers the same low rates to all workers, even those in hazardous industries such as coal mines or steel mills, and requires no physical examination to enroll. This organization also recognizes the benefits of low-cost, preventive care and establishes a series of medical, dental, and optical clinics as well as sanitariums for members who need a longer, therapeutic rest. For working people these clinics offer some of the only affordable health care around.

Imagine, too, it is the height of the Great Depression, and Hoovervilles dot the streets and parks of most American cities. In Detroit, Michigan, official unemployment hovers near 40 percent (not reflected in the figures are those "lucky" enough to work one or two days a month; they are counted as employed). Every other household in many cities faces foreclosure and eviction, swelling Hoovervilles to bursting, but the response from the White House, state house, and city hall is that prosperity lurks just around the corner, and any government "handout" would kill one's work initiative. Therefore, no federal or state programs cushion the disaster, although in Toledo, Ohio, private charities dole out three cents' worth of soup a day, sending the unemployed into the streets to search for that elusive prosperity, or even a job. A little starvation, evidently, is a small price to pay to ensure that "free market" principles and government austerity are enforced.[2]

But alongside President Herbert Hoover's bromides, what if your fraternal society recognizes that sending a member to an affiliated dentist or sanitarium, writing a check when he develops black lung, or paying a "death benefit" to his survivors is not enough to ensure the health of its members? Just think, your insurance company actively lobbies for federal unemployment insurance, old age pensions, effective workers' compensation laws, and jobs programs to ensure your health and that of your lodge brothers. You are proud of your insurance company, which for twenty-five years has carried on the fight to lobby for universal health care, printing booklets calling for full medical coverage for all Americans. Imagine.[3]

This insurance company is more than fantasy; since its inception in 1930, the IWO was an active lobbyist on behalf of its members for its entire existence. It pressed the government to move forward with what it termed "social security," and after some of the society's program was enacted, the IWO continued prodding the government in progressive directions, calling for an expansion of Social Security to cover federally funded medical care. The IWO also recognized that the health of its working-class members was bound to the right to a living wage, safe and reasonable working conditions, and fair treatment on the job. Consequently, it forcefully advocated for industrial unions, and with the advent of the Congress of Industrial Organizations (CIO), IWO members became some of the most effective organizers for the CIO. In 1937 Philip Murray, president of the Steel Workers Organizing Committee (SWOC), wrote praising the Order's work for the CIO.[4] Following World War II, the IWO continued to champion union rights, pushing for repeal of the Taft-Hartley Act, which required union officers to swear they were not Communists and placed other restrictions on labor's rights.[5]

The IWO was also committed to multiracialism during an era when segregation governed most of American society, either in its terroristic Jim Crow manifestation below the Mason-Dixon Line, or in the urban North with its informal apartness in residence, job site, and schoolroom. White-instigated terror erupted whenever whites perceived blacks had trespassed beyond their "place," whether in spectacle lynchings from Marion, Indiana, to Sherman, Texas, and beyond, or urban race riots in cities such as Chicago and Detroit when black people bought houses or enjoyed parks deemed off-limits.[6] In the IWO, however, white ethnics were enrolled alongside African American and "Spanish" members (Puerto Ricans in New York and other eastern cities, Mexicans in California)—in the 1940s Detroit even had an Arabic lodge. In 1951 Black Muslims testified that the IWO was one of the only places they found racial brotherhood, and surely the IWO was one of the few organizations of any kind in America with Jewish, Polish and Hispanic Catholic, and black and Arabic Muslim members on its rolls.[7]

Black members in particular appreciated the Order's low-cost insurance since most for-profit insurance companies of the era refused to write policies for black people, or if they did, they charged inordinately higher rates than for European Americans, and for inferior coverage. Vice President Louise Thompson organized black and white sharecroppers into IWO locals in the South and recalled that her fellow African Americans appreciated the nondiscriminatory insurance coverage—and dignity as humans—they were afforded in the IWO. She proudly recalled, too, that in Chicago and elsewhere Ukrainian and African American women cooperated as mainstays in interracial lodges in the heart of a de facto segregated city. Black newspapers such as the *Baltimore Afro-American* approved of the IWO's groundbreaking ways.[8]

But the IWO, which conceived of itself as a militant lobbying organization and not simply an insurance concern, went further in championing racial equality. IWO-sponsored rallies, pamphlets, and petitions called for antilynching legislation, abolition of the poll tax, a permanent Fair Employment Practices Committee (FEPC), the abolition of Jim Crow segregation, and complete racial social equality. Members of the Order targeted segregated baseball almost a decade before Jackie Robinson joined the Dodgers, and IWO lodges lobbied in cities such as Detroit for open-housing laws at a time when other white ethnics fire-bombed the houses of blacks who sought to dwell in "whites only" neighborhoods. The IWO orchestrated campaigns that targeted discriminatory practices by banks and insurance corporations, and during campaigns to integrate housing noted that corporate as well as federal funds were used to bolster segregation in places such as New York's Stuyvesant Town. To be sure, the Order wrestled with the white chauvinism of some of its members, but its overall commitment to integrated membership and advocacy of racial justice were enlightened policies far ahead of their time.[9]

Order members also lobbied on foreign policy, demanding the United States stand up to fascist provocation from Spain to Czechoslovakia to Ethiopia. Thompson made a well-publicized tour of the Spanish Republic in support of the defenders against fascism, and IWO rallies raised money for medical supplies and ambulances for Francisco Franco's foes and Ethiopians battling to remain free.¹⁰ With the U.S. entry into World War II, the IWO did everything it could to aid the Allied war effort, establishing an IWO Front Line Fighters Fund (FLFF) to send care packages to American GIs and orchestrating campaigns by their Slavic members to deliver war relief to Poland, Czechoslovakia, and the Soviet Union. As part of the broad Popular Front coalition of liberal and left-wing Americans of various affiliations, the IWO supported President Franklin Roosevelt's war policies, especially the call by his vice president for a postwar "Century of the Common Man" securing the Four Freedoms to all peoples. Many IWO members were instrumental in the creation of the American Slav Congress (ASC), "an organization of organizations" that united various Slavic groups in support of the war effort. The Slav Congress, like the IWO, pushed for the opening of a second front to take some of the heat off the Soviets, had plenty of praise for Red Army victories such as Stalingrad, and advocated an enduring Soviet-U.S. friendship.¹¹

Following the war the IWO argued for continued Soviet-American friendship and opposed remilitarization and the bellicose turn in America's foreign policy. Within months Moscow went from valued ally to pariah, a shift that the Order saw as needlessly aggressive and lamentable. While the organization sought to steer foreign policy in a more idealistic direction, it extended its demand for racial equality abroad, too, calling for the extension of self-determination and democracy to colonized parts of Asia and Africa. Warnings were published on the folly of supporting French efforts to hold onto its colony in an obscure place called Vietnam.¹² The wartime Atlantic Charter, outlining the Allies' commitment to postwar national self-determination, had to apply to Asia and Africa, too, or the Cold War would continue to heat up. While this may seem far afield from its mandate to write life insurance policies, the Order argued that a peaceful, saner foreign policy without nuclear mushroom clouds eternally looming over policyholders' heads could only improve citizens' health.

For all its militant lobbying for racial equality, social programs, and union rights, the IWO was unusual in other, pleasurable ways. Imagine that your insurance carrier also offered members a chance to join choral groups; orchestras; mandolin clubs; theater troupes; and baseball, basketball, gymnastics, and bowling teams. Imagine a life insurance society with lending libraries and ethnic dance performances, and you might be ready to join the IWO.

And the government would label you a subversive. For despite all its good works, the IWO was led by Communists, and by 1947 such a label was anathema. Whatever the merits of strong industrial unions, universal health care, workers' economic security, and racial equality (and many conservatives were not that sympathetic to these causes in any case), the taint of communism led to the IWO's extirpation through the combined efforts of the Federal Bureau of Investigation (FBI), Justice Department, House Un-American

Activities Committee (HUAC), and New York State Insurance Department. Some of the strongest advocates for black civil rights, anticolonialism, and economic justice had their voices stifled, and these causes were set back for years as the limits of the politically possible were narrowed after "red" perspectives were stilled.

Although the IWO contained Communists, among both grassroots members and national leadership, the organization embraced members from a wide political spectrum. To be sure, with the opening of the Communist Party USA (CPUSA) archives in Moscow, scholars have convincingly demonstrated that there was more contact and coordination of policy between officials of the CPUSA and Moscow than was previously acknowledged by American Party members, and the top echelon of the IWO was in contact with the national Party as well as at times the Communist International, or Comintern. Certainly, the Kremlin endeavored to stay apprised and, aspirationally, in control of all facets of Party work. In May 1926, for example, the secretary of the Comintern wrote to the U.S. Party asking for twice monthly reports on its activities, noting that "exhaustive reports on such questions as . . . work among the Negroes will be particularly valuable."[13] Such letters from the Kremlin may be the smoking gun for those inclined to see the American Communist movement as a tightly controlled project directed by the Comintern, and such documents certainly suggest that the Party was cooperating with the USSR to a far greater extent than left-wing activists between the 1930s and 1950s publicly allowed. The scholarship of John Earl Haynes and Harvey Klehr has, as Maurice Isserman has noted, done a service by affording a fuller picture of the degree to which American Communists looked to Moscow for guidance.[14]

Yet scholars of the African American freedom struggle such as Erik Gellman, Erik McDuffie, William Maxwell, Jacqueline Castledine, Dayo Gore, and others have countered with strong evidence that when it came to civil rights, activists within the Communist Party (CP) and its allies often acted out of deep commitment, and did so with a great deal of local initiative, not cynical manipulation by or subordination to Moscow.[15] Recently, organizations such as the National Negro Congress (NNC) and the Civil Rights Congress (CRC) have received sympathetic treatments demonstrating the praiseworthy nature of these groups, which in the late 1940s were targeted as un-American for containing or associating with Communists. Likewise, the American Committee for Protection of Foreign Born (ACPFB), another organization, like the IWO, on the Attorney General's List of Subversive Organizations, has been rehabilitated by Rachel Buff as a progressive defender of immigrants' rights.[16] Communists were only one element of these organizations, which were pursuing laudable goals.

Similarly, within the IWO, there is no evidence of espionage, nor was control by the CP, to say nothing of the Kremlin, ironclad. Party control of the Order was aspirational, not actual. And from the Order's earliest years, many officials argued that it was necessary to adapt revolutionary or Marxist rhetoric and aspirations to suit more closely the actual needs of the workers they sought to enroll. The Order grew organically to meet the goals of the members. Likewise, white ethnics in the Party's language branches exhibited a great deal of initiative, independence, even vituperation, in arguing with Party superiors when they felt they knew what would best serve the working class. The robotic servants of the Party or Kremlin are absent straw men when it comes to the language branches and the IWO lodges that succeeded them.

Indeed, a multivocal conversation on what shape the Order would take and how revolutionary it could or should be seems to always have taken place between Party leaders, Order officials, and lodges' ordinary members. The members of many lodges made of their Order the kind of grassroots organization that would serve their needs, not Moscow's or CPUSA General Secretary Earl Browder's. Rather than deride CP-affiliated organizations as "Communist transmission belts," as many conservatives did between the 1940s and 1950s, and as some recent scholars continue to argue, this book demonstrates how the IWO was attractive to members because it effectively advocated programs that benefited working-class people.[17]

Focusing solely on Communist connections, strong as they sometimes were, fails to address what the IWO was doing on the American ground, and what about its activities made this organization so attractive to tens of thousands of members. What was found lacking in 1930s–1950s America to cause tens of thousands of immigrants and ethnic Americans to embrace this organization?

To date the IWO has received scant attention from historians. Arthur Sabin's *Red Scare in Court: New York versus the International Workers Order* largely focuses on the Order's unsuccessful legal battle to remain afloat after running afoul of the New York Insurance Department.[18] Sabin, a professor of law, focuses on the legal fight involving the novel application of insurance law to the IWO, which the state dubbed a "moral hazard" for advocating subversive ideas. While this story is important, and certainly a sobering tale of the restriction of free speech rights, Sabin devotes only twenty-five pages (less than one-tenth of his book) to the leisure, political, and civil rights activities of the Order in the twenty years before its legal troubles developed. *Pluralistic Fraternity: The History of the International Workers Order* by Thomas Walker is a brief institutional history that offers little if any analysis of the Order's interracial composition and civil rights, labor, and peace activism.[19] Then, too, Walker seems to take at face value the deleterious nature of an Order ostensibly "dominated" by Communists, an assumption with which I take strong issue.

Roger Keeran has more usefully provided article-length studies of IWO members' vital role in organizing autoworkers during the rise of the CIO, and Tony Michels notes the vitality of the cultural activities of the Jewish Peoples Fraternal Order (JPFO), which launched the IWO by breaking away from the "right-wing" Socialists in the Workmen's Circle.[20]

In a similar vein, Timothy Johnson and Robin Kelley have demonstrated that the CP proved attractive to many black sharecroppers because of organizers' "hard, day-to-day organizing of people around their concrete needs, while agitating on the eventual need and right for majority rule." IWO organizer Thompson Patterson (Louise married William Patterson in 1940), too, found black and white croppers, as well as industrial workers, receptive to her message because the Order offered tangible relief in times of crisis. In this formulation rigid ideological adherence to Marxism of some organizers was immaterial, as sharecroppers embraced one of the few groups willing to better their lot.[21] It was the group's satisfaction of day-to-day, lived imperative needs for Depression-bound members that attracted most recruits. Espousal of social, economic, and racial reforms by the Order resonated with members; this group embodied a progressive spirit of Americanism, not a subversive cabal. To dismiss members as the latter is to ignore what the IWO, and other left-wing organizations, meant to members themselves, who found the Order's message attractive and believed it was advancing their own life goals.

By 1947 the IWO drew 180,000 working-class members from across the political spectrum.[22] To be sure, Order members were prone to be sympathetic to progressive causes, but rather than serving as dupes of the Kremlin, members avidly embraced these organizations' goals because they found the promise to further working-class desires such as strong unions, Social Security, and racial equality appealing.

While this left-wing organization served the needs of working-class white, black, and Hispanic members, the program it proposed—workplace democracy, universal health care, and most especially full racial equality—was anathema to conservatives such as FBI director J. Edgar Hoover, HUAC chairmen Martin Dies and John Rankin, and Attorney General Tom Clark. The IWO was labeled subversive not because it posed a threat to the United States vis-à-vis Moscow, but in some measure because it advocated multiracial democracy and fuller labor participation in the democratic process. The very policies that proved attractive to many members to a large degree alarmed the solons of the segregated, corporate-friendly status quo, and this, rather than any impending security threat, doomed the IWO.

The liquidation of militant organizations such as the IWO was not just a calamity for these groups' members; the clampdown restricted the limits of "permissible" dissent for all Americans. Political dialogue on racism, segregation, and corporate dominance of America's economy shrank considerably after the left-most outliers were so visibly punished. Members lost jobs, while others faced prison; foreign-born members were deported, while prominent native-born members of the IWO such as singer-actor-activist Paul Robeson and artist Rockwell Kent were refused passports by the State Department for more than eight years for their vocal advocacy of civil rights.[23] Landon Storrs argues that the imposition of loyalty oaths, HUAC hearings, and Smith Act restrictions on left-wingers had a chilling effect on all government employees, and from the late 1930s into the 1960s progressives of all kinds, even those with no Marxist affiliations, tacked to the right out of fear of firings or worse.[24] How vocal would exponents of reform have been after watching friends and relatives in the Order labeled pariahs and punished? The Bill of Rights became a thinner reed for all Americans under such conditions, with this evisceration excused as necessary for national security. In our own age of Homeland Security, these questions still have relevance, even if the targets of federal surveillance, discipline, and punishment are by and large no longer Italian, Jewish, Polish, and African American "reds" but new official pariahs.

From 1947 until its demise, as the IWO was fighting for its life, it downplayed connections to the CP. While this may have been the only plausible defense strategy available, in concealing its red heritage the IWO was too coy by half. The IWO was indeed the brainchild of the CP, and many of its national officers such as General Secretary Max Bedacht were top-ranking officials of the CP (in the late 1920s, Bedacht had served as acting chairman of the Party and then led its Agitational Propaganda—"Agitprop"—Committee and also openly ran on the Communist line for U.S. senator from New York). Many Communists in the IWO made no bones about their CP membership, although their commitment to revolutionary socioeconomic change was largely dedicated to what could be achieved through persuasion, not coercion or violence.

The larger question, however, is whether the well-publicized Communist affiliation of some (and certainly not all) officials negated all the group's activism and turned this group automatically into a "transmission belt" for Kremlin purposes as alleged. Was every member of the Order engaged in union-building or civil rights activism tainted because of the beliefs of some IWO executives? From 1947 to 1954, when the Order was liquidated by action of the New York State Insurance Department, anti-Communist activists argued that this was the case. This book argues that a thorough examination of the writings, actions, and words of IWO members as contained in the Order's records deposited at New York University, Cornell, and other repositories tells a different story. My mining of extensive primary sources on the IWO reveals that the organization's thousands of members displayed commitment to racial and social justice, legitimate, worthy causes for which they fought, not slavish loyalty to foreign spymasters.

The "red" heritage of the IWO does not negate the validity of the causes it espoused. Moreover, even militant advocacy of worthy causes with which well-connected conservatives disagreed was not subversive behavior. An examination of the IWO's own primary sources in the archives reveals left-wing advocacy, not espionage, but during the red scare, roots in the CP invalidated members' free-association and political lobbying rights.

The idea for a multiethnic, interracial fraternal order was indeed hatched within the language division of the CP. Communist sympathizers split with the Jewish Workmen's Circle in 1930 and allied with the Hungarian Workers' Sick Benefit and Educational Federation and Slovak Workers Society (SWS) and other groups to form the IWO. But already in the 1920s within the CP's language branches, members exhibited a stridently independent militancy regarding industrial unionism, black civil rights, and other matters that often put them at odds with the CP's national leadership. These strains of independence continued after the IWO's creation. While it was the aspiration of the Party's leadership to direct all aspects of the language branches' activities, the independence they exhibited suggests that, as Michels and Paul Buhle argue, ethnic agendas were more salient to Jewish, Slavic, and other immigrant Communists than the dictates of the central leadership.[25]

African Americans and Hispanics, too, knew of the discriminatory depredations of bosses, commercial insurance brokers, and others to keep them in subordination and joined the interracial IWO for reasons that had little to do with Moscow. The pursuit of unionization and racial brotherhood of these fraternalists was based on their own experiences in America, firsthand brushes with brutal anti-immigrant xenophobia, bosses' divide-and-conquer racism, and violent strikebreaking in mines and mills. Many of the people who after 1930 flocked to the IWO fashioned their own agendas, based on their own lived experiences in America. Just as Rosemary Feurer argues Communists often won a following in the United Electrical Workers (UE) because they were effective advocates for members, many working people found the Order addressed their needs, so red labels were overlooked.[26]

To be sure, the members of language fraternal societies who later joined the IWO often agreed that the CP's plans and directives could benefit them. But when they disagreed, they expressed views and acted independently of higher-ups' decrees. James Green has argued that the grassroots militant workers of the CIO prodded John L. Lewis to become a more militant labor leader than he might otherwise have been and that their insurgency from below was the real motivator for the CIO's organizing success.[27] The same could be said about the Communists who created the IWO. They had to adjust their aspirations and hopes for complete control of the IWO to the agendas of members, some of whom argued that an overemphasis on hardcore Bolshevik rhetoric would repel potential IWO members, others of whom prodded leaders to be more confrontational on racial equality, industrial union organizing, and other matters dear to their hearts. I hope to demonstrate that the archival records reveal a grassroots membership capable of expressing far more independence than the narrators of robotic Communist control allowed. Tight control of the IWO may have been the goal but aspirations did not match up with reality.

Unaddressed, too, by the courts, which upheld the IWO's liquidation, was whether members' free-association rights could be trampled because of the political affiliations of some Order officers. Was the liquidation, with the loss of an organization and its lobbying activities and insurance coverage, permissible because of the beliefs of some of its officers? The crimes of some Republicans or Democrats have not forced the dismantling of organizations they have headed.

This book integrates the labor and socializing aspects of the IWO with its strongly articulated racial egalitarianism, for the organization was a pioneer in linking labor, foreign-policy, and civil rights agendas in one progressive vision for America. This work, then, also returns multiracialism to our examination of the Left. The IWO was one of the few organizations in which Jewish, Slavic and Italian Catholic, Hispanic, African American (including Black Muslim), and Arabic leftists worked side by side in pursuit of racial and workplace justice.[28] Again, this commitment to what we might today call multiculturalism was one of the main markers of the IWO's so-called subversive un-Americanism in 1947, at least for conservatives. This work enhances our understanding of the early, radical roots of multiculturalism.

In this regard, *"A Road to Peace and Freedom"* seeks to fill a gap in the urban history and birth of the Right literature. Thomas Sugrue, Thomas Philpott, Arnold Hirsch, Andrew Diamond, Karen Miller, Robert Self, and Kevin Kruse have accurately charted the depths of white ethnic resistance to black integration and equality, but these authors by and large omit the significant "prophetic minority" of white ethnics in groups such as the IWO who were committed to working with black and Hispanic activists in pursuit of racial and working-class justice. The work of such leftists building interracial solidarity has largely gone unremarked in the historiography, which has focused on the white-defended neighborhoods, those violently resisting integration through Sugrue's "crabgrass-roots politics."[29]

Unquestionably, most white ethnics bitterly resisted cooperation with African Americans in neighborhoods or on job sites. There was, however, an interracial coalition possible, built by left-wing immigrant and second-generation Slavic, Greek, Italian, and Jewish Americans working alongside African American and Hispanic comrades on social legislation and battles for racial equality. Enrollees in left-wing groups such as the Slav Congress and IWO not only resisted the psychic (and financial) "wages of whiteness," aptly identified by W.E.B. Du Bois and explored in the works of whiteness studies scholars such as David Roediger.[30] IWO members worked on interracial civil rights campaigns decades before the enactment of the Voting Rights and Civil Rights Acts. The activism of IWO members wed campaigns against anti-Semitism and other causes to an explicitly antiracist policy on behalf of African American civil rights; my work intervenes to suggest that it was possible for some of the white ethnics James Barrett and Roediger term "inbetween people" to incorporate progressive race thinking into their white consciousness.[31]

To be sure, even within the IWO racial egalitarianism was put to the test. White chauvinism was a recurring problem, but unlike in more mainstream organizations of the 1930s to 1950s, it was one that the Order endeavored to address, even if many members often fell short of enlightened goals. There were failings on this count, and others; missteps and arrogance were not unknown in the Order and other left-wing organizations, and by midcentury even militant white ethnics were beginning to take for granted the racial privilege from which they, but not other Americans, benefited. Some IWO members exhibited not so much racism as unthinking white privilege, which has proven more tenacious in the nation at large. Still, IWO members' activism indicates another, interracial world was possible between the 1930s and 1950s. While many white Detroiters, for example, violently resisted black incursions into segregated neighborhoods, black and white leftists assisted black families with their moves into unfriendly terrain through interracial house-painting parties.[32] Indeed, the government's destruction of the IWO and other interracial, leftist organizations arguably forestalled enactment of black voting and civil rights for a full twenty years. This book fills this omission in the scholarship.

Largely because of its commitment to interracial organizing and union activism, the IWO was branded subversive in 1947. The IWO asserted its right to free speech and association and pursued remedies through the courts as it unfurled the Bill of Rights in its defense—to no avail. The Order was deemed a "moral hazard" and liquidated by New York's Insurance Department. Members lost their jobs, some were imprisoned, and many foreign-born members were deported. The suppression of left-lying dissent spelled out just how narrow were the parameters for critiques of racism, class inequities, or America's militarized foreign policy. This narrowing of the politically possible has had enduring effects, and this exploration of the IWO has sobering lessons for today on the limits to dissent in times of permanent national emergency.[33]

This book, then, is designed to uncover what activities the IWO pursued, why these activities landed it in trouble, whether these activities really were a threat to U.S. security, and how the Order defended itself against being labeled subversive.

"*A Road to Peace and Freedom*" begins with an analysis of the birth of the IWO in the language division of the CP. Chapter 1 looks at these language-group fraternal societies among Jewish, Italian, Hungarian, and Slavic leftwingers. Already in the 1920s members of these ethnic fraternal societies were militant advocates of industrial unionism, programs such as Social Security, and multiracial equality, agendas that would find full flowering in following decades. Moreover, as Michels, Buhle, Al Gedicks, and others have pointed out, these ethnic leftists were quite independent from centralized Party control. They balked at calls from the CP for "Americanization" or "Bolshevization" (strict top-down centralized control and obedience to Party superiors' directives).[34] Leftist immigrants exhibited a great deal of assertive independence in pursuing agendas that suited their own needs.

Chapter 1 continues to trace the chronological history of the IWO, its birth and growth. The IWO was born in the CP's desire to amalgamate pre-existing left-wing mutual societies such as the Independent Workmen's Circle and the SWS. Accident and death policies were the main draw of this insurance consortium, but from its onset the IWO envisioned itself as a militant lobbying group preparing the proletariat for a coming workers' state.

The nature of U.S. communism changed over the course of the IWO's lifetime. There were less calls for revolution and more faith in a social-democratic Popular Front from around 1935. By World War II, and into the 1940s and early 1950s, the IWO was openly lobbying, rallying, and petitioning for or against legislation that members believed was beneficial or pernicious. Never was this organization engaged in espionage, for if these were spies, they were the most inept spies on the planet. The Order openly publicized meetings and rallies and signed public calls for them in widely circulated newspapers. Agents of the Office of Strategic Services' (OSS) Foreign Nationalities Branch (FNB) admitted in 1944 that while the IWO's national leadership might desire to see Soviet-style socialism established in America, there was little evidence they were engaged in illicit or revolutionary activities to bring this goal about. They were working through the expanded parameters of the Popular Front coalition, where it was possible to believe Roosevelt's commitment to enacting the Four Freedoms would be carried forward following the war.[35]

In the depths of the Great Depression, with no relief from capitalist parties anywhere in sight, the Order did little to disguise its militancy. With the enactment of New Deal reforms, however, and recognizing that many members were unsympathetic to hard-core Bolshevik rhetoric, the IWO deemphasized class conflict by the late 1930s. As the New Deal progressed, and just as important, the Comintern shifted to a Popular Front strategy of cooperation with the most progressive bourgeois elements, the Order shifted from a more militant call for a workers' state and hostility to U.S. capitalism. The earlier conviction of a need for a revolution was, by the late 1930s and early 1940s, tempered by calls to win the greatest social and political goals for members via vigorous lobbying. While some scholars argue that such a switch masked continued Communist ideology, I argue that the Order's members embraced a Popular Front coalition with Roosevelt's Democrats.

During World War II, the Order avidly supported the Soviet-U.S. alliance, only to discover following the war that the rapidly freezing Cold War rendered their continued commitment to left-wing domestic policies and Soviet-U.S. cooperation "subversive." An examination of the internal records of the IWO demonstrates that the group had a sincere faith that it would have an enduring place in the United States following World War II.

Chapters 2 through 5 depart from the chronological format to take up, thematically, the activism of the IWO, for it was the substance of the Order's activism, not any actual subversive threat, that was unpalatable to conservative politicians. It makes more sense, therefore, to consider this activism thematically and not strictly chronologically.

Chapter 2 examines the IWO's economic goals, for aside from writing insurance policies for members the Order also lobbied for Social Security, enacted in 1935, and universal health care, still pending, among other programs. IWO members were instrumental in building the unions of the CIO. Order members were some of the most determined activists for workplace justice.[36]

Asserting that the crises of capitalism could not be overcome through immigrants' self-financed accident and sickness policies, the Order's leaders argued, "The workers must meet [the crises] by fighting for a full measure of Social Insurance. . . . They must meet it by fighting against unsanitary and unsafe working conditions in the mills, mines and factories. They must meet it by fighting for a condition in which the life and the welfare of the worker will be the guiding principles of government policies and not the profits of the capitalists as are now."[37] While early pamphlets spoke of a coming workers' state and looked with favor on a Soviet model, even such campaigns laid out legislative strategies, not violent subversion of the government.

For class reasons, too, the IWO proved attractive to many enrollees. Those workers who had been beaten down as late as 1941 at the Ford Motor Company's River Rouge plant when they sought a union contract or a living wage did not spurn IWO organizers who offered them assistance. IWO activists played an instrumental role in turning CIO unions into effective deliverers of material improvements to industrial workers.

By the 1940s they were advocating legislative ameliorations to working people's plight, a reflection of the greater possibilities for social change born of the New Deal. Shortly after World War II, the IWO lobbied for the Wagner-Murray-Dingell Bill, which would have enacted universal health insurance. The IWO continued to call for such measures as a guaranteed annual income and recognized that inadequate housing and lack of affordable health care severely affected African Americans and other minorities, and thus vocally advocated full racial equality.[38]

Commitment to racial justice was always part of the IWO's mission, and Chapter 3 examines the Order's civil rights activism. From its onset the IWO condemned segregation "as a vicious anti-working class policy of the bourgeoisie." The IWO enrolled black and white members in English-language lodges, and even Hungarian and other ethnic lodges sometimes enrolled black members. The Order engaged in campaigns to end segregation and participated in the American Crusade against Lynching as well as other interracial lobbying campaigns to dismantle Jim Crow. Early IWO meetings took up collections and launched letter-writing campaigns on behalf of the Scottsboro Boys and Angelo Herndon and continued to agitate on behalf of victims of racialized justice until the Order's liquidation.[39] The IWO opened its doors to African Americans, including Muslims who defended the Order as a true seat of brotherhood; Arabs in the Detroit area; Puerto Ricans enrolled in Cervantes Fraternal Society lodges, alongside Jewish, Italian, and Slavic members. Thompson served as IWO vice president at a time when other fraternal organizations excluded African Americans entirely. The IWO was one of the only organizations open to all races and faiths in 1930s–1950s America.

To be sure, lobbying to end segregation and lynching, and for the enactment of a permanent FEPC, sometimes ran up against the racial prejudice of some members. During World War II, IWO headquarters had to defuse a row between Detroit Italian members who opposed open-housing laws, angering black lodge brothers. As in other areas of its activism, the Order's members made miscues, but compared to the violent anti-integrationist vigilantism of many conservative white ethnics, IWO members exhibited a commitment to multiracialism far ahead of their time.[40]

Important causes such as workplace justice or ending Jim Crow preoccupied Order members, but lodge meetings were never dull or prosaic affairs. IWO member Robeson frequently serenaded the Order's anti-Jim Crow rallies, but even for ordinary members, meetings were lively events.[41] Chapter 4 focuses on the social aspect of the IWO, for the Order offered a panoply of entertainment, sports, and educational activities to cultivate the mind and body. "Greetings to Comrade Basketball!" the IWO Youth Section magazine *The New Order* enthused, and integrated baseball, basketball, and gymnastics teams were on offer "to build up a healthy body and a healthy mind, a strong conscious fighter for the working class." Years before big league baseball's integration the IWO circulated petitions urging this course.[42]

The Order sponsored a national orchestra and choir, and local lodges ran their own theaters, bands, and choruses, too. Entertainment often had a didactic, class-conscious purpose. The IWO's Workers' Schools ran classes on ending "Negro oppression" but also sessions on organizing workers. In one of these the teacher advised, lodges "should look for interesting and colorful techniques. A chorus or mandolin orchestra in national costume on a sound truck could attract a lot of attention."[43]

Plays, too, carried militant messages. Solidarity Lodge sponsored the Harlem Suitcase Theater, which featured works by Langston Hughes dramatizing rent strikes and antilynching campaigns and gave actors such as Robert Earl Jones their first professional break. The IWO Freedom Theatre presented *Let's Get Together*, which an FBI agent said contained "vehement attacks against private business" and a musical number, "'Willie and the Bomb' (about the A bomb)." A Ukrainian Society play, *All Our Yesterdays*, included vignettes of a "Negro being killed by a police officer without provocation . . . interspersed with audience participation bits." During World War II, other Ukrainian lodges presented plays glorifying pro-Soviet partisans. Social and entertainment venues carried class-conscious messages.[44]

As Ukrainian actors recognized, the wartime alliance with Russia afforded radicals an opportunity to make a case for a more social-democratic America, but also an enduring Moscow-Washington friendship. Chapter 5 examines the foreign-policy goals of the IWO. Here the Order's fealty to CP lines and Soviet interests did at times have costs. Although the IWO and its members sounded early warnings of the dangers of fascism and avidly participated in campaigns to assist Ethiopia and Spanish Loyalists in their fight against it, in August 1939 the Order supported the Soviet switch to neutrality with the signing of the Soviet-German Nonaggression Pact. This embrace of a message that "the Yanks are not coming" to aid Great Britain and France in World War II had costs and revealed some of the blind spots that the Order's leaders retained vis-à-vis Moscow. Still, a sizable number of IWO members immediately condemned the new neutrality, as well as the IWO leaders who embraced it, suggesting that the Order's 188,000 members did not move in lockstep on foreign policy or other matters. The IWO's foreign-policy zigzags sometimes were abrupt, though, and suggest an overcredulous embrace of the Soviet Union.

Once the United States and the USSR became tenuous allies, the IWO found itself on surer footing. During World War II, thousands of IWO members joined the ASC, a new "organization of organizations" hoping to cement Slavic American support for the war. Like the Order, the Slav Congress was capacious enough to include Communists and people of many other political stripes. Both groups avidly participated in blood drives, Russian War Relief campaigns, and the IWO Front Line Fighters Fund, which raised money and sent care packages to members of the armed forces. In apt Popular Front iconography, the IWO's Polonia Society featured homages to "our ancestors, the pilgrims," urging members to send Thanksgiving dinners to soldiers overseas.[45]

Both the IWO and Slav Congress were forceful advocates of opening a second front in Western Europe to aid the Red Army, but they also continued their calls for racial justice in America. Commitment to racial equality was internationalized, too, for both organizations advocated independence for colonized nations in Africa and Asia. The Order asserted that the Atlantic Charter had to apply to India, no matter what Winston Churchill thought, while Slovenian American journalist Louis Adamic prophetically warned the Slav Congress that Indochina would not stand for attempts to maintain French colonialism.[46]

Following the war the IWO continued to lionize America's recent ally, the Soviet Union, and called for a continuing partnership. The credulity of many IWO officers regarding Joseph Stalin's commitment to the spirit of Teheran, espousing freedom for all areas liberated from the Nazis, can certainly be deplored. But members believed in the wartime coalition and regarded red-baiting as a far graver sin. During World War II, members of the IWO were dedicated to the Popular Front "win-the-war coalition" and presumed their position in progressive American life was secure. Confident of its place in the wartime coalition, the IWO urged the FBI to prosecute conservative "Fifth Columnists" such as William Randolph Hearst for the treasonous poison they spread, an ironic call, for the FBI was surveilling the Order throughout the war. With congratulatory telegrams from Roosevelt in hand, left-wingers felt assured of their place in the Popular Front. The Order advocated postwar cooperation with Moscow but was quickly at odds with Washington's stigmatization of the Soviets.[47]

When they found themselves targeted for red-baiting, Order members seemed genuinely shocked, couching their defenses in the Bill of Rights, believing free speech included even views anathema to the rapidly expanding national security state. Although heartfelt, this defense strikes one as a bit naïve, for the IWO knew it was being targeted by conservative politicians. Then, too, the invocation of free speech rights was somewhat one-sided, as during World War II the Order had called for prosecution of right-wing opponents such as Hearst for expressing "treasonous" critiques of U.S. policy. Nor did the IWO have much sympathy for Trotskyists' civil liberties.[48]

As an officer of the OSS observed regarding the IWO, its members were vituperative in labeling those with whom they disagreed "fascists" and treasonous, and noted such heated rhetoric only inflamed and distorted the political dialogue in Polish and other ethnic communities.[49] The Order forcefully advocated wartime unity and loyalty to the nation-state and tarred as traitors or fascists those who did not adhere to what it perceived as properly progressive Americanism. During the Cold War, this loyalty cudgel was turned on members' heads.

Leftists were soon to learn how narrow the options were for critiques of U.S. policies. Chapter 6 documents the sporadic efforts the Order faced to suppress it. In 1940 HUAC illegally raided the IWO's Philadelphia offices, while throughout World War II, the FBI and OSS continued writing reports on the group, sending informants to lodge meetings and rallies throughout the country.[50] Real trouble came for the Order in 1947 when it was placed, along with the Slav Congress and hundreds of other organizations, on the

Attorney General's List of Subversive Organizations. "Red" members of both the Order and Slav Congress were barred from government employment, up to and including work in the Hammond, Indiana, post office. Private employers fired members, and others, cowed into silence, quit their IWO fraternities in droves.

Other members begged the Order not to send them copies of its magazine, fearing authorities were keeping an eye on all suspicious "foreigners." Members were right to worry. The government sought multiple times to deport Stanley Nowak, an official in both the IWO and Slav Congress who was also a Michigan state senator. The Supreme Court finally put a halt to that effort in 1957, although other IWO and ASC members were deported.[51]

More ominously, elected officials in the IWO were placed on the FBI's "Internal Security" list. Congressman Vito Marcantonio, Nowak, and Slav Congress president Leo Krzycki were to be herded into concentration camps in the event that the president decided there was a "national emergency." IWO leaflets aptly wondered just who was "un-American" in Cold War America.[52]

By 1951 the IWO faced liquidation by the New York State Insurance Department after it was deemed subversive, a death warrant the Order unsuccessfully fought through the courts. The Insurance Department offered a novel interpretation of the actuarial term "hazard" (as in a financially unstable society) in now labeling the IWO a moral and political hazard. Even though the Order demonstrated that its finances were impeccable, a *New York World-Telegram and Sun* headline scoffed, "Their Books Balanced, But Politics Were in Red." The Order was mocked in other print media as well.[53]

Chapter 6 also examines the strategies that the IWO employed as it sought to defend its rights of free speech and association. Parades on newly created Bill of Rights Day in 1947 heard speakers ask, "What do men know of loyalty who make a mockery of the Declaration of Independence and the Bill of Rights?" Rhetoric accompanied by images of Thomas Jefferson, a bound and gagged Statue of Liberty, and cries of "when did dissent become un-American?" were deployed, and members were urged to write to elected officials demanding relief.[54]

The IWO orchestrated defense campaigns to protect members facing deportation, decrying the injustice of expelling activists with American-born wives and children for expressing their political beliefs. "Family values" were deployed to attempt to protect the foreign born. The Cold War's stigmatization of left-wingers had traumatic effects for families facing firings, deportations, and jail. Conversely, the IWO was quick to point out that some of the "Displaced Persons" entering the United States had unsavory records of collaboration with Adolf Hitler's Third Reich, "some of the worst fascist and pro-fascist scum of Europe," while some of the leftists targeted by the government were decorated U.S. Army veterans.[55]

The Order continued to fight liquidation through the courts until the Supreme Court declined to review the case. Legal strategies were deployed in tandem with rallies, letter-writing campaigns, and appeals from the IWO Policyholders Protective Committee, and voices of grassroots members demonstrate the depth of commitment to working-class militancy and the IWO. A Black Muslim member wrote, "I have found true fraternalism and racial equality in the organization, which I am proud to support and belong to."[56] All appeals were unsuccessful, and an insurance society—and much more—expired because of the political beliefs of its officers.

The Conclusion to *"A Road to Peace and Freedom"* briefly notes the continuities between the Old Left and the New Left, for while the IWO was dismantled, some former members continued their progressive activities. Former IWO members hosted an annual Workers' Bazaar in Detroit through the 1960s. At one 1966 event, Order veterans and others heard activist-historian Herbert Aptheker explain the folly of America's move toward active involvement in Vietnam.[57]

In summarizing the book, the Conclusion stresses that the IWO pursued legitimate political and social goals. While the group contained Communists, it also contained, as members argued to no avail, people of all political stripes who genuinely believed a capacious Popular Front coalition could continue after World War II. The suppression of left-wing dissenting views on economic egalitarianism and racial equality had deleterious effects for the entire country, and Bill of Rights protections were brushed aside by a government entering a Cold War security state mentality from which it has yet to emerge.

As the IWO faced government-ordered execution, an African American woman from Los Angeles joined many other members in defending the organization she believed had protected her interests so well: "What I liked best about the Order was the fact that it really practices brotherhood and democracy," she wrote. "All persons of all creeds and races are together in perfect unity. . . . I would like to ask the court to please let us have the <u>one organization</u> which is helping all people regardless of race, creed, or color to live and grow through mutual assistance which is Universal Brotherhood."[58] Such effective, militant, and democratic interracialism as exhibited in the IWO was another casualty of Cold War red-hunting. We are still waiting for an effective advocate for the causes this letter writer and her IWO brothers and sisters held so dear.

1

"A Practical Demonstration in Democracy"

The IWO

Throughout 1953 letters begging for assistance streamed into the IWO from across industrial America. Many of these were addressed to the custodians of the Joseph R. Brodsky Welfare Fund, established to assist members with medical bills. The secretary of the SWS in Guttenberg, New Jersey, wrote of the plight of "a member for 33 years of our lodge. . . . He is 64 years old and unable to work, because his health is ruined. He tried to get work but in his age and condition they would not give any. But he has to eat and he has to pay for his room, but how? The lodge is trying to help but that is not enough."[1]

Another secretary spoke up for Sister Katy Hlavenko, who "is 100% disabled from work. She is unable even to comb her hair. This Sister submitted to two expensive operations without relief. She suffers with chronic arthritis." Equally heartfelt stories of a sixty-two-year-old widow living on a monthly pension of $27.27 and "therefore . . . very much dependent on the help from the Welfare Fund" came in, along with appeals for assistance for a coal miner injured in 1945 and subsequently unable to work. The secretary stressed, "He needs help very badly."[2]

Custodians of the welfare fund's meager resources received many such letters. Even in the prosperous 1950s, after workers had begun to enjoy some benefits of Social Security, unemployment insurance, and unionized contracts—reforms the IWO had played a large role in championing—many aging industrial workers still lived in precarious economic circumstances.[3] The IWO sought to cushion the worst of industrialism's blows. The secretary of the SWS lodge in California, Pennsylvania, alerted the head office to the case of Olga Coben, who "got sick over a year and a half ago. She is paralyzed, so that she will never be able to work. She is in a hospital for a long time all ready [sic]." The IWO heard of a similarly distressed member who had "suffered a stroke on the right side. She cannot move her hand and her right leg has a brace. Most of the time she spends sitting down. Her husband . . . had to quit work for four months in order to . . . take care of her. They are requesting help."[4]

Even with New Deal legislation in place and the Brodsky welfare fund available to members, security was uncertain, as the Slovaks of the coal town of Lansford, Pennsylvania, could attest. There Frank Schubak's claim for an injury was returned with a request for further explanation. The IWO's Sick Benefit Department wrote, "On the surface, this disability is a very prolonged period for the diagnosis indicated by the doctor."[5]

In this instance relief was forthcoming, for the secretary explained the particulars of Schubak's case. "The thing is, he was crippled in the finger at work, and he was under company treatment by the company doctor through 'compensation' when it was announced that he was already healthy and could go to work," the secretary explained. After Schubak had been back at work for two or three weeks, the secretary went to visit him and discovered "his whole hand was wrapped up in bandages. He said that his blood was poisoned." His whole arm had turned black. The secretary surmised the hospital was receiving a kickback from the company doctor to hasten injured workers back onto the job. A check for fifteen weeks' sick benefits was sent in June 1953.[6]

As the initial letter raising questions about the "very prolonged period" of Schubak's sickness suggests, in performance of their insurance-society duties IWO officers scrupulously guarded their meager treasury. In this regard, IWO officers behaved like officials of other ethnic fraternal societies. Still, many IWO officers were sympathetic to a Marxist outlook, so there was always a chance a personal appeal noting corporate malfeasance (as with a company doctor prematurely hastening an injured worker back into the coal pits) would gain a sympathetic hearing. Prior to the unionization of much of the coal fields, deadly and debilitating accidents were widespread, and ethnic self-insurance fraternal societies were often the only recourse immigrant miners had.[7] In 1920 in Guttenberg, New Jersey, the SWS (later affiliated with the IWO), likewise heard of the plight of Frank Galba, "soon to be forever blind" as the result of a work injury.[8] Similar hazards were documented in the nation's steel mills and auto plants, where lost limbs, lost eyes, and ailments related to toxic chemicals were common.[9] Such woes brought home the grim nature of life in industrial America.

The level of trust that members placed in the IWO was touching. Isaac Galperin of Brownsville, Brooklyn, wrote in search of an electric blanket, "wholesale or at a place like a[n] I.W.O. laboratory where I can get a certain percentage off." General Director of Organization Dave Greene replied, "The IWO has no laboratory" but reported that bargains on electric blankets were available at S. Klein's on Union Square. Some members had such faith in the IWO that they sent their doctor's bill to headquarters as well as requests to put them in touch with Soviet doctors who could cure them. In February 1951 Greene replied to Stella Fidyk, "The IWO is in no way connected, medically or otherwise, with the doctors of the Soviet Union, and we have no contact with them." He suggested, though, that Fidyk "get in touch with some of the doctors who have serviced our membership. . . . [T]hey may be in [a] position to help you with your medical problem."[10]

The example of a member writing to the fraternal insurance society in search of an electric blanket suggests that by 1953, over the course of more than two decades, members had "regarded our Order as the head of a big family" that, as one member attested, was "always together in good times and bad." As Fidyk's plea to be connected to Soviet doctors indicates, members knew of the leadership's Communist affiliation. In 1934 Bedacht, general secretary of the Order from 1933 until 1946, had run as CP candidate for senator in New York. For many members, however, more important than leaders' politics was the tangible relief the Order could deliver—$10 sick benefits or a tip on a discount electric blanket—together with relief on the macrolevel, in leading campaigns for social legislation to sand the rough edges off industrial conditions.[11]

What such letters suggest is that by 1953 the IWO was not the radical threat envisioned by red-baiters but an organization—left-wing, to be sure— catering to the desperate detritus of industrial America, people like Schubak and Galperin looking for a little comfort, security, or maybe even dignity as they wrestled with all-too frequent disability, industrial accidents, and, inevitably, economically perilous old age. Such dire circumstances, rather than any international Communist conspiracy, may have explained the appeal of the IWO for such people.

The IWO was founded to meet the grassroots demands of working men and women for quality health care and insurance as well as to help them articulate their organic demands for substantive relief from the state on matters such as social insurance and union rights. The Order embraced, too, albeit imperfectly, an interracial membership that shared a vision of a racially egalitarian working class. From its earliest years, African Americans, Hispanics, and other non-Europeans, along with Southeast Europeans, were instrumental in the IWO's growth. While the IWO was born in the meetings of American Communists, it grew through demonstrated commitment to members' needs. It could not have been otherwise, for the building blocks of the Order, militant workers, were often stridently independent, determined to ensure that the organizations to which they belonged met their needs, even if this meant arguing with their supposed leaders. This is the saga of the IWO, a fraternal organization that boasted, "It protects the worker as an individual," which for the 1930s was in and of itself a radical idea.[12]

"Capitalism Itself Is a Case of Crime"

The IWO was a consortium of self-insurance fraternal societies with a different, Marxist paternity. But in its focus on providing financial relief to destitute, sick, or injured members, the IWO was following in a long line of mutual benefit organizations. Slovak immigrants, for example, established the National Slovak Society (NSS) in 1890, while other people for whom faith was more central established religious fraternal organizations. The more devout were wary of some societies. In Philadelphia, according to one observer, the local Slovak Gymnastic Union *Sokol* was reputed to be "not communist exactly, but kind of like non-believers." Still, this individual hastened to add that in the 1920s she and other Catholic and Lutheran teenagers nevertheless socialized with, even belonged to, the ostensibly radical *Sokol* lodge.[13]

Other ethnic groups established similar secular and faith-based mutual benefit societies. Jewish immigrants often formed *landsmanshaftn*, self-insurance benefit societies that brought together immigrants from the same hometown or region. Some more militant Jewish immigrants scorned the societies as parochial. Politically radical immigrants found a more palatable refuge in the branches of the Workmen's Circle, founded in 1892 on a nonpartisan albeit socialist basis. It was from the Workmen's Circle that Communists would lead a walkout that led to formation of the JPFO, the precursor to what became the IWO. But in their militancy these "splitters" were not alone. Some branches exhibited radical allegiances openly, as in Harlem, where one lodge displayed portraits of Mikhail Bakunin, Karl Marx, and Ferdinand Lassalle. For other Jewish immigrants, the Workmen's Circle, while undeniably permeated with all stripes of socialism and radicalism, was more valued as a means of building some security for those in the cyclically unsteady garment industry.[14]

All these organizations offered members a full panoply of entertainment and social events, but the main draw was accident and burial insurance, with good reason. Prior to the enactment of state workmen's compensation laws and, more importantly, the federal Social Security Act in 1935, such ethnically defined fraternal societies were often the only institutions that stood between injured workers, or the families of those killed on the job, and destitution. For a small monthly dues payment, members were guaranteed a weekly sick benefit if illness or injury prevented them from working. One could also purchase a death policy that provided a payout to survivors to cover funeral expenses. It was in free-market industrial conditions that the ethnic mutual benefit societies flourished.[15]

Fraternal organizations pooled members' meager resources to provide sick benefits as a measure of protection. But this was a bandage continually at risk of fraying. Dangerous work and negligible help from government or employers meant workers often called on lodges for aid. In 1929, the secretary of Philadelphia's Slovak Catholic *Sokol* lodge remarked that thirty-five of ninety-five members were drawing sick benefits. Most members worked at the oil works and gasworks of South Philadelphia, sites prone to industrial accidents and work-related illness. In his monthly report, the secretary noted the plight of a lodge brother hospitalized after falling from an oil tank. At the nearby Rusyn lodge of the Greek Catholic Union, Steve Sinchak was awarded $5 sick pay in 1925 after being burned by a fire wall. Similar high rates of accidents and death occurred in other fraternal organizations.[16]

Immigrants quickly noticed the rough bargain they had made by moving to industrial job sites in the United States, and they were not hesitant to critique the deplorable features of unregulated free-market capitalism. Slavic coal miners in the anthracite fields of eastern Pennsylvania were quick to employ militant rhetoric when facing wage cuts and perceived injustices from the coal companies, and lodges of fraternal organizations such as the Polish National Alliance took up collections in support of strikes. Slovaks in Philadelphia and elsewhere often used lodge collections to send support to *štrajkujúci* (strikers) throughout the country.[17]

Even nonsocialist fraternal societies could rise in indignation when particularly egregious suppressions occurred. In the aftermath of the Ludlow Massacre, in which National Guardsmen operating at the behest of the Colorado Fuel and Iron Company attacked a tent colony of striking immigrant miners and killed two women and eleven children, the NSS's newspaper angrily denounced the use of troops in strike suppression.

What particularly galled the editors was that the bloodshed came at the same moment other troops were being deployed to Mexico's Vera Cruz. "There is no crime that capitalism cannot even imagine, for capitalism itself is a case of crime," the editorial thundered. "The only difference between the war in Mexico and the war against workers in Colorado is that the Mexican soldiers didn't kill innocent women and children, but in Colorado they did." The writer asserted, "The workers of the United States have nothing against the workers in Mexico, nor do the workers in Mexico have anything against U.S. workers." A month after the Ludlow Massacre, the real enemy seemed easy to identify: "Well, therefore, what war does concern our workers?—Who wants to take a guess!"[18]

Fraternal organizations, then, did not limit themselves to piecemeal, individualized responses to members' sickness but often engaged in politicking on behalf of systematic reforms, the kinds of campaigns for which the IWO would later be condemned. Immigrants attracted to Marxism saw the problem as one of untrammeled capitalism and similarly worked through mutual benefit societies to aid their fellow workers in more transformative ways.

Following the founding of the CP in 1919, comrades focused on organizing in ethnic fraternal organizations as a way of reaching immigrant workers. The CP's approach to the fraternal societies mirrored its efforts within labor unions. Just as the CP initially sought to "bore from within" existing unions before embarking on a campaign to build dual, militant industrial unions, Communists first sought to build factions within existing fraternal societies to win them to the most militant position possible.

As early as 1922 Lithuanians within the Party were urged to join fraternal organizations "heretofore used by the Lithuanian bourgeoisie to achieve its political undertakings." A Left bloc was conceived as moving the societies to a more working-class orientation. Sometimes, though, it was grassroots ethnic members who issued calls for fraternal organizing. Latvians complained to the Party executive committee that they "[could not] count upon the active support of the Party members of New York" and urged a campaign to organize within Latvian labor and fraternal organizations. The following day the Party's Latvian Agitprop Bureau sent out a letter to all Latvians in the Party urging them to reach out to labor and "language workers' societies" on a nonpartisan basis and "engage them in the various united front campaigns over the various issues."[19]

The Party's Language Department periodically solicited information from various groups on their progress in recruiting members within existing benefit societies, and the news was often discouraging. The South Slavic Bureau urged that a responsible editor be found, as the current editor was deemed "an incurable opportunist" who was hindering attempts to organize militant factions within the Slovenian benefit societies to counter "social-democratic leadership." Matters did not improve three years later, when the bureau submitted estimations on the minimal number of Party members and those it could deem sympathetic to its cause in the fraternal organizations. In the Slovenian National Benefit Union, of 68,000 members only a hundred were Party members. The Party's strength in the Serbian benefit society was "impossible to state."[20]

The 1926 report "Mass Work among the Jugo-Slavs" noted formation of the "Progressive Bloc" within the Croatian Fraternal Union (CFU), with fifty-one lodges said to be under the Party's "complete control" and twenty "in which we have a minority." More than twenty thousand members of the CFU were now said to be under the leadership of the Progressive Bloc, although in the Slovenian society the situation was worse. Only thirty Party members could be found, as the society's Socialist leaders had conducted "a vicious and provocative campaign . . . to drive the Communists out of the organization."[21] Optimistic assertions of "control" in Language Department and ethnic bureau reports may have been attempts to boost organizers' morale in the face of less than encouraging numbers, as in the Slovenian case.

Initially, the Party had held out great hopes for gaining influence among the "petty bourgeois elements and workers" in the 140,000-member Workmen's Circle, the Socialist-led Jewish fraternal society. Communist sympathizers formed a left-wing *Verband* (bloc) within the circle, the Language Department informed the Comintern, but were compelled to "make a retreat under the attack of the rightwing Socialist Elements." Although the *Verband* was disbanded, the Language Department overoptimistically believed the maneuvers by the Socialists had won support for peace in the Circle and strengthened the standing of left-wingers in this important Jewish benefit society. While the tens of thousands of "petty bourgeois elements and workers" of the Workmen's Circle were tempting ground for recruiting, as with Croatian, Hungarian, Slovak, and other fraternalists, the Party was stymied here, too.[22]

The opening of the CP archives in Moscow reveals that the U.S. party *was* consulting with the Comintern about its plans to organize within fraternal societies. Still, the Language Department's report to Moscow shows that recruiting came at the initiative of U.S. comrades. Descriptions of the establishment of a progressive bloc of forty delegates and reaching out to build a further coalition of like-minded fraternalists at the Croatian convention suggest that the nature of Communist activity was lobbying to win support and persuading delegates to vote for resolutions that might benefit them (putting the convention on record as supporting federal unemployment legislation, for example). While red-hunters characterized Communists' efforts to elect members to positions within the CFU as "subversion," other fraternalists might argue that winning elections at national conventions and lobbying for desirable social legislation were demonstrations of democracy in action.[23]

There were reasons immigrants might welcome Communist support. The year of the Language Department report on the fraternal societies, 1926, saw bitterly contested strikes in the textile mills of Passaic, New Jersey, and coal fields of Pennsylvania. While state police were deployed to suppress strikers with tear gas and tanks, CP organizers in Passaic directed the strike seeking to prevent wage cuts and speedups. Slavic strikers in Passaic and the coal fields slighted strikebreaking police forces by referring to them as the "Cossacks," while Hungarian organizer Emil Gardos compared scabs (strikebreakers) to monkeys, to which the president of the Passaic Central Labor Union exclaimed, "If I were a monkey I would shoot the man that compared me to a scab." When a priest told striking parishioners in Bentleyville, Pennsylvania, that "he would rather see Old Nick come to his church than a scab," Bethlehem Steel promptly shut off his church's water and electricity and evicted strikers' children from a playground built on company land.²⁴ On the floor of Slovak and Croatian conventions, delegates might have thought of worse epithets than "Communist" when they considered their plight.

Such delegates' sense of democracy was different from that of the corporate private police agencies, the detested Coal and Iron police, establishing a contested terrain prioritizing free speech and working people's rights over tear gas and property rights. Many Southeast Europeans were also "those without a country," people with enduring transnational ties.²⁵ Even immigrants who did not join a Marxist organization often regarded a stay in the United States as temporary, for as Mark Wyman demonstrates, for many ethnic groups, the rates of return migration neared 50 percent. Such people were pragmatically loyal, embracing institutions and assets from across the Atlantic that were likely to improve their lot in a factory or even a country they might be leaving in a few years.²⁶ In such situations looking to a transnational institution such as the Comintern for advice may not have seemed all that heretical. This was especially the case for, as the Finnish Bureau of the CP reminded comrades, "a party which was born in the purgatory fire of the revolutionary civil war, the class war" was "entitled to give advice and guidance to us."²⁷

Trouble "in the Land of the Billionaires": Working through the Fraternal Organizations

The Party continued to look to the benefit societies as a means of reaching, and helping, workers with their material needs. In 1930 Frank Borich of the South Slavic Bureau proposed a plan "on the question of unemployment in the Croatian Fraternal Union." Borich had earlier alerted the Party's central committee that "thousands of workers in these fraternal societies are not able to pay their dues and they are faced with expulsions from the organizations. These unemployed workers are coming to the meetings of these organizations demanding that the lodges should wait for dues and thereby the workers themselves are raising the questions of unemployment at the meetings." Despite this, Borich noted that not one of the more than thirteen hundred South Slavic lodges in the country had done anything to alleviate members' destitution. He argued that the South Slavic Bureau "should immediately work out the program for those unemployed members . . . unable to pay their dues." Borich argued that leftists should make motions to "reduc[e] the pay of Bureaucrats and to use this . . . in part for the funds for the dues of unemployed members in CFU."²⁸

Boleslaw Gebert, later head of the IWO's Polonia Society, was at this meeting and endorsed Borich's plan. He further proposed, "We should raise the question of taxing the bourgeois elements in the C.F.U. and use this tax for dues of unemployed; . . . we should raise the question of reducing the wages of Bureaucrats." Gebert added that these steps should be taken "to develop the sharp struggle among workers in C.F.U. for the Social Insurance." Social insurance was later a frequent demand of the IWO and its ethnic organizations. A program seeking unemployed members' dues relief was adopted at the meeting.[29]

The following month, the Language Department echoed this call for all fraternal societies. "No wages, no dues!" they demanded. "We piled up the funds for our organization! . . . All funds over the minimum sick and death benefit fund be turned into unemployment dues fund!" They echoed earlier calls for enactment of social insurance and unemployment legislation as well as an end to evictions.[30]

Rather than opportunistic, Party factions might have seemed, to the unemployed, responsive to their genuine needs and grassroots demands. Borich, after all, noted that in the South Slavic societies people out of work were already complaining of the injustice of having to continue paying dues. The complaints came from workers first, only then spurring Borich and other left-wingers to recommend a solution. With unemployment lines growing exponentially, Communist South Slavs' plans for gaining influence within the ethnic societies might have seemed, at least to some people, charitable, not devious.

Party officials frequently expressed such demands for more systemic amelioration of workers' suffering. In his 1930 report to the Party, "The Work of the Communist Fractions in Fraternal Organizations," Marcus Jenks admitted that thus far, "language organizations . . . have served as a hindrance to the development of the work of the Party."[31] Jenks explained that many mutual societies

> are an aid to the capitalists and government, because in reality they help to divert the struggle of the workers from fighting for social insurance and social laws in general. Who does not know that in this, the land of the billionaires, in America, there is no social insurance for workers, and also less protection of the lives of the workers than in any other capitalistic country in the world. And to a large extent it is due to the fact that there is no struggle going on for the establishment of laws for social insurance for workers, unemployment aid etc. By being a member of some mutual aid society, the worker hopes to be taken care of in case of illness, to be buried in case of death—and that is all.[32]

A marginal cushion of small weekly sick benefits, Jenks added, tended to divert the masses from the struggle for their interests against the capitalists. Still, the benefit societies should be entered by Party members "not only in order to collect a few dollars, but for the purpose of extending its influence and of drawing in more and more workers into the revolutionary movement. We must use these organizations to develop the class consciousness of the members."³³

Unfortunately, Jenks's analysis did not lead to large recruiting successes for the Party. Party officials' aspiration and assertion of "control" of the fraternal organizations often conflicted with ethnic bureaus' own assessments of the situation. Bedacht confessed in a letter to General Secretary Jay Lovestone, "Now as to [the] Italian situation. It is rotten. Our N.Y. fellows work at cross purposes to me." Bedacht worked with Luigi Candela, later president of the IWO's Italian Section, but other Italian comrades were derided as hopeless. "I am inclined to take a fatalistic attitude. Let the crash come. We close our eyes, stuff our ears and hold our breath. And when the noise and dust of the explosion is over we will count the victims."³⁴

While reports to superiors sometimes asserted Party "control" over certain fraternal lodges or progressive blocs within national organizations, other communications indicate this was always more aspirational than actual. Members of fraternal organizations exercised a great deal of independence and balked at directions from Party officials that they regarded as unwise. The general secretary before Lovestone, C. E. Ruthenberg, told the secretary of the Hungarian faction that all work and decisions within the Hungarian Workers' Sick Benefit and Educational Federation first had to be approved by the Party Hungarian Bureau. Ruthenberg noted that comrades in the society had been alerted to this three months before, but their independence persisted. The society, which four years later would amalgamate with the IWO, had elected a secretary they knew their supposed Party masters disliked. Five weeks later Ruthenberg complained that delegates to the society's convention were still acting independently, submitting amendments to the convention without consultation. Party member delegates even went so far as to publicly attack the Party's Hungarian Bureau, critiquing attempts to control the society.³⁵

Michels has noted that for Jewish immigrants in the Party, ethnic organizations and the community's own agendas were often more important than programs and pronouncements of Party leaders. Gedicks adds a similar independence and prioritization of Finnish concerns, even among radicals, long bedeviled Party efforts to enforce discipline. Indeed, in 1923 Bedacht wrote to Ruthenberg that while some "Finnish may be drawn into our party," they were more likely to "degrade into social clubs and relief organizations for Karelia," the Finnish region of the Soviet Union. Hungarians were similarly obdurate.³⁶

Jacob Zumoff has argued that in the 1920s much more internal democracy existed in the CP and the international Communist movement than would later be the case. This was true in the various language bureaus affiliated with the Party. The minutes of a 1929 Boston Estonian Workers Mass Meeting documents a grassroots protest against the Party's attempted takeover of the Estonian-language newspaper *Uus Illu* and "attempts to sling mud at all Workers' Clubs that are not controlled by [the] Party, forgetting at the same time that the majority of readers of *Uus Illu* are non-partisan proletarians." The Estonians declared, "We are not satisfied with such rough bourgeois ways."[37] Far from being automatons accepting of Party discipline, many radical immigrants jealously guarded their prerogatives to think and act for themselves.

Aside from the question of minimal Communist numbers in the fraternal organizations, even before the Depression the perilous financial state of many societies was cause for concern. In 1927 the Hungarian Workers' Sick Benefit and Educational Federation was already under scrutiny from several state insurance societies as to its actuarial soundness. The secretary of the Hungarian Bureau characterized this as a dual assault by "capitalist insurance societies and the state itself" but thought it might become an advantage if the various ethnic fraternal societies could be convinced to merge into a larger mutual benefit society with greater assets. A crisis might become progressive fraternalists' opportunity. Three years later the movement, known as amalgamation, would lead to the creation of the IWO.[38]

Draining "the Swamp": The Birth of the Order

Factional fights in the Workmen's Circle hastened the creation of the IWO. In 1950 Lucy Davidowitz wrote an unsympathetic "History of the Jewish People's Fraternal Order." In 1930 the JPFO was the founding kernel of the IWO, which was created, she wrote, after left-wingers within the Circle were unsuccessful in attempts to steer that society closer to the CP. Two years later, the IWO amalgamated with the Hungarian Workers' Sick Benefit and Educational Federation and then Slovak and Russian working people's societies (Figure 1.1).[39]

Records of the Jewish Fraction of the CP's Actions Committee and the Party's Language Department confirm that the IWO was the brainchild of Party leaders dissatisfied with their lack of progress in reaching workers in established societies.[40] But while Davidowitz, who was writing at the height of the Cold War, cast the IWO as an organization solely dedicated to furthering a Communist revolution, the minutes of these meetings reveal a more nuanced story. Within the Independent Workmen's Circle, left-wingers sought to build coalitions that would serve the social and economic needs of potential allies. Once it was decided to establish the IWO, organizers realized that if they were to attract workers to this new insurance society, they were going to have to use persuasion and appeals to the economic self-interest of potential members.

Figure 1.1 In 1940 the American Russian Fraternal Society (ARFS) celebrated its twentieth anniversary as well as the tenth anniversary of the IWO, which had amalgamated many preexisting ethnic fraternal societies. The ARFS was confident that a social-democratic America was on the horizon.

Source: Souvenir book, ARFS/IWO anniversary, IWO-CU, box 49.

The left-wingers at first sought to work with other progressives in the Workmen's Circle, seeking to gain some representation on committees. In 1927 the Party's Jewish Fraction's Actions Committee chose not to put forward a complete slate of Communist candidates for the Circle's executive, reasoning, "The most important thing at present is to make clear to the membership, that all the left wing wants . . . is to have representatives on committees." The Actions Committee added that it would even forego an endorsement from the Circle's Committee for Peace, as "this would give another opportunity to the right wing to label the Committee for Peace as a Toy in the hands of the communists." Working to persuade Circle members to grant some left-wingers a few committee seats seemed the better course. When the Party pushed for proportional representation on all Circle committees, though, the Committee for Peace, which was struck to try to work out some accommodation between Socialists and Communists, balked. Party sympathizers then declared, "Because of the brutal attitude . . . towards the left wing, the Workmen's Circle reached its present critical stage."[41]

Party members continued working within the Circle into 1929, but letters from organizers sent to rally left-wing branches attest to the demoralization and disorganization in Buffalo, Cleveland, Detroit, and elsewhere.[42] Attempts to reconcile with the "right wing" (Socialist) leadership of the Circle came to naught and according to the Socialists who remained within the Circle may never have been very sincerely pursued.

The particulars of the IWO's split from the Circle depended on where one sat on the Communist-Socialist divide. Rubin Saltzman, general secretary of the JPFO, later remembered "those difficult, but happy, days twenty years ago when we laid the foundation for the birth of our International Workers Order." Saltzman characterized the departure from the Circle as lamentable, "a great sorrow to us that we were forced to leave an organization which we had helped build, an organization to which most of our delegates had devoted the best years of our lives" even as he recounted his pride in the IWO's growth.[43]

The Socialists who remained in the Circle had a different take on the split. A lengthy letter to the Socialist newspaper *The Call* suggests the vitriol that lingered over the internecine Left battles. "The IWO mud slingers have for many years made a target of the Workmen's Circle," the article began. "Whoever is acquainted with the battle that was conducted by the 'lefts' in the Workmen's Circle knows well the crooked means they employed to seize control of the property and institutions of the Workmen's Circle." The article listed Communist confiscation of the Workmen's Circle Harlem Labor Lyceum and Camp Lakeland, as well as several Yiddish schools, as particular outrages that "the principles of working-class ethics" prohibited the Circle from contesting in court. The writer in *The Call* mocked the self-serving way the Communist *Morgen Freiheit* congratulated the leftists "for their 'great struggle' to emancipate the membership of the Workmen's Circle from this 'bourgeois-minded reactionary organization.' . . . They could not remain in the Workmen's Circle because it had become (so said the '*Freiheit*' and its flunkeys) a stagnant, malodorous swamp, an organization of bosses, scabs, and counter-revolutionaries." More than twenty years after the split, however, a charter member of the JPFO deposed less vituperatively, "The issue on which the split took place was that of local lodge autonomy."[44]

Whether it was with Saltzman's regretful sorrow or Socialists' curses on their heads, by late 1929 left-wingers decided there was no place for them in the Circle and set about creating a new society. The founders of the IWO alleged that the Workmen's Circle, "formerly a predominantly workers' organization, is rapidly becoming bourgeois, so that by now no less than a half of its members consists of merchants, shop-keepers, small manufacturers, etc. . . . [T]here is no possibility of wresting that control from the hands of the reactionary elements." Moissaye J. Olgin, editor of the *Morgen Freiheit*, argued that the Circle had become so overrun with "bourgeois" officers that continued fighting to transform the Circles into genuine workers' organizations was "so much wasted breath." Of the new IWO he predicted, "The first exodus is not to be the last one. The army of workers marching out of the reactionary Workmen's Circle will have left a great deal of discontent and potential rebellion among those who stay." The breakaway Party members were urged to continue working "to rally the proletarian membership and to take it out of the Workmen's Circle . . . until only the bourgeoisie is left in the Workmen's Circle, which, with the disappearance of the workers, will sink into complete insignificance." Thousands of people were enrolled in the new Order in October 1929 alone, and Olgin was confident of the success of this new organization "following the policy of the revolutionary class struggle and constituting one of the sources of power for the working class against capitalism."[45]

As Olgin's homages to the "revolutionary class struggle" indicate, the IWO primarily oriented itself toward workers in the Marxist orbit. But as the Order was looking to enroll as many working men and women as possible, to achieve financial stability but also to reach the critical mass necessary to achieve some of its social and racial programmatic aims, the organization reached beyond Party members and sought to appeal to as broad a mass of workers as possible. As such, the IWO's relationship to and sympathies for the CP were left a little ambiguous.

In 1931 Olgin published a Yiddish pamphlet explaining the benefits of the IWO. In *Der Internatsyonaler Arbeter Ordn: Geshikhte, Program, Taktik* (The International Workers Order: History, Program, Tactics), Olgin characterized the IWO as a "class-struggle" organization that should support the CP's activism. While he said the Order did not dictate to which political party its members should belong, he added that if a branch contained "not only the majority but even a significant minority favor[ing] the Socialist Party, the International Workers Order will have to investigate the situation most energetically and take the necessary steps." He further asserted, "It is already clear that the I.W.O. must look upon the Communist Party as the only labor party in the United States." Although there was much institutional endorsement of the Party by the IWO, Olgin nevertheless noted that individual members were not beholden to every decision of the Party, nor did they have to join. Still, he asserted, "Whoever says he can be a leftist, even though he is not concerned with the Communist Party, is not a leftist, but a petty-bourgeois weakling. . . . The International Workers Order . . . recognizes the Communist Party as the leading organization of the working-class, the brain, the will, and the fighting force of the working-class."[46]

The attitude of the Order's officers seems to have been endorsement of the Party without requiring all members to join. Many IWO officers such as General Secretary Bedacht, JPFO Secretary Saltzman, and Gebert of the Polish Section were active in the Party, and many lodges made a concerted effort to get individual members to contribute to collections for causes such as the *Daily Worker*.[47] The IWO was careful, however, not to use corporate funds for such purposes. It seems to have followed a policy of endeavoring to lead individual members to endorse Party causes via advocacy and persuasion, not strict control. In this respect the IWO already prefigured the Popular Front policy that the Party at large practiced after 1935: working in cooperation with as broad a progressive coalition as possible to achieve desirable social-policy, civil-rights, and foreign-policy objectives.[48]

To be sure, the IWO was not for everyone. The Order barred those who had been employed as strikebreakers or private detectives. When an Omaha, Nebraska, lodge secretary wrote in 1943 seeking advice on how to expel a member who had been reported strikebreaking, headquarters cautioned that state insurance authorities had advised that expelling a scabbing member who had paid his dues was unlikely to be allowed by the courts. Bedacht, though, said it was permissible "to place him on trial . . . and to fine him a maximum of $99.99." In this way, he wrote, "the organization gets rid of the undesirable person, because these fines are never paid," and other members are educated "on the principles of the organization." In 1948 a woman was expelled from a Ukrainian lodge in Youngstown, Ohio, "for supplying information about workers to stool pigeons, etc." Strikebreakers were not the kind of members the IWO desired.[49]

While Democrats, Republicans, even Socialists, could be tolerated, sometimes followers of Leon Trotsky were beyond the pale, echoing Communists' failure to defend Trotskyists' civil rights. In 1932 the Socialist Workers Party's newspaper, *The Militant*, reported that a Chicago lodge had expelled three members for their sympathy toward the Trotskyists. When Comrade S. Solomon asked for a reason, he was told, "You expelled yourself." The chairman said that "he personally [would] use everything possible to see that these three comrades should not be reinstated. . . . [T]hey were too critical of the Communist party and the Third International." Other lodge officers, however, defended the trio and called for their reinstatement, suggesting that not all early IWO members demanded ideological conformity. The three appealed to national headquarters, "condemn[ing] such action against comrades on principle as it narrows down the I.W.O. to a mere sect. We thoroughly understand and approve the necessity of the I.W.O. as a workers' fraternal organization based on the class struggle and recognize the principles of the Soviet Union," they wrote, but argued that if the IWO were "to fulfill its historic mission it must be of a broad mass character and must govern itself by the principle of democratic centralism. All forms of bureaucracy must be ruthlessly put down." The Chicago squabbles indicate that while some IWO officials sought conformity, other members conceived that if the organization was to succeed, it had to be organized on a broader, left-wing basis.[50]

In 1931 *The Militant* also reported on "the lengths to which the Stalinist bureaucracy will go in order to prevent workers from discussing the vital problems of the revolutionary movement" within a Chicago lodge. Sam Hammersmark, "the Stalinist watch-dog in the branch," was derided for getting the John Reed Branch of the IWO to vote down a proposal to allow Hugo Oehler of the Left Opposition to speak on Moscow's five-year plan. In Worcester, Massachusetts, the Party's Central Control Commission recommended that the secretary of a Russian lodge be exposed as a "purveyor of Trotskyite poison in the working-class movement." A head of a Hungarian lodge and singing society was likewise "recommended for exposure in [the] *Daily Worker* as a self-seeker, who allied himself with the Trotskyite counter-revolutionists and who stole organization funds."[51]

The prosaic charge of misusing funds was a frequent lament in nonideological immigrant societies, too. But while such cases suggest that some ideological conformity was expected from officeholders, grassroots Russian and Hungarian members evidently did not care or know about lodge members' Trotskyism and elected their secretary on the basis of other considerations. The IWO was bigger and broader than the factional fights preoccupying national Party leaders.

The "Most Important Effort": African American Organizing

While Walker argues that the IWO was always limited in its appeal beyond New York and remained an overwhelmingly Jewish organization, IWO records indicate that it was reaching out to many other ethnic and racial groups across America from its founding.[52] Already in 1934 African American Communist Thompson was organizing black as well as white sharecroppers into IWO lodges in Alabama, Georgia, Louisiana, Tennessee, and other parts of the South. The interracial sharecroppers' lodges were hailed as "an excellent thing, a real achievement for the Order." As a black woman engaged in interracial organizing, Thompson faced enormous difficulties, even dangers. She reported to Bedacht that Atlanta authorities "raided the homes of our IWO comrades, and stated that the IWO would have to go also." Atlanta police were sure "Eureka," the name of an IWO lodge, was actually a secret red password. The "fascist gang" scared some black members into quitting the IWO, and Thompson herself was jailed in a raid on a Birmingham union meeting while helping start lodges there. She was perturbed when the Communist press publicized her imprisonment, as she believed this would make her organizing more difficult. Thompson was interrogated in Birmingham by the infamous Eugene "Bull" Connor, but her case was later dropped. Despite these hurdles, she sent in frequent reports of newly established adult and youth branches among black Southerners. "I think that this branch will grow very nicely," she wrote of one Alabama lodge. There, she had some success organizing black people who had formerly been in the black nationalist Universal Negro Improvement Association (UNIA) until becoming disillusioned with the Garveyite movement. This correspondence suggests that the IWO often drew on organic counterracist traditions within the communities to which it reached out and that even in Alabama it did not have to hide its militant working-class, interracialist light under a bushel. Still, in some states the IWO faced legal hurdles. Although lodges of black members were established in Norfolk and elsewhere in Virginia, the Order was denied an insurance license by the state since it did not adhere to the requirement that benefit societies be racially segregated.[53]

Nevertheless, in the 1930s the IWO continued to stress "work among the Negro masses is a most important effort," preparing "special propaganda folders" to help organizers enroll black members. Lodges in Richmond, Portsmouth, Norfolk, and New Orleans were cited as proof of the success in reaching black people, "the most exploited masses of American workers." Thompson, for one, was sold on the Order, reflecting decades later with some bemusement that she appreciated that on her tours black and white miners and other workers were, in 1934, willing to accept leadership from a black woman. Thompson was gratified in "seeing their not only willingness but eagerness to accept leadership from a Negro woman." When she relocated to Harlem, Thompson was again glad support for her leadership from Jewish and Slavic comrades was not just rhetorical. "These people weren't only talking about unity, they were practicing it." In Alabama, too, Thompson won adherents for the Order when she persuaded miners' wives to support a strike. Miners told Thompson, "If you will help us win this strike by winning our women for the strike, we will promise to put the IWO over the mountain when we get back to work." Thompson later in the decade reached out to Hungarian and Czech miners and steelworkers. In these campaigns she promised women that as wives of workers, the IWO and the CIO would benefit them, too. Elsewhere in the country such as Chicago, where Thompson Patterson relocated with her husband, CRC president William Patterson, she noted that black and Ukrainian women were the mainstays of interracial lodges such as the South Side's Du Sable Lodge. Thompson would later become an IWO national vice president.[54]

The IWO's social program is explored more fully in Chapter 2. Here it should be noted, though, that there was something masculinist about the IWO approaching women recruits as wives first and not as wage earners in their own right or neglecting to appeal to them on their own economic or other needs. Nevertheless, Czech and Hungarian men and women following an African American woman into the Order was a groundbreaking achievement in Jim Crow America. Many women and men were receptive to Thompson's message in steel or coal towns such as Rankin and Homestead, Pennsylvania, for as Thompson noted, "where the young people of Homestead had only the bar and poolroom as places to gather, the IWO became the logical center for healthy cultural experience." In many such places the

IWO hall became an affective center of solidarity, for "the social life in many company towns had been the saloon on the corner until we organized IWO centers." The company town's grip was broken, or at least loosened, by the arrival of the IWO.[55]

Other black people, Thompson recalled, appreciated the Order's nondiscriminatory insurance. Commercial carriers offered substandard coverage to blacks at extremely higher premiums. The IWO later publicized the findings of the New York Legislature: "Negroes in Harlem are paying 208% more on their insurance policies and 372% more on cash surrender values than white persons." Thompson recalled the appreciation Southern black people had for the IWO as an antidote to "white insurance agents weaving their way through the black community. . . . Standing there in all their arrogance and white supremacy and collecting the nickels, dimes and quarters or fifty-cent pieces from black folk that netted them a policy anywhere from $100–150." Thompson appreciated the IWO because "there was a cultural program, but from a practical side, and being a very practical minded person myself, this organization had something to offer." After being hired by the Order, "in a very short time" Thompson "was out in the field seeking to bring into this International body, my own people." In 1934 providing affordable quality insurance protection to black workers was in and of itself a revolutionary concept.[56]

A "Patient and Persistent" Campaign: Making the Case to the Workers

Early reports on the progress of the IWO stressed the importance of recruiting efforts among Mexican workers, "Negroes," Chinese and Japanese workers, as well as young people, who, it was hoped, could be recruited from IWO youth branches into the Young Communist League (YCL) and Young Pioneers. The importance of reaching second-generation ethnic Americans was recognized, too, for it was noted that many younger workers would have difficulty attending lodge meetings conducted in Slovak, Magyar, and other languages of their parents. English-language lodges were created for these workers.[57]

Moreover, amalgamation with other, non-Jewish ethnic benefit societies was achieved through persuasion, not coercion. Fraternal members were reached via newspaper editorials, traveling lecturers, and debates in national fraternal society conventions. These methods were deployed to convince people of the advantages of uniting in a larger multiethnic and multiracial IWO. The IWO's creators stressed the need to persuade fraternalists of the advantages of amalgamating into the multiethnic IWO, appealing and tailoring lodges to the material needs of potential members. At meetings in

September 1930, the necessity of publishing editorials and articles in foreign-language papers arguing for the benefits of amalgamation was stressed. The main points of these editorials were to be "the struggle for unemployment, accident, sick, and old age insurance and death benefit on the line of the Party's Social Insurance policy." Every foreign-language bureau was also to send organizers "to visit all the fractions and branches to win them over for the amalgamation."[58]

The Language Department argued that workers had to be convinced via slogans such as "unite to fight for full insurance for the entire working class." This campaign had to proceed "without mechanically speeding and enforcing the amalgamation." The department further stressed that new IWO lodges "must be organized in the form as the workers desire to have them." Workers' own interests and agendas had to be addressed if the Order was to get off the ground. Organizers and editorialists were advised to deploy "facts to prove to masses, that amalgamation is in their interest, as well [as] working-class interest." This process of convincing potential members could sometimes be frustrating, and in the department's view only the Yugoslav Party press was devoting enough attention to the amalgamation campaign in the fall of 1930.[59]

In many early IWO lodges, Party members were already outnumbered by non-Marxists who joined for strictly instrumental reasons. At the IWO's first convention, Philadelphia's twenty-five-person delegation did not include a single Party member, and minimal Party membership in the Russian and Slovak societies was cause for alarm. In 1933 Hungarian Bureau secretary Gardos noted the success of Hungarian IWO lodges in Detroit in enrolling black members, Spanish miners in Whitman, West Virginia, and "building branches of all nationalities" in Logan Valley, West Virginia, but lamented that in many large IWO lodges there was not a single Party member. Only with great difficulty were members in Trenton, New Jersey, composed mostly of "church people," prevented from sending delegates to a Democratic Party victory celebration. Despite its founders' aspirations, the IWO quickly became a mixture of ideological members and those less convinced of the Communist cause. In later years many members asserted that it was the necessity of finding affordable insurance that attracted them to the IWO, confirming the Party's assessment of the situation in the early 1930s.[60]

Builders of the Order hoped that the severity of the Depression could sway workers of the need for a united, multiethnic fraternal society. In January 1931 the Language Department announced a plan issued in its report "Building of the Working Class Mutual Aid Organizations." Increasing "Americanization" of various immigrant groups, the report's author argued, enabled unity of action to overcome common problems. "This process of unification of the ranks of the different foreign language speaking groups," the report said, "is especially hastened as a result of the crisis, by the need for

[a] unified struggle for bread and butter." The depth of workers' suffering was not ameliorated by the existing ethnic fraternal societies, which had invested their treasuries in commercial real estate, banks, and other capitalist ventures, and thus been drained of assets just at the time when working-class members needed help most. The IWO, a working-class mutual benefit society, was held up as the salvation of the workers, for only in such an organization "can they draw the full benefit made possible by the mutual aid organizations controlled by the workers themselves and struggle jointly with the rest of the working class for full social insurance." With the Depression lengthening, the IWO appealed to workers' self-interest in pushing amalgamation.[61]

The January 1931 report focused primarily on efforts to amalgamate the Jewish members of the IWO with the "Hungarian, Slovak and Russian Mutual Aid Organizations," but the importance of organizing branches for the "millions of Mexican workers" was stressed, too, anticipating the interracial, multiethnic structure the Order assumed. Already in November 1930 a Los Angeles organizer was setting up Japanese and "Spanish" lodges. By the late 1930s, eleven language branches existed within the IWO, and the Order's monthly magazine printed articles in Polish, Slovak, Ukrainian, Carpatho-Russian, Russian, Croatian, Romanian, Yiddish, Italian, and Spanish as well as English to reach its multiethnic members. The virtues of amalgamation, the 1931 report argued, could be achieved "without mechanically forcing the amalgamation" by working through ethnic fraternal organizations and "carry[ing] through this joining when the majority of the membership is really convinced that this is in their interest."[62]

Ethnic groups were granted "full language autonomy," with "the form of the local organization . . . decided upon by the members themselves." Immigrants from the same ethnic group were to be afforded their Polish, Slovak, and Hungarian lodges, but English-language lodges were encouraged for reaching second-generation white ethnics as well as potential African American members. James Ford, the Party's African American vice-presidential candidate in 1932, reported on the IWO's success in organizing English-language lodges for black and white members, particularly highlighting the IWO's success in reaching three hundred members in Harlem. Provision was also made for IWO branches "according to the place of work," or "according to the trade." In New York lodges for longshoremen were established as well as Teamster branches. Ford also presented a plan in 1932 to bring the IWO to the railroad workers of Detroit, expressing optimism that the Order's superior benefit package would win over this group. By 1935 the Order's Buffalo organizers reported on efforts to reach German, Polish, and Italian workers in their own language lodges, but they also established an English-language lodge for "Americanized" workers at Bethlehem Steel.

Workers' own organizational preferences were given wide latitude. A multiethnic framework was flexible enough to allow affiliation based on occupational status or in interracial English-language lodges, too.[63]

Organizing efforts within the SWS demonstrate the manner in which ethnic workers were convinced to amalgamate. Prior to the national convention of the SWS, whose delegates were to vote on whether to amalgamate, meetings were scheduled between the city committees of IWO and SWS lodges, and Czech and Slovak factions in New York and Newark "in order to explain the task before the comrades concerning the amalgamation program." Proponents of amalgamation anticipated the opposition of some members. The Language Department's Amalgamation Sub-Committee issued a pamphlet in English "containing questions and answers regarding the problem of the amalgamation." The SWS newspaper *Rovnosť ľudu* "shall immediately translate, print, and publish it in two or three issues of the paper. The different mutual organizations shall print this pamphlet in their own language." While the pamphlet was being prepared, Saltzman made a speaking tour to Pittsburgh, Cleveland, and Chicago "to take up with the Jewish, Slovak, Hungarian and Russian comrades the problem of amalgamation." In addition, an outline was prepared "containing answers to the arguments opposing the amalgamation" to assist organizers in swaying members in favor of the IWO. Articles were to be written by both Party and nonparty members in places where SWS lodges had reservations.[64]

Some of the speaking tours delivered dispiriting results. Comrade Tuhy reported of his talks at SWS lodges, "Among miners too much drinking. The Branches work very little, on many places not at all." Although Tuhy was criticized for his excessively bleak outlook, it was thought advisable to send Comrade John Zuskár to an SWS convention in Charleroi, Pennsylvania, to counter opposition to amalgamation. Zuskár evidently was an effective advocate, for "although there was only one Party member on the Conference," his motions for amalgamation prevailed.[65]

When some Slovaks still balked at accepting amalgamation, the "unclarity" of arguments put forth by IWO proponents was faulted. The Language Department told Gebert that among the Slovaks it was not just opposition from members that impeded amalgamation, but that "the whole problem was discussed only at the top . . . and no real measures were taken to propagandize the members of the organizations through convincing arguments." SWS members were urged "to go down to the branches and to the individual workers who are opposed to the amalgamation and bring convincing arguments to them. They must understand that the campaign for amalgamation must be a patient and persistent one which will convince the members of the organizations." To ensure "unclarity" did not persist, a committee was tasked with bringing examples of all the arguments of workers opposing amalgamation "and to work out in detail all the answers which will clarify the workers on all technical problems that are being brought forward." The necessity of translating an English pamphlet explaining the wisdom of joining the IWO was raised.[66]

Rovnosť ludu was faulted for refusing to print letters from SWS members opposed to amalgamation. The editor was told to answer such objections "in a clear and convincing manner and not in an aggressive tone." It was recommended that he devote "a special column for discussion on this subject in which the correspondence and articles of those workers opposing the amalgamation shall be printed and of course the articles that are answering them also." Order leaders invited opponents to submit articles to Party journals, using a democratic forum to win converts rather than authoritarian control, which allegedly permeated all Communist-initiated organizations in 1931.[67]

At other moments Slovaks were chastised for not doing enough for the cause of amalgamation and for not working in concert with Hungarian and other ethnic groups. This was regarded as a particular shame, for the IWO had already established a dental clinic by July 1931, with a full-scale medical clinic on the horizon. If Slovaks recruited more proponents of amalgamation "it is clear that here also there are big possibilities for medical assistance of the members." Revolution may have been the ultimate goal, but appeals to the tangible benefits of dental clinics and affordable medical care would be the tools to reach the blue-collar masses.[68]

In arguing for the IWO, other fraternalists were advised to discuss the plight of the tens of thousands of unemployed workers whom the IWO could help. The real selling points were that "a united fraternal organization would be in a position to give to the workers more benefits with no extra payment. We would also be in a position to organize medical centers, sanitarium and other important features in the fraternal field." A united left-wing "mass fraternal movement would be in a position to carry on an intensive campaign to insure the workers at the expense of the government."[69]

The advantages of mass lobbying for relief from Depression-era ravages likely proved attractive to thousands of people with nothing but sick pay from near-destitute fraternal societies on which to rely. While later scrutinizers of Communist influence in the IWO would highlight organizers' rhetoric of "the revolutionary labor movement," they would ignore the degree to which organizers focused on convincing and persuading members of the wisdom of uniting in such left-wing societies. To be sure, the campaign to win ethnic fraternal societies was well coordinated and planned, with leaflets setting out the arguments in favor of the IWO translated and run verbatim in various foreign-language Party papers. Red-hunters cast this as evidence of a Kremlin-led conspiracy. But it can just as easily be interpreted as a sophisticated lobbying campaign on behalf of a cause that members themselves found worthy.[70]

"I Would Grind Him to Dust": Independent Leftists

It was necessary to appeal to workers' self-interest and persuade them of the IWO's virtues, for left-wing immigrants frequently balked at control from above. Members of Communist foreign-language branches exercised willful independence, talking back to supposed Party superiors when they believed they were wrong. Among left-wing Jewish workers, the ethnic community and its concerns were often of more central concern than the agendas and pronouncements of the Party's leadership. Jewish members from New York infuriated Party leadership by even writing to Stalin questioning Moscow's policies.[71]

"Red" Finns also were committed to autonomy, even if they supported world communism, and retained tight control of Finnish Workers' Clubs, cooperatives, and their newspaper, *Tyomies*. Radical Finns prizing autonomy resisted amalgamation of their benefit societies into the IWO until 1940. Jewish and Finnish comrades caused headaches for the Party's central leadership when they refused to turn over control of their children's camps to the Party's Young Pioneers. Party leaders in Minnesota and Michigan reported that they hoped to raise funds for *Daily Worker* subscriptions through Finnish festivals, but the red Finns refused to donate. In Hancock, Michigan, workers expressed "passive resistance" toward plans for an open-air demonstration they considered ill-advised. In Superior, Wisconsin, members of the left-wing Finnish Club voted 61–2 to bar use of their facilities to those siding with the Party in its attempt to control *Tyomies*. At the paper, editorial staff went on strike rather than accept the firing of a nonconformist employee.[72]

Comrades likewise objected when the Party directed them to put up their Lithuanian hall as collateral to bail a colleague out of jail, while "four party members also spoke and voted against the decision of the party." They asserted that "the party had no right or authority to control the paper as far as its business is concerned." Comrade J. Buivydas, one of the majority opposing Party instructions, went even further. "I would have spoken against this motion even if Comrade Stalin himself was there. The party wants to destroy our institution as it has already destroyed many of them. The party wants too much control." Buivydas's independence was not punished. At the following meeting he was nominated by the Lithuanian Bureau secretary as one of the comrades recommended for study at the Moscow University for Western Minorities, even after refusing to carry out Party orders.[73]

In 1932 members of the Bulgarian Workers' Mutual Benefit and Educational Society of Detroit wrote to the *Daily Worker* demanding that the Party reprimand Comrade Bocho Mircheff after he rudely commandeered the $18.75 they had raised to assist with the funerals of workers killed in the hunger march to Ford's River Rouge plant. "Why this took place?" the Bulgarians demanded in halting English. "In the organization is a private property?

Is Comrade Mircheff a dictator in Detroit?" If the Party did not act, the Bulgarians vowed to do everything they could to expose the "clique" of Mircheff and his allies. Cases such as these suggest ethnic comrades were not willing or required to don ideological strait jackets.[74]

This stubborn independence continued throughout the IWO's life. In 1950 a Baltimore member of the Garibaldi Society reported to his national secretary, objecting to a call for participation in a national conference of the CRC, "These are matters that don't concern us; those four blockheads who are in New York do it simply for propaganda, and to protect the policies of that beggar Stalin who is trying to conquer other peoples and to enslave them, just as he has already enslaved his own entire people. . . . [I]f I could get him in my hands, I would grind him to dust." Evidently, many Baltimore Italians in the IWO were no fans of world communism's leader, nor did they have any problem mocking or dismissing the Order's national leadership when they disagreed with its agenda.[75]

Officials of the IWO often recognized their membership was a sometimes unwieldy combination of left-wing believers and more apolitical or even conservative members. Gebert discussed some of the difficulties in building the IWO's Polish American Section, which he said many conservatives had joined simply as a cheaper form of life insurance. During World War II, Gebert worried that many Polish lodges had reactionary majorities more sympathetic to the conservative London Polish government in exile than to the social-democratic foreign and domestic goals of the Order. Conversely, Bedacht had to remind Croatians that it was necessary during wartime to work with more moderate political strains within the IWO in order to maximize the allied effort. From the Left and Right, opinionated IWO members talked back and caused problems for their leaders.[76]

On other occasions, even when IWO members were more sympathetic to Party leadership, they did not hesitate to question specific policies they considered ill-advised. In 1932 Gardos of the Hungarian Bureau objected to attempts of Party members to intervene and influence votes at the IWO's national convention. Gardos submitted "a sharp protest against the leading committee at the I.W.O. convention because of . . . the irresponsible and bureaucratic practices they followed." The delegates had voted to allow the democratic election of the Order's language section secretaries, as well as to allow "housewifes" to join and be eligible for a lower $4 weekly sick benefit, only to have a Party member overrule the convention's majority vote on both issues. Gardos demanded that the matters be put to a referendum of all Hungarian IWO members, warning "if things will remain as steam-rolled through, we are going to lose much more than the dollars. I am sure that after all those beautiful talks about democracy, . . . the leading comrades in the I.W.O. will understand this."[77]

Such heavy-handed interference, Gardos said, would serve "maybe more than the very artificial throwing in of the Scottsboro boys to 'cool off' people," suggesting not every member was sympathetic to the Order's early support for black civil rights. The main criticism, though, was directed at the Party's suborning of democracy within the Order. Gardos called this "another link of that heavy chain around the neck of the Party. We have had too much of this irresponsibility from the top, too much of this bureaucratic handling of comrades like pawns on a chess-board, too much music to be faced by us, lower functionaries, because the conductors . . . do not practice what they talk." He warned, "Unless there is going to be a change . . . on the top, our work is going to suffer tremendously."[78] Problems with democratic centralism arose almost immediately, but just as quickly, members pushed back to defend grassroots democracy.

In 1935 Luigi Candela, president of the Order's Italian Society, likewise appealed to Browder when he disagreed with the majority decision of the Italian Bureau. "I feel that if I don't appeal I would be committing a crime against our movement," he wrote. "The decision of the majority did not convince me that I am wrong." Candela objected to making the focus of a proposed national Italian Congress unemployment insurance, believing the main topic should be opposition to Benito Mussolini's war in Abyssinia. He argued that an antiwar focus would "develop and strengthen our united front of Italian and Negro workers in this country."[79] While the IWO devoted a great deal of energy to both social-policy and antifascist lobbying, the point remains that Order officials, even those in the Party, were not shy in speaking back to the powerful when the majority did not convince them they were wrong.

African American members of the IWO also exhibited independence, which sometimes got them in trouble with national officers. In 1945 Harlem Solidarity Lodge 691 sought and received headquarters' permission to expel Charles Stevenson because during a meeting he "had associated our leaders with the worst reactionaries in the country." The charge stemmed from a eulogy of Roosevelt that Stevenson had delivered. In appealing his expulsion, Stevenson admitted that he had criticized "the peculiarly obstructive role which Brothers Bedacht, [William] Weiner, . . . and certain other groups played in one of the most dangerous crises in the history of our country and of the world." He referred to opposition by the Order's leaders to Lend-Lease and the National Service Act in 1940–1941, adding, "At that time so fraught with peril for our country, these groups popularly used the presumptuous slogan, 'The Yanks are not coming.'" He asserted, "The attitude of these leaders . . . caused many a defection from the progressive and so-called left-wing movement. The remarks might have been unpleasant to hear—and perhaps, even indiscreet, but are nevertheless true."[80]

The abrupt turn to an antiwar position following adoption of the Soviet-German Nonaggression Pact in August 1939 was indeed cause for great dismay among many leftists. While most Party members fell in line with the new position rejecting aid to Great Britain in an imperialist war, others saw this as evidence of a Party cynically manipulated to serve the interests of Moscow. In any case, though, this abrupt change in the Party's position did not go unchallenged within the IWO, as Chapter 5 shows at greater length.[81]

Stevenson defended his right to free speech as outlined in the Bill of Rights, suggesting that by 1945 Order members had inculcated Popular Front Americanism as well as left-wing militancy. While Stevenson praised the "magnificent accomplishments of the progressive movement, including the International Workers Order, during the 1930's," he stood by his right to dissent. He cited leaders of the Order who in other contexts had defended constitutional free speech rights and wanted to know "what is wrong about a dissenting member of an organization subject to the laws of the land, making statements of fact and criticisms of the leadership of said organization." Stevenson pointed out that he had not "taken some oath or obligation as a member of some ultra political or other group, thus surrendering to them the power over my person and beliefs. I owe allegiance only to America in the support and maintenance of my human rights." Similar homages to the Bill of Rights would be deployed by the IWO during its castigation by the attorney general as subversive.[82] Stevenson's private letters to his lodge mates and Order executives suggest this fealty to American principles was heartfelt, not calculated.

Stevenson was also charged with frequently "attempting to show that the leadership of the Order does not have the interest of . . . the people of this community at large," suggesting that for all the Order's ostensible commitment to interracialism, tensions remained between some African American members and national leaders. In the Harlem lodge, it seems, Stevenson was not alone in finding fault with leaders, for Solidarity Lodge's officers wrote to their membership charging his "continued defiance of the chair" caused other members to act similarly. The case of Solidarity Lodge suggests that the Order contained many shades of progressivism not always in accord with the opinions of the national leadership.[83]

"It Protects the Worker as an Individual": Growth of the Order

The pro-IWO message proved convincing. Already in 1930 more than twelve thousand members were enrolled. Although eleven thousand of these members were Jewish, and the need to expand into a truly international organization was emphasized, the presence of twenty-four English-speaking youth branches as well as Italian, Ukrainian, Polish, Greek, Romanian, Armenian, German, Latvian, and Spanish lodges was held as a promising sign. The amalgamation with the Hungarian Workers' Sick Benefit and Educational

Federation and coming mergers with Slovak and Russian societies were expected to boost the IWO's membership past thirty thousand. A "hindrance" to the Order's growth, however, was "the too frequent collection of money," which kept members from attending meetings.[84]

In this regard the IWO's problems echoed the language branches of the Party. In 1935 Anthony Bimba, an organizer for the Lithuanian Bureau, complained, "Unless this avalanche of all sorts of letters, instructions, tickets and 'mobilizations' is stopped, all our talk of retaining members in the party will be in vain. Don't you see that? Can't you see that?" The constant "peddling of all kinds" at meetings was driving new members away. Within the IWO, members balked, too, at frequent collections for the *Daily Worker* and other causes, with one member saying he was not a ticket agency. This reaction is another indicator that many members joined for the sick benefits and not necessarily the working-class militancy the IWO hoped to cultivate.[85]

With the IWO striving to keep collections to a minimum, the Order began to grow. Saltzman, secretary of the JPFO, noted that the Order had enlisted Portuguese, Mexican, Greek, Ukrainian, and other language branches and would have grown even faster in its first year but many indigent workers could not afford the dollar for a medical examination or keep current in their dues, and the Order was not yet in a position to assist needy recruits. Nevertheless, Saltzman noted that the establishment of medical departments, dental clinics, and specialists departments in Chicago, Philadelphia, and New York, as well as eighty schools in which six thousand children were given a "working-class revolutionary education," drew new members. As reference to revolutionary education suggests, the Order was conceived as "an important part of the revolutionary working class movement."[86]

The IWO made a concerted effort to reach out to an interracial constituency, a revolutionary course in the 1930s. Most benefit societies remained racially segregated, and private insurance companies charged African Americans inordinately higher rates for inferior coverage. "When I found out the IWO gave cheaper insurance to the Negro people without discrimination," a black member from Jersey City attested, "I became a builder of the IWO," a sentiment other black members echoed. As a result, African American newspapers such as the *Baltimore Afro-American* and *Chicago Defender* gave extensive, favorable coverage to the IWO's campaigns to enroll black people on an equal footing. The IWO was "insurance against Jim Crow," Sam Roberts of the National Education Department told the *Afro-American*, linking the favorable coverage afforded black members to the Order's extensive lobbying and activism to defeat racial segregation.[87]

Unlike commercial carriers and other benefit societies, as early as 1931 the IWO stressed the need to enroll black members in English-language lodges, also recruiting Spanish-speaking workers such as Mexicans and Puerto Ricans in their own branches. Japanese, Chinese, Cape Verdean,

Brazilian Portuguese, Greek, and Arab-speaking workers were also enlisted. Black small businessmen in Portsmouth and Norfolk, Virginia, were recruited into interracial English-language lodges, while the national secretary of the Hispanic Cervantes Fraternal Society near the end of World War II reported, "We have organized several fraternal schools, some with over twenty lectures given by prominent people. We organized the only school to train Puerto Rican and Spanish speaking women to work in ladies auxiliary of our order. Some of them today are prominent in trade union, civilian defense and other civic work." Portuguese and Cape Verdeans sat together in IWO workers' clubs in New England.[88]

Frank Gevize, a Syrian man living in Detroit, wrote the IWO with plans to organize among the forty thousand Arabic speakers in his city. General Director of Organization Sam Milgrom wrote back telling Gevize that his lodge "could conduct its meetings in either Arabic or English depending on the wishes of the members." As part of its voluminous file on the IWO's Detroit Section, the FBI confirmed that an Arabic lodge was functioning by December 1945. Cubans in the Ybor City neighborhood of Tampa also established a lodge.[89]

As Chapter 3 more fully explores, efforts to build an interracial civil rights program within the Order were not without "white chauvinist" hurdles. Nevertheless, these efforts were often appreciated, as when a Black Muslim from New Haven wrote the Order detailing the discrimination he faced from private insurance companies and sought guidance in establishing an African American IWO lodge. While the IWO endorsed his plan, he felt his efforts were not given enough financial support. The Order's limited resources were explained to him, but some tension remained. Still, other Black Muslim teachers attested that the IWO was one of the few organizations in which they had experienced brotherhood and racial equality. The IWO was one of the only organizations in midcentury America with Black Muslim, Arabic, Hispanic, and white ethnic Catholic and Jewish members.[90]

The IWO grew to include sixteen nationality societies with, by 1947, 188,000 members.[91] "These different national societies are united not only to achieve the aims of better insurance, better sick benefits, and better medical aid," Saltzman said, in a summary that aptly captures the multiple interests of the IWO:

> They have also united to help labor improve its conditions, to integrate their own national cultures with the cultural life of our country, to fight against race prejudices and race discrimination, to defend the rights of minorities, to protect foreign born against persecution, to fight for the rights of the Negro people in our country, to fight to preserve the cherished traditions which the American Revolution has bequeathed to us, the traditions embodied in the Declaration of Independence and Bill of Rights.[92]

Until 1944 the Order had a centralized structure even though many lodges conducted meetings in Slovak, Italian, Yiddish, and the like. Near the end of World War II, however, the IWO adopted a plan granting greater autonomy to nationality societies. Some groups adopted new names reflecting ethnic pride. The Italian American IWO became the Garibaldi Society, Spanish lodges were rechristened the Cervantes Fraternal Society, and African American members founded the Douglass-Lincoln Society. An agent of the OSS tasked with keeping an eye on the Order speculated that this greater autonomy was a reflection of the CP's recent decision to disband and reformulate as the Communist Political Association, a lobbying group for progressive causes. Order officials reassured the agent, however, that the change to greater ethnic-group autonomy reflected the desire of the members, many of whom had experienced heightened ethnic pride as a result of the resistance fights in Yugoslavia, Poland, and elsewhere and predated the changes to the CP. It was hoped this would "transform each of the sections into 'a mass membership society' and the Order . . . into one of the largest and politically most effective in America."[93]

The agent noted that most IWO members accepted the reorganization, believing it would better allow members to satisfy communities' needs and tap into ethnic pride they were sure would continue growing after the war. State Senator Nowak of the Michigan IWO concurred, telling an OSS agent that the "revival of the nationalistic spirit" spurred by the war had to be channeled by the IWO. He believed that formerly, too much centralization left "no room for individual nationality sections or, for that matter, for individual initiative. . . . The central committee acted more as a political party than as a fraternal order. If anyone disagreed with their policy, they applied disciplinary measures. Now their aim is to place a greater responsibility on the shoulders of the leaders of different nationality groups."[94]

In alluding to "disciplinary measures," Nowak perhaps was thinking of events such as the Chicago expulsion of Trotskyites. He hoped more autonomy for groups such as the Polonia Society would make it more palatable to American workers. The society's Henry Podolski concurred that giving more decision-making authority to the nationality societies was actually the path to Americanization, expressing confidence that each nationality group would bring its second and third generations into the Order. The OSS agent reported, however, that other members had reservations, feeling America was on the path to unity and any move to ethnic particularism would be counterproductive.[95]

A few years later, a lodge president from Los Angeles put it more forcefully. In resigning his office, lawyer Jack Greenhill argued,

> Discrimination is discrimination, no matter how it is disseminated, whether in the form of a cudgel or in sugar coated pellets; it is discrimination just the same. To disjoin or to encourage our members

or anyone to split into Jewish, Slav, Croatian, Negro or what-not is aiding and abetting discrimination, our enemy. For the I.W.O., after years of unity . . . to advocate national or sectional groups by color, race or creed, shows a flare toward atavism and it can only result in the opposite of what we have struggled for.[96]

He insisted, "We must go back to our first principles—the achievement of universal cooperation—and not lose ourselves in mere factional mumblings." Although the JPFO tried to persuade Greenhill that "the national group orientation . . . will make our best contribution to the 'one world' concept and to the Brotherhood of Man," he remained adamant. "Minorities, as we have them, are the fruits of oppression from ignorance," Greenhill argued. "To perpetuate minorities in any form, in any group, under any name, will and must tend to preserve the minority evil." He characterized ethnic particularism as "the mole which undermines solidarity and . . . foreign to the I.W.O. that I joined and trust in."[97]

Another problem the Order confronted was the difficulty in reaching second-generation members, and in this regard the move to a greater emphasis on autonomous nationality societies may have been counterproductive. Already in 1941 Executive Secretary Herbert Benjamin lamented, "Most of our nationality group leaders will not or cannot conduct business in English, even though 40% of new members are now native born." In 1945 the Polonia Society's Gebert told OSS agents that his society had lost members over the last year. He noted that Polish benefit societies were losing membership due to their emphasis on "Polish-speaking elements," but only a quarter of Polish Americans knew the language, and "Americanized or second-generation Polish-Americans are not attracted by those organizations." Gebert still felt his society was in a better position to grow since it would pull in members from labor unions.[98]

The Order's move to a greater emphasis on nationality group organizations, though, ran counter to the tides of assimilation, or at least acculturation, by American-born white ethnics. General Secretary Bedacht recognized the problem, stressing in 1946 that it was imperative to attract younger, American-born members, either to nationality sections or English-language lodges. In 1947 the SWS likewise reported on meetings with American-born members to build English-speaking lodges, but these efforts met with little success. In the 1940s, with an increasingly native-born workforce no longer as completely reliant on fraternal-society benefits after the coming of Social Security and other New Deal reforms, the IWO, like many ethnic fraternal societies, faced challenges to its growth that it found difficult to solve.[99]

Problems of reaching the second generation did not preclude more than 180,000 working men and women from joining the Order. For many the chief attraction was low-cost insurance and affordable medical care rarely available elsewhere in industrial America. The FBI and OSS both acknowledged the Order provided benefits and coverage at low cost to its members, with the FBI noting that the IWO began a 1941 membership drive by boasting "it protects the worker as an individual. It gives him funeral-insurance, sick-benefit, and medical care, all at a low cost." Gardos earlier stressed the Order's provision of free medical and hospital care for needy members. Larger cities such as New York, Detroit, and Philadelphia maintained medical clinics, which became the Order's chief selling point for many members. Nathan Shaffer of the New York committee acknowledged that in his city most members joined not for ideological reasons but because of "the general appeal we make, namely the benefits we offer to the workers in this country," benefits, he noted, "better and more attractive than most fraternal organizations." Shaffer reported on plans for organizing a day nursery and a medical consulting service, which he felt would attract working men and women. The New York Medical Department, with its Specialists Department, Dental Department, and arrangement with pharmacies for low-cost drugs for members, was a "well-paying source of revenue for the City Central Committee," suggesting Communist or not, Shaffer was attentive to the bottom line. At a time when many working-class people had no recourse for health care save underfunded public hospitals derided as "butcher shops," the provision of clinics proved attractive.[100]

By 1937 the New York Medical Department was "operating a Birth Control Center in the interests of the membership of IWO and all of their friends." Shaffer noted, "This Birth Control Center is one of the finest and best equipped in . . . New York," run by "an outstanding woman physician who has been associated for many years with the Margaret Sanger Clinic." The center kept night hours, too, "to accommodate the working woman who is in no position to come to the Center during working hours." In an era when disseminating birth control information was still criminalized as "pornography," the IWO was ahead of other medical facilities in providing working women with quality health care.[101]

Here the IWO was responding to the demands of militant women workers. Even in smaller cities radical women made access to birth control and better maternal health care central demands. In 1932 the South Slavic Women's Educational Club of Cudahy, Wisconsin, passed a "Resolution on Protection of Motherhood and Childhood." Declaring "information on birth control is being withheld from working-class mothers, by the capitalist government in order to guarantee a large labor supply for further exploitation," and "that women never can be socially and economically independent so long as they have to bear continually recurring pregnancies, nor have sufficient strength and enthusiasm to bring up a family as they should, and continue their work in industry," the South Slavic women demanded "reliable and non-injurious birth control information" as well as "maternity homes, vacations before and after childbirth, social insurance, and other measures protecting motherhood and childhood" and birth control for the working class. In 1936 Lithuanian Communists echoed calls for birth control access. African American organizer Thompson appealed to coal and steel town mothers in this vocabulary, too, selling the IWO to blacks and whites as a purveyor of a "healthy cultural experience" as well as medical clinics.[102]

Throughout the 1940s the IWO championed *Our Plan for Plenty*, which reminded workers, "Battleships will not ward off the attacks of destitution and old age." This plan advocated greater federal social programs but also reminded workers of the benefits of joining the IWO. The plan's relevance to African Americans was stressed in special brochures. Similarly, a 1949 advertisement in the *Sunday Worker* combined a promise to American Labor to keep fighting racial discrimination and reactionary foreign and domestic policies with an explanation of the insurance and health benefits the IWO provided. The Order's "low-cost insurance" offering "one low rate for all occupations (coal miner and shoe clerk pay same premium)" was an attractive offer at a time when many private insurers barred workers in hazardous industries from all but the most minimal coverage. Likewise, the absence of racial discrimination ("No Jim Crow in the IWO") was an atypical, attractive practice.[103]

The IWO also publicized the opening of "America's first interracial hospital," Harlem's Sydenham Hospital, and arranged screenings of a film narrated by José Ferrer, *The Sydenham Plan*, for New York lodge members. "It's a practical demonstration in democracy," the IWO said of interracial public health care facilities such as Sydenham. "This is the formula for a better America—This is the formula for a better world!" The delegates to the JPFO's 1944 convention heard Montana Senator James Murray, proponent of universal health care, declare, "Medical Care is one of the necessities of life which a democracy should provide to all members of the community." Members of the IWO were receptive to this message, but until such time as Congress saw fit to agree, they relied on IWO medical facilities to take care of their needs.[104]

Members pointed to insurance and medical benefits as features that caused them to join. Salvatore Spampinato attested that he and twenty-five other young Italian men from a New York social club with "no insurance benefits of any kind" affiliated with the IWO in 1936. He served as a member of the Order's Medical Board for New York, where he "had supervision over the doctors servicing the Order, and had authority to inquire into any grievance presented by any Brother or Sister, and add doctors to or take them off of the list, which authorized doctors servicing the Order." Another member proudly reported, "The Medical Plan provides a family physician to members at half his regular fee and in addition has many specialists—internists, heart, eye, etc., available at greatly reduced rates."[105]

African American members especially appreciated the affordable insurance as well as the interracial solidarity in an organization with "No Jim Crow in the IWO." The Reverend S. M. Harden of Chicago wrote to Milgrom telling him that the IWO's Du Sable Lodge had recruited the members of his church by addressing problems of "crowded schools, inadequate housing, improper health facilities." "Your battle for health and social security, your culture activities are indeed wonderful!!" Harden enthused. The reverend praised the "social and educational programs" of the Order but was particularly grateful that "the I.W.O. provides the greatest amount of insurance protection for the entire family, at the lowest possible cost. Security through insurance is something that my people have never known."[106]

Other African American members attested that they joined when each discovered, "I could obtain more reasonable rates and under an equal standing, without discrimination; I dropped the Metropolitan Life Insurance Company policy which I had carried because I learned that they pursued discriminatory practices against my people." James Moorer of Jersey City similarly praised the IWO for its affordable insurance, but beyond that he regarded it as "the one insurance company in America which does not have one rule for me, a Negro, and another rule for white members. The I.W.O. has proven to me that there are white people in America who really believe in democracy for all." Moorer might have been thinking of someone like the Italian immigrant Angelo Poggioni, who affirmed that "the principal appeal of the society . . . is the complete lack of discrimination in its treatment and dealing with the various nationality groups. Affiant . . . enjoys being a member of a society that treats all people as equals."[107]

Comprehensive medical clinics might not have been available outside of larger cities, but the dearth of quality, affordable care or insurance meant members from smaller towns turned to whatever services the local lodge provided as one of the few options available. In 1939 coal miner Vuko Draskovich of Alton, Illinois, sent long, vitriolic letters to the IWO describing his fifteen-year-long battle to get disability compensation from the "Big Shots Money Hungry and Dollar Patriotic forces." Draskovich's claims for injuries suffered in the mines and on a Works Progress Administration (WPA) job came to naught, but he thanked the IWO for providing him with sick benefits. So grateful was Draskovich he immediately sent his first $36 in benefits back to the IWO to aid the children of the executed Julius and Ethel Rosenberg, IWO members convicted of atomic espionage. In smaller towns the IWO was often the only source of affordable medical care, a service much appreciated by members.[108]

IWO leadership took the provision of benefits seriously. The booklet *Guiding Policy for the Communists in their Leadership and Work in the International Workers Order* stipulated provision of "effective fraternal insurance" was the first duty of the Order's leaders; only the delivery of an "effective immediate solution" to the problem of workers' lack of social security would win workers' allegiance. "An approach to the problems of leadership in the Order which makes it appear that the supplying of fraternal benefits ... is merely an excuse for the organization, and not its purpose, will shut the door of the organization to the broad mass." While hard-core Marxists sometimes derided the IWO as a mere insurance company—Thompson remembered such slights from her friends in the Party when she took a job with the IWO—other times it was recognized that the effective provision of benefits was the best way for the Order to be successful. By providing needed services to victims of industrial America, it was perhaps no wonder the IWO attracted tens of thousands. The organization served its membership when industrial employers and private insurance companies turned their backs.[109]

To be sure, the IWO's 1934 constitution spoke of a coming workers' state in which revolutionary provision of social security would finally be realized. But while in January 1934 Bedacht urged a New York IWO conference to "serve the memory of Lenin" and disseminate "a Leninist understanding of the tasks of our Order among all of our members," the Marxism of leaders soon collided with the pragmatism of local lodges and even national officials. In 1938 the IWO fended off an attempt by Massachusetts to deny a renewal of its insurance license. Counsel Joseph Brodsky warned, "Our organization, like Caesar's wife, must be above all suspicion." To ensure this was so, Brodsky recommended political literature or campaigns be kept at arm's length, and finances be impeccable. He argued, "We must realize that we are attacked because we are the organization that we are. . . . [W]e must learn to carry on in a manner least harmful to ourselves."[110]

This leavening of the overtly Marxist nature of the IWO may have reflected the CP's switch in 1935 to a Popular Front accommodation with progressive workers from an earlier ultra-militant "Third Period" strategy (which forecast an imminent workers' revolution in Depression-ridden America). Within the IWO itself, however, voices urging a less Marxist approach were plentiful. In reply to a 1941 request from headquarters for information on local branches, Jerome Koch of Petaluma, California, said in his lodge most members "have been recruited on [the] basis of need for insurance and have no interest in political activity." Koch argued that the hard-bore political line was counterproductive and that those who stressed Marx or Lenin at every turn "have lost touch with the very people they are trying to reach; they have forgotten how to play . . . in times like these. . . . Until we make up our minds to be one thing or the other we aren't going very far."[111]

Other members confirmed Koch's assessment. Antonio Carneiro of the Bronx said that the Portuguese members of his lodge only joined for the benefits and were not interested in progressive principles. In Youngstown, Ohio, "some members are more interested in gambling than culture," while in the Hungarian lodge of Milwaukee, "those people have joined only as a purpose of the insurance and not as a labor organization, they are not developed intellectually, so cannot and do not want to understand the meaning of explanation about the necessity of word (labor) which word they interpret and connect with communism." They needed "some new capable elements, of Hungarian heritage one that would be able to oppose our Hungarian (Aristocracy)." The respondent, however, did not see any such elements within the lodge's two hundred members. Meanwhile, K. Raisin of Norwich, Connecticut, bluntly told headquarters, "No active members in our lodge. All are petty bourgeois, interested only in making money."[112]

Headquarters might have wondered what had become of class consciousness, for many IWO members, from Petaluma to Norwich, were already chasing the American dream, or at least a modicum of working-class security, rather than a Marxist education. New Deal reforms such as Social Security and the Wagner Act, which, as Chapter 2 shows, the IWO was instrumental in securing, may have already been steering some members into the middle class and out of the Order.[113]

Officers, too, sometimes exhibited a tight-fisted guardianship of the treasury. When organizers requested the Order's help in paying for indigent African Americans' funerals, Bedacht was having none of it. "The International Workers Order does not conduct funerals," he wrote. "It has a contract with a funeral director who conducts its funerals. This contract calls for a definite price. The IWO cannot get any funeral below that price. Nor can it undertake to pay [for] the funeral for those who cannot pay that price." He said funerals could only be provided to IWO members who had paid for them, not all workers, adding, "We do not yet control the mint and print our own money." Rejecting the provision of free funerals, he concluded, "Certainly the IWO cannot undertake this obligation. The members of the IWO have enough to do to finance this obligation for themselves."[114]

Administrators of the Sick Benefit Department were likewise tight-fisted when needs exceeded resources. They denied a claim for a member as he had not been totally disabled for seven consecutive days and reminded another that he had been "granted a sick benefit option on the specific condition that he would not be entitled . . . for any disability due to a hernia or any condition directly connected with it." His claim was therefore denied. With only a limited treasury, the frugal Order's abstract sympathy for the working class did not prevent it from scrupulously denying claims.[115]

The Order's fiscal prudence was appreciated by an accountant member, though, who noted that it "restricted its investments to municipal, state and Government bonds . . . providing the best yield." The OSS, too, praised the "stability of their investment basis" that "offered real competition to not only other foreign-language group fraternals but also to the larger American insurance companies." Agents also spoke of the IWO as exhibiting a "dual personality," in which there was a "transitional recognition of American capitalism," but with "retention of ultimate socialistic intent and ideal." Of IWO leaders, an agent remarked, "They are equally vocal in the language of 'Americanism' and of 'socialism.' Which is their preferred tongue, I leave to others." The need to provide tangible benefits to members in a financially sound mutual society, plus commitment to the Popular Front, tilted much of the IWO's rhetoric toward "Americanism."[116]

The IWO was quite "American," too, for as in other fraternal societies, petty squabbles and financial irregularities disrupted lodges. Louis Singer of Brooklyn was accused of ignoring a debt to a lodge brother who loaned him $40 to get his carpentry business off the ground. Singer said he did not owe anything to the man, as he had done work on his antique chairs. Still, the IWO declared that he owed the money. When Singer ignored this decision, he was expelled from the Party and his lodge until he made good on the debt. Miner Bruno Jasczcak of Logan, West Virginia, was expelled as a "financially irresponsible and dishonest individual." "He collected initiations and dues from IWO members (about $85) and failed to turn them in to the IWO; he took $15 from an IWO branch to pay for funeral flowers, but never paid the bill; he ran up unpaid *Daily Worker* bills to the sum of $29.13." John Virag had to flee West Virginia after he arrived at a meeting excessively drunk and attacked a friend who had slept with his wife. When lodge brothers tried to separate them, Virag pulled a gun. The leader of the Ukrainian Section was likewise charged with drunkenness, sleeping with members' wives, and making anti-Semitic remarks. The full range of human foibles was on display in the Order, whatever its aspirations for working-class militancy.[117]

For all the peccadillos, what made the IWO exceptional was the depth of its commitment to agitating for better living standards and racial justice; provision of a full range of cultural, educational, and athletic activities; and advocacy of an anticolonial, peaceful foreign policy. As in any other organization, not every member participated in all the IWO's activities, but its activities on behalf of social justice and racial equality, I argue, are what caused the government to target it for prosecution, not supposed control by a foreign Communist conspiracy. The next four chapters take up the causes for which the IWO battled, beginning with its efforts to transform the workers' "economically insecure position in Capitalist Society."[118]

2

A "Plan for Plenty"

The IWO Tames Capitalism

From its onset the IWO envisioned itself as a militant lobbying group preparing the proletariat for a coming more social-democratic workers' state. As such, the Order lobbied for Social Security, enacted in 1935, and universal health care, still pending, among other programs. The Order also played an instrumental role in organizing industrial unions.[1]

In the depths of the Depression, with no relief from capitalist parties anywhere in sight, the Order did little to disguise its militancy. It was not hard to see where General Secretary Bedacht's ideological heart lay. A poster advertising two 1932 speeches by Bedacht on the IWO's aims was subtitled "The Chaos of Capitalism." The poster promised a stem-winding lecture by the German-born Communist on this topic. "Capitalism is in the deepest crisis in its history, the world over," the poster asserted.

> American capitalism, perhaps the most ruthless and brutal in the world, has thrown 10 million workers of all classes out of work. These millions of jobless workers, with 30 million dependents are without food and clothing. They are hungry. . . . [N]o less than 50 million human beings [are] on the verge of starvation in this, the richest country in the world. But there is food in abundance. The Five Year Plan of the Soviet Union, has no provision for destruction of foodstuffs which could be consumed by millions of hungry people. Only the capitalists are capable of such a crazy plan. But you must come and hear Max Bedacht on this subject.[2]

Such declarations made apparent the IWO's communist roots, but in 1932 it was hard to argue with Bedacht at the enormity of the free market's failure.

Fifty million starving humans in the depths of the Depression might plausibly have labeled the free market "chaotic."

Assertions that starvation had been overcome in 1930s Russia were overstated, to say the least.[3] Still, while the characterization of the Soviet Union in glowing terms was perhaps naïve, the IWO was not alone in praising Moscow in the early 1930s. American reformers such as Lincoln Steffens praised the country where "the future works," and even Henry Ford admired the five-year plans that seemingly vaulted the USSR into industrial preeminence at a time when most American factories stood idle.[4] The failings of President Hoover's free-market palliatives to solve the Depression gave Bedacht a sympathetic hearing.

Bedacht's lectures were in line with the Order's early declarations of principles, which spelled out the degree to which the IWO saw itself as engaging in a militant political program going beyond mere provision of sick benefits. While the IWO's campaigns laid out legislative strategies, not the violent subversion of the government, as J. Edgar Hoover, Congressman Martin Dies, and others soon alleged, the Order was unapologetically dismissive of capitalism's inadequacies, which in the early 1930s seemed all too apparent. "The I.W.O. recognizes that the need for mutual help to the workers grows out of their economically insecure position in Capitalist Society," its 1933 "Declaration of Principles" asserted. "Capitalism tells him, you must work if you want to live! But it does not guarantee him work. It refuses him work when he gets old. It does not guarantee him means of life when he is sick or disabled. In such cases it leaves him to beg, at the same time it declares begging morally degrading and legally impermissible."[5]

Asserting the crises of capitalism could not be overcome through self-financed accident and sickness policies, the Order's leaders countered,

> The workers must meet [the crises] by fighting for a full measure of Social Insurance such as the workers' political rule has established for itself in the Soviet Union. . . . They must meet it by fighting against unsanitary and unsafe working conditions in the mills, mines and factories. They must meet it by fighting for a condition in which the life and the welfare of the worker will be the guiding principles of government policies and not the profits of the capitalists as are now. Such a condition exists only under the political rule of the workers.[6]

An even more explicitly revolutionary appeal was made in a Yiddish "Declaration of Principles" published in the first edition of *The Spark*, the IWO's official magazine. "The International Workers Order follows the line of class struggle," readers learned. The Order, *The Spark* announced, "refuses to restrict itself to narrow domain of 'benefit' and 'cemetery.' . . . It declares itself to be an integral part of the proletarian class front against capitalism. It declares it to be the aim of the working class to overthrow the capitalistic order, and to establish a socialistic order in its place." The declaration added, "The I.W.O. recognizes that the road to the liberation of the working class leads through Sovietism."[7]

Again, the Marxist grounding of the IWO was not concealed. But so, too, in 1930 prosperity—or even adequate relief for the unemployed, homeless, aged, or sick—seemed nowhere near "just around the corner," to paraphrase Herbert Hoover's favorite Depression-curing nostrum. In a time of mass unemployment, proliferating Hoovervilles, and police suppression of workers' strikes, the IWO militantly advocated for substantive relief measures such as unemployment insurance, federal old age pensions, effective workmen's compensation, and industrial unions to aid working Americans. Rather than focus on the revolutionary rhetoric in early IWO declarations of principles, as anti-Communist investigators would do, a more accurate picture of the Order develops by examining the organization's actions in advocating more robust social programs to protect American workers. Many, although certainly not all, of the social programs they demanded were enacted during the New Deal, and it was the militant demands of men and women in the streets, thousands of IWO members among them, that forced the Social Security Act, Wagner Act, and other progressive measures onto the national agenda.[8]

The components of the IWO's social agenda that were not enacted are important to note, too. The organization envisioned a more wide-ranging, social-democratic economy, one that articulated a conception of social security that included universal health insurance, a guaranteed annual income, generously funded neighborhood health clinics, and the valorization of working people as creators of the nation's wealth. The IWO articulated this vision in its 1940s pamphlet, *Our Plan for Plenty*. This plan sought not just piecemeal protections but comprehensive security from free-market capitalism's ravages.[9] While much of the IWO's rhetoric and iconography valorizing working people fits squarely in a masculinist, left-wing tradition, the Order spoke to, and employed, African American and female workers as in a halting, mid-twentieth-century way the organization reached out to women and minority workers. The IWO prefigured, if it did not always perfectly achieve, intersectionality, and prefigured, too, the militant social-justice activists of the 1960s, 1970s, and beyond. Its message must have resonated, for at its height it enrolled 188,000 members in an interracial Order.

Hungry Workers Fed with "Jails and Bullets": The Fight for Social Insurance

Among the most urgent crises facing the country in the IWO's founding years was the mass unemployment to which Bedacht alluded, and the lack of "social insurance" for those discarded Americans. In many parts of industrial America, the Depression was only an exacerbation of the periodic downturns that had brought seasonal unemployment and lack of relief. Communist organizers had responded to these crises, as when they organized rallies in 1928 at Cleveland's Public Square featuring a Christmas tree with "garbage from the market place" for the unemployed ignored by city fathers.[10]

With the onset of the Depression, though, attention to the needs of the unemployed intensified. In October 1931 Bedacht took to the lecture circuit, appearing at the invitation of IWO Lodge 161 of Duluth, Minnesota, to speak on "The Capitalist Crisis and the Workers' Problems." Chief among these, according to the IWO's leader, was unemployment, which already affected "15,000 able bodied workers" in Duluth who, along with their families, faced starvation. Those lucky enough to still have a job faced "one wage cut after another," he asserted, before exhorting workers to organize as the only means of fighting for "cash relief for the unemployed workers." The following month Bedacht spoke in Buffalo on "Workers Mutual Aid and the World Economic Crisis." Ever since the crash, he said, workers' marginal existence had become even worse. He argued that the only solution was social insurance, to guarantee both income and health care in times of need. The IWO also urged workers to "support the National Hunger March to Washington" and "demand all war funds for unemployment insurance."[11]

From its inception the fight for legislation to alleviate the suffering of the unemployed was one of the main tenets of the Order, and for IWO "builders," a central recruiting tool in soliciting new members. As early as 1930 leaders demanded unemployment insurance paid for by the government, years before mainstream politicians embraced this goal. A 1932 draft program labeled the Order "a fighter for social insurance for the American working class," noting, "Never in the history have the workers of the United States had greater need for mutual help than now. The present economic crisis demands of the workers most categorically to organize mutual help among themselves. It demands . . . the establishment of Social Insurance." Although the draft also asserted, "Our International Workers Order must become a bridge for the American workers onto the battlefields after class struggle," the battle it envisioned was a union recruiting drive.[12]

Although in 1932 the IWO pledged to work to build up a revolutionary commitment among its members on the need for government unemployment insurance and old age pensions, the memorandum stressed, "The International Workers Order is a genuine organization whose actions are determined by the decisions of its own members." Party fractions operating within the IWO were also given guidelines: "These fractions must win the membership of the IWO for revolutionary policies but the fraction cannot force these policies upon the membership against their will." The IWO's memorandum argued, "Our task is not to dictate to these workers what to do; our task is to win them for our proposals."[13]

Since these memoranda were for internal dissemination by the CP's fractions in the IWO, it seems the emphasis on the need to persuade workers and take instruction from members on what policies they found most desirable was genuine. In the case of social insurance and the need to alleviate the problems of the unemployed, many workers were in agreement.

In the depths of the Depression, workers demanding relief were indeed shot by panicky police and soldiers, most famously at Anacostia Flats, Washington, when the Bonus Army of unemployed World War I veterans was repulsed by troops under Douglas MacArthur's command. In 1932 Hungarian branches of the IWO denounced the repression that greeted Unemployed Council demonstrations, asserting, "Hungry workers are fed with police clubs, jails and bullets." The Hungarians charged that "workers resisting wage cuts, are terrorized by hired thugs, police and the capitalist courts. Volleys are fired upon workers who ask for bread. But the problem of unemployment and mass misery cannot be solved by these methods." Discontent with the hollowness of free-market assurances of prosperity's return, and the police clubs greeting those who remained unconvinced, was growing.[14]

To mobilize its members behind demands for unemployment insurance, the Hungarian IWO pursued a policy of cooperating with fraternal societies under more "reactionary" leadership. Gardos of the Party's Hungarian Bureau reported that the IWO had fought for the "release of frozen funds in the bank" to aid unemployed people in Easton, Allentown, and Bethlehem, Pennsylvania, was organizing laid-off steelworkers and miners in a campaign to demand federal unemployment insurance, and was recruiting for this cause in Akron around the "Salvation Army Flop House." The IWO worked with other CP organizations such as the Trade Union Unity League and Unemployed Councils in various locales on campaigns for social insurance. On a national level, in January 1934 the Hungarian IWO took part in the Washington Conference on Social Insurance. Similar conferences were held for African American IWO members, and discrimination against foreign-born workers by relief agencies was decried.[15]

Early calls for a "united front" on social insurance suggest that the periodization of Communist cooperation with non-Marxist progressives as beginning only with the 1935 espousal of a Popular Front needs to be rethought. Even in 1930, Polish and Ukrainian IWO members were instructed to build a united front on a campaign for an unemployment and insurance bill. To be sure, this may have been only a tactic, and only palatable so long as Communists directed the movement. During the campaign Italians in the IWO cautioned against letting the "movement for social insurance . . . [fall] into the hands of the bourgeoisie." Perhaps to prove their bona fides, the Italians ended their meeting "by singing the 'International' and the 'Bandiera Rossa.'"[16]

Polish militants in the IWO were also at the forefront of mobilization to enact social insurance and worked with more conservative ethnic societies in the January 1934 Washington Conference on Social Insurance. Podolski, who would later be an official in the Polish Section of the IWO, noted that fifteen delegates from their Polish organizations had attended the conference and had managed to assemble other Polish organizations in support of a bill for federal social insurance. "These delegates authorized the Polish Chamber of Labor to act in their name in the struggle for social insurance," Podolski wrote. The chamber went further, introducing into the conference a resolution endorsing a "Right to Work Bill." Unlike similarly named bills designed to weaken labor unions, the Polish Chamber's bill made it a crime not to hire workers because of their race, religion, ethnicity, or political beliefs and contained provisions designed to give workers access to any livelihood for which they were qualified. The measure had been introduced into Congress after pressure from left-wing Polish groups, Podolski said. Philadelphia Poles busily organizing new IWO lodges were instructed to concentrate on lobbying for the social-insurance bill. He also urged them to work with more conservative organizations but not assume more mainstream groups would do all the work on behalf of unemployment insurance. Communists, within and outside of the IWO, did not seek to dominate campaigns for unemployment relief, but tried to work with larger Polish organizations on behalf of a worthy common purpose.[17]

Talk of revolution was mostly political, espousals of militant, nonviolent agitation. When blood was shed, it was mostly law-enforcement officers who deployed guns or clubs. In January 1931 an interracial unemployment demonstration was broken up by Chicago police officers, causing consternation for the Party when B. D. Amis answered "all right" to police demands that he name names of Party superiors. Hearings looked into whether Amis had breached security, but a comrade said it was understandable that Amis had responded the way he did: "I have seen Comrade Amis at our unemployed demonstrations. . . . I know he was in the thick of the fight and that a few times he was brutally beaten up; I have seen myself how the cops beat him. We must remember that in Chicago particularly the terror against the Negro workers is great."[18]

For a while it was feared that Amis, who had "received a beating almost up to the point of unconsciousness," would be rendered blind due to this police terror. Lieutenant Barker later threatened to take Amis and black organizer Harold Williams "for a ride." Under such circumstances, his defender felt it excusable that Amis had answered "all right" when police torturers demanded information.[19]

Anti-Communists argued that Stalin's terror was something people such as the Chicago Unemployed Councils should have known about. Perhaps they should have, though these activists were too busy dealing with homegrown terror of U.S. police torturers to look farther afield. Communists who advocated civil rights for black people in the early 1930s were particular targets of municipal torture, and in that era the word "terror" was explicitly deployed to refer to state-sanctioned violence against the left. Amis and other activists in the Unemployed Councils recognized the intertwining of racial and class oppression. Thompson, too, faced the force of Jim Crow violence when she lent the IWO's support to strikes in Atlanta, Alabama, and elsewhere in the South in the 1930s. Police broke up an interracial meeting in support of strikers in Birmingham with a good deal of force, although police treated the light-skinned Thompson more gently, perhaps assuming she was white judging by an officer's admonishment that the Communists would be all right if they did not mix with black people. As Mary Helen Washington argues, "It is quite clear why the Party attracted blacks in Chicago, especially during the Depression." The commitment of organizers such as Amis and Thompson in facing up to capitalism's racism "were beacons of light to the African American community."[20]

The IWO sought to deliver tangible relief to the jobless by collecting food for the hungry in between demonstrations for more systemic relief. Two decades later, when the Order faced the threat of liquidation as a "moral hazard," members offered affidavits that spoke of collecting food and clothing for the jobless during the Depression, as well as lobbying for social insurance, as some of the most prized activities of their time in the IWO. Greene noted that charter members could recall the organization's "struggle for unemployment insurance and social security in the early '30s—now the law of the land." SWS president Helen Vrábel likewise reminded members of the struggles they had engaged in to ensure enactment of the Social Security Act when reviewing the SWS's campaign for universal health care.[21]

Sometimes the IWO's engagement in hunger marches caused trouble within its own ranks, from prosaic matters of dollars and cents. Bedacht sought the intervention of the National Committee of the Unemployed when an IWO organizer asked sympathizers in Jacksonville, Florida, to contribute in aid of a national hunger march to Washington. "Comrade Berenhaut," a man sympathetic to the march, wrote "since only a few of us are still making a living and nothing but a living, we decided that we would already stretch a point if we would contribute $15." The IWO organizer seemed satisfied with this, but a week later came back to Berenhaut saying he needed a truck to get the hunger marchers to Washington. Berenhaut and a few other comrades managed to scrape together $46 for rental of a truck but had to guarantee its owner it would be returned. Unfortunately, the truck was abandoned in Washington by the IWO marchers, who wrote to Berenhaut that "the truck will remain in Washington until hell freezes over, that it was a lousy truck anyway, that the gear case was wrecked." An irate Berenhaut wrote the IWO's national office seeking restitution, exclaiming, "I wouldn't expect such a dirty deal even from Al Capone's men." He added, "I am long enough in the movement to swallow such slaps in my face but the young movement here in Jacksonville will not outlast this affair if it is not settled.... We are willing to be used but not abused."[22]

Hoping to salvage the IWO's reputation, Bedacht wrote the National Committee of the Unemployed that the truck had to be returned and "such irresponsible behavior" ended. "Some comrades seem to think that the taking serious of obligations we undertake is an anti-revolutionary bourgeois quality that a good revolutionary must get rid of," he wrote. "What this leads to can be seen here.... When we started out, we had five friends, when we got through we have five embittered and antagonized former friends."[23]

If "property is theft," to quote a popular anarchist cry, such cavalier treatment of other comrades' items would do nothing to build the movement. Still, the story of the shabby truck and Berenhaut's stress over raising even $46 suggests that conservatives' fears of a tightly disciplined left-wing conspiracy were greatly exaggerated, in the 1930s and by historians examining the CP thereafter. The IWO, and other militant left-wing organizations, were often strapped for cash. Such squabbles suggest that the anti-Communist movement mischaracterized a sometimes disorganized, often underfunded Left as "a conspiracy so immense."[24]

In pushing for an effective social insurance bill, various groups cooperated with the IWO in publicity and lobbying campaigns. Left-wing Lithuanians maintained "constant contact" with the IWO as they translated the Worker's Bill for Social Insurance, the Frazier-Lundeen Bill, into Lithuanian and arranged for their newspaper to publish the bill as a pamphlet. The Frazier-Lundeen Bill went farther in providing relief to unemployed, aged, and disabled workers than the eventually enacted Social Security Act. African Americans in the Order, too, championed Social Security, with the *Baltimore Afro-American* approvingly publicizing an IWO Conference on Social Security; other black organizations were joining the IWO at this conference, and the paper urged its black readership to support the Order's drive for this legislation. Thompson represented the IWO at a New York Urban League "Conference on Industrial and Labor Problems" in Harlem. Thompson appeared on a panel addressing "Employer-Employee Relations. How Shall the Worker Obtain Security?" Perhaps because security for the family could be, in mid-twentieth-century terms, foregrounded as a domestic concern, women in the IWO often played a role in advocating for social security. Then again, Thompson's notes on her copy of the Urban League program indicate that she spoke on "pressure of need for unionization to protect the job," "traditional position of the Negro as a marginal worker," and "Union the medium thru which Negro can overcome these hurdles," suggesting that the Order's officers were attentive to the particular "hurdles" people of color faced. The IWO played a role in pushing politicians and other progressives to enact as comprehensive a social safety net as possible.[25]

An IWO flyer, *Why Not Social Insurance?* framed the pertinent question as one of the free market's inadequacies. "The worker has only wages as a source of livelihood. When disabled because of sickness, accident, childbirth, old age, etc., . . . [h]e and his dependents face privation. This privation is caused by the method of operation of present-day society. It is therefore the duty of society to relieve it." While committed to mutual aid, the IWO's author labeled "the problem of economic insecurity . . . much too big to permit a complete solution by mutual aid." Only the government had the means to redress the miseries of capitalism, the writer argued. Moreover, he emphasized, "Society must approach this problem not as one of charity, but as a duty of the government toward the working masses." At a time of 25 percent official unemployment in cities such as Detroit, one can understand that, whether red or not, the Order's recruiting drives sounded attractive to many workers. And while Communists hoped the IWO would attract workers to the Party, they admitted that "the basis on which the masses will test Communist leadership in the Order is its ability to organize the most effective immediate solution of the problem which brings them into the organization." The Order would be judged by its lobbying campaign's results.[26]

The IWO was ahead of its time in critiquing the demeaning features of traditional outdoor relief, too. As Michael Katz, Frances Fox Piven, and Richard Cloward argue, one of the key features of welfare provisions in the United States has been to deliver the minimal support possible in maximally demeaning circumstances. Families' living arrangements, consumption patterns, and overall moral worth were assessed by deliverers of supposed charity to separate truly deserving sheep from shiftless goats.[27] The author of *Why Not Social Insurance?* however, was having none of it. "It is a disgrace that an unemployed, destitute worker is treated as a miserable beggar," the writer proclaimed.

> He is adjudged a pauper. When he asks for relief, his antecedents are investigated, his morals are gone into, his religious beliefs are inquired into, his politics are checked up. A worker who for many years of his life has done useful work, . . . made the things society needs to live, is investigated just because he committed the "crime" of being unable either to find or to fill a job. In very many cases he is investigated by a useless parasite who never in his life did any useful work and who holds a political sinecure.[28]

Rather than this moralistic scrutiny, the writer said workers unable to find employment "are entitled to maintenance by society on the same level on which they did maintain themselves while working," anticipating later proposals for a guaranteed annual income. This IWO pamphleteer concluded that by taxing the profits of the wealthy and corporations, and reducing needless military spending, adequate relief could be provided for the jobless.[29]

In its denunciation of moralistic means testing for welfare applicants, the IWO prefigured by three decades the rise of the National Welfare Rights Organization, which, as Premilla Nadasen and George Lipsitz demonstrate, engaged in militant lobbying to increase cash, food, and furniture allowances for the poor as guaranteed rights, not grudging handouts.[30]

Such analyses might have been uncomfortable for capitalists to hear during the Depression, but not inaccurate. For workers still awaiting substantive relief from the government, such paeans had resonance and explain the popularity of the Order, which by 1940 had grown to enroll more than 180,000 Slavic, Italian, Puerto Rican, black, and other workers.

Early social-insurance drives were closely coordinated with the CP. Bedacht called "the building of the IWO . . . one of the most important tasks of the Communist Party," in a 1933 *Daily Worker* article, hailing "an organization that allows Communist leadership to drive its roots into the uncharted depths of the American working masses." Nevertheless, such campaigns laid out legislative strategies, not violent subversion of the government, as some soon alleged. It was leafletting and lobbying, not bomb throwing, that predominated in IWO campaigns to transform capitalism. Based on internal IWO records such as letters, recruiting pamphlets, and minutes of meetings, it is clear that members were confident the old economic system was on its last legs and that they could quite soon enact a more humane social system without need of violence. As Bedacht reminded a New York conference, "To a degree our Order is a school."[31]

Education went on in public, as when Louis Kovess of the CP Language Department wrote an editorial urging workers to join the Order and spelled out the need for unemployment insurance. Despite more than eight million unemployed, and risk of deadly industrial accidents for those lucky enough to find a job, minimal old age relief in states such as New York was only "a promise of 'You'll get pie in the sky when you die.' Are there many workers living up to the age of 70 years . . . under the strains of a murderous speed up system, to get this miserable Pension? Very few."[32] Under such onerous conditions the IWO's school drew many apt pupils.

"Evicted by the Coal Barons": Helping the Dispossessed

Beyond legislative demands, IWO lodges orchestrated campaigns to help strikers or destitute workers thrown out of their houses. Already in 1931 New York lodges competed to provide the most boxes of food, milk, and other necessities for families of striking coal miners, with "the comrades or sympathizers . . . who collect the greatest amount . . . given a trip to the strike field." New York's IWO lodges had already advanced the Strike Committee $2,000, and now they were encouraged to do more. Williamsburg lodges responded to the evicted miners' plight, although one organizer complained that when he showed up at one Brooklyn lodge with a miner to state his case for assistance, lodge officers refused to grant him the floor. Better results came from Newark, New Jersey, where the IWO Center became a collection site for shoes and clothing "for these heroic strikers and their children." Newark members were informed that four thousand miner families had been evicted onto the roads and highways, and truckloads of clothing and shoes were sent for the needy families of miners. Closer to the coal fields, Massillon, Ohio, hosted a "Big Picnic and Dance" at Utopia Hall to aid homeless miners. "Evicted by the Coal Barons," posters declared. An illustration of a despairing mother with her child was captioned, "She Is Hungry, Answer Her Cry!" Another interracial audience in aid of miners was told by a National Miners Union (NMU) speaker, "You miners must not starve quietly."[33]

As Randi Storch notes, during the Depression the CP and its affiliates won a reputation in Chicago's Black Belt as effective advocates for the dispossessed. When an eviction notice arrived, African American mothers told their children, go and "find the Reds!" As the actions of the IWO, NMU, and Unemployed Councils demonstrate, the same summonses could be heard throughout industrial America. Lashawn Harris writes, too, that the anti-eviction and unemployed campaigns of the CP gave agency to African American working-class women during the Depression at a time when few other venues for leadership existed and the class-based and racial-justice messages of the Party resonated with them.[34]

Women from all ethnic backgrounds found leadership within the IWO. Thompson, for example, became an IWO vice president in 1938 after organizing interracial IWO lodges among Deep South sharecroppers and other workers.[35] And Vrábel became president of the SWS. Women, too, were active in eviction prevention, although those engaged in these anti-eviction campaigns sometimes ran into trouble. In 1951 Russian immigrant and IWO member Clara Dainoff faced deportation proceedings after the Order had been labeled a subversive organization by the attorney general. The Justice Department noted that Dainoff had been arrested twice, in 1931 and 1933, on disorderly person charges. The first charge stemmed from a "Bread Strike" as Dainoff and other women picketed a bakery they said had raised the price of a loaf from five to twelve cents; the second charge related to "a mass arrest of persons watching an eviction." Both charges were dismissed, and Dainoff was allowed to remain in the United States. However, activism on behalf of those facing starvation or eviction that may have seemed rational and desirable in the Depression came back to haunt many IWO members.[36]

This activism sometimes fell into gendered norms. As supposed guardians of the home, women such as Dainoff may have been expected to be at the forefront of anti-eviction drives. Then, too, by stepping outside of received gender norms as nurturers, disturbing bakers' and landlords' peace, such women often enraged authority figures and brought the wrath of the law, or sometimes, as with Thompson's African American peers in the South, state violence on their heads. As Kali Gross has written, women, especially African American women, who behaved "unnaturally" were perceived to have abdicated the "protections" of their gender and deemed "legitimate" targets for repression. While Dainoff and other women such as the Polish activist Stella Petrosky, likewise targeted for deportation, might be said to have benefited from white privilege, in the 1930s Slavs, too, were also often denigrated as atavistically suspect beings, "dangerous women." Especially when they contested against capitalism, Dainoff and others seem to have aroused the state's ire as menacing "amazons."[37]

Dainoff's actions were typical of the IWO, which collaborated with CP-affiliated organizations such as the Unemployed Councils and the NMU, which targeted miserable living conditions even as they sought to prevent evictions and organize industrial workers. In Michigan's Upper Peninsula, the NMU distributed shop papers decrying more than 60 percent unemployment, demanding "immediate unemployed relief" but also adequate housing for miners in outlying "locations," where "the miserable Hovels of miners as dreary as the 'DOG TOWNS' of Czarist Russia are the only homes for the miners, wooden houses with leaking roofs, with the wind sweeping through under the floors doors and the windows." Degradation could only cease when workers ended company domination of their towns.[38]

The Copper Miner of Hancock, Michigan, derided meager welfare payments, expressing in verse idle miners' frustration:

Sing a song of "Welfare,"
A pocket full of tricks
To soothe the weary worker
When he groans or kicks.
If he asks for shorter hours
Or for better pay,
Little stunts of "Welfare"
Turn his thoughts away.

Sing a song of "Welfare,"
Sound the horn and drum,
Anything to keep his mind
Fixed on kingdom come.

> "Welfare" loots your pocket
> While you dream and sing,
> "Welfare" to your pay check
> Doesn't do a thing.³⁹

In March 1934 the IWO Youth Section magazine *The New Order* similarly satirized meager palliatives of the early New Deal when it published "The Soup Song," which was "written by unemployed workers in Detroit in the heat of their struggles against hunger and evictions." The song, sung in "Tempo: mockingly," began, "I'm spending my nights at the flophouse, I'm spending my days on the street, I'm looking for work and I find none, I wish I had something to eat."⁴⁰

These verses indicate that the relief measures of the early New Deal were looked on skeptically. To many labor activists, the National Industrial Recovery Act (NIRA) in particular seemed to favor industry and offer cartelization as the answer to unemployment. "Codes of Fair Competition" drawn up by industry insiders offered minimal protection to workers' wages, ineffective safety standards, and limited defense from the speedup, and the collective bargaining rights of Section 7(a) were quickly co-opted in management-directed employee representation plans. Other employers simply ignored the act's labor provisions, leading many on the Left to conclude that NIRA was an inadequate response to industrial workers' woes.⁴¹

As an alternative to the New Deal, the IWO pushed for greater institutional transformations of industrial America than the government was willing to deliver. Pronouncements dismissed the early New Deal as only more capitalist pablum; Chicago members mourned the accidental death of one of their own in a pamphlet, *Crushed to Death!* bitterly mocking the National Recovery Administration (NRA). "James Owens got an N.R.A. job and of course was laid off soon after. The N.R.A. did not guarantee him anything—no decent wages—no unemployment insurance—no security. It proves instead to be an empty bubble." Instead of shoring up corporations through industry-drafted Codes of Fair Competition, Bedacht urged an IWO conference to disseminate "a Leninist understanding of the tasks of our Order among all of our members."⁴²

In April 1934 delegates from the Philadelphia area pledged to continue their campaign for unemployment and social insurance and organized an open-air demonstration to compel their city council to endorse an unemployment bill. They also passed a resolution dismissing the NRA, which was "organized mainly to strengthen the power of big trusts and corporations" and had actually immiserated workers. When workers complained, the NRA became a "strike-breaking agency" for the "suppression of militant workers." "Fascism" was, they claimed, lurking behind the Blue Eagle.⁴³ The Blue Eagle decal, symbol of the NRA, served as a ubiquitous sign that cooperating businesses complied with Industry Codes of Fair Competition.

Opponents would continue to be branded "fascists" throughout the Order's life, and the overwrought nature of rhetoric sometimes limited the effectiveness of critiques. Still, in 1934 the NRA offered a meager solution to workers, and in Toledo auto-parts plants, Minneapolis Teamster halls, and San Francisco warehouses grassroots-led, wildcat strikes were met with state-sanctioned violence and little government sympathy. Under such circumstances the IWO was not alone in critiquing the early New Deal.[44]

Gebert and other leaders of the Polish Chamber of Labor circulated petitions demanding the insertion of unemployment insurance into the industrial codes governing conditions in steel, coal, textiles, and other industries. Gebert, who had been organizing coal miners on behalf of the Communist-affiliated NMU, would soon take a leadership role in the Polish Section of the IWO. Communists worried that Gebert was creating the false view, in their opinion, that with a little tweaking the industrial codes would be acceptable, but he did not see "what harm" such incremental improvements could do if such campaigns mobilized more workers. Another organizer worried that too blunt a condemnation of the NRA would scare away Polish workers. Even as Gebert and others pointed out the shortcomings of the industrial codes, they did what they could to add workers' protections to their administration.[45]

The CP also recognized that the NRA retained the racial stratifications permeating American industry, what David Roediger and Elizabeth Esch document as the remunerative "production of racial difference" by employers. Browder wrote critiquing a Seattle comrade's draft pamphlet on the NRA, that he "must insert a few words showing that the defense of the right of the Negroes, Japanese and Filipinos is an essential part also of the interests of the white workers, that the white workers in defending their colored brothers are defending their own interests." As Chapter 3 shows, the IWO, too, combined interracial solidarity and civil rights activism with its championing of labor's cause, a prefiguration of the later demand for intersectionality regarding racial and class equity.[46]

The ethnic press of IWO affiliates such as the SWS was deployed in the campaign against the NRA. Browder telegrammed the editors of *Rovnosť ľudu* urging them to "use [the] *Daily Worker* cartoon Evolution Eagle" mocking the NRA emblem. The NRA's Blue Eagle was a satirist's delight. Perhaps the Evolution Eagle was similar to a cartoon, "Very thin stew," printed the following year in the *Delco Worker*, a Communist shop paper in Dayton, Ohio. The "NRA Eagle" asks a worker, "Well what are you squawking about—you're still eating, aren't you?" To which the worker, wielding a frying pan, replies, "Yeah! You old buzzard—and tomorrow I may have to make eagle soup."[47]

Less satirically, posters urged women to fight against night work in mills cooperating with the NRA, while demonstrators exposed the "True Meaning of the NRA." Workers read that "savior Roosevelt" had forgotten the forgotten man in reconciling with Wall Street, while food workers in the Party's German Bureau distributed anti-NRA leaflets outside sausage factories. Militant ethnic workers such as these mocked the president for his supposed favoritism toward big business, a portrait at odds with many industrialists' demonization of "that man in the White House" as well as later lionization of Roosevelt by the IWO. Still, when industrial codes posited eighty-hour work weeks as fair conditions, many labor activists concluded that there was much to criticize about the Blue Eagle.[48]

"Steps in the Right Direction": On Board with the New Deal

By 1938 IWO officials were extolling the advances of the New Deal, even appropriating Roosevelt's language to condemn "economic royalists" who opposed the administration's programs and workers' unionization drives. Scholars of American communism have pointed to the rapid shifts in CP policy toward cooperation with "bourgeois, capitalist" parties beginning in 1935 as evidence of the American Party's subservience to the Comintern. Recognizing somewhat belatedly the danger that fascism posed, Moscow directed all Communist parties to cooperate with the most progressive political actors in their countries to stave off the fascist threat. The shift to the Popular Front certainly altered Communist perspectives on the New Deal and the prospects for social betterment arising from legislation enacted by non-Marxist parties, and this abrupt change was reflected within the IWO, too. For those conservatives who regarded the Order as tightly controlled by the CP, these sharp shifts were evidence that the IWO was little more than a "transmission belt" for Communist doctrine.[49]

The Socialist Party newspaper *The Call* also delighted in publicizing the IWO's "about-faces" as proof of its subservience to Moscow. "You boast that you participated in the fight for social security and other progressive legislation in the interests of the working masses," the Workmen's Circle Executive Committee addressed the IWO. "How long ago was it, however, when you ridiculed the Roosevelt social reform program? Everyone whom you then suspected of giving support to the New Deal was characterized by you as 'Social-Fascists.' . . . Soon thereafter there was a reversal in Communist policy and . . . you outdid yourselves in singing paeans of praise over anything and everything associated with the New Deal."[50]

The leaders of the Socialist Workmen's Circle contrasted their own pragmatic, steadfast support for the New Deal with the IWO's lack of constancy. Yet while leaders of the Circle may be forgiven their bitterness toward the IWO, more than the CP's tactical shift accounts for the IWO's growing embrace of the New Deal. What is rarely acknowledged in discussions of this shift by left-wing organizations such as the Order is that the Roosevelt administration altered after 1935, too, becoming more palatable to militant activists. The Second New Deal delivered more substantive programs, with the Wagner, Social Security, and Fair Labor Standards Acts advancing a more workers' rights-friendly, progressive approach than the First New Deal of the NRA. Whether the IWO was overclaiming to take credit for enactment of these measures, Order members could not help noticing the Second New Deal had substantively delivered tangible benefits worthy of support. From 1935, too, the president began critiquing the "economic royalists" opposing his programs, language that resonated with Order members weaned on antiplutocrat diatribes. Certainly the CP change to a Popular Front approach of working with liberal parties to forestall fascism affected the IWO. But the Democratic Party changed, too, at least in part in response to the activism and lobbying of organizations such as the IWO. Waves of strikes, demonstrations, and lobbying prodded the administration leftward, and it became more palatable. In this scenario the Popular Front was not a cynical, or manipulative *volte face*, rather an adjustment of attitudes toward "bourgeois, capitalist" political parties and actors who themselves evolved more progressive stances in response to militant demands to address workers' needs.[51]

While later red-hunters argued that these were merely cosmetic moves designed to conceal the IWO's true subversive, Marxist nature, I argue that the move to accommodate the possibility for social-democratic reform within America was heartfelt. As Koch and others noted in responding to IWO questionnaires about the strength of local lodges, many members joined the Order for pragmatic, insurance-based needs. When the New Deal began to satisfy, however imperfectly, these needs, members began to believe they could work with the Democrats. Charles Korenič and Helen Vrábel reminded the SWS that it was their own lobbying that had led to passage of Social Security and urged further lobbying to enact universal health care.[52] The Popular Front seemed to be delivering tangible results.

In the lead-up to the 1938 election, Bedacht embraced not just Roosevelt's program but his rhetoric. Using the president's favorite insult, he addressed members on the importance of "preventing the economic royalists from enslaving their workers by refusing their right to organize," and demanded to know were "the government, its army, its laws and its courts merely created for the protection of the rich and their possessions?" He answered his own question by calling on members "to use their votes to achieve a recognition of social responsibility of the government toward their problems.... [I]n the last analysis these problems are decided in the election battles... We must... be instrumental in selecting the right legislators who will listen to these demands and comply with the wishes and needs of the masses."[53]

Earlier calls for Leninist revolution dropped away, perhaps because IWO members had seen that militant demands had delivered tangible legislative programs, which were somewhat ameliorating the misery of workers. Although Bedacht admitted that "in the field of social legislation and social insurance some first steps have already been made," he lamented, "health insurance is still merely a dream. We must make it an imperative demand."[54] Until its demise the IWO lobbied for national health insurance, an advance America has still not been able to achieve.

The limits to actually existing Social Security, however, did not prevent the IWO from supporting the administration against its more conservative opponents. The fourth national convention "declared that the social program of the New Deal, despite its occasional inadequacy, covers in the main the social program of progressive fraternalism." Members were urged to support the program, as by August 1939 it had become evident that "the most reactionary forces of economic royalism in America are organizing against all social improvements." The IWO foresaw the coming elections as a crucial battleground in preserving or extending as much of the social-insurance agenda as possible. Under these circumstances in which "the naked profit interests of economic royalism try to kill the social conscience of America"—and even the New Deal's architects were backsliding—it was imperative to "remind the government of its social responsibility toward the people." By 1940 cutbacks to programs such as the WPA were decried by Order officials such as Congressman Marcantonio, but even when administration officials were faulted, the programs they had enacted were defended. The IWO in many cases became a more stalwart New Dealer than administrators already facing conservative pushback against the WPA and other programs.[55]

The IWO's embrace of Roosevelt, though, always remained pragmatic, a case of supporting the best alternative possible while still hoping for more systemic socialist change in the long term. In June 1944 an OSS agent reported that IWO officials said,

> We are under no illusion that "state capitalism," "monopoly control," "TVA," . . . security controls, etc. are socialism. But they are not incompatible with socialism, they are "steps in the right direction," and they merit our support. We will support those who will support measures which we regard as being progressively in line with a program which we would see achieved at greater speed, but which we are willing to now concede must and can be obtained only slowly and through evolutionary tactics.[56]

As Jefferson Cowie and others have argued, conservative business interests, as well as aggrieved white ethnic workers, were picking apart large elements of the New Deal consensus already in the late 1930s and 1940s. Under

Figure 2.1 Exhibiting the masculinist iconography of the Popular Front, the cover of *Security with FDR* featured virile working men confidently striding past factories with smoking chimneys, the result of President Roosevelt's New Deal, Vito Marcantonio argued.

Source: Vito Marcantonio, *Security with FDR* (New York: National Fraternal Committee for the Re-Election of President Roosevelt, September 1944), IWO-CU, box 49.

such circumstances the IWO believed it prudent to stand with the most progressive forces possible.[57] As Bedacht reminded his members in January 1940, "Economic royalism has always looked on social security legislation with hostile eyes."[58]

The president's enunciation of the right of all people to enjoy the Four Freedoms resonated with members, too. In backing the president's run for a fourth term, the IWO issued a pamphlet written by Vito Marcantonio, congressman and IWO vice president, with a foreword by Bedacht, *Security with FDR*. In emblematic, maculinist Popular Front iconography, the pamphlet's cover displayed determined black and white working men striding into the future past factories with fully smoking chimneys (Figure 2.1). Bedacht noted that the measures the IWO had supported in the past such as the Social Security and Wagner Acts, and its endorsement of a proposed national health insurance system, were embodied in Roosevelt's postwar vision for America. Marcantonio and Bedacht put the Order on record as supporting Roosevelt's reelection because of his articulation of a "new economic Bill of Rights." Individual IWO constituencies such as the Hispanic American Section committed to the president's reelection, too. Shortly after the war the

Figure 2.2 In making the case for its "Plan for Plenty," the IWO vowed that the depths of Hoover's Depression were conditions that would "Never Again" be tolerated.

Source: Joseph Starobin, *Never Again!* (New York: IWO, August 1945), IWO-CU, box 49.

IWO continued this campaign for economic security by issuing a second pamphlet in favor of universal health insurance. The cover of Joseph Starobin's *Never Again!*, in contrast to the earlier pamphlet, featured grim-faced apple sellers from the depths of Hoover's Depression. Starobin and the IWO made the case for enactment of the Wagner-Murray-Dingell Bill, a measure to extend Social Security to cover universal health insurance (Figure 2.2).[59]

The IWO further articulated this vision of greater security for all Americans in *Our Plan for Plenty*, a social-democratic manifesto for the country (Figure 2.3). The IWO's plan advocated a guaranteed minimum income of $1,200 per person among other reforms. In November 1940 a Russian lodge heard confirmation that the Order was drafting a petition to Congress "to make the minimum wage of the American worker $100 a month." "The politicians promised you everything before the election," a speaker said, "so now we will see if Mr. Roosevelt will keep his word and take care of the American workers as the American millionaire. $100 a month is not much, but it will give the lowest worker something to live on, because today no one can live on $300 a year like a human!" The IWO was determined to push the New Deal to its outer, leftward limits.[60]

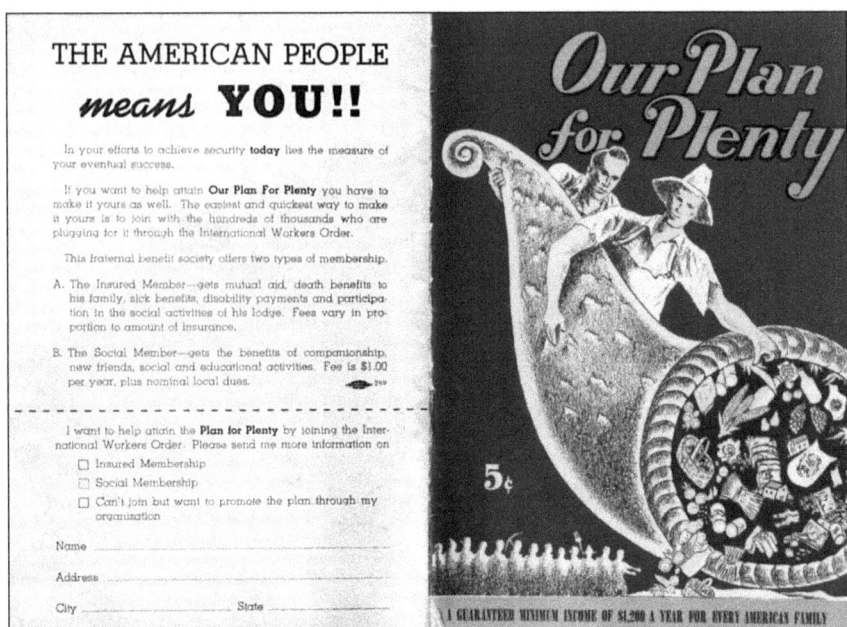

Figure 2.3 The IWO's "Plan for Plenty" in the 1940s featured universal health care and a guaranteed annual income for all Americans.
Source: IWO pamphlet, *Our Plan for Plenty* [ca. 1941], IWO-CU, box 5, folder 7.

"Health, Limbs and Lives": Occupational Safety

The Order recognized its payment of sick or accident benefits was only a bandage on the sores of industrial America. More systemic solutions to aid workers suffering from workplace injuries or toxic working conditions were advocated by the organization in its campaign to enact effective workplace safety legislation. A holistic campaign to sand the rough edges off of capitalism included efforts to document just how grim working people's health could be. As part of its support of labor unions, in 1938 the Order made plans "to establish a statistical department for research in workers' health," paying particular attention to "the problems of occupational diseases and hazards." Statistical information and "propaganda" was to be supplied to unions, while the Order engaged in lobbying to ensure adequate compensation for victims of industrial accidents and occupational hazards. Bedacht committed the Order to serving as "a brother-in-arms to the broad progressive political movement which . . . presses for the enactment of laws protecting the health, limbs and lives of the workers on the job."[61]

That the IWO's campaign for effective workmen's compensation might prove attractive is suggested by the case of George Palenchar, a coal miner from Powhatan Point, Ohio. When his back and shoulder were crushed in a mine accident in 1929, "the company doctor did not want to take him to the hospital. After several weeks elapsed the company doctor told him he could go back to work and he considered the wounds as little scratches." Palenchar could not continue working, and went to a private doctor who discovered his backbone and shoulder were cracked. However, Ohio's Industrial Commission deemed Palenchar only partially, temporarily disabled, and awarded him $6 a week, up to a maximum of $312. His lawyer told him, "I think you are fortunate in getting the amount that you are getting at this time." While Palenchar had a doctor's report indicating he was permanently disabled, his file also showed he suffered from "miners' asthma, . . . and that all of your trouble doesn't come from the injured back." In the 1930s coal corporations still evaded responsibility for most of their workers' accidents and diseases under the doctrine of "assumed risk." Perhaps with his lawyer's letter spelling out the realities of industrial capitalism in mind, Palenchar joined the CP. Other coal miners who turned to the IWO's welfare fund may have found the group attractive when assistance from the state proved so meager. A little democratic centralism may have seemed a small price to pay.[62]

With cases such as Palenchar's in mind, the IWO championed a mine safety bill in 1940. Bedacht wrote to Marcantonio, urging his support for a Federal Mines Safety and Inspection Act. Bedacht took particular interest in mine safety, since he noted a recent disaster in Bellaire, Ohio, had killed seventy-one miners, of whom "at least eight, and possibly ten of those killed, were members of our International Workers Order." He added that the Order, which enrolled thousands of miners, "is vitally concerned in the passage of legislation by Congress which will prevent such tragedies." He asked Marcantonio for a statement on the mine safety bill that could be used by the Order as part of a national campaign of support. Bedacht further told the congressman he would like to appear before the committee as a witness in favor of the bill. Grassroots IWO members lobbied for the bill, too. Victor Pöverk of Yukon, Pennsylvania, wrote to congratulate Marcantonio on his opposition to the HUAC chaired by archconservative Dies but also urged passage of the mine inspections measure. "As a coal miner and conscious of the grim fact that we have had two disastrous mine explosions in the last few months," Pöverk wrote, "I sincerely hope that you would do all in your power for the Federal Mine Inspection Bill." The miner enclosed a resolution supporting the bill passed by Yukon's lodge.[63]

So convinced were IWO members of their place in the progressive new political order that Italian lodges in East Harlem and the Bronx orchestrated rallies "against the Dies Committee, for the New Deal." Dante Alighieri and La Progressiva Lodges denounced the committee as "an agency for the propagation of anti-labor, anti-progressive and anti-New Deal sentiments behind the smoke screen of vicious red-baiting." The Italians were confident Marcantonio could scuttle the "Un-American Committee" and work to expand the WPA and other programs.[64] To IWO members the choice between an "un-American Committee" and progressive legislation was clear. Anti-Communism was deemed loathsome if it targeted individuals and organizations working to deliver safe workplaces, social security, and workmen's compensation.

"Helping the Entire Nation": The IWO and the Unions

Throughout its existence the IWO was committed "to act as a brother-in-arms to the militant trade and industrial unions."[65] Along with its campaigns on social legislation, the Order was committed to union drives before and then during the CIO's rise to prominence. In its first year, the IWO reported members in New Jersey, Pennsylvania, and Ohio aiding miners and metal workers. In the South these unionizing drives were coupled with commitment to interracial solidarity. As early as December 1930, IWO chapters in Birmingham and Chattanooga and Elizabethton, Tennessee, contributed volunteers and funds for organizing in textile and steel mills. When the IWO ventured south to aid union drives, it did not respect Jim Crow. Thompson successfully helped the IWO enroll black and white workers into Atlanta painters' unions, organized an interracial sharecroppers' lodge, and in New Orleans supported a strike by furniture workers. In the Crescent City, Thompson recalled, she attended a meeting of the faltering union: "When I went to the meeting that night, that was when I told them that if they wanted to win that strike, they had to take the 'Whites Only' clause out of their contract. I walked into this meeting of all white men and I felt kind of funny walking around, but I did it."[66]

Dispossessed miners and organizers faced real hardship when they demanded adequate wages or a safer work environment. Just a few years before the IWO's founding, a Pennsylvania judge prohibited the distribution of food to striking miners. In the NMU's journal, *The Coal Digger*, an unrepentant Anthony Minerich wrote, "A man who knew . . . of the clubbings by Coal and Iron and State police, . . . said 'Now I can understand why the statue of Liberty has its back turned towards the United States.'" As the IWO added its support to miners and other workers fighting for the right to unionize, assaults by Coal and Iron police, dubbed the "Cossacks" by Slavic immigrants, were fresh memories.[67]

In 1931 lodges throughout the country were mobilized to raise funds for striking miners, with the Order setting a quota of $6,000. German, Jewish, Russian, Polish, Ukrainian, and Lithuanian members of the IWO raised funds for the miners, although not without some difficulty. In Ridgewood, Brooklyn, the IWO waited so long to start a relief campaign in the German *Krankenkasse Verein* that Socialists beat them to the punch. "Then our comrades reminded themselves that there is a miners' relief campaign." Closer to the strike scene, CP organizer Steve Nelson noted problems developed when Comrade Almasoff of the IWO spoke before a nascent Jewish lodge in Wilkes-Barre, then demanded they pay a fee of $15 plus $10 travel expenses. The few IWO members in Wilkes-Barre had already committed to supporting the miners' strike, as well as financially contributing to a hunger march, so they and Nelson considered Almasoff's demands excessive. Nevertheless, the IWO continued to contribute to the miners' relief committee, which the committee gratefully acknowledged.[68]

Despite the problems organizer Nelson had identified with some anthracite country members, evidently the IWO proved an effective organizing apparatus for coal miners. In 1934 Nelson requested a Slovak organizer be sent into the eastern Pennsylvania coal region. Korenič provided the needed organizers and was also the conduit for sending Slovak members to the Gary and Chicago steel region to aid the Trade Union Unity League in building locals of the Steel and Metal Workers Industrial Union.[69] Thompson confirmed that political consciousness and commitment to unions was endemic to the Order, so that black and Latino organizers aided coal miners' unionization drives in West Virginia, and most of her IWO speeches in the South were before either union or church meetings. Such interracial union activism was a hallmark of her career with the IWO. In western Pennsylvania company towns, too, not only was the IWO hall the only social center for members aside from seedy saloons, it was often the only place to hold union meetings or discuss politics freely. She recalled in one western Pennsylvania town a "little Bohemian guy named Joe" in the IWO was able to get the first one hundred steelworkers to sign union cards. This was "typical of all these little mining towns that you went through. Aliquippa, Washington."[70]

Militant activism on behalf of destitute workers often led to arrest, and there is no doubt that some IWO activists engaged in union organizing were Communists. Gebert was a charter member of the CP, and the FBI began recording his speeches on behalf of bolshevism as early as 1919. In some of his speeches, agents noted, Gebert compared the oppression of industrial workers to British imperialism in India and Egypt, an early example of the CP's linking anticolonialism and class exploitation. He was reported as saying of capitalists, "We have to teach them the same way the bear is taught to dance." Not surprisingly, deportation proceedings were begun against him, although by 1922 the decision had been made not to deport. Gebert, later president of the IWO's Polonia Society, reported on his activities to the Comintern in 1932. Communism was near to Gebert's heart, and the fact he had once reported to the Comintern, although not known in the 1930s and 1940s, would have offered proof to anticommunists that they were correct in labeling the IWO he served a subversive organization.[71]

Yet this correspondence with the Comintern discussed his campaigns on behalf of the NMU, work designed to improve the lives of coal miners, not espionage. Gebert had reason to be concerned with the plight of coal miners, for he had labored as one in and around Nanticoke, Pennsylvania, after emigrating from Russian Poland in 1912. Not spying or subversion, but a shared commitment to bettering workers' lives through unionism seems to have drawn Gebert to socialism and, after 1919, to the CP.[72]

The criminal charge that hounded Gebert for sixteen years was not espionage but stemmed from his union activism on behalf of coal miners. As Gebert himself related, he was arrested on November 11, 1931, on criminal syndicalism charges "based on my participation in [a] strike of Orient Mines in Illinois in July and August 1931." Syndicalist charges were deployed frequently against strikers during the pre–Wagner Act years as well as infamously against Communist organizer Herndon for leading an interracial unemployment meeting, violating Georgia's segregation and antisyndicalist statutes. Thompson, too, ran afoul of segregation statutes when supporting an interracial miners' strike in Alabama as an IWO organizer. Often immigration and other authorities served as enforcers of the open shop. In Atlanta, too, interracial IWO lodges were prima facie dubbed subversive and in violation of Georgia's segregation and syndicalist statutes.[73]

In Gebert's case, his lawyer, David Bentall, pointed out that the CP was a legal party and wanted to know if an alien forfeited all right to criticize America's political institutions. He argued that if the deportation were upheld it would send a message to every alien laborer "the moment he sets foot on American soil he forfeits all right to think, reason or plan." As Daniel Kanstroom and Rachel Buff note, deportation proceedings were frequently deployed against militant labor activists such as Harry Bridges and Carlos Bulosan, answering Bentall's question. Although subject to deportation for these charges, action was continually deferred in Gebert's case, and as late as 1937 Roger Baldwin of the American Civil Liberties Union (ACLU) and Bentall were asking for some definitive decision, or at least return of his bail money. Finally, in 1941 the Immigration and Naturalization Service (INS) determined as the deportation was in abeyance, and as Gebert had admitted to membership in the CP up to 1939 and complied with the Alien Registration Act, no further action was contemplated, although the deportation order was only "in abeyance," not dismissed outright. As president of the IWO's Polonia Society, the threat of deportation hung over his head for his activism on behalf of Illinois coal miners. In 1947, when he voluntarily left to assume labor and diplomatic posts in Communist Poland, the IWO gratefully recalled the services he had offered in organizing CIO unions in auto and steel plants. Although in 1947 the Order's magazine, the *Fraternal Outlook*, made no mention of the still-pending deportation case, those who remembered that it stemmed from a Depression strike may have weighed Gebert's communism as less onerous a crime than state suppression of labor's free speech and association rights.[74]

Into the 1950s, when the IWO was under assault as a "subversive" organization, grassroots members pointed to the support shown to strikers as proof the Order was a praiseworthy organization. "During the miners' strike, I helped with my coal truck to deliver hundreds of food packages made up by the I.W.O. and distributed to needy miners' families," Anton Opara attested. "The Lodge does many other good deeds for the members who are in need." Charles Wasyluk agreed, noting, "During the coal strike when times were hard the I.W.O. sent food for the members of my lodge." The IWO, in coordination with the ASC of western Pennsylvania, had offered material and moral support to the miners' 1949 strike, continuing to advocate for safer working conditions and health standards for miners. In 1951 the IWO's treasurer, Peter Shipka, proudly asserted, "During strikes, such as the last miners' strike, we exerted every possible effort to help our members maintain their insurance. We stretched out the hand of fraternal assistance to our members in the coal strike, just as we always did in the past." The Order's Garibaldi Society more bluntly asserted, "We have given food to the children of IWO striking miners. Is this a crime?"[75]

Of course, many IWO members likely remembered only a few years before in western Pennsylvania a judge had indeed decreed feeding hungry miners against the law. In 1950 members still faced company retaliation when vocal in support of strikes. In West Virginia, members urged correspondents not to send them letters or literature through the mail, as officials in company-controlled towns still opened letters and punished employees who favored anything as "subversive" as unions. "We don't live here like people live in the cities," a member wrote Daniel Kasustchik of the IWO's Russian society. "You know that we live in Company houses, and we are supposed to do whatever the Company tells us to do." In some respects, the Wagner Act had changed little for workers, especially those favoring militant organizations labeled subversive, or those living in company-controlled towns. The company panopticon, though, may have made some people receptive to an organization preaching an alternative to capitalism. There was a reason to listen to the IWO, and it had nothing to do with espionage. IWO members often wore their defiance of antilabor injunctions as badges of honor.[76]

In other industries as early as the 1930s the IWO twinned its campaign for unionization with calls for racial justice, as when the CP's African American vice-presidential candidate, James Ford, led discussions in Detroit on how to bring the IWO to railroad workers and "how to get Negroes into unions" as well as the "struggle against growing spying and stool pigeons."[77] As Barrett, Roediger, and others have noted, black people had long been barred from most unions in the American Federation of Labor (AFL), stigmatized as a "scab race" prone to strikebreaking. This exclusion, though, made strikebreaking for some African Americans seem a rational act of self-advancement and provided employers with a ready pool of labor with which to eviscerate union strength as workers were played off against one another. The IWO's commitment to interracial solidarity is more fully examined in Chapter 3. It is important to note here, however, that the IWO, like earlier Communist-affiliated organizations, recognized that "wages of whiteness," the reformulation of Du Bois's concept, were poor recompense for white workers in industrial America when racism proved such a handy tool for bidding down all workers' wages.[78]

In the 1930s, Order organizers performed "exceptional work" on unionizing drives in steel, mining, and longshore industries. By 1935 in New York the IWO was participating in union drives among longshoremen and marine workers but also aiding campaigns for teamsters and workers in heavy metal trades. Money was raised to target marine work, which Gerald Horne and Howard Kimeldorf have written were notoriously corrupt and exploitive industries. The New York IWO pledged itself to "help out as much as possible in support of all strike struggles," in 1935 contributing "about $3,000" in support of various strikes by taxi, marine, metal, furniture, and office workers. Such help from the IWO was not always welcomed by established unions, however. Several IWO members were expelled from the United Mine Workers (UMW), and the Amalgamated Clothing Workers of America (ACWA) had "taken steps to decide on ways and means to destroy one of our Italian branches" in New Brunswick, New Jersey, after IWO clothing workers were "consider[ed] . . . a menace to the leadership." Still, organizers soldiered on. Thompson reported on union drives among building service workers, mechanics, and Pullman porters. In Harlem, she reported, the IWO had "recruited one member who sent us an invitation to participate in the Labor Day demonstration in Harlem." The IWO prepared a leaflet for distribution at this gala.[79]

Beginning in 1935, even many established unions such as the UMW and ACWA began to see the possibilities of organizing "unskilled" workers in industrial unions, and with the creation of the CIO late that year, labor leaders such as the UMW's John L. Lewis and Philip Murray began to collaborate with formerly stigmatized Communists, now valorized in the CIO for their dedication and organizational skills.[80]

In CIO campaigns the IWO proved instrumental. Rebecca Grecht wrote approvingly of "The IWO and the Steel Drive" in *The New Order*. Grecht reported that in the Pittsburgh, Cleveland, and Chicago steel districts "active leaders of the I.W.O. are serving as voluntary organizers to recruit steel workers into the union." The IWO sent speakers to address locals of the moribund Amalgamated Association of Iron, Steel and Tin Workers, urging old unionists to pour into the vibrant CIO. In the three districts, steelworkers in IWO lodges "are discussing the drive to unionize the industry, are holding general membership meetings, are trying to do their bit in this great campaign which will fundamentally affect the lives of the entire American working class." CIO speakers were invited to address IWO picnics, and "in McKeesport, the I.W.O. is officially on the Steel Workers Organizing Committee." The head of the CIO's Pittsburgh region "expressed his appreciation for the support the I.W.O. is giving the steel drive, adding that the I.W.O. has earned the respect of all the workers." With CIO support the IWO convened a national fraternal organizations' conference to harness benefit societies on behalf of SWOC. Incipient IWO campaigns for the steel union were noted in Buffalo and Philadelphia, too, and Grecht hoped similar drives could be begun in auto and textile industries.[81]

Not surprisingly, the *Daily Worker* praised the leadership the IWO provided to the steel campaign's Fraternal Orders conference. With the announcement that the United Ukrainian Toilers and CFU were joining the conference, the paper noted that more than twenty ethnic societies were slated to attend the meeting to be chaired by Gebert, who by 1936 was serving in the Polish Society of the IWO. The paper approvingly noted that women, too, were supporting the steel drive. In Chicago a women's auxiliary of an Amalgamated local issued a call for a similar fraternal conference on behalf of SWOC. Gendered language that asserted women's custodianship of the home was issued by the auxiliary to appeal to support for the union effort: "While the cost of living goes higher, our husbands' wages remain the same or are lowered. . . . We want better homes, better living conditions and educational opportunities for our children. How can we have these things unless our husbands, brothers, and fathers become organized into a powerful union of their own?" SWOC's Chicago regional director, Van Bittner, buttressed this call for a Midwest fraternal conference by appealing to gender norms, too, asserting that "the steel workers are fighting for their families, and 'those whom we love dearer than life itself, the children of the steel industry.'" Normative, nuclear-family values were evoked on behalf of the steel union's campaign. A second *Daily Worker* article on the Fraternal Orders conference cheered the multiethnic nature of SWOC's support, arguing that unlike in the failed 1919 steel strike, the bosses were proving unable to divide the workers based on ethnic origin.[82]

Other IWO organizers advocated for unions in similarly gendered language. Sadie Doroshkin asked Thompson to recommend a black woman steelworker who could serve as an IWO spokeswoman on a national tour, while Thompson told female audiences in West Virginia and Ohio that as "as wives of workers, women, too, would benefit from the union." Thompson also commented that Ukrainian women and others were some of the leaders in IWO centers supporting union drives. Thompson herself would later run Chicago's Du Sable Center, a largely African American IWO lodge that also served as a relief center catering to black and white striking packinghouse workers and their families.[83] She therefore was not insensitive to the burdens of women workers. Indeed, she would play an instrumental role in the short-lived Sojourners for Truth and Justice, an African American women's organization that took intersectionality as its core principle, and which was financially supported by the JPFO's Emma Lazarus Women's Federation. In 1952 Thompson, as well as other Sojourners, declared, "Negro women, as women, as Negroes, and as workers are the most oppressed group of the whole population in the United States." This organization's assertive articulation of intersectionality—the Sojourners declared at their Eastern Seaboard Conference, "We will not be trampled upon any longer!!"—is ably explored by Gore. The IWO, too, often spoke to racial and gender oppression, while at other times, when appealing to women as "miners' wives," it privileged male concerns and lent primacy to "traditional" breadwinners in the CIO.[84]

Within the CIO, Murray acknowledged the importance of the IWO, writing in *The New Order* on the "patriotic" service that fraternal organizations provided. Murray argued that the IWO was "helping the entire nation" because only unionized workers possessed the purchasing power, "the key to prosperity," that would lift the country out of its economic morass.[85]

In 1937 Murray sent a congratulatory letter to Bedacht: "The Steel Workers Organizing Committee takes this opportunity to express its appreciation for the splendid cooperation and support rendered by your organization to the campaign to organize the steel workers in an industrial union." He requested continuing help as SWOC took the fight to "Little Steel." Bedacht responded with a letter of his own, and along with Murray's note, it was promptly reissued as a brochure, *Two Letters about One Cause*.[86] In pledging his organization's continued support in building SWOC and other unions, Bedacht distinguished between piecemeal, voluntarist efforts in benefit societies and the broader, more systemic protections strong unions could provide. "The overwhelming mass of . . . our Order are workers," he wrote.

> They joined this workers fraternal Order because they expect it to help them meet the problem of their economic insecurity. It cannot be conscientiously claimed that any fraternal organization can solve this problem effectively. . . . Here, only strong, fighting labor unions can help. The remedy is not fraternal benefits, but better wages. We must, therefore and do teach our members that a good worker-fraternalist must also be a good unionist.[87]

While the IWO worked to build them, progressive labor unions quickly came under assault as destroyers of personal liberty and responsibility. In 1944 the National Association of Manufacturers (NAM) published a booklet warning of "statism" unless government and unions' assaults on "freedom" were curbed. As this booklet, *Victory for Freedom*, was deposited in the IWO papers, someone in the Order noticed a NAM-sponsored conference had assailed the Wagner Act and "the sprawling alphabetical agencies of government." NAM cautioned, "We are in grave danger of finding ourselves under some form of statism where freedom languishes, and men are controlled by government rather than controlling it." NAM warned, "The vision of liberty that once stirred the souls of men is fading, and is being replaced . . . by the delusion that personal freedom and security can be achieved by dependence on the state." The booklet's writer also derided "the disruptive forces of class antagonism" in asserting the sanctity of "individual responsibility, private property, and free competition." Of course, in 1944 many workers, in the IWO and out of it, had firm recollections of the kind of security a unionless free market had delivered to them during the Depression. Bedacht's letter was a cogent reply to conservative bromides telling workers that only "a strong, self-reliant, individualistic, intelligent people" could lift themselves out of tragedy, conservative antiunion messages that resonated in the 1930s and 1940s, only to resurface decades later.[88]

In 1937 *The New Order* reported that "the IWO continued to put its shoulder behind the steel drive," with local Fraternal Orders Committee conferences in "I.W.O. (and also CP) strongholds in Farrell and Ambridge, Pennsylvania," and further IWO organizing drives across the country were met by the joyous news that United States Steel had announced its willingness to negotiate. After this breakthrough members of the Order continued to work with SWOC to force the officers of Little Steel companies to sign union contracts. One of the founders of Russian and Carpatho-Russian lodges in Warren, Ohio, was also active in working to found a CIO local at Warren's Republic Steel plant. Peter Kostyshak recounted to the president of the IWO's Carpatho-Russian Society a lifetime encountering "among the workers, discontent and unjustice" before he discovered Marxism in the pages of the Russian socialist newspaper *Novy Mir (New World)* shortly before World War I. He joined the CP in 1927 and eight years later was in the CIO battle to crack Little Steel. During World War II, Kostyshak continued to work in both the CIO and IWO in Warren's Republic Steel.[89]

Republic Steel remained one of the most intransigent Little Steel corporations, vowing to keep unions out of its plants. The most notoriously violent confrontation between SWOC pickets and the open-shop Republic Steel occurred in South Chicago. There on Memorial Day weekend 1937, peaceful picketers were shot and clubbed by Chicago policemen deputized to guard the private property of Republic president Tom Girdler. Ten people were killed and at least another ninety injured as police attacked pickets, who Chicago officers said were preparing a violent assault on the plant. A Paramount newsreel film of the melee, quickly dubbed the Memorial Day Massacre, indicated that several of the picketers, as well as women and children accompanying the strikers, were shot in the back or clubbed as they fled the police assault. Paramount deemed the film too inflammatory, and it was pulled before it could be screened. It would, however, have a private command performance before the Senate Education and Labor Committee investigating the incident.[90]

SWOC pickets in Chicago had been led by Krzycki, vice president of the ACWA delegated to the steel drive. Krzycki, although not a member of the IWO, was a labor leader of prominence in the Polish community who had also been elected undersheriff and Milwaukee alderman as a Socialist. During World War II, he would assume the presidency of a newly created progressive organization, the ASC, to which thousands of Slavic IWO members flocked.[91]

Following the Memorial Day Massacre, Roosevelt famously disassociated himself from both SWOC and intransigent industrialists such as Republic's Girdler, blaming both for the bloodshed in Chicago. "A plague on both your houses," the president is reported to have said, enraging Lewis, who hastened to remind Roosevelt that he had been reelected the previous year due in part to labor's support.[92]

Militant Slavic, Italian, and other workers were more certain they knew where to apportion blame for acts of violence against picketers. In June 1937 the Polish newspaper *Dziennik Polski* ran a photo of picketers walking the line outside Republic Steel's headquarters while wearing gas masks. The picketers carried placards vowing, "Republic Steel will strike until Girdler gets ink and signs agreement." A second placard read, "Tom Girdler spent million dollars on tear gas & ammunition but no ink for signing agreement. Girdler's Strike for Ink?"[93]

Picketers were wise to wear gas masks. The Senate committee investigating "the Chicago Memorial Day incident" noted that police deployed tear gas provided by Republic Steel, which had stockpiled $50,000 worth of gas. The committee noted that ten pickets had been killed and approximately ninety members of the group injured, thirty by gunfire, when Chicago police alleged that the marchers crossing an open field were in fact an organized, paramilitary group determined to attack and occupy the plant. After hearing testimony and screening the newsreel, the committee found no grounds for police charges of imminent threat. The film showed "that the marchers were engaged in earnest and heated debate with the police" but provided "no evidence of physical threats or the frenzied disorder which the police describe." Rather, evidence indicated that picketers were talking with police officers and then abruptly clubbed, shot, and tear gassed, leading to "the general bewilderment and panic of the crowd." Cases of men being beaten until they were blind were detailed. The report further revealed that when Krzycki and other SWOC leaders had addressed the strikers prior to their march, there had been no incitement to riot, as police alleged. Rather, Krzycki had joked that the men looked suntanned, healthy, and well-fed. In general the report concluded, "The consequences of the Memorial Day encounter were clearly avoidable by the police." The official use of force "must be ascribed," the report declared, "either to gross inefficiency in the performance of police duty or a deliberate effort to intimidate the strikers."[94]

Articles in the magazine of the International Labor Defense (ILD) documented the company-initiated violence in more militant tones. Marcantonio, president of the ILD and officer of the Order, wrote on "The Menace of Vigilantism" through which companies targeted striking workers. He charged that "vigilantes [were] on the march against union men in steel" with "citizens' committees" deployed against picketers with the backing of Girdler. A photo accompanying the article showed a line of club-wielding vigilantes sent against CIO pickets. The article detailed the convening of a conference in Johnstown, Pennsylvania, that alleged that constituted authorities and elected officials had proven helpless "to protect American citizens in their inalienable right to work," and "therefore, as loyal American citizens we feel it is our patriotic duty to perfect a nation-wide organization whose functions it shall be to restore and protect those constitutional rights that have been taken from American citizens by certain unworthy officials." Marcantonio said such calls to take the law into their own hands masked the fact that picketers had been murdered in the Chicago melee, while another three had been killed in Massillon, Ohio, "for exercising their constitutional rights"—that is, striking. The "Johnstown Plan," as the vigilante convention called its manifesto, was deployed "not to organize and fight for decent living conditions," as the CIO was doing, "but to commit murder" and "prevent labor from organizing." Marcantonio warned such vigilantism was "a declaration of fascism." Under cover of protecting a "right to work," vigilantes actually violated the "fundamental and constitutional rights of labor" when they broke up picket lines, smashed food kitchens, and abetted murder.[95]

Popular Front activists often deployed charges of fascism against their enemies. Still, an accompanying article in *Labor Defender* described workers shot through the abdomen, suffering gangrenous or amputated arms and legs due to gunshot wounds, or committed to insane asylums because police had clubbed them so severely. A photo of some of the pickets with bandaged heads noted that the "Victims of Memorial Day Massacre" were "charged with conspiracy—to get shot!" Members of the ILD or IWO who had faced similar situations in strikes might have agreed with the characterization of strikebreakers as fascists and the Memorial Day Massacre victims as "the advance guard of democracy." Marcantonio's invocation of Paul Revere on behalf of the CIO summoned the spirit of the Popular Front, arguing left-wing unionism was the full flowering of the spirit of '76. In such tellings Memorial Day victims were the new patriots.[96]

Not everyone shared these interpretations. The arch-conservative *Chicago Tribune* accepted the police department's argument that a violent, Communist-inspired riot had been prevented by officers' timely actions. The *Tribune* charged that the mob had assaulted the police first and that Communists had plotted the violent event, all of which Senator Robert La Follette Junior's committee soon dismissed as a falsehood. Accompanying this story on page one was a cartoon of the photogenic Krzycki playing cards with a police officer. "Strike director" Krzycki grins over his cards, "armed rioting against forces of law and order" and "Mob Violence." "Which hand is bound to win?" the caption asks, while the policeman sighs, "Will he never learn that he can't win if he plays those cards?" Subtle it was not. A month later the *Tribune* ran another cartoon accompanying a second indictment of the "Communist" CIO: "Ghost from the old graveyard" depicts a bomb-carrying grim reaper striding past gravestones "French Syndicalism," "The Molly Maguires," and "The old I.W.W. Composed of assassins, dynamiters, wobblies, terrorists, bums, syndicalists, weary Willies and political castoffs. Departed this earth scorned by mankind."[97] While leftists regarded pickets as guards of honor, conservatives saw them as terrorists and exonerated the policemen who shot them. Terrorism was in the eye of the beholder.

The *Tribune*'s articles and anti-Communist cartoons demonstrate that even at the height of the CIO's success many Americans saw the consortium of unions as a foreign-inspired, radical threat. The paper's indictment by printing press prefigured the charges that would be leveled at Krzycki's ASC and other left-leaning organizations a decade later. Indeed, in 1949 when HUAC issued a voluminous report condemning the Slav Congress as subversive, one of the prime pieces of evidence cited was Krzycki's union background. "In 1937 Krzycki was a leading speaker at a Chicago CIO mass meeting featured by the Communist press, which resulted in rioting . . . near the strike-bound Republic Steel Corporation's . . . plant," the report charged, resurrecting the *Tribune*'s attacks.[98]

By 1949 HUAC members such as a young Richard Nixon may have forgotten, if they ever knew, the earlier Senate committee report proving "menacing" pickets had been mowed down with machine guns, many shot in the back as they were fleeing. The difference in political climates of 1937 and 1949 is clear when comparing the reports by La Follette (who had left the Senate after being defeated in a Republican primary by Joseph McCarthy) and Nixon. The same Congress that issued the condemnation of the Slav Congress had already passed the Taft-Hartley Act, severely curtailing the effectiveness of left-leaning unions of the sort in which Slav Congress and IWO activists enrolled.[99]

Whatever the *Tribune* or later un-American investigators thought of their activities, IWO members were actively engaged in union organizational drives and strikes from the late 1930s. Keeran has shown that the IWO, together with other Communist-affiliated organizations, was instrumental in building the United Auto Workers (UAW), while Feurer documents that some of the most effective advocates for a strong UE were Communists such as Bill Sentner.[100] In 1938 the IWO committed to working to expand CIO unions, declaring that emergency aid of the sort mutual benefit societies offered the "toiling people" could never "solve the problem of economic security." For that the IWO looked to unions.[101]

Ironically, the centrality of the IWO to CIO sit-down strikes was corroborated by the FBI and OSS. Both intelligence organizations maintained voluminous files on the IWO, Slav Congress, and other leftist organizations, and these files are treasure troves for documenting their labor activism and commitment to civil rights. An FBI report from December 1946, for example, cited a HUAC report of January 3, 1939, on the Order's central role in the CIO's sit-down strikes.[102]

Dies expressed little love for organized labor throughout his helmsmanship of HUAC and was quite vocal in branding the CIO a Communist-dominated organization. The recirculation of older reports of alleged subversive activity was standard practice at the FBI, setting up a Möbius strip of tainted behavior once a conservative politician charged one as "red." Still, while Dies and the FBI agent who cited him came to bury, not praise, the IWO, they confirmed articles in the *Daily Worker* and *The New Order* asserting the IWO's centrality in battles to win union rights in open-shop America.[103]

The FBI scrupulously recorded the IWO's part in battles to organize the anti-union Ford Motor Company. In 1941 the IWO commemorated the victims murdered during the Ford Hunger March of 1932, combining this memorial with a commitment to support UAW organizers who were continuing the union effort. When the UAW finally won a contract from Ford, *Tyomies*, a Finnish Communist newspaper, ran a story noting, "Ford Motor Company workers received IWO congratulations for their success after four long years of hard work in bringing the Ford Company in to the Union." The paper noted that UAW Ford Local 600's reply letter expressed gratitude for IWO support during the River Rouge campaign. *Tyomies* further noted that Lewis and Murray had also thanked the IWO for its assistance. The FBI also noted that the Polonia Society supported strikers, and four years later backed Richard Frankensteen's run for mayor of Detroit. Frankensteen was a UAW vice president who was severely injured in an assault by Ford's "Service Department" employees, hired gunmen who attacked organizers at the River Rouge plant in Dearborn in 1937. The attack on Frankensteen at the "Battle of the Overpass" became another rallying cry for the unionists, although Frankensteen's later mayoral campaign combining support for both unions and racial equality proved unsuccessful. The OSS similarly made note of the IWO's close cooperation with the CIO's Political Action Committee during electoral campaigns such as Frankensteen's run.[104]

After the UAW gained recognition at Ford, the IWO continued to assist the union. Hungarian and Slovak lodges were asked to intervene to prevent a threatened race riot at the River Rouge plant, fomented by "the bitter undercurrent of prejudice and intolerance stirred up in the campaign." The UAW again acknowledged the IWO's importance in establishing the union at River Rouge, and the letter sent out by the Hungarian and Slovak lodges stressed not just the importance of workplace democracy, but the necessity of avoiding a race riot in the community. The IWO continued to stress racial, not just class-based, justice in its union activities. While the term was not in vogue in 1945, the IWO was an early practitioner of intersectionality. Both class and racial justice were stressed by the Order.[105]

As with the Order's unemployment and anti-eviction work, in its union work the organization responded to grassroots demands. Ed Falkowski recorded his work on behalf of the Polish Section of the IWO in his diary. In February 1941 Falkowski also worked as a SWOC organizer in western Pennsylvania, where he noted numerous grievances bedeviling unionists. Grievances arose from the introduction of new labor-saving machinery, which reopened "the eternal problem of wage classification: new rates by reason of new machines are a never-ending cause of grievance." The new machinery was also accompanied by the introduction of "incentive rates . . . to speed up production." The old nemesis speedup was long fought through slowdowns as when UAW organizer and later IWO officer Nowak organized a "go slow" campaign at Detroit's auto plants in 1937.[106] Four years later Falkowski found similar resistance to speedups and "a hundred percent support" for the steel strike. His diary lists a mountain of complaints of workplace hazards, speedups, and unsanitary workplaces and company houses. In Bridgeville, Pennsylvania, only two showers and thirty-six wash basins served the plant's fourteen hundred men. Of the company houses in steel towns, Falkowski noted, "pressed paper walls, & ceilings, no furnaces, etc. No cellar, only what we dug ourselves. Rents: $18 a month—$7 would be too much."[107]

In commenting on the ubiquitous charge that the CIO was run by Communists, Falkowski rhetorically asked, "Radicals running this strike? Outside agitators? Why, it's the men that's been 18 and 20 yrs. in that plant that voted to put it across." He recorded the remarks of one such veteran steelworker: "'If standing by my constitutional rights means I'm a communist then by god I'm fourteen times a communist!'"[108]

Falkowski's sardonic question, "radicals running this strike?" indicates that IWO builders knew with what disdain they were regarded by "economic royalists." That these comments on grassroots support for the IWO-backed union campaigns appeared in Falkowski's private diary suggests they were not self-serving glosses on the legitimacy of Order activities. Rather, as with black and white coal miners, textile workers, and others who writers such as Robin Kelley and Steve Nelson argue welcomed the support that CP organizers gave them, here workers felt the IWO was delivering relief to heartfelt, organic industrial grievances.[109]

During World War II, the IWO, like most Communist-affiliated organizations, committed to the no-strike pledge, mandatory overtime, and other measures to demonstrate fealty to winning the war. Although after the war this commitment was interpreted as slavish loyalty to Stalin's Soviet Union, the pride IWO unionists took in their contribution to the war effort was palpable. The SWS, knowing how recently its members had been derided as "hunkies," now boasted that its members working in auto plants, steel mills, and shipyards were contributing to the war effort no less than the soldiers and sailors employing the guns, tanks, and ships they produced. The Slav Congress likewise proudly noted that 53 percent of employees in these wartime heavy industries were Slavs, a fact later reissued by HUAC as cause to worry at the strength of the IWO and Slav Congress.[110]

Commitment to helping the war effort, and the Soviet Union, did not always seamlessly translate into abandoning militant commitment to fighting for workplace justice. When coal miners engaged in a wildcat strike in 1943 to protest the rising cost of living, limits on miners' pay, and mandatory overtime imposed by the War Production Board, some members of the IWO felt compelled to support the action, criticizing the suspension of miners' rights "for the duration." SWS members supported the wildcatting miners near Charleroi, Pennsylvania, while a Carpatho-Russian member writing in support of the wildcat angrily rejected the argument the alliance with Moscow necessitated deferring the right to strike. "You said that today we have an all-national war and all should try to defeat fascism," he wrote to a lodge brother. "Nobody can tell what kind of war this will be tomorrow or the day after tomorrow. Capitalism, Imperialism, and Fascism, are a trinity; those thugs not only change their tactics from day to day, but their whole program. Therefore, we, the workers, must be on our guards against this trinity." Although such vituperative language was discordant in a time of supposed wartime unity, coal country Slavs recalled how only a few years before machine guns had been deployed against striking miners. Wartime unity thus may have seemed ephemeral, especially if laborers were perceived to be doing most of the sacrificing on its behalf.[111]

Other IWO members, though, condemned the UMW's wildcat. "As regards [John L.] Lewis, whom you defend," one Carpatho-Russian member wrote to a lodge brother,

> I can only say that he is nothing but a brutal ruffian, craving for fame and might, a defeatist and an appeaser.... In the Miners' Union the dictatorship is worse than Hitler's. The simple workers whom he robs are afraid to say a word. Mr. Lewis should submit to the jurisdiction of the [National] War Labor Board. This is in the interest of winning the war; our war, the war of the plain man against Nazi-ism—Fascism. No arguments can change that.[112]

Hyperbole of Lewis as "worse than Hitler" was the sort of rhetoric the IWO frequently employed to paint the world in Manichaean terms. But even the IWO was divided on the wisdom of adhering to the no-strike pledge, or backing the coal miners' wildcat strike. This member was evidently responding to a letter (not available in the archives) defending the wildcat, suggesting that during the war not every IWO militant abandoned defense of fellow workers' perceived interests, or found it all that easy to shift position simply because the CP directed him to do so.

"Did They Fight for This?" Labor on the Ropes

Following the war the IWO continued its support for militant unions and social justice but in an increasingly conservative political climate. As George Lipsitz has noted, 1946 saw more strikes than any previous year, as workers were determined to maintain the gains of the CIO's organizing drives and make up for wartime sacrifices. The memory of the rapidity with which World War I promises of a better bargain for labor had vanished in the wage cuts and layoffs of 1919–1921 steeled workers to guarantee there was no reprise after the second war. The IWO consequently supported General Motors strikers in 1946, sending greetings, money, and food. Societies reported on efforts in support of steel, auto, and "UE strikers in New Jersey, and many others." "Money was donated, women served in the kitchens, full cooperation was given to the trade union leaders," Slovaks reported of the steel strike in western Pennsylvania and Ohio. The Slovak *Ľudový kalendár* went even further, lionizing black and white striking steelworkers and UE pickets in East Pittsburgh as "the minute men of '46," as heroic as the soldiers of the American Revolution. But in many cases strikes were broken up by a combination of recalcitrant company officials and police and state actors who believed labor had gone too far. An alarmed Philadelphia lodge published a cartoon in its newsletter of mounted policemen clubbing strikers. "Did they fight for this?" the caption asked.[113]

During the midterm elections that year, a Republican majority was returned in Congress and the Taft-Hartley Act reined in wildcat and sympathy strikes, and allowed the president to order workers back to work in a "cooling off" period and decide which potential strikers had to continue working as a matter of national emergency. Most infamously, all union officials had to swear they did not belong to the CP; unions failing to file such affidavits were barred from protection of the National Labor Relations Board. Left-affiliated unions such as the UE and Mine, Mill and Smelter saw their membership plummet as bitter raids by rival unions ensued, and in 1949 the CIO expelled such left-affiliated unions.[114]

A Brooklyn lodge published an anti-Taft-Hartley broadside and cartoon of glum chain gang prisoners, "To be or not to be a slave?" Claiming the act would force labor to accept "whatever pay, no matter how low, Big Business jams down your throats," the broadside said the bill was "forging the chains for you right now. Here is the ugly face of fascism, clear and undisguised." Another Brooklyn lodge used its newsletter to rail against allegations that labor was a monopoly, pointing to the poverty, slum housing, and inadequate medical care most working people still faced in 1947. "Labor has a complete monopoly on all the ramshackle houses in the slums of all great cities." The editorial, reprinted from Mobile, Alabama, also cited labor's monopoly on all spots in poorhouses and charity wards "in too many unkempt city hospitals," with an additional "complete monopoly to suffer and to die for lack of proper medical attention because of the high fees of professional physicians." The editorial was accompanied by a cartoon from the York, Pennsylvania, *Gazette and Daily* of labor's secret weapon, a mighty fist, "Political Action."[115]

This assault on Taft-Hartley, with its critique of America's continuing slum and health care crises among the poor, imaginatively linked unions and activists in Brooklyn, Alabama, and Pennsylvania. By 1947 this institutional network for a Left politics of social movements, in which IWO members had access to a broad array of astute critiques of capitalism's inequities, was already imperiled by the architects of conservative measures targeting left-leaning labor unions as well as the IWO. The dismantling of such venues for critical, progressive political action, the IWO would argue, may have been the very deliberate point of such measures.

Headquarters issued action letters and resolutions against all antilabor bills introduced into the Eightieth Congress. "Keep America Free—Defend Labor's Rights," the IWO urged. The SWS sent protest letters to Congress against the attacks on unions and called instead for a strengthening of the Wagner and Norris-La Guardia Acts, while a Serbian IWO member wrote to President Harry Truman urging him to veto Taft-Hartley.[116]

Although Truman did veto Taft-Hartley (the veto was overridden), he had readily employed his powers to break up a nationwide railroad strike, threatening to run the trains with soldiers. Truman would later threaten to intervene to keep key industries such as railroads from striking during the Korean War. The IWO's ominous warnings of fascism marching into America must have at that moment seemed prophetic to some Order members. In 1947 the Cervantes Fraternal Society reported on its support of the tobacco workers' strike but also worried about Truman's strikebreaking powers. "In June of last year, President Truman tried to break the railroad strike," the society reported, "and almost at the same time the strike of the seamen. Invitations have been sent out to our delegates in order to discuss what can be done in the 'colony' . . . for their defense." Labor's powers were vitiated, and in 1947 the IWO was branded a subversive organization, at least in part, the Order argued, because of its unrepentant support for militant unions. In denouncing the IWO's placement on the List of Subversive Organizations, the Order declared, "We shall not submit passively to the efforts to impose a Taft-Hartley Act upon the fraternal movement and we shall not yield to the reactionary conspiracy to emasculate the liberty of the American people."[117]

By this point members of the IWO were beginning to ask what it meant to be "un-American," and to whom exactly one should be loyal. Philadelphia members watching such aggressive strikebreaking actions were not the only ones in the IWO asking "did we fight for this?" On the Order's twentieth anniversary, Greene recalled "our support of labor in the great CIO organizing drives" as one of the IWO's greatest achievements. The Order ran a full-page ad in the *Sunday Worker* before Labor Day 1949 saluting "the men and women in the factories, mines and mills, who are the source of America's riches." The ad featured a photograph of Philadelphia members preparing donations of canned food for striking UE workers, extolled the contributions to building CIO unions, and pledged to continue fighting on labor's side "for the repeal of the Taft-Hartley Act and against the reactionary drive aimed at the civil liberties of progressive Americans," as well as "to help end discrimination against Negroes, to abolish segregation and Jim Crow, to achieve the full equality of the Negro people in every sphere of life." As in so many of its campaigns, the IWO twinned espousals of racial equality with class-based drives to aid industrial workers.[118]

What the IWO regarded as a badge of honor, however, was quickly labeled a mark of opprobrium. In 1951 the *New York World-Telegram and Sun* ran an exposé of the Order condemning Bedacht's 1938 boast that in steel, auto, and rubber union drives, IWO members "were outstanding fighters and leaders." The provision of food and clothing to needy strikers was recast as an ominous threat to American industry: "Because of its ability to collect large quantities of clothing or food as well as money, the IWO paved the way for secret Reds to work their way into needy unions, particularly during organizing drives or strikes." Solidarity with fellow workers was now seen as part of a diabolical plot. Canned food for electrical workers took on ominous, red-tainted connotations.[119]

Near the end of World War II the CIO Political Action Committee, with which the IWO had so proudly participated, was already in the crosshairs of HUAC, which alleged that it was the brainchild of Moscow. Hostility to the very concept of organized labor is only thinly disguised in a March 1944 report. "While it is not the purpose or the province of our committee to enter into the question of wage demands," the report somewhat disingenuously stated, "the question comes within the jurisdiction of the . . . Committee . . . when such demands are merely a cover for subversive designs calculated to interfere with national security and war production." The report offered job actions by UE as examples of such subversive interference with national security.[120] Following the war the IWO would also be charged with such inimical interference as the Pentagon pursued policies with which these organizations disagreed. How to reconcile labor unions' rights to free association and collective bargaining when these newly won rights happened to interfere with a Pentagon-proclaimed national security emergency, soon to become open-ended, was never fully explained.

Out of step with the postwar political climate, the IWO continued to advocate universal health insurance. The Order had established medical clinics for members in larger cities, and even provided birth control clinics to women in New York. There, too, the city IWO Education Committee conducted, with Spanish-speaking lodges, a health survey of Harlem and lobbied for the opening of "additional health facilities" in "Spanish Harlem." These campaigns, though, were recognized as only stopgap measures, and throughout its existence the IWO called for government provision of health care. In its executive board meetings in 1938 and 1939, the IWO committed to working for what later became known as single-payer health care.[121]

Fortunately, the IWO had allies, one of whom, Senator Murray of Montana, introduced several bills between 1944 and 1947 extending Social Security to provide federally funded health insurance. "Medical Care is one of the necessities of life which a democracy should provide to all members of the community," he told approving delegates at the Jewish Section's 1944 convention. Bedacht's support for the bill was publicized in *Národné noviny*, the NSS newspaper.[122]

Bedacht countered opposition to government health insurance in his January 1944 article "What about Socialized Medicine?" in the IWO's *Fraternal Outlook*. In arguments that parallel the debates around "Obamacare" seventy years later, Bedacht said the federal plan would not preclude individuals from selecting doctors of their choice or turn doctors "overnight into undesirably sour and incompetent bureaucrats. We have a better opinion of American doctors." Bedacht noted that in the free market, millions of Americans were not really free to select a doctor of their choice as they could not afford private health care. The health care bill would at last "accept government responsibility for the health of the people," he wrote. "No fraternalist can find anything wrong with that." To clinch the argument, *Fraternal Outlook* ran an illustration of Federal Arts Project painter Emanuel Romano's modernist mural illustrating the benefits of "socialized medicine," an example of the IWO's collaboration with progressive artists (Figure 2.4).[123]

At war's end the IWO produced a pamphlet, *Never Again!* by CP member Joseph Starobin that made the case for "a National Health Insurance Fund to cover every man, woman and child in the United States. Out of this Fund, a man could call up any doctor he wanted." The pamphlet urged passage of the Wagner-Murray-Dingell Bill to close the country's "medical gap." One of the bill's sponsors, New York Senator Robert Wagner, wrote an introduction labeling his bill "an American Plan" and asking why Great Britain, Ven-

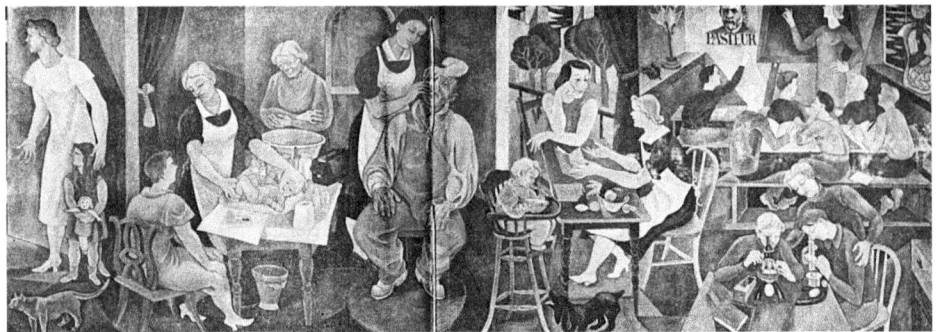

Figure 2.4 *Fraternal Outlook* made the case for universal health care's benefits for all Americans with an illustration by Federal Arts Project painter Emanuel Romano.
Source: Emanuel Romano illustration, in Max Bedacht, "What about Socialized Medicine?" *Fraternal Outlook*, January 1944, 16–17, IWO-CU, box 48.

ezuela, Uruguay, Canada, and Mexico were enacting similar plans, but not the United States. A cartoon by William Gropper showed a train, the "Wagner-Murray-Dingell Bill," laden with precious cargo—"health, medical and hospital care" and "$950,000,000 for hospitals and health centers"—hurtling "full speed ahead" toward Washington (Figure 2.5).[124]

The train was derailed by opposition of organizations such as the American Medical Association (AMA) and NAM, leveling charges of "socialized medicine," epithets already repeated in journals such as the Slovaks' *Národné noviny*. Grassroots IWO members, however, orchestrated lobbying campaigns for the bill, employing the technologies of mass communication on its behalf. Garibaldi Society member Philip D'Amato used broadcasts on WJLB by the Italian American Radio Club of Detroit to extol the health insurance proposal. Vice President John Middleton made the case for the act on radio. The IWO also hired United Film Productions to produce a short film, *Health and Security for America*. Lodges were urged to screen the film, which, "through photos, cartoons and spoken narration, explains what is contained in the two Wagner-Murray-Dingell Bills. It was produced by the Order as another weapon in our campaign to pass the bills." Milgrom wrote lodges, "This strip is the first of, what we hope to be, a series of films and film strips which will deal with the various problems confronting America and particularly those related to our program of fighting for health and security."[125]

Milgrom argued in supporting the measure that "insurance versus charity is the issue," discounting alternatives such as hoping individuals acquired private insurance. This, he argued, put the onus on poorly paid workers and let employers and the government off the hook. In 1947 Senator Murray again thanked the IWO for its cooperation. Support for universal health care

Figure 2.5 In 1945 the IWO publicized its support for the Wagner-Murray-Dingell Bill in pamphlets illustrated by artist William Gropper that showed this measure for universal health care hurtling "full speed ahead" toward Washington.
Source: William Gropper illustration, in Joseph Starobin, *Never Again!* (New York: IWO, August 1945), 8–9, IWO-CU, box 49.

was still a point of pride in Labor Day ads and public speeches in 1949 and 1950. Milgrom wrote an article, "Americanism and Loyalty," in the *Jewish Fraternalist* that listed commitment to universal health care as one of the IWO's patriotic measures. But as the Cold War deepened, support for universal health care was another marker, to many conservatives, of one's subversive nature.[126]

For all its support for the cause of labor, the IWO was not always on the side of striking men. In 1944 the JPFO cosponsored a full-page ad in the *Philadelphia Daily News*. "Philadelphia on Guard," the ad warned in condemning the "hate strike" by trolley drivers who had walked off the job rather than allow the hiring of black motormen. The strike was condemned as "treason against the American war effort" and "traitorous to the fundamental principles of American liberty and the right of all men to live and to earn their living—without discrimination." The ad charged that "ugly un-American forces" had instigated the strike and demanded a grand jury investigation.

Ironically, the JPFO would soon find itself branded un-American. But support for racial equality was adamant. The JPFO disseminated flyers in Yiddish and English calling for "Negro and White! Christian and Jew" to oppose the hate strike. The Philadelphia regional IWO declared, "A fleet of Nazi bombers could not have caused as much damage as has this treacherous 'stab in the back.'" While the IWO stood by the rights of labor, the cause of racial justice was equally central to its principles. The intersectional commitment that the Order demonstrated would not allow it to side with one racial component of the working class against another.[127]

As Sugrue, Hirsch, and others have shown, during the 1940s the defenders of white privilege violently resisted African Americans' citizenship rights in hate strikes and housing riots.[128] The IWO, however, maintained a commitment to interracial civil rights activism equally as fervent as its struggle for working-class justice, as its denunciation of the Philadelphia strike makes clear. In distinction to the more familiar embrace of white privilege by Southeast European Americans, the IWO forged a path of interracial solidarity, with thousands of "red" white ethnics taking that less-traveled road with their African American and Hispanic sisters and brothers. It is to this interracial civil rights activism that we turn next.

3

"We Dare Entertain Thoughts Not to the Liking of Present-Day Bigots"

Race, Civil Rights, and the IWO

In 1944 when white IWO members defended the rights and safety of black Philadelphia trolley drivers, they were often alone. Developing a white identity was a key component in Southeast European immigrants' American acculturation, and by World War II many immigrants had learned to distance themselves from black fellow workers through foreign-language newspaper reports of lynchings and race riots and other cultural productions delineating black people as impermissible outsiders. Many white ethnics also violently resisted black residential incursions into all-white ethnic neighborhoods.[1]

Scholars such as Roediger, Matthew Frye Jacobson, and Noel Ignatiev have noted the fraught history of white enmity toward black fellow workers, while nevertheless highlighting moments of interracial solidarity sporadically built by activists recognizing their necessity for overcoming a common plight in industrial America. Even if the larger trajectory saw white workers castigating black workers as illegitimate competitors, the work of such scholars suggests another, interracial world was possible.[2]

Radical white ethnics offered one such alternative. During the Popular Front of the 1930s and 1940s, members of the IWO, which avidly recruited African American, Hispanic, and even Black Muslim and Arabic members into its consortium of fraternal societies, endorsed anticolonial movements and black civil rights at home. The IWO carried forward the work on racial equality in which Southeast European and black comrades had been engaged during the 1920s. The SWS and other IWO lodges joined the "American Crusade against Lynching" and lobbied for an end to the poll tax and segregation. During World War II, other progressive-minded Slavs such as

Krzycki helped found the ASC, an organization that advocated civil rights for black people during and after the war as part of its campaign to make Roosevelt's Four Freedoms a reality.

Scholars of the African American freedom struggle such as Gellman, McDuffie, Maxwell, and others offer strong evidence that when it came to civil rights, activists within the CP and its allies often acted out of deep commitment, and did so with a great deal of local initiative, not cynical manipulation by or subordination to Moscow.[3] Other scholars such as Zumoff and Hakim Adi argue that during the 1920s and 1930s white Communists in the United States exhibited little appreciation of the onerous racism operating apart from class oppression to subordinate African Americans, and they had to be prodded by the Comintern to develop a program addressing the plight of black and colonized peoples.[4] The Comintern's May 1926 call for reports on what the CP was doing with regard to the "Negro" situation would suggest Moscow often felt the need to goad American comrades to facilitate racial equality.

A close look at the activities of radicals in the IWO and other organizations, though, reveals deep commitment to racial equality, even if comrades sometimes faltered or were unsure how to implement such a program. Letters, reports, and telegrams found in the CP's archives, as well as the papers of the IWO, strongly indicate that Party members and nonparty members of the IWO often acted on their own initiative when it came to agitating for black civil rights at home and anticolonialism abroad and were not passive or robotic recipients of orders radiating from Moscow, as those intent on denigrating American communism allege. Fixation on the degree of control by Moscow ignores, too, the admirable causes such as civil rights that black and white militants were working on, decades before nonradicals joined the movement.

Also striking is white ethnics' commitment to interracial solidarity in the IWO in the face of government red-baiting and many other white ethnics' indifference or hostility to black people's grievances. The IWO's record stands in stark distinction to the embrace of white privilege exhibited by most Americans of Southeast European descent. From the 1920s to 1950s, left-wing white ethnics sought to dismantle Jim Crow, end lynching and the poll tax, and foster racial equality. To be sure, activists in the IWO were often prone to missteps, sometimes exhibiting condescension or even what comrades called "white chauvinism"; by the 1940s courtesy of some of the social-welfare benefits for which the IWO had labored so hard, even progressive white ethnics were beginning to reap the advantages of unthinking racial privileges as they "worked toward whiteness" in relative comfort compared to African American and Hispanic comrades. One IWO member even moved to Levittown, Long Island, emblematic of the suburban racialized good life of which Roediger and others have written. Nevertheless, for all their miscues these left-wing white ethnics in the IWO represent the road not taken, the multiethnic path to racial equality.⁵

Combating Segregation Everywhere

From its founding the IWO was committed to combating America's racial caste system. Beyond accident and death policies the IWO envisioned itself as a militant lobbying group preparing the proletariat for a coming social-democratic workers' state. As such the Order lobbied for Social Security, enacted in 1935, and universal health care, among other programs, as we have seen.⁶

Yet the IWO did not privilege class issues over its work combating racism, for both causes were central to the Order's mission. Along with this early proletarian militancy went a 1932 declaration, "The International Workers Order condemns segregation as a vicious anti-working class policy of the bourgeoisie. It follows the leadership of the Communist Party in its struggle against this practice. To make this struggle ever more effective, the I.W.O. must carry on a continuous campaign within its own ranks, combatting the principle and ideology of segregation." The Order vowed that "continuous efforts must be made everywhere . . . to permeate all our white branches with Negro members and all our Negro branches with white members. This, and the mobilization of our branches to participate in the struggles led by the Communist Party, against lynching, against Jim Crowism, etc., must be the measures to transform backward workers that join the I.W.O. into advanced workers." The Order also warned, "Care must be exercised that infiltration of white members into Negro branches will not lead to the usurpation of the leadership of these branches by the white members." The Order orchestrated a fine balancing act between black members' autonomy and integration.⁷

Such commitment to fight against white supremacy was, not surprisingly, endemic to the IWO, for among radical immigrants, commitment to antiracism predated the Order. During the 1920s the SWS had already denounced lynching in its newspaper, *Rovnosť ludu*, as well as running exposés on "American imperialism," calling it "a history that has scandalized half the world." The Marines in Latin America and the Philippines were said to be "at the beck and call of Wall Street." Such leftist journals were some of the few places immigrants heard critiques of America's racialized new world order. John Bodnar and June Granatir Alexander have rightly identified immigrant newspapers as agents of acculturation to America, but in nonradical newspapers articles often exerted a racial tutelage on who was and was not fit for self-governance. Articles frequently derided nonwhite peoples' national aspirations, as when *Slovák v Amerike* applauded "a strict interpretation of the Monroe Doctrine" toward Haiti, Cuba, and Venezuela, and dismissed West

Africans as "ceaselessly restless savages" who did not appreciate the civilizing blessings of colonial rule. Conversely, in 1924 the Communist-affiliated *Rovnosť ľudu* sniped, "We heard a lot about German imperialism from the recently departed Woodrow Wilson, but not a peep about American imperialism in the Philippines, Haiti, Cuba, Puerto Rico, Santo Domingo, Mexico and elsewhere."[8]

In the 1920s white ethnics and African Americans in Party affiliates such as the All-American Anti-Imperialist League and the American Negro Labor Congress (ANLC) made the cognitive and agitational connections between fights against Jim Crow at home and imperialism abroad. ANLC officers also worked within UNIA, seeking to wean left-wingers away from a solely "Back to Africa" focus and cooperate with Party members as they worked to end racialized oppression in both the United States and colonized Africa. As Steven Hahn notes, many in UNIA saw the movement as "preaching preparedness" and said Marcus Mosiah Garvey "never did advocate for all Negroes to go back to Africa." As such many in UNIA may have agreed with the message the Party chairman sent them: "The rights of the Negro in Africa are not free for the taking. They have to be fought for, no less than the rights of the Negro in America." The ANLC's national organizer likewise made the connection between fighting for black civil rights in America and struggling against oppression in South Africa. It was grassroots American initiatives, not Kremlin directives, that pushed for forceful action, in this case looking to strangle apartheid in its cradle.[9]

Not only high-ranking Party officials sought to reach out to progressive UNIA members. In November 1926 B. Borisoff of Gary, Indiana, wrote to General Secretary Ruthenberg on the work he was doing to win over UNIA members "to the view-point of class struggle in America." Borisoff said in Gary and elsewhere the opposition group resisting Garvey's hegemony "is closer to us in its willingness to fight for the interests of the negro in America and to view this struggle as a class struggle." In Gary, he said, UNIA members "form a considerable part of the steel workers." Borisoff thanked Ruthenberg for names of black and Mexican workers, with whom he was beginning to organize. What is striking is to find a correspondent named Borisoff reaching out to black and Mexican fellow workers, to organize, not terrorize them. Many other Slavic, Irish, and Italian steelworkers in the aftermath of the failed 1919 steel strike scapegoated black people as impermissible intruders on whites-only job sites and neighborhoods, fire-bombing the homes of blacks who did not honor the color line. Here a "red" Slav looked to enlist black allies in the class struggle.[10]

Borisoff's efforts were not always appreciated by Gary comrades, but not because they resented a Slav reaching out to black people in UNIA. Rather, in 1927 the Party was contacted by Lake County, Indiana, Communists who complained that Borisoff had failed to publicize a "Negro" meeting in East

Chicago, among other derelictions. While many Slavs by the 1920s were joining other white Americans in resisting black people's advances at job sites or neighborhoods, radical immigrants faulted Borisoff for not doing enough for black fellow workers.[11]

Other comrades worked to organize non-Europeans. William Schneiderman had his hands full countering the AFL's denunciations of his Los Angeles comrades' work organizing black workers in unions as the establishment of "dual unions." The AFL opposed any attempt to organize this group, Schneiderman said, charging that "the Negroes were imported as scabs." Of course, many AFL craft unions exercised a strictly Jim Crow membership policy during the 1920s, and only a few militants such as Schneiderman sought to bring black members into the House of Labor. A few years later Thompson would similarly break New Orleans unionists' "whites only" clause on a mission from the IWO.[12]

In 1926 the Organization Department informed the ANLC that the Hungarian American Brotherhood's newspaper, *Új Előre,* had written, "One of our very good comrades, Joseph Szabo" of East Saint Louis was "working among Negroes in a machine shop" and, acting on his own, was "trying to propagate radicalism" among them. However, since Szabo was "not very fluent in English," his success was limited, and the department suggested that the ANLC send some copies of the *Negro Champion* to aid Szabo in his interracial organizing. Szabo's work "among Negroes" came just nine years after the infamous East Saint Louis white-on-black riot, in which other Southeast European immigrants had joined fellow whites with very different attitudes toward black people living in their city. The fellowship exhibited by Szabo, a member of the Hungarian fraternal society that would soon amalgamate with the IWO, and other members of the Left milieu stands in contrast to the actions of other white ethnics. As a veteran of the Industrial Workers of the World acknowledged in a 1924 letter, "The Negro and South European immigrant in the cities mix cutthroat competition."[13]

As the IWO would later affirm, racial barriers to self-determination or immigration had to fall. Fourteen years after Szabo's campaign, the IWO's African American vice president, Thompson, reported that the "Negro people" were united in their anticolonialism and were watching with great interest the campaigns of "the Indian National Congress which is leading the 350 millions of India to freedom from British imperialism." She noted that African American comrades in particular had "more than casual interest" in this struggle, as black people experienced imperialism as "a living issue" in Africa and the West Indies.[14] The IWO consistently linked civil rights activism at home to anticolonialism abroad.

Linkages between anticolonialism and advocacy of black civil rights persisted in the IWO. The Order included the Frederick Douglass–Abraham Lincoln Society for African Americans and the Cervantes Fraternal Lodge for Puerto Ricans as well as interracial English-language lodges. Although many lodges were ethnically defined, as Jewish, Polish, and Ukrainian members testified, interracial socializing and political activism was frequent. Moreover, by 1932 the IWO was working to recruit and enroll black people and second-generation white ethnics into integrated English branches, and such integrated branches continued until the Order's demise. As early as January 1931, leadership regarded it as essential that the organization "start to build English speaking branches of the IWO among the millions of white and Negro workers together." At the same time other ethnic insurance societies explicitly barred nonwhite membership, a policy in force as late as 1948. Conversely, the IWO's 1934 constitution and by-laws vowed to "organize agitation and cultural activities among its members with a view to creating . . . an understanding of the needs of these struggles to break down . . . the illusory barriers of race, creed and color, to establish among them the practices of class solidarity." While later versions of the constitution downplayed the Marxist class struggle, the commitment to interracial membership and black equality remained.[15]

As Chapter 1 notes, other races were actively recruited into the IWO, as when a Los Angeles organizer established Japanese and "Spanish" (likely Mexican) branches. Cape Verdean branches were created in New England after IWO organizers Jesús Colón and Sol Vail contacted Portuguese-speaking men in New Bedford, Massachusetts, and elsewhere. Cubans organized lodges in Tampa, while Arabic workers in Detroit and its vicinity established branches for their communities. The Cervantes Fraternal Lodge was established within the IWO for Hispanic members, and, as a Brooklyn member attested, instilled pride in Puerto Rican culture at a time when this community was denigrated by most white Americans.[16]

From its inception the IWO stressed the need to enroll black people in English-speaking lodges, where activists such as Thompson and Edward Nelson quickly exercised great autonomy. This is perhaps not surprising, for the Order was founded shortly after the CP promulgated its controversial Black Belt Thesis, arguing that as an oppressed national minority, African Americans had the right to self-determination up to and including creating a separate nation in the majority-black counties of the South. Critics derided the Party's thesis as having little purchase among black people themselves, and opponents such as Max Shachtman argued that the plans for a separate black nation ignored the hundreds of thousands of black people who had already migrated to northern industrial centers such as Detroit.[17] A careful reading of the CP's resolutions on the Black Belt Thesis suggests that the creation of a separate black nation was not an ironclad demand but rather a tactic, one option to be explored as part of "an intensive struggle [for] social and political equality." The Party continued to demand full equality for black people, even as it recognized "the right of Negroes for national self-determination in the South, where Negroes comprise a majority of the population." However, only where "the Negro masses put forward such national demands of their own accord" would the Party support such efforts. Racial equality was the larger goal. Moreover, counter to Shachtman's assertions, the Party recognized that many black people lived in the industrial North, where the "Negro question" could not be avoided. In the North, though, it was argued that black people should be recruited into the Party's existing organizations, where they could be trained as proletarian leaders.[18]

With such aims in mind, the IWO made organizing black members a priority. Party leaders such as B. D. Amis and James Ford worked with the Order to recruit black members in Harlem, Chicago, Detroit, Newark's Third Ward, and elsewhere. In Norfolk and Portsmouth, Virginia, in 1935, Alexander Wright established IWO branches consisting of black and Jewish small businessmen, while the IWO also established a toehold in Birmingham, Alabama, where members assisted in the Party assault on Jim Crow documented by Kelley.[19] A black IWO member named John Jefferson recruited with Thompson among black and white workers in New Orleans, which he saw as "an excellent field for the I.W.O." However, the promise of interracial harmony was not always so easy to achieve, even in the IWO or the Party. Two months after his efforts, Jefferson wrote to Clarence Hathaway, editor of the *Daily Worker*, charging that "white chauvinism, lily whiteism and Lovestonites" existed within New Orleans. "Comrades, there is a revolt brewing within the Party among the Negro comrades," Jefferson ominously warned, "whose rumblings you soon shall hear."[20]

The CP and the IWO certainly both exhibited "white chauvinism," as is addressed more fully in a later section. But even if Jefferson and other African American radicals sometimes grew disenchanted with the Order's commitment to interracial organizing, such activism—imperfectly implemented or not—was rare in 1935 America. Few other organizations enrolled Jewish, Slavic, Italian, and Hungarian members alongside African Americans, Arabs, and Hispanics, as was the practice in the Order. Thompson was gratified to see among members on her organizing tours "not only willingness but eagerness to accept leadership from a Negro woman." In Detroit local IWO officials worried that Scotch autoworkers would not take direction from a black woman, but Thompson reassured them and indeed won white workers' loyalty. In 1935 she became the Order's national secretary and in 1938 was elected a vice president. During the Order's reorganization in World War II, a black Douglass-Lincoln Society was founded to join the organization's ethnic societies such as the SWS and Cervantes Fraternal Society for Hispanic members. The interracial tent of the IWO was capacious and attractive enough to enfold Black Muslims in places such as Cleveland and New Haven. These members expressed their appreciation for the organization's racial equality and low-cost insurance policies available without discrimination.[21]

Beyond a multiracial membership—as important and unique as that was in 1930s America—the IWO was committed to substantive programs for advancing racial equality. Even as the IWO faced government prosecution, the Order's progressive stance on racial equality and black rights made it into the record. Cross-examination of state's witness George Powers brought out that "the IWO made a special appeal to Negro membership and supported . . . Negroes in Major League Baseball, the Anti-Poll Tax Amendment, anti-lynch legislation, and the Civil Rights Program." Powers also noted that when he was an IWO member in 1934, he collaborated with Treasurer Shipka in defense of the Scottsboro Boys, black Alabama teens sentenced to death for alleged rape of white women. During his cross-examination it came out that "even before Powers received his directive [from the Party] . . . the Scottsboro case was on the agenda of the IWO," suggesting that the group's members were genuinely concerned about injustices to Southern black people, not cynically using the issue for Communist advantage. Still, at the height of the red scare, vocal advocacy of black civil rights was regarded by many conservatives as subversive in and of itself. Powers admitted that some of what the IWO advocated may have had merit but saw the IWO's Scottsboro program as proof Moscow had been directing the Order to foment racial trouble.[22]

"Aiding the Scottsboro Defense with All Its Might"

As with many other anti-Communist opponents of the IWO, the testimony of the government's star witness alleging that the Order had stirred up racial animosity posits an irenic America of racial harmony that would have been news to many black and white members. What Powers did get right, though, was the rapidity with which the IWO took independent initiative in championing racial equality. This indeed was first exhibited in campaigns on behalf of the Scottsboro defendants. As early as May 1931 the IWO and foreign-language newspapers serving its members were mobilized in fundraisers on behalf of the Scottsboro defense team led by the ILD. This was to be expected, for one of the cocounsels in the case was Brodsky, lawyer for both the ILD and IWO. Radical ethnic communities such as Latvians and Slovaks organized mass demonstrations and editorialized in newspapers for the defendants' freedom. The Slovaks also raised funds for the ILD and wired protest telegrams to Alabama governor Benjamin Miller denouncing the legal lynching. It was reported, "The I.W.O. is taking steps to mobilize all of its branches to participate in this campaign led by the League of Struggle for Negro Rights [LSNR] and the International Labor Defense."[23]

Local lodges pitched in with this campaign, too. In July 1931 *The Spark* noted that the Providence, Rhode Island, youth branch was "aiding the Scottsboro defense with all its might." As Dan Carter notes, the ILD and its radical supporters were not squeamish about denouncing the legal lynching orchestrated by sham bourgeois justice in Alabama's courts. The LSNR advertised a "Save the Scottsboro Nine" rally planned for Cleveland with flyers featuring a cartoon of a black lynching victim hanging from the torch of the Statue of Liberty. That the case was more a racially tinged rape allegation, possessing little class-based element, was ignored by the ILD and other Communist-affiliated organizations. Haywood Patterson, Clarence Norris, and the other Scottsboro defendants were recast as stand-ins for all racially oppressed workers.[24]

As the nine young defendants faced retrials in Alabama, the IWO continued to demonstrate for the teens' release. In May 1932 Slovak lodges orchestrated protest meetings "against the lynch verdict in Scottsboro." The party instructed the IWO to coordinate mass meetings with other organizations such as the ILD and the LSNR. "Especially in Negro neighborhoods," the IWO was additionally told, "streets [and] buildings should be painted at night with slogans against lynching, 'The Scottsboro Boys Shall Not Die,' 'Death Penalty to the Lynchers.'" The Party carefully planned its spontaneous demonstrations denouncing lynch justice.[25]

While this directive gives the appearance that the IWO was merely the recipient of top-down instructions from the Party, at other times the Order's members needed little prompting in supporting the defendants. A 1934 Philadelphia regional convention passed a resolution for the release of the Scottsboro teens, Tom Mooney, a labor leader who had wrongfully been imprisoned for the 1916 bombing of a San Francisco Preparedness Day parade, "and all class-war prisoners." Black and white IWO members in Portsmouth and Norfolk, Virginia, raised funds and protested to aid the ILD defense campaign. As other racist cases caused scandal in the 1930s, the IWO linked them to the ongoing Scottsboro travesty. In New York in September 1935 Shaffer reported that the IWO had raised $1,000 for the defendants in Scottsboro as well as Herndon, who had been imprisoned for leading an interracial unemployment campaign in Atlanta. The convention of the IWO's Russian lodges heard reports of the eighteen recorded lynchings that had occurred in the first four months of 1933. A representative of the ILD congratulated the Russians for their "valuable assistance" and asked them to continue with their generous support for the ILD's expensive legal work in Scottsboro.[26]

Not every lodge was always as supportive of the ILD's defense campaign. Gardos complained that "the artificial throwing in of the Scottsboro boys" was doing a lot "to 'cool off' people" in the Hungarian Workers' Sick Benefit and Educational Federation.[27] Some Hungarians who had joined the IWO for the instrumental protection it offered may have regarded the plight of Patterson, Norris, and the other defendants as irrelevant to their lives. Gardos's letter suggests, too, a resistance from some Hungarians to constant directives streaming from Party headquarters. Other ethnic lodges, however, continued to rally and raise funds on behalf of the defendants.

James Miller, Susan Pennybacker, and Eva Rosenhaft have demonstrated that the ILD organized international support for the freeing of the "class prisoners" in Alabama. While Carter argues that the case never became as celebrated a rallying cry as the earlier campaign on behalf of the executed anarchists Nicola Sacco and Bartolomeo Vanzetti, an international speaking tour was arranged by the ILD, in which Ada Wright, mother of two of the defendants, traveled with Party functionary J. Louis Engdahl to address crowds in England, Germany, and other parts of Europe. Her denunciations of the racism and class oppression of the American South resonated with radicals but vexed the U.S. government and more conservative figures in Europe. When Irish president Eamon de Valera refused to permit Wright and Engdahl entry to the Free State, the Irish Workers' Club of New York, an IWO lodge, sent a resolution to de Valera condemning his actions: "You are influenced by and obey the order of American and British Imperialism. This is typical of your betrayal of the cause of the Irish workers and of all workers." While J. J. Mullally was congratulated on expressing the general IWO line supporting the Scottsboro defendants, he was taken to task by Party officials for labeling de Valera "an agent of British imperialism" as unlikely to gain a hearing with Irish workers in America or the Free State. The subtleties of Irish politics bedeviled the Irish Workers' Clubs, as other letters documenting attempts to enlist Irish Republican Army supporters in the IWO attest. The Irish intervention on behalf of the Wright tour, though, demonstrates an autonomy of action by IWO members, as did Gardos and the Hungarians' resistance to "the artificial throwing in" of Scottsboro. Order members chose to act—or not—in ways that made sense to their communities, not simply as receptors of Party instructions.[28]

International solidarity developed around Scottsboro, especially among colonial subjects. Arnold Ward of London wrote to ILD president Patterson noting that I.T.A. Wallace-Johnson, a Gold Coast activist-journalist, had taken an interest in the case and requested "more material on Scottsboro, but there are new laws just [being] enforced in West Africa. Muzzling the press. So if you send it on to us he might get it safer." Adi notes that Wallace-Johnson, like other African radical nationalists, often chafed at the insensitivity of the British CP, and Communists generally, toward the salience of racial liberation. Indeed, Ward also wrote to Patterson criticizing the activities of Trinidadian-born Communist apostate George Padmore, who "has sown the seed of dissension among the colonials here." The condescension of Ward and white British Communists such as Reginald Bridgeman, secretary of the League Against Imperialism, is suggested by Ward's slighting comment to the African American Patterson that in London "all the so-called

Negro leaders here are busy advocating some kind of race policy for Africa and the Africans." Such comments indicate, as Adi argues, that some Communists could often demonstrate a tin-eared, unsympathetic attitude to the *racial* oppression of black workers. Still, Bridgeman reached out to the ILD's Patterson to develop African American support for African colonial independence. Wallace-Johnson's call from West Africa for more Scottsboro material likewise marks an international solidarity among people of color that developed around this case.[29]

During the decades-long campaign to save the Scottsboro Nine, competing defense strategies of the tenuously allied ILD, National Association for the Advancement of Colored People (NAACP), and other legal teams were often on display. Nonradical lawyers argued that strident rhetoric of the kind exhibited at ILD rallies was less helpful than careful preparation of a defense in court, while the ILD argued that a "bourgeois" court could only side with the bosses and invariably deliver a legal lynching. It held that only militant demonstrations by the proletariat masses could "force" the courts to free the defendants. Samuel Leibowitz and other non-Communist defense counsel grew frustrated with these tactics, which they believed antagonized Alabama officials and caused them to dig in their heels rather than be perceived as surrendering to Communist pressure groups.[30]

After the state hastily freed four of the defendants in 1937, officials adamantly refused to parole or pardon the remaining five convicts. The case, Carter notes, faded from public consciousness, with even the ILD devoting less time to the matter. When the final convict was released in late 1950, little public notice was made of the event.[31]

The IWO, however, continued to display its Scottsboro militancy as a badge of honor. In 1948, the Order's office staff newsletter, *The Paper*, noted that shop chairman Grace Johnson had "served on the Scottsboro Defense Committee in Buffalo and was active in International Labor Defense and League of Struggle for Negro Rights." Already in the mid-1930s, New York City Council candidate Israel Amter noted that "the Communists made a national issue of the Scottsboro case, and the case of Angelo Herndon." Such militant activism, he argued, had saved the teens from the electric chair, but for their efforts "the whites have been branded 'Reds.'" As persecution of the IWO ratcheted up, members did not apologize for their stance on Scottsboro and support for antilynching campaigns but embraced them as emblems of true Americanism. Greene in 1950 addressed a Brooklyn rally, offering praise for embattled African American activist-entertainer Robeson, recommitting the Order to Negro-Jewish unity to end Jim Crow and lynching, and embracing "our honorable title of 'premature anti-fascists'" earned during campaigns such as Scottsboro. Greene pledged his organization to continuing fighting for more recent victims of racism such as the Trenton Six, convicted of murder by an all-white jury, and Willie McGee, a black man on Mississippi's death row for a rape conviction.[32]

Fighting "Strange Fruit on Southern Trees"

Lynching, the most brutal of America's racial atrocities, was an issue on which the IWO consistently lobbied, demanding federal measures to punish murderers of black people. In this the IWO followed the direction of the Party's antilynching activism. As early as November 1933 Browder telegrammed Gebert of the IWO's Polish Society and other Communist officials that "the increasing lynch wave signaling fascist development demands the broadest mass mobilization among Negro and white workers and the broadest united front approach to all working-class organizations." Throughout the 1930s and 1940s, the Party condemned "the Lynch Terror in the United States."[33]

As an interracial society, the IWO avidly contributed to the campaign to suppress the lynch terror. *Fraternal Outlook* frequently ran articles condemning racial atrocities in America and demanding national mobilizations to enact measures to end the lynching scourge. In March 1939 readers learned of another defeat of a federal antilynching bill by "a handful of pro-lynch and anti-New Deal Senators," whose filibuster killed the bill and "interfered with our whole democratic process." The article, "Strange Fruit on Southern Trees" by Emanuel Levin, employed the antilynching blues dirge that bitterly told of "Blood on the leaves and / Blood at the root, / Black bodies swinging in the Southern breeze / Strange fruit hanging from the poplar trees." Levin warned his readers, "This strange fruit is a gruesome warning of the poison that is eating at the very root of American democracy itself." He recounted the atrocities black people had faced during and after World War I in the East Saint Louis, Tulsa, and Chicago race riots in addition to "the Scottsboro boys' narrow escape from legal lynching" and Herndon's ordeal as "things which will always be remembered by the Negro people, as well as by progressive white people."[34]

Levin conceived of the fight for the Anti-Lynching Bill as "a basic part of the campaign to preserve and extend the democratic process of America" and preserve the rights of black and white sharecroppers and workers alike. In order to defeat Southern filibusters, he urged every IWO member to write to congressmen and senators enclosing the damning poem "Strange Fruit in Southern Trees" and demanding passage of the Anti-Lynching Bill "so that we will in some measure be free from the constant dread of a noose, a burnt tree, a dangling body filled with the bullets of a raging mob." Only united action by the "forces of progress and peace" such as the IWO could destroy the power of lynching's Senate protectors.[35]

The article's lumping together of blacks' lynching and the suppression of whites' collective bargaining rights as part of a united campaign by the boss class "to keep the living standards [of the South] at a pellagra level" suggests that many militant white ethnics still foregrounded class analyses and had trouble recognizing racial oppression as sui generis and abhorrent in its own right. Erstwhile black Communists such as author Richard Wright grew frustrated with this sometimes tin-eared, white-worker-centered materialist reading of black exploitation and pointed to such racial blind spots as leading to their parting with the Party.[36]

Nevertheless, even if its analysis was sometimes not as nuanced as could be hoped, the IWO was one of the few organizations in which mid-twentieth-century white ethnics consistently denounced lynching and other forms of black oppression. The militant stance of IWO publications stands in contrast to the complacency, if not outright acceptance of America's racialized status quo, exhibited by nonleftist ethnic newspapers such as the Slovaks' *Jednota*, *New Yorský denník*, and *Slovák v Amerike*. In the pages of such publications, immigrants learned to naturalize their place in America's hierarchy as deserving white people. Militants reading *Fraternal Outlook*, on the other hand, recognized lynching, Jim Crow segregation, and racial oppression as key ways bosses used race in "the production of difference" (to borrow Roediger and Esch's important concept) to fracture and weaken the working class.[37]

The IWO's insistence on linking racial oppression to a class analysis focusing on broader issues of economic exploitation was at variance, too, to the approach of more mainstream civil rights organizations such as the NAACP, which was much more accepting of the tenets of American capitalism. As Beth Tompkins Bates and Mary Helen Washington contend, the mainstream civil rights movement exemplified by the NAACP argued for integration into existing socioeconomic and political institutions, not transformation of these capitalist structures to address working-class grievances. While the IWO often foregrounded class, its stridency on racial issues such as anti-lynching, anti-poll tax, and an end to segregation campaigns arguably demonstrated true intersectionality, blending racial and class struggles. Washington notes that African American writers with Communist affiliations in the 1950s continued to swim against the inclusionist tide, seeking a broader transformation of the American economic and political landscape. So, too, for the IWO, opening a few slots in the middle class for black people was welcome, but only a piece of the struggle.[38]

The *Fraternal Outlook* also ran periodic exposés of the menace of the poll tax, although sometimes the racial aspect to disfranchisement was downplayed, with the poll tax instead derided as a threat to "the nation's war effort and unity." Other articles denouncing the poll tax, though, foregrounded the race issue, featuring vignettes of African American steelworkers, wives of soldiers, and female farmworkers who "contribute to the nation's food basket," but still were barred from the ballot box in the seven Southern states that maintained the poll tax. IWO organizers knew firsthand of the impediments the poll tax placed in the way of battlers for working-class justice. In 1932 Florida lodges of the IWO had pledged to pay the poll taxes of the men selected as that state's CP electors.[39]

Other *Fraternal Outlook* articles more explicitly demanded an end to segregation, with an article by General Secretary Milgrom shining a "Spotlight on Jim Crow" or demands that "The New Negro" be given justice after World War II. Milgrom's "spotlight," one of a series of articles, also shone on the IWO itself, where lamentable cases such as a Hungarian lodge shunning a potential black member mirrored the kind of "separate but equal" policies in the wider nation that the Order frequently condemned.[40]

For all their blind spots, militant white ethnics developed a sensitivity to racial oppression at odds with the consciousness of nonideological white ethnics. Leftist Slavs advocated an end to black oppression, which they characterized as a particularly pernicious manifestation of "the dictatorship of capitalism." In the late 1930s, the IWO was one of the few places in which a Slavic immigrant would hear defenses of black people's rights. The SWS's *Robotnícky kalendár* (Workers' Calendar) for 1937 ran a woodcut illustration of a lynching with the condemnatory caption, "'Democracy' in the South. Black citizens in the southern states of the U.S.A. until now have been vulnerable to white lynchers, because they haven't united with white workers." As in English-language publications of the CP, this equation gave little consideration to the racism of white workers, which may have stood in the way of class solidarity. Even this illustration showed not top-hatted millionaires, but overall-clad white workers rushing to the lynching tree. Still, such an unequivocal denunciation of lynch law was found only in leftist Slovak publications. The calendar also ran an exposé of "the treacherous Ku Klux Klan [KKK], which secretly organizes throughout the United States against the workers." In 1942, *Ľudový denník*, a Slovak version of the *Daily Worker*, published a cartoon of a soldier destroying a scarecrow labeled "poll tax." "The defeat of the poll tax is the triumph of democracy," ran the caption. That same day, *Ľudový denník* published an editorial, "The evil consequences of discrimination."[41]

After reading such condemnations, the IWO responded with various resolutions demanding antilynching legislation and other measures. The 1940 national convention passed a resolution branding "lynching ... an instrument of reaction used to keep the Negro people in bondage and to check the progressive forces of labor." The delegates further resolved, "As long as lynching continues ... the civil liberties of all the American people are jeopardized." All lodges were urged to petition their senators to support enactment of the Wagner-Capper-Van Nuys Anti-Lynching Bill. The Geyer Bill banning poll taxes was also backed by the convention, which pledged its support for the NAACP and NNC on these legislative campaigns. An identical resolution regarding the antilynching bill was passed seven months later at the IWO Anthracite District Convention.[42]

A year later, when the IWO's General Executive Board (GEB) pledged support for Roosevelt's Lend-Lease program and offered wholehearted support to the effort to defeat Hitler's forces, it nevertheless felt compelled to put forward a further resolution noting its "opposition to discrimination against the Negro people in the armed forces and defense industries of the land" as well as committing to the abolition of the poll tax "and other discriminatory laws." To be sure, the IWO sometimes dropped the ball, as when the Order, like other CP-affiliated organizations, absented itself from the March on Washington movement, partly perhaps out of enmity toward its Socialist leadership. Yet while critics of the Left argue that the CP and its affiliates suspended activism on behalf of African Americans "for the duration" as they devoted all their energies toward winning the war to save the embattled Soviets, the IWO never let up on its commitment to racial equality. In September 1941 it was demanding integration of the armed forces. The following year the IWO again denounced segregation in the armed forces and in defense work and called "upon the proper governmental agencies to prosecute as active traitors those responsible for such reprehensible acts as the terror against Negro soldiers and citizens," going further than Roosevelt was prepared to with his lukewarm issuance of the executive order creating the FEPC. It would be seven years before his successor began the armed forces' integration.[43]

Commitment to such race activism continued throughout the war. In February 1943 Bedacht reminded the board, "There are still many problems of conquering democratic rights for some sections of the American people, there is still the problem of defeating and ending discrimination, disfranchisement and lynch law against the Negro people in America. There is still the problem of enfranchising the poor working people in the South by putting an end to the poll tax." The board agreed but expanded the list of racialized oppressions that it committed the IWO to ending. All lodges and editors of *Fraternal Outlook* were instructed to do everything they could "to see that President Roosevelt's order #8802 is put into practice; to eliminate the poll tax, wipe out the blot of lynching, and the slanders against the Negro people in the movies, press and radio, and end Jim Crow policies in the armed forces." Local branches took this admonition seriously. The Bronx District Committee of the Jewish American Section of the IWO committed itself to "the struggle against the poll tax."[44]

"Clenched Fists and Determined Hearts"

During World War II, leftists in the IWO and the newly founded win-the-war umbrella group, the ASC, endeavored to harness patriotism and antifascist animus to a civil rights campaign. While other Poles and Slovaks (along with other white ethnics) attacked black people in the streets of Detroit and other urban battlegrounds, adherents of the Slav Congress called for racial unity and denounced the rioters as Hitler's apologists. "[Fifth columnists] will attempt to weaken and defeat us by dividing us among ourselves," Krzycki thundered to the first Slav Congress. "They will try to divide us from Americans who look back to other homelands. They will try to set us against Negroes. We will not be taken in. We will answer the sly whispers of the fifth columnists with clenched fists and determined hearts."[45]

Lodges of the Polonia Society, SWS, and Ukrainian-American Fraternal Union participated in the Slav Congress, so it is not surprising that the IWO likewise called for interracial solidarity as necessary to win the war. Already on February 8, 1942, the IWO's GEB passed a "resolution on Negro Rights," approving Roosevelt's creation of the FEPC, but again the IWO committed to going beyond what the president was willing or politically able to deliver in urging federal prosecution of lynchers and an end to segregation in the armed forces.[46] In 1942 the IWO also sent its lodge brother, Communist activist Patterson, as its delegate to the National Negro Labor for Victory Conference, determined to hold the government to its commitment to implement the FEPC.[47]

A permanent FEPC, the IWO believed, would guarantee "our Negro citizenry . . . taking an increasing part in the war effort both as fighting men and as soldiers of production" who would no longer face the "shameful practice" of industries' racial discrimination. The IWO demanded "full appropriations" for a permanent FEPC to ensure that "all forms of racial discrimination shall be ultimately abolished from the industrial life of our country." Ten months later the IWO singled out the poll tax and lynch terror for eradication, demanding an antilynching bill that "would bar all literature from the mails which promotes racial and religious hate." While the IWO did not explain how it would determine what letters sent through the mails promoted "hate" and how this could be prevented (and the irony of a left-wing organization demanding federal government intervention to prohibit the dissemination of ideas went unremarked), the Order again backed the creation of a permanent FEPC. To teach white ethnics the justice of these causes, the IWO began an "educational campaign in the nationality group societies, printing of pamphlets on the Negro question in a number of languages, and the direct involvement of members from these societies in the campaign." Candela guaranteed Italian Americans "could be won to aid in the fight for Negro equality" and committed his Garibaldi Society to winning "Negro" equality. A Republican attorney also endorsed the IWO's campaign of promoting racial brotherhood, suggesting that the wartime Popular Front was capacious. Requests for copies of IWO pamphlets such as *Democracy and the Negro People* came from African Americans throughout the South as well as correspondents in Saskatchewan, Canada.[48]

Near war's end white ethnics in the IWO remained committed to creation of a permanent FEPC, conceiving of racial discrimination as only the most pernicious end of a spectrum that encompassed anti-Semitism and anti-Catholic hatred. Members of the JPFO in particular saw the linkages between antiblack racism and the peril of anti-Semitism as all too apparent. In July 1945 June Gordon of the JPFO's women's branch, the Emma Lazarus Division, said, "The Fair Employment Practices Committee does not concern the Negro people alone." Countering zero-sum-gain rhetoric already building, which saw any policy aiding black people's advancement as coming at the expense of white people, Gordon noted, "The opponents of F.E.P.C. speak of it in terms of a gift to the Negro people at the expense of the white. Well, we are white; but we are Jews and we also suffer the effects of this policy of discrimination." She committed the JPFO to working "to put a stop to the sickness of racism." Arguing that the poison of racism in America was the kind of discrimination that had led to "the Maidenek [sic] and Lublin furnaces," Gordon called on Congress to vote for continuation of the FEPC. The Emma Lazarus Division would remain defiantly unrepentant in linking anti-Semitism and racism in the postwar world as Cold War militarism escalated and the demonization of America's erstwhile ally, the Soviet Union, increased. "War Propaganda Feeds Anti-Semitism and Its Monstrous Big Brother—White Supremacy," Gordon declared in a February 1950 "Bulletin on Women and Peace in Celebration of the 6th Anniversary of the Emma Lazarus Division."[49]

The Emma Lazarus Division became a financial supporter of the Sojourners for Truth and Justice, an African American women's group combating racism and segregation at home and imperialism abroad. The Sojourners, in which Thompson Patterson of the IWO was an officer, linked racial, gender, and class oppression, too, in an early and unapologetic demand for intersectional liberation. One 1952 Sojourners action sought to expose the horrors of South African apartheid, picketing and petitioning at the UN and South Africa's embassy. The Sojourners joined the Council on African Affairs (CAA) in endorsing a nationwide campaign of civil disobedience that the African National Congress (ANC) was conducting and sent letters of solidarity to women in the ANC as well as to white women trade union leaders "who have loyally supported the African people's struggles." Bertha Mkize was congratulated for leading demonstrations against the recently enacted pass laws, and for her declaration, "Whatever they call us, Communists or anything else, we must fight this tyranny to the end." The letters sent to Mkize and three other South African women, coauthored by Thompson Patterson, told them,

> We have been inspired by the example of militant action on the part of African women. We realize that our fight for freedom in the United States is inextricably linked to the struggle against the tyranny of

the white supremacists not only in South Africa but throughout the entire Continent. We further recognize that these struggles for full freedom on the part of colored women in Africa, Asia and in these United States must lead to the complete emancipation of women throughout the world."[50]

A surprised Mkize wrote back from Durban, "Your unexpected letter was received with the greatest pleasure. It is sweet and very encouraging that you have made it possible the link with you we have always wished for this side of the world." She wrote, "Please, give the love of the African women to the Negro women in the States," signing her letter, "Yours in Sisterhood."[51]

The CAA, under the leadership of Robeson, forcefully linked racial terrorism in the United States and South Africa four decades before the United States got around to disapproving of apartheid. A CAA flyer declared, "Racism Threatens Us in South Africa as Here." In reference to white riots that broke out when the first black person attempted to move into a Chicago-area city, the flyer added, "It's not as far as you think from Cicero, Illinois, to Odendaalsrust, South Africa, where police recently machine-gunned African men and women." Declaring that U.S. corporations benefited from both Jim Crow and apartheid, the CAA supported the South African campaign to oppose unjust laws, which was "contributing directly to OUR struggle for democratic rights and peace." The CAA urged people to sign petitions calling on the U.S. government to support the African people, not the apartheid Pretoria regime.[52]

The spirit of intersectionalism, as well as global antiracism, lived on in IWO members such as Thompson, Robeson, and Gordon who targeted racism at home and abroad. By the early 1950s, however, the leftist Emma Lazarus Division, Sojourners for Truth and Justice, CAA, and IWO were under assault for their political ideology and unapologetic calling out of racist imperialism, both U.S. and South African models. Their very support for black people's civil rights in any context was eyed suspiciously by many guardians against "un-American" ideas.[53]

Like Gordon, some Italian IWO members recognized fellowship with black members due to their common enemies. When Josephine Picolo of Brooklyn wrote to arch-segregationist Senator Theodore Bilbo of Mississippi in 1945 urging support for a permanent FEPC, she received a snide reply addressed to "Dear Dago." Picolo turned to the Garibaldi Society president, Congressman Marcantonio, for assistance. The *New York Daily News* reported, "Vito Demands Bilbo Apology on 'Dago' Note," but Bilbo instead wrote the congressman that when he called a Dago a Dago, no insult was meant. The Mississippi senator was in turn denounced by Marcantonio for "spewing out race hatred." "Now that the war is over you are Hitler's inconsolable political male widow," he wrote. Marcantonio assured Picolo, "I shall keep after this rat and the other domestic fascists until they are driven out of public life by an enraged democracy."[54]

The IWO and CRC did what they could to remove Bilbo from the Senate. An "Oust Bilbo Now!" campaign was begun by the CRC, while the IWO secretary stressed "the need for intensifying" the drive to remove the senator, twinning this campaign with lobbying for a permanent FEPC. Shaffer of the JPFO New York City committee organized a parade in the Garment District to demand Bilbo's impeachment, labeling him a menace to progressive democracy, and the IWO circulated petitions calling for the senator and fellow Mississippian congressman John Rankin's ouster for "spreading the dangerous seeds of anti-Semitism and other forms of hate propaganda in Congress." An IWO meeting at Philadelphia's Bok Vocational School passed a resolution demanding Bilbo's ouster, declaring him "the leading exponent in America of the Nazi theory of racial and religious superiority." Meanwhile, an FBI agent noted that a meeting of the IWO City Committee in Detroit presided over by national officer Milgrom passed around "We Accuse" petitions. The agent noted, "At the head of these sheets was . . . condemnation of . . . Bilbo for his attacks 'on the negro, the Jewish, and the Italian people and other minority groups.'" The agent further noted that Picolo, the woman insulted in Bilbo's original "Dear Dago" letter, was conducting an IWO-backed national speaking tour.[55]

The IWO and CRC were unsuccessful in their attempts to remove Bilbo from the Senate; he still retained his seat when he died of cancer in 1947. Nor did they change his or many white Mississippians' minds on the need for an FEPC. Although Bilbo's views were repugnant to the IWO, the effort to squelch his speech ironically bore some resemblance to the campaigns soon to be directed at the organization, the CRC, and other "un-American" advocates. In any event, many other Americans were more comfortable with the Mississippi defender against race "mongrelization" than with left-wing believers in civil rights, as Marcantonio learned from letters addressed to "dear wop" telling him, "you are a white man stay with your own color" and "three cheers for Bilbo, the forgotten white man's friend."[56] The IWO's demands for racial equality may seem to have been prescient and praiseworthy from the vantage point of seven decades; in 1945 they were still the outliers.

Even as it faced government prosecution, as late as 1952 the IWO still demanded the creation of a permanent FEPC, a measure Congress would never take. Citing an Urban League survey revealing "shocking examples of job discrimination against Negro Americans," the IWO urged enactment of a "compulsory FEPC" to secure "equal treatment for all Americans based on the democratic foundation of our Bill of Rights and Constitution," and asked all its lodges to "cooperate with civic, religious, social, and other community organizations" to secure the FEPC and end the "vile practice" of racial discrimination. By 1952 the Popular Front was a distant memory, and the IWO found few allies with which to cooperate. Within a few years the modern civil rights movement would win heralded victories such as the Brown school integration decision, but the Old Left bridge to a class-based racial justice campaign represented by the IWO had already been severed.[57]

When the national campaign sputtered, local lodges lobbied for fair employment and civil rights legislation on a statewide basis. From Trenton, Morris Forer wrote to Middleton about his lodge's participation in a Mercer County Legislative Conference in support of a state FEPC bill. With the cooperation of the IWO and the New Jersey Independent Voters' League, the bill was introduced into the legislature the day after the conference. Forer hoped to tie in the IWO's support for the FEPC with a celebration of Negro History Week. In order to make the Trenton gala a success, Forer sought to secure a prominent speaker such as Communist novelist Howard Fast or Harlem congressman Adam Clayton Powell Jr. Forer said he hoped the Negro History Week celebration would be an opportunity "to enroll Negro members into the Order."[58]

In Detroit, too, the IWO tried to defuse discontent among white residents, even some members of its own Garibaldi Society, over plans to place black people in public housing projects planned for white neighborhoods such as Oakwood. Part of this campaign involved lobbying in Lansing for enactment of a state FEPC. This campaign, though, was entered as one more damning indictment in the FBI's voluminous file on the IWO. The FBI agent in Detroit noted of the IWO, "It was ascertained that the headquarters office had sent a telegram to Michigan State Legislators on July 12, 1945, stating that '10,000 members in Detroit are strongly in favor of Fair Employment Practices Legislation' and urged the passing of the FEPC Bill." The sneering "ascertained" suggests that the FBI was probing for secret, "evil" purposes of the Order, when this organization had gone on record as supporting efforts to secure for African Americans their constitutional rights and had openly sent letters to legislators urging them to support the Michigan bill. Such activity is otherwise known as petitioning one's elected officials for redress of grievances. The FBI, however, also worriedly noted that the Michigan IWO had previously held a picnic—again this publicly advertised, open event was easily "ascertained"—at which a speaker "pleaded for the rights of the Negro" and circulated a petition calling for integrated battalions in the armed forces.[59]

At least one legislator was receptive to the IWO's plea for a civil rights agency, for state senator Nowak was also the Order's Michigan president. When some Grand Rapids businessmen objected to the bill for a permanent state FEPC that he had introduced, Nowak countered that he was merely trying to secure equal opportunity for all Michiganders regardless of race or national origin. He wrote, "If there is no discrimination in employment of people because of race or national origin, as some of the writers claim, then there is no reason to fear the bill, as certainly a law against discrimination would not apply. The fact that so many employers of labor strenuously protest against a Fair Employment Practice Bill adds evidence in favor of such legislation." As to charges the bill was Communist-inspired, Nowak noted that one of the FEPC's most prominent sponsors was the Catholic bishop of Grand Rapids. Nowak would continue to support black civil rights, first as a New Deal Democrat and then in his Progressive Party runs for Congress, noting on his campaign flyers that he had walked picket lines to protest Detroit's segregated lunch counters. The charge made by state's witnesses and FBI agents that progressives such as Nowak were opportunistically exploiting racial tensions for their own nefarious purposes seems specious when one reflects that, as Sugrue has noted, many other Detroit-area white people would have been repelled by, not attracted to, Nowak's championing of racial equality. That Nowak publicized his positions on these issues indicates that he, and the Michigan IWO he led, acted out of principle, not cynicism.[60]

During World War II, the ASC also endorsed civil rights for American blacks and, like the IWO, was active in antilynching and poll-tax campaigns. In Gary, Indiana, ASC member Katherine Hyndman, a Croatian immigrant, became involved with the Gary Civil Liberties Committee. After the war the ASC's journal lionized Hyndman, also a member of the IWO, as "an outstanding advocate of equal rights and the betterment of race relations" who "helped to settle a hate-strike of white citizens against Negro citizens in Gary. . . . [H]er efforts laid the groundwork for more harmonious relations between the groups." Officials of the IWO such as Thompson Patterson, too, endorsed Hyndman's efforts to promote racial brotherhood in her city when she worked to counter the white boycott of integrated schools. These efforts on behalf of school integration (and her left-wing affiliations) would later earn Hyndman prosecution and an attempted deportation. Hyndman suggested that this was because "we dare entertain thoughts not to the liking of present-day bigots."[61]

At its 1943 conference, the SWS equated segregation with Hitler's reign in Europe. "The enemies of the common people always use laws and the courts to incite the differences between the various religions, races and national groups, and thus are the common people divided and cast down into fascist slavery," its "Resolution against Race Discrimination and Anti-Semitism" began. "We are now seeing that anti-black laws in the U.S., just like the Nazis' anti-Semitic laws . . . is the best means of installing in America a similarly bloody fascist regime." The SWS consequently condemned all antiblack or anti-Semitic laws, and "call[ed] for strict punishment of all racial and ethnic unrest and slurs and riots." "We call on all workers, in order to strengthen understanding and cooperation between the various national groups, to work and engage in educational campaigns among those who either out of ignorance or as a result of the work of subversive elements, are hoodwinked by such racist laws." The following year, the SWS convention passed a similar "Resolution on Negroes" that equated American racism to the Hitlerism that had overrun Europe. The convention "ended with a call for an end to discrimination against Negroes, an end to Jim Crow and poll tax, and that as fast as possible, Negroes be integrated into all sections of American life."[62]

The IWO cooperated in an NNC-initiated national boycott of the Noxzema Company because it refused to hire black people, a campaign cheered on by the African American *Chicago Defender*. The *Baltimore Afro-American* approvingly reported on an IWO antidiscrimination rally and Marcantonio's introduction of a bill barring discrimination against blacks, Jews, and Italians in war work. Saltzman of the JPFO similarly demanded army base recreational facilities be integrated. Although the adjutant general of the army curtly replied to Saltzman, "The War Department has maintained throughout the emergency and present war that it is not an appropriate medium for effecting social readjustments," the commitment of the JPFO to ending racial discrimination contradicts the critique that Communist-affiliated organizations put their civil rights advocacy on hold in pursuit of a pro-Soviet "win the war" strategy.[63]

While during and after the war many white ethnics violently resisted black attempts to integrate neighborhoods, the ASC and IWO countered the hegemonic white narrative and built cross-racial alliances while preserving members' discreet, ethnic identities. Arnold Hirsch and other scholars are certainly correct that the majority of white ethnics fiercely resisted advancements of black people on shop floors and neighborhoods. The actions of the Slav Congress and IWO, however, give evidence that left-wing white Americans sought to implement an alternative model of interracial harmony. Ukrainian organizer John Mykytew wrote from Detroit of his contacts with black UAW official Shelton Tappes and the Reverend Charles Hill regarding Mykytew's "recruiting drive among the Negro people." Although his enthusiasm struck some black members in the IWO as a bit condescending, he wrote the national office in untutored English, "You have no Idie how much I am happy to work among the Negro people. . . . I am also sure we will build up I.W.O. by recruiting thousands in to I.W.O. Here in Detroit 100,000 Negro we must get them in to I.W.O. by half." In a 1951 affidavit, Herman Schlossberg of Los Angeles deposed, "In the course of my membership in the Order, I have taken in more than one hundred members, including Brothers and Sisters of all races and creeds." Many IWO members regarded the organization's interracialism as a badge of honor.[64]

The IWO's Polonia Society likewise published a Polish pamphlet supporting black civil rights, while various other IWO societies campaigned for passage of federal antilynching legislation. In October 1942 Mario D'Inzillo of the Garibaldi Society wrote the Justice Department, New York senators

Wagner and Mead, and President Roosevelt urging passage of antilynching legislation as well as anti-poll tax bills. D'Inzillo even lobbied Mississippi governor Paul Johnson on antilynching legislation.[65]

Individual Slavic societies carried forward the fight for civil rights. Benjamin Davis, first black man as well as first Communist on New York's city council, wrote to Gebert in 1947 praising his Polonia Society's work for civil rights as well as its campaign against lynch law, while the June 1947 convention of the Serbian American Federation passed a resolution demanding a permanent FEPC.[66]

Although the term was not used, we might regard these efforts as early multiculturalism, in which members celebrated their Slavic, Italian, and Jewish cultures (often denigrated in 1930s and 1940s America) but also took part in social affairs with black and Hispanic leftists. ASC conventions featured all the Ukrainian mandolin orchestras one could stand, but the congress also proudly sponsored appearances by Robeson at its national conventions. Robeson performed at the Order's rallies and took part in the group's civil rights campaigns. He also served on the Prisoners Relief Committee of the CRC, which, together with the IWO, sponsored a vacation at JPFO-affiliated Camp Kinderland for the four children of Willie McGee in 1950. Other relief committee members included Nowak, head of the Michigan IWO and Slav Congress.[67]

Many East European members highlighted the group's commitment to interracial solidarity. In 1951 Kalyna Popow of a North Philadelphia lodge deposed in her affidavit that in addition to sponsoring Ukrainian dance recitals and art exhibits, her lodge held celebrations during Negro History Week and Brotherhood Week. Frances Slowiczeck of a Polonia Society lodge in Hamtramck, Michigan, said "many of our activities were conducted in conjunction with other youth groups of other nationalities, such as Jewish, Ukrainian, Russian and Negro." While many white ethnics organized vigilante squads as black people moved into white urban enclaves, Popow and her comrades celebrated Brotherhood Week.[68]

Negro History Week celebrations continued as mainstays of the IWO, even as government prosecution accelerated. The Order's Douglass-Lincoln Society still sponsored Negro History Week observances in 1953, featuring Slavic dance troupes as well as African American actors and choral singers. Douglass-Lincoln Society executive secretary Nelson stated, "the society hoped to contribute, in however small a way, to the over-all objective of complete equality for the Negro people, economically, socially and culturally." The society's Negro History Week celebration was "in keeping with the principles of the interracial fraternal order which calls for day-to-day action on a year-round basis to secure a greater mutual understanding between Negro and white." The press release for the celebration on Harlem's Lenox Avenue carried the ominous caveat that the IWO had been liquidated by order of the

New York State Department of Insurance, and therefore "this press release is, pursuant to court order, sent solely upon the responsibility of the Executive Committee of the IWO." Celebrating "Negro History" or racial brotherhood in such a context could be translated into defiant political theater, or ominous subversion, depending on one's political point of view.[69]

By the early 1950s, charges of communism and subversion had been broadly leveled at many advocates of racial brotherhood by segregationist members of the HUAC for years. One such person, HUAC chairman Rankin of Mississippi, regarded any program seeking to aid African Americans as part of a nefarious Communist plot. During World War II, Rankin had read into the *Congressional Record* a denunciation of "one of the most vicious movements that has yet been instituted by the crackpots"—namely, "trying to browbeat the American Red Cross into taking the labels off the blood bank they are building up for our wounded boys in the service so that it will not show whether it is Negro blood or white blood." Rankin denounced this as "one of the schemes of these fellow travelers to try to mongrelize this Nation." This was the chairman of the committee weighing the "un-American activities" of advocates of racial equality, a farce that caused some witnesses such as the IWO's most famous black member, Robeson, to publicly discount the committee's legitimacy when called before it.[70]

"Just Plain Americans": Wartime Interracial Activism

During World War II, despite Rankin and his ilk, Popular Front interracialism became so accepted among progressive white ethnics that *Národné noviny* even publicized "Calypso Song of 'The Common Man,'" a tribute to Vice President Henry Wallace's speech envisioning an anticolonial, egalitarian world forged by continuing commitment to the Four Freedoms. "Sir Launcelot Pindar, calypso singer from Trinidad, has written a new song that he wants all the people to hear," the article said in describing the song about the multiracial American fighting forces battling to bring about fascism's defeat and democracy's full flowering. "Another of his recent songs is 'Defenders of Stalingrad,'" the article noted. This homage to left-wing calypso concluded, "As in days of old Launcelot is a modern troubadour singing of heroic deeds of the people, promulgating democratic ideals and spreading the seeds of hope for a better world."[71]

Even in the middle of the war, racism leveled at Japanese Americans was also pilloried by members of the IWO. On July 4, 1944, Ethel Stevens of Oakland, California, addressed a National Conference of the General Lodges on the Japanese Americans enrolled in her lodge. Stevens decried "the persecution the Japanese Americans had been subjected to because of the work of the Associated Farmers, who were opposed to allowing them to remain as first class citizens, because of business rivalry." Stevens stressed, "in the main, these people were loyal, hard-working Americans, and . . . this persecution was eminently unfair to them."[72]

Stevens was echoing the words of Communist John Pittman, an African American columnist, who two years earlier had editorialized in the *Pacific Citizen* that "prejudice, predatory motives" lay behind the "attack on U.S. Nisei." "What possible service will be rendered the Allied war effort by depriving American-born Japanese now in evacuation camps of their citizenship," Pittman demanded. Such a policy would do nothing to win the war but rather damage U.S relations with the colonized peoples of Asia, embitter Japanese Americans, and "give Tojo another argument with which to convince the peoples of Asia that they have nothing to gain by supporting our cause." Pittman was not hesitant to oppose racism during the war, even if institutionally the CP as well as other progressives argued for tabling discussion of civil rights and other "distractions" until after military victory. Lamentably, neither the CP nor the IWO directly condemned the internment of Japanese Americans, but individual members such as Stevens and Pittman denounced the concentration camps.[73]

Rather than curtail the rights of Japanese, Marcantonio proposed a bill to remove the bar on Asian naturalization, a move earning him congratulations from the Japanese American Committee for Democracy. Many white commentators still opposed Asian immigration, expressing an almost atavistic fear of "race mixing" should the ban be lifted. "It is the inherent desire of the colored race to break down, and bastardize the white race, communism notwithstanding," C. R. Wilmer, president of the National Sociological League of the Bronx wrote. In arguing for the maintenance of the Asiatic Exclusion Laws, Wilmer asked, "Would you my dear Mr. Marcantonio want to see your sister, or daughter married to a Negro, a Chinaman, a Jap or a Filipino??? I am definite sure that you would not. Yet you seem to advocate legislation that will indirectly incur this very condition." Marcantonio continued to press his bill and met with "Hindu, Chinese and Japanese groups" to coordinate lobbying. Perhaps most gratifying to Marcantonio were letters of support from Japanese Americans in relocation camps. "I believe that I am expressing the innermost feelings of all the 110,000 evacuees (90% of whom are citizens) in saying that we are greatly heartened and encouraged in the knowledge that you have the vision and courage to look at fundamental issues realistically," George Yoshioka wrote from a camp in Amache, Colorado, "and that you have taken steps to correct an unjust condition that has existed for these many years." A second letter commending him for his work on behalf of "loyal Japanese Americans" and "other forgotten little people" was sent by Bob Takahashi, interned at Camp McGehee, Arkansas.[74]

Ever since war's end, progressive Americans have lamented the failure of their countrymen to defend the civil liberties of Japanese Americans, with the U.S. Supreme Court's Korematsu decision upholding the constitutionality of the internment camps regarded as a particularly egregious dereliction of duty. Progressives in the IWO, as well as Communists such as Pittman, evidently did not subordinate support for racial equality and defense of civil liberties to the primary goal of winning the war.[75]

In 1944 *Národné noviny* was also pressing the anticolonial issue. "Maybe a time will come when the Atlantic Charter will also enter into force among the countries of colonial peoples," an editorialist wrote on the occasion of Mohandas Gandhi's release from prison. "Surely the crowds of millions of people would disagree with the British and butt in that the Atlantic Charter must be applied all over the world—and not just to the big shots."[76] IWO vice president Thompson had also already faulted Great Britain for retaining colonial control over India and Caribbean possessions and then asserting that it was fighting a war on behalf of cherished freedoms. Much has been made of the CP's switch to a stance in favor of American neutrality in World War II following the August 1939 signing of the Soviet-German Nonaggression Pact, but to African American activists there was little incentive to back Great Britain's war if this fight preserved the subjugation of nonwhite peoples. The struggle of the Indian National Congress, and nationalism in Africa and the Caribbean, were the "living issues" that interested black activists such as Thompson, not propping up Churchill's government.[77] White members of the IWO such as Nowak also argued that the fight for freedom had to extend to self-determination for people of color. In a radio broadcast in August 1941, he commented,

> In point one of the program agreed upon by President Roosevelt and Prime Minister Churchill, we are told that neither the United States nor Great Britain will seek aggrandizement, territorial or other. In my humble opinion, much more should be said on this question. Not only that the nations fighting Hitler should not desire to acquire any new territory, but a clear statement as to the future of such colonial nations as India. We cannot effectively fight Hitler's imperialism as long as we condone the subjugation of any nation by another.[78]

Just after the war, the ASC's George Pirinsky echoed this call for "a forward-looking colonial policy" to aid nonwhites in their "emancipat[ion] . . . from any imperialist domination."[79] Left-leaning Slavs joined with African Americans and other progressives in pressing the boundaries of the Four Freedoms to cover people of color at home and abroad.

"Stop the Ku Klux Terror!" Defending Black Neighbors

Not every white ethnic worker embraced interracial solidarity. In recalling the Slav Congress's efforts to calm Detroit following the June 1943 race riots, Pirinsky reminded readers that his organization had been one of the few East

European groups unequivocally to condemn the white assault on blacks. "The American Slav Congress by its very nature is averse to racial bigotry and prejudice," Pirinsky stressed. "Imbued with the philosophy of dynamic democracy, it joined hands with the labor movement and other liberal groups in sharply condemning these disgraceful and dangerous riots. It spoke out vigorously against the Slav Negro baiters, most of them innocent dupes who swallowed the vicious propaganda of native fascists." The ASC sponsored a Slav Day rally in nearby Hamtramck, at which five thousand attendees heard Slavic luminaries "castigate the fomenters of racial disorders in the sharpest terms. Sharing the platform with them was a youthful Negro leader, Shelton Tappes, secretary of Ford Local No. 600, UAW, who described the Detroit riot as Hitler's last effective weapon. . . . Practically the entire City Council of Hamtramck, the most Polish city in America, attended the rally."[80]

Progressives had their hands full countering those who condoned attacks on black people. Even before the riots, in Detroit white people of many ethnicities had already challenged the planned opening of Sojourner Truth Homes, a public housing project that they feared was designed for black residents. A Polish priest inveighed against the invasion of "the niggers" as a riot ensued to prevent the homes from being opened. The IWO worked to counter the influence of Polish American congressman Rudolph Tenerowicz, who had "made himself the initiator and leader of an anti-Negro movement which culminated in bloodshed when attempts were made to rob the Negro people of Detroit of the Sojourner Truth housing project." The IWO backed a primary challenger who favored open-housing laws and other progressive measures.[81]

The FBI provided further evidence that the IWO and other left-wing organizations were working to smooth the integration of black people into fiercely defended "whites only" neighborhoods. In its huge file on Marcantonio, a Detroit FBI agent wrote to Director J. Edgar Hoover in 1943 that he had found a letter in the wastepaper basket of the Detroit CP headquarters from "Pat," asking Marcantonio about Tenerowicz's "pro-fascist and vicious speech in the House . . . in connection with the Sojourner Truth Housing Project in Detroit." The letter rifled from Communist garbage pails labeled Tenerowicz's speech "a compendium of stool pigeons' reports, Dies Committee misinformation and other concocted material provided by the KKK in defense of the Klan's subversive attack against the Negro people here." The letter writer also noted that the congressman had charged he had evidence "Negro and radical elements" had "deliberately incite[d] both Negro and Whites" during the Sojourner Truth riots. The writer wanted to know if Tenerowicz could be forced to reveal his sources. In 1941 the FBI had already proposed that Marcantonio, a duly elected, sitting congressman, be held for custodial detention should the FBI deem that internal security warranted the roundup of "subversives," although an assistant to the attorney general reminded Hoover, "Being a citizen the Congressman naturally is not subject to internment as an alien enemy in the event of war." In 1950 the FBI again recommended this congressman be targeted for preventive detention, in part due to his militant advocacy of black civil rights. That the FBI weighed the possibility of rounding up elected congressmen might give respecters of civil liberties pause. That defenders of black civil rights, not the apologists for white housing rioters, were labeled possible "internal security threats" suggests advocacy of racial equality itself marked one as subversive in the eyes of conservative officials in 1940s America.[82]

Despite FBI surveillance, progressive Slavs, Italians, and others carried on with their civil rights advocacy. In the aftermath of the 1943 Detroit antiblack riot, the IWO issued news releases and letters to its members blaming the riots on "Nazi-led KKK attempts to divide the people." *Národné noviny* published articles in which Marcantonio faulted "the government of all race rioters," and Congressman Samuel Dickstein blamed the "KKK riot" on far-right agitators such as HUAC chairman Dies. Three weeks later the paper published an English-language editorial from the *CIO News* arguing, "Race Hatred Is Sabotage." *Národné noviny* also reprinted a CIO editorial asserting that "job discrimination, poll-tax denials of political rights, [and] unequal community treatment of racial minorities" were "some of the dark spots in American life where race hatred is bred." Still, the editorial was sure the riots were the work of Hitler's agents provocateurs, suggesting that some writers were unwilling to acknowledge Slavs could be both anti-Hitler and violently antiblack.[83]

Nowak continued to advocate for black people's access to adequate housing outside of the constricted ghetto of Detroit's Paradise Valley, despite fierce opposition from many of his white ethnic constituents. At a December 1944 meeting, Nowak emphasized "the necessity of integrating the negro into full citizenship and the problem confronting progressive forces in opposing efforts to prevent negro housing in Dearborn." Nowak worked with the IWO to pressure Dearborn to provide public housing available to African Americans.[84]

When white residents continued to resist black people's movement into their neighborhoods, up to and including firebombings in places such as Chicago and Detroit, members of leftist organizations expressed solidarity with African Americans in ways large and small. But even tiny acts of interracial solidarity were cause for official alarm. The CRC organized interracial house-painting parties for black homeowners facing angry mobs in 1948 Detroit. When the first black family moved into the 3400 block of Harrison Street, Detroit police reported that five white men were observed helping to paint the house and that "materials and labor used in the painting of this house are free of charge to the new owner." It was unclear which element of this ad hoc celebration alarmed the red squad more, black-white fraternization or fear that the donated paint and services might undermine the American capitalist system. The following day, the red squad noted that two picket lines appeared outside the Wayne County Building. "One picket line is made up of about 11 white women and 1 white man, all residents or home owners on Harrison Street . . . , who are opposed to the Negroes who purchased homes. . . . The other picket line is made up of men and women, white and colored, representing the Michigan Chapter of the Civil Rights Congress and the Progressives of America (Youths for Wallace)." Not surprisingly, only the names of the latter, pro–civil rights picketers were recorded by the red squad. Vigilante defenders of "whites only" neighborhoods often had the support of the forces of law and order. Interracial house painters were, however, colored red.[85]

The violence that greeted black home buyers was more than rhetorical. Arthur Price of the CRC of Illinois invited Marcantonio to a parade and demonstration to demand open-housing laws. The call came following the latest firebombing of a black family's home, something that had occurred weekly in the past few years as black people "moved into formerly lily-white communities." The "organized terrorizing" spurred the CRC to distribute flyers demanding, "Stop the Ku Klux Terror in Chicago" and "Put a Halt to Terrorism against the Negro People!" The mob that broke into the Johnson home on S. Lawrence Avenue and set the house ablaze with oil-soaked rags was countered by the solidarity of the CRC, which was quickly labeled a subversive organization for its interracial activism.[86]

The IWO cooperated with other left-wing organizations such as the CRC—not surprisingly, since IWO vice president Louise Thompson Patterson was married to CRC executive secretary William Patterson—and Order officials urged members to back up rhetorical commitment to black equality with tangible actions. In publicizing IWO celebrations of Negro History Week and Brotherhood Week, Middleton reminded members in New York, "Inter-racial unity is not something to be worn like a Sunday suit of clothes— on certain special days of the year. By our <u>daily</u> deeds we of the I.W.O. labor to stamp out prejudice and discrimination and strive to help attain full equality for all groups of the American people."[87]

There was no guarantee, however, that every IWO member would take the message of racial equality to heart, especially when it came to residential integration. In Detroit, Reverend Charles Hill, an IWO member and candidate for city council, complained that Garibaldi Society members bitterly opposed his call for open-housing laws and resisted building public housing open to black people in white neighborhoods. An IWO official wrote to General Secretary Milgrom that Hill was just about to quit the Order over his Italian brothers and sisters' white chauvinism.[88] Milgrom apologized but also to some degree excused the Italians' resistance:

> I am sorry that Reverend Hill takes the attitude that he does. . . . I hope he realizes that we are a fraternal organization and that our basic problem is to educate our membership. After all when a member joins the Order he comes in with all the baggage of his prejudices.

> Even while in the Order so many of our members . . . are reached with our education on the Negro question only with great difficulty. . . . I am sure we can convince Reverend Hill that the leadership of the IWO is conscious and is fighting for a definite policy which necessarily will come across difficulties in accomplishment. . . . I am sending out copies of [the] pamphlet "Complete Equality" to each member of the Garibaldi Society in Detroit.[89]

The Garibaldi Society's Candela traveled to Detroit to soothe his compatriots' resistance to integration, but Michigan IWO officials remained unimpressed by Candela's efforts.

Perhaps as a counter to some of its recalcitrant members, the IWO's Michigan leadership demanded Detroit's city council reverse itself and provide black people with public housing in formerly all-white neighborhoods. The IWO issued press releases backing Hill's attempt to become the city's first black councilman, but the reverend was unsuccessful in his bid. The Order also issued a news release "condemn[ing] the un-American attitude expressed by those members of the Common Council who voted against the proposed Negro housing project in Oakwood" but was silent on the opposition of its own Garibaldi Society members.[90]

The FBI, keeping tabs on IWO lodges in Detroit and elsewhere for its own purposes, detailed the troubles the Garibaldi Society members caused with their opposition to neighborhood integration. In 1945 the bureau noted that the IWO's recent decision to grant greater autonomy to its language federations ironically gave the Italians more latitude to balk at black housing rights, and an informant revealed that "some of the Italian IWO people had signed a petition opposing negro housing." A meeting of all the Italian lodges in the city was called, and the IWO worked with the Delray Communist Club to secure black peoples' housing rights. The FBI agent echoed IWO official Eleanor Broady and noted Candela's visit to the Motor City "to rally the Italian lodges behind the program for negro housing in the Oakwood section." It was regarded as "a 'black eye' for the IWO that the city council had voted down the housing project for negroes and that a fight must be undertaken to persuade them to reverse their position."[91] Within the fraught relationship to housing integration we can see the beginning of the white ethnic backlash to the New Deal coalition once race entered the picture.

Similar to Hill, Nelson of the IWO's Douglass-Lincoln Society complained in a 1950 letter to a *Daily Worker* columnist, "I was unfavorably impressed by the opening of your column . . . on Abdoulay Diallo. You opened by describing him as 'a slight, dark skinned young man,' and continued as though there was something incongruous in this 'dark-skinned young man' being influential, and giving reaction the jitters. Whatever your intentions, this kind of description . . . is a typical stereotype such as we encounter in commercial publications but which has no place in progressive journalism."[92] The Left did not always deliver on its rhetorical commitment to racial equality.

"Racist Poison": Battling White Chauvinism

Indeed, from its earliest days the problem of "white chauvinism" was a recurring nightmare for the Party and affiliates such as the IWO. A celebrated show trial involved August Yokinen, who was called to task for refusing to allow black comrades to use the sauna and swimming pool at Harlem's Finnish Progressive Hall. As with so many other radical immigrants, his "red" tendencies were at war with his whiteness. At Philadelphia's Slovak Hall, the SWS was one of the shareholders, but the hall's 1921 charter stipulated the building was "available for rental by all other groups, but Negroes were excluded because it was feared that their cleanliness standard would not measure up to that of other groups." Even if Slovak Communists expressed racial solidarity, they raised no objection to a color bar at their hall; the rationale of a black person's lack of a "cleanliness standard" suggests some immigrants had internalized racialized phobias. *New Yorský denník*, a Slovak daily, likewise featured a "joke" contributed by a reader in which a black man asks his son why he is barred from swimming with white kids. "Because, Papa, they were white before they went swimming, and they want to stay white."[93]

In New York, however, what is telling is that after Yokinen recanted his white chauvinism, black comrades rallied around him. When the government endeavored to deport Yokinen, the Party-affiliated LSNR held massive Save Yokinen rallies in the Bronx. The league wrote to Yokinen and expressed solidarity, asserting that it was because he had recanted white racism and publicly committed to working for black rights that the government was persecuting him. The Party's efforts failed to prevent the deportation. But even while Cyril Briggs, Harry Haywood, and others in the LSNR noted similar white chauvinism incidents elsewhere, this biracial rallying around the Finn suggests that when white people rejected their racial privilege and recanted, black comrades accepted and embraced them, imperfect vessels though they were.[94]

The IWO, too, found itself uncomfortably confronting vestiges of white racism in the early 1930s. Lithuanians, Ukrainians, Jews, and Croatians, among others—the potential constituents of the IWO's language sections—were chastised for exhibiting "the crassest manifestation of white chauvinism," as S. M. Loyen put it regarding South Slavs in Detroit.[95]

After boldly asserting the Order's commitment to racial equality, the author of a 1932 report on organizing Negro branches nevertheless allowed that the organization might have to turn a blind eye to some members' lingering prejudices. "The I.W.O. would defeat its own purpose of reaching the backward masses ... if it would insist that applicants for membership in the I.W.O. must all be free from the bourgeois poisons of racial or national prejudices. Such a policy would change the I.W.O. from a united front mass organization for mutual help into an organization of radicals only." The IWO often found itself striking a delicate balance between commitment to civil rights and turning an indulgent (if not quite blind) eye to the "bourgeois" race phobias of members such as the Detroit Italians who infuriated Reverend Hill.[96]

Problems of white condescension periodically surfaced, as when Philippa Stowe of Harlem wrote to the IWO of her mistreatment by an organizer:

> I feel compelled to tell you that I cannot join at this time. ... I do wish to be fair, but I am unable to determine ... whether the objectionable conduct of Mr. Sol Winnick was his own idea or a part of the program of the International Workers Order. His conduct, although subtle, was insulting and degrading, and I do not know whether it was intended to express disrespect for my race or merely for my sex. At any rate, I am convinced that your organization would fare better without the services of Mr. Winnick and I am especially anxious that he and his kind should not have the opportunity to corrupt the Negro People and our young.[97]

The Manhattan District of the JPFO conducted a special hearing on the "racist poison" in its organization, and pledged Winnick would not be able to visit any prospective recruits or hold any office in the JPFO until he recanted his improper advances and recognized "the need for fighting against discrimination and for the rights of the Negro people." The District Committee implemented an education campaign to achieve Jewish and black unity in the fight for racial equality.[98]

Winnick's transgressions were not unique. Charges of discrimination against "Negro employment" and guests were leveled at IWO-run summer camps such as Camp Lakeland and Camp Kinderland, and guests wrote complaining of the lack of attention paid to the plight of Robeson at Kinderland in 1949. That year, too, Secretary Milgrom wrote in the *Fraternal Outlook* of a new Croatian lodge in Canton, Ohio, that voted "not to rent its hall to Negro organizations. This resolution transformed the ... Hall ... from a progressive fraternal center into a Jim-Crow, lily-white center." "We bowed our heads in shame," Milgrom said, even as he realized many other IWO lodges were exercising segregation though they did not formally vote to ban black membership. "Jim Crow practices, in the absence of a formal decision," Milgrom wrote, "are no different and no more tolerable than formal resolutions barring Negroes." Milgrom thus recognized de facto segregation was no less insidious than formal Jim Crow statutes, a distinction rarely acknowledged in 1949 or for decades to come. After Milgrom and national Croatian Society secretary Leo Bacich paid a visit to Canton, the Croatians rescinded their Jim Crow resolution, but the secretary was not satisfied. He argued that all the halls, social centers, and recreation facilities of all IWO lodges had to be made available to all races and arguments of "practical" impediments such as the loss of business from some white people had to be rejected. "Full equality for everybody depends on the full social, political and economic equality of the Negro people," Milgrom concluded.[99]

In such a stance Milgrom was far ahead of most 1940s white Americans and, sadly, even outpaced many IWO members. The FBI confirmed some of the Order's own findings of white chauvinism, as when an informant related to the bureau that Polish and Ukrainian lodges in Muskegon, Michigan, were taken to task for not wanting to rent their halls "to any clubs that have Negro members because the people who live close to the halls don't want Negroes in the neighborhood." Here the IWO members deflected the Jim Crow decision away from themselves onto "the people who live close to the halls," an example of the kind of "practical" consideration underlying segregation that Milgrom deplored in the Croatians of Canton. Not all members lived up to the tenets of racial solidarity that the IWO espoused.[100]

Of course, such problems were more likely to arise in an organization committed to interracialism than in a more conservative ethnic fraternal society. There black attendance at one's lodge was simply unthinkable, and thus no squabbles over "white chauvinism" ever arose. If the IWO and other left-wing groups had been as opportunistic in recruiting naïve workers into their midst as anti-Communist investigators alleged, they might have ignored white ethnics' racism, instead of condemning it. Surely such a tactic would have reached more Poles, Ukrainians, and Croatians in places such as Canton and Muskegon than determinedly calling out white chauvinism as the IWO did.

On the national level, the IWO and Slav Congress leadership continued to advocate for black equality, a policy a Connecticut Black Muslim appreciated when he wrote to the IWO applying for membership. In its 1946 "Resolution on Lynch Terror," the IWO's General Council endorsed the "newly organized American Crusade to End Lynching['s] pilgrimage to Washington, D.C." to secure a federal antilynching bill. The IWO redoubled its recruiting efforts among black people in Harlem and Chicago, while General Secretary Bedacht called for an end to "Negro persecutions" and lynching, warning, "If the peddlers of racist poisons are not stopped, it will be only a matter of time before we have Oswiecim's and Dachau's in America, even though their names will be spelled differently." Writing in the ASC's journal, Adamic equated U.S.-backed colonialism in Asia and Africa with segregation at home, prophetically warning that black people would no longer accept ghettoization and "crumbs falling off the white man's table." "Until there is a clear and steady advance toward equality," he said, "there will be strikes and race riots, here." Gellman, Gore, and others have noted that leftist activists pointed out the international oppression that people of color suffered and have argued black civil rights and anticolonial struggles had to be twinned. The IWO made the linkage between colonial subjugation and civil rights at home, too. Weeks after World War II ended, Milgrom remarked that the "Negro community . . . is now the greatest test for America, and just like the colonial people will become the first barometer of real or phony victory, so will the oppressed nation, the Negro people in America, become this barometer." Many in the Order found America's commitment to both domestic and international civil rights lacking.[101]

The IWO came by its linkage of domestic racial equality and anticolonialism naturally, for the 1930s electoral campaigns of the CP, which the IWO frequently endorsed, equated American racism to the oppression of African and Asian colonialism. This occurred perhaps nowhere as trenchantly as in a 1932 pamphlet raking the Republican presidential candidate over the coals. *Herbert Hoover: Slave Trader, Negro-Hater, Jim Crow Expert* detailed the president's expertise in extracting mining labor from Chinese and "Khaffir" laborers toiling in near-slavelike conditions during his engineering career in Australia, China, and South Africa. The millions Hoover made in his business career came at the expense of colonized laborers and were also linked by the Party to the segregationist policies that his "lily-white" Republicans had abetted in America. The pamphlet thundered,

> A slave-driver in Australia and China; a slave-trader in Africa; the upholder of segregation and peonage in the Mississippi flood; the man who helped Harvey Firestone put across his gigantic land-steals in Liberia; the man who shipped marines and bombing planes to quell the revolts in Haiti; the president who has most consistently selected Negro haters and Negro-baiters to fill high office; the high mogul of the Lily-Whites—this, briefly, is the story of President Herbert Hoover.[102]

As Roediger and Esch document, Hoover had built his reputation as a mine-engineering entrepreneur in large part on his expertise in managing laborers' "racial differences" to extract maximum profits. In 1932 it was left to the CP and affiliated groups such as the IWO to expose the links between racism at home and colonial subjugation abroad.[103]

While the IWO's strategies regarding foreign policy are covered in greater extent in Chapter 5, astute assessment of linkages between domestic racism and support for imperialism abroad continued into the 1950s. Even after the IWO was liquidated and members ordered not to associate with one another, the FBI noted that Polish former members met in Detroit's Polish

Labor Democratic Club, "in lieu of the former IWO clubs," where in June 1954 they heard Thomas Dombrowski address members on "Indo-China's fights for its independence not because they received orders from Moscow but because there were uprisings in Indo-China long before Soviet Russia existed." That same month members of the JPFO read an editorial in *Jewish Life* condemning America's encroachment into Indochina's affairs. The magazine approved of Indochina's "fight to free that land of colonialism," asserting, "We have no business . . . to prevent Asian lands from achieving" independence. It would take the State Department at least another twenty-five years to accept this view.[104] The IWO kept up its international critique of racialized capitalism and oppression in all its manifestations.

The Order championed breaking racial barriers in small ways, too. The IWO congratulated itself as one of the first organizations to agitate for the integration of Major League Baseball; even a hostile witness acknowledged such lobbying occurred as early as 1934. Thompson noted that the *Daily Worker* was calling for integrated baseball by 1940, and the IWO distributed leaflets in South Chicago making these demands. In December 1943 Robeson, IWO officials Ernest Rymer, Sam Patterson, and Eugene Konecky, as well as an IWO labor delegation, presented a petition to baseball commissioner Kenesaw Mountain Landis "urging abandonment of Jim Crow in the big leagues"; Thompson had earlier met with William Wrigley, owner of the Chicago Cubs, to lobby for the same cause. Although it would have been fascinating to witness the Robeson-Landis encounter, the answer from baseball management was not encouraging. The IWO continued pressing for change. In 1945 eastern Pennsylvania lodges demanded an investigation into "Jim Crow Baseball," while in New York, Jewish lodges were represented on the Metropolitan Interfaith and Interracial Coordinating Council, which orchestrated an End Jim Crow in Baseball campaign. This campaign planned interracial demonstrations outside the Polo Grounds and Ebbets Field on game days (no mention was made of Yankee Stadium, which for proletarians may have been regarded as a lost cause). These demonstrations were called off after Mayor Fiorello La Guardia promised to speak to the Giants and Dodgers owners about beginning to look into integration.[105]

Prominent IWO members such as Marcantonio continued to demand that baseball integrate, earning the congressman vituperative hate mail. "Why under high heaven were they placed in darkest Africa as savages and cannibals?" a writer from Tennessee wanted to know, but even Willard Weiss, a serviceman from New York, saw this plan as "a big mistake." "We see where you give them some rights and before you know it, you or anybody else may have a granddaughter that is colored," Weiss explained. "Think of it that way," he wrote, "or maybe you think that would be alright [sic]." Phobias of social equality were also expressed by Bill Werber, former Major Leaguer with the Cincinnati Reds and other teams. Werber wrote to Marcantonio objecting to his interference. "The attempt to create pressure for the hiring of negro players through the use of the Press and Investigating Committees does the negro a great disservice since it builds up more antagonism against his cause than if his advancement were merited through natural selection," Werber wrote, echoing the false meritocratic argument often deployed against any effort to rectify America's racial imbalances. Werber worried about social equality, questioning whether Southern big leaguers would accept proximity to black players in showers or Pullman cars. He suggested that only if both white and black people accepted the proposal should it be put forward, giving a veto power to intransigent whites. Werber's stance, and the many other letters caustically faulting Marcantonio's support for integrated baseball, indicates just how exceptional support for integration was. Then, too, Werber did not die until 2009, suggesting that the racism the IWO battled, at the Polo Grounds and elsewhere, is not so remote a phenomenon as some now imagine.[106]

When the Cleveland Indians, the first integrated American League team, won the 1948 pennant, Milgrom sent a telegram to club president Bill Veeck, "greeting the victory as a 'victory for American democracy.'" "International Workers Order, the only interracial fraternal organization," Milgrom extolled, "cheers the Cleveland triumph as a victory for true fraternalism and real Americanism. Here's hoping you win the World Series." With the help of black Hall of Famer Larry Doby, the Indians did. Integrated IWO teams played games and passed petitions through the stands demanding all of baseball abolish the color line.[107]

While the IWO advocated other unpopular positions such as atomic disarmament, continued cooperation with the wartime Soviet ally, and vigorous union rights, it was in no small measure because of its antiracist activism that the group was placed on the Attorney General's List in 1947 and investigated by HUAC. Both the attorney general and three chairs of HUAC were Southern segregationists, including Mississippi's Rankin, scourge of integrated blood banks and "race mongrelization."

The IWO nevertheless continued its civil rights activism in an atmosphere of anti-red hysteria. IWO president Rockwell Kent accepted an offer to have his organization join the "National Emergency Civil Rights Mobilization," only to receive a letter from the NAACP's Roy Wilkins telling him that the IWO "is not one of the organizations invited to participate in this Mobilization." Even though the IWO had been mounting interracial support of black civil rights for almost two decades, by 1949 the Order's assistance was unwelcome to the staid NAACP. Wilkins may have been reacting to red-baiting of the mobilization by arch-segregationists such as Rankin, who denounced the rally's participants as "red fronts," leading to the exclusion of 410 registrants by the mobilization's credentials committee. Milgrom and Kent nevertheless urged individual members to attend the mobilization rally even if the Order institutionally had been blackballed, suggesting their organization was genuinely interested in furthering black civil rights and not just subverting the campaign for Communist gains. Other internal letters between IWO officials not meant for public consumption likewise speak of the group's dedication to furthering black civil rights, calling into question Harold Cruse's famous conclusion that Communists were only cynically interested in using the civil rights issue to further unsavory ulterior motives.[108]

Facing condemnation as subversive, the IWO remained defiant. As part of its appeal of the liquidation order, in 1951 the IWO solicited affidavits from members nationwide, and in many of these the Order's commitment to interracialism stands out. Miklos Petri, member of a Hungarian lodge in the Bronx, stated, "The most important thing about the IWO is that it does not discriminate against any people because of nationality, color, or religion, and we want to have peace with everybody. I am very proud of the fact that we have two Negroes in my Lodge. There is no other organization in America like the I.W.O., which provides social, fraternal, and economic benefits to all people of all races and colors."[109]

Black members confirmed this story of interracialism. Pecola Moore of Los Angeles appreciated the insurance she would not have been able to purchase in the segregated private market: "Being an American Negro (so called), I have been helped beyond words to tell. The fellowship of help through the fraternity and sick benefits is a blessing to the poor and distressed persons. I would not have been able to pay a doctor; nor buy the medicines, to say nothing of paying for a home call from a physician, had it not been for the help of this organization."[110]

But Moore added, "It was not the medical service features of the Order that primarily made me wish to join." She attested,

> What I liked best about the Order was the fact that it really practices brotherhood and democracy. The Brothers and Sisters in my Lodge hold picnics, socials, lectures and many kinds of educational activities, and all persons of all creeds and races are together in perfect unity. My lodge has on many occasions fought for issues important to the Negro people. . . . Each year we celebrate Negro History Week with wonderful programs. I would like to ask the court to please let us have the <u>one organization</u> which is helping all people regardless of race, creed, or color to live and grow through mutual assistance which is Universal Brotherhood.[111]

In defending their Order, national officers pointed out that private insurance corporations, which stood to benefit from the liquidation, had millions of dollars invested in segregated housing developments, even as they discrimi-

Figure 3.1 The segregation of Stuyvesant Town, a New York housing development built with insurance company funds, was exposed and contrasted with the IWO's racial egalitarianism in the *Jewish Fraternalist*.
Source: Max Taber, "Stuyvesant Town for Whites Only," *Jewish Fraternalist*, February–March 1950, 6–7, IWO-CU, box 46.

nated against black policyholders by charging exorbitant rates. Treasurer Shipka charged that the liquidation effort was motivated at least partially by private insurance corporations who "are preparing the greatest insurance grab in the history of our country . . . $100,000,000 of insurance and $7,000,000 of your money could very well be used by any insurance company to invest in Jimcrow housing or other enterprises." The *Jewish Fraternalist* and the Douglass-Lincoln Society's newspaper echoed this charge. Insurance company investment in New York's segregated Stuyvesant Town in particular was roundly condemned by black and white IWO members (Figure 3.1).[112] Evidently, such arguments from the Order's officers were favorably received by many ordinary lodge members; the testimony of black members such as Moore offers strong evidence that for many people, leftist affiliation was irrelevant if the organization made good on its commitment to civil rights.

Jumal Ahmad of Cleveland, "a local teacher in the Ahmadiyya Mission of the Moslem faith," recounted, "I had trouble with my life insurance company, and I was recommended by a friend to join the International Workers Order where I, as a Negro, did receive equal treatment." Ahmad added, "I have found true fraternalism and racial equality in the organization." Jewish, Slavic Catholic, and Black Muslim members rallied to the interracial order.[113]

Robeson, among many other IWO members, remained defiant. The singer-activist told segregationists on HUAC they had nothing to teach him about true Americanism. The "great Negro singer and fighter," as the Slav Congress termed Robeson, remained a fixture at ASC and IWO celebrations.[114] Even as both organizations worked to achieve tangible civil rights and other social policy advances, they offered a panoply of stimulating and educational entertainment, musical and theater offerings and sports teams in an interracial, progressive milieu. The entertainment venues, to which we now turn, were liberating sites of counterhegemonic culture, a respite from HUAC's America.

4

"A Mandolin Orchestra . . . Could Attract a Lot of Attention"

Interracial Fun

With its commitment to union and civil rights activism, the IWO offered more to its members than life insurance. But when they put down their picket signs, members could also, if they liked, spend almost all their leisure time at their local IWO lodge. A wide array of recreational activities was on tap to fill every hour of a worker's day with class-conscious fun. The pages of IWO publications such as *The Spark* and *The New Order* from the early 1930s illustrate how comprehensive the organization's social network could be, reporting on amateur dramatic societies, mandolin orchestras, and workers' choirs as well as youth branch members attending summer outings such as boat rides, swimming parties, or trips to Communist summer camps like Camp Nitgedaiget and Camp Kinderland. Lodges hosted "interesting programs of song and poetry," "chalk talks" on current events, and drama festivals where they collegially competed against other theater troupes. They held costume balls and picnics and competed in IWO sports leagues in basketball, baseball, football, even tennis. Classes were offered to sportsmen and sportswomen in gymnastics, tumbling, wrestling, and boxing. IWO lodges screened films and then discussed their class-conscious messages; they sponsored folk-dancing troupes, art classes, and essay and fiction contests for aspiring writers. The IWO's magazines themselves were outlets for members looking to break into working-class journalism. Members showed up at lodges, then, not only to collect accident pay, visit a dental clinic, or buy life insurance. The hours of the week were filled with working-class fun.[1]

As a working-class fraternal society, however, the IWO offered fun with a purpose, for the organization's founders regarded recreation not as a diversion to blunt the rougher edges of workers' misery but as a tool with which to educate its members that another world was possible. The editors of *The New Order* declared, "Our chief aim is to give expression to the athletic, social, and cultural requirements of the young workers and working class student."[2] A Yiddish "Declaration of Principles of the International Workers Order" published in *The Spark* was blunter in its commitment to culture:

> The I.W.O. recognizes one field in which it can develop a particularly fruitful action—viz.: the field of culture. The Order realizes that culture is a potent instrument in the hands of the bourgeoisie to enslave the toiling masses, and that when the bourgeoisie, through its schools, press, institutions of adult education, and the bourgeois "intelligentsia," purports to "carry the light to the masses," in fact it purveys them with such information, and influences their kinds in such manner, that they might become faithful servants of the capitalistic order. The I.W.O. therefore, declares it as its duty to not only develop its members culturally, but to develop them <u>in a proletarian way</u>, i.e., to give them such culture as will clarify their minds, fortify their wills, strengthen their ranks, mobilize them for the fight against the capitalistic order, elevate them to the dignity of builders of a new society.[3]

The Order thus envisioned its choirs, drama troupes, and baseball teams as a counterweight to the hegemonic power of mass entertainment, which it alleged was buttressing the harmful status quo. As the editors of *The New Order* promised, "Out of the chaos of a crazed, ballyhooed, boss driven American Culture, there has arisen a Proletarian Culture which is fast approaching the day when it can 'thumb its nose at its Bourgeois predecessor.'"[4]

It is not clear whether every lodge member who showed up for social events was as thoroughly committed to deploying play scripts as weapons against the existing social order as leaders may have hoped. In defending the IWO, many members stressed the pleasure they received from celebrating their ethnic cultures in Slavic, Hungarian, Jewish, Puerto Rican, and other ethnic theater and dance troupes. The very entertainments designed to drive out the "ballyhooed, boss driven American Culture" served as a pleasurable respite from often drab, exhausting, or even dangerous days in industrial job sites and neighborhoods. In IWO theater groups, revelry, not revolution, may have prevailed.[5]

For their own different reasons, agents of the wartime OSS and IWO treasurer Peter Shipka highlighted the plethora of entertainment venues the organization offered that kept many members active. In 1944 an FNB officer of the OSS wrote to FNB director DeWitt Clinton Poole, "In fulfillment of one of its announced aims the IWO pursues a diversified program of social-cultural activities," listing song, dance, drama festivals, sports, and summer camps as some of the cultural practices "skillfully put to the service of IWO's political program." The IWO's National Film Division, a concert bureau, and dancers and singers in Ukrainian, Russian, Polish, and African American troupes helped the IWO "spread its message and gained new adherents to its viewpoints," the agent wrote. He also cited a *Daily Worker* article that asserted of the IWO's cultural program, "When you give people a chance at self-expression, . . . you are doing a valuable thing for them, a thing they appreciate. Whether they participate as actors or as audience, sharing a cultural experience creates a bond and makes them willing to listen to what you have to say."[6]

Through its cultural activities the IWO offered an emotional pedagogy, dramas and musical groups that endeavored to create an affective community that instilled in actors and audience a cathartic redemption for their otherwise often marginalized workers' lives. These feelings of power flipped the larger society's status hierarchies, so that "unskilled workers," racially and ethnically stigmatized communities, could reclaim a valorized sense of something large and noble. A cheerful mood prevailed as IWO members contemplated revolution. Both the OSS and the *Daily Worker* shared the assumption that, whether on stage or in the audience, attendees at IWO cultural events were absorbing the desired proletarian message.

For his part, Shipka, in helping IWO officers prepare their appeal of New York's liquidation order, characterized entertainment activities as designed to foster pride in ethnic heritage. He told the Order's defense team, "The Order attempts to encourage the preservation of the cultural heritages and artistic values developed over the years and through the generations by the peoples of the different countries of the world and brought with them to the United States." Among the IWO's activities encouraging such "cultural heritage and artistic values," Shipka listed sports competitions such as "national baseball, soft-ball, boxing, bowling, soccer, ping-pong, swimming and other tournaments, . . . track and field events, and outdoor and indoor games and the like." The Order also "encouraged the development of groups in dramatics, choruses, social and interpretive dancing, orchestras, bands and photography."[7]

Many amateur actors and dancers also likely participated in the Order's more overtly political campaigns. Still, in its entertainments the IWO went beyond denunciations of capitalist misery or explicit demands for Social Security or an end to Jim Crow and allowed many working-class members to perform and celebrate their often denigrated ethnic cultures before valorizing and appreciative audiences of their peers. In this regard the IWO carried forth a venerable tradition of left-wing immigrant *Vereinswesen* (associational life) where members could make sense of their lives on their own terms, and maybe have fun doing it, too.

"Something to Think About" and "Good Peppy Music"

In carving out a left-wing working-class recreational space, the IWO carried on the work of the CP, which likewise sought a space in which recreation would develop a transformative class consciousness. As Marxist theorist Antonio Gramsci and even Marx himself noted, cultural institutions are often contested spaces. So, too, as the IWO's Yiddish "Declaration" perceived, cultural institutions are often employed to buttress the socioeconomic elite and a society's status quo. Schools, literature, popular songs, and other cultural productions often inculcate lessons that society is just and those who are in political and economic command are there because they earned it or that the social order is "natural."[8] However, this hegemony, Gramsci recognized, was imperfect and in constant need of shoring up—or tearing down if one believed wealth has been unfairly appropriated or maldistributed. In moments of crisis the same cultural productions—plays, schools, and musical groups—are deployed by adherents of social movements to harness discontent to imagine that another world is possible.

As sociologists of social movements recognize, so too, activists quickly realized they had to "weave together a moral, cognitive and emotional package of attitudes" if they were to win converts. "Cognitive liberation," James Jasper argues, "is probably more important for its bundle of emotions than for any 'objective' information about odds of success. 'Liberation' implies heady emotions." Ann Swidler, too, argues that social movements are often most effective when they transpose group allegiances and cultural symbols into new causes. The members of the IWO took these messages of the transformative possibilities of leisure to heart, continuing a tradition of left-wing immigrant culture that combined class militancy with recreational activities. While in the 1920s and during the Depression CP activists offered lengthy and intricate expositions on Marxism at their rallies, heavy on the cognitive side, they did not slight the emancipatory appeal to emotions and fun. Education and entertainment mixed as left-wing rallies employed singing societies and theater troupes to preach a new gospel of Marxism via cultural institutions with which Jewish, Italian, and Slavic workers were familiar.[9]

During the early twentieth century, radical immigrants made plenty of room for dancing while advancing the revolution. As Michael Denning notes, after the New Deal took hold in the 1930s, a "laboring" of popular culture developed in which working-class agendas and themes flourished in theater, art, literature, and music. What is less frequently noticed, though, is that radical immigrants began this "laboring" of popular culture in obscure radical sites long before their proletarian themes were given the imprimatur of more celebrated tastemakers. Moreover, entertainments of the CP and its affiliates were often interracial affairs, as organizers recognized the multiracial nature of the American proletariat that the Party sought to recruit. From the CP's inception, Slavic, Italian, and Jewish workers made common cause with black and Hispanic fellow workers, even if they frequently struggled to overcome their "white chauvinism." This at a time when crossing or questioning the color line was regarded by many white Americans as the most subversive activity of all. Members of interracial CP affiliates worked to advance industrial unionism, support for the Soviet Union, black civil rights, even revolution, but they also envisioned pleasure itself as a means of dismantling the grim capitalist status quo. The CP refashioned various ethnic traditions as props of the Left's "sequestered social sites" and paid attention to the need to engage the emotions and hearts of rally attendees, not just their intellects. As earlier agrarian radicals had built a "movement culture" enabling them to envision the possibility of ending their suffering, radical immigrants employed dance troupes, theater societies, and singing groups to serve as their own proletarian schoolrooms.[10] This leftist sociocultural infrastructure was didactic, but proletarian pastimes also built solidarity and morale among those who envisioned a coming workers' state.

Early on left-leaning organizers recognized the necessity of promising entertainment at rallies, but the proletarian cause was at the forefront; this was fun with a class-conscious purpose. As a flyer for a 1922 May Day celebration sponsored by the United Toilers of America put it, "Our Workers' Holiday is not a day of rest and play; it is a day of struggle. The class-conscious worker greets this day with gladness and hope of victory, while the oppressors and exploiters of the workers await this day, grinding their teeth with rage and mortal fear." The Toilers' lengthy text went through a list of proletarian grievances before vowing, "We will refuse to allow ourselves to be killed by overwork." They then offered the carrot to go along with the Hammer and Sickle stick: a not-to-be-missed May Day celebration with entertainers in English, Lithuanian, Russian, and Polish at Detroit's International Workers' Home.[11]

While such left-wing rallies stressed the need to educate workers on their true proletarian mission, comrades nevertheless also recognized the need to leaven the education with a bit of fun. Members of the Communist-affiliated National Textile Workers Union were told that "educational activity must not be of a dry-as-dust manner," and use of movies, theatricals, dances, and sports was urged to enhance the effectiveness of recruiting meetings. Communists seeking to organize Chicago steelworkers offered a play, *Steel Strike*, by the Workers' Cultural Federation, but promised "good peppy music" and "dancing! dancing!" as well. Similarly, Communist mine workers promised a "Full Day of Fun" for a rally at Nanticoke's Sans Souci Park to "make September 1st the Workers' Day"—"amusements, sports, entertainment, carnival, dancing"—and a speech by Communist vice-presidential candidate Ben Gitlow. It cannot all be entertainment.[12]

During the 1926 coal miners' strike, party factions in western Pennsylvania's UMW promised "fun and education at Labor Chautauquas" that "left the folks with something to think about and a lot to laugh at in pleasant recollection." The program "sandwiche[d] speeches and lectures on the labor movement between gay layers of music and song." On the bill were musical comedy sketches from a sister act, songs, jazz combos, and "Thumine's Boys' Band, from Sykesville—the same that jazzed up the miners' march and mass meeting at Du Bois." A schoolteacher from Sagamore composed songs and organized women's auxiliaries to help picketers. The *U.M.W. Bulletin* promised "no better fun anywhere," even though the Chautauqua proved only a brief bright spot in yet another violently squashed strike. Comrades knew what sociologists of social movements later realized, that emotions, which Jasper argued "have disappeared from models of protest," had to be engaged no less than the intellects of those one sought to recruit.[13]

As scholars have reminded us, the carefree Roaring Twenties were also, for many workers, the era of wage cuts, speedups, lockouts, and the violent suppression of strikes.[14] But all was not grim for the class-conscious worker. Throughout the late 1920s and into the early 1930s, festive entertainments such as the coal-camp Chautauquas offered a respite from the workaday world. Carnivalesque settings, as for Bakhtin, were often possible moments of liberation from, and subversion of, the established order. The CP hoped these festivities would not be brief reprieves from the dominant order but the catalyst for a transformative social movement. Left-wing workers thus frequently offered celebrations in relief of threatened strikers or to remind workers of some revolutionary anniversary that might eventually save them from bosses' Gatling guns. A 1926 "Gala Concert at Coney Island Stadium" promised an "Orchestra of One Hundred, Chorus of Two Hundred Voices, 50 Ballet Dancers," to raise funds for the starving children of striking Passaic textile workers. In an appeal that began, "The Bosses Hell No!," the International Workers' Aid arranged to send striking textile workers' children to the International Workers' Camp in Morristown, New Jersey. James Scott has argued that the marginalized poor can often only gain advances through sly, under-the-radar acts of resistance, some of the only "weapons" available to the weak. By reclaiming prominent sites of mass entertainment and amusement such as Coney Island for airing workers' causes, leftists engaged in a defiantly public transcript.[15]

Lenin Memorial meetings in Philadelphia and Detroit featured "Interracial Choruses of 300 Voices" presenting "revolutionary music." Posters for the gala at Detroit's Danceland Auditorium reminded concertgoers that "Lenin, like Karl Marx, . . . taught the workers of this country that the workers in the white skin cannot be emancipated so long as the worker in the dark skin is enslaved." An election rally at Danceland also featured not just Bedacht lecturing on the "issue in the election—class against class!" but an "excellent revolutionary music program."[16]

In times of economic crisis, these counterhegemonic spaces qualified as sites of potential liberation. After years of breadlines and soup kitchens, rallies with three hundred interracial singers or dance parties probably seemed liberating—or threatening, depending on one's perspective. Considering, too, the fear that interracial dancing or singing evoked in the forces of law, order, and the segregated status quo, the very transgressive act of "mixed" dancing may have been part of the fun of a night at Danceland. The very act of such public defiance achieved one of the workers' goals.[17]

The forces of law and order saw such interracial celebrations as threatening, subversive occasions. In Clifton, New Jersey, IWO members participated along with three hundred other black and white radicals in a mixed-race dance sponsored by the Ramblers Sports Club of the Labor Sports Union of America. When news of the affair reached the city's police chief, he arrested the hall's owner and fined him $27 for allowing a mixed-race dance. "We won't stand for mixed dances in Clifton," Chief Holster declared. The Ramblers' black president was also arrested and beaten up in nearby Passaic for walking with a white woman as he collected funds for the *Daily Worker*. A protest meeting was slated for the same hall where the offending interracial dance occurred, but when the masses arrived the doors were padlocked. Undeterred, "300 Negroes and whites held their meeting in the street, and marched singing to the headquarters of the International Labor Defense and the Unemployed Council. Members of the National Textile Workers Union, the Workers International Relief, the International Workers Order, the Young Communist League and the Communist Party were among the marchers."[18]

As Victoria Wolcott has shown, entertainment venues such as amusement parks, bowling alleys, and dance halls were some of the most fiercely defended icons of racial segregation. Fears of race-mixing on the dance floor evoked phobias of sexual contact and social equality. That the dancers in Clifton were celebrating on an interracial dance floor, among fellow believers in leftist causes, was doubly offensive to upholders of the status quo.[19]

Other galas celebrating the ninth anniversary of the Russian Revolution, seventh anniversary of the founding of the Workers (Communist) Party, or the birthday of the *Daily Worker* featured "elaborate musical programs" or dancing, along with speeches by prominent comrades such as William Z. Foster, who would become general secretary of the CPUSA in 1945. While the workers learned their proletarian canon, they made time to polka, for as the organizers of one workers' picnic promised, a "good time [was] assured." Lithuanian, Russian, and Ukrainian Workers' Clubs in Philadelphia pooled their mandolin-playing and singing talents for "an Evening of Joy and Inspiration." The International Orchestra, the *Freiheit Gesangs Verein* (Freedom Singing Society), the Pioneer Chorus, the Saint Paul Workers Orchestra, and the Young Workers' Mandolin Orchestra all did their best to keep this revolutionary promise.[20]

As Ron Eyerman and Scott Barretta note, there is nothing intrinsically radical in folk music. Some of the earliest proponents of folk music espoused conservative politics and saw the revival of "pure" culture as an antidote to the menace of industrial America. Even Henry Ford, enemy of unions and proponent of mass-produced assimilation, sponsored old-time fiddle contests at Greenfield Village. Other Italian folk dancers or Polish singers were bulwarks of conservative white ethnic parishes. It was the progressive organizational framework of Pioneer choruses and May Day celebrations that infused leftist connotations into the folk music at these "evenings of joy and inspiration."[21]

Immigrants heard something other than laissez-faire choruses at venues such as the Labor Lyceum. Francesca Polletta and James Jasper write of the vitality of "institutions removed from the physical and ideological control of those in power" for building social movements contesting the status quo. In a similar fashion, African Americans in Detroit deployed the swing clubs of Paradise Valley as a safe space in which to hear critiques of hypersegregated America as well as enjoy themselves. So, too, members of left-leaning drama clubs and singing groups were more than entertainers, for through their artistic endeavors they sought to teach a pleasing lesson of the justness of revolutionary struggles. In January 1925 the Lithuanian Working Women's Alliance of America reported, "One of its main activities is to organize the Lithuanian Workers' children into groups, teach them singing and dramatics (of a working class character) . . . and to give them a class conscious understanding of their position in society." Groups that later affiliated with the IWO such as the SWS established dramatic unions and schools to teach workers' theater, while in Harlem proletarian playwrights such as Paul Peters lectured at the Harlem Workers School on "the Negro and the Working-Class Theater." Members of Workers' Dramatic Unions saw their proletarian theaters as antidotes to the escapist fare of commercial theater. Jewish comrades held "a trial on the 'Burlesque Theater,'" which was presumably found guilty. Songs of class consciousness were effective recruiting tools. At a June 1931 meeting of the South Slav Singing Society, members "took up the question of affiliating with the Friends of the Soviet Union."[22]

Still, those more interested in aesthetics sometimes drowned out radical vocalists. "Among the Ukrainians the situation is very deplorable," Lovestone complained regarding work in Connecticut. "Instead of being the leader in the Ukrainian colony," the party faction was "gradually becoming an adjunct of the Ukrainian singing societies." Lovestone ruefully concluded, "our own very small group is gradually being absorbed by the backward mass and drawn into the swamps."[23] Such a lament shows there was no guarantee that the instructive message of comrade-entertainers reached the audience. The problem of reader-response—how do we know that every recipient imbibes the author's "lesson" in just the way that she planned—affected singing Ukrainians and other comrades, too. As Lawrence Levine has argued, during the early twentieth century working-class people were not passive recipients of the entertainments offered by Hollywood or America's radio networks. They chose the movies or radio programs they patronized and reinterpreted pat, happy endings to make them more plausible and applicable to their own lives. Something similar occurred in workers' entertainment venues. The cultural experiences, assumptions, and life narratives of particular immigrants and communities affected whether these singers would find Lovestone's intended lessons appealing. Maybe Connecticut Ukrainians just liked to sing.[24]

That Ukrainians showed up at a Communist singing society or a coal miners' Chautauqua suggested at least some sympathy to the message underlying songs and skits. Then again, there was no guarantee that attendees heard what the comrades wanted them to hear. In tiny outposts such as Pennsylvania coal patches, the militant Chautauqua might have been attended as one of the few sites of fun, or for instrumental nonmilitant reasons—they were fund-raising in support of strikers. Likewise, the singers who bedeviled Lovestone had their own complex reasons for singing their songs. Fellowship may have been enjoyed without inculcating the complete Bolshevik message of songs.

Sometimes the frequency of entertainments became a problem. Among larger Party units such as the Jewish Bureau, there were so many social affairs that the *Freiheit* Mandolin Orchestra was told to reschedule its concerts so it would not conflict with other entertainments; the orchestra countered that Communists gave its organization insufficient publicity. In 1946 Detroit, an organizer for the IWO, approached once too often to buy tickets for the "dance," snapped that he was not a ticket agency. When this organizer discovered the new dance was a fund-raiser for the *Daily Worker*, he sheepishly asked the solicitor to mail him a letter that he could send out to various IWO lodges. Anthony Bimba likewise complained that the incessant demands on the recreational time of new converts to the Party was leading to high dropout rates. The new member, Bimba argued, "hates to come to the meetings because he sees nothing else at these meetings but leaflets, tickets, peddling of all kinds." He warned, "Unless this avalanche of all sorts of letters, instructions, tickets and 'mobilizations' is stopped, all our talk of retaining members in the party will be in vain. Don't you see that? Can't you see that?"[25] There was only so much fun the proletariat could be expected to endure.

Competing recreational events sometimes caused friction. In 1930, Candela of the Party's Italian Bureau, later head of the IWO's Garibaldi Society, complained that an Italian fund-raising picnic was ordered canceled because it conflicted with another event deemed more important by the New York district. Candela was already incensed because the Party's summer camp, Camp Nitgedaiget, still had not paid *Il Lavoratore* for the ads it had run. Candela protested that there was no way he could keep the paper running if the Party did not allow him to raise money or collect on past-due bills. "Are we going to take action ourselves and make a scandal?" he asked.[26]

Camp Nitgedaiget in upstate New York (Yiddish for "carefree") was another counterhegemonic space, where class-conscious children and adults escaped tenements and enjoyed recreation far away from bosses' prying eyes. Already in 1928 the camp promised prospective vacationers swimming, baseball, and theatricals. Another red camp, Camp Wocolona near Monroe, New York, advertised its offerings in *New Masses*: "Baseball and Revolution." In between innings, campers were urged to "join the *New Masses* artists, writers, and their friends and enemies, in a discussion of 'The Intellectual and the Labor Movement.'" Artists and writers such as Mike Gold, Lewis Mumford, and Hugo Gellert participated in the debate. The following year Nitgedaiget billed itself as "the Workers' Rest Home," promising "physical and mental recreation" in a "Proletarian Atmosphere." IWO revelers later patronized "red" camps such as Nitgedaiget, Kinderland, and Lakeland.[27]

For all the baseball and polemics, the camps often had trouble paying their bills. In 1932 the Hungarian IWO complained that Nitgedaiget had failed to pay for ads in *Új Előre*. Perhaps as a result of such practices, at another red camp, the JPFO's Camp Kinderland, director Saltzman and members of the camp's board of trustees were expelled from the Party for several months due to the $10,000 deficit and unpaid bills they had allowed to accumulate.[28]

Despite financial woes, red camps were some of the few places workers could rehearse narratives countering the dominant society's message that free-market capitalism was the all-American way. While children of laborers escaped with their parents from crowded dwelling spaces for a few weeks in the woods, they learned to conceptualize a different way of ordering industrial society. Outside of the camps, in the pre–New Deal era, Vice President Calvin Coolidge reminded readers of *Good Housekeeping* magazine that "non-Nordic" immigrants were imperiling the nation and that immigration restrictions were necessary to "safeguard not just the present but the future" of the nation. Other authority figures acted more directly and brutally on the non-Nordics of the land, as when policemen, private detectives, and state police squads—aptly dubbed "Cossacks" by Slavic miners—broke up strikes from the textile mills of Passaic to the coal fields of Pennsylvania through generous doses of tear gas and machine-gun bullets.[29]

Workers' children flocked to camps to learn alternative ways of conceiving of their place in America. A teenager wrote that she had never thought much about racial brotherhood before her parents sent her to Camp Wo-Chi-Ca, a Port Murray, New Jersey, camp owned by the leftist Furriers' Union. At Wo-Chi-Ca (shorthand for "Workers' Children's Camp") this teenager first heard of the IWO and "learned, for the first time, how all people, regardless of race, color, or creed live together as one large happy family.... I learned that Negro and white are equal, and that is something I never knew or had thought about." This camper returned home vowing to enroll in the IWO to do her bit for "cleaning up slums, doing away with racial discrimination."[30]

Competing narratives of workers' spaces were on display in a *Detroit Free Press* article reporting on a 1930 raid on a red camp. "We have had this place under observation for weeks," Prosecutor Norman Orr said. "It is the breeding ground for communism in the state. Impressionable young children are taken from the poorer home in Detroit, taught fiery communistic songs, told stories of 'brutality of the bosses,' and assured that the way to end these conditions is through opposition to all law and order." But while Scott has argued that subalterns can often only be effective in pursuing counter-narratives to the ruling class through surreptitious "hidden transcripts," Detroit workers openly advertised their camp with "huge signs bearing the legend 'Workers' Camp'" at several entrances. The salience for subalterns of "sequestered social sites," as Scott puts it, meant Detroit comrades and others valued their camps and workers' halls. But perhaps the defiant publicization of their alternative spaces, on view to all of society's authority figures, was in and of itself part of the camp's fun.[31]

In Detroit the raided children wore their class-conscious allegiances openly. "To the children, the raid was an exciting experience," the article continued. "Apparently under the direction of adults, they shouted communistic songs at the raiders as they searched the barracks, offices and dining rooms on the farm." Among the subversive articles seized was a "crude childish drawing" that "portrayed a man labeled 'Boss,' swinging a cat-o-nine-tails over the bare back of a worker. 'Don't be a Slave' was the caption lettered over it."[32]

A Different "Source of Americanization"

The flowering of class-conscious recreation came with the founding of the IWO. From its onset the IWO privileged the fostering of the ethnic and racial cultures of its members. The 1938 constitution recommitted the Order to interracialism: "The cultural heritage of every one of the many national and racial groups which make the American people has contributed to and enriched the life and traditions of our country. Our Order endeavors ... to make the same culture and traditions a source of Americanization of education, recreation and happiness for its members. The Order thus hopes to become a stronghold of unity and progress of mankind."[33]

From its inception the Order offered a broad range of integrated recreational activities. The youth magazine *The Spark* documented the baseball team organized by the Providence Youth Branch, which "is aiding the Scottsboro defense with all its might," while the Chicago Youth Committee organized three youth branches, including a "Negro" one on the West Side. In some locations "white chauvinism" had to be overcome, but as early as July 1931 the John Reed Youth Club of Jersey City "repudiated the stand that they took on the Negro question," and interracial organizing ensued. Providence members also produced the play *It's Funny as Hell*. Philadelphians meanwhile formed an IWO Band and Workers International Relief Mandolin Orchestra, celebrating these achievements by singing the "Internationale." New Yorkers supported an IWO symphony orchestra as well as a Dramatic Festival (won in 1934 by lodges of the Russian Society for their entry, *Broadway 1934*, even though it was noted that audience members disagreed with the judges and preferred *The Earth Moves*, enacted by Lodge 404). Jewish lodges in the Bronx sponsored theater groups and "talks on the motion picture." An article on "Sports in the IWO" critiqued professional sports as just another way to enrich millionaire owners, whereas the aim of IWO baseball, basketball, and gymnastics teams was "to build up a healthy body and a healthy mind, a strong conscious fighter for the working class."[34]

In 1934 *The New Order* noted the development of baseball leagues in Los Angeles, where black, Hispanic, and white teams competed against each other. The IWO fielded integrated teams in Canton, Ohio, even though many lodges were ethnically defined as Slovak, Hungarian, or Jewish. There, IWO teams competed in the Stark County baseball league, breaking the color line thirteen years before Jackie Robinson. In Los Angeles the IWO also competed in tennis tournaments, at track and field meets, and in boxing, wrestling, and gymnastics. A similar array of teams for men and women was on offer in Chicago, Buffalo, Brooklyn, and other cities. *The New Order* congratulated the Berkeley, California, lodge, when, because no gyms were provided by the city, a member constructed basketball nets and gymnastics equipment on his own. These "sports shorts" in the paper were accompanied by an illustration of a worker-athlete punching a fat, top-hatted millionaire in the gut.[35]

A similarly anticapitalist counter–Boston Marathon was held in 1935 to "demonstrate against new war plans," while prior to that, in 1932, a workers' counter-Olympics was slated for Chicago. The lily-white South African athletics squad, as well as the exclusion of colonial nations such as India at the real Olympics, came under particular condemnation. For leftists, sports were a political act.[36]

At a 1951 New York state trial, Powers offered as evidence of the IWO's Communist hazard its 1934 campaign to integrate baseball as well as its work defending the Scottsboro teens, "the Anti-Poll Tax Amendment, anti-lynch legislation, and the Civil Rights Program." At a time when Southern segregationists were running the HUAC, integrationist fraternization, to say nothing of activism, was suspect.[37]

Even in small ways, the IWO championed the breaking of racial barriers. Integrated IWO baseball teams played games and passed petitions through the stands demanding baseball abolish the color line. Other IWO members wrote homages in their magazine, *The New Order*, to "Comrade Basketball," while IWO members joined an Interfaith and Interracial Coordinating Council planning an End Jim Crow in Baseball Day with demonstrations slated for the Polo Grounds and Ebbets Field. As noted, the protest rallies, which were to have included members of the IWO's Jewish Division, were called off when the mayor agreed to meet with representatives of the council to seek a means of integrating baseball.[38]

In 1941, perhaps due to the influence of the many Slovak IWO members, *Národné noviny* ran a comic strip by Joe Dujka, "The Numbskull Nine," about an integrated baseball team whose star was the dark-skinned Latino Carlos Kelly. In one strip a fan taunts Carlos, "Throw the Foreigner Out! G'wan back to Brazil Nut! Go peddle your bananas!! You Havana Honky!" At which point the star's girlfriend wallops him. When the fan asks "Why, lady?" she replies, "I pinch hit for my Carlos." A few weeks later she joins the team as a player. And as noted, IWO secretary Milgrom greeted the integrated Cleveland Indians' world championship "as a 'victory for American democracy.'"[39]

The IWO's Puerto Rican Cervantes Fraternal Society played an important role in fostering Latino culture where members "maintain[ed] our fraternal affiliations with one another and with our national hereditary culture." Peter Moreno of Brooklyn deposed in an affidavit, "We have programs of native music and dancing in national costumes," and he noted that Cervantes supported "a young folk's baseball league called 'Luis Olmo League.' . . . They are very proud to be the only Puerto Rican baseball league in this country." The Cervantes Fraternal Society also sponsored a concert by flamenco dancer Trini Romero at Carnegie Chamber Music Hall, to which all IWO members were invited.[40]

Teams competed for Eastern and Western District championships in basketball and baseball and held national meets timed to coincide with IWO conventions. In 1939 Hazleton, Pennsylvania, won the Eastern District basketball championship and played a Chicago team in the national finals. IWO president William Weiner was honored to throw the ball for the first tipoff. The African American *Chicago Defender* publicized these tournaments, too—in one case an interracial New York team, the Lincoln Brigadiers, proudly touted its members' service to Republican Spain. Local ethnic lodges such as the SWS of Detroit also slated sports teams, fielding a bowling team in 1947, even as it fretted over being able to fund such a team (the national SWS board started a fund to assist the Detroiters). Other IWO members fondly recalled bowling teams in Los Angeles and Philadelphia.[41]

Such revelry did not cause comrades to lose sight of serious issues. General Secretary Bedacht urged his organization to "redouble ... efforts for the defense of the Negroes in America against lynching." "Song, drama, living newspapers, interracial children's pageants and numerous other forms of cultural activities," he reminded the Order, "while they can educate and unify all groups, are at the same time very satisfying and attractive mass entertainment." The *Chicago Defender* ran an article in 1936 in which Thompson urged the "race" to tune in to IWO radio broadcasts of plays, songs, and musical numbers dramatizing "the furtherance of social security." The following year the IWO presented "a jubilee concert and pageant in New York. . . . [I]ts prologue presented three characters for three different periods in American history: 1776—Jefferson, 1861—Lincoln, 1937—A Communist leader." During the Popular Front, the CP cast communism as Americanism updated to the twentieth century, and the Order presented tableaus that night of "Economic exploitation of the 18th century," "Capitalists united against the working class," "1886—the trial of the labor leaders," "Crisis of 1929," and 1937's *deus ex machina*, "The Communist Party calls for a united front."[42]

Theater groups were some of the mainstays of the IWO, designed to educate and entertain peers on industrial unions, militarism, and black civil rights as well as to summon a usable past for the comrades. Philadelphia lodges as early as 1934 sponsored dramatic societies that performed plays such as *The Bulls See Red* and *Recruit*. These plays, the first of which presumably pitted the police ("bulls") against the comrades, as so often occurred during the early years of the Depression, was supplemented in the Philadelphia lodge by "classes in Marxism." In Chicago a citywide "speakers and drama bureau" offered training to lodges looking to start theater groups. While an IWO National Youth Day in Passaic featured militant theater productions, smaller cities such as Elizabeth, New Jersey, sometimes had to make do with performances by "a Chorus of Youth" that "sang some revolutionary songs" in lieu of a theater group.[43]

New York also supported an IWO symphony orchestra. In 1936 organizer Bob Jacoby greeted the convention of New York City IWO branches "and appealed to the membership ... for support for the orchestra." In this respect the IWO was carrying forth the earlier work of the Workers Cultural Federation of the New York District, which in 1931 was urged by Paul Keller, director of the Federation of Workers Choruses, to "get a stronger political content into our music" and "to develop the emotional side of our propaganda." The affective work of the IWO was not neglected. The Federation of Workers Choruses was having some success in this regard among various white ethnic singing groups and noted the development of the symphony orchestra later led by the IWO's Jacoby. But Keller was less satisfied with the minimal development of brass bands and mandolin orchestras, which he believed could provide the music at mass demonstrations and strikes "to lead the workers to victory." Keller was confident such brass bands could be developed in Brooklyn and the Bronx: "We have enough latent material." Evidently the IWO agreed, for throughout the 1940s it continued to organize concert tours of Slovak and Ukrainian choirs and mandolin orchestras, although as anti-Communist fervor heated up in smaller towns such as Charleroi and Bentleyville, Pennsylvania, "getting halls (and holding them once gotten) is becoming a nightmare." Still, with the IWO the show went on.[44]

The IWO even touched on higher culture if it thought it could make a revolutionary point. *The New Order* reported on the destruction of Diego Rivera's mural at Rockefeller Center because of the offending inclusion of a portrait of Lenin. John D. Rockefeller was "so conscious of the inharmony in the situation that he had the mural destroyed—a pure case of vandalism. But Mr. Rockefeller would not get clubbed on the head or dragged into prison for such an offense." *The New Order* happily reported, though, that Rivera "has photographs of his work and intends to restore his masterpiece." They congratulated the muralist, too, for declaring, "My object was attained when the painting was destroyed. I thank the Rockefellers for its destruction because the act will advance the cause of the labor revolution. The assassination of my work will bring about a wider dissemination of the teachings of Lenin among the workers, so that it is a victory for the proletariat."[45]

"Our Plays for the People": Revolutionary Theater

IWO drama groups were another popular means of dissemination of the revolutionary message. Throughout the country theater troupes were active in performing militant works. Boston Latvians in the IWO celebrated a "Lenin Memorial Celebration Program" by performing a play, *January 9th*, about the failed 1905 Russian revolution. Chicago Croatian Socialists in the Dramatski Zbor "Nada" were not above satirizing their own stigmatization as dangerous bomb-throwers, as when they presented *Risen from the Ranks, or From Office Boy to President*. This parody of a Horatio Alger story features Oswald Sapp, a rural rube who applies for a job with the Amalgamated Pretzel Co. Industrial harmony, however, is disrupted by a baroquely bewhiskered anarchist dressed in red, who proclaims, "I am Kachooski, the young Bolshevik agitator from Moscow!" (Bwah hah hah!) Kachooski shows up with his infant son, who is similarly bearded. "Yes, even in Russia the babies have whiskers. In fact, they are born with them." Kachooski organizes the Amalgamated Pretzel Benders' Union and ruins Mister Millionbucks. Oswald, though, invents a pretzel-bending machine so the workers can be fired.

The union is broken, and Oswald marries Mister Millionbucks' daughter at the play's "happy" end.[46]

Prior to the Popular Front, the Croatians performed other plays mocking the palliatives of FDR's New Deal, as in *The Forgotten Man*, where, to the tune of Roosevelt's chipper campaign song "Happy Days Are Here Again," the "Paytriot" sang: "What we need's another war, / For life's become an awful bore, / Oh what the hell's the army for, / What we need's another war!" The pop songs of Tin Pan Alley likewise were refashioned, as when "I'm Forever Blowing Bubbles" was reworked into a sardonic refrain of the Reconstruction Finance Corporation's bailout of Wall Street but decidedly *not* the Forgotten Man. Popular culture proved a malleable tool when wielded by Socialist theater troupes.[47]

The theater had a political purpose not just in educating the audience but to give emotional and material comfort to those on strike in desperate times. A YCL actor from Newark wrote to Party activist Pat Toohey offering the services of his Newark Collective Theater comrades. He proposed "a full evening of theater to help the strikers" in Camden, offering the courtroom scene from *They Shall Not Die!* and *Waiting for Lefty*, "two very effective and entertaining pieces." The fund-raiser, he wrote, would "undoubtedly prove successful in more ways than one."[48]

Plays championing black civil rights were performed, too. The *Rebel Arts Bulletin*, whose motto was "Art to Serve Labor," provided Chicago Croatians with a series of "Plays on Negro Life," including *Angelo Herndon* by Langston Hughes, *Trouble with the Angels* by Bernard Schoenfeld (from the article by Hughes), *Angelo Herndon Back in Atlanta* by Elizabeth England, and *Bivouac* by Paul Peters, in which "a Negro Threatened with Lynching Is Saved Through the Militant Action of Friends and Sympathizers." In Chicago radical Czechs took up the theme of black liberation, performing *When Slavery Was in Bloom in America*, a play lionizing abolitionists John Brown and Frederick Douglass. As Rebecca Hill notes, it was only on the Left that Brown was valorized as a masculinist, militant defender of racial equality, cast as a liberator and not, as many Americans were taught, an unstable, violent disturber of the peace.[49]

One of the most interesting IWO theaters was Solidarity Lodge's Harlem Suitcase Theater, in which Thompson brought the plays of her friend, African American poet Hughes, before working-class audiences. The IWO had already published some of Hughes's "revolutionary verse" in dime booklet form as well as sponsoring a lecture tour for him, "A Negro Poet Looks at a Troubled World." In 1938 Solidarity Lodge founded the Harlem Suitcase Theater, so named, Thompson said, because "we wanted a theater with few props, . . . that we could carry it around in a suitcase and do our plays for the people." The first play performed was written especially for the Suitcase Theater by Hughes, a send-up of black oppression, *Don't You Want to Be Free?*

that dramatized a lynching and black and white workers' realization they had to work together to throw off class-based subordination. Thompson recalled this play "was about as far as we went with agit-prop," and the play portrayed Jim Crow insurance agents (familiar to Harlem members who had entered the IWO to escape them) and wary characters who denounced agitators as radicals. Audience participation was encouraged as actors and playgoers worked through their class conflicts and racialized oppression. A "Member of Audience (rising)," is sure rioting will solve nothing, but ultimately black and white workers harmoniously work out their differences and in song invite the audience to join them in fighting for justice. The first cast was entirely composed of IWO members from Solidarity Lodge and its youth group, some of whom later enjoyed professional acting and dancing careers, most notably Butterfly McQueen and Robert Earl Jones, James Earl's father. Thompson recalled Jones as a powerful actor, "but he never did his lines the same way twice. We'd see a different show every night."

Don't You Want to Be Free? was first performed at Solidarity Lodge's own headquarters, ironically housed above a restaurant that refused to serve black people. It was then performed at the Harlem YWCA and then the same Finnish hall where Yokinen had earlier gotten into trouble for barring black people. At one 1939 performance, Hughes's play was paired with Frank Wilson reading from *God's Trombones* and Sierra Leonean Asadata Dafora "interpreting African Dance Rhythms." Other plays offered by the Harlem Suitcase Theater were similar agit-prop vehicles, such as Hughes's *Blues to Now—and Then Some!* and an opera with music by James P. Johnson and a book by Hughes. Thompson also fondly recalled satires of saccharine contemporary treatments of black America. *Limitations of Life* sent up the film *Imitations of Life*, while *Em-fuehrer Jones* got in a few digs at Berlin by way of Eugene O'Neill. The Suitcase Theater spawned other IWO experiments in leftist theater in Saint Louis, Los Angeles, Nashville, and elsewhere, and fostered other troupes such as the Newark Collective Theater and the Lincoln Players in Cleveland, the Trenton New Theatre, and the Montreal New Theatre. *Don't You Want to Be Free?* was later performed at the black Atlanta University as well as in Nashville and New Orleans. *Freedom Road* was later performed by an IWO theater troupe at the Du Sable Center when Thompson relocated to Chicago.

Unfortunately, the Harlem Suitcase Theater did not last long, partially a victim of its own success. Thompson spoke of "the influence of commercial theater on people's theater" as a factor that led to the Suitcase Theater's rapid demise. "Everybody had his eyes, or her eyes, on going to Broadway. . . . Everybody either was going to Broadway physically or imitating Broadway in the type of production which you did. Why do we always have to be in overalls or aprons. We want to do musical comedy or we want to do Noel Coward." She remembered how "some of the bitter arguments we had as the thing developed was the kind of plays we chose." Some actors favored plays such as those done by "Gilbert and Sullivan amateurs" over class- and race-conscious dramas. Such squabbles suggest the politics of respectability played out, even in Solidarity Lodge. The Suitcase Theater's constitution admonished actors to "refrain from entering the theatre intoxicated or with liquor on your breath. Not only is it a bad reflection on your theatre, but annoying to the person playing opposite you." Still, for a brief moment the Harlem Suitcase Theater offered exciting theater that also addressed the problems of the black and white working class.[50]

The IWO utilized theater throughout its lifespan. "The IWO Treasure Chest of Tools" listed songs and plays available to lodges nationwide. During World War II, the OSS noted the effectiveness of theater troupes such as the Harlem People's Art Group and the Polish People's Theater in spreading the IWO's message. The latter troupe "has never failed to impress upon its audience Poland's need of Soviet friendship. A pageant entitled 'Tribute to the Fighting Forces of Istria,' written by IWO National Activities Director Carol Fijan, aroused the Istrian community to memorialize Congress and the President in behalf of the recognition of Tito." During the war Slovak and Polish groups dramatized the Nazi massacre at Lidice, Czechoslovakia, and performed "a play dealing with the Polish partisans," which was even "favorably accepted upon being performed in Catholic Church auditoriums."[51]

Following World War II, the dramatists were still at it, only now the targets were once again capitalists, returning the IWO to the kind of proletarian culture the Order's founders had envisioned in the early 1930s. *Let's Get Together*, produced for the IWO Freedom Theatre, included "vehement attacks against private business" (in the words of the G-men tasked with keeping an eye on the Order) such as Pete Seeger's "Banks of Marble" and another musical number, "'Willie and the Bomb' (about the A bomb)." A Ukrainian Society play, *All Our Yesterdays*, was "a play with audience participation designed to turn the theatre into a political meeting." Vignettes included a "Negro being killed by a police officer without provocation . . . interspersed with audience participation bits." The play ends in triumph as the comrades win a court order against Americans Unlimited, "a fascist organization." During World War II, the Ukrainians also presented a play glorifying pro-Soviet partisans. Not to be outdone, the SWS produced *Keep Up!* by František Končinský, a "play on the suffering of women in war time," set "in the future" during a war between "proletarian" Eastern Europe and "capitalist" Western Europe. Near play's end several characters are cautiously optimistic that war will be abolished once and for all. But then "The United Warmongering States of America declared war on Europe." "The play ends with one of the characters proclaiming 'with inner fire': 'Yes, keep up! But this cry should not only be the cry of madmen—this cry must come from the entire wretched and oppressed world. . . . Comrades! Keep up!' to which a voice from the audience replies: 'We shall keep up!'" Another play by Končinský performed in Slovak was titled simply *A Picture of Good Revolutions in History*.[52]

The plots of these plays rehearsed for workers' situations with which they were likely all too familiar—strikes, police brutality, the pettiness of bosses and landlords—and thus to some extent they were performing their own lives for their fellow workers on stage and in the audience. Surely Chicago steelworkers could have guessed the basic plot of *Steel Strike*. But plays such as *Keep Up!* and, more famously, Clifford Odets's *Waiting for Lefty*, offered as a play to benefit strikers in Camden, were proletarian realism with a twist. In Odets's play assembled workers were berated not to wait for Lefty, a savior from beyond the proscenium, who was not coming this or any other night, but to organize and agitate themselves. Moreover, working-class audience members were adept at fashioning and critiquing entertainments into usable models. Levine notes that during the Depression moviegoers were part of "an interactive, independent social entity," and that in the 1950s television viewers in Boston turned implausible soap operas into satires through their mocking commentary. Similarly, IWO dramagoers were not passive recipients of the plays they watched. They had the option of seeing Hollywood movies or catching Jack Benny on the radio (and on other nights maybe they did). Their attendance at Communist or other left-wing entertainment venues thus already demonstrated some degree of choice and affinity with the message they were likely to hear. But the exhortations to "keep up!" urged attendees to bring their own thoughts and interpretations to the theater.[53]

While some of these postwar plays trod heavily on American toes, IWO organizers nevertheless endeavored to employ as raucous a spectacle as possible to attract recruits. A "National Training School" stressed seminars in "Rights of the Negro People, Equality," but also honed lodges' ability to harness lively entertainments to political campaigns and membership drives. Folk dance groups were to make appearances on Labor Day, May Day, and ethnic holidays such as Italians' Columbus Day or Poles' Kosciuszko Day. "When the lodge carries out a civic action it should look for interesting and colorful techniques," teachers advised. "A chorus or mandolin orchestra in national costume on a sound truck could attract a lot of attention. . . . [T]he use of national costumes will multiply the effectiveness of the work."[54] The IWO sought to instill progressive Americanism in its members, but at other times it did not slight the ethnic particularities of its Italian, Polish, and other members.

"Enrich Our American National Culture": Ethnic Pride Meets Radical Patriotism

Many Order activities privileged the valorization of ethnic culture over the assimilationist-homogenizing tendencies of such American pastimes as baseball games. The Order sponsored ethnic folk dancing troupes such as the Radischev Russian Folk Dancers or dance groups associated with the Emma

Lazarus Division, the women's branch of the JPFO. Slovak IWO members composed "The Song of Hope," with lyrics in Slovak and English, in praise of the ASC, while African American members of the Order's Douglass-Lincoln Society sang songs such as "Swing Low, Sweet Chariot" in performances designed to valorize their often denigrated culture. In 1950 General Secretary Milgrom wrote to Kent, artist and IWO president, on the reprise of "the already famous Ukrainian cultural festivals" that "will express not only Ukrainian culture, but certain aspects of American culture, integrated into the Ukrainian festivals." The melding of ethnic and American cultures and causes on these occasions was common. When the SWS held jubilee festivals to celebrate its thirtieth anniversary, the proceeds from concerts in Pittsburgh, Cleveland, and Chicago featuring the Radischev dancers and other Slavic performers were dedicated to funding a memorial to Roosevelt in Banska Bystrica, site of the Slovak Uprising against Nazi occupation.[55]

Other times, more explicitly ethnic agendas were pursued, as when the JPFO memorialized the Warsaw Ghetto martyrs on the anniversary of the uprising or took part in a Polo Grounds pageant celebrating "The Birth of the Jewish State." SWS lodges held a bazaar to benefit *Ľudový denník*. Radio listeners in western Pennsylvania enjoyed old country music broadcast on SWS's Slovak Radio Hour; during World War II, the SWS received a letter from West Homestead, "Please play a polka for Mrs. Marie Pavasko," as her son was serving in the military. During the war, Detroit African Americans could listen to IWO radio programs on "Negro history, folklore, etc.," too. The IWO expanded these ethnic appeals when it created the People's Radio Foundation, which pledged "Freedom of the air! Honest labor news!" The People's Radio Foundation promised to "chase out the black cats of radio censorship on Friday the 13th of December, 1946," by presenting "three radio plays that were banned from the air," including one billed as "A Smashing Attack upon Lynching Which Is Taboo on the Networks." As the Cold War heated up, in 1947 the Slav Congress, too, planned a radio program for western Pennsylvania called "Keep America Free." Earlier, it had been easier for radical Slavs to get a hearing. During the war, for example, the People's Radio Foundation had broadcast a complimentary life of Josip Broz Tito, liberally quoting Adamic on the need for the United States to continue supporting the Yugoslav partisan leader.[56]

Affidavits supplied by IWO members indicate a privileging of the ethnic cultural offerings of their lodges. This was not, however, a rejection of American culture but a refashioning of what American culture ideally could mean: a multiethnic, politically progressive and racially inclusive nation of nations. Such a capacious vision of America, though, was in itself often regarded as dangerously radical. Into the 1940s, many old-stock Americans still questioned the fitness of Jewish, Slavic, and Italian Americans, while more stridently denouncing African American and Hispanic calls for inclusion. Proudly celebrating one's non-WASP heritage in an organization that asserted the necessity of racial equality was an attempt to change the terms of what it meant to be a real American.[57]

Some lodges balanced attention to Slavic folk singing and dancing with American sports teams—baseball and basketball most prominently. While it is difficult to determine whether some younger white ethnics chose not to join the IWO due to its emphasis on Old World culture, we do know that within the Order both Americanized and ethnic entertainments were on offer. While IWO officials already in the early 1940s were lamenting the difficulty in retaining the second generation, and the Radischev Folk Dancers may have had a hard time competing with Frank Sinatra for the loyalty of some younger members, thousands of other American-born women and men enrolled in Jewish schools, Italian theater troupes, and Polish dance circles.

Moreover, ethnic and American cultures were seen by many members as mutually reinforcing. Members frequently spoke of the way ethnic theater and song enhanced their appreciation of American culture. Alexander Smoley attested that his "principal interest is the Russian cultural program in which the lodge engages," citing his participation in choral, dance, and drama groups. He added, though, "I firmly believe that the IWO is helping to enrich our American national culture by preserving for Americans of foreign extraction the cultures of the nations from which so many Americans have sprung. It is because of that conviction that I have assisted in organizing in our lodge children's dramatic activities in the Russian language and costume." Lewis Marks asserted that the Jewish Children's Schools his lodge ran taught not just Yiddish literature and Jewish history but "an appreciation of the heritage and contributions of Jews to American history." His lodge's programs also participated in Brotherhood Week celebrations warning of the twin perils of anti-Semitism and racial discrimination and segregation, so his brand of Americanism likely did not mesh with that of HUAC luminaries such as Rankin. Anna Mazurak believed the Ukrainian choral and drama groups in which she participated and similar programs "of other I.W.O. lodges are adding to the national culture of the American people by preserving the culture of the various national groups which make up the bulk of our people." A Russian member noted that his lodge's choral, dance, and dramatic groups performed at veterans' hospitals among other places, asserting, "We believe that in helping to preserve and develop our appreciation of our national origins, our lodge is also helping to enrich the content of American culture."[58]

A New Yorker echoed this belief: "While we take pride in our loyalty to, and love for, the United States, we are also proud of our national origin and of the great people from which we have sprung. Through our lodge we help to keep alive an appreciation of the contributions which the Carpathian

Russians have made and are making to this country." Slavic Americans were, to borrow Roediger and Barrett's term, "inbetween peoples" and certainly benefited to a far greater extent than non-European Americans from the largess of the New Deal and other privileges that came with being "white on arrival." Still, in a deepening Cold War, Russian and other Slavic customs and people were often viewed suspiciously. And older IWO members likely remembered it was not that long ago that sociologists sneered, "A Pole can live in dirt that would kill a white man."[59]

In such a context, IWO music groups were some of the few places working-class Slavs might gain celebrity. Louis Oroby, who said he had been a "worker" at the Hotel New Yorker for fourteen years, also noted, "I am very proud of my activities as a singer in the nationally famous Radischev Choir. There is not a corner in the City of New York, scarcely a single church where I did not sing with the Radischev Choir during the last world war. I owe to the IWO the wonderful experience that I have had in the cultural activities of the Order." Ewa Morawska notes that it was only through service to one's ethnic parish or fraternal that Slavic immigrants gained status, respect, and honors "mainstream" society withheld from working people. Such internal status markers were provided to progressive immigrants via performing groups such as the Radischev Choir, which entertained at many IWO galas.[60]

Milton Schiff of the JPFO's Tom Paine Lodge (a telling blend of progressive American patriotism and Jewish identity) wrote that he belonged to the JPFO's Fraternal Songsters, which performed at Jewish hospitals in the Los Angeles area. Max Lange attested that his lodge raised funds for Mount Sinai and affirmed the JPFO's Jewish *schules*, which gave children "an opportunity to learn the history, traditions and culture of the Jewish people and to integrate their background with their studies in American history and literature so as to make them well rounded citizens."[61]

Hispanic and African American members appreciated not just the leisure-time opportunities the IWO provided but also the expansive space the Order opened up for them on occasions of inclusion that valorized them as worthy Americans in ways few other 1940s venues fully afforded. Another Los Angeles resident, Catherine Ales, spoke approvingly of her lodge's "programs of Mexican culture, especially for the children." In an era when denigration of Hispanic Americans was widespread, and only a few years after the travesties of the Zoot Suit Riots and the framing of Mexican Americans in the Sleepy Lagoon murder case, Ales asserted the dignity of Mexican American culture, noting her IWO lodge annually "takes part with other organizations in Cinco de Mayo festivities celebrating Mexico's national holiday." Peter Moreno of Brooklyn likewise declared that in his lodge of "first and second generation Puerto Ricans," "while we yield to no one in our love for the United States, we maintain ties of affection for our native Puerto Rico and its people. Our lodge plays an important role in maintaining our . . .

national hereditary culture. . . . We teach our young ones to respect and honor the land of their origin." African American James Moorer of Jersey City, too, appreciated the venues his IWO lodge afforded him for learning of black peoples' contributions to a nation that still relegated him to third-class citizenship.[62]

Certain ethnic groups within the IWO ran their own summer camps, such as the JPFO's Camp Kinderland, Finnish camps in Michigan, the Russians' Arow Farm on Long Island, and a Jewish summer camp run by the JPFO near Brampton, Ontario, for Detroit-area children. Although these camps also often welcomed African American children, sometimes groups balked at sharing their camps and thus diluting the ethnic cultural aspect of camp programs. Even American activities such as baseball or basketball occurred in the cultural milieu of radicalism, as when Camp Wocolona, as noted, promised "Baseball and Revolution." And sometimes baseball occurred in interracial competition or among fellow ethnics still ostracized by Major League Baseball, as when black or Puerto Rican lodges fielded teams, but not in the good old, whites-only way.[63]

In such circumstances assimilation did not occur in a straight line. IWO members, especially American-born members often still marginalized as not quite belonging, endeavored to reclaim American heritage for themselves. Certainly in the 1940s this was the perception of many "mainstream" commentators regarding African Americans and Hispanics, but even Jewish and Italian IWO members were aware that congressmen dismissed their groups as "mongrelizers" of the nation.

During World War II, the space for the IWO to appear in such national costume opened up, as calls for black civil rights, cooperation with the Soviet Union, and providing for the needs of the forgotten man and woman gained credence with a broader public. Ukrainian member John Myketew boasted of his success recruiting "Negro" members to the Order and went on to propose an accordion orchestra that would "be dressed up in Russian Cossacks uniform, play Red Army songs. You see, I think that by July Fourth [the] Red Army will celebrate Victory over Hitler so we the delegates also will celebrate." In this instance the ethnic particularism of Slavic members, and valorization of Cossack uniforms, tenuously meshed with wartime patriotism. Progressive Americans could still openly celebrate the Soviet allies on July Fourth for a few more years.[64]

The wartime alliance also afforded an opportunity for the IWO's Liberty Singing Society to appear at an IWO Four Freedoms rally in Detroit's Belle Isle Park. Attendees heard addresses by state senator Nowak, UAW organizer Paul Boatini, as well as African Americans Reverend Hill and Ferdinand Smith (of the National Maritime Union), calling for the opening of a second front in Europe and an investigation of the Detroit race riot that had begun in Belle Isle Park two months previously. An OSS agent noted, "The Liberty

Singing Society, a well-known Detroit leftwing group, ... specialized in Yiddish folk songs and in songs from the Soviet Union. They sang this time a song in praise of General Voroshilov."[65]

In 1943 Slovaks paid homage to an egalitarian world with "Calypso Song of 'The Common Man.'" As noted in Chapter 3, Pindar's salute to a multiethnic assemblage of "just plain Americans" was a radical notion when conservative politicians such as Bilbo and Rankin excoriated blacks, Jews, and "Dagos" bent on "mongrelizing" America as part of an ostensible Communist plot. The connection between Trinidad and progressive Slavs was not as exceptional as it seems. By World War II, militants were immersed in interracial social networks. *The Sunday Worker* advertised the grand opening of Harlem's Club Calypso alongside ads for a Robeson concert for the JPFO (at which the 300-voice JPFO chorus as well as Jewish and Palestinian folk dancers performed) and a Weenie Roast for the Fighting South to benefit black and white striking tobacco workers in Winston-Salem, North Carolina. Black members of the IWO celebrated Negro History Week with a program of drama and music, arguing "the Negro people should not learn less about others, but more about themselves." On the bill with African American entertainers were Slavic folk singers such as Vera Nickoloff. The president of the black lodges said his group "hoped to contribute, in however small a way, to the over-all objective of complete equality for the Negro people, economically, socially and culturally."[66]

In 1944 Marcantonio, president of the Garibaldi Society, joined Adam Clayton Powell Jr., Communist New York councilman Davis, and the National Maritime Union's Smith in sponsoring a "Negro Freedom Rally." "VICTORY over Fascism—Jim Crowism—Anti-Semitism," ran the rally's poster. It also proclaimed: "EQUALITY Everywhere—in the armed forces.—Jobs for ALL.—The right to vote." Organizers promised "speakers of national prominence, great artists, and a stirring new pageant 'New World A-Coming,'" featuring Duke Ellington and dancer-choreographer Pearl Primus. Ellington had earlier performed at the Party's 1930 second annual interracial dance classic—itself a subversive act so far as Jim Crow America was concerned. In between musical sets, Foster of the CPUSA spoke to the dancers. Such mixing of class-conscious instruction and entertainment by celebrities was frequent, as when Hughes, already making a name for himself in the Harlem Renaissance, recited with other poets at the Third Annual International Red Poets' Nite Dance Bacchanal in December 1928 or when during World War II Woody Guthrie serenaded a Brighton Beach American Labor Party Spring Festival along with the "Stage for Action Players" and an appearance by the ASC's Krzycki. As Denning notes, the Popular Front era enabled many leftist pivots within the laboring of popular culture, and such celebrations indicate that even mainstream culture could be reappropriated in multiracial, left-wing spaces for progressive purposes.[67]

Likewise, Robeson joined Smith and others in sponsoring together with "Spanish organizations" and the Joint Anti-Fascist Refugee Committee a Fiesta Republicana in honor of "the valiant Spanish people who are sabotaging Franco's aid to Hitler." The Fiesta, slated for a park in Queens, offered "a colorful program of Spanish and American entertainment, dancing, games and outstanding speakers." In June 1939 a similar "Gran Acontecimiento Artistico Cultural" (Grand Cultural Artistic Event) was celebrated by the IWO's Club Obrero Español, with flamenco artists, ballet dancers, singers, and guitarists performing on behalf of the Committee for Democracy in Spain. A Detroit "Spanish Fiesta" hosted by IWO lodges and the Friends of the Abraham Lincoln Brigade was crashed by an FBI agent, who reported that the hundred or so in attendance was a "chiefly German" crowd enjoying "plenty of German music and dancing." The affair was "supposed to be for the benefit of the 'boys' who fought in Spain."[68]

After the war, antifascist interracialism continued, as when the national leader of the Russian society urged local lodges to book a talk by Charles Burrows, an American-born black man brought up in Moscow. Burrows was traveling the country in 1949, lecturing on "The Fight for Peace." The IWO made the case for demilitarization in the Cold War, but under less auspicious circumstances than when it had called for an antifascist UN coalition a few years earlier.[69]

As Chapter 3 demonstrates, this interracial socializing sometimes ran into the problem of "white chauvinism." Complaints from black Order members in Detroit were sent to headquarters about Myketew's condescension, suggesting racial harmony in the IWO was sometimes more aspirational than actual. As early as 1932, an Italian man complained of "white chauvinism" at a Communist summer camp near Boston, a charge repeated in 1949 by a Bronx member of the JPFO regarding the dearth of black guests or staff at IWO's Camp Lakeland.[70] Of course, such problems were more likely to arise in an organization committed to interracialism than in a more conservative ethnic fraternal society. There, black attendance at one's lodge was simply unthinkable, and thus no squabbles over "white chauvinism" ever arose.

The IWO's entertainments, however, never exhibited the racial myopia other leftist revelers sometimes displayed. As late as 1932 in Milwaukee, for example, the Socialist Party advertised for its chief fund-raiser, an annual winter carnival minstrel show. The Socialist *Milwaukee Leader* noted that the beloved Socialist minstrel shows dated back to a 1904 fund-raiser for the Socialist Educational Fund featuring prominent politicians such as Emil Seidel, later Milwaukee's first Socialist mayor and 1912 vice-presidential running mate of Eugene Debs. The *Leader* urged readers to attend the 1932 minstrel show, featuring local Socialist luminaries such as Eugene Krzycki donning blackface and grass skirts to perform as "King Boola-Boo's Fiji Guard." The year's winter carnival featured "Original Georgia Minstrels

Captured by Cannibals—The Quintessence of Old-Time Minstrelsy." The advertisement promised "A Stage Full of Savages—Burrrr!" and also noted "ice cream and candies" would be provided by the Young People's Socialist League, a reminder that minstrel shows in the early twentieth century were often regarded as the height of gentility. Amateur blackface artist Eugene Krzycki was the son of national Socialist Party chairman Leo Krzycki, who in 1942 would become the inaugural president of the ASC. The Slav Congress would exhibit greater racial sensitivity in staging its entertainments, which often linked performances by African American entertainers such as Robeson with appearances by troupes such as the Radischev Russian Dancers. The Slav Congress also forcefully advocated for African American civil rights, so perhaps the annual burnt-cork winter carnivals can serve as a reminder of the complicated embrace of whiteness even among progressive white ethnics, who advocated equality in some contexts while also unproblematically conveying racist stereotypes on other stages. Still, for all their many racial blind spots, there is no evidence of IWO members enacting minstrel shows, and it is difficult to imagine them doing so.[71]

The IWO forged a celebratory interracialism where members saluted their Slavic, Italian, and Jewish cultures but also took part in social affairs and political rallies with black and Hispanic leftists. Ukrainian accordion and mandolin orchestras were twinned with African American performers. In 1941 Robeson shared the bill with the Radischev Russian Folk Dancers on IWO Day at the Civilian and National Defense Exposition (Figure 4.1). Following the war, the IWO joined other black and white organizations in supporting a Robeson concert on behalf of unionized clerical workers in Panama and that local's antidiscrimination program, while the Slav Congress featured Robeson alongside Slavic luminaries such as Adamic at its gala People's Festival. In 1950 the JPFO and the Douglass-Lincoln Society turned out in droves—at least sixteen thousand—for a Robeson concert demanding an end to segregation and enactment of an antilynching bill. Greene of the JPFO exclaimed, "Sitting side by side, Negro and white, Jew and Christian, all brothers and sisters of one big united fraternal family. What more effective demonstration of genuine democracy in action could you find anywhere in America!" That year Robeson teamed with the JPFO and Michigan Slav Congress to raise funds to send the children of Willie McGee to Camp Kinderland.[72]

Such interracial fun could not go unanswered by officialdom. In 1946 interracial dancing, singing, and acting appalled the FBI. An agent was aghast that at an ASC "Win the Peace" rally, a Russian woman in a Red Army uniform kissed Robeson. Informants also alerted the bureau that dance classes at the IWO's Detroit Polish Club were actually indoctrinating the eighteen students, for the teacher was "teaching them how to secure new members by propaganda, sports, dances and politics." A similar IWO dance

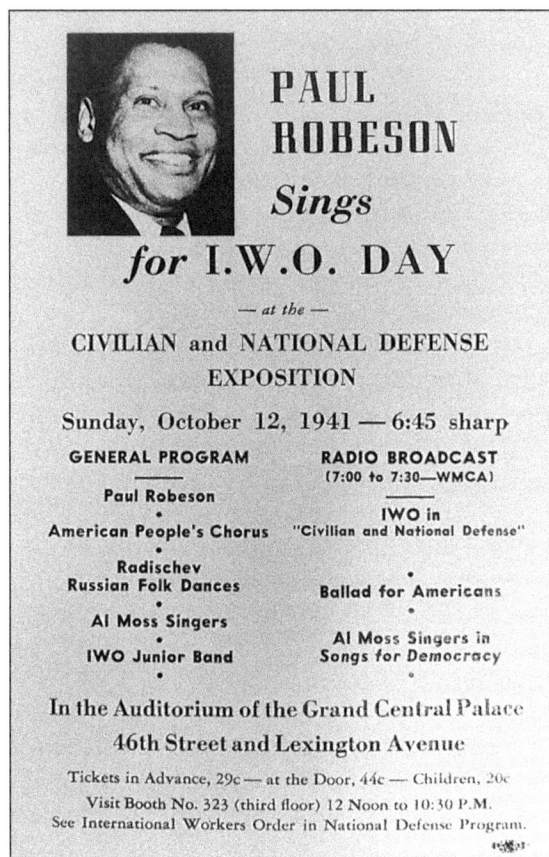

Figure 4.1 Actor-activist Paul Robeson, the IWO's most famous African American member, frequently appeared alongside Slavic American entertainers such as the Radischev Russian Folk Dancers, as during IWO Day at the 1941 Civilian and National Defense Exposition.
Source: Flyer, *Paul Robeson Sings for IWO Day*, IWO-CU, box 49.

class at Detroit's Slavonia Club was also more nefarious than it appeared, for "a considerable number of youths are drawn by the pretext of dancing."[73]

Even by the FBI's suspicious lights, not all IWO dances bore such subversive fruit. An informant reported on a social evening held in 1939 by Detroit's Patrick Henry Lodge in the back of Joe's Barber Shop. "Very poor crowd and very little spending of money," he wrote. "There were about 20 persons there. Sold very little beer. Everybody was saying—'I wonder what's the matter with this party? Where is everybody?'" He concluded, "This Party was a FLOP in every sense of the word." Another 1939 IWO party in Detroit drew an interracial crowd (which attracted the notice of Detroit police), but the gist of the meeting was less exciting: "Whiskey, beer and sandwiches were on sale. For nearly three hours the crowd sat around and told smutty stories."[74]

Even if the content of such meetings was more Rotary Club than revolution, the IWO nevertheless was deemed subversive. In response, dozens of Order members offered affidavits defending the group for its interracial solidarity. Lodges that engaged in Ukrainian and Polish dance recitals and art exhibits also held celebrations during Negro History Week and Brotherhood Week and sponsored interracial youth activities.[75]

Many black members affirmed this "complete and sincere equality of treatment with member of other races" at lodge venues such as Camp Robin Hood. A black woman from Los Angeles appreciated the interracial "picnics, socials, lectures and many kinds of educational activities" that promoted "perfect unity." To many red-baiting congressmen, such joyous expressions of "social equality" were nothing short of un-American. The most prominent African American member of the IWO, Robeson, stated that the Order had been placed on the Attorney General's List of Subversive Organizations because of its work to end segregation: "In our great Order we live and practice equality and brotherhood of man all the year 'round. . . . That's what Tom Clark, Rankin, and other hatchet men of reaction don't like about the IWO. Their . . . blacklists are aimed at the people's organizations fighting Jim Crow and segregation, fighting American-style fascism, fighting for peace."[76]

Leftists sometimes leavened indignation with satire. Detroit police reported on the 1949 New Year's Eve social of the Michigan CP, an event likely attended by some IWO members. The officer reporting on the red revels seemed alarmed to note that of 290 attendees, 120 were "Negroes." The policeman also reported, "During intermission, a pumpkin (ridiculing the HUAC spy investigation) was auctioned off, with auctioneer Harry Boskey stating that a secret formula was contained within." When the winner claimed his pumpkin, "Formula disclosed 'Season's Greetings.'"[77]

Michigan Communists, of course, were riffing off Whittaker Chambers's infamous hollowed-out pumpkin, which contained, or so an ambitious young Congressman Nixon asserted, microfilmed proof that Communist spies had infiltrated the State Department. But here the encoded message—"Season's Greetings"—came not from Alger Hiss but advocates of civil rights and strong unions. Leftists knew their activities were often caught under the panopticon of surveillance, so perhaps the pumpkin was a subtle dig at the undercover policeman in attendance, not just a morale booster for besieged activists. When activists knew they were being spied on by the "un-American" state around the clock perhaps they had to have a sense of humor.[78]

Robert Putnam has lamented the decline of associational life in an America where everyone "bowls alone," without considering the coercive role anticommunism played in ending the party for politically engaged Americans.[79] To be sure, by 1950 ethnic fraternal lodges, even nonradical ones, faced stiff competition from television and Hollywood as they tried to keep their bands, choruses, and theater societies going. While the triumph of mass consumer culture played a role in ending the participatory theater troupes, mandolin societies, and sports leagues of ethnic America, the progressive, counterhegemonic variety acts of groups such as the IWO were not simply victims of assimilation or television.

As IWO members built interracial alliances while working for civil rights, a more peaceful world, and workplace justice, they often found it difficult to find a place in which to have their fun. Slavs who screened films praising the Soviet Union often faced enmity from more conservative ethnic peers. The secretary of a Ukrainian lodge in Edwardsville, Pennsylvania, wrote the national office, "Ever since we showed a film *Mannerheim Line* in February 1941 we are attacked from every corner now. We also received a note to move from the hall after May 15th . . . but we hope that the storm will pass, sometime."[80] With Moscow still widely condemned for its nonaggression pact with the Nazis, and any thought of an alliance still a distant dream, a Soviet film defending the Red Army assault on Finland was a tough sell for coal-country Ukrainians.

Once the United States and the Soviets became wartime allies, no matter how tentatively, IWO bookings for films defending Russia began to improve. As an OSS agent noted in 1944, "The National Film Division of the IWO . . . is the largest distributor in the United States of Soviet films." During the war the Film Division ran a "Special Summer Offer" to all lodges, offering feature films at $25 per showing, or $22.50 if three or more films were ordered. Lodges could choose among nine "Films for Victory" such as *Ukraine in Flames* and *Leningrad Music Hall*. In May 1945 Milgrom was informed that large crowds had attended screenings of *Battle for Russia* in Carnegie and Homestead, Pennsylvania. The following year, however, with the war ended and the Soviet Union rapidly relegated to enemy nation, a Detroit screening of *Battle for Russia* had to be canceled because a hall could not be obtained.[81]

Films praising the Soviet Union had always offended many in the ethnic communities in which IWO lodges were situated, as Edwardsville Ukrainians could attest, and perhaps the wartime alliance had only been a respite from such hostility. For the IWO such blackouts became increasingly common. While Slovaks in Aliquippa, Pennsylvania, still managed to find a place to screen a film about orphans in postwar Czechoslovakia, when lodges sought to show films more explicitly praising the Soviet Union they had trouble finding a hall. In 1947 Flint and Lackawanna, New York, lodges encountered difficulties securing a place to screen films. Lackawanna wrote, "Most of the hall administrators are Poles and (members of) the American Legion, and Russia is not in good with relations with America. . . . Here the reaction runs high everywhere." The Russian society president wrote back agreeing that reaction and hostility to Moscow were in the ascendant, but arguing "now more than ever it is necessary to demand that such Soviet moving pictures are shown to Americans." He was confident when viewers saw the picture, "they [would] palpably see themselves that the Soviet Union and the Soviet people do not prepare for war."[82]

The IWO's defense of the Soviet Union and its other foreign-policy positions were some of its most unpalatable policies so far as more conservative Americans were concerned. Sympathy toward the Soviet Union engendered much public hostility, and eventually government prosecution, but IWO advocacy of freedom for colonized African and Asian peoples also was out of step with conservative Americans and ruffled State Department feathers. It is to the IWO's contentious activism regarding international relations that we now turn.

5

Foreign Policy and the IWO

When the officers of the IWO addressed matters of foreign policy, it was not difficult to see where their hearts lay. General Secretary Bedacht made no secret of his admiration for the Soviet Union and his belief that working people would benefit were the United States to develop a foreign policy less antagonistic to Moscow. In 1931 Bedacht wrote a booklet for the *Daily Worker* refuting "Anti-Soviet Lies" that were, he charged, part of "The 'Holy' Capitalist War against the Soviet Union" and its five-year plan. "In recent months anti-Soviet propaganda has reached a point of hysteria," he charged. "Anti-Soviet documents emerge from the laboratories of capitalist forgers faster than ever." He offered to "supply an accurate and reliable gauge for the detection of anti-Soviet lies."[1]

In 1931 the Hoover administration still adamantly refused to grant diplomatic recognition to Moscow, even as the grinding economic malaise of America's Depression led many people to look with favor on alternatives to the free-market capitalist model. Bedacht's booklet established a comparison with the Soviet Union, whose solution to depression, centralized economic planning and alleged worker self-governance, seemed attractive to many destitute workers and preferable to the brutal suppression of strikes in America. Even many affluent Americans outside the orbit of the IWO such as Henry Ford, William Bullitt, and Lincoln Steffens in the early 1930s found much to admire in the Soviet Union.[2]

In the early 1930s, the IWO praised the Soviet Union as a model America might emulate if "a full measure of Social Insurance such as the workers' political rule has established for itself in the Soviet Union" were to be obtained. Among its many complaints with the early years of the New Deal, the

Philadelphia District plenum lamented in 1934 that "the conditions of the workers are growing worse," partly since "the government is spending millions of dollars for war preparations, as all other capitalist countries, especially aiming to attack the Soviet Union, the only living example of the workers' and farmers' rule."[3]

After the mid-1930s, the IWO would temper its demands for a revolutionary reordering of the American domestic economy, as Chapter 2 demonstrates, offering qualified support to Roosevelt's measures to combat the "economic royalists" as the best evolutionary path to socialism America was likely to see.[4] Even after support for a Soviet economic model was downplayed, however, the organization's leaders were fairly steadfast in supporting the Soviet Union and opposing militarism in the United States, casting the latter as a graver threat to world peace until the Order's dissolution in 1954. The consistency with which the Order supported Moscow's foreign-policy positions left the organization vulnerable to charges of subservience to the CPUSA, or more ominously, the Kremlin. At the very least, other observers were struck by the credulity of a group that for more than twenty years accepted virtually all the USSR's assertions to peaceful intentions.

Yet in its international advocacy, the IWO presented many positions the Order's multiracial membership regarded as attractive and beneficial, not to some distant global power but to themselves. The IWO was founded as fascist and authoritarian regimes came to power in the homelands of members. Members warned of the spread of fascism, and the Order rallied its members to combat the threat of Nazi Germany. When Mussolini's troops invaded Ethiopia and Japanese troops overran Manchuria and the rest of China, the IWO's anticolonial stance was linked to its antifascist message, and IWO members soon thereafter joined other leftists in supporting Loyalist Spain in its campaign to repel Franco's fascist-backed forces. Even the IWO's support for the Soviet Union during the 1930s was often framed as endorsing that nation's call for a united front of America, European powers, and Moscow against the dangers of Nazi Germany, calls for an antifascist alliance that largely went unheeded. In its insistence, too, on an anticolonial foreign policy offering independence to Asian, African, and Latin American peoples, the IWO was advocating policies attractive to its multiracial members and offered a broader conception of what national, and international, policies would be beneficial to them.

Following U.S. entrance into the war, the IWO, with its support for a coordinated allied antifascist effort and commitment to independence for all captive and colonized nations, was at last working in tandem with the Roosevelt administration's stated goals. For a few years, the IWO's admiration of the Soviet Union was palatable, although shortly after VJ Day, the Order's continuing commitment to irenic relations with Moscow, opposition to authoritarian regimes in favor with Washington, and support for colonial independence movements quickly ran afoul of the hardening Cold War consensus. In the late 1940s and 1950s, the IWO argued that it was merely advocating a continuation of wartime allied cooperation and a demilitarized, peaceful world. But the IWO's view of a nonnuclear, cooperative foreign policy was already passé.

Still, throughout its existence, the IWO took as part of its mission to safeguard the well-being of its members an advocacy of a less bellicose, colonialist foreign policy, and for more than twenty years thousands of people not yet inured to a permanent state of wartime alert and a nuclear-overarmed Pentagon supported an alternative approach to world relations. A survey of the IWO's actions in conceiving of a possible, better-ordered world, suggests why so many people found the organization's foreign-policy positions so appealing.

"Every One of Us Loves the Entire Russian Nation"

Although the IWO's primary function was the issuance of insurance policies for its working-class members, the organization had an expansive notion of its mission to protect the health and well-being of working people. A world hurtling toward war, with fascism and militarism on the rise, imperiled the health and well-being of IWO members, and so during the 1930s the Order did what it could to combat these developments.

At its national convention in 1938, the IWO passed a "Resolution on the Soviet Union" that greeted "the strengthening of the democratic institutions and the progress of the socialist construction achieved by the Soviet Union." The resolution claimed that this strengthening had enabled the Soviet Union to establish "complete economic security for the toilers," which was the objective of the organization's own "workers' fraternalism." Assertions that the USSR had achieved both perfect democracy and economic security for its people would have been hotly contested by other commentators, even on the Left. Kenyon Zimmer notes that already in the 1920s Jewish anarchists returning from Russia recounted the brutal imprisonment of those resisting Bolshevization as well as suppression of the Kronstadt uprising. During the 1930s, too, other immigrants denounced any notion of the Soviet Union as a workers' paradise. In 1934 the United Ukrainian Organizations of the United States published its exposé, *Famine in Ukraine*, documenting the state-orchestrated Ukrainian famine reported in newspapers, including the Yiddish Socialist *Daily Forverts*, citing writers who had discovered peasants who were "driven to cannibalism." The booklet concluded, "the application of Communist theories to agriculture has certainly been disastrous." When Ukrainian organizations in the United States tried to publicize the terrible situation, it charged "Communistic bodies in America" of hiring "common thugs" to break up "the Ukrainian anti-Soviet demonstrations staged to present the Ukrainian cause before the American public."[5]

Officers of the IWO can certainly be condemned for their uncritical acceptance of Moscow and unwillingness to examine evidence of atrocities such as the Ukrainian famine. Still, although the United States had established diplomatic relations with Moscow in 1933, the Order correctly noted much hostility toward the USSR continued to emanate from the West, and they often dismissed such condemnations of the Soviets as capitalist saber-rattling. At the IWO's fourth national convention, the pro-Soviet resolution charged "enemies of labor" within the USSR with sabotage and linked them to the "lies and anti-Soviet war conspiracies" at home. The resolution congratulated "the Soviet masses with their victory over the enemies within their own country," an oblique reference to the recently concluded Moscow show trials, and pledged to "defeat the fascists in America" who opposed the USSR. "This is in the regular function of our Order," the resolution's authors argued, "because the enemies of labor in America are identical with the enemies of the Soviet Union." The IWO had a point in linking these issues. The Ukrainian authors of *Famine in Ukraine* had cited an author who had written on the famine in *Nation's Business*, an organ of the U.S. Chamber of Commerce, just the sort of capitalist paper the IWO accused of spreading anti-Soviet lies. The Chamber of Commerce, too, was already at work propagandizing against the Wagner Act, Fair Labor Standards Act, and other New Deal measures beneficial to IWO members, making it easy for leftists to imagine a link between anti-Soviet critiques and a reactionary big-business cabal. "Because of this," the IWO's resolution concluded, "the Convention considers sympathy and support of the Soviet Union a natural function of every member of the Order."[6]

Critical links, too, were drawn between support for the Soviet Union and the IWO's enmity toward the alarming rise of fascism. The fourth national convention also offered a "Resolution on Fascist Aggression" that cataloged the militarism of Italy, Germany, and Japan, which had already brought war to Spain and China and threatened to extend the reach of fascism elsewhere. The IWO pledged to continue acting to combat aggression, declaring, "The threat of fascism against the peace of the world can be met only by collective efforts of the democratic countries." The convention praised Soviet foreign minister Maxim Litvinov's call "for a unification of the democratic peoples for their protection against fascism," asking members to write the president and congressmen urging adoption of "collective security" against this threat.[7]

Various ethnic lodges worked to extend support for Moscow to as broad a community as possible. In 1937 the IWO's Russian Section issued a call to other Russian fraternal societies, including those affiliated with the Russian Orthodox church, urging "unity of action in the fight for peace, against the warmongers." "War preparations are now being made in Europe and in Asia against our Fatherland—the Soviet Union," the society's officers wrote to the leaders of Russian fraternal societies. "We have lived in America for many years, but every one of us loves the entire Russian nation beyond the ocean."

They urged a united defense of Russia as "the greatest force in the world to save us from war." The Russian Section proposed "unity of action . . . on the broadest democratic basis," and welcomed any suggestions by the various groups' leaders for amending the IWO's proposals.[8]

There may have been limits, however, to the IWO's broad-mindedness. Two months before issuing this appeal, Russian secretary Kasustchik noted "the unmasking of the disgraceful activities of the Trotzkyists in the USSR, as well as the trial in the popular case against same," a veiled reference to the Moscow purge trials. Kasustchik denounced the "disgraceful propaganda" against the Soviet Union he said was spread by Trotskyists and White Russians in order "to disseminate hate against our Fatherland among the Russian toilers." For all the IWO's calls for a united front in defense of Russia, or in combating fascism, the Order's enmity with Trotskyists, or those even further from the fold, suggests that there were limits to the IWO's tolerance of free speech or dissent when it came to critiques of the USSR.[9]

Then again, even a hostile state's witness against the IWO would in 1951 admit under cross-examination that during the late 1930s, "the 'hands off Russia' or 'defend the Soviet Union' campaigns" occurred during a period when "the United States relations with the Soviet Union were good." Powers added that he believed the IWO's "slogan 'defend the Soviet Union' grew up as a result of the rising Fascist menace during this period."[10] The bounds for cooperation between the IWO and even religiously based Russian fraternalists had expanded by 1937, and not every supporter of cooperation with the Soviet Union, in the IWO or out of it, was necessarily a Communist.

"The Bloodstains of Its Deeds": Antifascist Activism

As Powers was later forced to allow, the fascist menace was alarmingly on the rise, and there was much on the world stage to concern working-class militants during the IWO's first decade of existence. As early as August 1932, the German-born Bedacht was warning, "Open Fascist Dictatorship Threatens the German Workers!" Bedacht addressed a meeting in New York's heavily German Yorkville section. Although Adolf Hitler would not assume power for another five months, he had already made an impressive showing in a 1932 run for the German presidency. Posters for the rally presciently warned, "The bankers, big industrialists and land owners are ready to make Hitler chancellor of Germany," and that "this attempt to set up an open fascist dictatorship of blood and terror" would "drown the working class in a sea of blood." Posters for the talk augured, "A Hitler dictatorship in Germany means immediate war on the Soviet Union and world war," although they also blamed German and American Socialists for contributing to fascism's rise, an indication of the battles on the Left that impeded a genuine united front against fascism.[11]

Bedacht had been warning of the ominous rise of German fascism even years before the creation of the IWO. In a November 1924 article, "In the Catacombs of Democracy," he complained that while leftist protesters had been imprisoned or murdered, "the perpetrators of the Kapp putsch, ... very few of whom have ever been brought to justice, have all been pardoned," while 540 army officers involved in the attempted takeover had never been punished. Meanwhile, "the participants in the Hitler putsch in Munich are all free, with the exception of one, and all over Germany they are publicly feted as heroes."[12] Bedacht saw the rise of fascism as the reaction of bourgeois democracies to a militant working class:

> Wherever Dame Democracy feels herself crowded by masses who no longer consent to accept the phrase for the substance, the lady calls for aid on her twin brother, Fascism. While Democracy strangles free speech and free press in the name of the law, Fascism chokes them in spite of the law. While Democracy covers its crime under a cloak of virtue, Fascism openly revels in the bloodstains of its deeds.[13]

Condemnation of parliamentary democracy as an only slightly better behaved strangler of workers' rights was in line with the Party's revolutionary stance in the 1920s, and likely to find little acceptance outside the immigrant Left. Still, commentators such as Bedacht were some of the few writers warning as early as 1924, and into the 1930s, of the fascist threat. That few were listening to this early "premature anti-fascist" is lamentable.

Once the Nazis assumed power, the IWO continued to alert Americans to the fascist menace. Hungarian lodges worked with other Hungarian progressives on an "anti-Nazi united front campaign," while S. M. Loyen, who worked with South Slavs in the IWO as well as the CFU, was instructed to alert these groups to the dangers of fascism spreading from Germany to Yugoslavia. Non-Communist progressives such as Adamic drew the same conclusion after a trip to his native land, and from the 1934 publication of his book, *The Native's Return*, warned of the authoritarian strains in King Alexander's Yugoslavia. Adamic frequently wrote on this danger and addressed IWO meetings and, after 1942, ASC gatherings on the fascist menace to Europe.[14]

The IWO sought to unite with other leftists in as broad an antifascist coalition as possible. Doroshkin of the English language branches wrote to Thompson, who was on an organizing trip to Birmingham, Atlanta, and other Southern cities, asking if she could "recommend an IWO woman member" to send as a delegate to a Women's Congress against War and Fascism planned for Paris. Doroshkin wrote, "It would be good if we can find a woman comrade in the South, one who is a steel worker, a sharecropper, or generally a good proletarian negro or white comrade." She added, "Such a tour would be an excellent thing both for the campaign against war and fascism and for building the Order." Three years later Thompson attended a Paris antifascist congress as a delegate of both the Order and the NNC, a left-wing black civil rights organization. This conference brought together delegates from French colonial Africa and black people from the United States, linking the injustices of European fascism and colonial subordination. Thompson also traveled to Spain following the 1937 antifascist World Congress to provide IWO assistance to the Spanish Loyalists defending Madrid from Franco's Nazi-supported revolt. The IWO's interracial activism extended to international defense of fascism's victims.[15]

Not every IWO member could contribute to the antifascist struggle on such a lofty level. A Chicago shop paper, the *North Side Workers News*, reported in 1934, "IWO Gives Generously to Heroic German Communists." Rogers Park's IWO branch "voted to give 15% of all affair profits to the German C.P.," whose members were some of Hitler's first victims. In Rogers Park, however, the depth of members' commitment perhaps outstretched their pocketbooks; the brief article noted that branch members' "voluntary contributions already total $3.66." Similarly, Andy Hromiko of Tarentum, Pennsylvania, sent his contribution of $2.35 to the CP of Italy "to fight against Mussolini and his Italian fascism." Hromiko felt compelled to do his best for this purpose after he saw that some IWO lodges sent $3 to support the Italian antifascists. Even if it was not yet fashionable, and the amounts they could contribute were often minimal, IWO members were not afraid to exhibit "premature anti-fascism" as they worked to stem the totalitarian tide.[16]

In larger cities it was possible for the IWO to make more substantial contributions to progressive antifascist campaigns. In June 1935 the IWO cosponsored a United Anti-Nazi Conference at New York's New School for Social Research. The IWO and the ILD joined with non-Marxist leftists such as activist-writer Waldo Frank and the ACLU's Arthur Garfield Hays in inviting "All Friends of Freedom, Peace, Justice" to discuss actions that would "back the German people in their struggle against Hitler fascism." From this conference arose plans for a series of anti-Nazi marches and demonstrations in New York to call for the United States to boycott products made in Nazi Germany as well as a boycott of the Berlin Olympics. But the Anti-Nazi Federation of New York, in which the IWO participated, had trouble securing public venues. Frank complained to Mayor La Guardia when the group was denied a permit for public rallies and a People's Parade against Nazism to Columbus Circle. "To refuse permission will inevitably stamp him as having taken sides against the Cause of Democracy which the people of New York wish to defend in peaceful demonstration," Frank wrote the mayor.[17]

The managers of Luna Park in Brooklyn similarly reneged on a commitment to rent the amusement park's arena for an anti-Nazi rally. The park's board of directors vetoed the agreement because they "feared a riot might ensue because of their German patronage." The Anti-Nazi Federation issued a news release decrying the ban as "a startling indication of how far-reaching the effects of the Nazi terror are." The park's managers evidently worried many German American revelers would not find an anti-Nazi rally amusing.[18]

Into the 1970s amusement parks and other recreation sites marketed themselves as safe, conflict-free spaces offering virtually all-white patrons a respite from the harsher realities of industrial cities. In effect this policy of safe spaces often meant barring African Americans from visiting such parks; park managers often argued that they had no other option because of the violent disturbances white patrons caused when black people tried to use public amenities.[19] Luna Park's 1935 reluctance to offend the perceived pro-Nazi sensibilities of its German American patrons indicates public amusement parks also erected barriers to prevent ideological conflicts within their gates.

Throughout the 1930s, though, the Order worked to expose the dangers of fascism. In March 1936 a resolution was passed calling on members to boycott stores selling Nazi-made goods. All members were "urged . . . to actively participate in the mass picketing of such stores to the end that Nazi goods shall not be sold in the city of New York." The Order's fears of the international reach of fascism were apparent as this resolution was followed by one denouncing the murder of labor leaders by the police of Brazilian dictator Getúlio Vargas. The IWO sent telegrams to the governments of Brazil and the United States demanding an investigation into the death at the hands of Vargas's police of a U.S. citizen suspected of sympathy with the Brazilian labor movement.[20]

By 1938 the IWO was working with other progressive organizations to publicize the danger of fascism. Ben Gold, Communist president of the International Fur and Leather Workers Union, reached out to the IWO as president of the Jewish Peoples Committee for United Action against Fascism and Anti-Semitism. Gold sought the IWO's financial assistance for a planned National Unity Conference in New York. Since the IWO's president, Weiner, was vice president of the Jewish Peoples Committee, it is likely the Order donated to this anti-Nazi conference. By this point the Popular Front coalition combating the growing power of Nazi Germany had expanded so that the Jewish Peoples Committee, headed by a Communist union president and endorsed by the IWO's Jewish Peoples Schools, also listed as sponsors Republican and Democratic congressmen. In 1938, too, the IWO held outdoor New York rallies to call on the United States to curb Hitler's growing might; Thompson, the Order's African American secretary, addressed one such enthusiastic rally of three thousand, demanding steps to thwart "the Nazi terror." And when the Nazis unleashed the Kristallnacht on German Jews, Secretary Saltzman of the Jewish Section wrote to Roosevelt expressing "gratitude for the outspoken condemnation you expressed of the Nazi atrocities against the Jewish people." Saltzman welcomed the recall of the U.S. ambassador but urged further acts such as a trade embargo "to show the present rulers in Germany that America condemns a reversal to the Middle Ages."[21]

As an internationally minded, multiracial organization, the IWO also endeavored to alert the country to the fascist threat in Asia and Africa and took care to warn African Americans of the true nature of militarist Japan. In the spring of 1938, Solidarity Lodge inaugurated its Harlem Community Center with a series called Seminars in Negro History. The Sunday seminars were followed by swing dancing, another example of the IWO's blending of activism and leisure. In announcing the seminars, however, Solidarity Lodge stressed the urgency of African Americans developing "a correct understanding" of world upheavals. The threat posed by Japan merited particular attention, as the IWO feared propaganda asserting that Tokyo was the protector of the world's colored peoples was gaining a hearing. To counter this narrative, the center scheduled a lecture by Max Yergan of the NNC, "A Negro Views the Tokio-Rome-Berlin Axis." The lecture brochure noted Yergan "has an intimate knowledge of African and Far Eastern affairs and will answer the question of Japan's role in the destiny of the darker people."[22]

Judging from other material prepared by Harlem Communists, the Solidarity Lodge likely made sure its speakers came to criticize, not praise Japan. Although not every member of the IWO's Harlem lodge was a Communist, and Yergan would in a few years resign from the NNC over differences with the Party, the Harlem Community Center's director, Thompson, made no secret of her Party affiliation. In 1938 both Yergan and Thompson agreed on the need to counter pro-Japanese sentiment in African American neighborhoods such as Harlem. In February 1938 the Educational Department of the Harlem Division of the CP prepared a book on "material for discussion" regarding *The Sino-Japanese War and the Negro Question* to help counter "misguided pro-Japanese sympathies among a large section of Negroes." As examples of such worrisome support for Japan, the book cited editorials in the *Baltimore Afro-American* endorsing Japan's invasion of China and a syndicated column by the NAACP's William Pickens, who asked, "Well, who in the name of the Lord ought to be master in the Orient, if not the Japanese or some other Oriental Race?" Tokyo's propaganda claiming that "Japan is the champion and defender of the darker races" was evidently swaying some people.[23]

As a countermodel for African Americans, the authors proposed Chinese resistance to Japanese invasion as anti-imperialism worthy of emulation. The authors derided the *Baltimore Afro-American*, which dismissed China as the "Uncle Tom of Asia," and pointed to the subjugation of captive peoples in Korea and Taiwan as well as Tokyo's support for imperial partition of Shanghai as proof that "Japan helps to bear the 'White Man's Burden' in Asia." The book's authors rejected Japanese arguments that China was not ready for self-government as a replication of European colonialists' arguments belied by Chinese resistance to invasion.[24]

This 1938 book is evidence, too, that African American Communists looked quite early to revolutionary China as a model to emulate in their own struggles at home and abroad. Robeson Taj Frazier argues that the U.S. CP remained Eurocentric in locating the seat of world revolution in Moscow and discounting anticolonial movements by Chinese and other people of color. In the 1950s, Frazier argues, African American radicals chafed at this model and began looking to Beijing as their lodestar. Works such as *The Sino-Japanese War and the Negro Question*, however, indicate that Chinese and other non-European freedom struggles were central to militant black people within the Communist milieu long before the late 1950s.[25]

What really gave the lie to Japanese leadership of nonwhite peoples was its abandonment of Ethiopia "when Fascist Italy launched its piratical invasion." The book's authors argued that when Japan extended recognition to Mussolini's "Ethiopian Empire" and made alliance with Germany and Italy, any pretense of Tokyo leading the darker races was revealed as a sham. Tokyo's collaboration with "Mussolini, the man who raped Ethiopia and shed the blood of tens of thousands of Negro men, women and children," sealed the question of whether African Americans could support Japan. In 1938, three years after Italy first threatened it, Ethiopia remained for black militants a rallying cry of fascist aggression and colored people's abandonment by the world's nations. At the IWO's Harlem Community Center, too, the sponsors of the Seminars in Negro History linked Japan's aggression in China to Italy's conquest of Ethiopia and a broader pattern of fascist ascendancy.[26]

Members of the IWO often took an active role in combating racial oppression at home, and now they linked domestic atrocities to imperialism abroad. As with their domestic activism, IWO members often went beyond rhetorical commitment. In defending Ethiopia, and to an even greater extent, Spain, many Order members put their bodies on the line.

"Mussolini Hurls a Burning Torch into the World"

The threats that Il Duce leveled at one of only two independent black African nations in early 1935 rallied militants to Ethiopia's defense. The Harlem Workers' Center invited "Negro and White, Workers and Professionals, Garvey followers, etc." to hear James Ford, African American member of the CP's Central Committee, discuss "The Communist Position on National Minorities." As at the later IWO Seminars in Negro History, it was promised that Ford's talk would link "the Negro as the oppressed Minority Nationality in the U.S.A.; Abyssinia as an oppressed Nation threatened by Italian Fascist terror." As the Harlem Workers' Center was only six blocks north of IWO Solidarity Lodge, it is likely Order members turned out to hear Ford's thoughts on the threat to Abyssinia/Ethiopia; the attempt by the IWO to recruit followers of UNIA was a long-standing one.[27]

It is not surprising that Ford twinned oppression at home and colonial depredations in Ethiopia, especially when attempting to reach out to Garveyites. Within the IWO, however, even Italian and other white members prioritized defending Ethiopia. In an appeal to Browder, Candela, president of the IWO's Italian Section, urged that the focus of an upcoming Italian congress should not be social insurance but rather a program "against the war adventure of Italian Fascism in Ethiopia as part of our general struggle against war and fascism in America." Focusing on opposition to Mussolini's war plans in Ethiopia would be a means to "strengthen our united front of Italian and Negro workers in this country." Candela proposed expanding interracial demonstrations of blacks and Italians to protest Mussolini's militarism "as soon and where the situation ripens," suggesting "more agitational work, demonstrations in front of Italian Consulates, in front of Italian papers, institutions and prominent personalities which are for war against Abyssinia." By August 1935 lodges of the IWO in Syracuse and Rochester were organizing "Hands Off Ethiopia committees" and "laying special emphasis on the Italian and Negro organizations."[28]

By the fall of 1935, Syracuse lodges could have joined an ongoing IWO campaign to support Addis Ababa. Rebecca Grecht replied to her Party comrades answering a *Daily Worker* editorial that appealed for medical aid to Ethiopia. Grecht wrote that the Medical Departments of the Order "in whatever cities they are established" would be enrolled in this campaign; she listed departments in New York, Chicago, Boston, Los Angeles, Cleveland, Detroit, and Philadelphia. The IWO's New York Committee, she noted, was also soon to enlist all the doctors and dentists in its Medical Department in "setting up a committee to cooperate with the American Committee for the Defense of Ethiopia and to get pledges of financial contributions from them." The druggists cooperating with the Medical Department were to form a committee to acquire drugs to ship to Ethiopia. Individual IWO members, too, were asked "to approach their neighborhood druggists for contributions of supplies." Doctors in various cities were approached and asked for donations to the cause. Thompson similarly reported on the Ethiopian campaign Harlem members were orchestrating in September 1935, a campaign that Ford remarked was enabling the IWO to become "a unifying force in the community."[29]

As Grecht noted, the IWO was responding to appeals from the *Daily Worker*. The support shown to the besieged African nation in the Communist press, and through organizations such as the IWO's Medical Department, might be contrasted with condescending coverage in mainstream newspapers. The *New York Sun* assured readers, "Harlem Quiet in African Crisis." "The Italian-Ethiopian dispute is being reflected in Harlem these days," the reporter noted, "but the observer who would study the reaction must have his eyes skinned and his ear to the ground. There are no tom-toms beating on Lenox Avenue and New York's Negro population is not advancing with shield and assegai upon the unoffending residents of nearby Little Italy." Instead, the reporter found only small groups of men asking what the "rest of the civilized world" would do if Mussolini declared war. For the *Sun*, by implication, the civilized world did not include Ethiopia, and maybe not even Harlem. Of course, the paper said, "the Harlem Communists . . . are raising the usual rumpus." The paper also noted that UNIA was calling for a thousand African American recruits to fight for the defense of Ethiopia.[30]

Only the Left raised much of a "rumpus" on behalf of fascism's victims. The week before Grecht wrote of the IWO's medical campaign, the Party issued a call to a September 7th Union Square rally defending Ethiopia. "Mussolini Hurls a Burning Torch into the World!" posters proclaimed, urging New Yorkers to defend "the only independent Negro nation," which was "about to be ravaged by fascist imperialist Italy!" warning, "Ethiopia threatens to become the Sarajevo of the new world slaughter!" Left-wing militants saw war clouds gathering over Union Square in the fall of 1935.[31]

Even in smaller locales the invasion of Ethiopia spurred left-wing activism. From Norfolk, Virginia, organizer Alexander Wright wrote, "The Ethiopian situation is also hot. The I.W.O. campaign is on." As Kelley has noted, the war in Ethiopia, and the fact Communists were some of the few people vocally protesting the fascist attack, led many Southern African Americans to give the Party a positive reception. In Virginia, the IWO participated in a newly created Richmond Committee for the Defense of Ethiopia. While elsewhere in the country pro-Ethiopia demonstrators demanded all Italian-owned stores be boycotted and cried, "Let's Run the Italians Out of Harlem," in Richmond the committee kept the focus on "the barbaric war of Italian Fascism" and avoided ethnic animus. A bit overoptimistically, the Richmond committee asserted, "The Italian people . . . are not deceived by the adventurist spouting of Mussolini and his Fascist hirelings. The Italian people are against this war of rapine, from which they have nothing to gain. In numerous actions, they have demonstrated their opposition to this war which is pregnant with the spark of a new world conflagration." In Birmingham, Communist organizer Bill Moseley similarly worked to defuse black people's enmity toward Italians. He reported of "a growing sentiment among the Negroes for the boycott of the small Italian-American grocers who do business in the Negro neighborhoods." To counter this tension, Moseley and comrades distributed flyers "To the Negro People of Birmingham" urging, "Boycott Italy, not the Italian Storekeepers." Arguing that Italian immigrants had come to the United States to escape persecution, the flyers said, "They are treated with contempt and called 'dagoes' by the same ruling class which calls Negroes 'niggers' and oppresses them." The flyers urged people to boycott products from Mussolini's Italy but not to stigmatize fellow workers who happened to be Italian.[32]

IWO organizers certainly had a difficult task maintaining black-Italian unity on the fraught issue of the war in Ethiopia. In issuing his call for the founding of the NNC, John P. Davis linked international fascist depredations to domestic oppression, parallels especially evident to African American militants. Thompson served as well on the board of the NNC, which consistently made the connection between domestic segregation and colonialism and fascist war overseas. Robeson later recalled as chairman of the left-wing CAA, "Yes, all Africa remembers that it was [Soviet Foreign Affairs minister] Litvinov who stood alone beside Hailie Selassie in Geneva, when Mussolini's sons flew with the blessings of the Pope to drop bombs on Ethiopian women and children. Africa remembers that it was the Soviet Union which fought the attempt of Smuts to annex Southwest Africa to the slave reservations of the Union of South Africa." In such contexts of abandonment by Western colonial powers, it was perhaps understandable that leftist African Americans remembered the Soviet Union with gratitude.[33]

For leftists the fascist war against Spain quickly overshadowed the defeat of Haile Selassie. The IWO would periodically recall its long-standing support for Ethiopia, as when during World War II an IWO FLFF rally publicized its $500 contribution to the Ethiopian World Federation among the other money it had raised for Russian War Relief and other funds as part of its campaign to "Give 'Til It Hurts Hitler!"[34] Still, the war in Spain soon preoccupied and involved members of the IWO to a greater extent than the African crisis.

"First Ethiopia and Now Spain!"

In July 1936 military forces led by Franco began their uprising against Spain's leftist Popular Front coalition government. Franco's forces were quickly aided by Nazi Germany and fascist Italy, while the United States, Great Britain, and France remained neutral in the fight. Washington imposed an arms embargo on both sides, which effectively disadvantaged Loyalist Spain. Only the Soviet Union sent military assistance to the Loyalist government, although bitter rivalries between Spanish anarchists and Communists wracked the Loyalist forces.[35] For all the internecine bloodshed on the Left, however, men and women in the IWO answered the call to defend Spain, enlisting in the Abraham Lincoln Brigade and other contingents of the International Brigades fighting against fascism or contributing money and goods to aid the Loyalists despite America's embargo.

The IWO's Italian Section joined in an Italian Anti-Fascist Committee rally and "Mass Protest Meeting against Mussolini's Invasion of Democratic Spain." "First Ethiopia and Now Spain!" posters for the demonstration proclaimed; to enrage antifascist attendees, the posters reproduced *New York Times* headlines reporting, "Italians Boastful of Malaga Victory" and "Press Hails Downfall of the Loyalist Port as New Fascist Achievement." Attendees were promised a "Special Showing of the Dramatic Film Document, 'Spain in Flames'" and urged to "Support the Garibaldi Battalion!" This military unit consisted of Italians and Italian Americans who traveled surreptitiously to Spain to fight. Evidently, IWO members were found in their ranks, for when a rally "to Support American Boys of the Lincoln Brigade in Spain" was held at New York's Stuyvesant High School, Marcantonio as well as the Italian Section secretary addressed the crowd. Flyers featured determined fighters from both the Lincoln and Garibaldi Battalions.[36]

Militants from many backgrounds were drawn to support the Loyalist cause. The most prominent Slavic American fighting in Spain was Steve Nelson, Croatian immigrant, who a few years earlier had been recruiting miners into the IWO in eastern Pennsylvania. In 1937, too, Gizella Chomucky, a Slovak IWO member from Philadelphia, worked through another of her fraternal societies to raise funds for "the Spanish Loyalists" ($5 was sent in April 1937). Perhaps Chomucky and her peers were responding to appeals in the *Robotnícky kalendár* of the IWO's SWS, which gave extensive coverage to the Spanish fight for democracy and the "workers' militia men and women, leading the battle against fascism." The Slovaks contrasted the Spanish and their international working-class allies to domestic "fascists," such as newspaper magnate Hearst, "Hitler's friend." The ease with which the IWO labeled its ideological enemies fascists, or even un-American, was a lamentable trait that later left the Order vulnerable when charges of anti-Americanism were leveled at it from the Right.[37]

While the CP declared, "unity the need of the hour!" regarding Spain, it nevertheless continued to denounce "the Trotskyites, whose fascist connections have been proven in the Soviet Union and Spain, and whose underworld gangster alliances have been shown in Minneapolis, USA." The allusion to the leading role that Farrell Dobbs and other members of the Socialist Workers Party took in the successful 1934 Teamsters strike indicates the long-standing enmity the CP expressed toward its domestic rivals, which would even result in Communists' support for the prosecution of Dobbs and other Socialist Workers Party members under the Smith Act for alleged advocacy of violent revolution. Within Spain, too, calls for a united front clashed with defense of the violent suppression of anarchist organizations such as Barcelona's Partido Obrero de Unificación Marxista (POUM), which already in 1937 Communists were asserting was "an armed rebellion against the Peoples' Front Government." Bloody infighting among competing leftists in Spain affected Lincoln Brigade combatants, too, as when Sam Baron, U.S. Socialist reporting in Spain for the Socialist newspaper *The Call*, was arrested and "charged with the high crime of 'Trotskyism.'" The head of a committee charged with securing Baron's release called the charges "ludicrous." Such a characterization was likely to enflame Communists, not rally them to Baron's cause. The violence directed at anarchists and others was indicative of the fratricide of the Left in Spain and the United States, but the CP asserted that the suppression of POUM and other deviationists was necessary to defeat the fascists.[38]

Members of the IWO who later turned state's witness provided evidence that the Order was deeply involved in the campaign to defend Spain. While he admitted under cross-examination that "there was a large body of American opinion, outside of the Communist, who supported the democratically elected Government of Spain," Powers testified in 1951 that campaigns on behalf of the Loyalists "were brought into the National Committee of the IWO by fraction members, they were approved in the National Committee, and then they were passed down through the various channels of the IWO." The IWO contributed to Loyalist Spain by "distributing literature, soliciting funds from the lodges, purchasing of ambulances and recruiting men to fight against Franco." Powers said he handed the names of other IWO leaders to the CP to facilitate the recruitment of IWO members to go fight against Franco.[39]

The IWO was unapologetic about recruitment of its members to fight in Spain. In 1938 the general secretary proudly reported on the Order's rapid response to "the needs of the Spanish people in their life and death struggle against fascism," noting many members, including "a member of our National Executive Committee, Brother Tom Goodwin," went overseas to fight. In addition nearly $50,000 was donated by members to send ambulances, food, medicine, and five thousand sweaters to aid the Loyalist cause. The Polish Section, too, remembered its contribution to Madrid's defense as one of its proudest moments in the fight "to halt German-Italian-Japanese aggression." At the end of World War II, the Poles hailed "members volunteering for service in the International Brigades which fought fascism on the Spanish soil" as its most outstanding contribution. Junior Section leader Jerry Trauber stressed the Order's commitment to the Spanish cause, too, listing "the Abraham Lincoln Battalions of the Loyalist Armies in Spain" as well as Left-patriotic icons Frederick Douglass and Tom Paine as the kind of "real Americanism" the IWO was teaching its children.[40]

Even those who did not fight for Spain contributed to the cause. In 1937 Thompson traveled to Spain with other African Americans, ostensibly as a press correspondent covering the Loyalist cause, touring relief hospitals and battlefields. Before arriving in Spain, Thompson had attended an antiracism conference in Paris as a delegate of the IWO and the NNC, suggesting the linkages the American Left made between antiracist activism at home and the fight to dismantle colonialism abroad. Although Robert Reid-Pharr argues that African Americans fighting in Spain were required to perform constricting, masculinist roles as brave leftist global freedom fighters, gender norms that bled the complexity of their Republican service from the saga, Thompson complicates this narrative.[41] She championed black men fighting for the Loyalists and freedom but also brought "nurturing" gifts of ambulances and medicine to Madrid, combining the templates of both Florence Nightingale and Ida B. Wells. Once in Madrid, Thompson joined poet Langston Hughes, Lincoln Brigade soldier Walter Garland, and Communist Harry Haywood in delivering radio addresses on what the Loyalist fight meant to antiracist, anti-imperialist blacks in America. These speeches were rebroadcast to the United States. Thompson said she felt a kinship with the Spanish people fighting fascists because

> they are fighting oppression, and I come from a people whose oppression is centuries old. I am a part of their feeling against the Italian fascism which has participated in the devastation of their country, because we in America felt keenly the devastation of Ethiopia by the same forces. I sense their determination to maintain democracy in Spain, because in America we Negroes have been striving for democratic rights since the days of slavery.[42]

The African Americans fighting fascism were welcomed in Spain, she added, and "one encounters none of the racial prejudice so characteristic of one's own country.... The conclusion can only be, therefore, that all of us who as minority peoples are victimized by fascism, all of us who believe in the principles of democracy, have the duty of supporting this fight of the Spanish people with all that we have. It is our common struggle."[43]

On her return to the United States, Thompson and other participants made a speaking tour for the IWO to raise funds for the Loyalists. She spoke to both black and white groups of the "many, many black soldiers" fighting for the Spanish Republic. Thompson spoke in Harlem at her home lodge as well as at a reception at the University of Chicago. IWO lodges in smaller cities such as Cleveland and Grand Rapids also hosted fund-raising talks by Thompson. Moved by her accounts of the interracial International Brigades' heroic defense of the Republic, IWO members contributed funds to purchase ambulances "in the name of black Americans" as well as to contribute "money, milk and food" for the refugees from Malaga and other cities captured by the fascists. During one IWO-sponsored appearance in New York, she optimistically declared, "A courageous, determined Spanish people— behind their unified government and army, supported by the liberty-loving anti-fascist forces of the world, no Franco, no Hitler, no Mussolini can conquer." She recollected that she had made so many addresses for the IWO that she felt "it's coming out of my ears," although she regarded the three weeks touring Spain as one of the transformative events of her life. As Thompson later recalled of the ferment around Spain, "People began taking sides."[44]

The urgency of the crisis caused the IWO to set aside ideological differences and work with non-Communists on behalf of Spain. Thompson participated in a Lift the Embargo conference in Washington with non-Communists of the NNC such as A. Philip Randolph and Yergan, although CP figures such as Robert Minor and *Daily Worker* editor Clarence Hathaway attended as well. The German-American Committee for Spanish Relief wrote Bedacht in February 1938 thanking him for the IWO's financial contribution to its relief campaign. The committee, on whose board sat Albert Einstein as well as the widow of Socialist congressman Victor Berger, hoped it could count on the IWO's continued financial support for its relief work, since as of January 1938 it had only $900 on hand for direct Spanish relief. The following month the Medical Bureau and North American Committee to Aid Spanish Democracy wrote to Bedacht relaying the multiple cablegrams it was receiving daily on the bombing of Loyalist ambulances and mobile hospital units. The emergency spurred the committee to call "a meeting of all groups backing the Spanish Loyalist cause in this country, irrespective of any particular viewpoint." Bedacht as well as CP leader Browder, Socialist Party chairman Norman Thomas, and anti-Communist ILGWU official Charles Zimmerman were invited to devise "emergency measures" to ensure medical aid reached the battlefront. While in different contexts Bedacht and other Communists had denigrated the contributions of "social fascists" such as Thomas, by 1938 the crisis in Spain led the general secretary to work with Socialists and other leftists to deliver medical assistance.[45]

The IWO had to tread carefully in its support of the Loyalist cause, for not only was the Republic unpopular with more conservative Americans, direct aid to Madrid violated America's Neutrality Acts, which embargoed aid to either side in the conflict. IWO official and congressman Marcantonio, whose East Harlem district contained many Hispanic constituents sympathetic to the Madrid government, introduced bills seeking to lift the embargo to no avail. The Order's activities caught the attention of the FBI, and also the Massachusetts Department of Insurance, which in 1938 attempted to revoke its insurance license because of alleged improper use of corporate funds to support the Loyalist cause. General Counsel Brodsky proved in court, however, that the IWO had used none of its corporate funds to support the Spanish government; funds were raised through voluntary contributions of individual members. The IWO dodged a bullet when Massachusetts courts determined the Order had not violated the terms of its insurance license.[46]

As the military situation in Spain grew more desperate, the IWO turned its attention toward helping refugees from Franco's assaults. In New York the IWO's Spanish Society as well as Marcantonio participated in fiestas for the children of Loyalist Spain and "for the benefit of the embattled people of Spain who are fighting against terrific odds to preserve those same civil rights that every American enjoys." In June 1939 IWO members receiving the Order's monthly magazine, *Fraternal Outlook*, found a full-page back-cover ad urging readers in English, Yiddish, Italian, and Russian to donate to the Spanish Refugee Relief Campaign. Donors could contribute $1.50 or $3 to provide a basic-needs package to refugees, or send $50 to support ten refugees for a month. Those IWO members able to aid the cause more broadly were asked to donate $75 "to bring 1 refugee to a new life in Latin America" or send in $800 (almost certainly the commitment of a lodge, not a single individual) to provide "monthly upkeep of American Mobile Dispensary for supplying medical treatment to refugees." The following month *Fraternal Outlook* published a story by Dorothy Parker on "Spain's Refugees in France" documenting the 440,000 victims of "starvation and betrayal" who had fled the victorious fascists.[47]

Although a lingering commitment to the defeated Spanish Republic remained, after the summer of 1939, the Spanish Loyalist cause was given less of a hearing. Facing the immediate dilemma of the long-feared world war against fascism, members of the Order confronted another challenge. With the Soviet Union's dramatic announcement of a nonaggression pact with the recently despised Nazi enemy, the European war was suddenly redefined as an inter-imperialist war that was none of the United States' concern. As in other Communist-affiliated groups, this policy reversal caused turmoil in the IWO.

"A Bombshell Has Burst over Our Party"

The surprise announcement in late August 1939 of the Molotov-Ribbentrop Pact, committing Moscow to neutrality in the war, quickly followed by Hitler's invasion of Poland, led to a rapid reappraisal of the world situation by the CPUSA and the leadership of the IWO. The war was now characterized as a struggle between rival imperialist systems and therefore none of working-class Americans' fight. Officials in the IWO and other organizations advocated American neutrality in the war, which they cast as a struggle of bankrupt imperialist-capitalists versus their mutant fascist stepchildren. The rapidity with which warnings of the Nazi menace were replaced by assertions that "the Yanks are not coming" was regarded as evidence that the IWO, the American League against War and Fascism, the YCL, and other like-minded organizations were automatons taking their orders directly from the Kremlin.[48]

Isserman has argued that most Party members, while disillusioned or angry at the change, followed the adjusted line as the only alternative once Great Britain, France, and even the United States made it clear they had no interest in cooperating with the Soviet Union in an antifascist coalition. The nonaggression pact, and Moscow's noninvolvement for almost two years in the war against the Nazis, may have caused some private grumbling, Isserman argues, but American Party adherents and their allies felt they had few other organizations that strenuously advocated for their causes and so for the most part accepted the changed line on neutrality.[49]

Yet the reaction of a significant number of leftists to the new line seems to have been not acquiescence but outrage. The IWO contained, as noted, many non-Communists in its ranks, but even in other organizations such as the YCL (to which many IWO Junior Branch members belonged), opposition to the abrupt calls for neutrality were raised. While IWO officials defended the calls for America to stay out of the war, grassroots members sometimes rejected such reasoning. And even when IWO officials defended neutrality, they endeavored to frame this call as an extension of the Order's anticolonialist stance, asking why Americans should be expected to redeem Great Britain's Caribbean, African, and Asian empire.[50] Such reasoning may have resonated, particularly, with the Order's African American members.

On the very day the Wehrmacht stormed into Poland, "A Group of Members of the Communist Party and the Young Communist League" made their opposition to the new policy known. "A bombshell has burst over our Party," the young oppositionists wrote, portraying the confusion of Party members over the nonaggression pact. Party members were "absolutely stunned and bewildered" and "sympathizers and so-called fellow travelers" were said to be already abandoning the Party and its organizations. The letter writers rejected the explanations of the *Daily Worker* and argued that hundreds of comrades felt the same way. They also lamented that the previous Communist advocacy of "collective security is dead.... The French-English-Russian alliance is dead. The Stalin-Hitler Pact puts us in the position of saying everything is white which we yesterday claimed was black." While other writers from the IWO would quickly note that the leaders of Great Britain and France had acted far too minimally on Soviet calls for a collective resistance to fascism, and even the YCL members admitted having little faith in Neville Chamberlain and Édouard Daladier, their bitter denunciation of the pact makes it clear that many American leftists resisted the swift move to neutrality.[51]

The YCL oppositionists noted that this letter was just the latest in a series they had written opposing the pact and that they had also recently objected to a decision by their organization to back a strike of WPA workers. They asked how this pact could possibly be explained to the average American worker, who would conclude that Nazis and Soviets were just different sides of the same coin, and they predicted a wave of reaction would ensue in unions that would use the pact as an excuse to hound out Communists. Instead of "applauding and yelling approval of everything that comes from the leaders," the YCL writers demanded more democracy in the Party. We have already seen that Party members often exercised independence when they believed their comrades had acted unwisely. Still, the dilemma that many Americans faced in September 1939 is suggested by the YCL's admission that neither collective security with conservative French and British premiers holding Moscow at arm's length nor isolationism was palatable. The Soviets joining in Great Britain and France's war in September 1939 would likely have been an equally repugnant *volte face*, for the writers declared "no faith in the democratic capitalists who oppress hundreds of millions of colonial people."[52]

In the IWO the switch to neutrality also was angrily denounced by many members. Grassroots Jewish members issued a Yiddish pamphlet near the end of 1939 criticizing the Soviet Union for signing the pact. *Der Stalin-Hitler Opmakh un der Internatsyonaler Arbeter Ordn* (The Stalin-Hitler Pact and the International Workers Order) was issued by a committee of IWO members and addressed to "all Order members and Leftist Jewish workers." "Where are we going?" the IWO members demanded. "Where are the leaders of the International Workers Order leading us?"[53] In a demonstration of the kind of independence Order members showed on social and economic matters as well, the pamphlet's authors urged readers to "ponder on the situation":

> We know that the leaders of the Order are Communist leaders. Until now we have followed them and supported the Communist Party, because we believed that they were leading us on the path of progress and Socialism. But now the Communist leaders have suddenly turned in an opposite direction, in the direction of cooperation with Hitler and Hitlerism. Now they are supporting the partnership between Stalin and Hitler in their war against the democratic countries and support the Hitler peace-maneuvers.[54]

Nonparty IWO members were willing to follow Communist officials' lead when it seemed these positions served one's interests. When members saw wrongheadedness, or worse, they were not hesitant to denounce those leaders. The Popular Front membership of the IWO did not move in lockstep on the nonaggression pact or any other policy.

Nor did Jewish dissidents cede the field to leaders with whom they disagreed. Joining with staff members of the *Morgen Freiheit* and others, IWO members formed a League against Fascism and Dictatorship and vowed to stay in the Order and fight. They urged other IWO members to fight the

Communist leadership on the pact, too. "Do not allow the handful of bureaucrats and their handymen, who have turned the order into a private business of theirs, lead you by the nose and talk in your name," they argued. "You no longer dare remain passive."[55]

Not many members remained passive. Many resigned in disgust at Stalin's pact, while others stayed and complained. In 1941 local branch secretaries lamented a decline in membership due to critical coverage of the Party in capitalist newspapers, especially since the start of the war. A Denver Jewish lodge's secretary noted social affairs that previously attracted four hundred attendees now saw only a handful, and few new faces. "When the world situation was more or less 'normal,'" he wrote, "it was comparatively easy to approach a person to join the IWO," but now most people stayed away from the group's events. A Finnish secretary from the Bronx added, "Our large drop in membership was a result of the Finnish-Soviet war last year." When another lodge in Edwardsville, Pennsylvania, showed the Soviet film *Mannerheim Line*, which defended Stalin's Finnish war, the secretary reported, "we are attacked from every corner now." While it had likely never been easy for this Ukrainian lodge to defend the Soviet Union, the abrupt turnaround in Moscow's foreign policy in 1939–1941 compounded the problem.[56]

In late 1940 the IWO's New Jersey district convention felt compelled to address the Order's "Special Problem," the fallout from the USSR's neutrality. Brother Landy admitted to the Newark assembly that "the ills of our Order" started with the signing of the "Soviet-Nazi Trade Pact," and that a decline in membership had resulted. He defended the pact, however, as part of Moscow's overall peace policy, even as he admitted "the enemies of the Order" had created dissension among Jewish, Slovak, and Polish members. Landy argued that the "liberating actions" of the Soviets could be contrasted with the Nazi aggression in Poland. His report failed to reflect that the decline in IWO membership might have been at least partly because many Jewish, Polish, or other Slavic members did not regard the Red Army invasion of Poland as any more benevolent than Hitler's. Still, the New Jersey report indicates not all IWO members were as reflexively supportive of the nonaggression pact and its aftermath as Brother Landy.[57]

In Harlem, too, African American local officials expressed opposition to the IWO's newfound determination to keep America out of the war. Stevenson, who had served as an officer in Solidarity Lodge 691, later criticized the national leadership, which had "bitterly assailed the Alien Registration Act; The National Service Act; The Lend Lease, as a 'dictatorship bill,' and other aid to Britain, coupled with the acquisition of Island and other bases, as imperialistic and war-mongering." Referring to the two years before America entered the war, Stevenson said, "At that time so fraught with peril for our country, these groups popularly used the presumptuous slogan, 'The Yanks are not coming.'" Although Stevenson ran afoul of national leaders such as Bedacht for his criticism of their opposition to Lend-Lease between August 1939 and June 1941, a significant number of the members of Lodge 691 backed Stevenson's right to criticize the national leadership.[58]

Another fixture of Solidarity Lodge, however, provided a different take on the war. Thompson joined other Order officers in supporting the turn to neutrality. She characterized the Order's anti-interventionist stance as a continuation of long-standing commitments to peace and anticolonialism. At a time when the two chief opponents of the Axis were Great Britain and France, the two largest occupiers of Caribbean, African, and Asian colonies, arguments that the world war was a battle to prop up imperialism and therefore none of America's fight may have resonated with at least some African Americans and Hispanics in the IWO.

In November 1939 Thompson told a Milwaukee audience that people had to keep the country out of war and ensure there were no "evasions of the neutrality act." Three days later Detroit police took note of Thompson's appearance at a "Rally for Peace and Civil Rights," where she lauded Bedacht and Stalin but attacked England and France and called on the American people to maintain neutrality and peace. The police informant added, "A movie short . . . was then shown with Joe Stalin, leading his Red Army, which drew the house down but when the American Flag was shown on the screen for a minute, no applause followed." Thompson also wondered whether Roosevelt was following in the footsteps of Woodrow Wilson, perhaps an appeal to the sentiment, widespread in late 1939, that World War I had been a pointless conflict despite soaring rhetoric to make the world safe for democracy.[59]

The following year Thompson was more explicit on the anticolonialist argument for not coming to Great Britain's aid. Thompson asked of black Americans, "Can they work up any enthusiasm about going to fight for democracy thousands of miles away when their desire for democracy is denied at home?" listing the failure of Congress to pass antilynching and poll-tax measures. Her main argument for why black people should back neutrality, however, was that "imperialism and its effects are for them a living issue as it bears down upon the backs of the black people of Africa and the West Indies," whether of British or Italian subjugation. She pointedly raised Great Britain's continued rule over 350 million people in India in arguing that for people of color the war was not much of a fight for freedom. It would be another three years before Great Britain grudgingly committed to self-determination for its colonies, the last of which was only relinquished twenty years after the war's conclusion. African Americans in the IWO such as Thompson may have had reason to look at Great Britain's cause skeptically.[60]

Such critiques were arguably extensions of the IWO's long-standing condemnation of colonialism, and in this respect the speeches in 1939–1941 advocating neutrality in Great Britain and France's war were not a big departure in foreign-policy alignment. To be sure, the sudden assertion that America stay out of a fight against Hitler struck even many IWO members as an unpardonable change of direction, as we've seen. But African Americans and other members of the Order had also heard from their officers on the need to liberate the colonized subjects of Great Britain, especially oppressed India; the urgency of freeing Cubans and Filipinos from the vice grip of dollar diplomacy; and the need to work for Caribbean and West African freedom. Thompson and other Order officers also served on the board of organizations such as the NNC that assertively advocated these causes. For such members immediate embrace of Great Britain's war might have seemed just as abrupt a change of policy as advocacy of neutrality in 1939.[61]

Thompson later recalled that arguments about "the pact between Stalin and Hitler and things of this kind" only caused dissension at IWO headquarters, but when she traveled to lodges in West Virginia, Ohio, and Pennsylvania, she noted that "you never had any of these problems when you went into areas to work with the people. The workers, they understood." These sentiments, expressed more than forty years after the events recollected, may have glossed over the tensions within the IWO over Russia's neutrality, as the remarks of some lodge secretaries indicate. Nevertheless, some workers may have regarded the IWO's good works as outweighing the leaders' discussion of events in Europe.[62]

Vrábel, too, told the SWS national convention, "The war that is now going on in Europe is a war of plunder, a war for markets, a war which has as its sole aim the decision as to which of the murderers, despots, politicians, financiers shall control how much of the world's surface." Although inclusion of "financiers" in her list of rogues tipped off her Communist sentiments, in June 1940 many nonleftist Americans regarded the European conflict as none of their business, too. Vrábel went further, listing fascist conquest of Ethiopia, Manchuria, Albania, Spain, and Czechoslovakia, aided and abetted by French and English inaction, and wondered how these nations could now profess to be defenders of democracy and civilization. After the Munich agreement ceded parts of Czechoslovakia to Germany, she added, London and Paris likewise ignored Moscow's calls for an alliance because the Western democracies hoped Hitler would in time destroy the Soviet Union. The hostile unwillingness of Western democracies to cooperate with Moscow led to the signing of the nonaggression pact, she suggested, a move "that caused such rage and nightmares for Chamberlain, Daladier and Roosevelt . . . because at least for the time being it thwarted their plans for the fomenting of a German-Soviet war." While perhaps overstated, the Western democracies had been cool to Russia's warnings of a fascist menace and less than vigilant in standing up to the Nazis. The Soviets were not the only ones to effect a rapid switch in foreign policy in the summer of 1939.[63]

Bedacht echoed Vrábel's critique of the imperialist hypocrisy of Great Britain, France, and the United States following World War I and likewise mocked the conversion of British Nazi sympathizers such as Lord Halifax into advocates of a new war supposedly about democracy and not preservation of Great Britain's colonial system. Bedacht said, "We are asked to believe the unbelievable. We are requested to believe that the Hitler-lovers of yesterday, the Lord Halifaxes, and our own [William] Knudsens, Fords and Dieses, have transformed themselves today into staunch and uncompromising haters of Nazism." He noted American and British politicians and industrialists had failed to stand up for Spain or Ethiopia; instead, he charged they "whistle[d] nonchalantly when Mussolini's legions overran Abyssinia." The "fat 'defense' contracts" bestowed on Henry Ford, he reminded the IWO, went to the holder of a Nazi medal who was also "the disseminator in America of Hitler's barbarous racial teachings." Under such circumstances, Bedacht argued, the rush to war should be resisted.[64]

In April 1941 Executive Secretary Benjamin tapped into this isolationist sentiment when he asserted, "Americans, immigrants all want peace." He told an IWO assembly, "We are here to give expression to the vast and overwhelming majority of Americans that our country shall not be dragged further into the war between the rival groups of imperialists for a redivision of the world." Benjamin charged that the only Poles, Czechs, and Slovaks calling for U.S. intervention in the war were those under the domination of the Polish government in exile or those "guided by the Czecho-Slovak consulates in the United States." He charged that the groups sympathetic to Hitler's puppet Slovak Republic of Monsignor Jozef Tiso were engaging in industrial spying and subservient to a foreign power. These charges of foreign domination, leveled at the IWO's ideological enemies, would later be hurled at the Order by the FBI and other red-hunters.[65]

"We Have Changed Our Attitude toward the War"

IWO officials' loyalty to the neutrality stance of the Soviet Union attracted the U.S. government's notice, as the OSS's FNB remarked, IWO president Weiner "zigzags with the Party line." Socialist foes in the Workmen's Circle also mocked the IWO's changes with every "last aircurrent from Moscow."[66] Further zigzags soon came.

Within days of the June 1941 Nazi invasion of the Soviet Union, officials of the IWO revived earlier calls for a multinational antifascist coalition. State senator Nowak of the Michigan IWO, who must have found it a difficult job selling his fellow Poles on the Nazi-Soviet pact, used his Polish-language radio broadcast just seven days following the invasion as an opportunity to resume speaking on the need for a coalition to defeat Nazism abroad as well as fascist tendencies in all capitalist nations. "Our role in America must be to work towards greater co-operation between all the nations and all the peoples, including the Soviets," Nowak said. But the rights of colonized peoples were also stressed by Nowak. Even as he urged working with the British and Soviets, he told his radio listeners that the accidental allies had to pledge themselves not just to defeat the Nazis but to work "towards the establishment of the right of all nations to their independence, including even those nations which are today subject to Great Britain, such as India." A month later Nowak welcomed Roosevelt and Churchill's establishment of war aims precluding territorial aggrandizement but said "a clear statement as to the future of such colonial nations as India" was needed. "We cannot effectively fight Hitler's imperialism as long as we condone the subjugation of any nation by another."[67]

The following month IWO's National Education Department rushed into print its "Speaker's Guide on the Soviet-Nazi War." The guide argued that the Soviets had been forced to sign the nonaggression pact when Great Britain and France showed no interest in Russia's entreaties for an antifascist coalition. The Soviets had gained a year and a half "breathing room," enabling them to rearm to be in a better position when the Nazi invasion came. "Events have confirmed the wisdom of this policy," the guide said, even as in July 1941 the Red Army faced catastrophic defeat on the battlefield. Little good was said of "the Munichmen in England and America," on whose inaction Hitler was counting when he invaded the Soviet Union. But the guide's authors asserted, "The entrance of 200,000,000 Soviet people into the war cannot help but change the character of the war as this powerful anti-imperialist force enters the fight with the one and only object of wiping fascism out and destroying German Nazism." The old war of "imperialist aims" had been supplanted by "a just people's war against Hitler," the authors added. The Soviet's fight, they suggested, was also America's fight, and all Order members were urged to build full support for the British-Soviet coalition.[68]

A month after the Nazi invasion, an FBI informant reported that members of the Polish Workers' Solidarity Lodge in Milwaukee were told what had started as an imperialistic war was now "a war of the laboring masses against Fascism." In August the IWO in Detroit held a "Smash Hitlerism" rally, the proceeds of which went to aid the British and Soviet people. A speaker charged each Michigan lodge with contributing to a fund to send cigarettes to the soldiers fighting Hitlerism "as well as . . . raise $100,000 for medical supplies to be sent to the Soviet Union and her allies." The same officials who a few months earlier had denounced the war as a fight to preserve British imperialism now explained that the war had taken a new turn. Vrábel of the SWS said, "We have changed our attitude toward the war, because the history of the war has changed." Benjamin similarly argued that the attack on the workers' state by Hitler justified a change in position on the war.

Benjamin spoke of support for Moscow but also said the changed nature of the war necessitated that the United States become allies of Great Britain. He added, though, "we must be critical allies" who would hold London to its "avowed policy," presumably regarding democracy and its colonies. He acknowledged that prior to June 22 the IWO often "unduly antagonized" people by calling for neutrality but now hoped the organization could work with other groups and people who saw the need to defeat Hitler.[69] Such rapid reversals may have raised eyebrows, but then again many nonleftists in 1941 America also shifted from isolationism to support of intervention as events unfolded overseas.

Even before the United States entered the war, the IWO mobilized its members behind the fight. The Soviet ambassador thanked an Italian lodge in Greenwich Village "for their warm feelings toward the Soviet Union and their support of the Russian people in its present fight against Nazism" and conveyed the hope that Italy would soon throw off the "Hitlerite" yoke. The IWO mobilized its members as early as August 1941 in a campaign to send "twenty million cigarettes" to British and Soviet soldiers. The State Department informed General Counsel Brodsky that as the president had not declared the USSR a belligerent nation, the Order was free to solicit relief contributions for Soviet soldiers, but the organization would have to apply under the Neutrality Act to register as a relief organization if it wished to aid British troops. The IWO did register, and a newly created FLFF provided clothing, blankets, food packages, radios, Victrolas, and cigarettes to Allied soldiers beginning in the fall of 1941. By February 1942 more than $200,000 in goods were sent overseas, and the IWO also contributed toward drives of established organizations such as the Red Cross. The FLFF continued sending care packages to U.S., British, Soviet, and other troops throughout the war.[70]

As the United States extended Lend-Lease to the Soviets and inched toward war, the IWO gained access to public space to a greater degree than when it had been a lonely voice for assistance to Ethiopia or Spain a few years before. Robeson joined other IWO members in entertaining visitors to IWO Day at the Civilian and National Defense Exposition in midtown Manhattan. Two months before Pearl Harbor, Robeson joined the Radischev Russian Folk Dancers, the Al Moss Singers, and the IWO Junior Band in performances broadcast over radio station WMCA. Talks were also presented on "the IWO in Civilian and National Defense," and listeners were urged to visit the IWO's booth to learn of its national defense program. The Order endeavored to place itself firmly in the mainstream of national defense efforts and, in line with its showcase appearance at the exposition, soon published a booklet titled *Air Raid Blackouts First Aid: A Handbook for Civilians in Wartime*. By late 1941 thousands of members were registering for civilian defense and buying defense bonds.[71] And with the formal entrance of the United

States into the war, the IWO enjoyed four years in which its foreign-policy goals mirrored, at least ostensibly, those of the government.

"Give 'Til It Hurts Hitler"

The tenuous alliance of the United States and Russia enabled the IWO to recast its actions as support for American democracy as well as wartime unity, but the organization continued to emphasize support for Moscow, a policy that caught the attention of the FBI, OSS, and other authorities and revealed some of the competing war aims and tensions between the allies. While still stressing support for the Soviets, the Order's officers now characterized their activities as motivated by "concern for our country, our common homeland as Americans." The FLFF, which sent care packages to soldiers fighting the Axis, now reconfigured its work to place greater emphasis on aiding the soldiers of America, "which ha[ve] first claim on our loyalty and devotion." Already by February 1942 the FLFF had conducted two national fund-raising tours, with more in the works. Ethnic societies were redirected to contribute to a common fund, rather than sending aid solely to the armies of their old homelands. Still, local districts were given wide latitude on where the aid they raised would be directed, and thus many FLFF packages were sent to Red Army troops, Polish and Czech partisans as well as U.S. and British soldiers (Figure 5.1).[72]

A pamphlet, *The Story of the Front Line Fighters Fund*, told of the funds raised for soldiers "from the Philippines to the frozen steppes," comprising the "Yanks, Tommies and the Red Army" as well as guerrilla forces in Asia and Eastern Europe. The FLFF noted that it had contributed more than $10,000,000 to the American Red Cross's War Fund Drive and sent fifteen thousand woolen garments, millions of cigarettes, and hundreds of radios and phonographs to the troops. The FLFF asserted that its primary concern was American troops, but that as its members had roots in many of the countries battling Hitler, and "the struggle is global, indivisible," it would continue to aid Soviet and other soldiers, too. Poles, Slovaks, Jews, Ukrainians, and others in the IWO were urged to send more funds to "this melting pot of war relief." Donors were urged to "Give 'Til It Hurts Hitler" in sending Solidarity gifts, "salutes from friends in far-off America," to British, Russian, Czech, Polish, French, Greek, and other soldiers. Another FLFF poster called for donors to "Help Them Save Freedom" and depicted a soldier striding past a tank with dollar coins as its tank treads. The "medical supplies, food, cigarettes and warm clothing" the FLFF sent, the poster implied, were the ammunition needed to defeat Hitler (Figure 5.2).[73]

The poster's metaphor was literalized in a JPFO campaign to raise money to buy tanks for the Red Army. Saltzman met with Soviet ambassador Litvinov, who gave the campaign his full support. A flyer advertising the fall

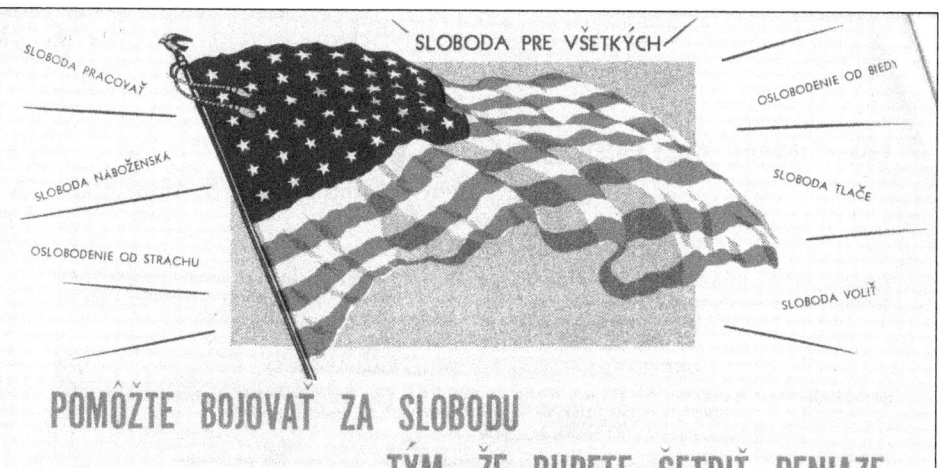

Figure 5.1 During World War II, patriotic American icons were used in appeals to ethnic group members to buy war bonds and help the fight for freedom. The IWO combined ethnic particularism with American patriotism throughout the war.

Source: Flyer, "Pomôžte Bojovať za Slobodu tým, že Budete Šetriť Peniaze" [Help the Fight for Freedom, Buy War Bonds], IWO-CU, box 15, folder 3.

Figure 5.2 The IWO's Front Line Fighters Fund sent care packages to American and Allied soldiers but also raised money to purchase tanks for the War Department. Here the metaphor is literalized as tanks ride to victory on treads composed of contributed coins.

Source: Poster, "Help Them Save Freedom," IWO-CU, box 16, folder 26.

1942 campaign in English and Yiddish reported on the $100,000 raised by the JPFO for the purchase of ten tanks. Saltzman hoped to have the tanks named for Jewish heroes and the IWO itself, although the flyer also noted that if it proved impossible to ship weapons to the Soviets, the JPFO's contribution would be "diverted to the purchase of medicines, hospital equipment, warm clothing, portable movie projectors and portable radio stations." "Every Jew has a burning desire to help smash Hitlerism!" the leaflet declared. "Every Jew should take part in this holy action!" Individual JPFO members who answered this appeal were awarded "honor certificates" celebrating their gifts to the Red Army. Local members responded in creative ways. A birthday celebration for an eighty-year-old IWO member in Los Angeles promised all proceeds of the affair would go toward "a tank for the fighting Red Army." In Oakland a mass meeting responded to the call, "Tanks for the Red Army, Death to the Nazis."[74]

Even though Moscow was allied with the United States, the JPFO's campaign to send military hardware explicitly earmarked for the Red Army seemed to belie the Order's earlier assertions that America was the land "with first claim on our loyalty." The campaign, which was publicized via pamphlets showing the JPFO's contributed tanks setting Hitler on the run, was opposed by other organizations less certain of the commitment of the Soviets to democracy or Jewish welfare. The campaign also caught the attention of the FBI, which noted, too, "Negro" contributions to the FLFF in aid of black U.S. soldiers.[75]

Other campaigns were conducted on surer, patriotic footing. The fund developed a "Servicemen's Welfare" campaign, which sent holiday care packages to IWO members in the armed forces. Flyers listed the number of servicemen from each ethnic society and showed an appreciative soldier enjoying the IWO's gift. Potential donors were urged to "put him first on your Xmas List!"[76] Ethnic and American patriotic appeals were linked in calls to send Thanksgiving dinner to IWO servicemen. In best Popular Front fashion, a Polish-language appeal linked the Polonia Society to the spirit of American patriotism. Claiming the Mayflower passengers as spiritual ancestors of left-wing Order members now fighting fascism, Bedacht wrote, "The pilgrims, our ancestors, came from the old world to America in pursuit of freedom and a better life. . . . [T]hey celebrated the first Thanksgiving as a celebration of that search, and their triumph over the elements, adversity and tyranny." He argued that it was only fitting to support the fund bringing "a few moments of happiness" to those fighting "tyranny and oppression." At another FLFF rally IWO members including Ohio state president Anthony Krchmarek gathered on "George Washington's Birthday to re-dedicate ourselves to the ideals of liberty for which our forefathers fought." Jacobson argues that World War II was one of the moments Slavs, Jews, Italians, and other white ethnics began to claim icons of American history as "our forefathers," but left-wing militants made this imaginative leap, too. Patriotic appeal to pilgrim ancestors, even if printed in Polish, were likely less controversial than calls to buy Red Army tanks (Figure 5.3).[77]

The IWO also enthusiastically contributed to government war bond drives, blood donor campaigns, and other relief efforts, although often with an emphasis on assistance to the Soviet allies. Treasurer Shipka estimated that by war's end more than $30 million in war bonds were purchased by Order members, and noted that "the Order and its subordinates received numerous commendations, certificates and awards for its patriotic participation in such activity." The Order printed leaflets in languages such as Slovak urging members to "Help the Fight for Freedom, Buy War Bonds." Members recalled government citations their lodges earned for blood drives, bond subscriptions, and Civilian Defense work. An ambulance was also purchased for the War Department. An IWO member in Detroit was enlisted to make radio appeals in Polish for the Red Cross blood drive. Vrábel of the SWS recorded pro-Allied radio addresses that the government's Office of War

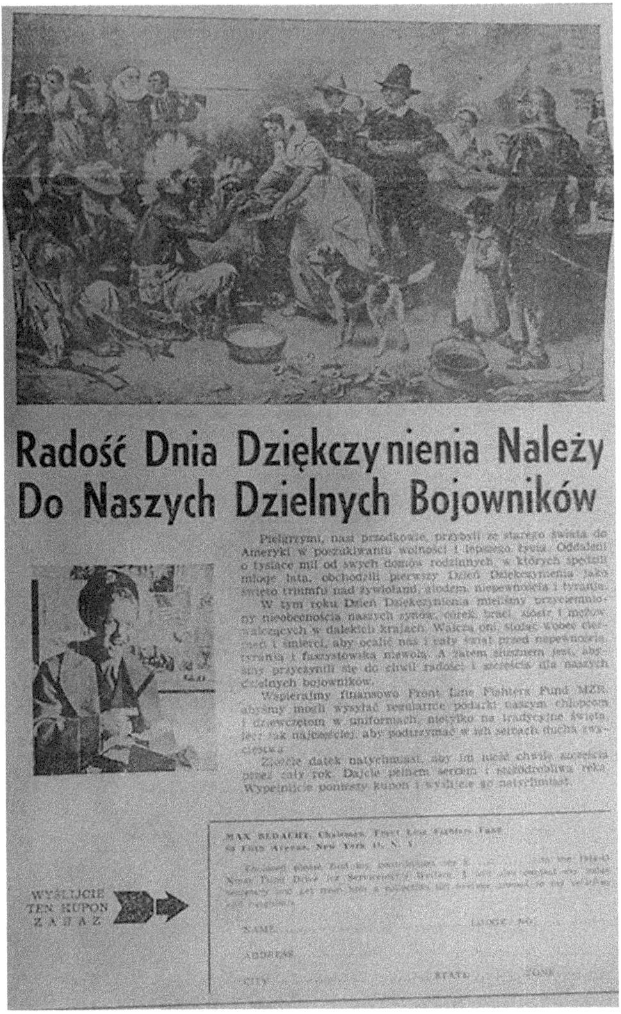

Figure 5.3 The IWO urged members, in Polish, to contribute to the FLFF during World War II. The IWO argued that, like the pilgrims at Plymouth, Polish IWO members in the armed forces were fighting against "adversity and tyranny."
Source: Max Bedacht, "Radość Dnia Dziękczynienia Należy do Naszych Dielnych Bojowników" [The Joy of Thanksgiving Belongs to Our Brave Warriors], *Glos Ludowy,* November 25, 1944, 6, DB-WSU, box 5, folder 5–29.

Information (OWI) broadcast to occupied Europe. When the editor of the conservative Catholic newspaper *Jednota* complained about this, the OWI reprimanded not Vrábel but her critic. The wartime alliance opened up space for IWO participation in civic culture it had previously not so broadly enjoyed.[78]

IWO members made sure their contributions were commemorated as Slavic contributions to the war effort, as when the Order participated in Detroit's All-Slav Blood Donors' Parade on the first anniversary of the bombing of Pearl Harbor. The FBI recorded that an IWO member was heard to remark that 95 percent of the Poles participating in the parade were members of the Order. The member contacted the Red Cross to make sure the IWO got credit for its large participation; he was a little irked, though, that the ASC, which had organized the parade, had not thought to have a photographer present. The IWO was also planning a concert "based on the battle songs of the Allied nations," with Polish singers, to coincide with the start of the Red Cross's next blood drive the following February.[79]

As the Servicemen's Welfare campaign of the FLFF attests, the IWO was proud of its members in the armed services. On Memorial Day 1945, the Slovak and Croatian Sections published memorial honor rolls of their members who had perished in the conflict. Following the war, as the IWO's patriotism and loyalty to America were already being questioned by professional Cold Warriors, Shipka noted that in addition to $30,000,000 in war bonds purchased and other civilian work in aid of the war, around ten thousand members and fifteen thousand husbands, sons, and daughters of members served in the armed forces during the war. More than three hundred members were killed in combat, "and hundreds more suffered wounds and received citations and medals for valor."[80]

In attesting to the Order's merits as liquidation loomed, local members recalled the sacrifices they, like other Americans, had made through wartime service. Dora Friedkas of the Bronx testified that both of her sons, "raised in the youth section" of the IWO, had been killed during the war. Both had volunteered for service even though they could have claimed medical exemptions. "The devotion of my two boys to the service of their country and the devotion of my deceased husband resulted from their membership in the IWO," Friedkas said, and she hoped she could be buried near her sons in the military section of the IWO cemetery in Pinelawn, Long Island. Rubin Cravetz of Philadelphia similarly spoke of a son killed in Normandy interred in an IWO cemetery. Another member spoke of his thirty-three months' service in an anti-aircraft battalion in the European and Mediterranean theaters, where he earned five battle stars, and added, "My IWO activity was one of the important features of American life to which I hoped to return during my years of military service.... Among the precious freedoms for which we fought was the freedom of association."[81]

Some IWO enlistees, though, were interrogated about their political affiliations, barred from promotion, and even expelled from the service. The most notorious case was the treatment of Dale Zysman by the navy. Zysman, a member of the IWO as well as a teacher and vice president of the militant Teachers Union of the City of New York, had been dismissed by the board of education in late 1941 at the instigation of the state legislature. While appealing his dismissal, Zysman enlisted in the navy days after Pearl Harbor. He made no secret of his work both with the Teachers Union and as an IWO organizer in New Jersey. After a newspaper story revealed that a "red" teacher was now infiltrating the armed forces, Zysman was cast out of the navy. The Teachers Union began a campaign to appeal this action to the secretary of the navy, "urging him to prevent the setting of this precedent of excluding militant representatives of organized labor from the service." Congressman Marcantonio of the IWO's Italian Section took up Zysman's case with both the New York Board of Education and Secretary of Navy Frank Knox. The IWO passed resolutions, too, decrying Zysman's discharge "without cause other than the suspicion of some officials that he held minority political views" as "an unwarranted reflection upon Brother Zysman's patriotism and a denial of his constitutional rights, suggest[ing] the influence of anti-labor, pro-fascist tendencies in the ... Federal Government." The IWO urged members to write the navy secretary demanding Zysman's reinstatement. Marcantonio told Knox, "It is indeed a travesty on our Victory effort to prevent Americans from fighting and dying for their country ... because they are the targets of Quislingistic stool-pigeons and of the domestic counterparts of the [François] Darlans and other Vichymen." Marcantonio, not known for pulling his punches, demanded an end to red-baiting in the navy as counter to America's interests.[82]

The IWO's quick leap to suspecting fascist actors at work inside America indicates that the Order's old suspicions of American capitalism died hard and were not quite subsumed in calls for wartime unity. Still, the IWO was correct to see conservative forces at work limiting left-wingers' advancement in the armed forces. Marcantonio fielded letters from artist Kent, later president of the IWO, who complained that his son was being prevented from attending officers' candidate school because of his and his father's political affiliations. The congressman took up the case with the president, and Kent thanked him for promising the "domestic fascists are not going to get away with this stuff." IWO vice president Middleton, too, tried to intervene with the U.S. Civil Service Commission when he learned a civil service applicant was being questioned about his membership in the Order.[83]

Following the war IWO members reacted with seemingly genuine shock at the vitriol of anti-Communist rhetoric and prosecutions as an abrupt fracturing of the wartime democratic coalition to which they believed they had contributed. Those who remembered the Zysman case or other incidents of thwarted military careers might not have been so surprised.

"Opening of a Second Front Now"

The IWO, and the ASC to which its Slavic sections affiliated, enthusiastically supported the war effort, but sometimes these organizations' agendas placed extraordinary emphasis on assisting the Soviet Union. Nowhere was this more noticeable than in insistent calls for the immediate opening of a second front.

For two years the IWO and ASC insisted the "opening of a second front now is imperative," recalling this was the policy of the president and U.S.

generals, too. Sometimes calls were moderate, as when in April 1942 the first Slav Congress meeting "was able to temper proposed resolutions so that the one adopted called for the opening of a Second Front only when the military leaders of the United Nations thought it advisable." OSS agents noted, "The resolution's final wording was thus far less pro-Soviet than the speech made . . . by Lord Beaverbrook, whose demand for the opening of a Second Front was featured by the *Detroit Free Press*." Even though the ASC's executive secretary, Pirinsky, was an open Communist, the OSS concluded, "no excessively pro-Soviet resolutions were adopted." Two months later the IWO greeted the Allies' "plan for the setting up of a Western front as an imperative immediate problem of the war. It calls upon its . . . members to do whatever is in their power to hasten the realization of this Western Front." The Order's *Fraternal Outlook* publicized local efforts to push for a second front, as when Chicago IWO members held an All-Slav rally at Soldier Field featuring costumed Ukrainian marchers carrying placards reading "Open 2nd Front Now, Defeat Hitler in 1942!" as well as portraits of Roosevelt, Stalin, and Churchill. Polish members met in a Hamtramck, Michigan, park to appeal for "the immediate opening of a second front." An FBI agent could not help noting, "The speakers lauded the struggle put up by the Russian Army, but no one on the platform, or in the audience seemed to be American enough to notice that the American Flag was displayed incorrectly, the Stars and Blue Field being on the left side. The Flag itself was none too clean, and after the meeting it was dumped into a panel truck."[84]

Dirty flags aside, sometimes these calls for an invasion of Western Europe to take the heat off embattled Soviet forces were couched in patriotic American rhetoric, as when Detroit IWO members hosted a Four Freedoms rally at Belle Isle Park. The rally of six thousand also celebrated the anniversary of the signing of the Atlantic Charter and inspected an ambulance the Michigan IWO had purchased for the U.S. Army. The ambulance was draped with a sign declaring, "Everything for Invasion of Europe Now!" While the IWO had been denied a permit to sell war bonds in the park, it distributed pledge cards on which attendees promised to buy what the Order called "Invasion Bonds." Thirty-five thousand dollars in pledges were announced.[85]

As the opening of the western front was continually delayed, the IWO and Slav Congress often expressed frustration, and suspicions, that something more nefarious than military logistics was at work. The delay, IWO officials concluded, could be attributed to conservative, even fascist "appeasers" and "fifth columnists" at home whose defeatist attitudes and actions were selling out America's Soviet ally. The Russian-American Section issued a leaflet declaring, "Opening of a Second Front Now Is Imperative." The leaflet recalled, "Promises were given. Agreements were entered into. Assurances were made. Still no Second Front is entered into." The leaflet argued that the second front would benefit not just Moscow but also the United

States, as it would prevent Hitler from seizing natural resources and shorten the war in Europe and Asia. Suggesting those who expressed anything less than wholehearted support for a second front were secretly sympathetic to the Nazis, the leaflet declared that the UN coalition should not be allowed to "fall victim to the mean, insidious pro-Hitler propaganda aiming to disrupt our National Unity."[86] In demanding a second front, the IWO also questioned the patriotism of those with whom it disagreed, a troubling calling out of "fifth columnists" more than a little similar to the charges of subversion that would be leveled at the Order by anti-Communists in a few years.

At the Hamtramck rally with the dirty American flag, ASC petitions were passed around, calling on the president to open the second front immediately. Those who disagreed were painted as enemies sowing dissension among loyal Americans. An IWO official told the crowd, "Our arm chair generals and type writer generals say that the opening of the second front should be left to the general staff, and they should pick the time and place." He added, though, that something more than military pragmatism was at work. "I have heard rumors that the Allies want to wait so that the Russian army will be weakened by Hitler, then the English and American armies will take the offensive against him." Nowak, head of the Michigan IWO, more ominously told the crowd, "There are so many Officers in our army who are comrades of Hitler, and who have been advising our President against the opening of this front." When some people in the crowd heckled Nowak, he derided them as "tools of Hitler."[87]

The IWO's "Win the War Statement" quoted the *Detroit Free Press* in suggesting "perhaps an element of politics . . . explains the very delay in going to Russia's rescue." The IWO demanded to know, "Who is playing politics with the lives of our boys?" arguing that aiding the beleaguered Red Army would shorten the war and save American lives. Citing General Joseph Stilwell on the necessity of a second front, the IWO took the fight to the home front and urged a vote against "appeasement" to elect a "Win the War Congress." By labeling Republicans "appeasers" and suggesting they had deliberately sabotaged the second front, the IWO suggested something un-American lurked in the opposition party. Frustrated members of the American-Russian Section executive committee saw failure to aid the "heroic Red Army," which had "delivered mortal blows" at Stalingrad, as the work of "black forces of the reactionaries in America." The IWO's executive board also regarded the continual delays as the work of "appeaser enemies of the American people" and derided calls to leave government to businessmen and war to military men as antidemocratic. Resolutions were passed demanding an immediate second front as "there can be no valid reason for further delays." The Order pressed for "passage of a measure to halt the Fifth Column" allegedly sowing national disunity. Those urging delay in opening the Western European front were targeted as committing a "Crime against the State." In wartime dissent or any disruption of a unified national purpose was castigated by the IWO as work of "fifth columns," a troubling precedent of more reactionary witch hunts to come.[88]

Although gratified at reassurances that the United States would preserve the civil liberties of aliens and foreign-born citizens during the war, the IWO declared, "We likewise approve the actions of the FBI in dealing vigorously with fifth columnists." Although the IWO was already in the crosshairs of the FBI, and would not be happy with broad prosecutorial powers for the government in other contexts, the Order amazingly asserted, "We pledge our wholehearted support and cooperation in all such cases of ferreting out and disposing of spies and saboteurs active among the national groups." These charges of "spying" and "sabotage" would quickly be turned against the Left. IWO members in the armed forces similarly wrote headquarters to demand something be done about the "poisonous pro-fascist press," especially "the renowned Hitler-decorated Mr. Hearst" who was "sabotaging the war effort" and, the writer promised, would not "escape the wrath of the men and women of the armed forces." The IWO might later have regretted giving the FBI ammunition in an open-ended war against subversion. The Slovak *Národné noviny* likewise insisted the attorney general and FBI "quarantine ruthlessly the leprosy of William Randolph Hearst."[89]

The ASC, too, used the coercive language of enforced loyalty to support the win-the-war coalition. After the inaugural Congress, supporters published articles in *Národné noviny* charging, "Various quislings, who mocked or also ignored or boycotted the congress should now ask themselves: 'Am I worthy of the freedoms that this country provides me?'" If such people could not recant their opposition to the ASC and recognize that by so doing they had damaged the U.S. war effort, "then they are not loyal citizens, but traitors to our national government." A second writer argued that critics of the Slav Congress would face the wrath of "these million Slavic workers" who would "work together with the FBI (G-men)" to stifle disloyal critics, who "should stop talking, or we'll notify the G-men about these hopeless Hitlerist Slovaks, who should be turned over to the authorities. Your Hitlerists may not know it, but such talk is 'Fifth Column activity,' treason, which is the most unfaithful thing a citizen can do and worse than the things about which Germany boasts." To distinguish their support for the war from supposedly disloyal conservatives, seventy thousand IWO members in the Slav Congress pledged "the loyal and active support of our membership to our beloved country and to our government and place unreservedly our organization, our labor and our lives at the service and disposal of our country."[90]

The Slav Congress would later laud the government's prosecution of Socialist Workers Party members as "seditionists" under the Smith Act, which broadly criminalized those who wrote or spoke in favor of a change in

America's form of government. During the war militants' advocacy of democracy and right to dissent was lamentably selective.[91]

By pledging "unreserved" loyalty, the Slav Congress and IWO reinforced the government's and public's expectations that citizens should always pledge unreserved loyalty to a government. Demands to punish one's ideological enemies were troubling, but these calls for punishment of "fifth columnists," combined with expressions of loyalty to the government in its prosecution of the war, are ironic, too, considering that the FBI and other agencies were already monitoring the IWO and ASC for alleged subversive activity. By suggesting that the Bill of Rights could be contingent on demonstrations of loyalty and unreserved support for the president in times of national emergency, the IWO and ASC were acceding to the tools that the permanent national security state would vigorously deploy against their own organizations in a few years. In the late 1940s, the Order argued that dissent was a legitimate American tradition. During World War II, however, the IWO did not see it that way and regrettably advocated just such restraints on dissent.

"Yalta Is the Major Issue": Support for Soviet War Aims

The IWO supported, too, Soviet aims for the reorganization of postwar Eastern Europe. While in this regard the Order's leaders may have been overly credulous in believing Moscow's assertions of democratic and peaceful intentions, support for cooperation with the Soviets in rebuilding Europe was in line with official U.S. policy as reflected in agreements worked out at wartime conferences in Teheran and Moscow. The OSS's FNB, tasked with explaining the internecine battles of U.S. ethnic communities to the government, issued a July 1944 report saying the IWO considered "Teheran the key to reorganization." The Order, the FNB agent said, interpreted Teheran to mean support of Russia's policies, especially in the countries of members' origin, as well as doing what they could to preserve favorable American-Russian relations in the postwar world. "More concretely though less openly stated," the agent added, "it signifies support of a position of dominant influence for the USSR in Eastern Europe and a recognized role for the USSR in world affairs on a par with Great Britain and the United States." The IWO supported the Yugoslav partisan leader Tito, offered "praise of Soviet-Czechoslovak collaboration," and critiqued Poland's government in exile. By 1944 all these policies were endorsed by the Roosevelt and Churchill administrations, even if grudgingly; the IWO was not an outlier in these respects.[92]

In rejecting the London government as reactionary, the IWO likewise mirrored the U.S. government, which also favored the Polish partisans cooperating with the Soviets and resettlement of the Polish-Soviet border along the Curzon Line, with Polish territorial compensation in German-held East Prussia. Polish IWO rallies backed the "Polish Patriots" organized as a fighting force in the USSR and derided the exile government as full of reactionaries interfering with active Polish resistance to Nazism. Although such policies angered many Polish Americans, who regarded the territorial dismemberment of their homeland as a betrayal and capitulation to the USSR, the Roosevelt administration championed these policies, and the IWO congratulated Secretary of State Cordell Hull for his role at the Moscow Conference supporting them. The OSS did not seem to notice that the Curzon Line readjustment, which granted a large area of eastern Poland with many Ukrainian residents to the Soviet Union, had already been recommended by the League of Nations twenty years before the IWO supported this stance.[93]

The OSS did acknowledge that the IWO devoted a seemingly inordinate amount of time to a "self-conscious" defense of the USSR during the war but admitted that "on closer analysis" this was due to "psychological and personality factors" rather than a result of "direct communique or 'directives' from Moscow." Thus, the OSS reported that IWO members believed the Soviets had no territorial ambitions aside from the stated adjustments in Eastern Poland, Bukovina, and the Baltics and that it had no desire to permanently occupy other countries such as Czechoslovakia and Hungary. OSS agents also reported that IWO members were certain while the Soviets wanted to make sure no permanent anti-Communist bloc of nations was created after the war, it was uninterested in spreading its Socialist system by any means other than persuasion. These beliefs may have been naïve, but even the OSS admitted they arose out of members' genuine sentiments, not as a result of espionage or control by the Kremlin. IWO members might have desired a Socialist world, but they did not advocate or plot a violent revolution to bring this about. Instead, the OSS reported that it was adherents of the Polish government in exile who were receiving money and directives from London to disseminate propaganda among Polish Americans supportive of the conservative regime of Prime Minister Stanisław Mikołajczyk. One Polish American union official, approached by an agent of the exile government, demurred that the propaganda campaign would be expensive. "Don't worry, there will be a lot of money for this purpose," he was allegedly told. Conservative Poles, not Communists, seem in this instance to have been implicated by the OSS in attempts to interfere in internal U.S. affairs.[94]

As more conservative Polish Americans argued that Poland should retain its eastern territories, the Order's *Fraternal Outlook* defended the justice of the USSR's claim to more secure borders and recounted the history by which Poland's Marshal Józef Piłsudski had repudiated the judgment of the League of Nations for the Curzon Line and forcibly annexed parts of the Ukraine in 1921. The article by the IWO's Edward Falkowski reported on an IWO-initiated conference of Poles meeting in Cleveland that endorsed

Allied support for the Curzon Line and said only reactionary Polish Americans were grumbling about this. In defense of the justness of the Soviet position, Falkowski cited foreign-policy experts such as the *New York Times*' Arthur Krock, who wrote that the Curzon Line had been violated by Polish military invasion, and Walter Lippmann, who in the *New York Herald Tribune* said only the border claimed by the Soviets "has moral standing as a basis of discussion."[95]

Even the *New York Times* echoed this need for Soviet-American postwar cooperation and accommodation of Moscow's security needs. In January 1943 the newspaper published an assessment by Wendell Willkie, the 1940 Republican presidential candidate, of the need to cooperate with Russia following the war to ensure a lasting peace. Moscow's need for dependable countries on its borders that would not seek to undermine the Soviet system had to be supported, and the country's legitimate security needs had to be respected by the United States and other nations. Willkie, who had been a utilities company president before his presidential run but was now serving as Roosevelt's unofficial goodwill ambassador touring Allied nations, stressed, "Russia is a force to be reckoned with. . . . Such a power, such a people, cannot be ignored, nor disposed of with a high hat." Two years later, after the conclusion of the European war, the *Times* again emphasized the need for postwar cooperation with the Soviet ally. Journalist C. L. Sulzberger offered an appraisal of Soviet aims in light of their horrific wartime casualties, "considerably more than 20,000,000 lost to the German war god." Sulzberger detailed the destruction, too, of sizable parts of the Soviet countryside in arguing that Soviet demands for more secure borders and dependable neighbors were justifiable.[96]

When even Republican corporate executives and mainstream journalists defended the Soviet position, one cannot fault the IWO for doing likewise. Following the February 1945 conference at which Roosevelt and Churchill acceded to Stalin's position on the Curzon Line in return for a pledge to allow democratic elections in postwar Poland, Bedacht proclaimed, "Yalta is the major issue." "We must help to turn the current military cooperation of the peoples and nations for victory, into an economic and social cooperation for the construction of a lasting peace and the accomplishment of economic security," he said, echoing non-Communists such as Willkie. In 1945 the Ukrainian Section likewise reported on its "great campaign" that spring to win U.S. support for the Yalta conference's recognition of the new Soviet-Polish border, hailing "the reunion of all Ukrainian lands and people into the Ukrainian Republic."[97] Although more bellicose than Willkie or Sulzberger, IWO members' support for the Soviet position was not an isolated or extreme view at war's end.

Not every American was happy with Yalta, however, or the IWO. As Robert Szymczak has written, conservative Poles were furious with the U.S.

government during the war, and especially after Yalta, for its perceived sellout of the Polish government in exile and accommodation of Soviet demands. While the OSS's FNB seems to have regarded conservative East Europeans as equally troublesome as the IWO, other government officials already watched the Order warily. Only weeks after the European war's conclusion, FBI Director Hoover sent a confidential letter to the State Department on the "Alleged Plans of U.S.S.R. for Control of Europe." According to the director, Gebert of the IWO's Polish Section had been heard to boast that once elections were held in Poland, "Yalta would be a thing of the past" and neither Great Britain nor the United States would enjoy any influence in Eastern Europe. According to a "confidential informant," the director further related, "Gebert declared that . . . Russia intends to handle affairs in all the other European countries, and intends that the United States will have no part in the affairs of Europe."[98] The reliability of Hoover's information is difficult to ascertain, nor is it clear if Gebert was expressing his hopes or beliefs, or if he was actually privy to Moscow inside information. Hoover's communique is an indication, however, of how quickly IWO positions and U.S. government foreign policy diverged.

"All Part of the Imperialist Game": The Cold War

The IWO quickly lost its optimism for a continuation of the wartime alliance. Unlike Hoover, however, many IWO members attributed the rapidly developing enmity to U.S. and British determination to preserve imperial hegemony. In December 1945 the *Jewish Fraternlist* stressed that "America must continue the Roosevelt policies of international collaboration," adding the Soviet Union's program was able to "show all the peoples of the world the road to a life of peace and freedom." Domestic social-democratic advances and racial equality could only flourish in a spirit of enduring international cooperation, the article—and the IWO itself—argued. That same month a speaker at the JPFO's national convention warned of the strained Big Three relations and talked of a coming "third world war." This was due, he said, to America's "embark[ing] on the path of imperialism with the desire to dominate the policies and markets of the world." Great Britain was supported by the United States, too, in "strangling the people's movements in India" and elsewhere, which, the speaker said, was "all part of the imperialist game."[99]

The rapidity with which European powers and the United States reneged on their wartime commitment to the Atlantic Charter right of self-determination for colonized peoples was one of the biggest disappointments for the IWO and Slav Congress, which continued to advocate liberation for African and Asian nations. Both organizations participated in a 1946 Win the Peace Conference, cochaired by Robeson. The conference committed to "maintenance of Big Three unity" and thwarting the "economic royalists" who were already beating "drums of war against the Soviet Union." The conference also passed resolutions asserting that "the colonial peoples everywhere, and the new democracies of Europe, shall be permitted to exercise their right of self-government without outside interference." Specific resolutions called on the United States to foreswear military alliances and bases in Latin America, grant independence to the Philippines and Puerto Rico, and end racial discrimination in the Panama Canal Zone. U.S. support for British and Dutch military action in Indonesia was condemned in a resolution calling on the United States to support independence for Jakarta, "founded on the principle of self-determination." A resolution demanded UN pressure on Great Britain to grant complete independence to India. Another resolution declared, "It is imperative to break the conspiracy of international silence surrounding the question of freedom for the 150 million colonial subjects of Africa, held in bondage. . . . The war-time promise of self-determination for all peoples must be fulfilled in Africa as in every other part of the world." The conference's organizers were certain these measures could avoid further conflict, for, as they declared, "The tree of liberty needs only the sunshine of peace to make it flower; it has been watered with enough blood."[100]

As blood continued to flow, the IWO and Slav Congress continued their commitment to colonial liberation. In 1946 Pirinsky, executive secretary of the Slav Congress, wrote of the unfulfilled promise of the war: "In Indonesia, Indo-China and Greece allied troops mobilized for the defeat of the Axis have been used to shoot down people whose only crime is that they believe in the principles of the Atlantic Charter and are fighting to throw off foreign domination." He said that Slavs who had recently experienced their own homelands' subjugation supported "a forward-looking colonial policy which will enable the so-called backward peoples to emancipate themselves completely from any imperialist domination." The Slav Congress's monthly magazine ran articles by Adamic and Pirinsky advocating independence for colonized peoples in Burma, India, Indonesia, the Congo, and Indochina. Adamic perceptively noted that such struggles were linked with the rising black civil rights movement at home and that both domestic and international liberation struggles had to be supported. "The Negro-White situation here now is part of the color and colonial questions in the world," he declared. The SWS agreed. "Put an end to the exploitation of colonial peoples," ran a cartoon in 1947's *Ľudový kalendár* in which a clueless British lord asks his butler, "What's new in India?" "Everything's the same, your excellency," the butler replies. "In Calcutta they're rebelling, in Delhi strikes, and in Bengal the people are starving to death."[101]

The Order continued to support democratic rights for Asia. In 1954 IWO members were reading defenses of the Indochinese freedom struggle in far-off Vietnam at least a decade before the antiwar cause became popular. The JPFO magazine *Jewish Life* cited Senator Wayne Morse of Oregon, who said,

"What you have to face is that for decades the people of Southeast Asia ... are making it clear that they are going to fight on until there is an end of western domination of southeast Asia." The journal added that the war in Vietnam was "a fight to free that land from colonialism.... Our own country was created in the struggle to throw off colonial domination. We have no business a century and a half later to prevent Asian lands from achieving the same victory." In Detroit IWO Poles similarly heard speeches defending the justness of the Vietnamese freedom struggle.[102]

Gore has documented the extent to which radical African Americans in the early Cold War era linked the domestic civil rights struggle to a commitment to colonial liberation abroad. African American figures in the IWO such as Robeson and Thompson Patterson were at the forefront of efforts to champion freedom struggles in Africa, the Caribbean, India, and elsewhere and in the 1950s continued these campaigns in new organizations such as the Sojourners for Truth and Justice, the CAA, and *Freedom* magazine. In 1952 Thompson Patterson engaged in a campaign through the Sojourners urging the United States and UN to condemn South Africa's system of apartheid. The Sojourners, who were supported by the IWO's Emma Lazarus Division, also sent letters of support to ANC women organizing peaceful anti-apartheid campaigns in Durban, Johannesburg, and other cities. Robeson, too, condemned the continuing colonialism through his work with the CAA. He declared, "Ho Chi Minh is the Toussaint L'Ouverture of Indo-China," referencing the liberator from earlier French colonialism in Haiti. Robeson spoke as early as 1955 on "Our Disgrace in Indo-China," asking, "Shall Negro sharecroppers from Mississippi be sent to shoot down brown-skinned peasants in Vietnam—to serve the interests of those who oppose Negro liberation at home and colonial freedom abroad?" African American activists from the IWO carried the cause of colonial liberation into the 1950s.[103]

But what should be remembered, too, is the militant white members in the IWO and Slav Congress who also made this international connection and combated Jim Crow at home and racist colonialism abroad. While most Slavic, Italian, Jewish, and other white ethnics of this era thought little of the fate of colonized Africans or Asians, the IWO and Slav Congress were supporting liberation movements around the globe.

"Anglo-Saxon Crusade against the Soviet Union"

If most American policy makers were uninterested in supporting colonized peoples' independence movements, after World War II it was also soon apparent that Washington was rapidly expressing a new coolness toward the Soviet Union. Members of the IWO were not alone in noticing how quickly many Americans and Britons turned hostile toward their erstwhile ally. In the summer and fall of 1945, *Národné noviny* reported that Assistant Secretary of State Sumner Welles said Great Britain already advocated rearming Germany as a defense against the alleged Soviet threat, and ex-prime minister Churchill was warning of a "red menace" to Eastern Europe, just nine days after war with Japan had concluded. The same day that *Národné noviny* reported Churchill's call for a "new defense" against the Soviet threat, the paper noted a ceremony at Philadelphia's Slovak Hall honoring the fifty million Slavic victims of "German barbarism."[104]

The IWO mobilized to resist the remilitarization of the United States, Great Britain, and Western Europe, which it perceived as a betrayal of the plans for postwar Big Three cooperation and bellicose attempts to marginalize the Soviet Union. When Churchill made his "Iron Curtain" speech alleging Soviet plans to dominate all of Eastern Europe and calling for an Anglo-American alliance to defeat this drive, the IWO termed the speech the opening salvo in World War III and a resuscitation of a "military-fascist system of 20th-century enslavement," an "Anglo-Saxon crusade against the Soviet Union."[105]

As the British and Americans reintegrated West Germany into the anti-Communist bloc of nations, the Polonia Society called on its lodges to work energetically "against the reconstruction of militaristic and imperialistic Germany." The Slav Congress, too, in 1951 noted the rehabilitation of former Wehrmacht officers and the rearming of West Germany as threats to peace, telegramming Truman in outrage at America's "freeing the Nazi beasts who murdered our GI's and tortured and killed millions of our Slav kin who fought so bravely for our common victory over Nazi Germany." IWO members on the Slav Congress's board signed this telegram denouncing the freeing of Nazis such as General Franz Halder and Ilse Koch and demanded "the punishment of those responsible for the brazen leniency towards Nazi war criminals and . . . cartelists who paved the way for Hitler's aggression."[106]

The *New York Times* noted the rapidity with which former Nazi officials were placed in positions of authority regarding education, military affairs, and other matters. The rearmament and reemergence of industrial cartels alarmed the *New York Post* and, the newspaper reported, the Soviet Union, too. By 1951 *U.S. New and World Report* published an interview with a German military expert on how the Soviet Union could be defeated. The expert was Colonel General Heinz Guderian of Hitler's Wehrmacht, and his advice was to rearm Germany and allow it to invade the Soviet Union. Under such circumstances it was perhaps understandable that IWO members rallied for German disarmament under the theme "No Truck with Hitler's Heirs."[107]

The proclamation of the Truman Doctrine in support of authoritarian Greek and Turkish governments allegedly fighting against Communist takeover was likewise denounced by the IWO as an attempted "cordon sanitaire" around the Soviet Union and the imposition of an "American Century" in which Wall Street and the Pentagon would dictate to the world. The Slovak and Polish Sections lobbied against aid to Greece and the Marshall Plan as measures bypassing the UN and the Soviet Union and, in the case of aid to Greece, assistance to a military dictatorship brutally suppressing its left-wing opponents in a civil war. The IWO backed the American Council for a Democratic Greece protesting U.S. military aid for the monarchy. The JPFO vehemently denounced the slaughter of partisans, who a few years before had been the most determined allies in resisting German and Italian occupation of their homeland. "Today we stand aghast and alarmed at the turn of events which swerves America from the road of wartime unity with our allies towards the disaster of World War III," the JPFO declared, citing the chief rabbi of Athens as lauding the partisans, now targets of Truman's military hardware.[108]

The IWO's Hellenic American Brotherhood condemned the slaughter in members' homeland. "Civilized people the world over are shocked and enraged by the criminal execution of hundreds of Greek anti-fascist patriots by the firing squads of the monarcho-fascist Athens regime," the brotherhood announced. "Since the institution of the Truman Doctrine in Greece, the slaughter and oppression of the Greek people has become the most serious problem of the American people first, and of the entire civilized world." Citing the execution of "more than 1,400 heroic fighters for democracy, including women and priests," the brotherhood declared, "These crimes must be stopped." The IWO demonstrated at the Greek consulate in New York, but the United States continued to provide military aid for the partisans' suppression.[109]

Other IWO sections argued that a more materialistic motive than support for "freedom" undergirded the extension of military aid to Greece and Turkey. HUAC noted that *Glos Ludowy*, the newspaper of the Polonia Society, stated, "Aiding these two undemocratic governments has an objective with an 'oily touch,' to hold the middle east pools grabbed by English and American companies." The Slav Congress reprinted *New York Post* editorials that cited the exponential growth of American military ventures. The *Slavic American* quoted the *Post*'s condemnation of U.S. militarism in Greece, China, Turkey, and other parts of the world, musing, "We are exporters of death to parts of the world which have only corpses for export; fear and hate have so unseated our reason that we no longer have patience enough to examine the problems or to find the honest answers. Bullets have become our cure-all; the patent-medicine on which we rely for the solution of every difficulty."[110]

The IWO and the Slav Congress also condemned the United States for allowing many European refugees with unsavory wartime records to enter the country as displaced persons (DPs). In September 1946 the Order's General Council passed a "Resolution on Quisling Immigration" that opposed the increasing immigration of "reactionary, quisling and fascist elements from American and British zones of occupation in Europe." The council urged the administration to halt this trend and called on the IWO's ethnic societies to compile data and documentary evidence on the wartime records of potential immigrants. The council pressured the government to establish a civilian screening committee "truly reflecting the anti-fascist, democratic viewpoint of the majority of American people, which shall be in charge of screening in DP camps . . . in order to weed out open fascists and war criminals and send them back to their own countries." Camps should stop hiding fascists masquerading as DPs, and the IWO demanded "democratic" ethnic societies in the United States be consulted on the admission of refugees.[111]

Six months later Milgrom told the council, "Fascist elements among the Croatians, Ukrainians, Serbians, Romanians, [and] Poles, who openly and flagrantly betrayed our country during the war, are today honored guests of our State Department. Thousands of fascists who fought side by side with Hitler, today receive honorable admission to America." Local lodges noticed the welcome given to former Nazis even as they complained about the long delays Jewish refugees faced in emigrating to the United States. *The Patriot*, newsletter of JPFO Haym Solomon Lodge in Philadelphia, recounted how more than one hundred scientists who had worked for the Nazi war machine were now being admitted to assist the U.S. military; it also reported on Congressman Adolph Sabath's questioning "why we allow not only these scientists who worked for Hitler, but Nazi maneuverers and entrepreneurs to come into this country, too?"[112]

Decades later the Nazi or fascist collaborationist past of some 1940s entrants would be exposed, and several people would be deported to their European homelands for trial, but immediately following World War II the IWO and Slav Congress were lone voices condemning the admission of such people. Perhaps not coincidentally, as Chapter 6 shows, in the ten years after World War II, the United States also actively pursued deportation cases against many of the group's members whose leftist and trade-union backgrounds ran afoul of the government's Cold War policy. In 1947 South Philadelphia's JPFO pointed out the hypocrisy of deporting people for their political opinions while welcoming Nazi scientists into the country.[113]

Even as they were labeled subversive organizations, the IWO and Slav Congress continued to denounce the lenient emigration policy for rightists. "The doors of America are flung wide open to some of the worst fascist and pro-fascist scum of Europe," Pirinsky of the Slav Congress complained. The experience of Chicago IWO members illustrates the differential treatment authorities afforded to left- and right-wing immigrants by 1949 as well as the deepening political rift in many East European communities over issues of communism and fascism. A Lithuanian IWO meeting, called to offer support to the editor of the leftist newspaper *Vilnis*, who was facing deportation, was taken over by force by a group of two hundred Lithuanians, mostly recently arrived DPs. They "proceeded to conduct the meeting by singing fascist songs and shouting fascist phrases in Lithuanian." It took an hour for the IWO to persuade Chicago police to come to the scene, and when officers arrived they said there was nothing they could do about the intruders, so the meeting had to be disbanded. Soon after, the letter writer reported, "the fascist Lithuanians marched out in storm trooper fashion."[114]

Use of the epithet "scum" to refer to right-wing DPs, now rechristened by the State Department reliable anti-Communists, was regarded by officials as evidence of the organization's subversive nature, but leftists remained unrepentant. Shipka cited "speeches and articles in the *Fraternal Outlook* concerning the Truman Doctrine, the Marshall Plan, articles which express great concern over the drive to war, and propose that in the interests of America and world peace, our country shall negotiate with the Soviet Union and settle all outstanding differences." He added, "These quotations prove further that we expressed opinions against bringing to this country fascist scum, and giving them a free hand to poison the nationality groups of America with the irresponsibly criminal idea of 'Throw the atom bomb now!' So we did write this. What's wrong with it?" Of course, by 1951 the government had developed amnesia about the pro-Hitler collaboration of Ukrainian DPs to whom Shipka was referring ("whitewashed into democratic saints" was the phrase he used). During the Korean War, though, IWO criticism of America's expanding Pentagon budget and atomic arsenal was deemed impermissible.[115]

Several IWO officials made postwar tours of Eastern Europe and declared that they found no evidence of an aggressive war machine, but rather countries rebuilding from the devastating war. Saltzman reported in the *Fraternal Outlook*, "After everything I saw in Europe, the lie of the war propaganda in America—which implies that there is a threat to the security of the U.S.—stands exposed as the biggest hoax of the century." As Frank Kofsky has documented, the war scare talk disseminated by Truman and his cabinet in 1947–1948 was based on a very selective, sometimes fabricated reading of his own military and embassy officials' less alarmist dispatches. Analysts told the administration that while the Soviet Union was economically devastated and stood little genuine military threat to the United States, there was at least a theoretical possibility that by ignoring all civilian rebuilding the Soviets could devote all their resources to mounting a credible military threat sometime in the next decade or more. In selling to Congress a national emergency that necessitated the Truman Doctrine and Marshall Plan, and an exponential growth in military spending, the president and his aides cherry-picked dispatches to turn these diplomatic caveats into proof of the certain existential threat the Soviets posed to freedom itself. As Truman's old Senate friends told the president, in order to sell the Marshall Plan to Congress, he had to scare hell out of the American people. He did.[116]

Pirinsky similarly condemned the establishment of NATO, wondering how long the United States would stand for it "if the Soviet Union were forging military alliances with Canada, Mexico and Cuba, and were arming them to protect themselves from the United States!"[117] A dozen years later, when Soviet missile bases were discovered being built in Cuba, Pirinsky had his answer.

Convinced that Cold War saber rattling was leading toward atomic warfare, the IWO committed to the 1950 Stockholm Peace Conference. President Kent and JPFO president Albert Kahn attended the conference, which pledged to outlaw the A- and H-bombs and declared "the first to use these hellish weapons will be branded as war criminals." Kent argued in an open letter to the IWO that "the unhampered continuation of the Cold War" would lead "toward its inevitable climax—the atomic holocaust." The Polonia Society and other IWO sections gathered signatures for the Stockholm Peace Pledge and hailed the millions of signatures collected in Communist Poland. The Polonia Society's *Glos Ludowy* ran the text of the Stockholm appeal outlawing the first use of atomic weapons and provided instructions on where to send petitions. Expressing a kind of one-worldism increasingly out of favor in Cold War America, the Polonia Society passed a resolution pledging, "On our part, we promise to support the Stockholm appeal, as we do not wish that Chicago, New York and Pittsburgh or Warsaw, Cracow, Wrocław and Łódź be destroyed by the atomic bomb."[118]

As Marian Mollin has demonstrated, fear of atomic war was prevalent in postwar America and hastened the development of a broad, grassroots peace movement containing many constituents besides Communists. The IWO released a letter from a nine-year-old New York student, who wrote, "Ever since I've heard about the Hydrogen Bomb over the radio and heard the terrible things that could happen to the people and to the cities if it were dropped . . . I wonder if it is worth studying my lessons and planning for the future. . . . I would like to know if there is going to be a future for us."[119] These were the kinds of uncomfortable questions that by 1950 the IWO was stridently asking as it sought a more peaceful foreign policy of international cooperation, demilitarization, and support for anticolonial freedom movements.

Such questioning of America's foreign-policy direction in a time of permanent militarization, preparedness for a global war that never quite arrived, was the final impermissible act that earned the IWO the labels "un-American" and "subversive." The IWO had already enraged many conservatives by forcefully advocating for strong unions and more equitable social policies as well as racial equality. Postwar advocacy of a more peaceful, cooperative foreign policy, one that did not rely on a military response to all disagreements, simply added to these "crimes." The IWO was about to learn how narrow the parameters were for permissible dissent in an America on permanent state of wartime alert.

6

"A Fraternal Order Sentenced to Death!"

Government Suppression

At the end of 1947, the IWO was struck by a thunderbolt. Attorney General Clark released a list of organizations that the federal government labeled subversive. Ostensibly, the Attorney General's List of Subversive Organizations was to be used solely to determine the loyalty of federal government employees; however, members of enumerated organizations, even those not employed in government service, were soon targeted by other agencies such as the INS and Internal Revenue Service (IRS) and faced punitive action by private employers, landlords, and municipal governments. Mechanisms for disciplining and punishing those deemed subversive were hydra-headed—an open-ended, self-perpetuating campaign of harassment and intimidation developed in which each official sanction was used to justify another punitive measure. By March 1948 the Attorney General's List expanded to include 196 organizations, including the IWO and all "its subdivisions, subsidiaries and affiliates" such as the Polonia Society, SWS, and Douglass-Lincoln Society of black members. For the IWO this marked the beginning of a seven-year-long, state-sanctioned execution.[1]

The branding of the IWO as subversive, which came with no explanation or evidence as to how such a determination had been made, seems to have genuinely come as a shock to its officers. Kent, Shipka, and Milgrom penned a joint letter to all members, declaring "the Attorney-General committed an act that might well be considered a new Pearl Harbor against the civil rights of the American people." The officers said, "Without hearing or warning, the Attorney-General, Tom Clark, took it upon himself to question the loyalty of our Order," and they reassured members that legal steps were being taken to lift the designation. Saying the "insult against our organization cannot go by unchallenged," the officers called on the "dear members" who "know best through your daily activities the loyalty and devotion you and your organization have displayed in the service of our country" to defend the Order and thereby preserve "the democratic way of life and freedom of association, secure from 'police-state' interference." They urged every lodge to adopt a resolution denouncing the list and to send copies to Clark as well as congressmen and senators; lodges were also asked to enlist members who were veterans to publicly declare their opposition to this violation of the freedoms for which they had fought. The tenor of these minutes, as well as the letter quickly answering Clark's subversive designation, suggests that leaders of the IWO were genuinely outraged to find themselves the recipients of stigmatization.[2]

Local units took up the leadership's challenge. The FBI noted that the Order's "Reaction to Subversive Listing" included articles in the Polonia Society's newspaper denouncing "the despotic and scandalous declaration by the Attorney General." *Romanul American*, organ of the Romanian Section, echoed the national leadership's denunciation of Clark's "Pearl Harbor against the liberties of the American people." Romanian Section president George Vocila reassured the Romanians that the IWO had secured an injunction to block implementation of the list and was "determined to take legal action against any newspaper which in any illegal way may write something detrimental to our organization or its members." Vocila declared that Clark's list "means to borrow a page from the Nazi and Fascist book." In June 1948 the Poles' *Glos Ludowy* called IWO members to attend "Protection of American Liberties" rallies in ten cities. Ethnic societies were instructed by Secretary Milgrom to write to "trade union leaders, professionals, scientists" and other ethnic elite to solicit support for the IWO's defense. One such leader, Congressman Marcantonio, was in an advantageous position to make his displeasure known. This IWO vice president read into the *Congressional Record* a denunciation of the attorney general's action, which "denies every element of democratic procedure and fair play." "The IWO has proven its loyalty with deeds," he declared.[3]

Less well-placed members agreed. A nineteen-year postal employee from Brooklyn who was a member of the JPFO wanted to know what the IWO was doing to fight the subversive designation, as the government's loyalty investigations would target her, especially as she had held numerous offices in her lodge. She wrote the IWO's national office that she could not imperil her post office pension but nevertheless wanted to remain loyal to the IWO and needed to know "does the national IWO plan to fight this attack upon itself? I am not the only one looking for an answer to this question," noting "members in our lodge have already dropped out because of the scare."[4]

In smaller communities tensions between those determined to fight against Clark and "the Fascist regime of the Un-American Committee" and those fearing for their safety and livelihood was even greater. An Italian secretary from New Kensington, Pennsylvania, wrote the Garibaldi Society's national secretary, "What with this hunt of the 'reds,' I had another half dozen members who refused to pay because they were afraid." The writer added, "Let us hope that 1948 will be the year of World Progressivism. Only then will we have Peace, Liberty and Work." Vito Magli replied that the dedication of members such as the secretary guaranteed that "Clark will not easily get away with it. Our members are honest people who have seen us and know well who we are, and how near to our heart their interests are."[5]

For every member cowed into silence, another stepped up to condemn the list. In February 1948 one JPFO lodge sent a blistering letter to Clark promising his distortion of facts and "violation of the constitutional rights of all free peoples . . . shall not go unanswered." Reciting the racial and ethnic egalitarianism of the IWO, as well as its war-service record, the petitioners said, "We do not expect medals for our deeds, these things were done, because we are, and shall always be in the midst of the fight, to preserve our Democratic Ideals, which you have seen fit to abuse." The petitioners urged Clark to live up to the ideals of Lincoln, Jefferson, and Roosevelt, the Constitution and Bill of Rights, and become a good American. The language of un-Americanism was flipped against Clark by unrepentant JPFO members, who demanded a "public apology."[6]

For such avid defenders of the IWO, the national office published speaker's guides explaining "Loyalty Order Violates Constitution." Members were reminded "The IWO Battles for Tomorrow" by teaching its Junior Branch children the principles of American democracy and training them to emulate Lincoln, Jefferson, and Douglass. "Who can question the loyalty of leaders who teach the children these things?" the Junior Branch guide asked. It was suggested lodges add "Democracy Hours" to their programs in which children could study the principles of the Constitution and Bill of Rights. Along these lines, in December 1947 the IWO issued a press release celebrating Bill of Rights Day, pointedly noting that regarding the Subversive Organizations List, historian Henry Steele Commager had commented, "What do men know of loyalty who make a mockery of the Declaration of Independence and the Bill of Rights?"[7] IWO activities in the wake of the Order's branding as subversive suggest a heartfelt sense of aggrieved surprise and indignation that their type of progressive Americanism could be called into question. Responses to the subversive listing indicate that by 1947 many members were convinced they had won a place in the American mainstream, which they believed was capacious enough to contain racially egalitarian progressives.

Perhaps the renewal of red-hunting season should not have come as such a shock. As noted, many of the campaigns of the IWO were scrupulously recorded by FBI agents turning the state's panopticon on them. The Order was the subject of official anti-Communist scrutiny well before Clark compiled his list, surveillance of which many IWO officers were warily cognizant. Indeed, while by late 1947 many officers and grassroots members believed they were legitimate and accepted components of a progressive American social order, if they had reflected on earlier episodes they might have recalled that their organization had often been the subject of hostile government interrogation. Only a few years earlier speakers had warned of the despotism capitalist legislatures and courts frequently levied against a people's fraternal society. Following World War II, Order members had seemingly accepted the permanency of a cooperationist coalition on the Left of American politics and had forgotten their own warnings of the suppression often visited on workers' organizations. When Cold War prosecutions began, the IWO's amnesia left it alarmed and vulnerable to what it cast as red-hunters' "un-American" ways.

"Like Caesar's Wife": Above Suspicion

If they had reflected on the IWO's own not-so-distant run-ins with the coercive forces of state suppression, Order members might not have been so surprised. As early as June 1932, Saltzman sent out a letter warning of the pernicious effects of the Dies bill, which provided for the deportation of a foreign-born resident who "believes in, advises, advocates or teaches the overthrow by force or violence the Government of the United States." Saltzman saw this measure as "the highest mark of vicious anti-foreign born legislation" as well as a criminalization of thought, pointing out that mere belief in a different form of government was sufficient to begin deportation. He urged IWO members to act to ensure this "white terror legislation" sponsored by Texas congressman Dies, later chair of the HUAC, would not pass.[8]

Saltzman saw the Dies bill as an assault on the working class, and he was right to worry. As Buff and Kanstroom both document, the wide latitude afforded the INS, and the later Smith Act's broad definition of advocacy of forcible change of government to include belief, speech, and writing in favor of almost any alteration to the free-market status quo, meant deportation proceedings were often instituted against militant trade unionists.[9] Indeed, Gebert, later president of the IWO's Polonia Society, was ordered deported in 1931 after his conviction in Illinois on criminal-syndicalist charges for daring to speak in support of a coal miners' strike. Although Gebert had been under surveillance since 1919 for his inflammatory anticapitalist speeches, his crimes were those of speech and thought, not revolutionary or violent actions. Gebert's deportation was never implemented, but when he voluntarily returned to Poland in 1947 the government's criminalization of his union activity still hung over his head. IWO Secretary Milgrom, too, had been ordered deported in 1935, although to a country refusing to take him, so this order sat in abeyance until reactivated during 1951's red scare.[10]

Organizers for the IWO encountered state suppression when they sought to enroll workers. In 1934 Thompson reported to the national office that black people in New Orleans were wary of the IWO after the red scare was reported in the black press, and members she had enrolled dropped out. That year, too, raids were conducted by Birmingham and Atlanta police on the homes of black people who had joined the IWO. Thompson was jailed in Birmingham after she visited a meeting of striking miners during her IWO recruiting work in that city. She was furious with the coverage of her arrest in the Communist press, as this made it even more difficult to convince Alabama's African Americans to join the Order. The enormity of the potential dangers facing an African American organizer, or member, of the IWO in 1930s Alabama may be gauged by the fact that Thompson was interrogated by Eugene "Bull" Connor, who nearly thirty years later became infamous for his brutal suppression of civil rights activists. On her arrest, Thompson, who evidently could pass for a white person, was told by one Alabama police officer, "You know, the only thing wrong with these communists is they just like niggers too well." Suppression by the protectors of private property, and Jim Crow segregation, was not unknown by early IWO activists.[11]

By the mid-1930s miners such as those Thompson had supported were long familiar with state suppression, and even as some turned to the IWO they acknowledged the retribution authorities visited on them for speaking and acting against the status quo. Albert Fenely, an IWO member from Wendel, West Virginia, who was also active in his UMW local, informed Browder and other comrades that the company check weighman was taking down names of all noncitizen miners and that after the election local Democrats were going to take steps to deport them. Those active in the UMW were especially prone to deportation. He documented cases in his town in which fathers had been deported while their American-born wives and children remained behind, stories of family separation that would grow more frequent during the Cold War years. "Is that a humanity," Fenely asked of these family separations. "That's monstrous hell." Fenely sent a check in aid of the SWS and began subscribing to the SWS newspaper but cautioned that his mail should not be sent to Wendel as the company's agents monitored the mails. He instead gave a name and address in another town where letters should be sent. Foreign-born union activists and members of the IWO had to tread cautiously in deportation-prone 1930s America.[12]

More systemic threats to the IWO emerged. In July 1938 the organization was informed by the Massachusetts Commissioner of Insurance that he was refusing to renew their insurance license. The announcement came after an investigation by a committee of the legislature indicated that "the activities of the International Workers Order have definitely been of a Communistic nature." The commissioner reminded the IWO that in 1935 the Order had been granted its insurance license "with the understanding that neither the national organization nor any of its branches in Massachusetts will take part in Communistic activities and this shall be the ground of revoking the Order's license if it found that the Order indulges in such activities." Because he believed the IWO had ignored this promise, the commissioner peremptorily ordered it to stop conducting business in his state. Bedacht characterized the notice as one of the ways "reaction threatens our Order."[13]

General Counsel Brodsky offered more reassuring news. He was happy to report that the supreme court in Boston indicated it "would give no weight to the original letter issued by the Commissioner in 1935, which accompanied our original license. . . . The statute provides what a fraternal must do to get a license . . . the Commissioner cannot therefore add new conditions." The ruling that compliance with the business and actuarial stipulations for conducting insurance would govern the IWO's hearing, not the supposed political beliefs of officers, was an important victory, one that, thirteen years later, would not govern a similar court hearing in New York. As to the alleged "Communist political activities" of the Order, the Boston judge bluntly asked Massachusetts officials, "Do you mean that the I.W.O. cannot engage in Communistic activities but may engage in Democratic or Republican activities?" Six months later the court indeed cleared the IWO, ruling no corporate funds had been used for improper political activity and thus the Order was entitled to its Bay State insurance license.[14]

Brodsky, however, recognized his organization had narrowly avoided sanction and cautioned, "Our organization, like Caesar's wife, must be above all suspicion." The Massachusetts case, and a similar 1938 examination by the New York State Insurance Department, ended well. Brodsky was particularly cheered by the favorable outcome in New York, "where we happen to have at the present time a rather intelligent and liberal Insurance Department." In New York, he said, "We argued that while we were not a political organization . . . we nevertheless did have the right to interest ourselves in those issues which face all the people of this country—social security, a health program, etc." After much argument, New York insurance officials granted this point, and all talk of "communistic activity" was dropped. Still, the IWO's lawyer prophetically warned, "Danger signals . . . have been hoisted; let us pay attention to them." Brodsky cautioned that all collections must be scrupulously accounted for, and IWO publications had to make sure overtly political content or calls endorsing specific candidates were excluded. Only then could the IWO avoid pernicious scrutiny from Insurance Department officials, who often, he said, "hate our guts."[15] By the time the late 1947 round of red-baiting began, Brodsky had passed away, and the IWO, grown comfortable in its alleged place in a progressive American coalition, had seemingly forgotten his warning.

The IWO soon faced an even graver assault. The new HUAC under Dies launched an investigation of an extensive list of "alien" groups, the IWO among them. HUAC argued that the IWO was "possibly one of the most effective and closely knitted organizations among the Communist 'front' organizations," delivering its damning report in January 1939. The Order's support for Communist candidates for office, participation in "left-wing strikes" and recruitment of "foreign and radical elements" as well as Bedacht's leadership roles in the CP were offered as proof of the IWO's nefarious purposes.[16]

The IWO did not take HUAC's attacks lying down. The FBI noted that Vice President Middleton told a January 1939 Detroit meeting that while the Order had once been regarded as radical, un-American, and unpatriotic, he asserted, "Those who are against us are against progress, they are not Americans. We are the real patriots and the real Americans." Italian lodges held anti–Dies Committee rallies and circulated petitions denouncing its work. An East Harlem lodge demanded the Order's vice president, Marcantonio, turn the tables on Dies and begin an investigation of his committee, which "has behaved very suspiciously." They urged Marcantonio to "unmask their work." The lodge participated in a mass meeting "against the Dies Committee, for the New Deal," that was endorsed by the United Italian Committees of Harlem, suggesting the depth of anti-red-baiting animus in some ethnic communities.[17]

The IWO's monthly magazine, the *Fraternal Outlook*, ran exposés on "The Threat to Civil Liberties" posed by Dies. An article by Peter Morell was accompanied by a William Gropper cartoon of an evil top-hatted millionaire shredding the Bill of Rights: "Speaking of 'Un-American Activities,'" ran the caption (Figure 6.1). Dies was characterized as one of the "aspiring tin-horn fascists" who sought "to abridge the Bill of Rights." Morell saw Dies's committee as a plot to discredit the New Deal, and indeed, the Texas congressman held well-publicized hearings denouncing the WPA and federal theater program. Morell noted that after IWO officers such as Bedacht testified for more than four hours, all that was revealed was that "lo and behold, . . . the I.W.O. was a progressive, fraternal organization which welcomes all people into its membership regardless of their race, political creed or color." The following month the *Fraternal Outlook* published an article in Slovak wondering if there would soon be "Concentration Camps in America?" The article discussed "the threat of reactionary congressmen to the Bill of Rights," citing Congressman Sam Hobbs's bill with its proposed internment of foreign-born residents and Virginian Howard Smith's proposal to criminalize a wide manner of belief, speech, or writing that advocated a forceful change of government as well as plans to deport all foreigners in radical organizations.[18]

Despite Morell's praise of Bedacht's courageous testimony, the general secretary remained pessimistic about the threat the Order faced. "Congress

Figure 6.1 The *Fraternal Outlook* showed its opposition to HUAC with a William Gropper illustration of an opponent shredding the Bill of Rights.

Source: William Gropper illustration, in Peter Morell, "The Threat to Civil Liberties," *Fraternal Outlook*, November 1939, 5, IWO-CU, box 48.

is in a fair way to add to the division of our government: Legislative, Executive, Judiciary and a fourth one, fascist propaganda," he told a January 1940 meeting, "by perpetuating the arch-reactionary Dies Committee. Everything steers toward silencing and hogtying the American people into helplessness."[19]

Bedacht's virulent labeling of Dies's committee a "fascist" threat to American liberties was typical of the strident rhetoric employed by the IWO in denouncing its ideological foes. But perhaps in this case warnings were not so overwrought. In April 1940 agents of the Dies Committee raided the Philadelphia offices of the IWO, carting off a truck full of all manner of records including the names, addresses, and insurance policy information of Pennsylvania members. The impounded material sat in a Philadelphia warehouse after local IWO and CP officials filed suit against the Dies Committee, demanding the return of the confiscated material. A month later a federal judge ruled that the raid had indeed violated the IWO's rights, although he deferred on whether the seized records had to be returned immediately.[20]

To secure its papers as well as its rights, the IWO orchestrated a series of "Stop Dies" rallies enlisting speakers from an extensive group of progressive organizations such as the CIO, AFL, and ACLU. The *Daily Worker* reported on rallies in San Francisco, Los Angeles, and Jersey City; while the Communist newspaper reported that the Jersey City rally was addressed by Bedacht, who made no secret of his Party membership, it also noted that the CIO's regional director "call[ed] upon the people to stop Dies by building 'a labor movement strong enough to elect its own people to both Houses of Congress. That is the only way in which we will get real democracy in America.'" In San Francisco, California lieutenant governor Ellis Patterson urged the audience of a thousand to stop Dies's witch hunts. Patterson declared, "A man in public office who is not called a 'red' these days is not worthy of holding public office." Perhaps Patterson, a New Deal Democrat, was gratified by the inadvertent compliment paid to him when a witness before the Dies Committee labeled the Californian a "Communist."[21] Whatever Dies thought of Patterson, he was part of a broad spectrum of progressives that felt comfortable appearing at IWO anti-Dies rallies, perhaps because they saw the glibness with which the congressman deployed the epithet "Communist" as the real threat to democracy.

Such public rallies, in which more mainstream albeit progressive figures offered support to the IWO's court case, offered morale-boosting solidarity to grassroots members. Brooklyn's Tom Mooney Lodge 817 held an anti-Dies rally in the Bensonhurst section that attracted national secretary Thompson as well as speakers from the Communist-affiliated Fur Workers union and ILD, but also a representative of the ACLU. Public solidarity only thinly covered private anxiety, however. The Detroit Police Department's red squad, which seems to have shared information quite liberally with the FBI and other federal agencies, reported on a lodge meeting at which the Michigan district secretary and the energetic Thompson urged the lodge to have its group picture taken for publication in the *Fraternal Outlook*. Several members thought it was a good idea, but others hesitated. Nick DeKold worried that the Dies Committee might obtain the picture and said, "I wouldn't want them to get hold of my picture nor Angelo Gucci's picture for anything." He added, "We have jobs to protect." An undercover police agent reported that a black woman, "who claims to be a Socialist, said she didn't think that we, the IWO, had anything to worry about from the Dies Committee as our officials had gone before them and told them who we were." But when the lodge voted on whether to take the picture, only two voted yes, eight said no, and ten abstained. DeKold's anxiety that a lodge photograph might be captured in anti-Communists' panopticon swayed his brothers and sisters. That his fears were recorded in an undercover report to the Detroit police's Office of the Special Investigation Squad, suggests, too, that IWO members had good reason to suspect ubiquitous state repression.[22]

A Philadelphia judge eventually allowed the IWO to examine the seized records, records the *Daily Worker* argued were "essential to the proper operation and function of the business of [the Order]." Bedacht wrote to members of Congress urging them to rein in the Dies Committee, although the answers he received were not always helpful. Michigan Republican Clare Hoffman asked Bedacht, "Why not devote some of your energy and resources in an effort to insure liberty to the average American citizen as well as to the Communistic and subversive groups?" Marcantonio's response was, not surprisingly, more encouraging. Bedacht forwarded to Marcantonio a copy of the telegram he sent to Dies rejecting the congressman's assertion in the *New York Sun*, "If the International Workers Order has nothing to hide, then they will come in now and surrender those records and invite their publication." Bedacht replied that he would not accede in Dies's creation of a political blacklist, adding that when HUAC's agents raided the Philadelphia offices they had also seized such nefarious items as an American flag and "lantern slides on [the] life of Abraham Lincoln and other subjects." "We will never help you to persecute, to hound and to blacklist innocent people by volunteering to turn over names to your committee," Bedacht told Dies, adding, "Your statements intending to prove your vigilance in guarding Americanism would sound much more convincing if you yourself would respect the Constitution of the United States . . . instead of acting as an anti-labor propagandist."[23]

While the IWO regained control of its Philadelphia records, Dies's HUAC continued fishing for the organization's records. The FBI revealed that HUAC was still pursuing the Order's internal records the following year, noting, "The Dies Committee had subpoenaed the Michigan Commissioner of Insurance to furnish lists of names and addresses of IWO members." The IWO labeled this "an attempt to intimidate and terrorize labor unions and branded such activities as illegal and un-American." A federal judge sitting in Philadelphia had already concurred with the branding of such tactics illegal, if not exactly "un-American," but evidently this judicial decision did not forestall Dies's activities targeting the Order.[24]

More troublesome news came in the spring of 1941 when the national office asked lodge secretaries to respond to a questionnaire assessing membership drives and social and recreational activities. Secretaries were invited to offer "general remarks," broadly including "any of the problems of the life and activities of your lodge," and many respondents cited the deleterious effects of the Dies investigations. A Bronx secretary blamed "the critical times we live in" for his local's drop in membership. His lodge offered "the same and even better" activities as in previous years, but members stayed away "because many of them are afraid we are a communist organization." In Atlantic City the secretary reported there was "no activity" partly because members were targeted by the district attorney "as communists, and since they are small business men, they have to be very careful." The secretary of a Denver Jewish lodge mused, "There is no denying that the propaganda in the capitalist press against anything that is progressive has had a detrimental effect on the attitude of the average man or woman on the street. The red scare has made a good many otherwise fairminded persons crawl into their 'shell.'" He admitted, "Our hall has the name of being red and there are many who are simply afraid to go there," although the situation was better for Denver's Jewish lodge than among Russian and English lodges.[25]

Similarly, Elia Vitanoff of Madison, Illinois, wrote the national office that a man identifying himself as an FBI agent had shown up to investigate his branch. It is not surprising, then, that people interested in joining the Order such as a woman from Paterson, New Jersey, wrote with concerns she had been "told that this organization has communistic affiliations."[26] Who told her this was unclear, but newspaper reports documented the exploits of Dies, the FBI, and other investigators.

Still, for all the fears of red-hunting congressmen, as noted in Chapter 5, during World War II the IWO gained acceptance as part of a broad-based progressive coalition to a far greater degree than during the Depression, or than would be the case following the war. In such a win-the-war milieu, the Dies Committee's activities may have seemed like a minority view, the annoying remnants of a disappearing intolerance.[27]

This belief may particularly have been the case since the actions of other government officials seemed to lend legitimacy to the IWO and other progressive organizations such as the ASC. Paul McNutt, director of the War Manpower Commission, praised the Slav Congress in an address at the organization's inaugural convention, while Secretary of the Interior Harold Ickes made appearances at later Slav Congress conventions. Roosevelt, too, sent a letter congratulating the organizers of the Slav Congress on their patriotic efforts. The IWO was likewise valorized as an essential part of the win-the-war progressive alliance, as when it received commendations for its participation in blood drives and bond-selling campaigns, or when IWO and Slav Congress officials appeared at rallies alongside the mayors of Cleveland and Pittsburgh.[28] In such circumstances members of these organizations were perhaps justified in believing they were accepted and would continue to have a place in postwar America.

Not that IWO members escaped conservative scrutiny entirely. As noted, IWO organizer Zysman was fired as a teacher in New York and then ousted from the navy over his membership in this suspect organization.[29] Other times, though, the IWO was able to intervene and save members' government jobs. In the fall of 1941, an IWO member who worked in a federal agency in Washington wrote, "The Civil Service Commission, for the last 6 months, has been carrying on an inquisition, investigating, intimidating and then firing federal employees." The writer had been asked about his membership, and was pressed about whether he was "an instructor in arts and crafts in the Junior Section of the International Workers Order." The writer urged the national office "to put forth a strong demand that this sort of intimidation and persecution must be stopped."[30]

Vice President Middleton wrote to Civil Service Commissioner Henry Mitchell to enlighten him on the patriotic activities of the IWO and its exemplary record in support of the defense effort. Mitchell replied agreeing that civil service employees' membership in fraternal, labor, and religious organizations was no bar to government employment, but he reminded Middleton that Congress had authorized the barring from the civil service of anyone belonging to "any political party or organization which advocates the overthrow of our constitutional form of government." Consequently, Mitchell said investigators needed broad latitude to question applicants on the organizations to which they belonged. Mitchell's letter was quintessential bureaucratese, stating that IWO membership was in and of itself no bar to civil service employment while quibbling about the suitability of interrogating IWO members to discover whether they advocated the overthrow of the government. In subsequent years the IWO would emphasize only the first part of this letter, asserting that the government had expressly declared IWO membership did not preclude government employment.[31]

Indeed, the IWO widely publicized letters from government agencies written between 1938 and 1943, all stating that IWO membership was no impediment to government employment. These letters were offered as proof that the IWO was a reputable, patriotic organization. The Order even noted that U.S. Army Morals and Orientation officers had requested IWO literature to aid with soldiers' training. In September 1943 Counsel Brodsky wrote to the Civil Service Commission concerning Michael Skibo, who was dismissed from a War Department job because he was determined to be an "agent for the International Workers Order, which is a transmission belt for the Communist Party." William Hull wrote Brodsky that Skibo's termination was an administrative decision of the War Department and thus not subject to Civil Service Commission review. However, Hull provided Brodsky with the commission's opinion that IWO membership, "standing alone," had never prevented government employment. He added, "Mere fact of membership in, or activity in behalf of, the International Workers Order would play no part in the final determination of the case."[32]

Officers employed this letter as proof that the government endorsed the legitimacy of the Order. Four years later the IWO was abruptly labeled subversive. Members might have wondered what had changed in such a short time to justify this seemingly drastic government turnaround.

In the middle of World War II, officers of the IWO were confident that the red-baiting tide had turned. In a rousing speech to the IWO's national convention, frequently interrupted by "applause" and "laughter," Marcantonio gave a prediction: "I hope that the day is not far off when I will not be the only member of Congress who is a member of the International Workers Order. In fact, I am confident . . . very soon there will be less Dieses, less Rankins, and more members of the IWO in the halls of Congress!" The congressman added that in 1939 "the Dies Committee was going to destroy the International Workers Order." But "in 1944 . . . the Dies Committee runs to cover, the Dies Committee is dying, and the International Workers Order is growing."[33] Cheering delegates, who had just endorsed Roosevelt's reelection platform pledged to securing the Four Freedoms, might have been forgiven for so readily presuming reactionaries' demise. Their error soon became apparent.

The Subversive Listing: The People versus Tom Clark

The listing of the IWO as a subversive organization carried no explanation for how this determination had been made, nor was it backed with any evidence of actions allegedly threatening national security. Rather than rely on denunciatory resolutions alone, in June 1948 the IWO instituted a lawsuit in federal court. President Kent wrote to all lodges informing members that General Counsel Lee Pressman had filed suit "challenging Attorney General Clark's smear of the Order as unconstitutional and illegal." The suit asked the court to order the attorney general and federal Loyalty Board to remove the IWO from the list "and cease circulating it," and it also sought to prevent discrimination against any IWO member with a civil service job. Kent assured local lodges, "We are prepared to take our fight to the highest courts of the land." Consequently, lodges were urged to rush their donations to a $50,000 defense fund.[34]

Members responded with contributions of a buck fifty, a buck, or even fifty cents. Andy Hromiko of Curtisville, Pennsylvania, who thirteen years earlier had sent similar small donations to help fight Mussolini's fascists, now sent $3 from his coal mining lodge brothers. Their names and donations were enrolled on a petition featuring a woodcut of a defiant miner. Other members fought the battle with their words. Spiridou Comanita of Youngstown and Dorothy Tripp of Endicott, New York, informed the national office that they had written to the attorney general, congressmen, and Truman denouncing the subversive listing.[35]

The IWO also fought the battle against its subversive listing in "the court of public opinion," issuing news releases and pamphlets stating its case. Clark's methods of denying any notice or hearing to the Order were declared "themselves subversive of due process of law and of the Constitution." A news release demanded that Clark meet the IWO's lawyers in court to deliver any evidence of the Order's wrongdoing. The release argued that it was completely innocent, noting that earlier government decisions, such as the 1943

Civil Service Commission determination discussed previously, declared IWO membership no bar to government employment. Also mentioned were INS rulings in 1942 and 1943 stating "that the Order does not advocate force and violence or the overthrow of the United States Government 'or that it has ever done any of these things.'" All these precedents, the news release argued, as well as the Order's stellar war record and nondiscriminatory membership policy, required that the listing be overturned.[36]

A pamphlet designed to resemble a legal document was delivered to every IWO member spelling out the case against the listing. *An Indictment: The People vs. Attorney General Tom Clark Before the Court of Public Opinion* made the case "against the unconstitutional, dictatorial and arbitrary action" of Clark, denouncing "the un-American drive to suppress freedom of thought and association in the United States." The pamphlet's authors were confident that all members shared the shock at the "scandalous libel against the integrity, patriotism and loyalty of our IWO and its membership." The Attorney General's List, the IWO charged, was part of a "fascist" plan to "strangle democracy in our country." The pamphlet's authors surmised that "reaction" hated the Order because it practiced interethnic and interracial brotherhood and "reaction hates any organization which truly lives and practices the equality of peoples." The Order's efforts to extend social security to cover health insurance also led to reactionaries' hatred of the Order, although the pamphlet reminded members that "economic royalists" had hated Roosevelt, too. The IWO also alleged that its continued commitment to peaceful cooperation of all peoples, and the strengthening of the UN, had led to its stigmatization as subversive, commenting, "It is a sad day, indeed, when peace itself, and voices for peace, can be branded 'subversive.'"[37] The pamphlet dismissed allegations that the Order was controlled by Communists, noting,

> Our membership is of diverse political beliefs. . . . We do not ask anybody what political belief he holds, and we do not discriminate against anybody because of his political beliefs. Naturally there are Communists in our organization. Communists get sick, too, and die, and they need protection for their families. . . . Woe to a country or an organization which insists upon taking away bread and security from people whose thoughts may not conform to dictated standards![38]

"Don't let reaction's dirty paws touch the sacred temple of your guaranteed freedom of association, and your cherished Order," the pamphlet concluded.[39]

The JPFO's *Jewish Fraternalist* similarly noted that the IWO enrolled members with a variety of political beliefs and never interrogated members on their politics. The IWO examined members' "lungs but not the mind." The attorney general's opaque list was satirized in a cartoon in which Clark served as prosecuting attorney, judge, and all twelve jury men in the matter of deeming organizations subversive.[40]

In 1948 while some national officers such as Saltzman and Thompson Patterson made no secret of their CP membership, others such as Kent and Marcantonio were never Party members. Moreover, only a small minority of the IWO's overall 180,000 members were Communists. But in 1948 an organization with even a minority of its members in the Party was anathema to the Justice Department. Defenses of the lawsuit published in radical newspapers were noted by the FBI. A June 1948 article in *Glos Ludowy* noted rallies in ten cities to "defend people's right of freedom of association" and endorse the lawsuit against the Justice Department, but also to protest the Treasury Department's withdrawal of the IWO's tax-exempt status. This action came shortly after publication of the Attorney General's List, and like that action, the burdensome tax change was announced with no explanation or evidence of any wrongdoing on the Order's part. Indeed, as the IWO would point out in its court battles, its corporate record as a financially sound insurance organization had been consistently rated impeccable; now that its politics were unpopular it was being sanctioned. The Poles demanded a hearing from the Treasury Department on the withdrawal of the tax-exempt status.[41]

Prominent Americans were cited denouncing the Subversive List. Some of these celebrities were noted leftists, such as Robeson, who charged that the blacklists and other conservative measures "are aimed at the people's organizations fighting Jim Crow and segregation, fighting American-style fascism, fighting for peace." The actor-singer vowed, "We are going to fight this out to victory." Idaho senator Glen Taylor, vice-presidential running mate of Henry Wallace on the Progressive Party ticket, was less restrained in criticizing Clark for "tearing up the Bill of Rights and issuing lists of organizations that Wall Street and its military hangers-on didn't like. That isn't Americanism. That's the way they did things in Nazi Germany, and . . . Clark is acting like a Himmler. The Constitution of the United States doesn't provide for any Lord High Executioner of the people's liberties and we don't intend to have one sneak up on us behind our back."[42]

Taylor's intemperate remarks, as well as his left-wing alliance with the Progressive Party, which was supported by many members of the IWO, may not have convinced many conservatives of the justness of the Order's cause. Even former Justice Department officials, however, questioned the IWO's subversive listing. Former assistant attorney general O. John Rogge lamented the assertion that only "conservative" or even "reactionary" Americans were now acceptable as "true patriots" while "your own great workers' Order has been arbitrarily branded as a 'subversive' organization in . . . the completely illegal and unconstitutional decree" by Clark. Illinois congressman Sabath also tried to intervene with the Justice and Treasury Departments to remove the subversive listing and restore the IWO's tax exemption, without success, but he assured Kent he would try again.[43]

For all Sabath and Kent's efforts, no hearing was granted by either the Justice Department or the federal Loyalty Board. A memorandum prepared by the Order's lawyers summarized the attorney general's position. Clark asked the court to dismiss the IWO's lawsuit because, he claimed, "there is no controversy between the IWO and the defendants, including the Attorney General and the members of the President's Loyalty Board." He argued that the IWO had no standing to bring the suit, claiming only individual IWO members in the civil service who might be dismissed could do so. The decision of the IRS on the Order's tax status, as well as members' resignation or threatened resignation, or their denial of naturalization, were only "indirect and incidental" to placement on the Attorney General's List. Clark stated that the "published opinion and considered judgment of the Attorney General presents no justifiable controversy" and that he and the president had the right to express this opinion, a right neither the court nor the IWO had any standing to question. No deprivation of free speech or free association had occurred, Clark maintained, and thus the IWO had no case.[44]

The reaction from IWO headquarters was more appalled surprise. Molly Tallentire wrote to Kent, who was in the midst of his own Progressive Party run for Congress in New York state's Adirondack region, with gratitude for Sabath's interest in their case. She added, though, "As for the Attorney General's answer, aghast is just the word for the emotions that arise. That so-and-so claims he has done us no harm! He must have had a terrible set of parents; in fact, I believe his mother barks."[45]

Morale-building private sarcasm gave way to publication of a response in the JPFO's magazine, charging, "Department of Justice Evades Justice." Treasurer Shipka called the attorney general's refusal to answer in court "nothing more than the legal equivalent of hit-and-run driving. . . . [T]he Attorney General is trying to duck the responsibility of defending his action in court. First he hit us, now he is trying to run away." Shipka noted that Clark had refused to produce any evidence to back up his subversive listing and was therefore placing himself above the law. An "atomic chain reaction of an irresponsible smear" had led to the Treasury Department's adverse tax ruling, charges against members who were government employees, and members' naturalization applications being imperiled. These actions had "terrorized" the IWO's members, and Shipka appealed to the Constitution to defend citizens against "Lord High Executioners." The treasurer concluded, "We insist on our right to test this unconstitutional act. We shall continue our fight for democracy, for security and peace in the spirit and through the methods guaranteed by the Constitution and the Bill of Rights."[46]

"One of These Days the Hysteria Will Die Down and Light Will Appear Again"

Clark's dismissal of any harm individual IWO members faced as "indirect and incidental" to the listing was disingenuous. The vice president of a Washington, D.C., lodge wrote to headquarters at the end of 1948, "We lost a few members during the year because of the 'Red Scare.' . . . Those that dropped out were Government workers, but most of them continued their activity in the lodge unofficially."[47] Although individual government employees now feared retribution for public identification with the IWO, at least in some locals commitment to progressivism continued, despite such activities' increasing stigmatization.

In the face of government repression, IWO members continued their lobbying for an end to Jim Crow and other causes in which they believed, and in civil rights rallies they were also reassured through affective emotional solidarity that at least some Americans did not demonize them. A Polonia Society member reported in *Glos Ludowy* on her attendance at a Washington legislative conference to end racial segregation and discrimination. She was gratified to hear "a leading Negro delegate" say, "Communists don't have hooves and horns. Besides a person in the United States has just as much a right to be a Communist as I have to be a Republican." Such endorsements, however, were countered by anti-Communist luminaries. HUAC chairman John Wood of Georgia sent a letter warning every House member that the CRC members visiting Washington for a Freedom Crusade belonged to an organization on the subversive list and that their planned visits to congressional offices spelled trouble. Wood wrote his colleagues, "It is clear that the object of this mass demonstration is to intimidate the Government of the United States." In such a milieu those engaged in lobbying activities might as well have had "hooves and horns."[48]

Under such circumstances many Order members felt vulnerable and no longer able to be vocal advocates for justice. Government employees enrolled in the IWO were interrogated by the federal Loyalty Board to ascertain their fealty to the American way of life. While some people quit the Order to protect family in sensitive security positions, as when a Philadelphia member quit because his son was an engineer at a defense plant "closely watched by the FBI," more frequently the alleged subversive threat posed by the IWO was lower grade. In November 1948 Seymour Goldman, a postal employee from Harlem, faced an extensive series of "interrogatories" asking him about his affiliations and activities with the IWO, Artkino Films, and the CP. "Are you now, or have you ever been, in sympathy with any of the aims, purposes, or doctrines of the Communist Party or of Soviet Russia," he was asked. It would probably not have helped Goldman's case if he had pointed out that "aims and purposes" such as defeating Nazi Germany had quite recently been embraced by many other Americans, in and out of the Party. Of his time in the IWO, Goldman was required to "give a complete explanation of your membership therein, . . . your reasons for joining, the number of meetings attended, . . . whether you subscribe to the *Fraternal Outlook*, whether you agree with the policies expressed by the *Fraternal Outlook* with respect to Communism and Soviet Russia, and such other facts as may be pertinent."[49]

How any of this was "pertinent" to delivery of the mail was unclear, but such interrogatories were effective in driving mailmen out of the IWO. A man working at the post office in Hammond, Indiana, "of course . . . had to take a loyalty test." He asked that the JPFO stop sending him literature as "the Post-Office Department and the F.B.I. in Hammond have taken every name that receives a *'Fraternal Outlook'* and every Russian sounding name that receives literature or is in the directory." He hastened to add, "I don't want you to think that I have given up on my convictions or beliefs. I have not. I have to take precautions as to my job and as the only breadwinner in the family." This harried mailman ruefully concluded, "One of these days the hysteria will die down and light will appear again." A Slovak family with a son at the post office quit the IWO after the son was fired. Still, the father "pledged himself to pay his arrears once the storm is over" and also contributed $10 for defense of the Order. A Cicero, Illinois, federal employee likewise wanted his *Fraternal Outlook* subscription discontinued, refused to attend meetings, and asked that his membership be kept secret.[50]

The IWO had no doubt that postal workers were targeted not for their subversive activities but because of their militant advocacy of civil rights and union causes. A draft article for the *Fraternal Outlook* detailed the case of Arthur Drayton, suspended from the Philadelphia post office. "Although the alleged purpose of the government is to fire so-called subversives, its actual purpose is to punish the people fighting militantly for the rights of the Negro people," the draft quoted Drayton. Most of those fired from civil service posts, according to the United Public Workers, CIO, "have been fighters against racial bias and hold advanced views on racial matters." In a letter accompanying the draft, Abraham Chapman of the *Fraternal Outlook* noted that Drayton was the first black trustee of the National Federation of Postal Clerks and a poet and playwright whose work was published in the NAACP's *The Crisis* and IWO publications.[51]

To the IWO it was Drayton's championing of racial equality and workers' rights, not subversion, that led to his suspension, and there were grounds for suspicions. A Loyalty Board chairman in another government employee's hearing publicly remarked, "Of course the fact that a person believes in racial equality doesn't prove that he's a Communist, but it certainly makes you look twice, doesn't it." In later hearings before HUAC, Robeson flatly told Southern congressmen on the committee that he knew it was for his civil rights activism that he was regarded as "un-American." And union leaders such as the UE's Sentner who were too effective at advocating for their members' rights were chased from the CIO for being "reds." In 1950 grassroots activists in the IWO such as Drayton faced a double bind for their unpopular militancy on racial and class matters.[52]

Whether Clark thought it was "incidental" to his list, members rapidly dropped away from the Order. From Pennsylvania, Luigi Ciarafoni wrote to the Garibaldi Society's president that in his little village "they say we are of the Red Party" and that members were afraid of losing their jobs. The correspondent added that his business partners had told him "to quit his job or to quit the society" after they learned of his IWO membership. Because of the local red scare no one wanted to serve as lodge secretary, and the writer suggested transferring the members to a nearby lodge where perhaps the crackdown was not yet as fierce. The Garibaldi Society president wrote back to Ciarafoni refuting "these slanderers and their filthy accusations." "They say it about us because we don't want to shine the shoes of their masters, because we are for the defense of human rights, and nothing else," he wrote. He urged Ciarafoni and his brothers and sisters not to disband the lodge but stand and fight, and prove by their example the value the Garibaldi Society had for working people.[53]

Advice to coal-country members was easy to dispense from New York but hard to put into practice. FBI agents visited the home of a Polish secretary in Martins Ferry, Ohio, and coerced him into giving up monthly dues lists, much to the chagrin of Shipka. The Martins Ferry secretary wrote that FBI agents demanded he tell them which members were Communists, and when he answered that he did not know, "This angered them like angry dogs, (they told me) that they will be back, and if I do not identify the Communists I shall be arrested." Some local officers remained defiant in the face of red-scare tactics, as when a Miami Beach secretary participated in a CRC anti-Klan rally. After local newspapers "exposed" this public meeting and labeled both the IWO and CRC "Communist fronts," a Florida indictment hung over his head, but this secretary wrote to Saltzman, "Well, let them drop dead." Elsewhere FBI agents and police departments made off with records and membership lists handed over by intimidated lodges, and members suffered hardships as local doctors refused to examine them or fill out medical forms for this "Communist" organization, making it difficult to collect sick benefits. The national office gamely told members to "hold the fort."[54]

The fort was hard to hold in many places. A secretary reported that Italians in the Endicott-Johnson City-Binghamton area of New York felt "a certain hysteria . . . because of the intense anti-communist campaign" that was likely to lead to "investigations, reprisals, etc." Companies, the Chamber of Commerce, and the American Legion had seen to it that "the witch hunt is in full development." Italian leaders of the local IWO already had resigned, telling the writer, "It is a matter of our bread and of our future." The local secretary told the Garibaldi Society's national office, "I, on my part, have no words to persuade them. Can you do something?" and warned that "our reactionaries are capable of and prepared for everything."[55]

As the Cold War escalated, journalists and government officials argued that steps such as the Attorney General's List were necessary emergency measures designed to preserve America's freedom. Those experiencing the repercussions of these instruments of Foucauldian discipline and punishment might have been forgiven for seeing not so much freedom as repression in the IWO's demonization.[56] Conformity via anxiety took hold in many places such as Binghamton.

The government and corporate panopticon kept local IWO members in a high state of distress. Correspondents asked the head office not to send speakers who were CP members to visit their lodges, as such people were already, they said, on FBI and local police red-squad watch lists. The secretary of the Russian Society waspishly wrote back to a Pittsburgh branch, "We certainly did not think that a lecture . . . on the subject 'the fight for peace' could bring about the demolition of the premises, or any damage thereto." But in the Cold War there were no guarantees. Even in larger cities members dropped away.[57]

To be sure, some local officers had ties to the Party; the Binghamton-area secretary noted one resigning lodge president was "a fervent anti-fascist" and reader of Communist publications such as the *Daily Worker* and *L'Unita del Popolo*. But Party members were a tiny minority of the IWO's approximately 180,000 members, with Sabin estimating Party members as 3 percent of the Order's enrollees.[58] Still, even mundane correspondence from the IWO alarmed members in isolated places. A member from the coal patch of Elbert, West Virginia, nervously wrote to New York about the Russian books that were sent him. "We are not supposed, here, to have any Russian books, nor American ones, if they contain anything in favor of Russia," he wrote, adding that the day after the books arrived, "I was asked by the Company police what kind of books I received from New York." The U.S. mails were under the rigid control of the company's police, suggesting in many parts of America, despite ostensible gains of the New Deal, miners still lived in the corporate-dictatorial conditions that had prevailed in the 1910s and 1920s.[59] Now corporate hegemony had the added excuse of anti-Communism in deploying the management whip. Correspondent W. Sobol explained to the Russian Society in his company town that he had to do as the company demanded, "Or else, the Company policeman brings you a note, and within three days, you must move out. In other words, on whoever's carriage you ride, you have to sing his song . . . and that's what we do."⁶⁰

In Elbert lodges had no recourse but to meet in the company hall, providing the coal corporation with another means of controlling workers' thoughts, speech, and actions. Three East European lodges were allowed to use the company hall, but the Russian IWO lodge was not one of them. Members threatened with firing quit the IWO. The Russian Society secretary wrote back to Sobol, advising him to explain to management that the IWO was an insurance company and the Russian books were primers on IWO benefits, but Sobol said the remaining members did not want the books, "not even for nothing." Meetings of the lodge were impossible in this tightly controlled company town, where visitors coming to speak to the IWO were immediately accosted by company police at the town's single hotel.⁶¹

A similar tale was told by Ludwik Paluch, who quit as secretary of a Polish lodge in Enterprise, West Virginia, after the Justice Department interrogated him about his membership in what the agency called the "Communist" and "subversive" IWO. Enterprise was left with no secretary as everyone was too scared to serve. Paluch begged headquarters not to send him any more mail, as the town's post office would be watching him closely.⁶²

It is a fair question how much freedom coal miners, in the IWO or not, enjoyed even as late as 1950. For such people the company police state was the kind of "freedom" Clark and HUAC were enforcing. Perhaps "despotism" evoked for such IWO members images of the coal camps with which they were all too familiar, not Poland or Russia. Even in 1950, in places such as Elbert and all the country's West Virginias, perhaps it is not surprising that the IWO was still afforded support and a hearing, even if fear of punishment was increasing. For people such as Sobol and Paluch, fears of espionage summoned up not images of the IWO, but the coal company police busily opening one's mail.

In such a Cold War surveillance context, some lodges decided it was safer to destroy records rather than allow them to fall into authorities' hands. Lodges with many foreign-born members especially feared the INS would use proof of membership contained in lodge records to deny people naturalization, or even deport them. When a Russian lodge destroyed stacks of material, national secretary Kasustchik wrote, "We have been extremely amazed to learn that you burned the balance of the literature." He was "ashamed by this decision of your leadership. The Hitlerian fascists, as you know, used to burn progressive literature." He wished the literature had been passed along to members and their friends, not returned to the home office, "where it cannot be useful to anybody, lying around on the shelves."⁶³

Elsewhere the FBI noticed lodges were burning minutes books and membership and dues lists, and this destruction was regarded as proof that the Order had something nefarious to hide. Agents reported that western

Michigan lodges were instructed at a Party meeting in Grand Rapids, "Most of the IWO lodges keep minutes of meetings and of financial transactions and there is plenty in these minutes to prove them subversive, so it is best to destroy the minute books. All the Detroit lodges have already destroyed theirs and now keep the minutes on pads and five cent tablets." The G-men added, "The secretaries of the IWO lodges in Muskegon have already been instructed to burn their records and to withdraw money they have on deposit from the banks in the name of the IWO."[64]

Even assuming informants had accurately heard and reported what IWO members were told, admonitions that "there is plenty in these minutes to prove them subversive, so it is best to destroy the minute books" are subject to interpretation. It is indeed possible that somewhere in the ashes was proof Muskegon members were disloyal to the United States, feeding vital national security secrets to the CP and, ultimately, Moscow. But it is also plausible that by 1951 the speaker knew what the federal government regarded as subversive cast a broad net over civil rights lobbying, militant union activism, and petitioning and other activities on behalf of a more peaceful and cooperationist foreign policy and that lodge minutes likely would be used to condemn and prosecute members. The extensive IWO records that survived the era that historian David Caute aptly terms "the great fear" provide ample instances of dissent from the Cold War consensus, but no espionage or other demonstrably subversive activity. In Grand Rapids the speaker may have been acknowledging the government would likely use these records as "proof" in a very broad-ranging prosecution of anything smacking of dissent. These warnings are not necessarily evidence that the IWO knew it was actually up to no good, just that members feared the government would use these records to paint them as such.

Such fears may have been well-founded, especially when several municipalities enacted local subversive-registration ordinances, widening the scope of the Attorney General's List well beyond its application to civil service loyalty reviews. In 1950 Erie, Pennsylvania, passed an ordinance requiring members of designated "subversive" organizations to register with police. Secretary Kasustchik wrote to Erie's Russian lodge saying this "fascist ordinance about registration" also applied to the IWO, even though "our organization . . . absolutely never undertook and never will undertake, any criminal action against the town, its population, our country or our people." IWO vice president Middleton was dispatched to Erie to assist members with a campaign for "the repeal of this fascist aggression against progressive minded people." "I trust that none of you will remain just an observer," Kasustchik wrote the lodge, and whistled past the graveyard, "It must be believed that progress still is moving forward! And Reaction will not succeed in fooling all the people. Victory will be with the people." Still, the city's fearful Russians refused to pay dues, despite reassurances that they were enrolled in a perfectly legal fraternal society. The cloud of surveillance lifted somewhat with a temporary injunction suspending enforcement of the Erie ordinance.[65]

In Jacksonville, Florida, enforcement of the municipal "anti-Red" ordinance ended in tragedy. Alexander Trainor, an IWO member and the only registered Communist in the city, had been sentenced to ninety days in the City Prison Farm. While free on bail pending appeal, Trainor stabbed himself in the chest with an ice pick and fell from a second-story balcony. The IWO's secretary wrote to George Starr of the JPFO expressing frustration that Trainor had not been helped by the national "Welfare Fund," implying this omission may have led to his rash act. A defensive Starr wrote back, saying the IWO indeed cared about its small lodges and their members, but that the Joseph R. Brodsky Welfare Fund like other Order resources was rather limited. "Brother Trainor undoubtedly is in need of help but we are not in position to provide the help." Starr suggested Trainor apply for sick benefits regarding his stab wounds.[66]

"Glory and Honor to You, Who Drive the Pigs . . . Out of Our Garden"

Government suppression led some members to despair; others remained defiant. As the Order's troubles multiplied, a Russian member, "George" of Audubon, New Jersey, poetically assured "my friends, battling Committee" that he was committed to the fight: "Glory and honor to you, who drive the pigs with their long snouts out of our garden," George wrote. "As Comrade Stalin said, we will not surrender a single inch of our land to anyone; we, also, dear friends, should not surrender a single moment of the time we have given to our Organization, not a single cent of our money, to the low-down blood-suckers." He added, "Whatever effort and fight may be needed, drive these scoundrels away from our human effort."[67]

While the IWO had many progressives sympathetic to its goals, some members were shocked and irate as they tendered their resignations. In quitting, Morris Dubin said, "I cannot and will not be a member of an organization whose beliefs, doctrines or ideas are in any way contrary to those of my country." E. T. Besenyodi canceled his and his wife's memberships explaining he was doing so "because I am a good American; I love my country; I like my government." Besenyodi was certain Clark would not have made statements labeling the IWO subversive "unless he had positive proof to back them up." He bluntly wrote, "I am sorry I ever paid a damned cent into your organization."[68]

It was difficult to retain "conscientious, progressive people" within the Order under such conditions. This was how Solomon and Sarah Kleinberg of the Bronx characterized themselves in a letter to Pressman. On emigrating from Argentina, they had immediately enrolled in the JPFO. Now, however, they wanted to become U.S. citizens, but, "know[ing] the situation in this country, and that our Order is on Tom Clark's black list," they wanted to know if they should take out first papers—declaring their intent to become citizens—or if it was better to resign from the JPFO temporarily or if Pressman thought it more important that they remain in the Order and forego naturalization for the moment. The unasked question the Kleinbergs may have pondered was, would they have to travel even further than the Bronx to escape the government's Peronist tendencies?[69]

Thousands of foreign-born IWO members were particularly vulnerable: the INS deemed membership in the CP, or in any organization on the Attorney General's List, grounds for denial of naturalization, or, for those already naturalized, revocation of citizenship and deportation. The Smith Act was liberally used to argue that IWO members had been part of a group that advocated the forceful overthrow of the government, simply by disseminating Marxist ideas. By 1947 even people who had been brought to America decades earlier as children were scrutinized for Party membership or activities in the IWO, even if those associations had occurred many years in the past.[70]

The IWO alerted its membership to the "terrorization of the Yugoslav-American community of Farrell, Pennsylvania," by the INS, and joined with the ACPFB in demanding an investigation of the threat to progressive Yugoslavs. Two men were "harangued" and threatened with revocation of their citizenship if they did not cease their progressive activities. The IWO argued that the case of these citizens was only the tip of the coercive iceberg in Farrell, where "many non-citizens are told plainly that they will not be permitted to become citizens solely because of their membership in the Aria Singing Society, the Croatian American Civic Club, or local branches of the Croatian Fraternal Union and the International Workers Order." During World War II, the FBI indeed had spied on Slav Congress members for their suspect activities in the dreaded Aria Singing Society as well as the Croatian Glee Club of Gary, Indiana, and now the INS was targeting progressive Croatian singers. The IWO vowed to join the ACPFB in fighting this "attempted terrorization" of citizens and aliens alike. The IWO showcased the plight of one Farrell woman now threatened with denial of citizenship and deportation even though she had entered the United States in 1908 when she was three years old. Her two American-born sons had joined the U.S. Marines right after Pearl Harbor and one was still serving.[71]

Some tenacious members could prevail in their pursuit of naturalization. Philip Stasiukevich of Maynard, Massachusetts, successfully appealed the negative decision of the INS, when an appeals court in Boston ruled that the testimony of INS agent Joseph Apelman on Stasiukevich's "reputation in the community as being a Communist" was "man in the street" hearsay "of a particularly unreliable sort" and not sufficient evidence to prevent naturalization. Nor was mere membership in the IWO proof that Stasiukevich was bent on overthrowing the government. The judges further ruled that Apelman's testimony on the nature of the IWO was based on a cursory reading of HUAC reports, not actual knowledge of the organization. The court ordered a rehearing of the case, suggesting denial of naturalization had been in error.[72]

Stasiukevich was lucky to appear before judges who viewed with skepticism "man in the street" and "common knowledge" designations of applicants as "radical." In the 1920s courts applied such "man in the street," "common sense" logic to deny the right of immigration to Middle Eastern and Asian people "commonly known" to be "non-white."[73] But other IWO members were not as lucky, and pleas for assistance as the INS threatened them with denial or loss of citizenship indicate the psychic stress such aggressive interrogations exacted. A fearful Baltimore member wrote the Russian secretary that she had admitted she was an IWO member during her final citizenship examination, but when she wrote that the organization was a fraternal benefit association, the examiner crossed out her words. The secretary tried to reassure her that he had been naturalized during the war, and thus she likely would have no problem. But she wrote back that she had been called in for further questioning about her IWO membership, and immigration agents "asked whether our meetings were secret, whether we had any signal or secret catchwords among our members." She was then asked for copies of IWO literature. She requested that literature no longer be sent to her and that any further letters be sent to her daughter's address or the home of a friend. Under such grilling about the IWO's "secrets," this woman may indeed have felt the INS was engaged in a process of "terrorization."[74]

Slovak members seeking to naturalize were intimidated in ways that exhibited the full might of the state. An SWS member from Passaic, New Jersey, appearing at his mother-in-law's naturalization hearing "had quite some difficulties." The judge had a list of all Passaic SWS members and said that as long as the man remained in the organization his mother-in-law would never receive her citizenship papers. The hapless member said that if it were necessary, he'd resign immediately, but the judge demanded that he take an oath to that effect and threatened that if he did not resign, he would be fined $10,000 and jailed for five years. When the member's wife heard about this, she "tore up the policies and the dues books, went outside and burned it all," and told her husband if he did not resign she would leave him.[75]

Still, even in the face of deportation, or the combined wrath of judges and mothers-in-law, many grassroots members remained poetically defiant. "One thing they don't understand—our stubbornness. We are fearless people," a Carpatho-Russian member wrote his society's president. "Even if they deport me to the North Pole, among the Eskimoes, I shall show, by gesticulation, if needs be, to these Eskimoes the wrong we are being done by Capitalism. There too I shall prepare for the day of the overthrow of the oppressors of the working people. They will not get rid of us, no matter where they deport us!" Such indignant letters suggest the depth of radical immigrants' commitment to the Order.[76]

Other IWO members found the deportation threat a more sorrowful experience. Benny Saltzman, a Bronx housepainter and IWO member, faced deportation for his brief membership in the CP sixteen years earlier. Icons of family and wartime sacrifice, as well as homages to American values of freedom of speech and press, were deployed to defend Saltzman's right to remain in the country in which he had lived for thirty-nine years. The Trade Union Committee for Protection of Foreign Born publicized a sympathetic story by the *New York Post*, "'This Is Home and Here I Stay.'" "If they throw me out of the U.S., I'll be a man without a country," Saltzman told the *Post*. "This is my only home . . . the only one I want. I am proud of being an American." The article noted that Saltzman's wife and sons were American citizens and that one son had been killed defending American freedom at the Battle of the Bulge and another received a Purple Heart. Saltzman also bristled at inquisitions into what he thought or read, noting, "One of the crimes they accuse me of . . . is that I read the *Morning Freiheit*. Whose business is it what I read? This is America. Here we have freedom of speech. This is a shame against our flag." As for his brief membership in the CP in 1936, he said that he had freely informed the INS of this and that he had joined "to fight the racketeers in my painters union." A photo of the Saltzman family deployed the tropes of domesticity and wartime sacrifice on his behalf: "It is not enough that one son lost his life, another wounded and the third awaits a call to Service. Today, Sadie Saltzman is to be widowed, her two sons orphaned through the deportation of her husband Benny." The IWO offered constant, accurate denunciations of state ordeals by which free speech from the Left was beaten senseless, not so much defeated in the open marketplace of ideas. To defend its nonnaturalized members, the IWO mobilized a score of "stop deportation drive" rallies.[77]

In this and other cases, defense of IWO members was framed in narratives of family, domesticity, respectability, and wartime service or sacrifice to country. Nowak, former state senator and IWO and ASC leader in Michigan, also faced denaturalization and deportation for allegedly belonging to an organization that advocated the overthrow of the government. Decades later Nowak saw the humor in this harassment, for as an elected official, he said, "I was the government."[78] In the 1940s and 1950s, however, as the government twice sought to revoke Nowak's citizenship, his defenders were more alarmed than amused. Even after the IWO and Slav Congress had been destroyed, the government still sought Nowak's removal. To prevent this possibility, his defenders deployed symbols of Americanism and domesticity. *An American Family*

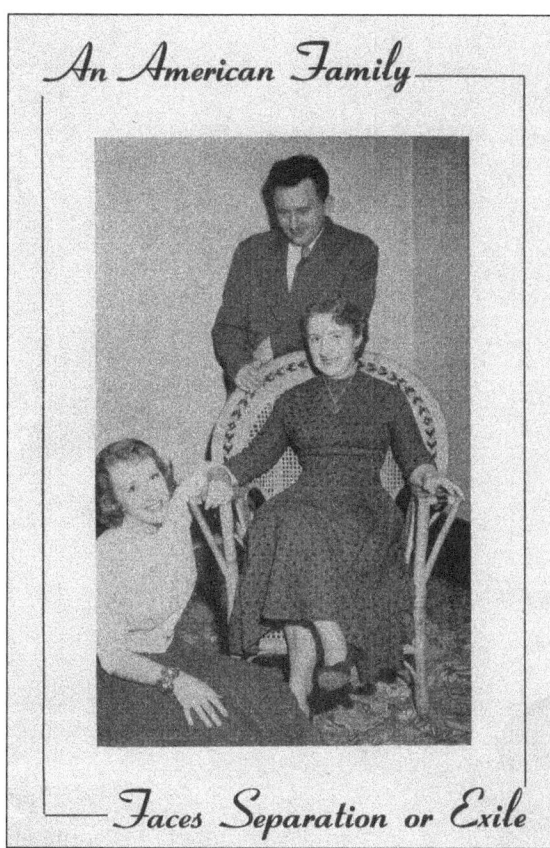

Figure 6.2 IWO members such as Stanley Nowak were targeted for denaturalization and deportation for their membership in "subversive" organizations. Defenders deployed images of domesticity to advocate for them.

Source: Pamphlet, *An American Family Faces Separation or Exile*, by the Stanley Nowak Defense Committee, April 1956, DB-WSU, box 7, folder 7–48.

Faces Separation or Exile, the title of one pamphlet read. It featured a photo of the former senator, his wife, and daughter. "The family is one of the most sacred of institutions, but many forces tend to break up families in America today," Margaret Nowak, Stanley's wife, wrote, citing the McCarran-Walter Act as the most pernicious of these forces. Margaret asserted that it was "simply because of their ideas" that people such as her husband faced deportation, noting Stanley's vigorous activism for the UAW and on behalf of the New Deal as the reason reactionaries were targeting him. While Nowak's service to the nation was not on par with the wartime service of Benny Saltzman's sons, Nowak's defenders cast his persecution as a result of his work building unions to guarantee a decent standard of living to Americans, a counternarrative of patriotism already coming under assault by the 1950s (Figure 6.2).[79]

The defense committee's pamphlet was replete, too, with homages to American icons such as minutemen, Franklin, Lincoln, and Jefferson, and the constitutional rights of freedom of speech and assembly, which were being denied the foreign born under the "draconian" McCarran-Walter Act. It cited, too, a call by UAW president Walter Reuther to "repeal the McCarran-

Walter Act or tear down the Statue of Liberty, because the two simply don't go together."[80]

Nowak may have brought the full force of the Justice Department down on his foreign-born head by refusing to be deferential to anti-Communist investigators. In his 1952 appearance before HUAC, he declared, "I find myself in complete disagreement with the committee's work and procedure. From its very inception this committee has been, in the words of the *Detroit Free Press*, 'the most un-American thing.'" Nowak condemned HUAC as a stick with which to beat organized labor. He also condemned HUAC's lax record with respect to "the Ku Klux Klan and Fascist or Nazi groups" and excoriated the committee, which "uses its Congressional power and prestige to intimidate people who have ideas different from those of the committee members." Nowak further condemned HUAC for its hounding of militant civil rights activists, joining fellow IWO member Robeson in faulting committee members' "un-American" endorsement of racial segregation and African Americans' disfranchisement. In 1952 parlance Nowak was a most uncooperative witness.[81]

Nowak's citizenship was eventually affirmed by the Supreme Court. His lawyers successfully argued that their client's militancy on behalf of industrial workers during the 1930s had to be understood within the tenor of that turbulent decade, "a period of ferment, unrest, change—of seeking for panaceas for our economic and social problems." The Depression, Nowak's lawyers argued, "was a period of free, open, vital, radical discussion. Ideas were freely advanced, vigorously defended and violently attacked. The language of the period was suited to its mood. Militant, radical, even revolutionary words and phrases became part of the current lingo." Even if Nowak had joined the Party, which neither he nor his defense team admitted, such militancy had to be understood within the tenor of the times, and not the very different context of the Cold War in the 1950s. As Buff notes, such a contextualized defense of uneasy times in which radical solutions gained a hearing was deployed by many defendants seeking to escape the "deportation terror." Nowak was one such successful defendant.[82]

Those foreign-born suspects that were eventually allowed to remain still experienced years of anguish, job loss, and imprisonment. Croatian-born Hyndman, who had led efforts to integrate the schools in Gary, Indiana, as well as organize steelworkers during her tenure with the IWO and ASC, was imprisoned pending deportation. Hyndman, who had been brought to America from Dalmatia in 1913 at age six, defended her effort to achieve integration as well as her other subversive ideas. In a letter to Eleanor Roosevelt, she asked, "Will we become a new type of displaced persons, banished from the United States because we dare entertain thoughts not to the liking of present-day bigots and witch-hunters?"[83]

Unlike Saltzman and Nowak, who stressed family and patriotism in arguing for the right to remain in America, Hyndman's defense was predicated on a riskier, more contested strategy: freedom of speech and thought in a time of national security conformity. Hyndman's question to the former First Lady aptly links the figure of the displaced person—welcomed to the United States so long as she or he was fleeing the right, State Department–approved government—to the country's criminalization and banishment of other people, those harboring supposedly dangerous thoughts. The criminalization of thoughts, not actions, was also underscored in Hyndman and the ASC's denunciation of her plight. Hyndman was eventually allowed to remain in the country.[84]

Similarly, in 1950 IWO executive secretary Milgrom was arrested and ordered deported, beginning a years' long fight to remain in the country. The arrest warrant listed one of Milgrom's "aliases" as "Little Caesar." The IWO immediately charged that their executive secretary's arrest was part of the "deportation hysteria" and vowed to fight the Justice Department's "un-American and unconstitutional tactics." Kent wrote to Milgrom that he saw his persecution as consistent with "the blueprint for fascism" that the Truman administration was preparing. A month later Shipka reported on the "attacks on the Order" represented by the attempted deportation of officials such as Milgrom, Andrew Dmytryshyn, and Peter Harisiades as well as a former member, Dr. Krishna Chandra. "The objective is the mass murder of civil liberties," he declared. Such deportation tactics, the IWO charged, were designed "to brand the 165,000 members as outcasts."[85]

An ailing Milgrom was imprisoned on Ellis Island as the IWO and ACPFB worked to secure his freedom and that of other IWO officers "subject to an intensified campaign of intimidation." Rallies of black, Jewish, and Slavic members demanded his freedom, and letters penned by Milgrom on Ellis Island—"already a concentration camp"—were sent to members with an appeal for wires to the attorney general pleading his cause. In December 1952 he was remanded to a hospital due to his medical condition, although the Justice Department pursued his removal from the country. Leaders of the IWO including Kent and African American minister Hill met with the commissioner of immigration, urging bail for the hospitalized Milgrom, who was still in "preventive custody" at Mount Sinai even though he had been bedridden for months.[86]

After nearly three years of litigation, the grievously ill Milgrom won his freedom. His lengthy ordeal was an example of what Hannah Arendt, in referring to stateless people, terms the fight for the right to have rights.[87] The sense of the IWO's lodges as an affective community, a safe haven where one could feel at home politically, socially, and emotionally, was one of the casualties of what the IWO had aptly labeled deportation hysteria. Through such campaigns of intimidation, red-hunters eradicated lodges' home-like loci of belonging.

Conversely, while some IWO members fought deportation, the government refused to allow other defiant leftists to travel abroad to argue for civil rights, nuclear disarmament, world peace, and other "subversive" concepts. American-born members of the IWO such as singer Robeson and painter-illustrator Kent had their passports pulled, effectively ending their careers. Foreign- and native-born members of the Order experienced the state's heavy hand as it policed their thoughts, writings, and actions.[88]

As other foreign-born members of the IWO faced deportation, the Statue of Liberty was once again enlisted in their defense. The Committee in Defense of Henry Podolski, an official in the Polonia Society, demanded to know, "Shall We Destroy the Statue of Liberty and Build Concentration Camps?" As the Hobbs, Mundt, McCarran-Walter and other bills contemplated indefinite detention of alien radicals, defenders of Podolski were right to ask if concentration camps were on the way. The IWO unequivocally defended Podolski as a victim of the "deportation delirium" and "a fearless fighter for democratic rights." If Podolski were removed from the country as "subversive," the IWO suggested an equally subversive document—the Declaration of Independence—should be torn up, as well.[89]

The defenders of IWO official Harisiades pointed out that another alien with strange ideas was likewise born abroad. They wanted to know if perhaps the Statue of Liberty should be deported, too, for after all, "Miss Liberty is a 'foreigner.' She was born in France and came to the United States in 1886. She symbolizes the ideals which the Justice Department today regards as 'subversive' and grounds for deportation. She represents the ideas of freedom and equality which the Justice Department is trying to make illegal for non-citizens and naturalized citizens to advocate." Harisiades's defenders admitted, "Of course, the idea of deporting the Statue of Liberty is ridiculous. It is shocking to any American. But, it is no less shocking to observe the manner in which the Justice Department treats decent, hard-working foreign-born Americans, . . . threatening to forcibly separate them from their families and friends." Leftists hoped the absurdity of the idea would cause citizens to pressure the government to give up its plan to deport more than thirty-five hundred foreign-born people stigmatized as subversive. The message here thus was morale-boosting—Lady Liberty is a progressive immigrant, just like me—as well as didactic, endeavoring to get Americans to alter a policy exposed as absurd. Such appeals sought to capture the flag of iconic American images and reframe the narrative for a progressive patriotism, for, as his defenders argued, "If Peter Harisiades is deported, the Statue of Liberty will be in the boat with him" and no American's freedoms would be safe (Figure 6.3).[90]

Such appeals to American traditions and icons rarely succeeded in preventing expulsion of noncitizens with unpopular beliefs. *Glos Ludowy* urged

Should Miss Liberty Be DEPORTED?

Miss Liberty is a "foreigner." She was born in France and came to the United States in 1886. She symbolizes the ideals which the Department of Justice today regards as "subversive" and grounds for deportation. She represents the ideas of freedom and equality which the Justice Department is trying to make illegal for non-citizens and naturalized citizens to advocate.

Ridiculous? Of course, the idea of deporting the Statue of Liberty is ridiculous. It is shocking to any American. But, it is no less shocking to observe the manner in which the Justice Department treats decent, hard-working foreign-born Americans, threatening to jail or deport them after they have lived most of their lives in this country, threatening to forcibly separate them from their families and friends.

The current deportation hysteria is in complete violation of the Bill of Rights, of everything Miss Liberty symbolizes. To date, more than 160 non-citizens in 21 states have been arrested . . . and the Justice Department says it will proceed against 3,500 more. The lives of these 3,500 non-citizens—and the future of American democracy itself—may be determined by the CASE OF PETER HARISIADES, which is now on the way to the United States Supreme Court as a test case in the deportation hysteria. If the Justice Department succeeds in its current deportation drive, no one—citizen or non-citizen—will be safe since the Bill of Rights will become meaningless.

Unbelievable? Turn the page and read the shocking story of this 1950 version of the Palmer Raids, which threatens your rights . . . which threatens to extinguish the Torch held high by the Statue of Liberty and then to put Miss Liberty herself on a boat headed for France, a victim of hysteria.

Figure 6.3 The defenders of Peter Harisiades, leader of the IWO's Hellenic American Brotherhood, wanted to know if another dangerous foreigner with strange ideas should be deported.
Source: Flyer, *Should Miss Liberty Be Deported? The Case of Peter Harisiades*, 1950, VM-NYPL, box 46.

readers to rally around Podolski as a patriot in the tradition of Lincoln, Jefferson, and Roosevelt. Such appeals fell on deaf ears. Both Podolski and Harisiades were deported as "undesirable aliens" to Poland; the Greek-born Harisiades spoke not a word of Polish but opted to accept asylum there rather than face imprisonment or execution in right-wing authoritarian Greece, a country he had left with his parents at the age of nine in any case.[91]

In labeling Harisiades and others "un-American," the Justice Department failed to answer a decided conundrum: Where had a nine-year-old Greek immigrant boy learned his "un-American" ideas? Unless he had been a particularly precocious and observant child, surely it was some experience of the inequities of industrial America, not Greek or other foreign conditions that gave rise to his education, labor militancy, and participation in the IWO's Hellenic American Brotherhood. His "un-American" ideas very much arose not from his foreignness, but his homegrown, American experience of proletarian exploitation.

For all the Justice Department's earlier assertions that aliens were being punished not for IWO membership but for their CP affiliation, in December 1951 a federal judge, in upholding Dmytryshyn's deportation, ruled even former IWO membership might now be grounds for expulsion. *Glos Ludowy* accurately warned a "Hitler knout" now hung over the heads of American residents with unpopular beliefs.[92]

A Moral and Political "Hazard"

By 1950 the Hitler knout to which *Glos Ludowy* alluded threatened not just individual members but the entire IWO. Execution came in the incongruous form of a New York State insurance examiner. Although audits of the IWO's finances had been conducted regularly, prior to 1950 these periodic reviews had focused on the finances of the organization. That year when insurance examiner James Haley filed his initial report, the IWO was again found to be financially impeccable. As legal scholar Sabin notes, "The State [of New York] never claimed any legitimate basis for action against the organization on financial grounds; the IWO was in excellent shape, running efficiently as an insurance company." But the IWO's very fiscal soundness was regarded as a danger in Cold War America, with fears that these insurance funds might be directed toward Moscow in time of war or national emergency.[93]

Although the IWO's finances were again deemed exemplary, Haley was tasked with writing a second report on the organization's "fraternal activities," marking the only time the New York Insurance Department used its regulatory powers to delve into the political program of a mutual benefit society. Here Haley and his department superiors moved beyond financial oversight and recast the actuarial term "hazard"—applied in every case both before and after the IWO report to a company with insufficient funds to cover policyholders or engaging in financial irregularities—to portray the Order as a moral and political hazard. Even here the Haley Report, delivered in May 1950, was ambiguous. Haley admitted that his examination of IWO publications such as issues of the *Fraternal Outlook* "disclosed no affirmative evidence of subversive acts," but he nevertheless regarded caustic criticism of U.S. foreign policy and consistent support for the Soviet Union as alarming. Criticism of the Marshall Plan and condemnation of red-baiting by Truman administration officials were cited as the sorts of "intemperate remarks" constituting "a concerted effort . . . to impugn the integrity of our country's President, his Cabinet and the Congress, specifically in their conduct of foreign policy." Haley allowed that such criticism might not be "an affirmative subversive act" but nevertheless asserted that "there may be discerned therein a plan to accomplish by indirection the same result as would be achieved by a direct subversive act."[94] Speech and writing in support of unpopular positions, or criticism of a particular president's policies, was turned into cause for punishment because a particular insurance examiner thought such speech and writings *might* lead others to a subversive act.

The Haley Report placed politics, not the IWO's impeccable finances, at the center of its condemnation. The Order's support for other organizations on the Attorney General's List, as well as its own listing, were held to constitute not just a hazard to the general public but also a hazard to the IWO's own members, who might be open to charges of disloyalty, or, as in the case of Dmytryshyn, deported solely for their IWO membership. Thus the punitive actions of government officials—attorneys general, congressmen, and INS officers—were cited as grounds for further punitive action against the IWO. The Order was a hazard to the public because its members might lose their jobs or face prison because the government did not like its policies.[95]

Haley argued that political advocacy by the Order went beyond the IWO's charter and recommended that the department liquidate the organization, the most extreme step available. Other, more incremental steps such as removal of officers deemed incompetent or steps to put the organization's books on sounder footing were not considered, evidently because as Haley himself admitted, his audits revealed no financial shenanigans, only political views he regarded as "alarming" and "intemperate."[96]

The IWO was quick to note the inconsistencies in Haley's report. In preparing for an Insurance Department hearing to show cause why liquidation should not be carried out, IWO lawyers pointed out that the Order's ads in left-wing newspapers to which Haley objected were a common practice by fraternal societies to recruit members. IWO officers noted that previous audits had not objected to such practices. In any case, as Shipka remarked, contributions to "so-called subversive organizations" represented only 0.05 percent of the IWO's total expenditures, and ads in suspect newspapers such as the *Daily Worker* and *Morgen Freiheit* were actually a good advertising investment for the Order in its recruitment of new members and not, as the department charged, proof that the IWO was a "transmission belt" funneling funds to the Party.[97]

As for the charges of Communist domination of the IWO, the Order's lawyers dismissed the issue as misplaced as well as illegitimate for a government regulatory body to raise. "The real question," the lawyers argued, "is not what the leadership of the Communist Party tried to do to the Order, but whether the Order through its own activities, violated the New York insurance law." The lawyers asserted, "In every large group there are those within it who seek to impress upon the organization their views." In a democratic organization such as the IWO, this was not proof of subversion but only a healthy exchange of views. "The examiner's real complaint," the lawyers charged, "is that the Order was a theatre for the expression of views to which he is hostile." Articles and speeches urging members to become "class conscious" were not, they argued, evidence of advocacy of the overthrow of the government by violent means, the broad Smith Act language that had seemingly been imported into insurance law and allowed an examiner to sniff out political and moral hazards within life insurance policies.[98]

Noting that the CP remained legal, the lawyers wanted to know, "Why was it proper for the Aetna, Guardian and the Prudential to give support to the Republican Party, and improper for the IWO to give support to the Communist Party." The Polonia Society likewise pointed out this lopsided imposition of a political litmus test. While their organization, which they said had never endorsed political candidates, was targeted for liquidation, "no insurance commissioners attack the Związek Narodowy Polski (Polish National Association [sic]) because their leaders publicly, in the columns of their house-organ, indorsed [sic] the Republican candidate to the Presidency in 1948." Only left-wing political speech was subject to censure.[99]

Of course, the IWO's case played out not just in a hearing room but in the Cold War public arena. The organization endeavored to steer the hearing back to the actuarial soundness of the Order. Officers pointed out that auditors had consistently praised their finances for more than twenty years, a fact reiterated by a Newark accountant in the Order who deposed that the organization had "restricted its investments to municipal, state and Government bonds because as a group, such securities offer greater safety." Shipka combated the attempt by several states to follow New York's lead and not renew the IWO's insurance license by noting, "Very few fraternal organizations... can match the 146 percent solvency of the IWO and the A-plus excellent condition of its insurance funds." Such arguments, though, were mocked by the conservative *New York World-Telegram and Sun*, whose headline writer scoffed, "Their Books Balanced, But Politics Were in Red." The paper likewise dismissed arguments that the IWO elected non-Communist officers by sneering that officers such as Marcantonio "could therefore serve as 'window dressing,' a familiar Commie trick." Repentant ex-Communist and professional testifier Louis Budenz piled on, condemning the Garibaldi Society, where "the boys worked like beavers to get out the vote for that now-defeated Stalin stooge, Marcantonio."[100]

Despite the IWO's argument that "the basic definition of 'public hazard' was being twisted beyond its plain and indicated meaning," the Insurance Department found that the IWO was too solvent and its ostensibly pro-Russian officers might find "some means to transfer its assets to that country." As Sabin notes, the IWO's very financial soundness was held to be a mark against it. In the hearing the IWO argued that "a finding of potential hazard which flows from the fact that the assets . . . are *too liquid*, is simply too incredible to dignify with discussion." Outside the hearing room, the IWO was less temperate, charging in the *Fraternal Outlook*, "They are trying to liquidate all of the people's rights" and "[their] objective is the mass murder of civil liberties."[101]

Nervous lodge officers worried that their treasuries would be confiscated by the state and that elderly members would lose their insurance coverage. The president of the SWS wrote to one officer in Binghamton, reassuring him that Shipka had promised "the storm will blow over without a disaster." The money that belonged to Binghamton's members was safe, he added, for "it's as they say, the devil is not all that black as they paint him, or McCarran isn't sending anyone to the gallows." The Slovaks' president concluded by advising, "I'd say carry on with the usual practice. . . . [I]t will have to be, stand up on your hind legs and don't worry, everything will be OK."[102]

The Slovak officer added, "It's when a village is sleeping that thieves can accomplish the most," and sleeping or not, the IWO was disappointed by the Insurance Department's December 1950 decision accepting Haley's recommendation to liquidate.[103] The matter then moved to New York County Supreme Court, where Judge Henry Clay Greenberg directed the IWO to show cause why liquidation of the Order should not proceed. An expedited trial process, which had always previously been employed so that a financially insolvent insurance company could prove its books were in order, was for the first (and as of the present, only) time deployed against an organization because of the unpopular beliefs of some of its officers. More ominously, Greenberg's order for the IWO to stand trial also restricted the Order not to enroll any new members or write any insurance policies as of December 14, 1950, and placed the Order under joint supervision of the state Insurance Department and its own officers. As of that date, any IWO expenditure of funds, save for its legal defense, required Insurance Department approval.[104]

The devastating effects of this order caused officers much anguish. Shipka wrote to defense counsel Raphael Weissman, "The Department has evidently intended to paralyze all functions of the organization." With the installation of Insurance Department officer William Karlin as coadministrator at IWO national headquarters, the government agency seeking the Order's liquidation had access to all its records, in effect giving the prosecution advance glance at the organization's defense strategy. SWS officer Joseph Schiffel instructed a Chicago member, "In case you want to write me anything of importance, . . . don't write to the General Office, but rather to my private address, as we have here a bunch of fellows from the [Insurance] Department, and every letter, even every slip of paper, goes through their hands; now, we must not give them additional material, you understand???" Considering the voluminous amount of IWO records that ended up in the Insurance Department files, Schiffel had reason to worry.[105]

To allay members' concerns, the IWO announced formation of the Policyholders Protective Committee. If the state cast the IWO as a moral and political hazard to its members, the committee asserted its allegiance to the Order and portrayed the organization as a defender of their property interests—that is, the equity they had built up in their insurance policies that might be reassigned to a commercial carrier if liquidation were upheld. The committee trekked to Albany to lobby Governor Thomas Dewey, Insurance Commissioner Alfred Bohlinger, and legislators to end the liquidation proceedings.[106]

Vice President Thompson Patterson reflected decades later that as an insurance company the IWO was always vulnerable to government regulation, and now that regulation was deployed to stifle political dissent. She remarked on the irony of the government seeking to confiscate the property of a soundly run, fiscally solvent left-wing organization, while alleged Communists defended private-property rights, commenting, "They actually stole it by declaring [the IWO] was a Communist front."[107]

In early 1951 rallies decried the liquidation action. At the Emergency Conference against the Liquidation of a People's Organization on New York's Lower East Side, resolutions viewed with "concern and alarm" the plan to "strip 162,000 IWO members of their insurance protection, sick benefits and burial rights and dissolve their . . . organization." The conference noted that the Insurance Department had consistently attested to the IWO's "excellent financial condition" and had never in twenty years "challenged the cultural, sports, social and civic activities of the IWO, since these are outside its jurisdiction." Red-baiting and war fears were being used, the conference charged, to break up an interracial people's organization that ably served the needs of its members; New York, not the IWO, was engaged in thought control. "If the Insurance Department can smash a going concern like the IWO," the conference warned, "then other government agencies can attempt to destroy groups which do not always agree with them. Our organizations, our civil liberties and our property rights are not safe if such precedents are established." The conference demanded liquidation proceedings be withdrawn immediately.[108]

The conference turned the tables on the Insurance Department, noting that while the interracial IWO offered low-cost insurance protection to black and white members alike, the department had ignored evidence that commercial companies charged black Harlem residents 208 percent more on their policies than white people. The conference demanded that the legislature investigate the department's failure to enforce antidiscrimination laws with respect to commercial insurers.[109]

The department had also violated the law, the convention charged, in denying the IWO permission to hold its scheduled eighth national convention. Judge Greenberg concurred with the Insurance Department's refusal, as coadministrator of the IWO, to permit the convention prior to the trial in New York County Supreme Court. The *New York Herald Tribune* quoted the department's lawyer as arguing, "It is clear that the sole function of the convention will be to carry out the instructions of the Communist Party. It may also be assumed that the entire aim of the convention will be to whitewash the International Workers Order."[110] The state seemed to argue simultaneously that the IWO was Communist-dominated and that a democratically run convention would likely choose new officers for the Order with no radical affiliation, thereby "whitewashing" the organization in time for its trial. Other commentators had cited non-Communist IWO officials such as Kent and Marcantonio as "proof" the CP had cleverly promoted some non-Communist officers, "a common Commie trick." Professional informant Budenz said Kent was promoted to president to lend "an air of intellectuality and gentility around the post" but still reliably supported the Communist line. The IWO was doubly damned if even the election of non-Communist officers was cited as proof of Communist domination.[111]

The emergency conference decried the banning of the convention—"a denial of fair play, a denial of justice, a denial of due process, a denial of the constitutional right of assembly, and an outrageous perversion of democracy"—while also pointing out that the Insurance Department was ordering the IWO to violate both its own constitution and New York laws that required mutual benefit societies to hold regularly scheduled conventions. The ban prevented 162,000 members from exercising their democratic rights to elect delegates to make vital decisions affecting "the future of their life insurance savings and protection, their sick and cemetery benefits, and the $110,000,000 in insurance policies and $7,000,000 assets of the IWO, which belong to them." Duly elected delegates to the suspended convention petitioned Greenberg to allow them to meet, arguing that the pending trial made it more crucial than ever that members' representatives be allowed to make decisions affecting the financial security of these working men and women. They asked Greenberg "a very simple question": "Will it not shame our nation in the eyes of the world to be forced to confess that conventions . . . are now to be banned by the court because a governmental authority is fearful that such meetings will make it more difficult to destroy them?" When the judge refused to lift the ban, the IWO wrote to the would-be delegates, reminding them again that this was a violation of New York insurance law "as well as the elemental democratic right of freedom of assembly" and called them to an emergency meeting to defend their organization.[112]

"Hitlerism with an Insurance Twist"

Prevented from assembling in their national convention, IWO members sought to sway New York through the Policyholders Protective Committee, rallying in seventeen cities and taking out ads in liberal newspapers such as *The Compass* to urge insurance superintendent Bohlinger to withdraw the liquidation order. The committee and many IWO members were particularly irked by what they regarded as a condescending letter from Bohlinger to all policyholders, in which as cosupervisor he urged members to continue paying dues so as not to let their coverage lapse. He added, "If liquidation is granted I will try to reinsure the present policyholders on as nearly the same terms as possible with some other insurance company or companies."[113]

Many members took umbrage at Bohlinger's pretensions of caring about their fiscal interests. Abraham Freeman of Boston wrote the superintendent on "February 22 Washington's birthday, . . . in memory of our great president," sarcastically asking him, "What have I done to merit your personal attention as to the security of my insurance?" Freeman reminded Bohlinger of the consistently favorable audits his own department had conducted of the IWO and asked how what had been fine during the war could now be construed as subversive. "If there is still left in you a semblance of a free-loving American then your conscience should prompt you to call off the case against the IWO," Freeman concluded, "and let . . . members and their families once more breathe the AIR of a free America." A lawyer who was an IWO member similarly saw in Bohlinger's letter a plan "to turn my insurance over to one of the monopoly insurance companies." He condemned interference in the Order due to the politics of some of its officers, telling Bohlinger, "I do not approve of Republicans, in fact, I believe most of them are a menace to the welfare of the people, and yet if I held your position, I would have no right to tell citizens [that] they may not associate with Republicans for fraternal or business purposes." A members' meeting declared Bohlinger's letter "a little masterpiece of arrogance and insult." "Dear Mr. Bohlinger," they wrote, "we did not ask your permission to join the IWO and we did not ask you to decide whether we should continue our membership. . . . So, thanks for nothing." A New York rally declared Bohlinger, not their interracial, working-class Order, the public hazard and demanded an end to the liquidation, which they called "Hitlerism with an insurance twist."[114]

Despite such solidarity the case against the IWO went forward in Greenberg's courtroom. To make its case that the Order was Communist-dominated and therefore a hazard, the Insurance Department called to the stand ex-Communists who by 1951 were carving out second careers as well-compensated government witnesses. At the height of the Cold War's red scare, such an impressive array of former Communists testifying against the IWO likely made the charges of subversion and foreign domination seem, to Greenberg, plausible. Nevertheless, the reliability of such paid witnesses, who were often caught in contradictory testimony from one trial to another, has been questioned by scholars such as Caute, who points out that the continued livelihood of witnesses at the IWO trial such as Mathew Cvetic and Budenz depended on their continually producing "an encyclopedic knowledge of the Communist movement across a vast country." Thus "they sold hunches or guesses as inside knowledge, supporting their claims with bogus reports of conversations and encounters." By the mid-1950s Cvetic was exposed as a perjurer and dismissed by the FBI and other government agencies as a particularly erratic, unreliable informant. Another witness against the IWO, Manning Johnson, had the previous year been caught perjuring himself in the deportation trial of longshoremen's union leader Bridges. In cross-examinations, the IWO's lawyers, too, drove home that the state's case relied on "kept" witnesses whose testimony seemed to contradict their earlier statements in other cases.[115]

The state's case confirmed what the IWO had never made secret: some of its officers were members of the CP (still a legal albeit beleaguered political party in 1951), and the Order had supported left-wing causes as part of its fraternal work. Powers testified that he had attended CP fraction meetings with IWO officers such as Saltzman, Shipka, Bedacht, Thompson, and others. In addition he testified to the IWO's campaigns on behalf of the Scottsboro defendants, enactment of social security and unemployment insurance, and integration of baseball and other civil rights measures, asserting such campaigns were begun in obedience to CP instructions. The Order's attorneys, however, pointed out that these campaigns predated Powers's IWO membership by four years and that lobbying for these causes began in the Order prior to Party support for the causes. And while the IWO had raised funds for causes such as the Scottsboro defense, this was always members' contributions and not from the Order's corporate funds. Moreover, the digest of Powers's testimony stated that "Powers spoke frequently at these meetings, but did not openly advocate the violent overthrow of the Government by force." Powers gave no testimony that any other IWO members had advocated violent overthrow of the government, the heart of the Smith Act, either. IWO attorney Weissman also got Powers to admit that some of the ostensibly subversive literature he said appeared at IWO meetings was readily available in bookstores and public libraries and that some of his testimony conflicted with his sworn statements during the Dmytryshyn deportation case. Powers's sizable payment of $25 a day for his testimony was also stressed.[116]

The IWO's democratic procedures were transformed into something nefarious in the testimony of Joseph Zach Kornfeder. Although he admitted that only a minority of IWO members were Communists, he claimed that the Party was able to maintain officerships by securing enough votes to get elected. While such advance planning and politicking for success during open elections might sound like democracy, anti-Communist advocates saw in such actions the hand of conspiracy and subversion. Although Kornfeder testified that the IWO had been created at the behest of the "Communist Internationale in Moscow," he admitted he had "not heard of any oral directives involving the IWO which were issued by . . . the Communist Internationale, nor has he heard of any written directives concerning the same subject matter and issued by . . . the Communist Internationale." Another disparity arose when Kornfeder testified as to a 1932 meeting of the CP's Central Committee "to discuss a slate of officers for the IWO." The witness was reminded by defense counsel that during the Dmytryshyn trial "he had stated that he did not recall ever having voted on a slate of officers for the IWO." It was then pointed out that Kornfeder had not been a member of the Central Committee since 1928, two years before the creation of the IWO. Defense attorneys further stated, "Kornfeder has never attended a convention of the IWO and is not qualified to say in what manner the National officers were elected." As evidence of Communist domination, such testimony seemed fairly thin.[117]

Other witnesses contradicted themselves, too. Simon Weber, who had been editor of the *Morgen Freiheit*, said the IWO had subsidized this Communist Yiddish newspaper but later admitted that the money came from members' individual donations. Weber, too, was hard-pressed to elaborate on the inner workings of the IWO, as he had left the organization fifteen years previously. Weber also admitted there was little subversive in the Order's support for extending Social Security, fair-housing legislation, slum clearance, and black civil rights. Star witness Cvetic named an extensive number of IWO officers as members of the CP's Nationality Commission but was at a loss to explain why, as defense counsel asked, he had not so identified IWO members in earlier testimony on the Nationality Commission before HUAC. Cvetic likewise had made no mention of the IWO in his earlier HUAC testimony on "the break down of the Communist Party operations in Pittsburgh," even though he now asserted western Pennsylvania IWO lodges were Communist-dominated. Defense counsel made much of Cvetic's generous payment by the government—he had garnered approximately $800 as a "kept" witness since May 1950—as well as his messy divorce proceedings and arrest for assaulting his sister-in-law.[118]

In presenting the IWO's defense, Weissman won some important concessions from insurance examiner Haley, who agreed that the organization had a democratic government structure, was not founded by the CP, was financially sound, and that he found no evidence of Smith Act violations or other advocacy of the violent overthrow of the government. Haley agreed, too, that most of the IWO publications that had influenced his finding of "hazard" had been written ten or more years earlier. As to these publications, defense witnesses such as Rubin Saltzman testified that their militant writings in IWO publications were not expressions of official IWO policy but merely the personal opinions of individual authors. As evidence that many IWO lodges contained members with a gamut of political beliefs, the defense submitted an article written by an Order member advocating the presidential candidacy of conservative Republican senator Robert Taft. Testimony on the IWO's medical programs was entered as evidence that the organization was a help, not a hazard, to both its members and working-class communities.[119]

Freedom of thought and association were at the center of the IWO's defense, with the organization's officers refusing, as a matter of principle, to "controvert" any connection or sympathy with the Communist movement in America. Greenberg, who was conducting the trial without a jury, had frequently asked IWO witnesses if they now rejected the Party, its political campaigns, and the support the Order once seemingly provided to Party newspapers. Defense counsel Weissman finally intervened, objecting to Greenberg's characterization of such alleged Communist connections as "damning" evidence. The Order's activities, "whatever they were, were legal, constitutional, open, proper, and not in the least damning." He argued that political questions "are utterly incompetent, irrelevant and immaterial,... a witch-hunt in an insurance matter." President Kent agreed; when questioned about why he seemed to agree with Communists in his writings, he suggested that perhaps he had found their arguments made sense but reminded the court that the U.S. and New York constitutions protected political beliefs.[120]

As part of its defense, the IWO submitted more than a hundred members' affidavits from throughout the country. Members attested to the Order's racial brotherhood, civil rights activism, and wartime service record as well as the organization's good works on domestic policy and the quality medical care and benefits and fellowship they derived. Affiants, too, addressed head-on the question of members' free-association rights and swore they had been exposed to nothing subversive or inimical to true Americanism in the Order. John Hrusovsky of Irvington, New Jersey, a charter member of the SWS, stated, "I know that nothing has been circulated that could by the widest stretch of the imagination be considered 'subversive' of our American democracy." Switching to the language of property perhaps suitable to an insurance-company trial, he added, "I consider my membership ... to be the most precious of all of my personal assets."[121] From Los Angeles, Salvatore Spampinato wrote,

> I wish to say no other company could begin to replace what the I.W.O. represents to me. I have been a member and an officer for so many years that I know it from A to Z, and I believe it to be a real expression of democracy, Americanism, and brotherhood. I have never seen to date in the I.W.O. ... when any person, right or wrong, might not freely express his opinion on any subject, and I have never seen any action taken save by free democratic vote of the rank and file. Because of the democratic character of its organization and because of the services and brotherhood which it furnishes to its members, I know the I.W.O. has a place in the community and in the country.[122]

Other members expressed "alarm and indignation" at the possible liquidation as well as the undemocratic suspension of the IWO's convention. A Philadelphian attested, "In the 21 years of my membership, I have never heard anyone advocate attacking our government or overthrowing it by force and violence." He added, "I say flatly" the IWO was not controlled by Communists. Dominica Alasina of Detroit attested that she saw no Communist literature or speakers at her lodge, adding, "I am a Catholic and I go to church and I would remember." Other members swore they had never seen as democratic an organization as the IWO and stated, "We decide for ourselves what we shall do and how we shall operate." A woman from Elizabeth, New Jersey, denied there were any suspect political activities at her lodge, which instead worked to keep the children of her industrial city in healthy and constructive activity and provide economic and medical security for older members. A Philadelphia Slovak branded allegations of Communist domination "a lie," attesting, "We do good work. It is a good organization." A Hungarian man from the Bronx echoed these sentiments as well as detailing the support his lodge had given to working people during the Depression and its commitment to combating racial discrimination. He ended his sworn statement, "I am upset and anxious about the present court proceedings against my organization, and I feel that this action is unjustified and wrong. We should be left alone; no one should interfere with us as we have done no wrong. Our objective has been to protect the poor, the working people, minorities, in the best interest of America." Dozens of IWO members saw nothing of a moral or political hazard in the organization to which they wished to belong.[123]

In May 1951 the Order's members seemed to gain a great advantage when the U.S. Supreme Court agreed with the IWO in finding its placement on the Attorney General's List unconstitutional. The law firm representing the IWO declared the ruling made it "illegal to discriminate against the International Workers Order or its members.... A refusal to permit ... any of its lodges to use a meeting place, to purchase radio time, or place advertisements in the public press because of this former listing would be a clear violation of law." The ruling was publicized in the *IWO News Bulletin*, while the Garibaldi Society sent the good news to all Italian lodges, expressing confidence that "this decision will no doubt have great effect upon the liquidation proceedings." The Garibaldi Society reassured members, "Your thoughts are your own." The opinion of Justice Hugo Black gave the IWO optimism that the liquidation threat would soon be over, for the jurist had written, "The executive has no constitutional authority, with or without a hearing, officially to prepare and publish the lists." Black found the subversive list to be punishment of "political beliefs and utterances," which he wrote "smacks of a most evil type of censorship." Since Haley had admitted the subversive list was "a prime mover" behind his condemnatory report, the IWO was confident that the liquidation case would soon collapse.[124]

Members were soon disappointed. The court had based its ruling on the absence of due-process hearings for organizations on the list. The federal government created a Subversive Activities Control Board (SACB), and with this veneer of administrative hearings in place, the subversive list continued into the Nixon administration. More immediately, government agencies ignored the ruling; the attorney general continued to authorize loyalty oaths for government employees and dismissal for those belonging to listed organizations. The INS, too, continued aggressive deportation proceedings against members or former members of the IWO and other listed groups.[125]

In late June Greenberg ruled in favor of liquidating the Order. Greenberg accepted the argument that the IWO was closely tied to the CP, noting the proletarian militancy of Order publications from the early 1930s as evidence of this. Although the judge allowed that after 1935 the tone of writings moderated, he concluded that the substance of the Order's Marxist aims remained the same. He noted that sixteen of the twenty-two current members of the IWO's executive committee, as well as nine of ten national officers, had been identified as members of the CP. Greenberg, however, did not comment on the fact that only a minority of the IWO's overall membership were Communists. While allowing that the Order's finances were in impeccable shape "at this time," Greenberg accepted the state's "take the money and run" argument—that the very liquidity of IWO assets made it possible that, in the event of a conflict with the Soviets, the organization's assets could be transferred to Moscow. The state's case was built on the supposition that the IWO *might* act at some *future* time to benefit foreign or domestic Communists. No evidence of such activity had been entered into the trial. Greenberg accepted the state's hypothetical argument, writing, "If the time arrives when there is a conflict between the interests of this country and the world of Communism, it is not beyond the realm of reasonable probability that the funds of this Order will be expropriated." To forestall that hypothetical, Greenberg confirmed the very actual expropriation of 160,000 members' millions in assets. The irony of militants, even Communists, fighting to protect private property from seizure by the capitalist state was nowhere reflected in the ruling.[126]

While Greenberg declared that policyholders' interests would be protected pending appeal, he nevertheless directed the Order to turn over all its papers to the Insurance Department. Administrator William Karlin followed through on this directive with meticulous thoroughness, demanding that the Order's accountant deliver "all the books, work papers, other papers, accounting reports..., tax reports..., documents, pamphlets, publications, accounts, files and other records" relating to the IWO and its sixteen ethnic societies as well as records from medical departments, schools, cemetery departments, camps, the FLFF, the JPFO Book Fund, and the Franklin D. Roosevelt Hospital Fund. The voluminous list of funds and departments might have suggested the breadth of the organization's good works, but Karlin was more interested in seeing to the Order's speedy liquidation. The Detroit JPFO secretary sardonically wrote that the sum total of her "records, books, etc., consist of a receipt book and a record of disbursements." The absurdity of the liquidation dragnet was apparent to some IWO members, even as the gravity of the threat was clear.[127]

"Will Justice and Liberty Still Call Themselves American?"

The IWO's lawyers continued to battle against liquidation, first in New York's appeals courts and then at the U.S. Supreme Court. In the Order's liquidation fight, all appeals were unsuccessful as jurists accepted the "present-day context of world crisis after crisis" as outweighing IWO members' free-association rights. Defense counsel Arthur Kinoy wrote that the New York State Appellate Court "in a conscious manner brushed aside all previous existing law in its efforts to uphold a political result."[128]

In demanding a rehearing, the IWO argued that the concept of "moral hazard had no basis in insurance law" and that the liquidation amounted to a state seizure of millions of dollars in private property—that is, policyholders' assets. New York's assistant attorneys general argued against a rehearing, maintaining once again the moral and political hazard posed by the Order, labeling the IWO "an arm of the Communist Party and the U.S.S.R." The state's move to liquidate, the petitioners argued, was brought because of "Communist and hence seditious activity" on the part of the IWO. In the state's petition, the economic hazard of a potential funneling of IWO funds to Communists abroad—again no evidence was presented of such a plan, only its possibility—was conflated with a broad moral hazard.[129]

In April 1953 the appellate court let the liquidation ruling stand. As the Order's lawyers petitioned the U.S. Supreme Court to consider their appeal, the Policyholders Protective Committee issued a pamphlet stating its case. *A Fraternal Order Sentenced to Death! The Strange Case of the International Workers Order* set forth the Order's good works and argued that it was only "the atmosphere of the Cold War with its loyalty oaths, subversive lists, [and] political persecutions" that had created "a political climate in which the traditional safeguards of constitutional rights are attacked and undermined and the right of free association trampled upon." The pamphlet asked, "Can decent Americans of all beliefs ... fail to see the charge of Communism as a smokescreen behind which sinister forces introduce the abhorrent principles of collective guilt, guilt by association and denial of constitutional rights?" More pointedly, the pamphlet asked, "Will the Supreme Court permit Censorship—Suppression—Confiscation?" adding, "The IWO may pass from the American scene ... , but will Justice and Liberty still call themselves American?"[130]

The IWO received its answer in October 1953 when the Supreme Court declined to hear the case. In the face of this death knell, many members remained adamant. Joseph Petercsak expressed "deep regret [at] the decision of the Supreme Court in connection with our Order. ... Our membership always regarded our Order as the head of a big family. We were together in good and bad times." The secretary of the Hungarian lodge of Hammond, Indiana, protested to the high court, "Our money is there and we feel that we have our rights."[131] The Policyholders Protective Committee sought a rehearing by the court. Individual lodges petitioned for this review, too, but the following month the petition for rehearing was denied. Shortly thereafter every member received a letter from the Insurance Department notifying them that their policies had been reassigned to the Continental Assurance Company of Illinois. Members could accept coverage with this commercial company or file for a cash payout, but the IWO, with its bands, choirs, and militant advocacy of workers' rights and racial justice, was done. The IWO had been liquidated.[132]

In December 1953 the Insurance Department informed members that, by court order, the department now had "sole supervision and control" of the Order's property and affairs. In subsequent months the department sold off and compensated lodges for their real property, as when a Russian lodge in Cliffside Park, New Jersey, was redeemed for its shares in Arow Farm, a summer camp, or IWO halls in the New York area were sold off. The IWO's lawyers continued filing objections to the department's "reinsurance program" as "a gigantic give-away plan. ... The Superintendent has casually tossed to the first comer millions of dollars of policy-holders' funds." When liquidation and assignment to Continental Assurance went ahead anyway, the Insurance Department quibbled over how much severance pay former

IWO officers were owed. Again, in this context it seems Communists were the defenders and a state agency the expropriator of private property.[133]

The department went beyond financial dismantlement. In his letter detailing members' options, Bohlinger cautioned, "Joining or maintaining any connection with any fraternal, cultural, social or other group which has been organized or which may be organized by former officers or leaders of the former IWO . . . may well be considered to be membership in a subversive or a Communist-front organization." *Jewish Life*, magazine of the recently expired JPFO, labeled this "new violation of free association" a "fascist piece of impudence." It printed a statement by nineteen former IWO officers that said this "crassest example of thought control" exposed Bohlinger's hypocrisy, since his department had argued that liquidation had nothing to do with members' civil rights. The editorial urged Americans to stand against "creeping fascism."[134]

A former IWO member was more colorful in denouncing the superintendent's warnings on any future associations. The Yiddish Communist *Morgen Freiheit* reprinted a letter to "Saint Bohlinger" in which "G. M." demanded to know, "Who gave you the right to tell me where I should belong? Do you imagine yourself riding high on Hitler's white horse, controlling my thoughts and my right of association. Do you really want to push yourself, with your stormtrooper's paws, into my head and my mind?" "G. M." asked Bohlinger, "Why do you stick your pig's snout in a matter that is none of your business?" and told him that despite these threats, he and his friends were building a new organization "for mutual aid, for culture for democratic rights." Many members did not gently accept liquidation.[135]

In a final, surreal development, even as the IWO fought liquidation in the courts, the attorney general determined that under the 1950 McCarran Act, the Order and all its members had to register as part of a "subversive" organization. The IWO fought this designation and was granted a hearing before the recently created SACB. However, the multiple government agencies orchestrating a punitive panopticon limited the Order's ability to defend itself. The Insurance Department, now running the Order's day-to-day business and scrupulously overseeing all expenditures, denied a request by its officers for funds to pay lawyers to represent them at the SACB "hearing." Lawyerless, the Order's officers boycotted the SACB hearing, and that body declared failure to attend an admission of guilt. When the IWO's officers attempted to appear for a second hearing, the SACB ruled that as the Insurance Department was now the sole administrator of the Order, former IWO officers Greene and Saltzman had no standing to appear or speak on the Order's behalf. The Insurance Department had removed them as officers the day before. In January 1954 the SACB, ignoring Greene and Saltzman's appearance at the second hearing, ruled that the IWO had twice failed to appear before the board, and therefore the subversive listing stood. In an ironic twist, in November 1954 an appeals court ruled that the IWO had been placed on the subversive list erroneously after all. From beyond the grave, the militant, interracial IWO, which had haunted the imagination of red-hunters, was exonerated—cold comfort to the members who were already deprived of their "big family," the IWO.[136]

Conclusion

The evisceration of the IWO and other left-wing organizations considerably narrowed the parameters for permissible debate in the United States. From its inception, the IWO envisioned a practical program to create a vibrant social-democratic state, one that could unapologetically demand government-funded universal health care and militant unions that guaranteed safe and remunerative employment for all Americans while valorizing the true creators of the nation's wealth. Beyond this concern, decades before it became fashionable for politicians and civic boosters to mouth homages to America as a gorgeous mosaic of multiculturalism, the IWO combated America's vicious Jim Crow segregation and endemic racism, practicing—with miscues, to be sure—a commitment to racial egalitarianism in an interracial organization. On the world stage, too, commitment to anticolonialism and a more irenic foreign policy became even more of an outlier position, earning government suppression not only of the IWO but also groups such as the CAA in which Order members like Robeson took the lead. Critiques of outsized Pentagon budgets and open-ended military adventures and calling out of American imperialism and fascism became voices in the wilderness in an America becoming intent on invading and quashing national aspirations from Vietnam to Iran to Guatemala when such aspirations collided with the new world corporate order.

The evisceration of the IWO also closed off an alternative road of interracial cooperation and alliance of black, Hispanic, and white ethnic working-class Americans committed to working for racial and economic justice for all the country's inhabitants, citizens and foreign-born residents alike. In mid-twentieth-century Detroit and Chicago, for example, firebombings and angry white homeowners violently challenged African American attempts to achieve full citizenship and dignity. But working-class Hungarians, Slovaks, Jews, Italians, and others in the IWO and other militant organizations were the resisters of white privilege, the practitioners—imperfect though they were—of racial equality and civil rights as well as economic justice. They hosted interracial house-painting parties and created "American Crusades against Lynching."[1]

It has become fashionable in academia to focus on the angry white ethnic turf defenders, those practicing "crabgrass-root politics" bent on defending neighborhoods and job sites from black incursions.[2] Certain politicians have recently dismissed such people as a "basket of deplorables." There is much to deplore in recent American political developments: perhaps warnings by members of the IWO of a growing American fascism now seem not so much overwrought as prophetic.

I hope I have demonstrated that more than tentative steps were taken toward an intersectional worldview that foregrounded racial as well as class-based oppression in one of the seedbeds of the Old Left. White ethnic members of the IWO and similar organizations—again, with many missteps, to be sure—did not have a blind spot on race. The terrorism visited on African Americans was viscerally condemned and combated. It was something they felt in their bones. The suppression of such organizations is to be more than lamented in our era of almost quotidian state-sanctioned violence against African American teens and hypermilitarization of policing of the boundaries between "us" and "them." Again, members of the IWO envisioned that another world was possible.

The ease with which all agencies of the state brushed aside Bill of Rights guarantees of free speech, press, and association for the members of the IWO resonates, too, in the present militarized crackdown on dissent. While FBI agents and police red squads kept voluminous records of the Order's activities in the 1950s, today the National Security Agency taps into billions of e-mails and cell phone calls; the uncharged, unsentenced, but very much incarcerated inmates at Guantanamo, or the U.S. citizens targeted for "surgical" assassination by drone, could likely attest that the modern security state is more than just a mild, take-your-shoes-off-at-the-airport annoyance. In the 1950s IWO members were being targeted for deportation or jail, and their organization was being liquidated because of their political beliefs. But their warnings of fascism coming to the United States struck many Americans as hyperbolic at the time. Now that we live in a country in which Chelsea Manning gets not a medal but life in prison for exposing tales of torture and mass murder in Iraq, and now that the freedom to dissent from the omni-observing, omni-condemning security state is imperiled by a candidate for Homeland Security chief calling for the shipment of three million U.S. citizen "troublemakers" to Guantanamo, perhaps it is time to reconsider, as the IWO once did, "Should Miss Liberty Be Deported?" Near the end of its state-sanctioned ordeal, the IWO's Policyholders Protective Committee asked if the government would "permit Censorship—Suppression—Confiscation?" and warned, "The IWO may pass from the American scene . . . , but will Justice and Liberty still call themselves American?"[3] Increasingly, the jury seems to be out on that one. We may all come to feel Kent and Robeson's pain.

To be sure, the liquidation of the IWO did not end the militant activism of all its members. Thompson Patterson continued her radical advocacy for African American equality in the Sojourners for Truth and Justice and then in other organizations into the 1990s. As early as 1954, Detroit Poles had ignored the admonition of New York Insurance superintendent Bohlinger not to associate with former fellow IWO members and were meeting in Polish political clubs that criticized America's incipient imperial adventure in Vietnam, among other topics. Former IWO members also heard Aptheker discuss the ongoing Vietnam War in the mid-1960s and ran a Detroit Workers' Bazaar through the 1960s. There, too, Polish former members of the IWO held fund-raising Halloween parties for rising African American politician Coleman Young; the city's first black mayor had roots in the militant Old Left, too. In 1973 an International Bazaar for Peace and Freedom was held at the same Detroit address that in 1936 police had noted was an IWO hall.[4] The links between the Old Left and the New Left were, as McDuffie and Gore note, sometimes strong.[5]

I argue that the government's intentional severing of the institutional homes for interracial activism such as the IWO made it that much more difficult for sustained campaigns of racial- and class-based justice to occur. The kinds of affective places, institutional homes where one was free to think, plan, and play with kindred spirits, represented by IWO halls, workers' schools, and children's camps, were dismantled. The thick network necessary for social movements to thrive was destroyed by the government, perhaps to make it that much harder to contest the status quo.

The Old Left of the IWO is gone, but the necessity to contend with the endemic racism, militarism, and shredded safety net are still with us. Provision of social goods such as universal health care for which the IWO once so forcefully advocated is as distant a dream as in 1947, perhaps more so now that the austeritarians control both major political parties. Vibrant, militant new social movements such as Black Lives Matter, the Standing Rock protest, and the pushback on corporate-friendly globalization give me cause for cautious optimism. I hope the story of the IWO, "a fraternal organization sentenced to death," demonstrates to present-day scholars, activists, and citizens that their intellectual ancestors once dreamed as they do that another world was not only possible, but imperative.[6]

Notes

INTRODUCTION

1. Peter Shipka, "Department of Justice Evades Justice," *Jewish Fraternalist*, November 1948, 3–4, box 46, International Workers Order Records, 1915–2002, MSS 5276, Kheel Center for Labor-Management Documentation and Archives, Cornell University [hereafter cited as IWO-CU]; Gedalia Sandler to Henry Wald of Atlanta, January 31, 1949, IWO-CU, box 31, folder 11.

2. Irving Bernstein, *The Lean Years: A History of the American Worker, 1920–1933* (Boston, MA: Houghton Mifflin, 1960); Zaragosa Vargas, *Proletarians of the North: A History of Mexican Industrial Workers in Detroit and the Midwest, 1917–1933* (Berkeley: University of California Press, 1999), 172–173.

3. IWO flyer, *Why Not Social Insurance?* [1932], reel 234, delo [folder] 3037, Records of the Communist Party USA, Microfilm 21, 966, Library of Congress [hereafter cited as CPUSA-LC]; "The Activities of the I.W.O.," [1932], CPUSA-LC, reel 234, delo 3037; "Report of District Plenum of IWO, April 29, 1934" [Philadelphia], CPUSA-LC, reel 287, delo 3709; Max Bedacht to Earl Browder, July 26, 1934, including suggested copy for an IWO election leaflet on Social Insurance, ibid.; "Lodge Program Civic and Community Events" [1940s], includes "Rights of the Negro People, Equality," and "Daily Schedule National Training School, September 3–11, 1949," with a call for universal health care, IWO-CU, box 4, folder 10. Sam Milgrom to "Dear Brother," February 28, 1946, IWO-CU, box 20, folder 5; Draft report of the General Secretary of the IWO, August 29, 1946, calling for passage of the Wagner-Murray-Dingell health care bill, box 1, folder 2, International Workers Order Records, Robert F. Wagner Labor Archives, Tamiment Library, New York University [hereafter cited as IWO-NYU].

4. Letter from Philip Murray, SWOC, commending the IWO for its support, April 13, 1937, and letter in reply from Max Bedacht, April 20, 1937, IWO-NYU, folder 43. Both letters made up the brochure *Two Letters about One Cause*, April 20, 1937, ibid. For the CIO, see Robert Zieger, *The CIO, 1935–1955* (Chapel Hill: University of North Carolina Press, 1995). For acceptance of Communists as effective organizers among

coal miners, see Steve Nelson, James Barrett, and Rob Ruck, *Steve Nelson, American Radical* (Pittsburgh, PA: University of Pittsburgh Press, 1981); and Rosemary Feurer, *Radical Unionism in the Midwest, 1900–1950* (Urbana: University of Illinois Press, 2006). Margaret Collingwood Nowak, *Two Who Were There: A Biography of Stanley Nowak* (Detroit, MI: Wayne State University Press, 1989) discusses Nowak's 1930s organizing activities for the United Automobile Workers.

5. Among other items targeting the Taft-Hartley Act, see Leo Krzycki to union members of the American Slav Congress, October 27, 1947, box 5, folder 3, International Ladies Garment Workers Union, Charles Zimmerman Papers, 1919–1958, MSS 5780/014, Kheel Center for Labor-Management Documentation and Archives, Cornell University [hereafter cited as ILGWU-CU, 5780/014]; "IWO Resolution against Anti-Labor Legislation" [1947], IWO-NYU, folder 6; Rockwell Kent, Sam Milgrom, and Peter Shipka to members [1947?], ibid.; Baltimore member of IWO Russian Section to Daniel Kasustchik, May 12, 1948, IWO-NYU, folder 40; and "Daily Schedule National Training School, September 3–11, 1949," includes sessions on defeating Taft-Hartley, IWO-CU, box 4, folder 10. *Lodge Log*, a mimeographed magazine of Jewish Peoples Fraternal Order (JPFO) Lodge 585, Brooklyn, April 1947, includes a cartoon and text, "To be or not to be a Slave," urging anti-Taft-Hartley Bill lobbying, IWO-CU, box 46. "Greetings to Labor by the IWO," *Sunday Worker*, September 4, 1949, 7, included the IWO's pledge to continue working for repeal of Taft-Hartley, box 2, folder 2-55, Don Binkowski Papers, Walter P. Reuther Library, Wayne State University [hereafter cited as DB-WSU]. FBI report, Detroit Polonia Society of the IWO, noting speech by Thomas Dombrowski of the IWO at a November 27, 1953, meeting of the Friends of the People's Press Committee, DB-WSU, box 5, folder 5-29.

6. James Madison, *A Lynching in the Heartland: Race and Memory in America* (New York: Palgrave, 2001); Amy Louise Wood, *Lynching and Spectacle: Witnessing Racial Violence in America, 1890–1940* (Chapel Hill: University of North Carolina Press, 2009); Christopher Waldrep, *The Many Faces of Judge Lynch: Extralegal Violence and Punishment in America* (New York: Palgrave Macmillan, 2002); Philip Dray, *At the Hands of Persons Unknown: The Lynching of Black America* (New York: The Modern Library, 2003); Robert Zecker, *Race and America's Immigrant Press: How the Slovaks were Taught to Think Like White People* (New York: Continuum, 2011), 12–49, 204–247; Thomas Philpott, *The Slum and the Ghetto: Neighborhood Deterioration and Middle-Class Reform, Chicago, 1880–1930* (New York: Oxford University Press, 1978); Arnold Hirsch, *Making the Second Ghetto: Race and Housing in Chicago, 1940–1960* (Chicago: University of Chicago Press, 1998); James Hirsch, *Riot and Remembrance: The Tulsa Race Riot and its Legacy* (Boston, MA: Houghton Mifflin, 2002); Thomas Sugrue, *The Origins of the Urban Crisis: Race and Inequality in Postwar Detroit* (Princeton, NJ: Princeton University Press, 1996); Andrew Diamond, *Mean Streets: Chicago Youths and the Everyday Struggle for Empowerment in the Multiracial City, 1908–1969* (Berkeley: University of California Press, 2009); Kevin Boyle, *Arc of Justice: A Saga of Race, Civil Rights and Murder in the Jazz Age* (New York: Henry Holt, 2004); Karen Miller, *Managing Inequality: Northern Racial Liberalism in Interwar Detroit* (New York: New York University Press, 2015). Cyril Briggs to Secretariat, Communist Party (CP), May 12, 1930, CPUSA-LC, reel 151, delo 1166. Brochure and poster, "Workers! Smash Lynching!" American Negro Labor Congress [1930], CPUSA-LC, reel 165, delo 2204.

7. FBI file, IWO, Detroit division, report on Arabic Section, December 10, 1945, DB-WSU, box 16, folder 16-36. For Black Muslims in the IWO, see Harold Peters to Metropolitan Life Insurance, February 2, 1945, Sam Milgrom to Peters, February 19,

1945, Peters to Milgrom, February 22, 1945, Peters to Milgrom, March 22, 1945, Milgrom to Peters, March 31, 1945, Peters to Milgrom, April 3, 1945, Milgrom to Peters, April 6, 1945, Peters to Dave Greene, May 14, 1945, and Sol Vail to Milgrom, October 5, 1945, IWO-CU, box 8, folder 2. Affidavit, Jumal Ahmad, Cleveland, April 1951, box 3, International Workers Order Case Files, MSS 5940, Kheel Center for Labor-Management Documentation and Archives, Cornell University [hereafter cited as IWOCF-CU].

8. Affidavit, Pecola Moore, Los Angeles, April 24, 1951, IWOCF-CU, box 3; "Report of the Officers Presented to the General Council, IWO, February 3 and 4, 1951," IWO-NYU, folder 18; Edward Nelson, "What the Attack on the Order Means to the Negro People," *The Defender*, April 1951, 1–2, IWOCF-CU, box 2. "Daily Schedule National Training School, September 3–11, 1949." An "Answer to Superintendent of Insurance Bohlinger, Adopted at Membership Meeting of the International Workers Order, March 7, 1951," IWO-CU, box 23, folder 4. An Emergency Conference of IWO members, ibid. "Resolutions, Adopted by Emergency Conference against the Liquidation of a People's Organization," February 10, 1951, IWO-CU, box 24. Max Taber, "Stuyvesant Town for Whites Only," *Jewish Fraternalist*, February–March 1950, 6–7, IWO-CU, box 46. Affidavit, Jumal Ahmad, Cleveland. Sadie Doroshkin to Louise Thompson, June 4, 1934, box 8, folder 8, Louise Thompson Patterson Papers, MSS 869, Stuart A. Rose Manuscript, Archives, and Rare Book Library, Emory University [hereafter cited as LTP-EU]; Max Bedacht to Thompson, June 7, 1934, ibid.; Interview with Louise Thompson Patterson [ca. 1950–1951], LTP-EU, box 8, folder 10; Thompson Patterson, interview by Linda Burnham, March 11 and 14, 1988, LTP-EU, box 27, folder 13; Thompson Patterson, interview by Mary Lecht [ca. 1980s], LTP-EU, box 28, folder 16; Interview with Thompson Patterson, June 2 and 9, 1987, LTP-EU, box 27, folder 8; Thompson Patterson, interview by Margaret Wilkerson, April 20, 1989, LTP-EU, box 28, folder 2. Samuel Roberts, IWO National Education Department, to *Baltimore Afro-American*, February 5, 1938, 4. See "What Will We Do If . . . ?" *The Compass*, January 20, 1952, 10, for publicity for a rally to support the IWO scheduled for January 26, 1952, IWOCF-CU, box 2.

9. Sam Milgrom to Eleanor Broady of Detroit, April 2, 1945, IWO-CU, box 7, folder 4. On Stuyvesant Town, see Nelson, "What the Attack on the Order Means to the Negro People."

10. Press release, "Anti-Nazi Federation of New York," "March against the Nazis!" November 21, 1935, CPUSA-LC, reel 300, delo 3938; Press release, "Anti-Nazi Federation," August 8, 1935, includes IWO participation in planned Madison Square Garden anti-Nazi, anti-Olympics rally, CPUSA-LC, reel 300, delo 3939. On Ethiopia, see Luigi Candela to Earl Browder and Central Committee of the CP, June 29, 1935, CPUSA-LC, reel 292, delo 3787; Rebecca Grecht to Polburo Central Committee of the CP, September 12, 1935, CPUSA-LC, reel 301, delo 3942; Pamphlet, *The Seminar in Negro History*, 1938 spring lecture series, Harlem Community Center of IWO, LTP-EU, box 8, folder 9; Invitation, IWO Solidarity Lodge 691, Harlem, reception dinner for Thompson reporting on her visit to Spain, October 20, 1937, LTP-EU, box 13, folder 9; Thompson radio speech, Station EAR, Madrid, August 27, 1937, LTP-EU, box 13, folder 9.

11. "Statement of National Committee, Italian-American Section, IWO, October 12, 1942," IWO-CU, box 10, folder 8; Flyer, WIN THE WAR—*Open That Second Front Now!* (1942) contains some of the numerous IWO calls for a second front, IWO-CU, box 19, folder 11. Minutes, Slovak Workers Society convention, July 4–6, 1944, IWO-CU, box 54.

12. Louis Adamic, "Conspiracy against Peace," *Slavic American*, Winter 1947, 5–6, 52.

13. Secretary, Communist International, to Central Committee of the Workers Party of America, May 7, 1926, CPUSA-LC, reel 40, delo 588.

14. Allen Weinstein, *The Haunted Wood: Soviet Espionage in America–The Stalin Era* (New York: Random House, 1999); John Haynes and Harvey Klehr, *Venona: Decoding Soviet Espionage in America* (New Haven, CT: Yale University Press, 1999); John Haynes and Harvey Klehr, *The Soviet World of American Communism* (New Haven, CT: Yale University Press, 1998); John Haynes, *In Denial: Historians, Communism and Espionage* (New York: Encounter Books, 2005); John Haynes, *Red Scare or Red Menace? American Communism and Anticommunism in the Cold War Era* (Chicago, IL: Ivan R. Dee, 1996). For the anti-Communist activism of the American Federation of Labor (AFL), see Jennifer Luff, *Commonsense Anticommunism: Labor and Civil Liberties between the World Wars* (Chapel Hill: University of North Carolina Press, 2012); Maurice Isserman, "Open Archives and Open Minds: 'Traditionalists' versus 'Revisionists' after Venona," *American Communist History* 4, no. 2 (2005): 215–223; and John Haynes and Harvey Klehr, "The Historiography of American Communism: An Unsettled Field," *Labour History Review* 68, no. 1 (April 2003): 61–78.

15. Jacqueline Castledine, *Cold War Progressives: Women's Interracial Organizing for Peace and Freedom* (Urbana: University of Illinois Press, 2012); Erik Gellman, *Death Blow to Jim Crow: The National Negro Congress and the Rise of Militant Civil Rights* (Chapel Hill: University of North Carolina Press, 2012); Dayo Gore, *Radicalism at the Crossroads: African American Women Activists in the Cold War* (New York: New York University Press, 2011); Daniel Katz, *All Together Different: Yiddish Socialists, Garment Workers, and the Labor Roots of Multiculturalism* (New York: New York University Press, 2011); William Maxwell, *New Negro, Old Left: African-American Writing and Communism Between the Wars* (New York: Columbia University Press, 1999); Erik McDuffie, *Sojourning for Freedom: Black Women, American Communism, and the Making of Black Left Feminism* (Durham, NC: Duke University Press, 2011); Hakim Adi, *Pan-Africanism and Communism: The Communist International, Africa and the Diaspora, 1919–1939* (London: Africa World Press, 2013); Minkah Makalani, *In the Cause of Freedom: Radical Black Internationalism from Harlem to London, 1917–1939* (Chapel Hill: University of North Carolina Press, 2011).

16. Rachel Ida Buff, *Against the Deportation Terror: The American Committee for the Protection of the Foreign Born and Immigrant Rights Advocacy, 1933–1982* (Philadelphia, PA: Temple University Press, 2018); Daniel Kanstroom, *Deportation Nation: Outsiders in American History* (Cambridge, MA: Harvard University Press, 2007).

17. Weinstein, *The Haunted Wood*; Haynes and Klehr, *Venona*; Haynes and Klehr, *The Soviet World of American Communism*; Haynes, *In Denial*.

18. Arthur Sabin, *Red Scare in Court: New York versus the International Workers Order* (Philadelphia: University of Pennsylvania Press, 1993).

19. Thomas Walker, *Pluralistic Fraternity: The History of the International Workers Order* (New York: Garland, 1991).

20. Roger Keeran, "National Groups and the Popular Front: The Case of the International Workers Order," *Journal of American Ethnic History* 14, no. 3 (Spring 1995): 23–51; Roger Keeran, "The International Workers Order and the Origins of the CIO," *Labor History* 30, no. 3 (Summer 1989): 385–408; Tony Michels, "Communism and the Problem of Ethnicity in the 1920s: The Case of Moissaye Olgin," *Contemporary Jewry* 25 (2011): 26–48; Tony Michels, ed., *Jewish Radicals: A Documentary History* (New York: New York University Press, 2012).

21. Timothy Johnson, "'We Are Illegal Here': The Communist Party, Self-Determination and the Alabama Share Croppers Union," *Science and Society* 75, no 4 (October 2011): 463; Robin Kelley, *Hammer and Hoe: Alabama Communists during the Great Depression* (Chapel Hill: University of North Carolina Press, 1990). See, too, Doroshkin to Thompson, June 4, 1934, and Bedacht to Thompson, June 7, 1934; Interview with Louise Thompson Patterson [ca. 1950–1951]; Thompson Patterson, interview by Burnham, March 11 and 14, 1988; Thompson Patterson, interview by Lecht; Thompson Patterson, interview, by Ruth and Bud Schultz, August 12, 1984, IWO-CU, box 27, folder 3.

22. News release, "IWO Challenges Constitutionality of Attorney General Clark's Report; Plans Legal Action," December 5, 1947, puts IWO membership at 188,000 members, IWO-NYU, folder 31.

23. Paul Robeson, *Here I Stand* (New York: Othello, 1958); Martin Duberman, *Paul Robeson* (New York: Knopf, 1988); Tony Perucci, *Paul Robeson and the Cold War Performance Complex: Race, Madness, Activism* (Ann Arbor: University of Michigan Press, 2012); Jordan Goodman, *Paul Robeson: A Watched Man* (New York: Verso, 2013).

24. Landon Storrs, *The Second Red Scare and the Unmaking of the New Deal Left* (Princeton, NJ: Princeton University Press, 2013).

25. Michels, "Communism and the Problem of Ethnicity"; Paul Buhle, "Historians and American Communism: An Agenda," *International Labor and Working-Class History* 20 (Fall 1981): 38–45; Paul Buhle and Robin Kelley, "The Oral History of the Left: A Survey and Interpretation," *Journal of American History* 76, no. 2 (September 1989): 537–550.

26. Feurer, *Radical Unionism in the Midwest*; Shelton Stromquist, ed., *Labor's Cold War: Local Politics in a Global Context* (Urbana: University of Illinois Press, 2008).

27. James Green, "Working Class Militancy in the Great Depression," *Radical America* 6, no. 6 (November–December 1972): 1–36.

28. *The Slavic American*, Winter 1947, 46.

29. Philpott, *The Slum and the Ghetto*; Hirsch, *Making the Second Ghetto*; Sugrue, *Origins of the Urban Crisis*; Diamond, *Mean Streets*; Miller, *Managing Inequality*; Kevin Kruse, *White Flight: Atlanta and the Making of Modern Conservatism* (Princeton, NJ: Princeton University Press, 2005); Robert Self, *American Babylon: Race and the Struggle for Postwar Oakland* (Princeton, NJ: Princeton University Press, 2003); Thomas Sugrue, "Crabgrass-Roots Politics: Race, Rights, and the Reaction against Liberalism in the Urban North, 1940–1964," *Journal of American History* 82, no. 2 (September 1995): 551–578.

30. W.E.B. Du Bois, *The Souls of Black Folk* (1903; repr., New York: Vintage Books, 1990); David Roediger, *The Wages of Whiteness: Race and the Making of the American Working Class* (New York: Verso, 1991).

31. James Barrett and David Roediger, "Whiteness and the Inbetween Peoples of Europe," *Journal of American Ethnic History* 16, no. 3 (Summer 1997): 3–44.

32. Detroit Police report, August 26, 1948, DB-WSU, box 2, folder 2-55.

33. Ellen Schrecker, *Many Are the Crimes: McCarthyism in America* (Princeton, NJ: Princeton University Press, 1998).

34. Michels, "Communism and the Problem of Ethnicity"; Al Gedicks, "The Social Origin of Radicalism among Finnish Immigrants in Midwest Mining Communities," *Review of Radical Political Economy* 8, no. 3 (1976): 1–31; Buhle, "Historians and American Communism."

35. Office of Strategic Services/Foreign Nationalities Branch (OSS/FNB) report, the FNB to the Director of Strategic Services, "Communist-Line IWO Reorganizes to

Emphasize Nationality," July 11, 1944, DB-WSU, box 4, folder 4-29; also see OSS/FNB report and letter, both July 17, 1944, "CFB" to "Dear Rodman" on the IWO's "dual personality" and Machiavellian nature, DB-WSU, box 4, folder 4-29; OSS/FNB report, "The Polish-American Section of IWO," February 10, 1944, DB-WSU, box 7, folder 7-53; OSS/FNB report, "The Polish American Left," June 16, 1944, DB-WSU, box 2, folder 2-53.

36. Letter from Murray, and Bedacht, *Two Letters about One Cause*.

37. IWO Declaration of Principles [1933], CPUSA-LC, reel 260, delo 3372.

38. Sam Milgrom to "Dear Brother" on IWO film strip "Health and Security for America," February 28, 1946, IWO-CU, box 20, folder 5; Draft report of General Secretary, IWO, August 29, 1946, IWO-NYU, folder 2.

39. IWO report on organizing Negro branches [1932], CPUSA-LC, reel 234, delo 3037; Affidavit, Miklos Petri, the Bronx, April 23, 1951, IWOCF-CU, box 3. On the American Crusade against Lynching, see Minutes, General Council meeting, September 7–8, 1946, IWO-NYU, folder 14. On Scottsboro, see "Digest of Testimony of Witnesses for the State in the I.W.O. Matter. January 29, 1951, to March 7, 1951," IWOCF-CU, box 4. Minutes, meeting of CP's District 2 Bureau, September 4, 1935, including an IWO report by Comrade Shaffer, CPUSA-LC, reel 294, delo 3811. Minutes, Language Department, CP, May 11, 1931, notes Scottsboro actions taken at IWO meetings, CPUSA-LC, reel 177, delo 2332; Letters, Charles Dirba, May 6, 1931, and Language Department to Czecho Slovakian Bureau, May 7, 1931, discuss IWO protests and fund-raising regarding Scottsboro, CPUSA-LC, reel 177, delo 2336.

40. Sam Milgrom to Eleanor Broady, IWO-CU, box 7 folder 4.

41. See ad for a Robeson appearance before JPFO rally in the *Sunday Worker*, June 3, 1947, 10, IWO-CU, box 27.1, folder 9; IWO press release, Negro History Week, February 5, 1953, IWO-CU, box 4, folder 6.

42. "Comrade Basketball," *The New Order*, 1935, cited in Paul Buhle, "Interview with Ernie Reymer of the I.W.O.," *Cultural Correspondence* 6, no. 7 (Spring 1978): 98–101; *The Spark*, July 1931, 30, 31, CPUSA-LC, reel 195, delo 2584; *The New Order*, March 1934, 14, CPUSA-LC, reel 287, delo 3709; "Report of District Plenum of IWO, Philadelphia, Sunday, April 29, 1934." Proceedings of the Fourth New York City Convention of IWO Branches, March 21–22, 1936, 3, CPUSA-LC, reel 305, delo 4050; A. Kanovsky, financial secretary, IWO Branch 521, Bronx, to "Dear Member," January 20, 1936, regarding theater and talk on "The Motion Picture," ibid. For integrated baseball leagues and campaigns, see *The New Order*, March 1934, 11; "Digest of Testimony of Witnesses for the State"; News release, "IWO Hails Cleveland Pennant Victory," October 4, 1948, IWO-NYU, folder 31. "Lodge Program Sessions 9 and 10 Civic and Community Events," "Daily Schedule National Training School, September 3–11, 1949," IWO-CU, box 4, folder 10; Ben Goldstein of the Metropolitan Interfaith and Interracial Coordinating Council, to "Dear Friend," July 19, 1945, box 46, Vito Marcantonio Papers, Manuscripts and Archives Division, The New York Public Library [hereafter cited as VM-NYPL]; Flyer, *August 19—End Jim Crow in Baseball Day* [1945], ibid.; Goldstein to "Dear Friend" and Goldstein to Mayor Fiorello La Guardia, both August 17, 1945, ibid.; John Joy of Negro Major American and National League Baseball Teams to Congressman Vito Marcantonio, May 3, 1945, ibid. For an IWO Puerto Rican baseball league, see affidavit, Peter Moreno, Brooklyn, April 24, 1951, IWOCF-CU, box 3.

43. "Lodge Program Civic and Community Events," "Rights of the Negro People, Equality," "Daily Schedule National Training School, September 3–11, 1949."

44. Evelyn Louise Crawford and MaryLouise Patterson, eds., *Letters from Langston: From the Harlem Renaissance to the Red Scare and Beyond* (Berkeley: University

of California Press, 2016), 142, 144–146, 148–158, 161–169, 189, 193, 202, 332. Script of show produced by the Freedom Theatre for IWO, *Let's Get Together* [1950], IWO-CU, box 26, folder 10; Synopsis of Ukrainian Society play, *All Our Yesterdays*, by Andrew Hertz, October 1948, and *The Partisans*, by M. Pilny, January 19, 1942, IWO-CU, box 26, folder 7; *Keep Up!* in synopses of SWS material [ca. 1950], IWO-CU, box 26, folder 5.

45. Ad, Front Line Fighters Fund, "Radość Dnia Dziękczynienia Należy do Naszych Dielnych Bojowników" [The Joy of Thanksgiving Belongs to Our Brave Fighters/Warriors/Soldiers], *Glos Ludowy*, November 25, 1944, 6, DB-WSU, box 5, folder 5-29. All translations from original languages, unless otherwise noted, are mine.

46. Adamic, "Conspiracy against Peace."

47. "Moral Lepers Like Hearst Peril Nation," *Národné noviny*, March 15, 1944, 5. See, too, pamphlet issued by National Negro Congress, deriding "our peanut Hitlers . . . the Talmadges, the Gerald L. K. Smiths, the Lindberghs . . .": *Negro People Will Defend America* (Washington, D.C.: National Negro Congress, 1941); IWO to Vito Marcantonio, telegram, February 4, 1943, VM-NYPL, box 47; Flyer, *Mass Meeting against the Dies Committee, for the New Deal* [English and Italian], January 29, 1939, La Progressiva Lodge 2501, IWO, ibid.; Petition against the Dies HUAC, from IWO Dante Alighieri Lodge 2579, Bronx [January 1939], ibid. For Roosevelt's congratulations to the ASC, see Roosevelt to Blair Gunther of ASC, telegram, April 25, 1942, DB-WSU, box 1, folder 1-17. For Slav Congress's disapproval of Truman's policies, see Leo Krzycki and Zlatko Baloković to Truman, telegram, March 7, 1946, DB-WSU, box 1, folder 1-18; George Pirinsky to Truman, October 11, 1946, ibid.

48. "Moral Lepers Like Hearst Peril Nation"; *Negro People Will Defend America*; IWO to Marcantonio, telegram, February 4, 1943.

49. OSS/FNB report, "Communist-Line IWO Reorganizes to Emphasize Nationality"; OSS/FNB report and letter, July 17, 1944.

50. Max Bedacht to Vito Marcantonio, telegram, May 3, 1940, copying Bedacht's letter to Congressman Dies, VM-NYPL, box 47; "IWO National 'Stop Dies' Drive Gets Mass Support," *Daily Worker*, May 15, 1940, 5, CPUSA-LC, reel 318, delo 4243; "IWO Calls an Anti-Dies Rally in Brooklyn," May 18, 1940, 5, ibid.; "Court Allows I.W.O. to Inspect Seized Files: Phila. Judge Orders Dies Permit IWO Inspection of Raided Material," May 17, 1940, 5, ibid.

51. Pamphlet, *An American Family Faces Separation or Exile*, by the Stanley Nowak Defense Committee [April 1956], DB-WSU, box 7, folder 7-48; "Statement of the American Slav Congress on the arrest of George Pirinsky," October 23, 1950, box 4, folder 4-2, Stanley and Margaret Collingwood Nowak Papers, Walter P. Reuther Library, Wayne State University [hereafter cited as NP-WSU]; ASC press release, 1950, decrying deportation orders against Pirinsky and other aliens, ibid.; Pirinsky to Nowak, October 10, 1949, NP-WSU, box 4, folder 4-16.

52. FBI report on Vito Marcantonio, May 6, 1954, DB-WSU, box 7, folder 7-19; FBI memorandum, "To: Mr. D. M. Ladd, From: Mr. A. H. Belmont, Subject: Vito Marcantonio, Security Matter—C," July 27, 1950, ibid.; FBI memorandum, "To: Director, FBI, From: SA, New York," November 25, 1950, ibid. An FBI file on Stanley Nowak, May 1, 1952, notes his peace activism and designates him an internal security threat, DB-WSU, box 7, folder 7-49. FBI report, to the Director, March 11, 1946, notes that ASC president Leo Krzycki should be interned in the event of a "national emergency," DB-WSU, box 4, folder 4-19.

53. Nelson Frank, "Their Books Balanced, But Politics Were in Red," *New York World-Telegram and Sun*, January 23, 1951, and "Among Reddest Red Nests," *New York World-Telegram and Sun*, January 20, 1951, IWOCF-CU, box 2. Louis Budenz,

"IWO—Red Bulwark: The Inside Story of an Outfit That Works Hand in Glove with the Communist Party and Which Now Faces a Crackdown That Is Long Overdue," *American Legion Magazine*, March 1951, reprint, IWOCF-CU, box 3.

54. News release, "IWO Challenges Constitutionality of Attorney General Clark's Report; Plans Legal Action," December 27, 1947, notes December 15 Bill of Rights Day celebrations, IWO-NYU, folder 31; Flyer, *Should Miss Liberty Be Deported? The Case of Peter Harisiades* [1950], VM-NYPL, box 46; Flyer, *Shall We Destroy the Statue of Liberty and Build Concentration Camps?* [Committee in Defense of Henry Podolski, ca. 1950], DB-WSU, box 8, folder 8-42; IWO press release, "IWO URGES ATTORNEY GENERAL TO ACT ON BAIL FOR FOLEY SQUARE DEFENDANTS," October 27, 1949, IWO-CU, box 48.

55. *Should Miss Liberty Be Deported?*; FBI report, IWO, Detroit division, November 20, 1953, DB-WSU, box 16, folder 16-38; "Appeal to Members of the Polonia Society—Don't Let Them Deport Henry Podolski," *Glos Ludowy*, September 10, 1949, 13, DB-WSU, box 16, folder 16-36. Minutes, English-speaking lodges, SWS meeting, September 1-2, 1946, IWO-CU, box 14, folder 4. "Cvetic Reveals More Names in Red Probe," *Pittsburgh Press*, March 15, 1950, 2; HUAC report, ASC, June 26, 1949, 54–55, https://archive.org/details/reportonamerican00unit. Quotation on fascist displaced persons as "the worst scum of Europe" is attributed to George Pirinsky in the Bulgarian-Macedonian newspaper *Narodna Volya*, January 14, 1949, cited in HUAC report, 63.

56. Affidavit, Jumal Ahmad, Cleveland, April 1951, IWOCF-CU, box 3.

57. Detroit Police, "Criminal Intelligence Bureau" report, February 16, 1966, Herbert Aptheker speaks against Vietnam War at McKie Memorial Library and Educational Center, as well as a flyer on Aptheker's "Eyewitness Report from Hanoi," DB-WSU, box 2 folder 2-55. FBI report—Stanley Nowak and the Polish Labor Democratic Club serving "in lieu of the former IWO clubs" [1954?], mentions June 11, 1954, meeting, DB-WSU, box 7, folder 7-55.

58. Affidavit, Pecola Moore, Los Angeles, April 24, 1951, IWOCF-CU, box 3.

CHAPTER 1

1. SWS Lodge 2002, Guttenberg, New Jersey, to IWO Joseph R. Brodsky (JRB) Welfare Fund, September 18, 1953, box 20, folder 17, International Workers Order Records, 1915–2002, MSS 5276, Kheel Center for Labor-Management Documentation and Archives, Cornell University [hereafter cited as IWO-CU].

2. Application to JRB Welfare Fund, from SWS Lodge 2074, July 17, 1953, on behalf of Katy Hlavenko, IWO-CU, box 21, folder 32; Application from SWS Lodge 2034, Bellaire, Ohio, November 30, 1953, on behalf of Rosie Vovea, IWO-CU, box 21, folder 20; Application from SWS Lodge 2048, Monongahela, West Virginia, April 21, 1953, on behalf of John Novichenko, IWO-CU, box 21, folder 28.

3. Jack Metzgar, *Striking Steel: Solidarity Remembered* (Philadelphia, PA: Temple University Press, 2000); Judith Modell and Charlee Brodsky, *A Town without Steel: Envisioning Homestead* (Pittsburgh, PA: University of Pittsburgh Press, 1998), 7, 8, 26–28, 134–143; John Strohmeyer, *Crisis in Bethlehem: Big Steel's Struggle to Survive* (Pittsburgh, PA: University of Pittsburgh Press, 1994), 64–77; Deborah Rudacille, *Roots of Steel: Boom and Bust in an American Mill Town* (New York: Anchor, 2010), 98–125; Sherry Lee Linkon and John Russo, *Steeltown U.S.A.: Work and Memory in Youngstown* (Lawrence: University Press of Kansas, 2002), 88–118; Ewa Morawska, *Insecure Prosperity: Small-Town Jews in Industrial America, 1890–1940* (Princeton, NJ: Princeton University Press, 1996); Stanley Aronowitz, *The Death and Life of American Labor: Toward*

a New Workers' Movement (New York: Verso, 2014), 59, 61–62, 71–83, 160–161; H. Luke Shaefer and Elizabeth Sammons, "The Development of an Unequal Social Safety Net: A Case Study of the Employer-Based Health Insurance (Non) System," *Journal of Sociology and Social Welfare* 36, no. 3 (September 2009): 179–199; Alan Derickson, "Health Security for All? Social Unionism and Universal Health Insurance, 1935–1958," *Journal of American History* 80, no. 4 (March 1994): 1333–1356; Michael Brown, "Bargaining for Social Rights: Unions and the Reemergence of Welfare Capitalism, 1945–1952," *Political Science Quarterly* 112, no. 4 (Winter 1997–1998): 645–674; Jill Quadagno, "Why the United States Has No National Health Insurance: Stakeholder Mobilization against the Welfare State, 1945–1996," *Journal of Health and Social Behavior* 45 (2004): 25–44.

4. SWS application to JRB Welfare Fund, September 18, 1953, from Mike Slavik for Olga Coben, California, Pennsylvania, IWO-CU, box 21, folder 33; Application to JRB Welfare Fund, September 24, 1953, from SWS Lodge 2011, Allentown, Pennsylvania, re: Eleanor Budihas, IWO-CU, box 21, folder 5.

5. Fanny Goldenzweig, IWO Sick Benefit Department, to A. Harvan, Lansford, Pennsylvania, May 8, 1953, IWO-CU, box 20, folder 19.

6. A. Harvan, Lansford, Pennsylvania, to Charles Korenič on behalf of lodge member Frank Schubak, June 1, 1953, ibid.

7. Mildred Allen Beik, *The Miners of Windber: The Struggles of New Immigrants for Unionization, 1890s–1930s* (University Park: Pennsylvania State University Press, 1996), 70–75; David Alan Corbin, *Life, Work, and Rebellion in the Coal Fields: The Southern West Virginia Miners, 1880–1922* (Urbana: University of Illinois Press, 1981), esp. 195–224; James Green, *The Devil Is Here in These Hills: West Virginia's Coal Miners and Their Battle for Freedom* (New York: Atlantic Monthly Press, 2015), 20, 64, 72–80, 170; Scott Martelle, *Blood Passion: The Ludlow Massacre and Class War in the American West* (New Brunswick, NJ: Rutgers University Press, 2007); Helen Papanikolas, *Buried Unsung: Louis Tiklas and the Ludlow Massacre* (Salt Lake City: University of Utah Press, 1982), 20, 38, 96, 140, 247; Thomas Andrews, *Killing for Coal: America's Deadliest Labor War* (Cambridge, MA: Harvard University Press, 2008); Daniel Letwin, *The Challenge of Interracial Unionism: Alabama Coal Miners, 1878–1921* (Chapel Hill: University of North Carolina Press, 1998); Thomas Dublin, *When the Mines Closed: Stories of Struggles in Hard Times* (Ithaca, NY: Cornell University Press, 1998), 27, 46, 58–60, 87, 109, 170, 201, 209–210, 231; Lon Savage, *Thunder in the Mountains: The West Virginia Mine War, 1920–1921* (Pittsburgh, PA: University of Pittsburgh Press, 1990); John Gaventa, *Power and Powerlessness: Quiescence and Rebellion in an Appalachian Valley* (Urbana: University of Illinois Press, 1980), 87–88, 172–175, 183–184.

8. Minutes book, SWS, August 24, 1920, IWO-CU, box 54. See, too, NSS Lodge 58, Peckville, Pennsylvania, monthly minutes book, December 16, 1917, February 10, 1918, June 9, 1918, and physician's note from A. J. Davis, M.D., February 15, 1918, pasted in NSS Lodge 58 minutes book, National Slovak Society records, Balch Institute for Ethnic Studies, Philadelphia [hereafter cited as Balch], Mss. 3447.

9. Zaragosa Vargas, *Proletarians of the North: A History of Mexican Industrial Workers in Detroit and the Midwest, 1917–1933* (Berkeley: University of California Press, 1999), 61, 100–105, 120–122; Beth Tompkins Bates, *The Making of Black Detroit in the Era of Henry Ford* (Chapel Hill: University of North Carolina Press, 2012), 64–65, 214–215, 253–254; Dan Georgakas and Marvin Surkin, *Detroit, I Do Mind Dying: A Study in Urban Revolution* (New York: Saint Martin's, 1975); Richard Feldman and Michael Betzold, eds., *End of the Line: Autoworkers and the American Dream, An Oral History* (Urbana: University of Illinois Press, 1990); Jerry Herron, *AfterCulture: Detroit*

and the Humiliation of History (Detroit, MI: Wayne State University Press, 1993); Mark Binelli, *Detroit City Is the Place to Be: The Afterlife of an American Metropolis* (New York: Metropolitan Books, 2012); Nelson Liechtenstein, *The Most Dangerous Man in Detroit: Walter Reuther and the Fate of American Labor* (New York: Basic Books, 1995), 141–142; David Brody, *Steelworkers in America: The Nonunion Era* (New York: Harper Torchbooks, 1960), 91–93, 100–101, 165–168; William Kornblum, *Blue Collar Community* (Chicago, IL: University of Chicago Press, 1974), 42–65; Linkon and Russo, *Steeltown U.S.A.*; Edward Greer, *Big Steel: Black Politics and Corporate Power in Gary, Indiana* (New York: Monthly Review Press, 1979); S. J. Kleinberg, *The Shadow of the Mills: Working-Class Families in Pittsburgh, 1870–1907* (Pittsburgh, PA: University of Pittsburgh Press, 1989), 27–40, 52–53, 76, 122–123, 173, 258, 265, 276–277; Metzgar, *Striking Steel*, 247; David Montgomery, *The Fall of the House of Labor: The Workplace, the State and American Labor Activism, 1865–1925* (New York: Cambridge University Press, 1987). See, too, death claims report by Dr. Petra Ivana Zeedick, head doctor of *Sojedenia* (the Greek Catholic Union) given at *Sojedenia's* 12th national convention, June 22, 1936, Balch, SPC 485.

10. Isaac Galperin to IWO, January 11, 1953, and Dave Greene to Galperin, January 26, 1953, IWO-CU, box 4, folder 6; Greene to Stella Fidyk, February 16, 1951, IWO-CU, box 4, folder 5.

11. IWO petitions to U.S. Supreme Court, "Translation," letter from Joseph Petercsak, October 23, 1953, box 3, International Workers Order Case Files, MSS 5940, Kheel Center for Labor-Management Documentation and Archives, Cornell University Library [hereafter cited as IWOCF-CU]; Booklet, *Why You Should Vote Communist— N.Y. State Ticket—for U.S. Senator, Max Bedacht*, 1934, box 11, folder 57, International Ladies Garment Workers Union, Charles S. Zimmerman Collection of Radical Pamphlets, 1914–1958, MSS 5780/178, Kheel Center for Labor-Management Documentation and Archives, Cornell University [hereafter cited as ILGWU-CU, 5780/178].

12. FBI report on *Glos Ludowy* [newspaper of the Polonia Society, IWO], May 17, 1941, 6, box 4, folder 4-42, Don Binkowski Papers, Walter P. Reuther Library, Wayne State University [hereafter cited as DB-WSU].

13. M. Mark Stolarik, *Immigration and Urbanization: The Slovak Experience, 1870–1918* (New York: AMS Press, 1989); R. Vladimir Baumgarten and Joseph Stefka, *The National Slovak Society 100 Year History, 1890–1990* (Pittsburgh, PA: National Slovak Society, 1990); Jozef Pauco, ed., *75 Rokov Prvej Katolickej Slovenskej Jednota, 1890–1965* [75 Years of the First Catholic Slovak Union] (Cleveland: First Catholic Slovak Union, 1965); *Americko-Slovensky Evangelical Lutheransky Kalendár Sion na Obyčajny Rok 1950* [American-Slovak Evangelical Lutheran Calendar Zion for the Year 1950], Pittsburgh; George Dolak, *A History of the Slovak Evangelical Lutheran Church in the United States of America, 1902–1927* (St. Louis, MO: Concordia, 1952). Quotes about the *Sokol* lodge are from Stephanie W., interview by the author, July 10, 1996, Hatboro, Pennsylvania.

14. Michael Weisser, *A Brotherhood of Memory: Jewish Landsmanshaftn in the New World* (Ithaca, NY: Cornell University Press, 1985); Hannah Kliger, ed., *Jewish Hometown Associations and Family Circles in New York: The WPA Yiddish Writers' Study Group* (Bloomington: Indiana University Press, 1992); Kenyon Zimmer, *Immigrants against the State: Yiddish and Italian Anarchism in America* (Urbana: University of Illinois Press, 2015), 37. Susan Glenn, *Daughters of the Shtetl: Life and Labor in the Immigrant Generation* (Ithaca, NY: Cornell University Press, 1990); Elizabeth Ewen, *Immigrant Women in the Land of Dollars: Life and Culture on the Lower East Side,*

1880–1925 (New York: Monthly Review Press, 1985), 246–249; Daniel Katz, *All Together Different: Yiddish Socialists, Garment Workers, and the Labor Roots of Multiculturalism* (New York: New York University Press, 2011), 36–37, 65–66, 118–119.

15. David Beito, *From Mutual Aid to Welfare State: Fraternal Societies and Social Service, 1890–1967* (Chapel Hill: University of North Carolina Press, 2000); Beito, "To Advance the 'Practice of Thrift and Economy': Fraternal Societies and Social Capital, 1890–1920," *Journal of Interdisciplinary History* 29, no. 4 (Spring 1999): 585–612; Matjaž Klemenčič, "American Slovenes and the Leftist Movements in the United States in the First Half of the Twentieth Century," *Journal of American Ethnic History* 15, no. 3 (Spring 1996): 22–43.

16. Vargas notes Mexicans in the industrial Midwest often faced the dilemma of making rent or grocery payments or keeping current on their dues in mutualistas providing a modicum of help for accident or disease. See Vargas, *Proletarians of the North*, 149–154. Minutes, Slovak Catholic *Sokol* Assembly 61, Philadelphia, May 5, 1929, Balch, Mss. 3499; Minutes, Greek Catholic Union Lodge 160, Philadelphia, February 8, 1925, Balch, Mss. 3337.

17. Victor Greene, *The Slavic Community on Strike: Immigrant Labor in Pennsylvania Anthracite* (Note Dame, IN: Notre Dame University Press, 1968), 199–203, 212. See, too, announcement of a celebration for "Johnny Mitchell Day" in a Rusyn church lodge, *Amerikansky Russky Viestnik*, October 17, 1912, Balch Microfilm Drawer 311. Minutes, Slovak Gymnastic Union *Sokol* Lodge 56, Philadelphia, May 3, 1914, Balch, Mss. 094. This same month, rooms were rented to the Slovak Socialist Workers' Section, which would later affiliate with the IWO. Minutes, Slovak Gymnastic Union *Sokol* Lodge 56, March 7, 1915, and November 5, 1913, Balch, Mss. 094; Minutes, Greek Catholic Union Lodge 160, Philadelphia, October 17, 1912, and March 11, 1928, Balch 3337. Minutes, Slovak Catholic *Sokol* Assembly 61, Philadelphia, December 2, 1928, Balch, Mss. 3499.

18. *Národné noviny*, May 21, 1914.

19. "Agitation and Propaganda among the Lithuanian Working Masses and Their Organizations," adopted by Conference of the Lithuanian Federation [1922], reel 8, delo 139, Records of the Communist Party USA, Microfilm 21, 966, Library of Congress [hereafter cited as CPUSA-LC]; Edward Tabban to Central Executive Committee of Workers [Communist] Party [1926], C. E. Ruthenberg, "To All Lettish [Latvian] Fractions and Members of the Workers [Communist] Party," May 18, 1926, and Tabban to Ruthenberg, May 28, 1926, CPUSA-LC, reel 50, delo 699.

20. Charles Novak to CEC, Workers Party, November 3, 1925, CPUSA-LC, reel 34, delo 501; Yugoslav Language Bureau Questionnaire [1928], CPUSA-LC, reel 109, delo 1454.

21. Report, "Mass Work among the Jugo-Slavs" [1926], CPUSA-LC, reel 65, delo 905; "To the Investigation Committee of the CEC, On the Workers' Progressive Bloc" in the CFU, February 4, 1926, ibid.

22. Report, Language Department to Comintern, October 12, 1926, CPUSA-LC, reel 40, delo 589.

23. HUAC, "Report on the American Slav Congress," June 26, 1949, 84–85, https://archive.org/details/reportonamerican00unit. See, too, J. Edgar Hoover, *Masters of Deceit: The Story of Communism in America and How to Fight It* (New York: Holt, 1958); and sources in Introduction, note 14.

24. "Report on Textile Industry, Passaic Situation," to CEC and Trade Union Committee, September 22, 1926, CPUSA-LC, reel 59, delo 815; Jacob Zumoff, "Hell in New

Jersey: The Passaic Textile Strike, Albert Weisbord and the Communist Party," *Journal for the Study of Radicalism* 9, no. 1 (2015): 125–170. "News Release Number 27," January 26, 1928, issued by the Pennsylvania-Ohio Miners Relief Committee, CPUSA-LC, reel 115, delo 1523. On the 1926–1927 Passaic textile strike and earlier labor disturbances in the city, see David Goldberg, *A Tale of Three Cities: Labor Organization and Protest in Paterson, Passaic, and Lawrence: 1916–1921* (New Brunswick, NJ: Rutgers University Press, 1989); General Relief Committee of Textile Strikers, *Hell in New Jersey: Story of the Passaic Textile Strike Told in Pictures* (Passaic, NJ: General Relief Committee of Textile Strikers, 1926); Albert Weisbord, *Passaic: The Story of a Struggle Against Starvation Wages and the Right to Organize* (1926; repr., New York: AMS Press, 1976); Paul Murphy, Kermit Hall, and David Klassen, *The Passaic Textile Strike of 1926* (Belmont, CA: Wadsworth, 1974); Zumoff, "Hell in New Jersey"; Martha Stone Asher, "Recollections of the Passaic Textile Strike of 1926," *Labor's Heritage* 2, no. 2 (1990): 5–23; Michael Ebner, "The Passaic Strike and the Two I.W.W.'s," *Labor History* 11, no. 4 (1970): 452–466; and General Relief Committee, "Textile Strike of 1926: Passaic, Clifton, Garfield, Lodi, New Jersey" (Passaic, NJ: General Relief Committee, 1926). On company control of church land in coal towns, see Beik, *The Miners of Windber*, 117–119.

25. Michael Miller Topp, *Those without a Country: The Political Culture of Italian American Syndicalists* (Minneapolis: University of Minnesota Press, 2001); Donna Gabaccia and Fraser Ottanelli, eds., *Italian Workers of the World: Labor Migration and the Formation of Multiethnic States* (Urbana: University of Illinois Press, 2001); Angelo Trento, "'Wherever We Work, That Land Is Ours': The Italian Anarchist Press and Working-Class Solidarity in São Paulo," 102–120, in Gabaccia and Ottanelli, *Italian Workers of the World*; Jennifer Guglielmo, *Living the Revolution: Italian Women's Resistance and Radicalism in New York City, 1880–1945* (Chapel Hill: University of North Carolina Press, 2010); Marcella Bencivenni, *Italian Immigrant Radical Culture: The Idealism of the Sovversívi in the United States, 1890–1940* (New York: New York University Press, 2011); Donna Gabaccia, Franca Iacovetta, and Fraser Ottanelli, "Laboring across National Borders: Class, Gender, and Militancy in the Proletarian Mass Migrations," *International Labor and Working-Class History* 66 (Fall 2004): 57–77. Zimmer, too, traces the transnational networks of journals, institutions, and personal connections among Italian and Jewish migrant anarchists. See Zimmer, *Immigrants against the State*.

26. Mark Wyman, *Round-Trip to America: The Immigrants Return to Europe, 1880–1930* (Ithaca, NY: Cornell University Press, 1993). For other examples of migratory, transnational industrial workers, see Robert M. Zecker, "'They Roamed All Over Fixing Things': The Migratory Tinkers of Slovakia," *Journal of American Ethnic History* 35, no. 1 (Fall 2015): 38–70; Dragon Ferko, "Slovenskí drotári v Rusku počas prvej svetovej vojny" [Slovak Tinkers in Russia during the First World War], *Slovanske Studie* 22 (1981): 179–192; Christiane Harzig, "Domestics of the World (Unite?): Labor Migration Systems and Personal Trajectories of Household Workers in Historical and Global Perspective," *Journal of American Ethnic History* 25, nos. 2/3 (Winter–Spring 2006): 48–73; Sharron Schwartz, "Bridging 'The Great Divide': The Evolution and Impact of Cornish Translocalism in Britain and the USA," *Journal of American Ethnic History* 25, nos. 2/3 (Winter–Spring 2006): 169–189; Robert Ostergren, *A Community Transplanted: The Trans-Atlantic Experience of a Swedish Immigrant Settlement in the Upper Middle West, 1835–1915* (Madison: University of Wisconsin Press, 1988); Joan Scott, "The Glass Workers of Carmaux, 1850–1900," in *Nineteenth-Century Cities: Essays in the New Urban History*, ed. Stephan Thernstrom and Richard Sennett (New Haven, CT: Yale

University Press, 1976); and Ken Fones-Wolf, *Glass Towns: Industry, Labor, and Political Economy in Appalachia, 1890–1930s* (Urbana: University of Illinois Press, 2007).

27. Statement of Finnish Bureau, CPUSA, December 29, 1929, CPUSA-LC, reel 119, delo 1567.

28. F. Borich, South Slavic Fraction, to Central Committee, CP, March 15, 1930, CPUSA-LC, reel 151, delo 1961; Minutes, "The Benefit Organizations" plenum, South Slavic Fraction, Workers Party, March 10–11, 1928, 3–9, CPUSA-LC, reel 109, delo 1454; Minutes, South Slavic Bureau meeting, October 1, 1930, CPUSA-LC, reel 162/1, delo 2161.

29. Minutes, South Slavic Bureau meeting, October 1, 1930.

30. Secretary, Language Department, to Secretariat, CPUSA, November 3, 1930, CPUSA-LC, reel 154, delo 2017.

31. "The Work of the Communist Fractions in Fraternal Organizations," excerpt from Com. Marcus Jenks' Report to Our Last Party Convention, 1930, CPUSA-LC, reel 154, delo 2018.

32. Ibid.

33. Ibid.

34. Max Bedacht to Jay Lovestone [ca. February 1925], CPUSA-LC, reel 34, delo 512.

35. C. E. Ruthenberg to A. Rostovsky, secretary, Hungarian Bureau, September 17, 1926, and Ruthenberg to Rostovsky, October 30, 1926, CPUSA-LC, reel 49, delo 694.

36. Tony Michels, "Communism and the Problem of Ethnicity in the 1920s: The Case of Moissaye Olgin," *Contemporary Jewry* 25 (2011): 26–48; Tony Michels, ed., *Jewish Radicals: A Documentary History* (New York: New York University Press, 2012); Tony Michels, *A Fire in Their Hearts: Yiddish Socialists in New York* (Cambridge, MA: Harvard University Press, 2005), esp. 217–250; Al Gedicks, "The Social Origin of Radicalism among Finnish Immigrants in Midwest Mining Communities," *Review of Radical Political Economy* 8, no. 3 (1976): 1–31. Max Bedacht to C. E. Ruthenberg, September 30, 1923, CPUSA-LC, reel 11, delo 185. See, too, Henry Piro, secretary, Finnish Bureau, to CEC and District Executive Committee No. 8, regarding "breach of Party discipline by certain Finnish comrades at Finnish Workers' Clubs District Convention in Waukegan," December 20, 1926, CPUSA-LC, reel 50, delo 706.

37. Jacob Zumoff, *The Communist International and U.S. Communism, 1919–1929* (Chicago, IL: Haymarket Books, 2014); Minutes, Boston Estonian Workers Mass Meeting, November 3, 1929, CPUSA-LC, reel 137, delo 1815.

38. Joseph Peter, secretary, Hungarian Bureau, to "Dear Comrade," September 19, 1927, and "Statement of the Hungarian Bureau on the Expulsion of Louis Basky" [1927], CPUSA-LC, reel 79, delo 1049.

39. Lucy Davidowitz, "The History of the Jewish People's Fraternal Order of the International Workers Order" [November 1950], TS, folder 8, International Workers Order Records, Robert F. Wagner Labor Archives, Tamiment Library, New York University [hereafter cited as IWO-NYU].

40. Minutes, Actions Committee of the Jewish Fraction of the Workers [Communist] Party, January 12, January 28, February 2, February 10, and March 23, 1927, CPUSA-LC, reel 87, delo 1180; Moissaye J. Olgin, "The Workmen's Circle Policy and the Renegade Trio," CPUSA-LC, reel 129, delo 1674; Minutes, Language Department meeting, October 29, 1929, CPUSA-LC, reel 129, delo 1680; H. I. Costrell to P. Smith, Language Department, September 9, 1929, CPUSA-LC, reel 129, delo 1683; Minutes, Language Department meetings, January 8 and September 18, 1930, CPUSA-LC, reel

154, delo 2014; "Minutes of the Meeting Held on the Amalgamation of the Sick Benefit Organizations Held on September 18, 1930," CPUSA-LC, reel 154, delo 2015; "Report of the Language Department C.C.—Unite to Fight for Full Insurance for the Entire Working Class" [September 1930], CPUSA-LC, reel 154, delo 2016.

41. Minutes, Jewish Fraction, Actions Committee meetings, February 2 and 10, 1927, CPUSA-LC, reel 87, delo 1180.

42. Costrell to Smith, September 9, 1929; H. I. Costrell to Central Bureau, Jewish Section, September 9, 1929, CPUSA-LC, reel 137, delo 1811.

43. Rubin Saltzman, General Secretary, JPFO, report, "Twenty Years of the International Workers Order," November 18–20, 1949, IWO-NYU, folder 3.

44. "For the Sake of Clarity—A Workmen's Circle Answer to the IWO from *The Call*, April 1940," 12, IWO-NYU, folder 8; Affidavit, Jacob Holmstock, Queens, April 24, 1951, IWOCF-CU, box 3.

45. Olgin, "The Workmen's Circle Policy and the Renegade Trio."

46. Quoted in Davidowitz, "History of the Jewish People's Fraternal Order," 1–2.

47. A letter inviting recipient to a "Vote Communist Banquet" at the New Star Casino lists Bedacht and Saltzman on the New York State Committee of the CP, September 18, 1933, IWO-CU, box 5, folder 1. Bill Gebert biography, April 15, 1932, sent by Gebert to the Executive Committee, Communist International, DB-WSU, box 4, folder 4-14. Rubin Saltzman, "The First Convention of the IWO," *Daily Worker*, May 30, 1931, 3, notes that the order's branches had collected "$5,000 for the central organ of the Communist Party, *The Daily Worker*" and "nearly $25,000 for the Jewish daily Communist paper, the *Freiheit*, which became the organ of the International Workers Order," DB-WSU, box 5, folder 5-29. See, too, Central Committee of CPUSA to all language-paper editors regarding a *Daily Worker* fund drive, March 3, 1933, CPUSA-LC, reel 245, delo 3123. See Slovak National Bureau to Central Committee, CP, September 11, 1935, in which the Slovak IWO's *Daily Worker* quota is set at $200, CPUSA-LC, reel 293, delo 3796.

48. "Digest of Testimony of Witnesses for the State in the I.W.O. Matter. January 29, 1951, to March 7, 1951," esp. testimony of Charles Baxter and Manning Johnson, 38, 100, 110, IWOCF-CU, box 4. For prominent non-Communist albeit progressive politicians who belonged to the IWO, see Gerald Meyer, *Vito Marcantonio: Radical Politician, 1902–1954* (Albany: State University of New York Press, 1989); Annette Rubinstein, ed., *I Vote My Conscience: Debates, Speeches, and Writings of Vito Marcantonio* (1956; repr., New York: Calandra Institute, 2002); and Margaret Collingwood Nowak, *Two Who Were There: A Biography of Stanley Nowak* (Detroit, MI: Wayne State University Press, 1989).

49. "Constitution and By-Laws of the International Workers Order, in effect January 1, 1948," stated, "No member of a private police force and no professional strikebreaker shall be accepted as a member of the Order," IWO-CU, box 1, folder 4. Max Bedacht to Daisy Bell Pike, July 2, 1943, IWO-CU, box 3, folder 12; Mary Markstrom to Sam Milgrom, December 5, 1948, and Joe Kamen to Milgrom, December 16, 1948, IWO-CU, box 8, folder 8.

50. "I.W.O. Expels Three for 'Trotskyites,'" *The Militant*, October 1, 1932, 4, reprint, IWO-NYU, folder 43.

51. "The Bureaucracy in the IWO," *The Militant*, October 31, 1931, 2, reprint, IWO-NYU, folder 43; Central Control Commission meeting, April 1, 1938, case of Paul Skers of Worcester, Massachusetts, and cases of William Farkas (Thell) and Rudolph Klein of Cleveland, Ohio, CPUSA-LC, reel 307, delo 4079.

52. Thomas Walker, *Pluralistic Fraternity: The History of the International Workers Order* (New York: Garland, 1991), 104–105.

53. Sadie Doroshkin to Louise Thompson, June 4, 1934, Thompson to Max Bedacht, June 4, 1934, Thompson to Bedacht, February 23, 1934, Bedacht, "To Whom It May Concern," regarding Thompson's credentials as an IWO organizer, February 24, 1934, Bedacht to [name blacked out], February 28, 1934, Doroshkin to Thompson, June 7, 1934, Bedacht to Thompson, June 7, 1934, Thompson to Doroshkin, June 9, 1934, Doroshkin to Thompson, June 12, 1934, Doroshkin to Thompson, June 20, 1934, Thompson to Doroshkin, June 19, 1934, Doroshkin to Thompson, March 9, 1934, Thompson to C. B. Powell, Birmingham, Alabama, attorney, May 21, 1934, Thompson to Doroshkin, May 21, 1934, Powell to Thompson, May 22, 1934, Thompson to Joseph Brodsky, May 21, 1934, Doroshkin to Thompson, May 23, 1934, and Powell to Thompson, May 28, 1934, box 8, folder 8, Louise Thompson Patterson Papers, 1909–1999, MSS 869, Stuart A. Rose Manuscript, Archives, and Rare Book Library, Emory University [hereafter cited as LTP-EU]; Louise Thompson Patterson MS autobiography, chap. 6, p. 11, LTP-EU, box 20, folder 5.

54. IWO, "Recruiting of Negro Workers" [ca. 1934], LTP-EU, box 8, folder 8; Interview with Thompson Patterson [ca. 1950–1951], LTP-EU, box 8, folder 10; Interview with Thompson Patterson, June 2 and 9, 1987, LTP-EU, box 27, folder 8; Thompson Patterson, interview by Margaret Wilkerson, April 20, 1989, LTP-EU, box 28, folder 2.

55. Interview with Louise Thompson Patterson [ca. 1950–1951]; Thompson Patterson, interview by Ruth and Bud Schultz, August 12, 1984, LTP-EU, box 27, folder 3.

56. "Resolutions, Adopted by Emergency Conference against the Liquidation of a People's Organization," February 10, 1951, IWO-CU, box 23, folder 4; Thompson Patterson, interview by Linda Burnham, March 11 and 14, 1988, LTP-EU, box 27, folder 13; Thompson Patterson, interview by Mary Lecht [ca. 1980s], LTP-EU, box 28, folder 16.

57. "Four Months Program of Work—Language Department—Building and Organizing the Communist Fractions in the Language Mass Organizations" includes a section titled "I.W.O." [1929], CPUSA-LC, reel 129, delo 1681; Report, Language Papers of the Party, October 3, 1930, CPUSA-LC, reel 154, delo 2016; Report, Language Department, "The Building of the Working Class Mutual Aid Organizations—A Plan for Immediate Action," January 6, 1931, CPUSA-LC, reel 177, delo 2334; Report from Language Department on Hungarian Workers' Sick Benefit and Educational Federation and other fraternal societies, the IWO [1931], ibid.; Report, Language Department, "Present Status of the IWO," April 15, 1931, ibid.

58. Minutes, Leading Fractions of the IWO meeting, September 28, 1930, CPUSA-LC, reel 154, delo 2015; Minutes, Language Department meeting, September 18, 1930, ibid.

59. "Report of the Language Department C.C."; Report, Language Papers of the Party, October 3, 1930.

60. Report, Language Papers of the Party, October 3, 1930; Hungarian Bureau Central Committee, "Report of the National Fraction Conference, December 11, 1933," CPUSA-LC, reel 247, delo 3175. For depositions of IWO members asserting the centrality of insurance coverage among their reasons for joining, see Affidavits, Abraham Kaplan, Boston, April 24, 1951, Lewis Marks, Roxbury, Boston, April 21, 1951, and Lazarus Jacovides, Boston, April 20, 1951, IWOCF-CU, box 3. Walker points out that immigrants were considered bad risks by many private insurance companies. See Walker, *Pluralistic Fraternity*, 16. Evelyn Louise Crawford and MaryLouise Patterson, eds., *Letters from Langston: From the Harlem Renaissance to the Red Scare and Beyond* (Berkeley: University of California Press, 2016), 110, 115, 127.

61. Language Department report, "The Building of the Working Class Mutual Aid Organizations—A Plan for Immediate Action," January 6, 1931, CPUSA-LC, reel 177, delo 2334.

62. "Building of the Working Class Mutual Aid Organizations"; H. Beck, Los Angeles, to Louis Kovess, Language Department, November 12, 1930, CPUSA-LC, reel 155, delo 2021. For multilingual editions of *Fraternal Outlook* from 1939 to 1943, see IWO-CU, box 48.

63. "The Building of the Working Class Mutual Aid Organizations"; On English-language lodges for second-generation workers, see Max Bedacht, "IWO Centers on Campaign for Unemployment Insurance," *Daily Worker*, October 8, 1934, 6, CPUSA-LC, reel 318, delo 4243; "Draft Four Month Plan of the Negro Department, October–February 1932," CPUSA-LC, reel 213, delo 2735; James Ford, "Report on Harlem," and N. Shaffer, "Report on the I.W.O.," to the District 2 [New York] Bureau meeting, December 28, 1935, CPUSA-LC, reel 294, delo 3811; James Ford, "A Week in Detroit, April 30 to May 7, 1932," CPUSA-LC, reel 231, delo 2984; CP, District 4, Buffalo, New York, to "Dear Comrades," July 16, 1935, CPUSA-LC, reel 294, delo 3826.

64. Minutes, Language Department, Amalgamation Sub-Committee meeting, June 15, 1931, CPUSA-LC, reel 117, delo 2332.

65. Minutes, Czechoslovak Bureau meetings, May 4, May 12, and May 27, 1931, CPUSA-LC, reel 191, delo 2553.

66. Language Department to B. K. Gebert, June 12, 1931, and Language Department to Czechoslovak Bureau, June 11, 1931, CPUSA-LC, reel 177, delo 2336.

67. Language Department to Czechoslovak Bureau, June 11, 1931. Zumoff, *The Communist International and U.S. Communism*; John Manley, "Moscow Rules? 'Red' Unionism and 'Class against Class' in Britain, Canada, and the United States, 1928–1935," *Labour/Le Travail* 56 (Fall 2005): 9–49; Kevin Morgan, "The Trouble with Revisionism: or Communist History with the History Left In," *Labour/Le Travail* 63 (Spring 2009): 131–155.

68. Comrade F. Brown, Language Department, "To All District Language Departments," July 25, 1931, CPUSA-LC, reel 177, delo 2334. Ad for the IWO Dental Department, "All Work Done under Personal Care of Dr. Josephson," *Daily Worker*, August 10, 1932, 2, CPUSA-LC, reel 318, delo 4243.

69. "To All Party Fractions in the Hungarian Workers' Sick Benefit and Educational Federation—Slovak Workers Society—Russian Mutual Aid Society of America and the International Workers Order" from Language Department [1931], CPUSA-LC, reel 177, delo 2334.

70. HUAC, "Report on the American Slav Congress," 13, 83–85; Hoover, *Masters of Deceit*.

71. Michels, *A Fire in Their Hearts*. See Jay Lovestone to J. Mindel, chairman, Central Commission, New York, September 15, 1927, regarding a letter that "Comrade Sura" had written to Stalin, CPUSA-LC, reel 75, delo 1017.

72. Gedicks, "The Social Origin of Radicalism." Paul Mishler, "Red Finns, Red Jews: Ethnic Variations in Communist Political Culture during the 1920s and 1930s," *YIVO Annual* 22 (1995): 131–154; Minutes, Language Department meeting, April 19, 1930, CPUSA-LC, reel 154, delo 2014; District Nine, Minneapolis, to "Dear Comrade," July 23, 1930, and Karl Reeve, Superior, Wisconsin, to Max Bedacht, January 10, 1930, CPUSA-LC, reel 161, delo 2120.

73. Minutes, Lithuanian Bureau meeting, December 18 and 26, 1930, CPUSA-LC, reel 162/1, delo 2160.

74. Bulgarian Workers' Mutual Benefit and Educational Society, Detroit, to *Daily Worker*, May 13, 1932, CPUSA-LC, reel 235, delo 3052. On the Ford Hunger March, see Vargas, *Proletarians of the North*, 178–179; Karen Miller, *Managing Inequality: Northern Racial Liberalism in Interwar Detroit* (New York: New York University Press, 2015), 183–184; August Meier and Elliot Rudwick, *Black Detroit and the Rise of the U.A.W.* (New York: Oxford University Press, 1979); Roger Keeran, *The Communist Party and the Auto Workers' Unions* (New York: International, 1980), 71–74; and Bates, *The Making of Black Detroit*, 144–145, 159–163, 176, 254. FBI report, IWO, Detroit division, December 31, 1946, 101, notes a "confidential informant" "made available . . . a leaflet . . . 'Come to the Memorial Meeting to Honor the Murder for the Cause of the Laborer [sic] Murdered by Ford,' . . . at the IWO Center at 8951 12th Street," DB-WSU, box 16, folder 16-37.

75. Giulio Giombi of Baltimore to Vito Magli, June 24, 1950, IWO-CU, box 25, folder 5.

76. Memorandum, Boleslaw Gebert to Max Bedacht on Polish American Section of the IWO, June 30, 1942, 3–4, IWO-CU, box 11, folder 1; Memorandum, Max Bedacht on the Croatian Fraternal Union's newspaper and the Croatian IWO [during World War II], IWO-CU, box 10, folder 1. Fragment of letter from Joseph Schiffel, n.d., IWO-CU, box 45, folder 6.

77. Emil Gardos to Earl Browder, June 29, 1932, CPUSA-LC, reel 214, delo 2752.

78. Ibid.

79. Luigi Candela to Earl Browder and Central Committee, CP, June 29, 1935, CPUSA-LC, reel 292, delo 3787.

80. Charles Stevenson to Executive Committee and Members of Lodge 691, IWO, July 19, 1945, and Stevenson to Max Bedacht, June 11, 1945, IWO-CU, box 8, folder 4; "To the Officers and Members of Solidarity Lodge 691—Charges against Brother Charles A. Stevenson by Brother Samuel G. Patterson," 1945, ibid.

81. Howard Brick and Christopher Phelps, *Radicals in America: The U.S. Left since the Second World War* (New York: Cambridge University Press, 2015), 25–32; Maurice Isserman, *Which Side Were You On? The American Communist Party during the Second World War* (Middletown, CT: Wesleyan University Press, 1982), 18–67.

82. Stevenson to Executive Committee and Members of Lodge 691; Charles Stevenson, "To the Board of Trustees, I.W.O. The following is the summary of my appeal from the decision of the Executive Committee of Lodge #691," 1945, IWO-CU, box 8, folder 4.

83. Beryle Banfield, president, and Maude Jett, financial secretary, "To the Members of Lodge 691, IWO," July 25, 1945, IWO-CU, box 8, folder 4; "To the Officers and Members of Solidarity Lodge 691—Charges against Brother Charles A. Stevenson." African American organizers and members in the IWO frequently felt that they had been slighted by the order's leaders: Robert Meyers of Baltimore to Sam Milgrom, April 5, 1946, Milgrom to Meyers, April 11, 1946, IWO-CU, box 6, folder 2; Philippa Stowe to headquarters, April 12, 1949, IWO-CU, box 4, folder 4.

84. Report, Language Papers of the Party, section titled "The I.W.O.," October 3, 1930, CPUSA-LC, reel 154, delo 2016.

85. Anthony Bimba to Organization Department, October 30, 1935, CPUSA-LC, reel 292, delo 3791. See, too, Zorach Aronson, Brooklyn, to Gedalia Sandler of the JPFO, December 16, 1948, and Sandler to Aronson, January 5, 1949, IWO-CU, box 25, folder 10; FBI report, IWO, Detroit division, December 31, 1946, 66.

86. Rubin Saltzman, "The First Convention of the IWO," *Daily Worker*, May 30, 1931, 3, DB-WSU, box 5, folder 5-29. For IWO optical clinics, see ad for William Vogel,

official IWO optician, *The Review*, March 17, 1941, CPUSA-LC, reel 316, delo 421, and ad for the IWO Dental Department, *Daily Worker*, August 10, 1932, 2, CPUSA-LC, reel 318, delo 4243. Language Department, Central Committee, CP, July 25, 1931, CPUSA-LC, reel 177, delo 2334. "Report of District Plenum of IWO, Sunday, April 29, 1934," Philadelphia, stipulated, "Doctors from different language sections, including a Negro doctor, to be in the Medical Department," CPUSA-LC, reel 287, delo 3709.

87. Dan Bouk, "The Science of Difference: Developing Tools for Discrimination in the American Life Insurance Industry, 1830–1930," *Enterprise and Society* 12, no. 4 (December 2011): 717–731; Affidavits, James Moorer, Jersey City, April 23, 1951, and Pauline Taylor, Youngstown, Ohio, April 1951, IWOCF-CU, box 3; Harold Peters to Metropolitan Life Insurance, February 2, 1945, IWO-CU, box 8, folder 2; Samuel Roberts, IWO National Education Department, to *Baltimore Afro-American*, February 5, 1938, 4; "Race Is Urged to Tune in Broadcast Series of IWO," *Chicago Defender*, October 3, 1945, 4, "IWO Plans New Negro Campaign," *Chicago Defender*, July 15, 1944, 16, and "IWO Plans Big Campaign for Negro Membership," *Chicago Defender*, December 23, 1944, 10.

88. Report, Language Department, "Present Status of the IWO," April 15, 1931, CPUSA-LC, reel 177, delo 2334; Letters from Alexander Wright, August 27, September 8, and October 4, 1935, CPUSA-LC, reel 298, delo 3882. Reports on questionnaires from ethnic groups to Organization Department, including Japanese and Chinese efforts to build IWO lodges, CPUSA-LC, reel 309, delo 4110. Outline for Dave Greene JPFO speech, Brooklyn, June 19, 1950, notes that the IWO's growth to 160,000 members came about because of growth in African American and Spanish as well as European ethnic lodges, IWO-CU, box 4, folder 5; Constitution and By-Laws of the IWO in Spanish [1938], IWO-CU, box 1, folder 4; Eleanor Broady to Louise Thompson Patterson, February 7, 1945, details the recruitment of African Americans into the IWO, IWO-CU, box 7, folder 3; Report, "The Hispanic American Section from January 1940 to January 1944" [at 1944 IWO convention], 4–5, IWO-CU, box 9, folder 8. *Fraternal Outlook*, October 1940, adds a Spanish section to the articles printed in various European languages, IWO-CU, box 48. Report, "Notes on the Portuguese and Cape Verdeans," n.d., IWO-CU, box 5, folder 5; Organizing Committee, Central Committee, to Jose Novo of New Bedford, Massachusetts, December 19, 1933, CPUSA-LC, reel 246, delo 3150. N. Economos to Greek Bureau of the Central Executive Committee, CP, March 30, 1932, notes the building of IWO lodges in Chicago, Hegewisch, and Pullman, Illinois; Gary and Indiana Harbor, Indiana, and Milwaukee, CPUSA-LC, reel 214, delo 2753.

89. Frank Gevize of Detroit to IWO National Office, April 6, 1945, and Sam Milgrom to Gevize, April 23, 1945, IWO-CU, box 6, folder 8. FBI report, IWO, Detroit division, "Arabic Section," 16, December 10, 1945, DB-WSU, box 16, folder 16-36. For Cuban IWO members in Tampa, see Homer Barton to National Election Campaign Committee, September 15, 1932, CPUSA-LC, reel 233, delo 3017. Gary Mormino and George Pozzetta, *The Immigrant World of Ybor City: Italians and Their Latin Neighbors in Tampa, 1885–1985* (Urbana: University of Illinois Press, 1987); Ferdie Pacheco, *Ybor City Chronicles: A Memoir* (Gainesville: University Press of Florida, 1994).

90. Harold Peters to Metropolitan Life Insurance, February 2, 1945, Peters to IWO, February 12, 1945, Sam Milgrom to Peters, February 19, 1945, Peters to Milgrom, February 22, 1945, Peters to Milgrom, March 22, 1945, Milgrom to Peters, March 31, 1945, Peters to Milgrom, April 3, 1945, Milgrom to Peters, April 6, 1945, Peters to Dave Greene, May 15, 1945, and Sol Vail to Milgrom, October 5, 1945, IWO-CU, box 8, folder 2. Affidavit, Jumal Ahmad, Cleveland, April 1951, IWOCF-CU, box 4.

91. News release, "IWO Challenges Constitutionality of Attorney General Clark's Report; Plans Legal Action," December 5, 1947, puts the IWO membership at 188,000

members, IWO-NYU, folder 31. Peter Shipka, "Department of Justice Evades Justice," *Jewish Fraternalist*, November 1948, 3–4, IWOCF-CU, box 46; Gedalia Sandler to Henry Wald of Atlanta, January 31, 1949, refers to the membership as 180,000, IWO-CU, box 31, folder 11. Outline for Dave Greene JPFO speech, Brooklyn, June 19, 1950, puts the IWO's membership at 160,000.

92. Saltzman, "Twenty Years of the International Workers Order."

93. OSS/FNB report, "Communist-Line IWO Reorganizes to Emphasize Nationality," July 11, 1944, DB-WSU, box 4, folder 4-29; OSS/FNB report on "Slav Groups" in the IWO, left-wing in the IWO, "BUTTS 642," April 1, 1944, DB-WSU, box 5, folder 5-30; Report on "All Groups" in the IWO, "BUTTS 648," April 3, 1944, ibid. For the OSS and immigrant communities during World War II, see Robert Szymczak, "Uneasy Observers: The OSS Foreign Nationalities Branch and Perceptions of Polish Nationalism in the United States during World War II," *Polish American Studies* 56, no. 1 (Spring 1999): 7–73.

94. OSS/FNB report, "Communist-Line IWO Reorganizes to Emphasize Nationality"; OSS file, "Report #940, Poles, Interview with Boleslaw Gebert, Detroit, Michigan, July 17, 1945," DB-WSU, box 4, folder 4-20; OSS/FNB report, "Subject: International Workers Order SL #595," June 27, 1944, DB-WSU, box 7, folder 7-53.

95. Ibid.

96. Jack Greenhill of Los Angeles to Ruby Karron, secretary, Lodge 488, Los Angeles, May 19, 1947, IWO-CU, box 32, folder 26.

97. Greenhill to Karron; George Starr to Greenhill, June 20, 1947, and Greenhill to Starr, June 5, 1947, IWO-CU, box 32, folder 26.

98. Walker, *Pluralistic Fraternity*; Herbert Benjamin, Executive Secretary, IWO, report, "Work among the National Groups," February 23, 1941, IWO-CU, box 5, folder 9; OSS file, "Report #940."

99. Draft report of General Secretary of the IWO, August 29, 1946, IWO-NYU, folder 2; Report, "Our Slovak Society," to IWO general meeting, March 16–17, 1947, IWO-NYU, folder 13. Milton Gordon, *Assimilation in American Life* (New York: Oxford University Press, 1964); June Granatir Alexander, *Ethnic Pride, American Patriotism: Slovaks and Other New Immigrants in the Interwar Era* (Philadelphia, PA: Temple University Press, 2004).

100. OSS/FNB report, "Communist-Line IWO Reorganizes to Emphasize Nationality"; Part of FBI report on *Glos Ludowy*. Emil Gardos to General Fraction of IWO, March 30, 1933, CPUSA-LC, reel 247, delo 3175. Minutes, District 2 Bureau [New York], CP meeting, September 4, 1935, includes report on IWO by N. Shaffer, CPUSA-LC, reel 294, delo 3811. The Philadelphia IWO also maintained a medical department. Max Bedacht to Vito Marcantonio, telegram, May 3, 1940, box 47, Vito Marcantonio Papers, Manuscripts and Archives Division, The New York Public Library [hereafter cited as VM-NYPL]; "Court Allows I.W.O. to Inspect Seized Files," *Daily Worker*, May 17, 1940, 5, CPUSA-LC, reel 318, delo 4243. Marcantonio's "Copy of following telegram sent to Martin Dies, Chairman, Investigating Un-American Activities," from Bedacht [May 1940], VM-NYPL, box 47. Affidavit, George Gombasy, Detroit, April 23, 1951, IWOCF-CU, box 3. For "butcher shops," see Mary Sch., interview by author, June 4, 1996, Philadelphia.

101. N. Shaffer to Charles Zimmerman, August 27, 1937, ILGWU-CU, 5780/014, box 17, folder 4; M. Horwitz to Vito Marcantonio, October 18, 1940, notes that the order's Medical Department also ran a birth control center, VM-NYPL, box 44. For Margaret Sanger and the criminalization of birth control information, see Andrea Tone, "Contraceptive Consumers: Gender and Political Economy of Birth Control in the 1930s," *Journal of Social History* 29, no. 3 (Spring 1996): 485–506.

102. Resolution, South Slavic Women's Educational Club of Cudahy, Wisconsin, May 21, 1932, CPUSA-LC, reel 235, delo 3052; Minutes, Lithuanian Central Bureau meeting, February 7, 1936, CPUSA-LC, reel 303, delo 3995; Interview with Louise Thompson Patterson [ca. 1950–1951].

103. IWO pamphlet, *Our Plan for Plenty* [ca. 1941], IWO-CU, box 5, folder 7; Ad, "Greetings to Labor by the IWO," *Sunday Worker*, September 4, 1949, 7, DB-WSU, box 2, folder 2-55. Synopses of SWS material contains a Slovak-language copy of *Our Plan for Plenty*, IWO-CU, box 26, folder 5; Resolution passed on "Negro Work in the IWO" at a conference of the IWO, April 8, 1941, stressed the relevance of the "Plan for Plenty" to African Americans, IWO-CU, box 19, folder 10. Outline for Dave Greene JPFO speech, Brooklyn, June 19, 1950, refers to the dissemination of the plan among JPFO lodges, IWO-CU, box 4, folder 5. Mike Hanusiak to Sam Milgrom, March 9, 1949, IWO-CU, box 8, folder 12.

104. Sherman Price of Film Publishers Incorporated to "Dear Friend" [1949] and one-page prospectus of film, IWO-CU, box 5, folder 5; Speech, Senator James Murray of Montana to convention, Jewish American Section, IWO, July 4, 1944, IWO-CU, box 27.1, folder 2. The short film *The Sydenham Plan* was released in 1949. On Sydenham Hospital, which New York mayor Ed Koch ordered closed as a budget-cutting measure in 1978, see Sharon Lerner, "The Outpatient Is In: A New Harlem Clinic May Be a Litmus Test for the Future of City Health Care," *Village Voice*, June 9, 1988, 63–64. The hospital was finally closed in 1980.

105. Affidavits, Salvatore Spampinato, Los Angeles, April 23, 1951, and Lewis Marks, Boston, April 21, 1951, IWOCF-CU, box 3. See, too, affidavit, Max Lange, Los Angeles, April 24, 1951, ibid.

106. Reverend S. M. Harden, Chicago, to Sam Milgrom [ca. 1945], IWO-CU, box 6, folder 13.

107. Affidavits, Pauline Taylor, Youngstown, Ohio, April 1951, James Moorer, Jersey City, April 23, 1951, and Angelo Poggioni, Cleveland, April 24, 1951, IWOCF-CU, box 3.

108. Vuko A. Draskovich of Alton, Illinois, to the International Workers Orders, August 27, 1953, Draskovich to IWO, August 31, 1953, Dave Greene to Draskovich, September 9, 1953, IWO-CU, box 4, folder 7.

109. IWO booklet, *Guiding Policy for the Communists in Their Leadership and Work in the International Workers Order* [ca. 1930s], IWO-CU, box 19, folder 6; Louise Thompson Patterson, interview by Linda Burnham, May 14, 1987, LTP-EU, box 27, folder 7; Louise Thompson Patterson, interview by Evelyn Louise Crawford, August 6, 1989, LTP-EU, box 28, folder 11.

110. "Constitution and By-Laws and Declaration of Principles," 1934–1935, IWO-CU, box 3; "Report, Max Bedacht to New York City Conference of IWO, January 20–21, 1934," CPUSA-LC, reel 287, delo 3709; Report, Joseph Brodsky, General Counsel of IWO, to General Executive Board [GEB], plenary session, September 10–11, 1938, IWO-CU, box 1, folder 5.

111. Edward Johanningsmeier, *Forging American Communism: The Life of William Z. Foster* (Princeton, NJ: Princeton University Press, 1994), 239, 259, 272–273; Zumoff, *The Communist International and U.S. Communism*, 242, 249–250, 267–268, 282–284; Jerome Koch, Petaluma, California, to IWO headquarters, April 11, 1941, IWO-CU, box 18, folder 13.

112. Questionnaires, Antonio Carneiro, Bronx, April 30, 1941, Nathan Chcel, Cleveland, and Harvey Gale, Chicago, all May 5, 1941, Helen Lane, Youngstown, Ohio,

April 16, 1941, Elsie Scheiber, Milwaukee, May 16, 1941, and K. Raisin, Norwich, Connecticut, May 2, 1941, IWO-CU, box 18, folder 13.

113. The Carpatho-Russian Society to "Dear Comrade John," December 1 and 17, 1943, IWO-NYU, folder 4.

114. Israel Amter for the International Labor Defense, Southern District, Memphis Section, to "Pat" [1932], CPUSA-LC, reel 233, delo 3017. Max Bedacht to J. Josephson, April 22, 1936, CPUSA-LC, reel 304, delo 4007.

115. IWO Sick Benefit Department to Paul Kovačič, secretary, Detroit Lodge 2012, SWS, July 21, 1953, IWO-CU, box 21, folder 6; IWO Sick Benefit Department to secretary, Lodge 2015, Binghamton, New York, February 2, 1950, IWO-CU, box 21, folder 8.

116. Affidavit, Jacob Zeitlin, Newark, New Jersey, April 24, 1951, IWOCF-CU, box 3; OSS/FNB report, "All Group, Reorganization of IWO," from "BUTTS 715," May 27, 1944, DB-WSU, box 5, folder 5-30; OSS agent "CFB" to "Dear Rodman," July 17, 1944, DB-WSU, box 4, folder 4-29; OSS/FNB report on "Slav Groups"; Report on "All Groups" in the IWO.

117. Minutes, Central Control Commission meeting, May 13, 1938, case of Louis Singer, District 2, of Brooklyn, CPUSA-LC, reel 307, delo 4079; Minutes, Central Control Commission meeting, January 11, 1936, case of Bruno Jasczcak, District 22, of Logan, West Virginia, CPUSA-LC, reel 303, delo 4002; Minutes, Central Control Commission meeting, June 2, 1937, case of William Powell, District 3, of Philadelphia, CPUSA-LC, reel 306, delo 4071; Ed Green, Oakland, California, to "Comrade Hanoff," March 2, 1936, CPUSA-LC, reel 303, delo 3977; Minutes, Central Control Commission meeting, May 9, 1939, case of John Virag [Szabo], District 13, of Butte, Montana, CPUSA-LC, reel 303, delo 4002; Morris Bonn of Pittsburgh to Max Bedacht, May 26, 1947, IWO-CU, box 15, folder 8; Peter Sokalch of Pittsburgh to IWO, April 11, 1946, IWO-CU, box 15, folder 18; Mary Mochanko of Pittsburgh to IWO, June 15, 1946, IWO-CU, box 15, folder 8. Other members complained that drunkenness of local IWO officers prevented them from collecting sick pay for mining accidents: Russian Lodge 3006, Curtisville, Pennsylvania, to "Dear Sirs," June 14, 1948, IWO-CU, box 21, folder 38. For problems of embezzlement in nonideological ethnic fraternal societies, see Robert Zecker, *Streetcar Parishes: Slovak Immigrants Build Their Nonlocal Communities, 1890–1945* (Selinsgrove, PA: Susquehanna University Press, 2010), 126–130, 184–185.

118. IWO Declaration of Principles [1933], CPUSA-LC, reel 260, delo 3372.

CHAPTER 2

1. IWO flyer, *Why Not Social Insurance?* [1932], reel 234, delo 3037, Records of the Communist Party USA, Microfilm 21, 966, Library of Congress [hereafter cited as CPUSA-LC]; "The Activities of the I.W.O." [1932], CPUSA-LC, reel 234, delo 3037; "Report of District Plenum of IWO, April 29, 1934" [Philadelphia], CPUSA, reel 287, delo 3709; Max Bedacht to Earl Browder, July 26, 1934, including suggested copy for IWO election leaflet on Social Insurance, ibid.

2. Poster, "Two Lectures! By Max Bedacht. International Workers Order and Its Aims and The Five Year Plan of Socialism and the Chaos of Capitalism" [1932], CPUSA-LC, reel 310, delo 4122; Flyer, *The Capitalist Crisis and the Workers' Problems* [1931], workers of Duluth hear lecture by Max Bedacht, CPUSA-LC, reel 310, delo 4122.

3. CPUSA Organization Department to Comrade Randolph on the "imaginary famine in Ukraine," December 18, 1933, CPUSA-LC, reel 246, delo 3150.

4. Lincoln Steffens, *Autobiography* (New York: Harcourt, Brace, 1958); Peter Hartshorn, *I Have Seen the Future: A Life of Lincoln Steffens* (Berkeley, CA: Counterpoint, 2011); Thomas Hughes, "How America Helped Build the Soviet Machine," *American Heritage* 39, no. 8 (December 1988): 56–67; Christine White, "Ford in Russia: In Pursuit of the Chimerical Market," *Business History* 28, no. 4 (October 1986): 77–104.

5. IWO Declaration of Principles [1933], CPUSA-LC, reel 260, delo 3372.

6. Ibid.

7. Translation from Yiddish, "Declaration of Principles of the International Workers Order," printed in *The Spark*, official organ of the IWO, vol. 1, no. 1, September 1930, 1, box 3, International Workers Order Case Files, 5940, Kheel Center for Labor-Management Documentation and Archives, Cornell University Library [hereafter cited as IWOCF-CU].

8. Irving Bernstein, *Turbulent Years: A History of the American Worker, 1933–1941* (Boston, MA: Houghton Mifflin, 1971); Lizabeth Cohen, *Making a New Deal: Industrial Workers in Chicago, 1919–1939* (New York: Cambridge University Press, 1990), 251–289; Robert Zieger, *The CIO, 1935–1955* (Chapel Hill: University of North Carolina Press, 1995), 13–21, 32–54; Arthur Schlesinger Jr., *The Coming New Deal: The Age of Roosevelt* (Boston, MA: Houghton Mifflin, 1958), 387–393.

9. IWO pamphlet, *Our Plan for Plenty* [ca. 1941], box 5, folder 7, International Workers Order Records, 1915–2002, MSS 5276, Kheel Center for Labor-Management Documentation and Archives, Cornell University [hereafter cited as IWO-CU]. See, too, IWO, *Promoting Security: Facts about the Role and Purpose of the International Workers Order* (New York: National Educational Department, International Workers Order, October 1940). FBI report, IWO, Detroit division, December 31, 1946, 253, box 16, folder 16-37, Don Binkowski Papers, Walter P. Reuther Library, Wayne State University [hereafter cited as DB-WSU].

10. Alfred Wagenknecht to Jay Lovestone, February 14, 1928, CPUSA-LC, reel 102, delo 1342.

11. *The Capitalist Crisis and the Workers' Problems*; Poster, "Workers Mutual Aid and The World Economic Crisis," and Bedacht speech, Sunday, November 22 [1931], Buffalo, "National Hunger March to Washington," CPUSA-LC, reel 195, delo 2584.

12. Secretary, Language Department, to Secretariat, CPUSA, "Unemployed in Mutual Aid Organizations," November 3, 1930, CPUSA-LC, reel 154, delo 2017; Draft, IWO, "Bedacht," CPUSA-LC, reel 195, delo 2584.

13. Memorandum, "The Activities of the I.W.O." [1932], CPUSA-LC, reel 234, delo 3037.

14. Irving Bernstein, *The Lean Years: A History of the American Worker, 1920–1933* (Baltimore: Penguin Books, 1966), 13–21, 32–54; Paul Dickson and Thomas Allen, "The Legacy of the Bonus Army," *Washington History* 19–20 (2007–2008): 87–96; Stephen Ortiz, *Beyond the Bonus March and GI Bill: How Veteran Politics Shaped the New Deal Era* (New York: New York University Press, 2009); Stephen Ortiz, "Rethinking the Bonus March: Federal Bonus Policy, the Veterans of Foreign Wars, and the Origins of a Protest Movement," *Journal of Policy History* 18, no. 3 (July 2006): 275–303. "Hungarian Mass Organization for the Defense of U.S.S.R." Resolution passed by "the Hungarian Workers' Benevolent and Educational Federation, Hungarian Section of the IWO" [1932], CPUSA-LC, reel 235, delo 3052. See, too, Report, CP to Comintern, "Unemployment Movement in the U.S.A.," December 2, 1930, for violence against Unemployed Council demonstrators, CPUSA-LC, reel 141, delo 1857. Bulgarian Workers' Mutual Benefit and Educational Society, Detroit, to *Daily Worker*, May 13, 1932,

on the Ford Hunger March, CPUSA-LC, reel 235, delo 3052; Leaflet, Italian Workers' Club, North Tonawanda, New York. Protest meeting held by the International Labor Defense (ILD) on January 7, 1932, CPUSA-LC, reel 233, delo 3016. See, too, Leaflet, *From Circulation Promotion Department, Daily Worker,* July 27, 1932, for reference to the Dearborn Hunger March massacre and Henry Ford's use of gangsters in his strikebreaking Service Department, CPUSA-LC, reel 247, delo 3159. On the Ford Company's anti-union tactics, see Beth Tompkins Bates, *The Making of Black Detroit in the Age of Henry Ford* (Chapel Hill: University of North Carolina Press, 2012), 144–145, 159–165, 210–211, 224–229, 232; Karen Miller, *Managing Inequality: Northern Racial Liberalism in Interwar Detroit* (New York: New York University Press, 2015), 183–184; Gregory Wood, "'The Paralysis of the Labor Movement': Men, Masculinity, and Unions in 1920s Detroit," *Michigan Historical Review* 30, no. 1 (Spring 2004): 59–91, esp. 65–66; John Brueggemann, "The Power and Collapse of Paternalism: The Ford Motor Company and Black Workers, 1937–1941," *Social Problems* 47, no. 2 (May 2000): 220–240.

15. Report, Emil Gardos to Hungarian Bureau Central Committee, on National Fraction Conference, December 11, 1933, CPUSA-LC, reel 247, delo 3175; "What Are the Tasks among the Foreign-Born Workers," July 22, 1933, from F. Brown, "To All the Language Bureaus," CPUSA-LC, reel 247, delo 3170. On Mexican deportations during the Depression, see Francisco Balderrama and Raymond Rodríguez, *Decade of Betrayal: Mexican Repatriation in the 1930s* (Albuquerque: University of New Mexico Press, 1995). "Many Delegates Expected at Workers Conference Sunday," *Baltimore Afro-American*, March 14, 1936, 14.

16. "Report of the Language Department C.C." [September 1930], CPUSA-LC, reel 154, delo 2016; Report of conference of Italian delegates to third convention of the IWO, May 7–9, 1935, IWO-CU, box 25, folder 5. Earlier, a Croatian comrade had similarly warned of a right-wing tendency in the tactics pursued in the Croatian Benefit Society: S. Zinich to Central Executive Committee, CP, March 16, 1926, CPUSA-LC, reel 50, delo 709.

17. Henry Podolski to Central Executive Committee, CP, January 2, 1935, CPUSA-LC, reel 292, delo 3792; Polish Chamber of Labor, "The Right to Work Act" text [1934], CPUSA-LC, reel 273, delo 3497; Henry Podolski of the Polish Bureau to "Comrade Mills" of the Philadelphia District Committee [1934], ibid. For conservative efforts to enact anti-union "right to work" laws, see Cedric de Leon, *The Origins of Right to Work: Antilabor Democracy in Nineteenth-Century Chicago* (Ithaca, NY: Cornell University Press, 2015).

18. "Hearing and Discussion of Case of Sol Harper, Amis and Question of White Chauvinism in Chicago," January 17, 1931, CPUSA-LC, reel 187, delo 2470.

19. Ibid. On violent suppression of strikes and demonstrations, see Steven Norwood, *Strikebreaking and Intimidation: Mercenaries and Masculinity in Twentieth-Century America* (Chapel Hill: University of North Carolina Press, 2002).

20. Sadie Doroshkin to Louise Thompson, June 4, 1934, Thompson to Max Bedacht, June 4, 1934, Thompson to Bedacht, February 23, 1934, Bedacht, "To Whom It May Concern," regarding Thompson's credentials as an IWO organizer, February 24, 1934, Bedacht to [name blacked out], February 28, 1934, Doroshkin to Thompson, June 7, 1934, Bedacht to Thompson, June 7, 1934, Thompson to Doroshkin, June 9, 1934, Doroshkin to Thompson, June 12, 1934, Doroshkin to Thompson, June 20, 1934, Thompson to Doroshkin, June 19, 1934, Doroshkin to Thompson, March 9, 1934, Thompson to C. B. Powell, Birmingham, Alabama, attorney, May 21, 1934, Thompson to Doroshkin, May 21, 1934, Powell to Thompson, May 22, 1934, Thompson to Joseph

Brodsky, May 21, 1934, Doroshkin to Thompson, May 23, 1934, and Powell to Thompson, May 28, 1934, box 8, folder 8, Louise Thompson Patterson Papers, 1909–1999, MSS 869, Stuart A. Rose Manuscript, Archives, and Rare Book Library, Emory University [hereafter cited as LTP-EU]; Louise Thompson Patterson MS autobiography, chap. 6, p. 11, LTP-EU, box 20, folder 5; Interview with Louise Thompson Patterson [ca. 1950–1951], LTP-EU, box 8, folder 10; Mary Helen Washington, *The Other Blacklist: The African American Literary and Cultural Left of the 1950s* (New York: Columbia University Press, 2014), 75–76.

21. Affidavits, Salvatore Spampinato, Los Angeles, Bice Diana, Detroit, Harry Rifkin, Detroit, George Frederickson, Detroit, Gus Doxakis, Detroit, and Jacob Balan, Highland Park, Michigan, all April 23, 1951, IWOCF-CU, box 3; Outline for Dave Greene speech, JPFO, Brooklyn, June 19, 1950, IWO-CU, box 4, folder 5; Minutes, General Council meeting, September 15–16, 1945, Helen Vrábel of SWS report, 7, folder 12, International Workers Order Records, Robert F. Wagner Labor Archives, Tamiment Library, New York University [hereafter cited as IWO-NYU].

22. Excerpt from Comrade Berenhaut of Jacksonville, Florida, to IWO [1932], CPUSA-LC, reel 234, delo 3037.

23. Max Bedacht to Israel Amter, National Committee of the Unemployed, December 24, 1932, CPUSA-LC, reel 234, delo 3037.

24. David Oshinsky, *A Conspiracy So Immense: The World of Joe McCarthy* (New York: Oxford University Press, 2005).

25. Minutes, Lithuanian Central Bureau meeting, January 28, 1936, CPUSA-LC, reel 303, delo 3995; "Many Delegates Expected at Workers Conference Sunday," *Baltimore Afro-American*, March 14, 1936, 14, ibid.; Patrick Selmi and Richard Hunter, "Beyond the Rank and File Movement: Mary van Kleeck and Social Work Radicalism in the Great Depression, 1931–1942," *Journal of Sociology and Social Welfare* 28, no. 2 (June 2001): 75–100.

26. *Why Not Social Insurance?*; Bernstein, *The Lean Years*, 254–259, 316–317; Miller, *Managing Inequality*, 124–125, 157–161; "Guiding Policy for the Communists in Their Leadership and Work in the International Workers Order" [early 1930s], IWO-CU, box 19, folder 6.

27. Michael Katz, *In the Shadow of the Poorhouse: A Social History of Welfare in America* (New York: Basic Books, 1996); Michael Katz, *Improving Poor People: The Welfare State, the 'Underclass,' and Urban Schools as History* (Princeton, NJ: Princeton University Press, 1995); Frances Fox Piven and Richard Cloward, *Poor People's Movements: Why They Succeed, How They Fail* (New York: Vintage Books, 1979); Frances Fox Piven and Richard Cloward, *Regulating the Poor: The Functions of Public Welfare* (New York: Vintage Books, 1993).

28. *Why Not Social Insurance?*

29. Ibid. On 1970s proposals for a guaranteed annual income, see Brian Steensland, *The Failed Welfare Revolution: America's Struggle Over Guaranteed Income Policy* (Princeton, NJ: Princeton University Press, 2008).

30. Premilla Nadasen, *Welfare Warriors: The Welfare Rights Movement in the United States* (New York: Routledge, 2005); Premilla Nadasen, "Expanding the Boundaries of the Women's Movement: Black Feminism and the Struggle for Welfare Rights," *Feminist Studies* 28, no. 2 (Summer 2002): 270–301; George Lipsitz, *A Life in the Struggle: Ivory Perry and the Culture of Opposition* (Philadelphia, PA: Temple University Press, 1988); Piven and Cloward, *Poor People's Movements*.

31. Max Bedacht, "The Place of the IWO in the Revolutionary Movement," *Daily Worker*, February 3, 1933, cited in Lucy Davidowitz, "The History of the Jewish People's Fraternal Order of the International Workers Order" [November 1950], TS, IWO-NYU, folder 8; "Plan for the International Workers Order for the Period from July to December 1934—Social Insurance Campaign" and "Report of Max Bedacht to New York City Conference of IWO, January 20–21, 1934," CPUSA-LC, reel 287, delo 3709; Max Bedacht, "IWO Centers on Campaign for Unemployment Insurance," *Daily Worker*, October 8, 1934, 6, CPUSA-LC, reel 318, delo 4243.

32. Minutes, Czechoslovak Bureau meeting, February 23, 1934, CPUSA-LC, reel 273, delo 3502. Language Department to Czechoslovak Bureau, September 2, 1932, CPUSA-LC, reel 213, delo 2747; Language Department to Chicago South Slavs, April 25, 1932, CPUSA-LC, reel 213, delo 2749; Language Department to Chicago South Slavs, April 27, 1932, ibid.; "Report of the Language Department C.C."; S. M. Loyen to Louis Kovess, December 26, 1930, CPUSA-LC, reel 155, delo 2021; "Status of Our Campaign for Unemployment Insurance," part of Unemployment Council report [1935], CPUSA-LC, reel 295, delo 3837.

33. Letter from Pittsburgh to "Comrades," June 8, 1931, regarding the national Pennsylvania Ohio West Virginia Striking Miners' Relief Committee, CPUSA-LC, reel 193, delo 2558; "Statement of Miners Relief of Williamsburg [Brooklyn], Section 6, by Joseph Lapidus" [1931], ibid.; Poster, "Workers of Newark!" which also publicized a state picnic for relief of miners, August 23, 1931, Unionville, New Jersey, CPUSA-LC, reel 193, delo 2561; Flyer, *Big Picnic and Dance—National Miners Union Benefit—August 30, 1931*, ibid.; Flyer, Mass Meeting, Slovak Hall, West Masontown, Pennsylvania, May 15, 1931, *Miners! Negro and White!* ibid. On the NMU, see Linda Nyden, "Black Miners in Western Pennsylvania, 1925–1931: The National Miners Union and the United Mine Workers of America," *Science and Society* 41, no. 1 (Spring 1977): 69–101; Walter Howard, "The National Miners Union: Communists and Miners in the Pennsylvania Anthracite, 1928–1931," *Pennsylvania Magazine of History and Biography* 125, nos. 1–2 (January–April 2001): 92–124; Walter Howard, *Forgotten Radicals: Communists in the Pennsylvania Anthracite, 1919–1950* (Lanham, MD: University Press of America, 2004); and Steve Nelson, James Barrett, and Rob Ruck, *Steve Nelson, American Radical* (Pittsburgh, PA: University of Pittsburgh Press, 1981), 87–92, 165–166.

34. Randi Storch, *Red Chicago: American Communism at its Grassroots, 1928–1935* (Urbana: University of Illinois Press, 2009), 113; Lashawn Harris, "Running with the Reds: African American Women and the Communist Party during the Great Depression," *Journal of African American History* 94, no. 1 (Winter 2009): 21–43.

35. Doroshkin to Thompson, June 4, 1934.

36. For Thompson's election, see "proceedings of the fourth national convention, IWO, April 30, 1938," IWO-CU, box 2, folder 2. "Oznámenia—Do Garfield, N.J. a okolia" [Notice to Garfield, N.J., and area], *New Yorkský denník*, February 11, 1937, 5, reported that Vrábel was delivering a speech in Garfield on "the situation in Europe and the threat of a new world war." As head of the SWS, Vrábel delivered a report to an IWO youth conference at IWO's fifth national convention, June 8–14, 1940, IWO-CU, box 3, folder 3. Deportations Proceedings, December 11, 1951, In re: Clara Dainoff, or Kraina Dainoff, or Rose Draina Dainoff, IWOCF-CU, box 1. See, too, Arthur Kinoy to Thomas Jones, January 8, 1952, enclosing two IWO decisions that may be useful in Jones's loyalty case, including that of Clara Dainoff, whom the INS adjudged an "innocent or nominal member" of the IWO and thus granted a suspension of deportation, ibid.

37. Doroshkin to Thompson, June 4, 1934; Kali Gross, *Colored Amazons: Crime, Violence, and Black Women in the City of Brotherly Love, 1880–1910* (Durham, NC: Duke University Press, 2006); Danielle McGuire, *At the Dark End of the Street: Black Women, Rape, and Resistance* (New York: Knopf, 2010); American Committee for Protection of Foreign Born, *"A Dangerous Woman": Stella Petrosky Held for Deportation* (New York: American Committee for Protection of Foreign Born, 1936); Edward Alsworth Ross, *The Old World in the New: The Significance of Past and Present Immigration to the American People* (New York: Century, 1914).

38. Shop paper, *The Copper Miner*, February 1932, CPUSA-LC, reel 227, delo 2948. For copper country conditions, see Gary Kaunonen and Aaron Goings, *Community in Conflict: A Working-Class History of the 1913–14 Michigan Copper Strike and the Italian Hall Tragedy* (East Lansing: Michigan State University Press, 2013); Arthur Thurner, *Rebels on the Range: The Michigan Copper Miners' Strike of 1913–1914* (Lake Linden, MI, John H. Forster Press, 1984); Larry Lankton, *Hollowed Ground: Copper Mining and Community Building on Lake Superior, 1840s–1990s* (Detroit, MI: Wayne State University Press, 2010); Larry Lankton, *Cradle to Grave: Life, Work, and Death at the Lake Superior Copper Mines* (New York: Oxford University Press, 1991); and Alison Hoagland, *Mine Towns: Buildings for Workers in Michigan's Copper Country* (Minneapolis: University of Minnesota Press, 2010).

39. Shop paper, *The Copper Miner*, February 1932.

40. *The New Order*, March 1934, 17, CPUSA-LC, reel 287, delo 3709. The song's unappetizing chorus was "Soo-up, Soo-up, They give me a bowl of soo-oo-up, Soo-up, Soo-up, They give me a bowl of soup!"

41. Cohen, *Making a New Deal*, 277–283, 292–294; Steve Fraser, *Labor Will Rule: Sidney Hillman and the Rise of American Labor* (Ithaca, NY: Cornell University Press, 1991), 284–289, 292–296.

42. Pamphlet, *Crushed to Death!* [1934], on NRA and James Owens, member of IWO Branch 589, Chicago, CPUSA-LC, reel 287, delo 3709; "Report of Max Bedacht to New York City Conference of IWO, January 20–21, 1934."

43. Philadelphia District Plenum of the IWO, April 29, 1934, CPUSA-LC, reel 287, delo 3709.

44. Bernstein, *Turbulent Years*, 217–317.

45. Organizing Committee Central Committee, CP, to John Williamson, December 20, 1933, regarding the Polish Chamber of Labor, CPUSA-LC, reel 246, delo 3150.

46. Secretary, CPUSA [Earl Browder] to Comrade Rapport of Seattle, January 13, 1934, CPUSA-LC, reel 245, delo 3143; David Roediger and Elizabeth Esch, *The Production of Racial Difference: Race and the Management of Labor in U.S. History* (New York: Oxford University Press, 2012).

47. Earl Browder to *Rovnosť ludu*, telegram, August 23, 1933, CPUSA-LC, reel 245, delo 3143. For the CP's take on the NRA, see Pamphlet, *What Every Worker Should Know about the N.R.A.* [September 3, 1933] by Earl Browder, in which Browder refers to the NRA as, among other things, "the Blue Buzzard," CPUSA-LC, reel 239, delo 3097. Shop paper, *The Delco Worker*, May 1934, Dayton, Ohio, CPUSA-LC, reel 283, delo 3650. Another shop paper offered a song denouncing the NIRA: "Nira, Nira, why, oh why, did you lie?" [NIRA poem], in the *Independent Worker*, "issued by Independent Packing Unit Communist Party" [1934], 2, ibid.

48. Poster, "We Appeal to All Men and Women—Fight Night Work for Women, Which Is Being Forced on Us by the National Recovery Act and the Misleaders of the A.F.L. and United Textile Workers Union" [1933?], CPUSA-LC, reel 191, delo 2556;

Flyers, *True Meaning of the N.R.A.* [Lawndale, Chicago, 1934], and *Workers of Strawberry Mansion, Negro and White* [Philadelphia], June 6, 1934, rally, CPUSA-LC, reel 283, delo 3649; Fred Wulf, German Bureau, to "Comrade Brown," Language Bureau, CPUSA, January 18, 1934, CPUSA-LC, reel 273, delo 3490; *NIRA Notes*, August 1, 1933, CPUSA-LC, reel 247, delo 3490.

49. Minutes, IWO GEB plenary session, September 10 and 11, 1938, IWO-CU, box 1, folder 5; Nigel Copsey, "Communists and the Inter-War Anti-Fascist Struggle in the United States and Britain," *Labour History Review* 76, no. 3 (December 2011): 184–206; Maurice Isserman, *The Death of the Old Left and the Birth of the New Left* (Urbana: University of Illinois Press, 1993), 11–17; "Digest of Testimony of Witnesses for the State in the I.W.O. Matter. January 29, 1951, to March 7, 1951," George Powers testimony, 27–28, IWOCF-CU, box 4. News release, January 30, 1951, charged Powers, the New York State Insurance Department's star witness, with perjury, IWO-CU, box 23, folder 4.

50. "For the Sake of Clarity—A Workmen's Circle Answer to the IWO," letter from the Workmen's Circle National Executive Committee, *The Call*, April 1940, 12, IWO-NYU, folder 8.

51. Cohen, *Making a New Deal*, 283–289; Bernstein, *Turbulent Years*, 318–351.

52. Jerome Koch, Petaluma, California, to IWO, April 11, 1941, IWO-CU, box 18, folder 13; Minutes, General Council meeting, September 15–16, 1945, IWO-NYU, folder 12.

53. Minutes, IWO GEB plenary session, September 10 and 11, 1938, speech by General Secretary Max Bedacht, IWO-CU, box 1, folder 5.

54. Ibid.

55. General Secretary Max Bedacht, report to GEB plenary session, August 26, 1939, IWO-CU, box 2, folder 3; IWO report, "Our Tasks" [1939], "Duties of Progressive Fraternalism," IWO-CU, box 2, folder 3; General secretary report to GEB plenary session, January 27, 1940, IWO-CU, box 2, folder 4; "Marcantonio Says WPA Cuts Lead to War," *Daily Worker*, May 18, 1940, 1 and 5, CPUSA-LC, reel 318, delo 4243. Landon Storrs, *The Second Red Scare and the Unmaking of the New Deal Left* (Princeton, NJ: Princeton University Press, 2013).

56. OSS/FNB report, BUTTS 730, June 9, 1944, DB-WSU, box 5, folder 5-30.

57. Jefferson Cowie, *The Great Exception: The New Deal and the Limits of American Politics* (Princeton, NJ: Princeton University Press, 2016); Elizabeth Fones-Wolf, *Selling Free Enterprise: The Business Assault on Labor and Liberalism, 1945–60* (Urbana: University of Illinois Press, 1994); Kim Phillips-Fein, *Invisible Hands: The Making of the Conservative Movement from the New Deal to Reagan* (New York: Norton, 2009); Kim Phillips-Fein, "'If Business and the Country Will Be Run Right:' The Business Challenge to the Liberal Consensus, 1945–1964," *International Labor and Working-Class History* 72 (2007): 192–215; Storrs, *The Second Red Scare*.

58. General secretary report to GEB, January 27, 1940, 15.

59. Vito Marcantonio, *Security with FDR*, sponsored by members of the IWO (New York: National Fraternal Committee for the Re-Election of President Roosevelt, September 1944), IWO-CU, box 49; Report, "The Hispanic American Section from January 1940 to January 1944," 4–5, delivered at 1944 IWO convention, IWO-CU, box 9, folder 8; Joseph Starobin, *Never Again!* (New York: IWO, August 1945), IWO-CU, box 49.

60. IWO pamphlet, *Our Plan for Plenty* [ca. 1941], IWO-CU, box 5, folder 7; National Educational Department, IWO, *Promoting Security: Facts about the Role and*

Purpose of the International Workers Order (New York: National Educational Department, IWO, October 1940), ibid. FBI report, IWO, Detroit division, December 31, 1946, 253, DB-WSU, box 16, folder 16-37.

61. Max Bedacht, "Policies to Guide the Order," January 19, 1938, 2, IWO-CU, box 2, folder 2.

62. James Henderson, lawyer, to George Palenchar, January 3, 1935, and Workmen's Compensation, the Industrial Commission of Ohio, Claims Section, to Palenchar, October 11, 1935, CPUSA-LC, reel 293, delo 3796; Palenchar's membership card in the CPUSA [1935], ibid.; Palenchar to Central Committee, CP [Organization Committee], November 14 and 24, 1935, ibid.; Central Committee of CP [Organization Committee] to Slovak Bureau CP, December 2, 1935, ibid.; Frank Steflik, secretary, Slovak Bureau CP to Organization Committee [1935], ibid. A. Harvan, Lansford, Pennsylvania, to Charles Korenič on behalf of member Frank Schubak, June 1, 1953, IWO-CU, box 20, folder 19.

63. Max Bedacht to Vito Marcantonio, March 21, 1940, and Victor Pöverk of Yukon, Pennsylvania, to Marcantonio, April 25, 1940, box 47, Vito Marcantonio Papers, Manuscripts and Archives Division, The New York Public Library [hereafter cited as VM-NYPL].

64. Flyer, *Mass Meeting against the Dies Committee, for the New Deal* [English and Italian], January 29, 1939, La Progressiva Lodge 2501, IWO, VM-NYPL, box 47. Petition against the Dies HUAC, from IWO Dante Alighieri Lodge 2579, Bronx [January 1939], ibid.

65. Bedacht, "Policies to Guide the Order," 1.

66. Hy Gordon to Earl Browder, December 22, 1930, CPUSA-LC, reel 151, delo 1960; "Language Department, Central Committee—Communist Party, to All Language Bureaus of the C.C.," July 8, 1931, CPUSA-LC, reel 177, delo 2334. See, too, Flyer, *Workers of Newark!* for an IWO-sponsored picnic, August 14–15, 1931, to raise funds in support of striking NMU coal miners, CPUSA-LC, reel 193, delo 2561; S. M. Loyen to Language Department, Central Committee, October 26, 1933, CPUSA-LC, reel 247, delo 3172; Thompson MS autobiography, chap. 6, p. 25. For Southern union drives by the CP, see Robin Kelley, *Hammer and Hoe: Alabama Communists During the Great Depression* (Chapel Hill: University of North Carolina Press, 2015).

67. Jay Lovestone to Alfred Wagenknecht, November 22, 1927, Wagenknecht to Lovestone, November 28, 1927, and Wagenknecht to Lovestone, December 19, 1927, CPUSA-LC, reel 80, delo 1066; *The Coal Digger*, February 15, 1928, 3 and 4, CPUSA-LC, reel 115, delo 1522. Victor Greene, *The Slavic Community on Strike: Immigrant Labor in Pennsylvania Anthracite* (Note Dame, IN: Notre Dame University Press, 1968); Mildred Allen Beik, *The Miners of Windber: The Struggles of New Immigrants for Unionization, 1890s–1930s* (University Park: Pennsylvania State University Press, 1996); Katherine Mayo, *Justice to All: The Story of the Pennsylvania State Police* (New York: G. P. Putnam's, 1916); James Green, *The Devil Is Here in These Hills: West Virginia's Coal Miners and Their Struggle for Freedom* (New York: Atlantic Monthly Press, 2015).

68. F. Brown, Language Department, "To All Language Bureaus of the C.C.," July 8, 1931, CPUSA-LC, reel 177, delo 2334. "Statement of Miners Relief of Williamsburg [Brooklyn]"; Organization Department to Jewish Bureau Central Committee, May 15, 1931, CPUSA-LC, reel 177, delo 2325; Letter from Pittsburgh to "Comrades."

69. Minutes, Czechoslovak Bureau meeting, May 9, 1934, CPUSA-LC, reel 273, delo 3502.

70. Interview with Thompson Patterson [ca. 1950–1951]; Thompson Patterson, interview by Mary Lecht [ca. 1980s], LTP-EU, box 28, folder 6; Interview with Thompson

Patterson, June 2 and 9, 1987, LTP-EU, box 27, folder 8; Thompson Patterson, interview by Linda Burnham, March 11 and 14, 1988, LTP-EU, box 27, folder 13; Thompson Patterson, interview by Ruth and Bud Schultz, August 12, 1984, LTP-EU, box 27, folder 3.

71. Bill Gebert biography, April 15, 1932, DB-WSU, box 4, folder 4-14; FBI report, "Boleslaw K. Gebert, Bolshevik Agitator," July 25, 1919, DB-WSU, box 4, folder 4-22; FBI report on Gebert at Detroit, "Report made by J. S. Apelman. Detroit, Mich. July 10, 1919," ibid. "Report made by J. S. Apelman. Detroit, Mich. July 8, 1919," ibid. Affidavit, County of Wayne [Detroit, 1919] by a witness in the Gebert deportation hearing, ibid.; Memorandum on Gebert deportation proceedings, from Bureau of Investigation "for the Acting Secretary," November 4, 1919, ibid.; Commissioner General of Immigration and a memorandum on B. K. Gebert attached to the deportation proceedings, October 13, 1919, DB-WSU, box 4, folder 4-23; FBI affidavit, Joseph S. Apelman, January 19, 1920, on Gebert, DB-WSU, box 4, folder 4-22; William Burns, FBI director, to Secretary of Labor, April 21, 1922, requesting the reopening of deportation proceedings against Gebert, DB-WSU, box 4, folder 4-23.

72. Bill Gebert biography, 1–4. Even from Poland in 1979 Gebert complained, "My health is not the best because of 'black lungs' a present of the anthracite mines, which I quit 60 years ago. I need not to say that for the black lungs I do not get one penny, because there was no compensation for that deadly effect." B. K. Gebert to Ed Falkowski, February 19, 1979, DB-WSU, box 3, folder 3-9.

73. Bill Gebert biography; American Committee for Protection of Foreign Born, "A Dangerous Woman"; Rachel Buff, *Against the Deportation Terror: The American Committee for the Protection of the Foreign Born and Immigrant Rights Advocacy, 1933–1982* (Philadelphia, PA: Temple University Press, 2018); Charles Martin, "The ILD and the Angelo Herndon Case," *Journal of Negro History* 64, no. 2 (Spring 1979): 131–141; Doroshkin to Thompson, June 4 and 12, 1934, Thompson to Doroshkin, June 9, 1934; Interview with Thompson Patterson [ca. 1950–1951]; Thompson Patterson, interview by Lecht.

74. Daniel Kanstroom, *Deportation Nation: Outsiders in American History* (Cambridge, MA: Harvard University Press, 2007); Buff, *Against the Deportation Terror*. "Brief by Alien" in Gebert's deportation proceeding [1931], DB-WSU, box 4, folder 4-23; Hearing on deportation of Boleslaw Konstantin Gebert, November 18, 1931, Benton, Illinois, ibid.; Roger Baldwin of the ACLU to Daniel MacCormack, Commissioner General of Immigration, November 28, 1934, W. W. Brown, assistant for MacCormack, to Baldwin, January 17, 1937, David Bentall, lawyer, to Department of Labor, January 26, 1937, and J. R. Espinosa, Chief Supervisor of Special Inspections, Department of Justice, to "Mr. Brown" of Immigration Service, October 20, 1941, ibid.; "Bon Voyage, Bill," *Fraternal Outlook* [1947], 18, DB-WSU, box 4, folder 4-14. See, too, Resignation letter, Boleslaw Gebert, August 11, 1947, IWO-CU, box 5, folder 12.

75. Affidavits, Anton Opara [Pittsburgh?], and Harry Bobey and Charles Wasyluk of West Leechburg, Pennsylvania, all April 1951, IWOCF-CU, box 3; Mike Hanusiak to Sam Milgrom, May 16, 1949, IWO-CU, box 8, folder 12; "Report of the Officers Presented to the General Council, IWO, February 3 and 4, 1951," by Peter Shipka, Secretary-Treasurer, IWO-CU, folder 18; C. Lippa, Acting National Secretary, IWO Garibaldi Society, to "Dear Member," April 26, 1950, IWO-CU, box 10, folder 10. See, too, "Workers Order Urges Seizure of Mines," *Pittsburgh Press*, March 23, 1945, 5.

76. Lovestone to Wagenknecht, November 22, 1927, Wagenknecht to Lovestone, November 28, 1927, and Wagenknecht to Lovestone, December 19, 1927. *The Coal Digger*, February 15, 1928, 3 and 4. Gustavo Caparoli of Arnold, Pennsylvania, to C. Lippa,

August 23, 1950, Lippa to Caparoli, August 28, 1950, and Ludwik Paluch of Enterprise, West Virginia, to IWO national office, February 6, 1953, IWO-CU, box 10, folder 10; W. Sobol of Elbert, West Virginia, to Daniel Kasustchik [ca. June–July 1950], IWO-CU, box 25, folder 1. For persistent company control of small coal towns, even after mines were unionized, see Beik, *The Miners of Windber*.

77. James Ford, "A Week in Detroit," April 30 to May 7, 1932, CPUSA-LC, reel 231, delo 2984.

78. James Barrett and David Roediger, "Whiteness and the Inbetween Peoples of Europe," *Journal of American Ethnic History* 16, no. 3 (Summer 1997): 3–44; Roediger and Esch, *The Production of Racial Difference*; David Roediger, *The Wages of Whiteness: Race and the Making of the American Working Class* (New York: Verso, 1991).

79. Hungarian Bureau Central Committee, December 11, 1933, report on National Fraction Conference, CPUSA-LC, reel 247, delo 3175; CP, District 4, Buffalo, New York, to "Dear Comrades," July 16, 1935, CPUSA-LC, reel 294, delo 3826; Part of letter from Tony Gerlach, January 31, 1935, CPUSA-LC, reel 296, delo 3851; Minutes, District 2 Bureau CP [New York] meeting, September 4, 1935, report on IWO by N. Shaffer, "additional report on the IWO" by Louise Thompson, CPUSA-LC, reel 294, delo 3811. See, too, Gerald Horne, *Red Seas: Ferdinand Smith and Radical Black Sailors in the United States and Jamaica* (New York: New York University Press, 2005); Howard Kimeldorf *Reds or Rackets? The Making of Radical and Conservative Unions on the Waterfront* (Berkeley: University of California Press, 1992). For the ACWA, see Fraser, *Labor Will Rule*; Daniel Katz, *All Together Different: Yiddish Socialists, Garment Workers, and the Labor Roots of Multiculturalism* (New York: New York University Press, 2011); Jo Ann Argersinger, *Making the Amalgamated: Gender, Ethnicity, and Class in the Baltimore Clothing Industry, 1899–1939* (Baltimore, MD: Johns Hopkins University Press, 1999); Karen Pastorello, *A Power among Them: Bessie Abramowitz Hillman and the Making of the Amalgamated Clothing Workers of America* (Urbana: University of Illinois Press, 2008).

80. Robert Zieger, *The CIO, 1935–1955* (Chapel Hill: University of North Carolina Press, 1995); Nelson, Barrett, and Ruck, *Steve Nelson, American Radical*; Staughton Lynd and Alice Lynd, eds., *Rank and File: Personal Histories by Working-Class Organizers* (New York: Beacon Press, 1973).

81. Rebecca Grecht, "I.W.O. in the Steel Drive," *The New Order*, September 1936, IWO-NYU, folder 43; "Fraternal Orders Backing Steel Drive to Meet Sunday. Pittsburgh Conference First of Series to Speed Campaign," *Daily Worker*, October 23, 1936, 3, DB-WSU, box 4, folder 4-14.

82. "Fraternal Orders Backing Steel Drive to Meet Sunday"; *Sunday Worker*, November 1, 1936, 6, *Daily Worker*, October 23, 1936, 3, DB-WSU, box 4.

83. Interview with Thompson Patterson [ca. 1950–1951]; Interview with Thompson Patterson, June 2 and 9, 1987; Thompson Patterson, interview by Wilkerson.

84. Sojourners for Truth and Justice statement in support of a Harlem Domestic Workers Union [1952?], LTP-EU, box 12, folder 17; Flyer, *Announcing the Eastern Seaboard Conference of the Sojourners for Truth and Justice, March 23, 1952*, LTP-EU, box 12, folder 18; Dayo Gore, *Radicalism at the Crossroads: African American Women Activists in the Cold War* (New York: New York University Press, 2011), 85–89.

85. Philip Murray, "Steel," *The New Order*, September 1936, 14, IWO-NYU, folder 43.

86. Letter from Philip Murray, SWOC, commending the IWO for its support, April 13, 1937, and Max Bedacht to Murray, April 20, 1937, IWO-NYU, folder 43. Brochure, *Two Letters about One Cause*, ibid.

87. Bedacht to Murray, April 20, 1937.

88. Fones-Wolf, *Selling Free Enterprise*; Phillips-Fein, *Invisible Hands*; Phillips-Fein, "'If Business and the Country Will Be Run Right'"; Cowie, *The Great Exception*; Storrs, *The Second Red Scare*. Booklet, *Victory for Freedom—A Program Adopted by the War and Reconversion Congress of American Industry* (New York: National Association of Manufacturers, December 1944), IWO-CU, box 46.

89. Article on steel unionization campaign, *The New Order*, May 1937, 6, IWO-NYU, folder 43; Peter Kostyshak to Michael Logoyda, September 30, 1944, IWO-CU, box 25, folder 2.

90. Zieger, *The CIO*, 62; Michael Dennis, *The Memorial Day Massacre and the Movement for Industrial Democracy* (New York: Palgrave Macmillan, 2010); Michael Dennis, *Blood on Steel: Chicago Steelworkers and the Strike of 1937* (Baltimore, MD: Johns Hopkins University Press, 2014); Carol Quirke, *Eyes on Labor: News Photography and America's Working Class* (New York: Oxford University Press, 2012); Carol Quirke, "Reframing Chicago's Memorial Day Massacre, May 30, 1937," *American Quarterly* 60, no. 1 (March 2008): 129–155; John Hogan, *The 1937 Chicago Steel Strike: Blood on the Prairie* (Charleston, SC: History Press, 2014). Pamphlet of Senate Report No. 46, Part 2, *Violations of Free Speech and Rights of Labor: Report of the Committee on Education and Labor Pursuant to S. Res. 266—A Resolution to Investigate Violations of the Right of Free Speech and Assembly and Interference with the Rights of Labor to Organize and Bargain Collectively—The Chicago Memorial Day Incident—July 22, 1937*, box 1, folder 3, Leo Krzycki Papers, MMS 276, University of Wisconsin—Milwaukee [hereafter cited as LK-UWM].

91. Eugene Miller, "Leo Krzycki: Polish American Labor Leader, *Polish American Studies* 33, no. 2 (Autumn 1976): 52–64. Pamphlet of Senate Report No. 46, Part 2; Obituary, "Leo Krzycki Dies at 84," *The Advance*, February 7, 1966, 4, LK-UWM, box 1, folder 1. Program of April 1942 inaugural ASC in Detroit, in which the IWO took out a full-page ad, "70,000 Members of the Slav-American Section of the International Workers Order Greet the Unity of the 15,000,000 Americans of Slav Extraction Gathered at This Historical Congress!" DB-WSU, box 5, folder 5-29.

92. Zieger, *The CIO*, 39–40, 62; Cohen, *Making a New Deal*, 303–304, 323, 340.

93. *Dziennik Polski*, June 9, 1937, 5, DB-WSU, box 13, folder 13-14.

94. Pamphlet of Senate Report No. 46, Part 2.

95. Vito Marcantonio, "The Menace of Vigilantism," *Labor Defender*, July 1937, 7, 15, CPUSA-LC, reel 306, delo 4074. For the history of "right to work" tactics by business, see de Leon, *The Origins of Right to Work*.

96. Jan Wittenber, "For the Families of Chicago's Dead and Wounded," *Labor Defender*, July 1937, 13, CPUSA-LC, reel 306, delo 4074; Marcantonio, "The Menace of Vigilantism." For CP deployment of concepts of American patriotism during the Popular Front era, see Earl Browder, *Who Are the Americans?* [pamphlet], CPUSA-LC, reel 303, delo 3983. David DeLeon, "The Popular Front CPUSA and the Revolution of 1776: A Study in Patriotic 'Marxism,'" (Humanities Working Paper 39, California Institute of Technology, 1979).

97. "Riots Blamed on Red Chiefs. Coroner Moves Today to Seize Mob's Leaders," with cartoon, "Which Hand Will Win?" *Chicago Tribune*, June 1, 1937, 1, DB-WSU, box 13, folder 13-14; "Ghost from the Old Graveyard," *Chicago Tribune*, July 2, 1937, 1, ibid.

98. HUAC, "Report on the American Slav Congress," June 26, 1949, 35, https://archive.org/details/reportonamerican00unit.

99. George Lipsitz, *Rainbow at Midnight: Labor and Culture in the 1940s* (Urbana: University of Illinois Press, 1994), 171–179.

100. Roger Keeran, *The Communist Party and the Auto Workers' Unions* (New York: International, 1980), Roger Keeran, "National Groups and the Popular Front: The Case of the International Workers Order," *Journal of American Ethnic History* 14, no. 3 (Spring 1995): 23–51; Roger Keeran, "The International Workers Order and the Origins of the CIO," *Labor History* 30, no. 3 (Summer 1989): 385–408; Rosemary Feurer, *Radical Unionism in the Midwest, 1900–1950* (Urbana: University of Illinois Press, 2006).

101. "Declaration of Principles," "activities of labor unions," July 1, 1938, IWOCF-CU, box 4; "Report to the General Executive Board, IWO, by the General Secretary," September 1938, IWO-CU, box 2, folder 2.

102. FBI report, IWO, Detroit division, December 31, 1946, 8–10, DB-WSU, box 16, folder 16-37.

103. Ellen Schrecker, *Many Are the Crimes: McCarthyism in America* (Princeton, NJ: Princeton University Press, 1998), 91–97.

104. FBI report, IWO, Detroit division, December 31, 1946, 101, "Activities in 1941," 103 on *Tyomies*, and 12 on the Polonia Society; OSS/FNB report, "Communist-Line IWO Reorganizes to Emphasize Nationality." Rubin Saltzman and Albert Kahn of the JPFO sent a letter to Sidney Hillman of the CIO's Political Action Committee congratulating the CIO for the part it played in Roosevelt's 1944 reelection: Saltzman and Kahn to Hillman, November 10, 1944, IWO-CU, box 29, folder 6. See Flyer, *Protest Ford Brutality Ford Fascism*, for June 5, 1937, rally at which Homer Martin, Frankensteen, and Krzycki were scheduled to speak, DB-WSU, box 6, folder 6-23. For the Battle of the Overpass and Frankensteen's campaign for mayor, see Bates, *The Making of Black Detroit*, 211; Zieger, *The CIO*, 99, 121, 242; Nelson Liechtenstein, *The Most Dangerous Man in Detroit: Walter Reuther and the Fate of American Labor* (New York: Basic Books, 1995), 83–87, 91, 217.

105. FBI report, IWO, Detroit, December 10, 1945, DB-WSU, box 16, folder 16-36.

106. Interview with Stanley Nowak [Detroit, March 30, 1983]. Tapes 177 A–C. Oral History of the American Left Collection, 1940–2011, OH.002, Robert F. Wagner Labor Archives, Tamiment Library, New York University.

107. Ed Falkowski diary, March 23, 1941, DB-WSU, box 3, folder 3-33.

108. Ed Falkowski diary, January 23, 1942, DB-WSU, box 3, folder 3-9; Falkowski diary, March 23, 1941, DB-WSU, box 3, folder 3-33.

109. Kelley, *Hammer and Hoe*; Nelson, Barrett, and Ruck, *Steve Nelson, American Radical*, 76–79.

110. See SWS meeting minutes, November 7, 1943, and February 27, 1944, on suggestion that members of the IWO in the state [Pennsylvania] should join the UE of the CIO, IWO-CU, box 54. For the ASC's assertion, see "Committee of American-Slav Congress Issues a Delegate Call," *Národné noviny*, March 25, 1942, 5. The quotation on Slavs is from Edward Alsworth Ross, *The Old World in the New*. For the stigmatization of Southeast Europeans as not quite white, see Matthew Frye Jacobson, *Whiteness of a Different Color: European Immigrants and the Alchemy of Race* (Cambridge, MA: Harvard University Press, 1998); Roediger, *The Wages of Whiteness*; Barrett and Roediger, "Whiteness and the Inbetween Peoples of Europe."

111. Maurice Isserman, *Which Side Were You On? The American Communist Party during the Second World War* (Middletown, CT: Wesleyan University Press, 1982), 136–138, 161–169; Art Preiss, *Labor's Giant Step: The First Twenty Years of the CIO, 1935–1955* (New York: Pathfinder Press, 1972), as excerpted in *The Militant* 69, no. 29 (August 1, 2005). SWS minutes, November 7, 1943; Harry Dutkanych of Stratford, Connecticut, to Carpatho-Russian Society, IWO, March 5, 1943, IWO-CU, box 9, folder 7;

"Carpatho-Russian National Society," letters from Carpatho-Russian IWO members [1943, and May 21, 1943], IWO-NYU, folder 4.

112. "Carpatho-Russian National Society" letter, May 21, 1943, IWO-NYU, folder 4.

113. Lipsitz, *Rainbow at Midnight*, 120–134. FBI report, IWO, Detroit division, December 31, 1946, 10; Affidavits, Bice Diana, Detroit, and Jacob Balan, Highland Park, Michigan, both April 23, 1951, IWOCF-CU, box 3; Reports of Croatian, Polish, and Slovak Societies to General Council, IWO, March 16–17, 1946, IWO-NYU, folder 13; Letter from Leo Krzycki, June 27, 1946, box 5, folder 2, International Ladies Garment Workers Union, Charles S. Zimmerman Papers, 1919–1958, MSS 5780/014, Kheel Center for Labor-Management Documentation and Archives, Cornell University [hereafter cited as ILGWU-CU, MSS 5780/014]. *Ľudový kalendár na rok 1947*, 100, 122. *Bombardier*, JPFO newsletter, Philadelphia, March 1946, IWO-CU, box 46. The 1949 HUAC report on the ASC noted the Congress's support for the General Motors strike as proof of its "subversive" nature.

114. Zieger, *The CIO*, 246–248, 277–293; Lipsitz, *Rainbow at Midnight*, 171–179, 191–201.

115. *Lodge Log*, April 1947, IWO-CU, box 46; Newsletter, Lodge 817 *Fraternalist*, December 1947, includes reprints of "Labor Is a Terrible Monopoly," an editorial from the *Mobile* [Alabama] *Labor Journal*, organ of AFL unions, and an editorial cartoon from Walt Partymiller, *York* [Pennsylvania] *Gazette and Daily*, IWO-CU, box 32, folder 55.

116. Action letter of the IWO, February 7, 1947, and "IWO Resolution against Anti-Labor Legislation" [1947], IWO-NYU, folder 6; ASC of western Pennsylvania, "Resolution on Anti-Labor Legislation," February 23, 1947, IWO-CU, box 13, folder 11; SWS meeting minutes, March 23, 1947, IWO-CU, box 54; Milan Draskovich to President Truman [1947], IWO-CU, box 13, folder 11.

117. Bill Wiese, "The 1946 Railroad Strike: Harry Truman and the Evolution of Presidential Power," *Public Voices* 11, no. 2 (September 2012): 77; Ralph Waldo Strickland, interview by LuAnn Jones, April 18, 1980, in Oral Histories of the American South, interview H-0180, Southern Oral History Program Collection (4007), University of North Carolina; Reports on 1946–1948 activities of Cervantes Fraternal Society, IWO, 7, IWO-NYU, folder 5.

118. *Bombardier*, March 1946; Affidavits, Diana and Balan; Dave Greene, JPFO speech, Brooklyn, June 19, 1950, IWO-CU, box 4, folder 5; Ad, "Greetings to Labor by the IWO," *Sunday Worker*, September 4, 1949, 7, DB-WSU, box 2, folder 2-55.

119. Nelson Frank, "Their Books Balanced, But Politics Were in Red," *New York World-Telegram and Sun*, January 23, 1951, IWOCF-CU, box 2.

120. HUAC, "Report on the CIO Political Action Committee," March 29, 1944, DB-WSU, box 11, folder 11-32; OSS/FNB report, September 11, 1944, included a *Pittsburgh Sun-Telegraph* editorial, "The Ill Wind from Moscow," September 11, 1944, DB-WSU, box 1, folder 1-15. Feurer, *Radical Unionism in the Midwest*.

121. Minutes, District 2 Bureau [New York], CPUSA meeting, September 4, 1935, includes report on IWO by N. Shaffer to District 2 Bureau meeting, CPUSA-LC, reel 294, delo 3811. The Philadelphia IWO also maintained a Medical Department. Bedacht to Marcantonio, telegram, May 3, 1940; "Court Allows I.W.O. to Inspect Seized Files," *Daily Worker*, May 17, 1940, 5, CPUSA-LC, reel 318, delo 4243; Marcantonio's "Copy of following telegram sent to Martin Dies, Chairman, Investigating Un-American Activities," from Bedacht [May 1940], VM-NYPL, box 47. Affidavit, George Gombasy, Detroit, April 23, 1951, IWOCF-CU, box 3; N. Shaffer to Charles Zimmerman, August 27,

1937, ILGWU-CU, MSS 5780/014, box 17, folder 4; New York City Central Committee of the IWO, M. Horwitz, Educational Director, to Marcantonio, October 18, 1940, notes that the Order's Medical Department also ran a birth control center and that Marcantonio and the IWO were fighting "for a hospital in the territory," VM-NYPL, box 44. Horwitz to Marcantonio, August 9, 1940, VM-NYPL, box 47. "Report to the General Executive Board IWO by the General Secretary," September 1938, 14–15; Minutes, IWO GEB plenary session, September 10 and 11, 1938, IWO-CU, box 1, folder 5; March 1939 plenary, 19–20, 25–26, IWO-CU, box 1, folder 6.

122. Speech, Senator James Murray of Montana to convention of Jewish American Section, IWO, July 4, 1944, 6–7 of convention program, IWO-CU, box 27.1, folder 2; "Gives His Views of Wagner Proposals," *Národné noviny*, March 8, 1944, 5; SWS meeting minutes, February 27, 1944.

123. Max Bedacht, "What about Socialized Medicine?" *Fraternal Outlook*, January 1944, 16–17, 28 and 30, with illustration by Emanuel Romano, IWO-CU, box 48. For Romano, see Paul Cappucci, "'A Blossoming of the Spirit': William Carlos Williams, Emanuel Romano, and the Authenticity of Artistic Expression," *William Carlos Williams Review* 29, no. 1 (Spring 2009): 15–27; "Emanuel Romano, 87, Dies; Painter and Book Illustrator," *New York Times*, November 16, 1984, www.nytimes.com/1984/11/16 /obituaries/emanuel-romano-87-dies-painter-and-book-illustrator.html.

124. Starobin, *Never Again!*

125. *Národné noviny*, December 14, 1949, 1, reported on the AMA's $3 million lobbying campaign to defeat "socialized medicine." H. Luke Shaefer and Elizabeth Sammons, "The Development of an Unequal Social Safety Net: A Case Study of the Employer-Based Health Insurance (Non) System," *Journal of Sociology and Social Welfare* 36, no. 3 (September 2009): 179–199; Alan Derickson, "Health Security for All? Social Unionism and Universal Health Insurance, 1935–1958," *Journal of American History* 80, no. 4 (March 1994): 1333–1356; Michael Brown, "Bargaining for Social Rights: Unions and the Reemergence of Welfare Capitalism, 1945–1952," *Political Science Quarterly* 112, no. 4 (Winter 1997–1998): 645–674; Jill Quadagno, "Why the United States Has No National Health Insurance: Stakeholder Mobilization against the Welfare State, 1945–1996," *Journal of Health and Social Behavior* 45 (2004): 25–44; Kathleen Doherty and Jeffrey Jenkins, "Examining a Failed Moment: National Health Care, the AMA, and the U.S. Congress, 1948–1950," paper presented at the 2009 Annual Meeting of the Southern Political Science Association, New Orleans. For opposition to "socialized" medicine in the 1940s, see Helen Fuller, "Playing Politics with the Health Issue," *The New Republic*, May 3, 1948; Donald Smith, "Social Security: The Wagner-Murray-Dingell [1945] Senate Bill 1050, H.R. 3293," *American Journal of Nursing* 45, no. 11 (November 1945): 933–936; "The ANA and the Wagner-Murray-Dingell Bill, S. 1606," *American Journal of Nursing* 46, no. 6 (June 1946): 373–376; Robert Rosenthal, "Organized Labor's Social Security Program: 1948," *Social Forces* 26, no. 3 (March 1948): 337–342. Philip D'Amato of Detroit to Sam Milgrom, January 8, 1946, and Milgrom to D'Amato, April 26, 1946, IWO-CU, box 7, folder 6; D'Amato to Milgrom, with ticket, April 19, 1946, IWO-CU, box 7, folder 7; Leaflet, *Labor Supports S. 1050—National Health Act. Hear . . . John E. Middleton* [1946], IWO-CU, box 9, folder 2; Stephen Bosustow of the United Film Productions to Sam Milgrom, February 9, 1946, IWO-CU, box 20, folder 3; Sam Milgrom to "Dear Brother," February 28, 1946, IWO-CU, box 20, folder 5.

126. "Confidential letter," May 8, 1947, Sam Milgrom to "Dear Brother," IWO-CU, box 4, folder 2; Sam Milgrom, "Report to the General Council IWO, March 1,

1947," IWO-NYU, folder 17; Senator James Murray of Montana to Max Bedacht, May 3, 1947, IWO-CU, box 3, folder 12; I. Isaacs of Detroit to Sam Milgrom, April 15, 1946, DB-WSU, box 5, folder 5-29; Minutes, IWO General Council meeting, September 15-16, 1946, 7, IWO-NYU, folder 12; Joint Conference of the New Jersey and New York Districts, SWS, February 8, 1948, IWO-CU, box 26, folder 5; Serbian Society report to IWO General Council, March 16-17, 1946, IWO-CU, folder 13; "Greetings to Labor by the IWO"; Outline for Dave Greene JPFO speech, Brooklyn, June 19, 1950, IWO-CU, box 4, folder 5; Sam Milgrom, "Americanism and Loyalty," *Jewish Fraternalist*, April 1948, 1-4, IWO-CU, box 46. The ASC also endorsed universal health care: George Pirinsky, *Slavic Americans in the Fight for Victory and Peace* (New York: American Slav Congress, 1946), 44.

127. Ad, "Philadelphia on Guard," *Philadelphia Daily News*, August 5, 1944, 5, IWO-CU, box 45, folder 1; Leaflet, *On Guard! Against Hitler's Attack!* in English and Yiddish, JPFO, Philadelphia, ibid.; News release, August 3, 1944, IWO of Philadelphia, ibid.

128. Allan Winkler, "The Philadelphia Transit Strike of 1944," *Journal of American History* 59, no. 1 (June 1972): 73-89; Thomas Sugrue, *The Origins of the Urban Crisis: Race and Inequality in Postwar Detroit* (Princeton, NJ: Princeton University Press, 1996), 17-88; Arnold Hirsch, *Making the Second Ghetto: Race and Housing in Chicago, 1940-1960* (Chicago, IL: University of Chicago Press, 1998); Lipsitz, *Rainbow at Midnight*, 69-94; Victoria Wolcott, *Race, Riots, and Roller Coasters: The Struggle over Segregated Recreation in America* (Philadelphia: University of Pennsylvania Press, 2012), 47-53.

CHAPTER 3

1. Robert Zecker, *Race and America's Immigrant Press: How the Slovaks were Taught to Think Like White People* (New York: Continuum, 2011); Thomas Sugrue, *The Origins of the Urban Crisis: Race and Inequality in Postwar Detroit* (Princeton, NJ: Princeton University Press, 1996); Arnold Hirsch, *Making the Second Ghetto: Race and Housing in Chicago, 1940-1960* (Chicago: University of Chicago Press, 1998); Thomas Philpott, *The Slum and the Ghetto: Neighborhood Deterioration and Middle-Class Reform, Chicago, 1880-1930* (New York: Oxford University Press, 1978); Andrew Diamond, *Mean Streets: Chicago Youths and the Everyday Struggle for Empowerment in the Multiracial City, 1908-1969* (Berkeley: University of California Press, 2009).

2. David Roediger, *The Wages of Whiteness: Race and the Making of the American Working Class* (New York: Verso, 1991); David Roediger, *Working toward Whiteness: How America's Immigrants Became White; The Strange Journey from Ellis Island to the Suburbs* (New York: Basic Books, 2005); David Roediger and Elizabeth Esch, *The Production of Difference: Race and the Management of Labor in U.S. History* (New York: Oxford University Press, 2012); James Barrett and David Roediger, "Whiteness and the Inbetween Peoples of Europe," *Journal of American Ethnic History* 16, no. 3 (Summer 1997): 3-44; James Barrett, "Unity and Fragmentation: Class, Race, and Ethnicity on Chicago's South Side, 1900-1922," *Journal of Social History* 18, no. 1 (Autumn 1984): 37-55; Matthew Frye Jacobson, *Whiteness of a Different Color: European Immigrants and the Alchemy of Race* (Cambridge, MA: Harvard University Press, 1998); Matthew Frye Jacobson, *Barbarian Virtues: The United States Encounters Foreign Peoples at Home and Abroad, 1876-1917* (New York: Hill and Wang, 2000); Matthew Frye Jacobson, *Special Sorrows: The Diasporic Imagination of Irish, Polish and Jewish Immigrants in the United States* (Berkeley: University of California Press, 2002); Noel Ignatiev, *How*

the Irish Became White (New York: Routledge, 1995); Eric Arnesen, *Waterfront Workers of New Orleans: Race, Class, and Politics, 1863–1923* (Urbana: University of Illinois Press, 1994); Jennifer Guglielmo and Salvatore Salerno, eds., *Are Italians White? How Race is Made in America* (New York: Routledge, 2003); Thomas Guglielmo, *White on Arrival: Italians, Race, Color and Power in Chicago, 1890-1945* (New York: Oxford University Press, 2003); Karen Brodkin, *How Jews Became White Folks and What That Says about Race in America* (New Brunswick, NJ: Rutgers University Press, 1998); Hasia Diner, *In the Almost Promised Land: American Jews and Blacks, 1915–1935* (Westport, CT: Greenwood Press, 1977); Catherine Eagan, *"I Did Imagine . . . We Had Ceased to Be Whitewashed Negroes": The Racial Formation of Irish Identity in Nineteenth-Century Ireland and America* (dissertation, Boston College, 2000); Glenda Gilmore, *Defying Dixie: The Radical Roots of Civil Rights, 1919–1950* (New York: Norton, 2008); Robert Orsi, "The Religious Boundaries of an Inbetween People: Street *Feste* and the Problem of the Dark-Skinned Other in Italian Harlem, 1920–1990," *American Quarterly* 44, no. 2 (September 1992): 313–347; Daniel Letwin, *The Challenge of Interracial Unionism: Alabama Coal Miners, 1878–1921* (Chapel Hill: University of North Carolina Press, 1998); Rebecca Hill, *Men, Mobs, and Law: Anti-Lynching and Labor Defense in U.S. Radical History* (Durham, NC: Duke University Press, 2008); Zecker, *Race and America's Immigrant Press*.

3. Jacqueline Castledine, *Cold War Progressives: Women's Interracial Organizing for Peace and Freedom* (Urbana: University of Illinois Press, 2012); Erik Gellman, *Death Blow to Jim Crow: The National Negro Congress and the Rise of Militant Civil Rights* (Chapel Hill: University of North Carolina Press, 2012); Daniel Katz, *All Together Different: Yiddish Socialists, Garment Workers, and the Labor Roots of Multiculturalism* (New York: New York University Press, 2011); William Maxwell, *New Negro, Old Left: African-American Writing and Communism Between the Wars* (New York: Columbia University Press, 1999); Erik McDuffie, *Sojourning for Freedom: Black Women, American Communism, and the Making of Black Left Feminism* (Durham, NC: Duke University Press, 2011); Dayo Gore, *Radicalism at the Crossroads: African American Women Activists in the Cold War* (New York: New York University Press, 2011); Minkah Makalani, *In the Cause of Freedom: Radical Black Internationalism from Harlem to London, 1917–1939* (Chapel Hill: University of North Carolina Press, 2011).

4. Jacob Zumoff, *The Communist International and U.S. Communism, 1919–1929* (Chicago: Haymarket Books, 2014), 298–305, 309, 331–332, 342–343; Hakim Adi, *Pan-Africanism and Communism: The Communist International, Africa and the Diaspora, 1919–1939* (London: Africa World Press, 2013), 258–281.

5. Roediger, *Working toward Whiteness*; Brodkin, *How Jews Became White Folks*; Ethel Levine to "Dear Sir," May 21, 1953, and Gedalia Sandler to Levine, May 22, 1953, box 32, folder 55, International Workers Order Records, 1915–2002, MSS 5276, Kheel Center for Labor-Management Documentation and Archives, Cornell University [hereafter cited as IWO-CU].

6. IWO flyer, *Why Not Social Insurance?* [1932], reel 234, delo 3037, Records of the Communist Party USA, Microfilm 21, 966, Library of Congress [hereafter cited as CPUSA-LC]; "The Activities of the I.W.O." [1932], ibid.; "Report of District Plenum of IWO, Sunday, April 29, 1934" [Philadelphia], CPUSA-LC, reel 287, delo 3709; Max Bedacht to Earl Browder, July 26, 1934, including suggested copy for IWO election leaflet on Social Insurance, ibid.

7. IWO report on organizing Negro branches [1932], CPUSA-LC, reel 234, delo 3037.

8. June Granatir Alexander, *Ethnic Pride, American Patriotism: Slovaks and Other New Immigrants in the Interwar Era* (Philadelphia, PA: Temple University Press, 2004); John Bodnar, *The Transplanted: A History of Immigrants in Urban America* (Bloomington: Indiana University Press, 1987); *Rovnosť ľudu*, March 8, 1922, 5, and February 8, 1924, 2. For coverage supportive of U.S. gunboat diplomacy, see *Slovák v Amerike*, May 11, 1900, 1, July 1, 1902, 6, February 28, 1905, 2, July 8, 1909, 2, May 30, 1912, 1, June 6, 1912, 1, January 30, 1913, 1, and August 5, 1913, 1; *New Yorkský denník*, February 12, 1915, 3; *Jednota*, December 9, 1908, 4; *Národné noviny*, September 30, 1915, 1 and 3. See, too, *Rovnosť ľudu*, March 8, 1922, 5. For antilynching coverage, see *Rovnosť ľudu*, February 20, 1925, 3, July 31, 1925, 8, June 26, 1925, 1, and May 5, 1926, 1. For anticolonial coverage, see *Rovnosť ľudu*, September 13, 1922, 6, October 6, 1925, 8, December 12, 1924, 1, and May 1, 1925, 1. Zecker, *Race and America's Immigrant Press*, 103–176; Jacobson, *Special Sorrows*.

9. "Report of the Committee on Negro Work" [1923], CPUSA-LC, reel 13, delo 207; Steven Hahn, *The Political Worlds of Slavery and Freedom* (Cambridge, MA: Harvard University Press, 2009), 115–162, quotation on 132. National Chairman, Workers Party, to UNIA, re: Fourth Annual International Convention of the Universal Negro Improvement Association, August 14, 1924, CPUSA-LC, reel 23, delo 359; Lovett Fort-Whiteman to Executive Committee, Communist International, April 21, 1926, CPUSA-LC, reel 40, delo 591; Fort-Whiteman to Charles Ruthenberg, August 7, 1925, CPUSA-LC, reel 34, delo 504.

10. B. Borisoff to Charles Ruthenberg, November 9, 1926, CPUSA-LC, reel 51, delo 728; Borisoff to Ruthenberg, November 18, 1926, ibid. On white-on-black violence in 1910s–1920s cities, see Philpott, *The Slum and the Ghetto*; Hirsch, *Making the Second Ghetto*; Kevin Boyle, *Arc of Justice: A Saga of Race, Civil Rights and Murder in the Jazz Age* (New York: Henry Holt, 2004); Charles Lumpkins, *American Pogrom: The East Saint Louis Race Riot and Black Politics* (Athens: Ohio University Press, 2008); William Tuttle, *Race Riot: Chicago in the Red Summer of 1919* (1970; repr., Urbana: University of Illinois Press, 1996); Jan Voogd, *Race Riots and Resistance: The Red Summer of 1919* (New York: Peter Lang, 2008); Zecker, *Race and America's Immigrant Press*, 204–247; James Hirsch, *Riot and Remembrance: The Tulsa Race Riot and its Legacy* (Boston, MA: Houghton Mifflin, 2002); Scott Ellsworth, *Death in a Promised Land: The Tulsa Race Riot of 1921* (Baton Rouge: Louisiana State University Press, 1982); Alfred Brophy, *Reconstructing the Dreamland: The Tulsa Riot of 1921; Race, Reparations, and Reconciliation* (New York: Oxford University Press, 2002); Edward Linenthal, "Remembrance, Contestation, Excavation: The Work of Memory in Oklahoma City, the Washita Battlefield, and the Tulsa Race Riot," in Marguerite Shaffer, ed., *Public Culture: Diversity, Democracy, and Community in the United States* (Philadelphia: University of Pennsylvania Press, 2008); Michael D'Orso, *Rosewood: Like Judgment Day* (New York: Boulevard Books, 1996); Vincent Franklin, "The Philadelphia Race Riot of 1918," *Pennsylvania Magazine of History and Biography* 99, no. 3 (July 1975): 336–350; M. Langley Biegert, "Legacy of Resistance: Uncovering the History of Collective Action by Black Agricultural Workers in Central East Arkansas from the 1860s to the 1930s," *Journal of Social History* 32, no. 1 (Autumn 1998): 73–99; Nan Elizabeth Woodruff, "African American Struggles for Citizenship in the Arkansas and Mississippi Deltas in the Age of Jim Crow," *Radical History Review* 55 (Winter 1993), 33–52. On the failed 1919 steel strike, see William Z. Foster, *The Great Steel Strike and Its Lessons* (New York: B. W. Huebsch, 1920).

11. "Report of the Committee Investigating Borisoff Case," Hammond, Indiana [1927], CPUSA-LC, reel 80, delo 1061; Letter of complaint, Lake County [Hammond, Indiana] comrades to Arne Swabeck and the District Executive Committee [1927], ibid. Dominic Pacyga, *Polish Immigrants and Industrial Chicago: Workers on the South Side, 1880-1922* (Columbus: Ohio State University Press, 1991); Dominic Pacyga, "To Live among Others: Poles and Their Neighbors in Industrial Chicago, 1865–1930," *Journal of American Ethnic History* 16, no. 1 (Fall 1996): 55–73; Philpott, *The Slum and the Ghetto*; Barrett, "Unity and Fragmentation"; James Barrett, *Work and Community in the Jungle: Chicago's Packinghouse Workers, 1894–1922* (Urbana: University of Illinois Press, 1987).

12. Joseph Stone to Earl Browder, March 31, 1925, CPUSA-LC, reel 34, delo 503; Minutes, Sub-Committee on Imperialism, May 21, 1925, CPUSA-LC, reel 36, delo 534; James Dolsen to Charles Ruthenberg, January 8, 1925, CPUSA-LC, reel 33, delo 497. On West Indian immigrants' activism, see Winston James, *Holding Aloft the Banner of Ethiopia: Caribbean Radicalism in Early Twentieth-Century America* (New York: Verso, 1998); on multicultural radicalism in California, see Scott Kurashige, *The Shifting Grounds of Race: Black and Japanese Americans in the Making of Multiethnic Los Angeles* (Princeton, NJ: Princeton University Press, 2010). William Schneiderman to C. E. Ruthenberg, May 14, 1925, CPUSA-LC, reel 33, delo 497. Barrett, *Work and Community in the Jungle*; Herbert Hill, "The Problem of Race in American Labor History," *Reviews in American History* 24, no. 2 (June 1996): 189–208; Eric Arnesen, "'Up from Exclusion': Black and White Workers, Race, and the State of Labor History," *Reviews in American History* 26, no. 1 (March 1998): 146–174; Maurice Zeitlin and L. Frank Weyher, "'Black and White, Unite and Fight': Interracial Working-Class Solidarity and Racial Employment Equity," *American Journal of Sociology* 107, no. 2 (September 2001): 430–467; Barrett and Roediger, "Whiteness and the Inbetween Peoples of Europe." Louise Thompson MS autobiography, chap. 6, p. 25, box 20, folder 5, Louise Thompson Patterson Papers, 1909–1999, MSS 869, Stuart A. Rose Manuscript, Archives, and Rare Book Library, Emory University [hereafter cited as LTP-EU].

13. Organization Department to ANLC, April 3, 1926, CPUSA-LC, reel 56, delo 784; Bennett of Seattle to "Dear Bill" [ca. January 1924], CPUSA-LC, reel 13, delo 207. Malcolm McLaughlin, "Ghetto Formation and Armed Resistance in East Saint Louis, Illinois," *Journal of American Studies* 41, no. 2 (2007): 435–467; Lumpkins, *American Pogrom*. On white worker competition with black workers, see Roediger, *The Wages of Whiteness*.

14. Resolutions passed and reports delivered, IWO national convention, June 8–14, 1940, IWO-CU, box 3, folder 2. Louise Thompson report, "The Building of Our English-Speaking Section," IWO national convention, June 8–14, 1940, ibid.

15. "Report of District Plenum of IWO, Sunday, April 29, 1934" [Philadelphia]; Language Department report, "The Building of the Working Class Mutual Aid Organizations—A Plan for Immediate Action," January 6, 1931, CPUSA-LC, reel 177, delo 2334; "Constitution and By-Laws of the Slovak Calvinistic Presbyterian Union [1948], National Slovak Society records, MSS SC188, Balch Institute for Ethnic Studies, Philadelphia [hereafter cited as Balch]; "Constitution and By-Laws and Declaration of Principles," 1934–1935, Declaration of Principles [1938], and "Declaration of Principles," January 1, 1942, box 3, International Workers Order Case Files, MSS 5940, Kheel Center for Labor-Management Documentation and Archives, Cornell University Library [hereafter cited as IWOCF-CU].

16. H. Beck to Louis Kovess, November 12, 1930, CPUSA-LC, reel 155, delo 2021; For multilingual editions of *Fraternal Outlook* from 1939 to 1943, see IWO-CU, box

48; Report, Language Papers of the Party, section titled "The I.W.O.," October 3, 1930, CPUSA-LC, reel 154, delo 2016; "The Building of the Working Class Mutual Aid Organizations"; H. Beck, Los Angeles, to Louis Kovess, November 12, 1930, CPUSA-LC, reel 155, delo 2021; Constitution and By-Laws of the IWO in Spanish [1938], IWO-CU, box 1, folder 4; Eleanor Broady to Louise Thompson Patterson, February 7, 1945, IWO-CU, box 7, folder 3; Report, "The Hispanic American Section from January 1940 to January 1944" [at 1944 IWO convention], 4–5, IWO-CU, box 9, folder 8; *Fraternal Outlook*, October 1940, adds a Spanish section to the articles printed in various other languages, IWO-CU, box 48. Report, "Notes on the Portuguese and Cape Verdeans," n.d., IWO-CU, box 5, folder 5; Organizing Committee, Central Committee, to Jose C. Novo of New Bedford, Massachusetts, December 19, 1933, on building Portuguese Workers' Clubs in New Bedford, Fall River, and Cambridge, Massachusetts, CPUSA-LC, reel 246, delo 3150. For Arabic lodges, see Frank Gevize of Detroit to IWO National Office, April 6, 1945, and Sam Milgrom to Gevize, April 23, 1945, IWO-CU, box 6, folder 8. FBI report, IWO, Detroit division, "Arabic Section," 16, December 10, 1945, box 16, folder 16-36, Don Binkowski Papers, Walter P. Reuther Library, Wayne State University [hereafter cited as DB-WSU]. Affidavit, Peter Moreno, Brooklyn, April 23, 1951, IWOCF-CU, box 3; Lorrin Thomas, *Puerto Rican Citizen: History and Political Identity in Twentieth-Century New York City* (Chicago, IL: University of Chicago Press, 2010); Carmen Teresa Whalen, *From Puerto Rico to Philadelphia: Puerto Rican Workers and Postwar Economies* (Philadelphia, PA: Temple University Press, 2001).

17. Max Shachtman, *Race and Revolution* (New York: Verso, 2003).

18. Negro Department, CPUSA, report to Political Committee, February 4, 1930, CPUSA-LC, reel 155, delo 2024; Executive Committee, Communist International, Moscow, to U.S. Party, on "Negro work," April 1930, CPUSA-LC, reel 141, delo 1855; Resolution of Negro Question in the United States, November 26, 1930, CPUSA-LC, reel 140, delo 1849; Letters from Alexander Wright, August 27, 1935, September 8, 1935, and October 4, 1935, on organizing African American small businessmen, as well as Jewish members, in English-speaking branches in Norfolk and Portsmouth, Virginia, CPUSA-LC, reel 298, delo 3882.

19. James Ford, "Report on Harlem" to the District 2 Bureau meeting, New York, December 28, 1935, CPUSA-LC, reel 294, delo 3811; FBI report, IWO, Detroit division, "Negro work," December 10, 1945, DB-WSU, box 16, folder 16-36; Report to IWO national convention, June 8–14, 1940, "On Organization and Plans," "Youth Conference," by Fannie Gardner records IWO plans to organize Negro youth in Harlem, the Third Ward of Newark, and South Chicago, IWO-CU, box 3, folder 3. Robin Kelley, *Hammer and Hoe: Alabama Communists During the Great Depression* (Chapel Hill: University of North Carolina Press, 2015); Timothy V. Johnson, "'We Are Illegal Here': The Communist Party, Self-Determination and the Alabama Share Croppers Union," *Science and Society* 75, no. 4 (October 2011): 454–479. Hy Gordon to Earl Browder, December 22, 1930, CPUSA-LC, reel 151, delo 1960; Zumoff, *The Communist International and U.S. Communism*, 353–363; Edward Johanningsmeier, "Communists and Black Freedom Movements in South Africa and the U.S.: 1919–1950," *Journal of Southern African Studies* 30, no. 1 (March 2004): 155–180.

20. "WGB" of New Orleans to Organization Commission, CP, July 23, 1935, CPUSA-LC, reel 298, delo 3899; John Jefferson to Clarence Hathaway, September 2, 1935, CPUSA-LC, reel 298, delo 3896. "WGB" then wrote to the Organization Commission of the CP dismissing Jefferson's charges: "WGB" of New Orleans to Organization Commission, CP, September 25, 1935, ibid. Arnesen, *Waterfront Workers of New Orleans*.

21. Broady to Thompson Patterson, February 7, 1945; Report, "The Hispanic American Section from January 1940 to January 1944," 4 and 5; Gevize to IWO National Office, April 6, 1945, and Milgrom to Gevize, April 23, 1945. FBI report, IWO, Detroit division, "Arabic Section," 16, December 10, 1945. "Proceedings of the fourth national convention, IWO, April 30, 1938," IWO-CU, box 2, folder 2. Interview with Louise Thompson Patterson [ca. 1950–1951], LTP-EU, box 27, folder 1. Harold Peters to Metropolitan Life Insurance, February 2, 1945, Peters to the IWO, February 2, 1945, Sam Milgrom to Peters, February 19, 1945, Peters to Milgrom, February 22, 1945, Peters to Milgrom, March 22, 1945, Milgrom to Peters, March 31, 1945, Peters to Milgrom, April 3, 1945, Milgrom to Peters, April 6, 1945, Peters to Dave Greene, May 15, 1945, and Sol Vail to Milgrom, October 5, 1945, IWO-CU, box 8, folder 2. Affidavit, Jumal Ahmad, Cleveland, April 1951, IWOCF-CU, box 4.

22. "Digest of Testimony of Witnesses for the State in the I.W.O. Matter. January 29, 1951, to March 7, 1951," IWOCF-CU, box 4. For Scottsboro defense and black Communists in Alabama, see Kelley, *Hammer and Hoe*.

23. Minutes, Language Department meeting, May 11, 1931, CPUSA-LC, reel 177, delo 2332; Charles Dirba to Language Department, May 6, 1931, CPUSA-LC, reel 177, delo 2336; Czecho Slovakian Bureau to John Mackovich, May 7, 1931, ibid. For Scottsboro case, see Dan Carter, *Scottsboro: A Tragedy of the American South* (1969; repr., Baton Rouge: Louisiana State University Press, 2007).

24. *The Spark*, July 1931, 30, CPUSA-LC, reel 195, delo 2584; Carter, *Scottsboro*, esp. 51–103; Flyer, *Save the Scottsboro Nine*, May 29, 1931, rally, Cleveland, LSNR, CPUSA-LC, reel 165, delo 2204.

25. John Mackovich to Central Committee, CP, May 6, 1932, CPUSA-LC, reel 214, delo 2766; "Directives on Scottsboro," Organization Commission, CP, November 29, 1933, CPUSA-LC, reel 246, delo 3147.

26. "Report of District Plenum of IWO, April 29, 1934," CPUSA-LC, reel 287, delo 3709; Minutes, District 2 Bureau meeting, September 4, 1935, report on IWO by N. Shaffer, CPUSA-LC, reel 294, delo 3811; Norfolk, Virginia, Independent Section, Section Committee meeting, September 8, 1935, CPUSA-LC, reel 298, delo 3882; Minutes, Russian Mutual Aid Society of America convention, 1933, IWO-CU, box 12, folder 4.

27. Emil Gardos to Earl Browder, June 29, 1932, CPUSA-LC, reel 214, delo 2752.

28. James Miller, Susan Pennybacker, and Eve Rosenhaft, "Mother Ada Wright and the International Campaign to Free the Scottsboro Boys, 1931–1934," *American Historical Review* 106, no. 2 (April 2001): 387–430; Susan Pennybacker, *From Scottsboro to Munich: Race and Political Culture in 1930s Britain* (Princeton, NJ: Princeton University Press, 2009); Carter, *Scottsboro*, 172–173; "Secretariat, Revolutionary Workers' Groups," to "Secretary, Irish Workers' Club, New York" [IWO affiliate], September 19, 1932, CPUSA-LC, reel 235, delo 3052. For efforts by the Irish Workers' Clubs to recruit Irish nationalists into the IWO, see Hugh McKiernan of Brooklyn to Comrade Murray, October 17, 1932, J. J. Mullally of Jersey City to "Comrades," November 5, 1932, and Mullally to "Comrades," November 10, 1932, CPUSA-LC, reel 235, delo 3052. Gardos to Browder. For an American appearance by Ada Wright, see Poster, "Save the 9 Negro Children," Ada Wright Scottsboro rally, May 31, 1931, Boston ILD, LSNR, CPUSA-LC, reel 194, delo 2576.

29. Arnold Ward to William Patterson, March 6, 1934, CPUSA-LC, reel 273, delo 3482; Reginald Bridgeman to Patterson, June 16, 1934, CPUSA-LC, reel 287, delo 3968; Adi, *Pan-Africanism and Communism*, 258–281; James, *Holding Aloft the Banner of Ethiopia*.

30. Carter, *Scottsboro*, 51–103.

31. Ibid., 399–415.

32. *The Paper*, FDR birthday issue [published by IWO headquarters office staff], January 1948, 3–4, IWO-CU, box 48; Israel Amter, "The Truth about the Communists" [1936], box 1, folder 79, International Ladies Garment Workers Union, Charles S. Zimmerman Collection of Radical Pamphlets, 1914–1958, MSS 5780/178, Kheel Center for Labor-Management Documentation and Archives, Cornell University [hereafter cited as ILGWU-CU, 5780/178]; Outline for Dave Greene JPFO speech, Brooklyn, June 19, 1950, and Outline for Madison Square Garden speech, IWO-CU, box 4, folder 5.

33. Earl Browder to B. K. Gebert and others, telegram, November 29, 1933, CPUSA-LC, reel 245, delo 3143; Meeting of District 5 Bureau [Pittsburgh], August 14, 1935, CPUSA-LC, reel 295, delo 3828; E. Owens, Anglo-American Secretariat report, "Lynch Terror in the United States—Save the Scottsboro Boys!" CPUSA-LC, reel 239, delo 3097.

34. Emanuel Levin, "Strange Fruit on Southern Trees—The Fight for the Anti-Lynch Bill," *Fraternal Outlook*, March 1939, 4–5, IWO-CU, box 48.

35. Ibid.

36. Levin, "Strange Fruit on Southern Trees." Maxwell, *New Negro, Old Left*; Amy Louise Wood, *Lynching and Spectacle: Witnessing Racial Violence in America, 1890–1940* (Chapel Hill: University of North Carolina Press, 2009), 4–5, 14, 50–52, 194–199, 212–218, 223, 225–226; Hill, *Men, Mobs, and Law*, 128–130, 134, 222–227, 230–231, 234; Kari Frederickson, "'The Slowest State' and 'Most Backward Community': Racial Violence in South Carolina and Federal Civil-Rights Legislation, 1946–1948," *South Carolina Historical Magazine* 98, no. 2 (April 1997): 177–202.

37. Zecker, *Race and America's Immigrant Press*, 12–49; Roediger and Esch, *The Production of Racial Difference*.

38. Mary Helen Washington, *The Other Blacklist: The African American Literary and Cultural Left of the 1950s* (New York: Columbia University Press, 2014); Beth Tompkins Bates, "A New Crowd Challenges the Agenda of the Old Guard in the NAACP, 1933–1941," *American Historical Review* 102, no. 2 (April 1997): 340–377.

39. "Opinion and Comment," *Fraternal Outlook*, September 1942, 8, offers a brief article on the Geyer Anti-Poll Tax Bill, IWO-CU, box 48; Lila Slocum, "Poll Taxes—Let's Abolish Them!" *Fraternal Outlook*, March 1945, 8–9, ibid.; Eva Gregg, "For Negro Rights," *Fraternal Outlook*, February 1944, 22, ibid.; Lila Slocum, "The New Negro and the Post-War World. Safeguarding the Gains of the Negro People Is the Problem of All the American People," *Fraternal Outlook*, December 1944, 6–7, ibid.; Homer Barton to National Election Campaign Committee, September 15, 1932, CPUSA-LC, reel 233, delo 3017.

40. Sam Milgrom, "Spotlight on Jim Crow," *Fraternal Outlook*, October–November 1949, 4–5, IWO-CU, box 48.

41. *Robotnícky kalendár na rok 1921*, 86; *Robotnícky kalendár na rok 1937*, 40, 45, 94; *Robotnícky kalendár na rok 1939*, 109–113; *Ľudový denník*, September 21, 1942, 4.

42. Resolutions passed at IWO national convention, June 8–14, 1940, IWO-CU, box 3, folder 2; Resolutions passed at Anthracite District Convention, November 9–10, 1940, Scranton, Pennsylvania, IWO-CU, box 8, folder 9.

43. Minutes, IWO GEB semi-annual plenary session, September 6–7, 1941, including resolutions passed, IWO-CU, box 1, folder 8; IWO GEB meeting, February 8, 1942, "Resolution on Negro Rights," IWO-CU, box 1, folder 9. For the CP and civil rights during World War II, see Maurice Isserman, *Which Side Were You On? The American Communist Party during the Second World War* (Middletown, CT: Wesleyan University Press, 1982), 117–119.

44. General Secretary Max Bedacht, "Our Civic and Organizational Problems," report to the IWO GEB, February 26, 1943, IWO-CU, box 2, folder 9; Proceedings of GEB, February 26–27, 1943, "Resolution on Negro Work," 20, IWO-CU, box 1 folder 10; Report by H. Shiller, secretary of the Bronx District Committee, Jewish American Section of IWO, to the Third Annual Convention of the Bronx District, March 27–28, 1943, 1270 Hoe Avenue, Bronx, IWO-CU, box 6, folder 3. See, too, Bedacht's further report to GEB, "On the Progress of the Order during the Year 1942," February 26–27, 1943, 3, IWO-CU, box 2, folder 8.

45. *Národné noviny*, April 29, 1942, 2.

46. IWO GEB meeting, February 8, 1942, "Resolution on Negro Rights," IWO-CU, box 1, folder 9.

47. Minutes, GEB, June 27, 1942, 1, IWO-CU, box 1, folder 9.

48. Proceedings, GEB plenary session, February 12–13, 1944, 7–8, 10–16, IWO-CU, box 1, folder 10; Minutes, General Council meeting, November 24–26, 1944, 5–6, 8, IWO-CU, box 1, folder 11; Rosa Walton of Macon, Georgia, to IWO, February 10, 1947, IWO-CU, box 20, folder 6; Rosilla King of Kamsack, Saskatchewan to IWO, January 28, 1947, IWO-CU, box 20, folder 7.

49. June Gordon, Emma Lazarus Division, statement of JPFO in behalf of FEPC, July 9, 1945, IWO-CU, box 28, folder 2; "Bulletin on Women and Peace in Celebration of the 6th Anniversary of the Emma Lazarus Division, 1950, by June Gordon," February 21, 1950, IWO-CU, box 35, folder 5.

50. Senora Lawson to June Gordon, July 17, 1952, Lawson to Louise Thompson Patterson, June 25, 1952, and Thompson Patterson to Lawson, June 23, 1952, LTP-EU, box 16, folder 14. Press release, Louise Patterson for the Sojourners for Truth and Justice, and Hilda Freedman, Emma Lazarus Federation, to UNESCO, July 8, 1952, LTP-EU, box 13, folder 2; Minutes, National Organizing Committee meeting, Sojourners for Truth and Justice, February 16, 1952, LTP-EU, box 12, folder 17; Summary of proceedings, Eastern Seaboard Conference Federation, Sojourners for Truth and Justice, March 23, 1952, LTP-EU, box 12, folder 18; Resolution, Council on African Affairs to the Conference of Sojourners for Truth and Justice, March 23, 1952, LTP-EU, box 13, folder 4; Charlotta Bass to South African Delegation to UN, April 5, 1952, and Sojourners for Truth and Justice, Bass and Thompson Patterson, to Ray Alexander, Johannesburg, South Africa, Baila Paige of Johannesburg, Bertha Mkize of Durban, and Minna Soga of East London, April 5, 1952, ibid. Gore, *Radicalism at the Crossroads*; McDuffie, *Sojourning for Freedom*.

51. Mkize to "Dear Friends" [of the Sojourners for Truth and Justice], April 20, 1952, LTP-EU, box 13, folder 4.

52. Flyer with petition, CAA, *Racism Threatens Us in South Africa as Here* [1952], LTP-EU, box 13, folder 37. See, too, Initiating Committee for the Sojourners for Truth and Justice to Congressman William Dawson of Chicago, September 15, 1951, regarding the Cicero Riot, LTP-EU, box 13, folder 5.

53. Gore, *Radicalism at the Crossroads*; McDuffie, *Sojourning for Freedom*.

54. Theodore Bilbo to Josephine Picolo of Brooklyn, July 1, 1945, Picolo to Vito Marcantonio, July 18, 1945, and Marcantonio to Bilbo, July 21, 1945, box 46, Vito Marcantonio Papers, Manuscripts and Archives Division, The New York Public Library [hereafter cited as VM-NYPL]; "Vito Demands Apology on 'Dago' Note," *New York Daily News*, July 24, 1945, ibid.; Bilbo to Marcantonio, July 24, 1945, Marcantonio to Picolo, July 24, 1945, and Marcantonio to Bilbo, July 25, 1945, ibid.

55. Civil Rights Congress pamphlet, *Oust Bilbo, You Can Do It Now . . .* [1945 or 1946], IWO-CU, box 46; Civil Rights Congress to Bessie Hillman, September 13, 1946,

DB-WSU, box 2, folder 2-15; "Report of Max Bedacht, General Secretary, to the General Council Meeting of the International Workers Order, September 7–8, 1946," folder 13, International Workers Order Records, Robert F. Wagner Labor Archives, Tamiment Library, New York University [hereafter cited as IWO-NYU]; Minutes, General Council meeting, September 15–16, 1945, 7–8, IWO-NYU, folder 12; Letter, from National Committee to Combat Anti-Semitism and the JPFO, November 12, 1945, with petition on Senator Theodore Bilbo, Representative John Rankin, and others, IWO-CU, box 30, folder 6; George Starr of the JPFO to "Dear Brothers and Sisters," November 18, 1946, IWO-CU, box 30, folder 7; Nathan Shaffer of the New York County JPFO, IWO, to Congressman Vito Marcantonio, August 30, 1945, VM-NYPL, box 48; Sol Rotenberg to Sam Milgrom, December 6, 1945, IWO-CU, box 8, folder 10; FBI report, IWO, Detroit division, December 10, 1945, 126.

56. Winifred Graham to Vito Marcantonio [1945], addressed to "My dear wop," VM-NYPL, box 46; Theodore Bilbo to Senate colleagues, September 4, 1945, ibid. See, too, Evelyn Louise Crawford and MaryLouise Patterson, eds., *Letters from Langston: From the Harlem Renaissance to the Red Scare and Beyond* (Berkeley: University of California Press, 2016), 270–272.

57. Resolution on the McCarran-Walter Law passed at IWO General Council meeting, September 13, 1952, and resolution on FEPC, IWOCF-CU, box 3.

58. Morris Forer to John Middleton, February 7, 1945, and David Vines to Forer, March 17, 1945, IWO-CU, box 8, folder 3.

59. Eleanor Broady to Sam Milgrom, March 22, 1945, IWO-CU, box 7, folder 4; FBI file, IWO, Detroit division, December 10, 1945, 21, DB-WSU, box 16, folder 16-36; FBI file, IWO, Detroit division, "Activities in 1942," December 31, 1946, 57, ibid.

60. State senator Stanley Nowak to Grand Rapids businessmen [1945?], box 5, folder 5-13, Stanley and Margaret Collingwood Nowak Papers, Walter P. Reuther Library, Wayne State University [hereafter cited as NP-WSU]; Flyer, *Nowak Is the Man! Help Blast Jim Crow—Loveland's* [1948], NP-WSU, box 4, folder 4-6; Press release, "Negro Leaders Praise Nowak's Record" [1948], DB-WSU, box 7, folder 7-50. For white ethnic resistance to integration, see Sugrue, *Origins of the Urban Crisis*, 22–23, 181–182, 189–190, 194–197, 231–242, 252–255; Diamond, *Mean Streets*, 150–168. For Michigan's FEPC campaign, see Sidney Fine, "'A Jewel in the Crown of Us All': Michigan Enacts a Fair Employment Practices Act, 1941–1955," *Michigan Historical Review* 22, no. 1 (Spring 1996): 18–66.

61. *Národné noviny*, June 7, 1944, 5. See, too, *Národné noviny*, February 2, 1944, 5, for Slav Congress's demand for the repeal of the Smith-Connally antilabor act. George Pirinsky, *Slavic Americans in the Fight for Victory and Peace* (New York: American Slav Congress, 1946), 29–30, 38, 44. "The Case of Katherine Hyndman—What Is True Americanism?" *The American Slav*, Winter 1949, 8. See, too, Katherine Hyndman to Sam Milgrom, April 26, 1945, IWO-CU, box 16, folder 22; Louise Thompson Patterson to Milgrom, telegram, September 24 [late 1940s], IWO-CU, box 6, folder 10; "History of the IWO and Role of the Fraternal Movement in the U.S.," September 1, 1949, pt. 3, p. 4, "Nationalism" and "Scapegoats," refers to the student strike in Gary, Indiana, where Ukrainian, Russian, Irish, and other white students went out on strike against going to school with "Negro" schoolmates, IWO-CU, box 17, folder 1. Postcard to attorney general, protesting jailing of Hyndman in Crown Point, Indiana [ca. 1947], IWO-CU, box 43, folder 7. Hyndman was allowed to remain in the United States. See 1970 oral history with Hyndman conducted by Staughton Lynd, box 3, Labor Oral History Project, Roosevelt University Archives; Susan Brown, "Katherine Hyndman: Region's Own Political Prisoner," *Northwest Times* [Gary, Indiana], June 2, 2003.

62. Resolution against race discrimination and anti-Semitism passed at the Slovak American Section [SWS-IWO] conference, September 5, 1943, IWO-CU, box 14, folder 6; "Resolution on Negroes," passed at national convention, SWS IWO, July 4–6, 1944, IWO-CU, box 14, folder 5.

63. "National Negro Congress News, news release, July 18, 1941. Fraternal and Youth Groups Cooperate in Nation-Wide Boycott of Noxzema Products," VM-NYPL, box 48; "Group Back Boycotting of Noxzema," *Chicago Defender*, July 26, 1941, 8; "Discrimination Protest," *Baltimore Afro-American*, July 29, 1941, 16, VM-NYPL, box 48; Major General J. A. Ulio, Adjutant General of Army, to Rubin Saltzman, September 21, 1944, replying to September 11, 1944, letter from Saltzman, IWO-CU, box 29, folder 6; Isserman, *Which Side Were You On?* 117–119.

64. Hirsch, *Making the Second Ghetto*; Philpott, *The Slum and the Ghetto*; Diamond, *Mean Streets*; Sugrue, *Origins of the Urban Crisis*; Letter from John Mykytew, June 15, 1944, IWO-CU, box 7, folder 1; Affidavit, Herman Schlossberg of Los Angeles, April 24, 1951, IWOCF-CU, box 3.

65. Sam Milgrom to Henry Podolski, December 18, 1944, IWO-CU, box 7, folder 2; Letters from Mario D'Inzillo, October 26 and 31, 1942, and Oscar Cox, assistant solicitor general, to D'Inzillo, November 6, 1942, IWO-CU, box 10, folder 8.

66. Councilman Benjamin Davis of New York to Boleslaw Gebert, May 29, 1947, IWO-CU, box 4, folder 2; Milan Draskovich convention notes, Serbian American Federation, IWO, June 15, 1947, IWO-CU, box 13, folder 11.

67. George Pirinsky, executive secretary of the ASC, report, "Program and Activities of the American Slav Congress," *The Slavic American*, Winter 1947, 30. Paul Robeson, "Big 3 Unity for Colonial Freedom," May 4, 1946, Madison Square Garden Rally on June 6, 1946, box 5, folder 2, International Ladies Garment Workers Union, Charles S. Zimmerman Papers, 1919–1958, MSS 5780/014, Kheel Center for Labor-Management Documentation and Archives, Cornell University [hereafter cited as ILGWU-CU, MSS 5780/014]. See, too, Flyer, *Paul Robeson Sings for IWO Day*, Civilian and National Defense Exposition, New York, October 12, 1941, IWO-CU, box 49. Lottie Gordon, director of the Prisoners Relief Committee, the CRC, to S. Davidovitch of Camp Kinderland, June 26, 1950, IWO-CU, box 43, folder 2.

68. Affidavits, Herman Schlossberg, Los Angeles, April 24, 1951, and Kalyna Popow, Philadelphia, and Frances Slowiczeck, Hamtramck, both April 24, 1951, IWOCF-CU, box 3.

69. IWO press release, Negro History Week, February 5, 1953, sponsored by Douglass-Lincoln Society of IWO, IWO-CU, box 4, folder 6.

70. Statement of Representative John Rankin of Mississippi, from the *Congressional Record*, May 28 [during World War II], A2141, IWO-CU, box 23, folder 7. Paul Robeson, *Here I Stand* (New York: Othello, 1958); Martin Duberman, *Paul Robeson* (New York: Knopf, 1988); Jordan Goodman, *Paul Robeson: A Watched Man* (New York: Verso, 2013), 90–95, 104–114, 227–242; Tony Perucci, *Paul Robeson and the Cold War Performance Complex: Race, Madness, Activism* (Ann Arbor: University of Michigan Press, 2012), 33–38.

71. *Národné noviny*, August 18, 1943, 5. Donald Hill, *Calypso Calaloo: Early Carnival Music in Trinidad* (Gainseville: University Press of Florida, 1993). In 1946 Pindar's song "Walk in Peace" was featured as the People's Song of the Week in the *People's Song Bulletin*. Thanks to Judith Smith for this.

72. Minutes, National Conference of General Lodges of IWO, July 4, 1944, IWO-CU, box 9, folder 1.

73. John Pittman, "Threat to Citizenship. Prejudice, predatory motives behind attack on U.S. Nisei," editorial, *Pacific Citizen*, July 9, 1942, 7, CPUSA-LC, reel 316, delo 4216a. Isserman, *Which Side Were You On?* 117–119.

74. Yoshitaka Takagi to Marcantonio, April 12, 1943, Marcantonio to Takagi, April 21, 1943, C. R. Wilmer to Marcantonio, May 28, 1943, Abner Green to Marcantonio, March 23, 1943, Bob Takahashi to Marcantonio, March 16, 1943, Marcantonio to Takahashi, March 24, 1943, George Yoshioka to Marcantonio, April 6, 1943, and Marcantonio to Yoshioka, April 13, 1943, VM-NYPL, box 46.

75. Kurashige, *The Shifting Grounds of Race*; Greg Robinson, *After Camp: Portraits in Midcentury Japanese American Life and Politics* (Berkeley: University of California Press, 2012).

76. *Národné noviny*, May 17, 1944, 6.

77. Resolutions passed and reports delivered, IWO national convention, June 8–14, 1940, IWO-CU, box 3, folder 2. Louise Thompson report, "The Building of Our English-Speaking Section," IWO national convention, June 8–14, 1940, ibid.

78. S. Nowak radio address, August 24, 1941, NP-WSU, box 3, folder 3-8.

79. Pirinsky, *Slavic Americans in the Fight for Victory and Peace*, 44.

80. Ibid., 15–17.

81. John McGreevy, *Parish Boundaries: The Catholic Encounter with Race in the Twentieth-Century Urban North* (Chicago: University of Chicago Press, 1996), 72–78; Sugrue, *Origins of the Urban Crisis*; Thomas Sugrue, "Crabgrass-Roots Politics: Race, Rights, and the Reaction against Liberalism in the Urban North, 1940–1964," *Journal of American History* 82, no. 2 (September 1995): 551–578; Eileen McMahon, *What Parish Are You From?: A Chicago Irish Community and Race Relations* (Lexington: University Press of Kentucky, 1995); Max Bedacht, report, "The IWO and Its Tasks," August 24, 1942, IWO-CU, box 2, folder 7.

82. FBI report, Vito Marcantonio, December 23, 1946, contains letter from Detroit FBI office to J. Edgar Hoover, May 18, 1943, regarding "Vito Marcantonio, Internal Security—C; Custodial Detention," which discusses a March 5, 1942, letter to Marcantonio plucked from the Detroit CP wastepaper basket, DB-WSU, box 7, folder 7-19. The FBI's extensive file on Marcantonio contains a July 21, 1941, "MEMORANDUM FOR MR. P. E. FOXWORTH" from Agent R. H. Kramer that proposed approval of a "Custodial Detention card relating to Vito Marcantonio," even though Kramer noted "the subject's position as a member of the House of Representatives, Washington, D.C.," ibid. Memorandum, Mathew McGuire, assistant to the attorney general, to J. Edgar Hoover, August 7, 1941, ibid. Marcantonio's FBI file also contains a letter from agent A. H. Belmont, July 27, 1950, explaining that as Marcantonio was still a congressman, he was not included on the FBI's Security Index, but that if he ceased to be a congressman, the issue might be revisited. Three weeks after Marcantonio was defeated for reelection, a letter was sent on November 25, 1950, from Director Hoover to the special agent in charge, New York, recommending a Security Index Card be created on Marcantonio, still sitting as an elected member of Congress, whose "business address" was listed as "United States House of Representatives." It was further advised that Marcantonio be detained should Hoover decide there was a national emergency. When Marcantonio was again running for Congress in 1954, the FBI still listed him as a subject for "internal security" roundup. FBI report, "May 6, 1954" on Marcantonio, "Character of Case: Internal Security—C," ibid. For Hoover's use of the custodial detention program, see Donna Haverty-Stacke, *Trotskyists on Trial: Free Speech and Political Persecution Since the Age of FDR* (New York: New York University Press, 2015), 36–37.

83. FBI report, IWO, Detroit division, December 31, 1946, 127, DB-WSU, box 16, folder 16-37. After the Detroit riots, the IWO published an appeal, "To All IWO Members, To the Negro People of Detroit," in the July 10, 1943, Communist paper, *Michigan Chronicle*; *Národné noviny*, July 7, 1943, 5, July 28, 1943, 5, and "Práca Piatej Kolony" [The Work of Fifth Columnists], editorial, June 30, 1943, 4.

84. FBI file, IWO, Detroit division, December 10, 1945.

85. Detroit Police report, August 26, 1948, DB-WSU, box 2, folder 2-55; Hirsch, *Making the Second Ghetto*; Diamond, *Mean Streets*; Sugrue, *Origins of the Urban Crisis*.

86. Arthur Price to Vito Marcantonio, August 18, 1949, VM-NYPL, box 47; Flyer, 1949 demonstration and parade, *Stop the Ku Klux Terror in Chicago*, ibid. William Patterson, *The Man Who Cried Genocide: An Autobiography* (New York: International, 1971); Gerald Horne, *Communist Front? The Civil Rights Congress, 1946–1956* (Rutherford, NJ: Fairleigh Dickinson University Press, 1988).

87. John Middleton "to all I.W.O. lodges in New York City," March 9, 1945, IWO-CU, box 8, folder 4. IWO leaders from the Hispanic Cervantes Fraternal Society, and Jewish, Hungarian, Slovak, Ukrainian, Russian, Carpatho-Russian, Croatian, Polish, and Finnish leaders endorsed an interracial brotherhood rally.

88. Broady to Milgrom, March 22, 1945, and April 5, 1945, IWO-CU, box 7, folder 4.

89. Milgrom to Broady, April 2, 1945, ibid.

90. News release, reprint of *Detroit Free Press* editorial from Thursday, March 22, 1945, IWO-CU, box 7, folder 3; IWO news release, October 17, 1945, "Rev. Charles A. Hill, IWO leader, Candidate for Detroit Council" [1945], IWO-CU, box 7, folder 5.

91. FBI reports, IWO, Detroit division, December 10, 1945, and December 31, 1946, 203.

92. Edward Nelson to Joseph Clark, February 21, 1950, IWO-CU, box 10, folder 3.

93. "A Statement of Several Negro Comrades Concerning Negro Work, Particularly by the League of Struggle for Negro Rights" [1931], CPUSA-LC, reel 195, dela 2585–2586; Christine Zduleczna, "The Czechoslovaks of Philadelphia," in *The Foreign-Born of Philadelphia* (Philadelphia: International Institute of Philadelphia, 1927); *New Yorkský denník*, April 7, 1923, 6. Zecker, *Race and America's Immigrant Press*.

94. Flyer, mass meeting, *Bronx, Negro and White Workers*, March 22 [1931], CPUSA-LC, reel 195, dela 2585–2586; League of Struggle for Negro Rights to August Yokinen, March 3, 1931, ibid.; For the LSNR, see "A Statement of Several Negro Comrades Concerning Negro Work"; "Stop the Persecution of Foreign Born Workers! (Stop Deportation of Yokinen)," March 22, 1931, CPUSA-LC, reel 195, dela 2585–2586; "The Fight for Yokinen Is for Every Negro and White Worker," "Statement of the National Committee for the Protection of the Foreign Born" [1931], ibid. Jacobson, *Whiteness of a Different Color*, 252–256.

95. S. M. Loyen, secretary, South Slavic Section, to Language Department, May 24, 1934, CPUSA-LC, reel 273, delo 3504. See, too, Report, "Mass Trial of Workers Expels White Chauvinists of Detroit" [1933], CPUSA-LC, reel 247, delo 3175; "Report of the Language Department C.C." [September 1930] in which Lithuanian IWO members in Chicago were taken to task for refusal to socialize with black members, CPUSA-LC, reel 154, delo 2016.

96. Report on organizing Negro branches [1932], CPUSA-LC, reel 234, delo 3037; "The Activities of the I.W.O." [1932], ibid.; "A Statement of Several Negro Comrades Concerning Negro Work."

97. Philippa Stowe to headquarters, April 12, 1949, IWO-CU, box 4, folder 4.

98. "The Fight against Poison in the Manhattan District, JPFO" [1949], IWO-CU, box 32, folder 65; Jack Goldman to Dave Greene, June 20, 1949, IWO-CU, box 4, folder 4.

99. Sam Friedlander to David Greene, September 7, 1949, IWO-CU, box 4, folder 4; Sam Milgrom, news release, "Let's Live Up to Our Principles," *Fraternal Outlook*, July 12, 1949, IWO-CU, box 48.

100. FBI report, IWO, Detroit division, November 20, 1953, 126, DB-WSU, box 16, folder 16-38.

101. Harold Peters to IWO, February 12, 1945, IWO-CU, box 8, folder 2; Minutes, General Council meeting, September 7–8, 1946, IWO-NYU, folder 14; George Starr, "To all Lodges in New Jersey, Philadelphia, Baltimore and Wash.," September 9, 1946, IWO-CU, box 30, folder 7; Draft report of General Secretary of IWO, August 29, 1946, IWO-NYU, folder 2; Report on Negro Rights, IWO General Council meeting, March 16–17, 1946, IWO-NYU, folder 13; Sam Milgrom report, "Development of Drive to Build the Order in the Negro Community," September 16, 1945, IWO-NYU, folder 16; Louis Adamic, "Conspiracy against Peace," *Slavic American*, Winter 1947, 5–6, 52; Gellman, *Death Blow to Jim Crow*; Gore, *Radicalism at the Crossroads*; Report, S. Cheifetz to Annual Convention of the JPFO, December 23, 1945, IWO-CU, box 27.1, folder 3. See, too, "Resolution on Indonesia" passed at the Win the Peace Conference, April 5–8, 1946, IWO-CU, box 22, folder 24.

102. Pamphlet, *Herbert Hoover: Slave Trader, Negro-Hater, Jim Crow Expert*, 1932, CPUSA-LC, reel 230, delo 2968.

103. Roediger and Esch, *The Production of Racial Difference*, 116–122, 142, 145, 149; "Appeal to IWO for Red Tag Days," *Daily Worker*, August 10, 1932, 2, CPUSA-LC, reel 318, delo 4243.

104. An FBI report mentions the Polish Labor Democratic Club meeting, June 11, 1954, DB-WSU, box 7, folder 7-55; "The Issue in Indo-China," *Jewish Life*, June 1954, 3, IWO-CU, box 53.

105. "Digest of Testimony of Witnesses for the State"; Louise Thompson Patterson MS autobiography, "Baseball Jim Crow," LTP-EU, box 21, folder 1; Eva Gregg, "For Negro Rights," *Fraternal Outlook*, February 1944, 22, IWO-CU, box 48; Morris Shafritz, "A Legislative Program," IWO Eastern Pennsylvania District, October 15, 1945, 3, IWO-CU, box 8, folder 10. Ben Goldstein, Metropolitan Interfaith and Interracial Coordinating Council, to Vito Marcantonio, VM-NYPL, box 46; Flyer, *August 19—End Jim Crow in Baseball Day* [1945], ibid.; Goldstein to "Dear Friend" and Goldstein to Mayor Fiorello La Guardia, both August 17, 1945, ibid.

106. D. E. James to Marcantonio, April 25, 1945, PFC Willard Weiss to Marcantonio, April 24, 1945, and Bill Werber to Marcantonio, April 28, 1945, VM-NYPL, box 46.

107. News release, "IWO Hails Cleveland Pennant Victory," October 4, 1948, IWO-NYU, folder 31; "Lodge Program Sessions 9 and 10 Civic and Community Events," "Daily Schedule National Training School, September 3–11, 1949," IWO-CU, box 4, folder 10.

108. Sam Milgrom to Rockwell Kent, December 7, 1949, Kent to Milgrom, December 10, 1949, Kent to the NAACP, December 10, 1949, Kent to Roy Wilkins, December 14, 1949, and Wilkins to Kent, December 21, 1949, IWO-CU, box 3, folder 9. "Civil Rights Rally Gets Rankin Treatment," *New York Compass*, January 17, 1950, VM-NYPL, box 48. Milgrom to Kent, January 11, 1950, and Kent to Milgrom, January 17, 1950, IWO-CU, box 3, folder 9. Lenn Davis to William Weiner, January 29, 1934, CPUSA-LC, reel 287, delo 3697. Liston Oak to John Peters [1934], ibid. Harold Cruse,

The Crisis of the Negro Intellectual (New York: Morrow, 1967). Cruse's thesis has recently been countered by Castledine, *Cold War Progressives*; Gellman, *Death Blow to Jim Crow*; Katz, *All Together Different*; Maxwell, *New Negro, Old Left*; and McDuffie, *Sojourning for Freedom*.

109. Affidavits from IWO members, April 23, 1951, IWOCF-CU, box 3.
110. Ibid.
111. Ibid.
112. "Report of Officers Presented to General Council, IWO, February 3 and 4, 1951," IWO-NYU, folder 18; Max Taber, "Stuyvesant Town for Whites Only," *Jewish Fraternalist*, February–March 1950, 6–7, IWO-CU, box 46; Edward Nelson, "What the Attack on the Order Means to the Negro People," *The Defender*, April 1951, 1–2, IWOCF-CU, box 2. "Daily Schedule National Training School, September 3–11, 1949," IWO-CU, box 4, folder 10. "Answer to Superintendent of Insurance Bohlinger, Adopted at Membership Meeting of the International Workers Order, March 7, 1951," IWO-CU, box 23, folder 4. Emergency Conference of IWO members, ibid. "Resolutions, Adopted by Emergency Conference against the Liquidation of a People's Organization," February 10, 1951, IWO-CU, box 24. *Morgen Freiheit*, November 16, 1951, 8, IWOCF-CU, box 2. "Built by Private Enterprise . . . BEGUN IN 1945 . . . Tenants Will Move in Soon. Government Building Project . . . BEGUN IN 1943 . . . Work Barely Started," *New York Journal-American*, June 5, 1947, 15.

113. Affidavits from IWO members, April 1951, IWOCF-CU, box 3. "What Will We Do If . . . ?" *The Compass*, January 20, 1952, 10, publicity for rally January 26, 1952, IWOCF-CU, box 2.

114. Perucci, *Paul Robeson and the Cold War Performance Complex*, 33–38; Goodman, *Paul Robeson*, 90–95, 104–114, 227–242; *The Slavic American*, Winter 1947, 30.

CHAPTER 4

1. *The Spark*, July 1931, reel 195, delo 2584, Records of the Communist Party USA, Microfilm 21, 966, Library of Congress [hereafter cited as CPUSA-LC]; *The New Order*, March 1934, CPUSA-LC, reel 287, delo 3709.

2. "What the Youth Section of the International Workers Order Is and Why Every Young Worker and Student Should Join It," *The New Order*, March 1934, 18, CPUSA-LC, reel 287, delo 3709.

3. Translation from Yiddish, "Declaration of Principles of the International Workers Order," printed in *The Spark*, vol. 1, no. 1, September 1930, 1, International Workers Order Case Files, MSS 5940, Kheel Center for Labor-Management Documentation and Archives, Cornell University Library [hereafter cited as IWOCF-CU].

4. "Partisan Review," *The New Order*, March 1934, 13, CPUSA-LC, reel 287, delo 3709.

5. Affidavits, Emil Betley, New York, April 1951, and Maxim Hayda, New York, Anna Mazurak, Bound Brook, New Jersey, John Uhrin, Los Angeles, Louis Oroby, New York, Jacob Holmstock, Queens, and Milton Schiff, Los Angeles, all April 24, 1951, Peter Moreno, Brooklyn, April 23, 1951, IWOCF-CU, box 3.

6. OSS/FNB report, FNB to the Director of Strategic Services, "Communist-Line IWO Reorganizes to Emphasize Nationality," July 11, 1944, box 4, folder 4-29, Don Binkowski Papers, Walter P. Reuther Library, Wayne State University [hereafter cited as DB-WSU].

7. Peter Shipka to Dave Greene, January 22, 1951, and complaint entered by Lee Pressman and Allan Rosenberg, February 15, 1949, box 23, International Workers Order Records, 1915–2002, MSS 5276, Kheel Center for Labor-Management Documentation and Archives, Cornell University [hereafter cited as IWO-CU].

8. David Forgacs, ed., *The Antonio Gramsci Reader: Selected Writings 1916–1935* (New York: New York University Press, 2000); "Declaration of Principles of the International Workers Order."

9. James Jasper, "The Emotions of Protest: Affective and Reactive Emotions in and around Social Movements," *Sociological Forum* 13, no. 3 (September 1998): 297–424, quotations on 410 and 416; Ann Swidler, "Culture in Action: Symbols and Strategies," *American Sociological Review* 51, no. 2 (April 1986): 273–286.

10. Michael Denning, *The Cultural Front: The Laboring of American Culture in the Twentieth Century* (New York: Verso, 1998). John Ott, "Graphic Consciousness: The Visual Cultures of Integrated Industrial Unions at Midcentury," *American Quarterly* 66, no. 4 (December 2014): 883–917; James Scott, *Domination and the Arts of Resistance: Hidden Transcripts* (New Haven, CT: Yale University Press, 1990); Lawrence Goodwyn, *The Populist Moment: A Short History of the Agrarian Revolt in America* (New York: Oxford University Press, 1978).

11. Flyer, Detroit City Committee of United Toilers of America, May Day 1922 celebration, CPUSA-LC, reel 9, delo 159. Paul Lafargue, *The Right to Be Lazy* (Chicago: Charles H. Kerr, 1975).

12. "Socials and Entertainments," in minutes, National Textile Workers Union national convention, New York, September 22–23, 1928, CPUSA-LC, reel 114, delo 1507; Ticket, *Steel Strike* by Workers' Cultural Federation, Chicago, December 10, 1932, CPUSA-LC, reel 227, delo 2948; Flyer, *Make September 1st the Workers' Day* [1928], CPUSA-LC, reel 112, delo 1485.

13. "Fun and Education at Labor Chautauquas in Mining Towns," in *Bulletin District Two*, UMWA, Clearfield, Pennsylvania, June 29, 1926, 3. CPUSA-LC, reel 66, delo 911. Jasper, "The Emotions of Protest." For western Pennsylvania coal miners' strikes, see Mildred Allen Beik, *The Miners of Windber: The Struggles of New Immigrants for Unionization, 1890s–1930s* (University Park: Pennsylvania State University Press, 1996), esp. 264–330.

14. Irving Bernstein, *The Lean Years: A History of the American Worker, 1920–1933* (Baltimore, MD: Penguin Books, 1966); Dan Georgianna and Roberta Hazen Aaronson, *The Strike of '28* (New Bedford, MA: Spinner, 1993); General Relief Committee of Textile Strikers, *Hell in New Jersey: Story of the Passaic Textile Strike Told in Pictures* (Passaic, NJ: General Relief Committee of Textile Strikers, 1926); David Goldberg, *A Tale of Three Cities: Labor Organization and Protest in Paterson, Passaic, and Lawrence, 1916–1921* (New Brunswick, NJ: Rutgers University Press, 1989).

15. Mikhail Bakhtin, *Rabelais and His World* (Bloomington: Indiana University Press, 1984); Ad, "Gala Concert at Coney Island Stadium, Swell the Movement for Passaic Relief," held August 28, 1926, *Textile Strike Bulletin*, July 30, 1926, 7, CPUSA-LC, reel 66, delo 913; Flyer, *Save a Child, 30,000 Undernourished Children of Passaic Appeal to You. International Workers Camp, Morristown, New Jersey*, ibid. Paul Mishler, *Raising Reds: The Young Pioneers, Radical Summer Camps, and Communist Political Culture in the United States* (New York: Columbia University Press, 1999); Judy Kaplan and Linn Shaprio, eds., *Red Diapers: Growing Up in the Communist Left* (Urbana: University of Illinois Press, 1998); James Scott, *Weapons of the Weak: Everyday Forms*

of Peasant Resistance (New Haven, CT: Yale University Press, 1985); Scott, *Domination and the Arts of Resistance*.

16. Poster, "Lenin Memorial Meeting," January 27, 1936, CPUSA-LC, reel 304, delo 4009; Poster, "To All Negro Workers of Detroit!" Lenin Memorial Meeting, Danceland Auditorium, Detroit, January 19, 1930, CPUSA-LC, reel 165, delo 2204; Poster, "Big Communist Election Rally," September 27, 1931, CPUSA-LC, reel 191, delo 2530.

17. Francesca Polletta, "Culture and Movements," *Annals of the American Academy of Political and Social Science* 619 (September 2008): 78–96, esp. 86–87. James Jasper notes that some early civil rights protesters took almost as much delight in defying and harassing the keepers of Jim Crow as in achieving substantive gains ("The Emotions of Protest," 416–417).

18. ILD press release, March 19, 1932, CPUSA-LC, reel 233, delo 3016.

19. Victoria Wolcott, *Race, Riots, and Roller Coasters: The Struggle over Segregated Recreation in America* (Philadelphia: University of Pennsylvania Press, 2012).

20. Flyer, *Come All! To the Ninth Anniversary of the Russian Revolution*, Paterson, November 6, 1926, CPUSA-LC, reel 63, delo 869; Flyer, *Second Annual Picnic Given by the Workers Party and Young Workers League*, July 4, 1926, ibid. Flyer, *Charter Fest and Celebration. To Hail the First Shop Bulletin Issued in Philadelphia and Presentation of Charters to the Shop Nuclei. April 16, 1926*, CPUSA-LC, reel 63, delo 876; Flyer, *International May Day Monster Mass Meeting and Demonstration, Philadelphia, May First, 1926*, ibid.; Flyer, *Celebrate the Seventh Anniversary of the Organization of the Workers* [Communist] *Party at the Summer Festival, Philadelphia, August 22, 1926*, ibid. Flyer, *Hail the* Daily Worker, Minneapolis, January 15, 1927, CPUSA-LC, reel 72, delo 976; Flyer, *Celebrate the Russian Revolution*, Philadelphia, November 5, 1926, CPUSA-LC, reel 63, delo 876.

21. Ron Eyerman and Scott Barretta, "From the 30s to the 60s: The Folk Music Revival in the United States," *Theory and Society* 25, no. 4 (August 1996): 501–543, esp. 507. For conservative use of ethnic culture among Southeast Europeans, see Matthew Frye Jacobson, *Roots Too: White Ethnic Revival in Post–Civil Rights America* (Cambridge, MA: Harvard University Press, 2006); Michael Novak, *The Rise of the Unmeltable Ethnics: Politics and Culture in the Seventies* (New York: Macmillan, 1972).

22. Francesca Polletta and James Jasper, "Collective Identity and Social Movements," *Annual Review of Sociology* 27 (2001): 283–305; Suzanne Smith, "'Boogie Chillen': Uncovering Detroit's African-American Cultural History," *Michigan Historical Review* 27, no. 1 (Spring 2001): 93–107; Suzanne Smith, *Dancing in the Street: Motown and the Cultural Politics of Detroit* (Cambridge, MA: Harvard University Press, 1999); "Report of Work among Women," January 1925, the work of the Lithuanian Fraction of the Workers Party among the Lithuanian Working Women's Alliance of America, CPUSA-LC, reel 65, delo 904; Questionnaire, Bulgarian Bureau, Workers Party, August 20, 1927, CPUSA-LC, reel 87, delo 1179; Language questionnaire, Czechoslovak [1931], CPUSA-LC, reel 178, delo 2337; "Proletarian Drama," spring term 1934 edition of *Harlem Student Worker*, 7, CPUSA-LC, reel 283, delo 3650; Language questionnaire, Czechoslovak; Minutes, Jewish Fraction, Actions Committee meeting, January 28, 1927, CPUSA-LC, reel 87, delo 1180; *F.S.U. News*, June 1931, CPUSA-LC, reel 195, dela 2580–2583.

23. Jay Lovestone to Ukrainian Bureau, August 20, 1926, CPUSA-LC, reel 55, delo 767.

24. Lawrence Levine, "The Folklore of Industrial Society: Popular Culture and Its Audiences," *American Historical Review* 97, no. 5 (December 1992): 1369–1399. For

how various readers interpret what they "consume" in the tabloid press, see John Carter Wood, "'Those Who Have Had Trouble Can Sympathise with You': Press Writing, Reader Responses and a Murder Trial in Interwar Britain," *Journal of Social History* 32, no. 2 (Winter 2009): 439–462.

25. Minutes, Executive Council meeting, Jewish Bureau, February 3, 1926, CPUSA-LC, reel 65, delo 898; FBI report, IWO, Detroit division, December 31, 1946, citing confidential informant on November 30, 1946, IWO meeting, DB-WSU, box 16, folder 16-37; Letter from Anthony Bimba, October 30, 1935, CPUSA-LC, reel 292, delo 3791.

26. Luigi Candela to Max Bedacht, August 18, 1930, CPUSA-LC, reel 151, delo 1961.

27. *New Masses*, July 1928, 15 and 24, DB-WSU, box 3, folder 3-23; Ad for Camp Nitgedaiget, "Spring Is Here with Its Beauty," *Daily Worker*, March 27, 1929, 3, CPUSA-LC, reel 318, delo 4243; Mishler, *Raising Reds*; Kaplan and Shapiro, *Red Diapers*.

28. Language Department to Central Control Commission, January 29, 1932, CPUSA-LC, reel 213, delo 2749; Minutes, CP Central Control Commission meeting, January 25, 1936, CPUSA-LC, reel 303, delo 4002.

29. Calvin Coolidge, "Whose Country Is This?" *Good Housekeeping* 72 (February 1921): 13, 14, 106, 109; Victor Greene, *The Slavic Community on Strike: Immigrant Labor in Pennsylvania Anthracite* (Notre Dame, IN: University of Notre Dame Press, 1968); Beik, *The Miners of Windber*; Katherine Mayo, *Justice to All: The Story of the Pennsylvania State Police* (New York: G. P. Putnam's, 1916); Scott Martelle, *Blood Passion: The Ludlow Massacre and Class War in the American West* (New Brunswick, NJ: Rutgers University Press, 2007); Helen Papanikolas, *Buried Unsung: Louis Tiklas and the Ludlow Massacre* (Salt Lake City: University of Utah Press, 1982); Thomas Andrews, *Killing for Coal: America's Deadliest Labor War* (Cambridge, MA: Harvard University Press, 2008); General Relief Committee, *Hell in New Jersey*; Goldberg, *A Tale of Three Cities*; David Alan Corbin, *Life, Work, and Rebellion in the Coal Fields: The Southern West Virginia Miners, 1880–1922* (Urbana: University of Illinois Press, 1981), esp. 195–224; James Green, *The Devil Is Here in These Hills: West Virginia's Coal Miners and Their Battle for Freedom* (New York: Atlantic Monthly Press, 2015); Bernstein, *The Lean Years*; Irving Bernstein, *Turbulent Years: A History of the American Worker, 1933–1941* (Boston, MA: Houghton Mifflin, 1970); Lizabeth Cohen, *Making a New Deal: Industrial Workers in Chicago, 1919–1939* (New York: Cambridge University Press, 1990).

30. *My Winter Camp*, flyer on Camp Wo-Chi-Ca [1942], DB-WSU, box 13, folder 13-3.

31. "Children's Red Camp Is Raided," 1, 3, *Detroit Free Press*, August 31, 1930, DB-WSU, box 12, folder 12-15; Scott, *Domination and the Arts of Resistance*; Polletta and Jasper, "Collective Identity and Social Movements."

32. "Children's Red Camp Is Raided," 1, 3.

33. IWO flyer, *Why Not Social Insurance?* [1932], CPUSA-LC, reel 234, delo 3037; "The Activities of the I.W.O." [1932], ibid.; "Report of District Plenum of IWO, April 29, 1934" [Philadelphia], CPUSA-LC, reel 287, delo 3709; Max Bedacht to Earl Browder, July 26, 1934, including suggested copy for an IWO election leaflet on Social Insurance, ibid.; "International Workers Order, Inc., constitution in effect July 1, 1938," IWOCF-CU, box 3

34. *The Spark*, July 1931, 30, 31, CPUSA-LC, reel 195, delo 2584; *The New Order*, March 1934, 14, CPUSA-LC, reel 287, delo 3709; "Report of District Plenum of IWO [Philadelphia] April 29, 1934." Proceedings of Fourth New York City Convention of IWO Branches, March 21–22, 1936, 3, CPUSA-LC, reel 305, delo 4050; A. Kanovsky, financial secretary, IWO Branch 521, Bronx, to "Dear Member," January 20, 1936, ibid.

35. *The New Order*, March 1934, 11.

36. Flyer, *Young Workers: Follow the Race to Demonstrate against New War Plans*, Labor Sports Union, Roxbury [Boston, 1935], CPUSA-LC, reel 195, delo 2591; National Counter-Olympic Committee letterhead: Tom Mooney, Honorary Chairman [1932], ibid.

37. "Digest of Testimony of Witnesses for the State in the I.W.O. Matter. January 29, 1951, to March 7, 1951," IWOCF-CU, box 4.

38. News release, "IWO Hails Cleveland Pennant Victory," October 4, 1948, box 1, folder 31, International Workers Order Records, Robert F. Wagner Labor Archives, Tamiment Library, New York University [hereafter cited as IWO-NYU]. "Lodge Program Sessions 9 and 10 Civic and Community Events," "Daily Schedule National Training School, September 3–11, 1949," IWO-CU, box 4, folder 10; *The New Order*, 1935, cited in Paul Buhle, "Interview with Ernie Reymer of the I.W.O.," *Cultural Correspondence* 6, no. 7 (Spring 1978): 98–101; Ben Goldstein to "Dear Friend," July 19, 1945, box 46, Vito Marcantonio Papers, Manuscripts and Archives Division, The New York Public Library [hereafter cited as VM-NYPL]; Flyer, *August 19—End Jim Crow in Baseball Day* [1945], ibid.; Goldstein to "Dear Friend" and Goldstein to Mayor Fiorello La Guardia, both August 17, 1945, ibid.

39. *Národné noviny*, September 10 and 24, 1941, both 6; "IWO Hails Cleveland Pennant Victory."

40. Affidavit, Peter Moreno, Brooklyn, April 24, 1951, IWOCF-CU, box 3; Poster, "Trini Romero in a Program of Spanish Dances" [ca. 1940s], IWO-CU, box 9, folder 13. For similar interracial activities, including flamenco performances, see Daniel Katz, *All Together Different: Yiddish Socialists, Garment Workers, and the Labor Roots of Multiculturalism* (New York: New York University Press, 2011), 158–159.

41. Minutes, March 1939 Plenary, IWO GEB, 26, IWO-CU, box 1, folder 6; *Chicago Defender*, March 29, 1941, 22. For baseball tournaments, see I. Isaacs to Sam Milgrom, April 15, 1946, DB-WSU, box 5, folder 5-29. SWS meeting minutes, March 23, 1947, IWO-CU, box 54; Affidavits, Milton Schiff, Los Angeles, April 24, 1951, and Mary Granich, Philadelphia, April 23, 1951, IWOCF-CU, box 3.

42. Draft report, General Secretary, IWO, August 29, 1946, 15, IWO-NYU, folder 2; *Chicago Defender*, October 3, 1936, 4; Lucy Davidowitz, "The History of the Jewish People's Fraternal Order of the International Workers Order" [November 1950], TS, IWO-NYU, folder 8. Maurice Isserman, *Which Side Were You On? The American Communist Party during the Second World War* (Middletown, CT: Wesleyan University Press, 1982); Steve Nelson, James Barrett, and Rob Ruck, *Steve Nelson, American Radical* (Pittsburgh, PA: University of Pittsburgh Press, 1981). For acceptance of leftists in the UE, see Rosemary Feurer, *Radical Unionism in the Midwest, 1900–1950* (Urbana: University of Illinois Press, 2006).

43. *The New Order*, March 1934, 15–16; *The Spark*, July 1931, 30.

44. Proceedings of Fourth New York City Convention of IWO Branches, 3; Paul Keller, director, Federation of Workers Choruses, "Report on Workers' Musical Activities in New York," June 14, 1931, CPUSA-LC, reel 194, delo 2579; Fannie Gardner, "On Organization and Plans to Youth Conference," report to national convention [June 1940], IWO-CU, box 3, folder 3; John Middleton to Sam Milgrom, February 1, 1948, IWO-CU, box 5, folder 2.

45. *The New Order*, March 1934, 8. Resolution, John Reed Club, May 11, 1933, declared destruction of the Rivera mural "an act of capitalist vandalism," CPUSA-LC, reel 260, delo 3384.

46. Translation of program, Boston Lettish [Latvian] Workingmen's Association, IWO, January 14, 1934, CPUSA-LC, reel 273, delo 3495; Miscellaneous play scripts, Dramatski Zbor "Nada" [Chicago Croatian Socialist Dramatic Group], Box 9, Dramatski Zbor "Nada" (Chicago, Illinois) Records, MSS 562, Immigration History Research Center Archives, University of Minnesota [hereafter cited as DZ-UM].

47. Miscellaneous play scripts, DZ-UM, boxes 4, 9.

48. Leo Tepp to Pat Toohey, July 29, 1935, CPUSA-LC, reel 292, delo 3774.

49. Miscellaneous play scripts, DZ-UM, box 9; Liston Oak to "Comrade Peters" [1934?], CPUSA-LC, reel 287, delo 3697; *Když Octroctví Kvetlo v America. John Brown* [When Slavery was in Bloom in America. John Brown], typewritten playscript, box 4, Czech-American Dramatic Society of Chicago (IL) Papers, MSS 503, Immigration History Research Center Archives, University of Minnesota; Rebecca Hill, *Men, Mobs, and Law: Anti-Lynching and Labor Defense in U.S. Radical History* (Durham, NC: Duke University Press, 2008), 27–68.

50. Evelyn Louise Crawford and MaryLouise Patterson, eds., *Letters from Langston: From the Harlem Renaissance to the Red Scare and Beyond* (Berkeley: University of California Press, 2016), 128–129, 142, 145, 149–152, 155, 161, 167, 229; Interview with Louise Thompson Patterson [ca. 1950–1951], box 27, folder 1, Louise Thompson Patterson Papers, 1909–1999, MSS 869, Stuart A. Rose Manuscript, Archives, and Rare Book Library, Emory University [hereafter cited as LTP-EU]; Thompson Patterson MS autobiography, chap. 8, "The Harlem Suitcase Theatre," LTP-EU, box 20, folders 6 and 7; Interview with Thompson Patterson, June 9 and 18, 1987, LTP-EU, box 27, folder 9; and Thompson Patterson, interview by Linda Burnham, February 19 and 24, 1988, LTP-EU, box 27, folder 10; Constitution, The Harlem Suitcase Theatre [sponsored by IWO Branch 691], LTP-EU, box 7, folder 4; Alice Evans, New Theatre League, New York, to the Harlem Suitcase Theater, September 29, 1938, ticket of Harlem Suitcase Theatre, Summer Season, *Don't You Want to Be Free?* July 16, 1939, advertising Frank Wilson and Asadata Dafora, and program, LTP-EU, box 7, folder 5; Palm card, Dr. Carter Woodson, talk at the Harlem IWO Community Center, LTP-EU, box 8, folder 9. Also, Easter Sunday Musicale, April 17, 1938, Langston Hughes's new play, *Don't You Want to Be Free?* ibid.; Sheet music, song "Let's Get Together" by Langston Hughes and Carroll Tate, from *Don't You Want to Be Free?* LTP-EU, box 20, folder 26; Script, *Don't You Want to Be Free?* in *One Act Play Magazine* 2, no. 4 (October 1938): 359–393, LTP-EU, box 20, folder 28.

51. "The IWO Treasure Chest of Tools," a list of plays and songs available from IWO, n.d., IWO-CU, box 13, folder 6; "Communist-Line IWO Reorganizes to Emphasize Nationality"; Report to IWO GEB, "On the Progress of the Order during the Year 1942," February 26–27, 1943, 27–28, IWO-CU, box 2, folder 8.

52. Script of show produced by the Freedom Theatre for IWO, *Let's Get Together* [1950], IWO-CU, box 26, folder 7; Synopsis of Ukrainian Society play, *All Our Yesterdays*, by Andrew Hertz, October 1948, *The Partisans*, January 19, 1942, IWO-CU, box 26, folder 7; *Keep Up!* in synopses of SWS material [ca. 1950], IWO-CU, box 26, folder 5. Another František Končinský play script, *Obraz z dób revolučných v jedomdejstve* [A Picture of Good Revolutions in History], is in IWO-CU, box 14, folder 4.

53. Levine, "The Folklore of Industrial Society," 1370, 1380, 1398; Herbert Gans, *The Urban Villagers: Group and Class in the Life of Italian-Americans* (New York: Free Press of Glencoe, 1962), cited in Levine, "The Folklore of Industrial Society."

54. "Lodge Program Sessions 9 and 10 Civic and Community Events" includes "Rights of the Negro People, Equality"; "Daily Schedule National Training School, September 3–11, 1949."

55. Flyer, *Paul Robeson Sings for IWO Day*, Civilian and National Defense Exposition, New York, Sunday, October 12, 1941, also featured the Radischev Russian Folk Dancers, IWO-CU, box 49; Affidavit, Louis Oroby, New York, April 24, 1951, IWOCF-CU, box 3; "Communist-Line IWO Reorganizes to Emphasize Nationality"; Ad, "Jubileum 30-ročného trvania Slovenského Robotníckeho Spolku—IWO," *Národné noviny*, November 7, 1945, 2, notes an appearance of the Radischev Russian Folk Dancers at a thirtieth anniversary jubilee celebration of the SWS; "Do Cleveland a okolia" [To Cleveland and area], *Národné noviny*, November 28, 1945, 2; *Národné noviny*, October 17, 1945, 2, contains notice of an SWS fund-raising concert in Chicago; Ad for performance by an Emma Lazarus Club dance group, *Jewish Life*, March 1954, 30, IWO-CU, box 53; Sheet music, "The Song of Hope," "Dedicated to the American Slav Congress," IWO-CU, box 26, folder 5; John Holton to "Dear Eddie" [Edward Nelson], May 27, 1949, IWO-CU, box 8, folder 1; Sam Milgrom to Rockwell Kent, January 11, 1950, IWO-CU, box 3, folder 10. A Slovak Gymnastic Union *Sokol* lodge in Leechburg, Pennsylvania, also donated to the SWS's campaign for a Banska Bystrica memorial to Roosevelt: ledger of income and expenses and minute book, December 30, 1945, box 4, Slovak Gymnastic Union *Sokol*, Lodge 255, Leechburg, Pennsylvania, Archives of Industrial Society, Series 79:26A, University of Pittsburgh.

56. JPFO "Program for Observance of Warsaw Ghetto Anniversary," April 1947, IWO-CU, box 36, folder 6. JPFO School and Cultural Committee, ibid.; Poster, "A Salute to the Jewish State in Palestine, May 15, 1948," IWO-CU, box 28, folder 6; Translation from Slovak, letter from Joseph Gurbal [1940s], IWO-CU, box 5, folder 3; Letter from Pavasko family of West Homestead, Pennsylvania [probably during World War II], ibid.; Minutes, SWS main board of western Pennsylvania, November 7, 1943, discussed a fifteen-minute SWS radio program that aired from Pittsburgh, IWO-CU, box 54; Flyer for People's Radio Foundation, IWO-CU, box 36, folder 7; Flyer, *Chase Out the Black Cats of Radio Censorship on Friday the 13th of December, 1946. People's Radio Foundation Presents Three Radio Plays That Were Banned from the Air*, ibid.; Letter from George Wuchinich, executive secretary, Western Pennsylvania Slav Congress, *Slavic American*, Winter 1947, 46; "'People to Remember': Weekly Series over Station WINS Sundays 10:00 to 10:15 p.m. Narrator: Foster Williams," TS, IWO-CU, box 36, folder 7. "Date: September 17, 1944. Subject: Josip Broz Tito," People's Radio Foundation, ibid.; Carpathian-Russian Society report to IWO General Council, March 16–17, 1946, notes a half-hour IWO radio program in the New York area that reported "on everything at home and abroad," IWO-CU, box 2, folder 14. FBI report, IWO, Detroit division, December 31, 1946.

57. Matthew Frye Jacobson, *Whiteness of a Different Color: European Immigrants and the Alchemy of Race* (Cambridge, MA: Harvard University Press, 1998); Denning, *The Cultural Front*; Jacobson, *Roots Too*.

58. Affidavits, Alexander Smoley, New York, April 25, 1951, Lewis Marks, Boston, April 21, 1951, and Anna Mazurak, Bound Brook, New Jersey, and Maxim Hayda, New York, both April 24, 1951, IWOCF-CU, box 3.

59. Affidavit, Emil Betley, New York, April 1951, ibid.; James Barrett and David Roediger, "Whiteness and the Inbetween Peoples of Europe," *Journal of American Ethnic History* 16, no. 3 (Summer 1997): 3–44; Thomas Guglielmo, *White on Arrival: Italians, Race, Color and Power in Chicago, 1890–1945* (New York: Oxford University Press, 2003); Edward Alsworth Ross, *The Old World in the New: The Significance of Past and Present Immigration to the American People* (New York: Century, 1914).

60. Affidavit, Louis Oroby, New York, April 24, 1951, IWOCF-CU, box 3; Ewa Morawska, *For Bread with Butter: The Life-Worlds of East Central Europeans in Johnstown, Pennsylvania, 1890–1940* (New York: Cambridge University Press, 1985).

61. Affidavits, Milton Schiff and Max Lange, both Los Angeles, April 24, 1951, IWOCF-CU, box 3.

62. Affidavits, Catherine Ales, Los Angeles, April 24, 1951, and Peter Moreno, Brooklyn, and James Moorer, Jersey City, both April 23, 1951, ibid.; Douglas Henry Daniels, "Los Angeles Zoot: Race 'Riot,' the Pachuco, and Black Music Culture," *Journal of African American History* 87 (Winter 2002): 98–118; Mauricio Mazon, *The Zoot-Suit Riots: The Psychology of Symbolic Annihilation* (Austin: University of Texas Press, 1984); Eduardo Obregon Pagan, *Murder at the Sleepy Lagoon: Zoot Suits, Race, and Riot in Wartime L.A.* (Chapel Hill: University of North Carolina Press, 2003).

63. Affidavit, George Frederickson, Detroit, April 23, 1951, IWOCF-CU, box 3; Minutes, Language Department meeting, April 19, 1930, noting Finnish and Jewish camps refused to cooperate with other groups, CPUSA-LC, reel 154, delo 2014. For Arow Farm, which took its name from the Cyrillic letters for American Russian Fraternal Society (ARFS), see Michael Singer, "Camp Witchhunt Tries Intimidating Guests," *Daily Worker*, August 25, 1955, 3, IWO-CU, box 53. For a history of Camp Kinderland, see I. Goldberg, "Camp Kinderland," *Proletarishe Dertziung* [Proletarian Education], 1, no. 6 (June 1935), the official organ of the National School Committee, IWO, IWO-CU, box 39, folder 11; History, "Camp Kinderland," n.d., IWO-CU, box 37, folder 7. For the Brampton, Ontario, JPFO camp, see FBI report, IWO, Detroit division, November 20, 1953, 304, DB-WSU, box 16, folder 16-38; *New Masses*, July 1928, 15 and 24, DB-WSU, box 3, folder 3-23; Affidavit, Peter Moreno.

64. John Myketew to Sam Milgrom, March 3, 1944, and Myketew to B. Gordon, June 15, 1944, IWO-CU, box 7, folder 1; Eva Gregg, "For Negro Rights," *Fraternal Outlook*, February 1944, 22, has a photograph of Myketew recruiting African American civil rights activist Reverend Hill into the IWO, IWO-CU, box 48. For the melding of ethnic and American identities in a nonradical context, see June Granatir Alexander, *Ethnic Pride, American Patriotism: Slovaks and Other New Immigrants in the Interwar Era* (Philadelphia, PA: Temple University Press, 2004).

65. OSS/FNB report, "RESTRICTED September 7, 1943. Event: FOUR FREEDOMS RALLY," DB-WSU, box 5, folder 5-30.

66. *Národné noviny*, August 18, 1943, 5. For Pindar, see Donald Hill, *Calypso Calaloo: Early Carnival Music in Trinidad* (Gainseville: University Press of Florida, 1993). *The Worker*, June 3, 1947, 10, IWO-CU, box 27.1, folder 9; IWO press release, Negro History Week, February 5, 1953, IWO-CU, box 4, folder 6.

67. Letter on "Negro Freedom Rally" letterhead, May 12, 1944, box 5, folder 2, International Ladies Garment Workers Union, Charles S. Zimmerman Papers, 1919–1958, MSS 5780/014, Kheel Center for Labor-Management Documentation and Archives, Cornell University [hereafter cited as ILGWU-CU, MSS 5780/014]; Poster, "Negro Freedom Rally," June 26, 1944, ibid.; Ad, "And Now the Dance Classic! Harlem Revels. 2nd Annual Inter-Racial Dance, Duke Ellington's Orchestra," *Daily Worker*, March 22, 1930, 4, CPUSA-LC, reel 318, delo 4243; Ad, Third Annual International Red Poets' Nite Dance Bacchanal, December 28, 1928, *Daily Worker*, December 26, 1928, CPUSA-LC, reel 91, delo 1228. Poster, May 5, 1945, Spring Festival, Brighton Beach American Labor Party, VM-NYPL, box 44; American Labor Party of the Bronx, to "Dear Friend," September 11, 1944, regarding a rally featuring both Leo Krzycki

of the ASC and ACWA and the Stage for Action Players, ibid. Denning, *The Cultural Front*.

68. Letter for Fiesta Republicana, June 22, 1943, ILGWU-CU, MSS 5780/014, box 5, folder 2; Poster and program, "Gran Acontecimiento Artistico Cultural" [Grand Cultural Artistic Event], June 25, 1939, Club Obrero Español, New York, VM-NYPL, box 47; FBI file on IWO, March 18, 1939, DB-WSU, box 5, folder 5-30.

69. Daniel Kasustchik to Lodge 3001, ARFS, November 4, 1949, IWO-CU, box 25, folder 1.

70. Andrian Anddrozzo, New York, to Secretariat, CP, September 20, 1932, CPUSA-LC, reel 234, delo 3032. Sam Friedlander, Bronx JPFO, to Dave Greene, September 7, 1949, and Philippa Stowe to headquarters, April 12, 1949, IWO-CU, box 4, folder 4. Eleanor Boady of the Michigan IWO similarly complained to headquarters of Italian comrades' resistance to housing integration in Detroit: Eleanor Boady to Sam Milgrom, March 22 and April 5, 1945, IWO-CU, box 7, folder 4. On resistance of Italian members of the IWO to housing integration in Detroit, see FBI report, IWO, Detroit division, December 31, 1946.

71. "Impromptu Minstrel Show—But Look at It Now," *Milwaukee Leader*, November 13, 1930, 5, DB-WSU, box 13, folder 13-16; "Guards of King Boola Boo," *Milwaukee Leader*, December 7, 1932, 2, DB-WSU, box 6, folder 6-5; Ad, "Socialist Winter Shows of 1932," *Milwaukee Leader*, November 27, 1932, 3, ibid.; "Socialist Winter Shows of 1930 Tomorrow!!," *Milwaukee Leader*, November 16, 1930, DB-WSU, box 13, folder 13-16; "Last Chance to See the Socialist Winter Shows of '32," *Milwaukee Leader*, December 9, 1932, ibid.; Letter from George Wuchinich, executive secretary of the Western Pennsylvania Slav Congress, on Robeson's performance at a Slav Congress People's Festival in Pittsburgh, *Slavic American*, Winter 1947, 46. Stephanie Dunston, "The Minstrel in the Parlor," *American Transcendental Quarterly* 16, no. 4 (December 2002): 241–256; Eric Lott, *Love and Theft: Blackface Minstrelsy and the American Working Class* (New York: Oxford University Press, 1993); Eric Lott, "'The Seeming Counterfeit': Racial Politics and Early Blackface Minstrelsy," *American Quarterly* 43, no. 2 (June 1991): 223–254.

72. George Pirinsky, executive secretary of ASC, report, "Program and Activities of the American Slav Congress," *Slavic American*, Winter 1947, 30. See *Slavic American*, Fall 1947, 17, for another Robeson appearance for the ASC. Robeson also performed on IWO Day, October 12, 1941, at the Civilian and National Defense Exposition in New York: Flyer, *Paul Robeson Sings for IWO Day*, IWO-CU, box 49. Letter from Ewart Guinier, regional director, United Public Workers of America CIO, Region 2, January 6, 1948, ILGWU-CU, MSS 5780/014, box 5, folder 4; Outline for Dave Greene JPFO speech, Brooklyn, June 19, 1950, and outline for Madison Square Garden speech, IWO-CU, box 4, folder 5; *Slavic American*, Winter 1947, 30, 46; Lottie Gordon, director, Prisoners Relief Committee of the Civil Rights Congress, to S. Davidovitch, Camp Kinderland, June 26, 1950, IWO-CU, box 43, folder 2.

73. FBI report on Paul Robeson, November 8, 1946, DB-WSU, box 9, folder 9-33; FBI report, IWO, Detroit division, November 20, 1953, 156, DB-WSU, box 16, folder 16-38.

74. FBI report on IWO, March 18, 1939, DB-WSU, box 5, folder 5-30; Detroit Police report, May 27, 1939, ibid.

75. Affidavits, Herman Schlossberg, Los Angeles, Kalyna Popow, Philadelphia, and Frances Slowiczeck, Hamtramck, Michigan, all April 24, 1951, IWOCF-CU, box 3.

76. Affidavits, Catherine McCastle, Cleveland, Jumal Ahmad, Cleveland, and Pecola Moore, Los Angeles, all April 24, 1951, ibid.; News release, July 8, 1948, excerpt from speeches by Paul Robeson and Senator Glen Taylor of Idaho opposing placing

IWO on Attorney General's List of Subversive Organizations, IWO-NYU, folder 31. For Robeson's denunciation of segregationist congressmen questioning his Americanism, see Tony Perucci, *Paul Robeson and the Cold War Performance Complex: Race, Madness, Activism* (Ann Arbor: University of Michigan Press, 2012), 66–73, 163–172. For fracturing of left-wing, interracial coalition around civil rights, see Robert Korstad and Nelson Liechtenstein, "Opportunities Found and Lost: Labor, Radicals, and the Early Civil Rights Movement," *Journal of American History* 75, no. 3 (December 1988): 786–811.

77. Detroit Police Department report, January 18, 1949, DB-WSU, box 2, folder 2-55.

78. Robert Zecker, *Race and America's Immigrant Press: How the Slovaks were Taught to Think Like White People* (New York: Continuum, 2011); Thomas Sugrue, *The Origins of the Urban Crisis: Race and Inequality in Postwar Detroit* (Princeton, NJ: Princeton University Press, 1996); Arnold Hirsch, *Making the Second Ghetto: Race and Housing in Chicago, 1940–1960* (Chicago: University of Chicago Press, 1998); Thomas Philpott, *The Slum and the Ghetto: Neighborhood Deterioration and Middle-Class Reform, Chicago, 1880–1930* (New York: Oxford University Press, 1978); Andrew Diamond, *Mean Streets: Chicago Youths and the Everyday Struggle for Empowerment in the Multiracial City, 1908–1969* (Berkeley: University of California Press, 2009).

79. Robert Putnam, *Bowling Alone: The Collapse and Revival of American Community* (New York: Simon and Schuster, 2000).

80. A. Prisiaznuk, Edwardsville, Pennsylvania, to National Office, IWO, April 24, 1941, IWO-CU, box 18, folder 13.

81. "Communist-Line IWO Reorganizes to Emphasize Nationality," "Social-Cultural Activity"; Flyer, IWO Film Department, Special Summer Offer [during World War II], IWO-CU, box 20, folder 3; "Abe" to Sam Milgrom, May 14, 1945, IWO-CU, box 16, folder 22; FBI report, IWO, Detroit division, December 31, 1946.

82. SWS national board minutes, June 2, 1946, IWO-CU, box 54; FBI report, IWO, Detroit division, November 20, 1953, 54, referencing a February 5, 1947, letter from Flint to IWO Film Division, DB-WSU, box 16, folder 16-38; N. Vashkevich of Lackawanna, New York, to Daniel Kasustchik, president, ARFS [ca. September–October 1947], and Kasustchik's reply to Vashkevich, October 9, 1947, IWO-CU, box 25, folder 1. The IWO also recommended progressive films to their members, as when Jesús Colón, president of the Cervantes Fraternal Society, favorably reviewed *Salt of the Earth*, the blacklisted film created by members of the left-wing Mine, Mill, and Smelters Union: Jesús Colón, "See *The Salt of the Earth*," *Jewish Life*, May 1954, 28, IWO-CU, box 53. *Salt of the Earth*, screenplay [1953] by Michael Wilson, commentary by Deborah Silverton Rosenfelt (New York: Feminist Press at the City University of New York, 1978).

CHAPTER 5

1. Max Bedacht, "Anti-Soviet Lies and the Five-Year Plan" [1931], box 12, folder 12-8, Don Binkowski Papers, Walter P. Reuther Library, Wayne State University [hereafter cited as DB-WSU].

2. Bedacht, "Anti-Soviet Lies and the Five-Year Plan"; Scott Martelle, *Blood Passion: The Ludlow Massacre and Class War in the American West* (New Brunswick, NJ: Rutgers University Press, 2007); Thomas Andrews, *Killing for Coal: America's Deadliest Labor War* (Cambridge, MA: Harvard University Press, 2008); Helen Papanikolas, *Buried Unsung: Louis Tiklas and the Ludlow Massacre* (Salt Lake City: University of Utah Press, 1982). Lincoln Steffens, *Autobiography* (New York: Harcourt, Brace, 1958); Peter

Hartshorn, *I Have Seen the Future: A Life of Lincoln Steffens* (Berkeley, CA: Counterpoint, 2011); Thomas Hughes, "How America Helped Build the Soviet Machine," *American Heritage* 39, no. 8 (December 1988): 56–67; Christine White, "Ford in Russia: In Pursuit of the Chimerical Market," *Business History* 28, no. 4 (October 1986): 77–104.

3. IWO Declaration of Principles [1933], reel 260, delo 3372, Records of the Communist Party USA, Microfilm 21, 966, Library of Congress [hereafter cited as CPUSA-LC]; "Report of District Plenum of IWO, April 29, 1934" [Philadelphia District, IWO], CPUSA-LC, reel 287, delo 3709.

4. OSS/FNB confidential report, "BUTTS 715, May 27, 1944," DB-WSU, box 5, folder 5-30; General Secretary Max Bedacht, report to GEB plenary session, August 26, 1939, box 2, folder 3, International Workers Order Records, 1915–2002, MSS 5276, Kheel Center for Labor-Management Documentation and Archives, Cornell University [hereafter cited as IWO-CU]; IWO report, "Our Tasks" [1939], "Duties of Progressive Fraternalism," ibid.

5. "Resolution on the Soviet Union," adopted at IWO national convention, April 23–30, 1938, IWO-CU, box 3, folder 1; Kenyon Zimmer, *Immigrants against the State: Yiddish and Italian Anarchism in America* (Urbana: University of Illinois Press, 2015), 143, 146–147, 160–163; United Ukrainian Organizations of the United States, *Famine in Ukraine* (New York: United Ukrainian Organizations of the United States, 1934), 5, 6, 12, 13, 21, 27.

6. "Resolution on the Soviet Union"; For conservative businessmen lobbying against the New Deal, see Kim Phillips-Fein, *Invisible Hands: The Making of the Conservative Movement from the New Deal to Reagan* (New York: W. W. Norton, 2009); Kim Phillips-Fein, "'If Business and the Country Will Be Run Right;' The Business Challenge to the Liberal Consensus, 1945–1964," *International Labor and Working-Class History* 72 (2007): 192–215; Jefferson Cowie, *The Great Exception: The New Deal and the Limits of American Politics* (Princeton, NJ: Princeton University Press, 2016); Elizabeth Fones-Wolf, *Selling Free Enterprise: The Business Assault on Labor and Liberalism, 1945–60* (Urbana: University of Illinois Press, 1994).

7. "Resolution on Fascist Aggression," adopted at IWO national convention, April 23–30, 1938, IWO-CU, box 3, folder 1.

8. President Wassily Popov and Secretary Daniel Kasustchik, Russian Section, IWO, "To all Russian Workers and Working 'Intelligentsia in America,'" n.d. [accompanying letter dated April 20, 1937], IWO-CU, box 25, folder 1. Minutes, American Russian Fraternal Society, April 3, 1937, ibid.

9. Excerpt, "From Minutes (February 27, 1937)," American Russian Fraternal Society, report from Kasustchik, IWO-CU, box 25, folder 1. For report on the Moscow purge trials in Slovak that accepted Trotskyist guilt, see "Osem sovietskych generálov obžalovaných a odsúdených na smrť pre zradu" [Eight Soviet Generals Indicted and Sentenced to Death for Treason], *New Yorkský denník*, June 13, 1937, 1. See "Statement by the International Communist Opposition. The Latest Events in the Soviet Union and Spain," June 25, 1937, for denunciation of Stalin's show trials and clampdown on dissent within the Soviet Union's Communist Party, box 41, folder 6, International Ladies Garment Workers Union, Charles S. Zimmerman Papers, 1919–1958, MSS 5780/014, Kheel Center for Labor-Management Documentation and Archives, Cornell University [hereafter cited as ILGWU-CU, MSS 5780/014]. Daniel Kasustchik report, "About Trotskyism," ARFS plenum, October 6 and 7, 1945, IWO-CU, box 25, folder 1.

10. "Digest of Testimony of Witnesses for the State in the I.W.O. Matter. January 29, 1951, to March 7, 1951," George Powers testimony, 27, 31, box 4, International

Workers Order Case Files, MSS 5940, Kheel Center for Labor-Management Documentation and Archives, Cornell University Library [hereafter cited as IWOCF-CU].

11. Poster, August 19 [1932], "Mass Protest Meeting. Open Fascist Dictatorship Threatens the German Workers!" CPUSA-LC, reel 230, delo 2968.

12. Max Bedacht, "In the Catacombs of Democracy," *Workers Monthly*, November 1924, 39–41, CPUSA-LC, reel 317, delo 4242.

13. Ibid.

14. Minutes, CPUSA Hungarian Bureau Central Committee meeting, January 8, 1934, CPUSA-LC, reel 273, delo 3489; Language Commission Central Committee to S. M. Loyen, April 5, 1933, CPUSA-LC, reel 247, delo 3172; Louis Adamic, *The Native's Return: An American Immigrant Visits Yugoslavia and Discovers His Old Country* (New York: Harper, 1934); John Enyeart, "Revolutionizing Cultural Pluralism: The Political Odyssey of Louis Adamic, 1932–1951," *Journal of American Ethnic History* 34, no. 3 (2015): 58–90.

15. Sadie Doroshkin to Louise Thompson, June 12, 1934, box 8, folder 8, Louise Thompson Patterson Papers, 1909–1999, MSS 869, Stuart A. Rose Manuscript, Archives, and Rare Book Library, Emory University [hereafter cited as LTP-EU]; Louise Thompson Patterson MS autobiography, chap. 7, "The Paris Conference and Spain," LTP-EU, box 20, folder 6; Interview with Louise Thompson Patterson [ca. 1950–1951], LTP-EU, box 27, folder 1; Louise Thompson Patterson, interview by Linda Burnham, March 9 and 11, 1988, LTP-EU, box 27, folder 12; Louise Thompson Patterson, interview by Louis Massiah for the W.E.B. Du Bois film project, 18, September 10, 1993, LTP-EU, box 28, folder 15. Thompson Patterson's FBI file cites an August 11, 1937, *Daily Worker* article, "Negro IWO Leader Sails for Paris Today to Attend Parley," on her attendance at the antifascism and antiracism conference: FBI, Freedom of Information Act (FOIA) file, Louise Thompson Patterson, New York, January 16, 1956, available at https://archive.org/details/LouiseThompsonPattersonFBIFile. Thanks to Ian Rocksborough-Smith for directing me to this source and to William Maxwell for making these files accessible.

16. "IWO Gives Generously to Heroic German Communists," *North Side Workers News* [shop paper], April 1, 1934, 5, CPUSA-LC, reel 283, delo 3650; Andy Hromiko of Tarentum, Pennsylvania, to "Dear Comrades," March 4, 1935, CPUSA-LC, reel 303, delo 3981.

17. Flyer, United Anti-Nazi Conference, June 29, 1935, the New School for Social Research, New York, CPUSA-LC, reel 300, delo 3939; News release, "Anti-Nazi Meeting to be Held Thursday Night in Madison Square Garden" [1935], ibid.; News release, "Anti-Nazis to Rally in Madison Square Garden on August 8th" [1935], ibid.; Flyer, *Anti-Nazi Federation of New York . . . March against the Nazis!* November 21, 1935, Madison Square rally, "For the Withdrawal of the United States from the Olympic Games Scheduled to Take Place in 1936 under Nazi Auspices!" CPUSA-LC, reel 300, delo 3938; News release, Ben Gold of the United Fur and Leather Workers Union petitions to allow Anti-Nazi People's Parade [1935], CPUSA-LC, reel 300, delo 3939; Waldo Frank to Mayor La Guardia, November 12, 1935, ibid. Pamphlet, *Keep the Saar Out of the Bloody Hands of Hitler Fascism!* [1934], CPUSA-LC, reel 288, delo 3722. In 1934 the Anti-Nazi Federation in New York ran a Saar Relief Warehouse for collection of food, clothing, and supplies for Nazi victims.

18. New release, "Luna Park Administration Refuses Use of Arena for Anti-Nazi Meeting," Anti-Nazi Federation of New York, August 18, 1935, CPUSA-LC, reel 300, delo 3939.

19. Victoria Wolcott, *Race, Riots, and Roller Coasters: The Struggle over Segregated Recreation in America* (Philadelphia: University of Pennsylvania Press, 2012), 58.

20. Proceedings, New York City Convention of IWO Branches, March 21–22, 1936, 8–9, "Resolution on Boycott of Nazi Goods" and "Resolution of Protest against the Murder of Victor Allan Barron, the Arrest of Luis Carlos Prestes and Threatened Deportation of Arthur Ewert by the Vargas Government of Brazil," CPUSA-LC, reel 305, delo 4050.

21. Ben Gold, president, Jewish Peoples Committee for United Action against Fascism and Anti-Semitism, to IWO, February 26, 1938, IWO-CU, box 37.1, folder 2; Program, "Louise Patterson Celebration, Sunday, September 16, 1984, New York City," LTP-EU, box 7, folder 6. The program book includes a photo of Thompson Patterson addressing the 1938 rally. Rubin Saltzman to Franklin Roosevelt, November 17, 1938, IWO-CU, box 29, folder 4.

22. Pamphlet, *The Seminar in Negro History*, 1938 spring lecture series, Harlem Community Center of IWO Solidarity Branch 691, LTP-EU, box 8, folder 9. In 1983 the Solidarity Branch also sponsored a lecture by Carter Woodson, founder of Negro History Week, indicating the link between civil rights activism and internationally minded anti-imperialism in the IWO. Palm card, April 10, 1938, IWO-CU, box 8, folder 9.

23. "The Sino-Japanese War and the Negro Question. Material for Discussion. Issued by the Organization Education Commission, Central Committee. February 3, 1938," box 7, folder 19, Matt N. and Evelyn Graves Crawford Papers, MSS 882, Stuart A. Rose Manuscript, Archives and Rare Book Library, Emory University [hereafter cited as CP-EU]. For Max Yergan's career with the NNC, see Erik Gellman, *Death Blow to Jim Crow: The National Negro Congress and the Rise of Militant Civil Rights* (Chapel Hill: University of North Carolina Press, 2012), 87, 155, 168, 171, 172, 177, 183, 192, 210.

24. "The Sino-Japanese War and the Negro Question."

25. Robeson Taj Frazier, *The East Is Black: Cold War China in the Black Radical Imagination* (Durham, NC: Duke University Press, 2015).

26. "The Sino-Japanese War and the Negro Question"; *The Seminar in Negro History*.

27. Poster, James Ford, Forum at Harlem Workers School, "The Communist Position on National Minorities," Sunday, January 13 [1935], CPUSA-LC, reel 299, delo 3905; Louise Thompson to Max Bedacht, June 4, 1934, LTP-EU, box 8, folder 8.

28. Luigi Candela to Earl Browder and Central Committee, CP, June 29, 1935, CPUSA-LC, reel 292, delo 3787. Zimmer notes that Italian anarchist communities in Paterson, New Jersey, and in New York and San Francisco also vocally opposed Mussolini's war in "Abyssinia" (*Immigrants against the State*, 121). "Control Tasks Approved at Recent District Plenum of District Four, CP" [August 18, 1935], CPUSA-LC, reel 294, delo 3826; Letter to "District #2 Organizer" [1935], CPUSA-LC, reel 294, delo 3816.

29. Rebecca Grecht to Polburo Central Committee, September 12, 1935, CPUSA-LC, reel 301, delo 3942; Minutes, District 2 Bureau meeting, CP, September 4, 1935, "Additional Report on IWO by Louise Thompson," CPUSA-LC, reel 294, delo 3811; James Ford, "Report on Harlem" to District 2 Bureau meeting, December 28, 1935, ibid.

30. "Harlem Quiet in African Crisis," *New York Sun*, July 18, 1935, LTP-EU, box 7, folder 3.

31. Thompson Patterson, "The Paris Conference and Spain," 6; "More Whites Than Negroes in Harlem Anti-War Parade," *New York World-Telegram*, August 3, 1935, LTP-EU, box 7, folder 3; Poster, "Mussolini Hurls a Burning Torch into the World!" Rally, Union Square, New York, September 7, 1935, CPUSA-LC, reel 299, delo 3906.

32. "A. W." [Alexander Wright] to "Dear Comrade," October 4, 1935, CPUSA-LC, reel 298, delo 3882. Paul Reid, American League against War and Fascism, to Communist

Party, USA, October 9, 1935, CPUSA-LC, reel 300, delo 3938. For other demonstrations, see *New York World-Telegram*, August 3, 1935, LTP-EU, box 7, folder 3. Robin Kelley, *Hammer and Hoe: Alabama Communists during the Great Depression* (Chapel Hill: University of North Carolina Press, 2015), 122–123; "Richmond Negroes Form Group to Aid Defense of Ethiopia," *Richmond Times-Dispatch*, August 27, 1935, CPUSA-LC, reel 298, delo 3883; Alexander Wright to "Dear Comrade Miller," August 27, 1935, CPUSA-LC, reel 293, delo 3882; Edward Dillon, "Harlem Drive upon Italians Stirs Disorder," *New York Daily News*, October 4, 1935, LTP-EU, box 7, folder 3; "The War Fever Strikes Harlem," *New York Daily News*, October 11, 1935, ibid.; "Harlem Quiet in African Crisis." Bill Moseley to "Comrade Brown," October 19, 1935, CPUSA-LC, reel 298, delo 3885; Flyer, *Boycott Italy, Not the Italian Storekeepers* [1935], ibid.; Clippings, "Police Caution about Boycott" and "Negroes Picket Italian Stores" [no papers named, ca. October 1935], ibid.

33. John Davis, *Let Us Build a National Negro Congress* (1936; repr., Washington, D.C.: National Sponsoring Committee, National Negro Congress, 1935), 27, box 1 folder 58, International Ladies Garment Workers Union, Charles S. Zimmerman Collection of Radical Pamphlets, 1914–1958, MSS 5780/178, Kheel Center for Labor-Management Documentation and Archives, Cornell University [hereafter cited as ILGWU-CU, 5780/178]. For the NNC's anticolonial activism, see Gellman, *Death Blow to Jim Crow*, 224–228, 233–234, 238–240, 249. FBI, FOIA file, Louise Thompson Patterson, Correlation Summary, July 19, 1955, includes report of FBI agent asking Thompson Patterson on November 30, 1953, about her presence at the founding convention of the NNC. The Correlation Summary also noted, "Mrs. Louise Patterson attended the National Convention of the National Negro Congress held in Detroit, Michigan, on May 30 to June 2, 1946, and was elected to the Executive Board of that organization." Chicago report, December 14, 1949, 16. See FBI report on Thompson Patterson, January 16, 1956, New York, for informants' reports on her activities on NNC's National Executive Board in 1941 and 1943, LTP-EU, box 11, folder 13. Paul Robeson, *The Negro People and the Soviet Union* (New York: New Century, January 1950), 4–6.

34. Pamphlet, *United Nations Front Line Rally*, IWO FLFF rally, Cleveland, Sunday, February 22, 1942, IWO-CU, box 22, folder 21. As an indication of the wartime acceptance of the IWO, Order vice president Kent shared the stage with Cleveland mayor Frank Lausche. IWO president William Weiner's message to General Board plenary session, February 7–8, 1942, IWO-CU, box 1, folder 9.

35. George Orwell, *Homage to Catalonia* (London: Penguin, 2003); Zimmer, *Immigrants against the State*, 168, 196–205.

36. Poster, "First Ethiopia and Now Spain! Support the Garibaldi Battalion!" [March 21, 1937 rally], ILGWU-CU, 5780/178, box 11, folder 2; Flyer, *Come to a Mass Meeting to Support American Boys of the Lincoln Brigade in Spain*, Friday, October 22, 1937, Stuyvesant High School, New York, box 45, Vito Marcantonio Papers, Manuscripts and Archives Division, The New York Public Library [hereafter cited as VM-NYPL].

37. Steve Nelson, James Barrett, and Rob Ruck, *Steve Nelson, American Radical* (Pittsburgh, PA: University of Pittsburgh Press, 1981), 183–239; Minutes, Czechoslovak Bureau meeting, May 9, 1934, CPUSA-LC, reel 273, delo 3502; Minutes, Slovak Gymnastic Union *Sokol* Women's Wreath 19, Philadelphia, April 4, 1937, Balch Institute for Ethnic Studies, Philadelphia [hereafter cited as Balch], Mss. 097; Affidavit, Gizella Chomucky, Philadelphia, April 24, 1951, IWOCF-CU, box 3; *Robotnícky kalendár na rok 1937*, 18–19, 58.

38. Flyer, *Unity—the Need of the Hour!* Communist Party of 10th Assembly District, New York, NY [1937], ILGWU-CU, 5780/178, box 5, folder 1; Jack Altman on arrest of Sam Baron, U.S. Socialist, in Spain, to "Dear Friends," November 8, 1937, ILGWU-CU, 5780/178, box 29, folder 7; Donna Haverty-Stacke, *Trotskyists on Trial: Free Speech and Political Persecution Since the Age of FDR* (New York: New York University Press, 2015); Orwell, *Homage to Catalonia*; Bryan Palmer, *Revolutionary Teamsters: The Minneapolis Trucker's Strike of 1934* (Chicago: Haymarket Books, 2013).

39. "Digest of Testimony of Witnesses for the State," George Powers testimony, 17, 27.

40. "Report of General Secretary Max Bedacht to national convention, IWO, April 23–30, 1938," 49, IWO-CU, box 3, folder 1; Translation from Polish, "The 13th Anniversary of the Polonia Society, IWO (Lecture prepared by the National Educational Division of the Polonia Society, IWO, to be used at meetings in October)," pencil marked "1945," IWO-CU, box 26, folder 3; "Resolution on Fascist Aggression," and Jerry Trauber, "Report on the Junior Section," IWO national convention, April 23–30, 1938, IWO-CU, box 3, folder 1.

41. Interview with Thompson Patterson [ca. 1950–1951]; Thompson Patterson, "The Paris Conference and Spain." Thompson Patterson's FBI, FOIA file cites an August 11, 1937, *Daily Worker* article, "Negro IWO Leader Sails for Paris Today to Attend Parley," on her attendance at the antifascism and antiracism conference. Robert Reid-Pharr, *Archives of Flesh* (New York: New York University Press, 2016), 42–71.

42. Louise Thompson, radio speech, Station EAR, Madrid, August 27, 1937, LTP-EU, box 13, folder 9.

43. Interview with Thompson Patterson [ca. 1950–1951]; Thompson, radio speech, Station EAR, Madrid. Walter Garland and Harry Haywood, radio speeches, LTP-EU, box 13, folder 9; Thompson Patterson, "The Paris Conference and Spain." Thompson Patterson's FBI, FOIA file, August 11, 1937, *Daily Worker* article, "Negro IWO Leader Sails for Paris."

44. Invitation, IWO Branch 691 [Solidarity Lodge, Harlem], reception dinner for Louise Thompson, reporting on her visit to Spain and the World Congress against Racialism and Anti-Semitism, October 20, 1937, LTP-EU, box 13, folder 9; Invitation, dinner for Thompson, December 1, 1937, at University of Chicago, ibid.; Nathan Shaffer, national executive committee, IWO, to Thompson, telegram, October 20, 1937, ibid.; Thompson Patterson, "The Paris Conference and Spain"; Thompson Patterson, interview by Burnham, March 9 and 11, 1988; Thompson Patterson, interview by Burnham, June 9 and 18, 1987; FBI, FOIA file on Louise Thompson Patterson, FBI report, Chicago, September 24, 1941, includes notation, "Among the miscellaneous papers in the file are throw-away circulars announcing a mass meeting entitled 'I Saw Spain' and listing Thompson as a speaker. The dates of these meetings were November 5, 1937, . . . Grand Rapids, Michigan, and November 2, 1937, . . . Chicago"; FBI report, Chicago, December 16, 1944. For African American soldiers fighting with the Abraham Lincoln Brigade, see Harry Haywood, *A Black Communist in the Freedom Struggle* (Minneapolis: University of Minnesota Press, 2012), 228–247.

45. Thyra Edwards to James Ford, January 26, 1938, LTP-EU, box 15, folder 29; Letter in German, from Deutsch-Amerikanisches Hilfskommittee for Spanish Relief, Professor Alfons Goldschmidt, to Max Bedacht, February 18, 1938, IWO-CU, box 3, folder 12; Harold Oram, Medical Bureau and North American Committee to Aid Spanish Democracy, to Max Bedacht, March 15, 1938, ibid.

46. Sántos Sánchez, president, Committee for Defense of Spanish Democracy, to Vito Marcantonio, telegram, January 6, 1939, VM-NYPL, box 47; M. Vargas Semprun,

Secretary of Propaganda, Comité pro Democracia Español, to Marcantonio, January 21, 1939, ibid. The FBI took note of Marcantonio's activities on behalf of Spain, too: FBI report, Vito Marcantonio, December 23, 1946, DB-WSU, box 7, folder 7-19. The Detroit Police Department's Literary Censorship Bureau made note of other IWO members' circulation of petitions urging the lifting of the embargo on Loyalist Spain: Report, Detroit Police, Literary Censorship Bureau, January 25, 1939, DB-WSU, box 2, folder 2-55. Report to the IWO GEB, plenary session, September 10–11, 1938, Brother Joseph Brodsky, General Counsel of the Order, IWO-CU, box 1, folder 5; Document, *Commonwealth of Massachusetts, International Workers Order v. Commissioner of Insurance*, March 6, 1939, IWO-CU, box 5, folder 12. Outline for Dave Greene speech, JPFO, Brooklyn, June 19, 1950, IWO-CU, box 4, folder 5.

47. Letters to Marcantonio: Eugenio Gavin, Comité pro Democracia Español, December 20, 1938, M. Vargas Semprun, January 21, 1939, Comité pro Democracia Español, June 2, 1939, and Marcantonio's reply letter, June 7, 1939, VM-NYPL, box 47; Poster, "Gran Festival organizado por el Comité pro Democracia Española (Afiliado a Sociedades Hispanas Confederadas)" [Grand Festival Organized by the Committee for Democracy in Spain (Affiliated with the Confederation of Hispanic Societies)], ibid. Ad, back cover, Spanish Refugee Relief Campaign, *Fraternal Outlook*, June 1939, IWO-CU, box 48; Dorothy Parker, "Spanish Refugees in France," *Fraternal Outlook*, July 1939, 6–7, 27, ibid.

48. Ellen Schrecker, *Many Are the Crimes: McCarthyism in America* (Princeton, NJ: Princeton University Press, 1998); Maurice Isserman, *Which Side Were You On? The American Communist Party during the Second World War* (Middletown, CT: Wesleyan University Press, 1982); Arthur Sabin, *Red Scare in Court: New York versus the International Workers Order* (Philadelphia: University of Pennsylvania Press, 1993); Thomas Walker, *Pluralistic Fraternity: The History of the International Workers Order* (New York: Garland, 1991). Charles Stevenson to Executive Committee and Members of Lodge 691, IWO, July 19, 1945, makes reference to editorials in *Fraternal Outlook* echoing the phrase, "The Yanks Are Not Coming," February 1940, 2 and 27, and May 1941, 25, IWO-CU, box 8, folder 4.

49. Isserman, *Which Side Were You On?* 55–82.

50. Louise Thompson report, "The Building of Our English-Speaking Section," IWO national convention, June 8–14, 1940, critiqued British rule of nonwhite peoples in India, the Caribbean, and Africa, IWO-CU, box 3, folder 2.

51. "To members of the Communist Party and Y.C.L. Only!" from "Comradely, A Group of Members of the Communist Party and the Young Communist League," September 1, 1939, ILGWU-CU, MSS 5780/014, box 41, folder 4; Report to Youth Conference, Helen Vrábel, executive secretary, SWS, at IWO national convention, June 8–14, 1940, IWO-CU, box 3, folder 3.

52. "To members of the Communist Party and Y.C.L. Only!"

53. Pamphlet quoted in Lucy Davidowitz, "The History of the Jewish People's Fraternal Order of the International Workers Order" [November 1950], TS, folder 8, International Workers Order Records, Robert F. Wagner Labor Archives, Tamiment Library, New York University [hereafter cited as IWO-NYU].

54. Ibid.

55. Ibid.

56. Questionnaires sent to IWO national office, Albert Steinberg, Denver, April 16, 1941, Sylvia Linna, the Bronx, April 14, 1941, and A. Prisiaznuk, Edwardsville, Pennsylvania, April 24, 1941, IWO-CU, box 18, folder 13.

57. Minutes, fifth annual convention, IWO New Jersey district, November 30–December 1, 1940, 2–3, "A Special Problem" by Brother Landy, IWO-CU, box 8, folder 3.

58. Charles Stevenson to Executive Committee and Members of Lodge 691, IWO, July 19, 1945, and Stevenson to Max Bedacht, June 11, 1945, IWO-CU, box 8, folder 4; "To the Officers and Members of Solidarity Lodge 691—Charges against Brother Charles A. Stevenson by Brother Samuel G. Patterson," [1945], ibid. Stevenson, "To the Board of Trustees, I.W.O. The following is the summary of my appeal from the decision of the Executive Committee of Lodge #691," [1945], ibid.; Beryle Banfield, president, and Maude Jett, financial secretary, "To the Members of Lodge 691, IWO," July 25, 1945, ibid.

59. "Urges People to Keep America Out of War," *Milwaukee Journal*, November 23, 1939, 17; Detroit Police, Office of Special Investigation Squad, report, Rally for "Peace and Civil Rights," December 2, 1939, DB-WSU, box 2, folder 2-55.

60. Thompson, "The Building of Our English-Speaking Section."

61. Central Committee CPUSA to all district language departments of Central Committee regarding foreign-language newspapers publicizing need for Indian and Filipino independence [1930], CPUSA-LC, reel 154, delo 2018; Resolutions on Cuba, Anti-Imperialist League, to IWO language federations and resolutions on Cuba, July 17, 1933, and October 24, 1933, CPUSA-LC, reel 247, delo 3170; Reginald Bridgeman to William Patterson, June 16, 1934, CPUSA-LC, reel 287, delo 3698; Gellman, *Death Blow to Jim Crow*, 224–228, 233–234, 238–240, 249; Davis, *Let Us Build a National Negro Congress*. As early as 1919 an FBI agent was reporting that Boleslaw Gebert, "Bolsheviki agent," was making speeches in Youngstown, Ohio, denouncing the continued British rule over "three hundred million of Hindus" in India and British control of Egypt as giving the lie to claims that the Allies had fought for democracy in World War I: FBI report, Arthur Barkey to G. Oliver Frick, July 25, 1919, DB-WSU, box 4, folder 4-22.

62. Louise Thompson Patterson, interview by Mary Lecht [ca. 1980s], LTP-EU, box 28, folder 16.

63. Helen Vrábel report to Youth Conference, IWO national convention, June 8–14, 1940, IWO-CU, box 3, folder 3. On British-Soviet diplomacy in 1938–1939, see Michael Jabara Carley, "End of the 'Low, Dishonest Decade': Failure of the Anglo-Franco-Soviet Alliance in 1939," *Europe-Asia Studies* 45, no. 2 (1993): 303–341; Hugh Ragsdale, "The Munich Crisis and the Issue of Red Army Transit across Romania," *Russian Review* 57, no. 4 (October 1998): 614–617.

64. Report of General Secretary to IWO GEB, February 22–23, 1941, New York City, 1–6, IWO-CU, box 2, folder 5; Report, Max Bedacht for IWO GEB, Winter 1941, IWO-CU, box 2, folder 4.

65. Herbert Benjamin, executive secretary, report, "Americans, Immigrants All Want Peace," IWO Conference on National Groups, April 6, 1941, IWO-CU, box 5, folder 9.

66. OSS/FNB report to Director of Strategic Services, "Communist-Line IWO Reorganizes to Emphasize Nationality," July 11, 1944, DB-WSU, box 4, folder 4-29; "For the Sake of Clarity—A Workmen's Circle Answer to the IWO from *The Call*, April 1940," 12, IWO-NYU, folder 8.

67. State senator Stanley Nowak's Polish speech, Radio Station WJBK, TS, Sunday, June 29, 1941, NP-WSU, box 3, folder 3-7; Nowak radio address, August 24, 1941, NP-WSU, box 3, folder 3-8.

68. "Speaker's Guide on the Soviet-Nazi War," National Education Department, IWO, July 18, 1941, IWO-CU, box 22, folder 20.

69. FBI report, IWO, Detroit division, December 31, 1946, DB-WSU, box 16, folder 16-37; SWS, "Excerpts from Report by Helen Vrábel" [1941 or 1942], IWO-NYU, folder 42; "Remarks of Brother Herbert Benjamin in discussion of the Resolution Meeting of the General Executive Board, IWO, September 6, 1941," IWO-CU, box 2, folder 5.

70. C. Oumansky, Embassy of the USSR, to B. Ricchebuono of "La Progressiva" Lodge, IWO, New York, August 8, 1941, IWO-CU, box 10, folder 8; Eldred Kuppinger, acting assistant chief, Division of Controls, Department of State, to Joseph Brodsky, August 15, 1941, IWO-CU, box 16, folder 26; Pamphlet, IWO FLFF, *We Gave Aid and Comfort* [October 1, 1941–January 31, 1942], IWO-CU, box 5, folder 8; Max Bedacht, general secretary, report to GEB, February 7–8, 1942, 1, 4, 7, IWO-CU, box 2, folder 6; Pamphlet, *The Story of the Front Line Fighters Fund*, and poster, "Help Them Save Freedom," IWO-CU, box 16, folder 26.

71. Flyer, *Paul Robeson Sings for IWO Day*, Civilian and National Defense Exposition, New York, Sunday, October 12, 1941, IWO-CU, box 49; Booklet, *Air Raid Blackouts First Aid: A Handbook for Civilians in Wartime*, introduction by John Middleton, IWO Director of Civilian Defense, IWO-CU, box 16, folder 6; John Middleton to Henry Mitchell, U.S. Civil Service Commission, November 5, 1941, IWO-CU, box 4, folder 1.

72. Bedacht, report to GEB; Report to GEB, "On the Progress of the Order during the Year 1942," February 26–27, 1943, 7, IWO-CU, box 2, folder 8. Affidavit, Milton Schiff, Los Angeles, April 24, 1951, IWOCF-CU, box 3.

73. *The Story of the Front Line Fighters Fund*; Leaflet, *Give Them Aid and Comfort, Solidarity Gifts for Soldiers Battling Hitlerism*, IWO-CU, box 16, folder 27; "Help Them Save Freedom." Unit of Czechoslovak Army in the USSR to IWO, telegram, November 21, 1942, thanking the Order for FLFF gift of 250,000 cigarettes, IWO-CU, box 16, folder 28; Letter "from a Major of the British Home Forces, to Women's Clubs of IWO," November 10, 1942, "appreciation of gift," IWO-CU, box 26, folder 10. Pamphlet, *United Nations Front Line Rally*, for rally in Cleveland, Sunday, February 22, 1942, in which IWO officials shared the dais with Cleveland mayor Frank Lausche at a fund-raising event, IWO-CU, box 22, folder 21.

74. Flyer, *Ambassador Maxim Litvinoff Declares Tank Campaign Has Full Approval of Soviet Government*, IWO-CU, box 29, folder 5; "Honor Certificate for Gifts to the Red Army," IWO-CU, box 16, folder 26; Ticket, "Celebration of the 80th Birthday of our sister Sarah Zaks, July 23, 1942" [Los Angeles], IWO-CU, box 38.1, folder 3; Flyer, *Tanks for the Red Army, Death to the Nazis*, meeting, September 6, 1942, Oakland, California, IWO-CU, box 45.1, folder 9.

75. Pamphlet, *A Crime against Jewish Unity—The Jewish Labor Committee Owes the Jewish Public an Explanation*, by Rubin Saltzman, National Secretary, Jewish American Section, IWO, IWO-CU, box 22, folder 23; FBI report, IWO, Detroit division, December 31, 1946, contains an informant's report that in November 1942 he had "obtained" three copies of the "throwaway" regarding the IWO Jewish Section's campaign to raise funds for ten Soviet tanks.

76. Flyer, *He fights for you—put him first on your Xmas List!* IWO-CU, box 16, folder 26.

77. Max Bedacht, "Radość Dnia Dziękczynienia Należy do Naszych Dielnych Bojowników" [The Joy of Thanksgiving Belongs to Our Brave Warriors], *Glos Ludowy*, November 25, 1944, 6, DB-WSU, box 5, folder 5-29; Pamphlet, FLFF, *United Nations Front Line Rally*, for rally in Cleveland, Sunday, February 22, 1942, IWO-CU, box 22, folder 21; Matthew Frye Jacobson, *Whiteness of a Different Color: European Immigrants and the Alchemy of Race* (Cambridge, MA: Harvard University Press, 1998). Letters of

gratitude, including thanks for shipment of the book *Russians Don't Surrender*, were sent to IWO headquarters from servicemen stationed in Europe, the Pacific, and stateside: John Vasilenko, Army Air Corps, to "Dear Sir," August 8, 1944, IWO-CU, box 9, folder 5; Sgt. Leo Spivack, New Guinea, 122nd Naval Construction Battalion, to IWO, "Dear Brothers and Sisters," May 21, 1944, IWO-CU, box 16, folder 27; Philip Shankman to "Dear Friends," November 15, 1944, ibid; Pvt. Carl Lieber, "Southern France," to Max Bedacht, postcard, November 24, 1944, ibid.; Cpl. Sol Gorelick, San Francisco, to John Middleton, October 7, 1944, ibid.

78. Peter Shipka to Dave Greene, January 22, 1951, IWO-CU, box 23, folder 1; Abraham Freeman of Boston to Alfred Bohlinger, Superintendent of Insurance, New York State, February 22, 1951, IWO-CU, box 23, folder 4; Greene to Mary Samsonick of Endicott, New York, November 6, 1947, IWO-CU, box 4, folder 4; IWO flyer in Slovak, *Pomôžte Bojovať za Slobodu tým, že Budete Šetriť Peniaze* [Help the Fight for Freedom, Buy War Bonds], IWO-CU, box 15, folder 3; Affidavits, Dora Friedkas, the Bronx, April 24, 1951, Lewis Marks, Boston, April 21, 1951, Jacob Balan, Highland Park, Michigan, April 23, 1951, Eugenia Czuprenski, Detroit, April 23, 1951, and Sebastian Bucola, Pittsburgh, April 1951, IWOCF-CU, box 3; "Office of War Information Reprimands Philip A. Hrobak, Editor of 'Jednota,'" *Národné noviny*, October 25, 1944, 5. Report of Vrábel to Bedacht on activities of the SWS, September 1943 and May 1944, 3, IWO-CU, box 15, folder 3. News release, "IWO Challenges Constitutionality of Attorney General Clark's Report; Plans Legal Action," December 27, 1947, noted that among millions of pieces of civilian defense literature issued by the IWO, the Order had issued two hundred thousand regulation air raid posters translated into thirteen languages, IWO-NYU, folder 31.

79. Memorandum for FBI file, March 25, 1943, on the December 7, 1942, All-Slav Blood Donors' Parade, DB-WSU, box 16, folder 16-36.

80. Honor rolls, Slovak and Croatian members of the IWO who were killed during World War II, IWO-CU, box 19, folder 5; Shipka to Greene, January 22, 1951; Greene to Samsonick, November 6, 1947; Pamphlet, *An Indictment: The People vs. Attorney General Tom Clark Before the Court of Public Opinion* [1947 or 1948], IWO-CU, box 4, folder 4.

81. Affidavits, Dora Friedkas, the Bronx, April 24, 1951, Rubin Cravetz, Philadelphia, April 23, 1951, and Alexander Smoley, New York, April 25, 1951, IWOCF-CU, box 3.

82. "Memoranda re: Dale Zysman, the New York Teachers Union, Charles Hendley, president, January 15, 1942," VM-NYPL, box 47; Vito Marcantonio to Albert Bonaschi and James McDonald, Trial Committee of the New York Board of Education, December 22, 1941, ibid.; Marcantonio to Secretary of Navy Frank Knox, January 16 and 21, and February 6, 1942, and Hendley to Knox, January 13, 1942, ibid.; "Facts in the Case of Mr. Zysman, ibid."; "Teacher Fired as Red Turns Up in the Navy," *New York Mirror*, January 10, 1942; "True to Form," *New York Teacher News*, editorial, January 13, 1942; Mr. and Mrs. David Liebler of Brooklyn to Knox, January 14, 1942, and Zysman to Marcantonio, February 11, 1942, VM-NYPL, box 47; Letter of appeal, Zysman to Knox, February 11, 1942, ibid.; "Resolution on Dale Zysman," IWO GEB meeting, February 8, 1942, IWO-CU, box 1, folder 9. Clarence Taylor, *Reds at the Blackboard: Communism, Civil Rights, and the New York City Teachers Union* (New York: Columbia University Press, 2011), 42, 223.

83. Rockwell Kent to Marcantonio, October 28, November 13, and December 14, 1942, Gordon Kent to Rockwell Kent, n.d., Marcantonio to Rockwell Kent, November

10, and December 23, 1942, Rockwell Kent to Senator Claude Pepper, December 13, 1942, Corporal Aaron Bindman to Marcantonio, November 13, 1942, Ann Ruth Yasgur to Marcantonio, June 4, 1943, W. A Stafford to Marcantonio, March 10, 1943, Sam Kovnat to Marcantonio, January 2, 1943, and Corporal Milton Wolff to Marcantonio, January 10, 1944, VM-NYPL, box 47; "Memorandum, Case of Technical Sergeant John Gates," ibid.; Gates to Marcantonio, January 7, and February 3, 1943, ibid. Middleton to Mitchell, November 5, 1941, and Mitchell to Middleton, November 21, 1941, IWO-CU, box 4, folder 1.

84. OSS report, ASC, May 2, 1942, DB-WSU, box 1, folder 1-22; Minutes, IWO GEB meeting, June 27, 1942, IWO-CU, box 1, folder 9; *Fraternal Outlook*, September 1942, 8, IWO-CU, box 48; FBI report, Polonia Society, IWO, August 7, 1942, DB-WSU, box 16, folder 16-36. Davidowitz, "History of the Jewish People's Fraternal Order,", 7, notes that the *Fraternal Outlook* in 1942 carried a streamer, "Open the Second Front," in almost every issue. Stanley Nowak radio addresses, July 25, August 2, August 23, 1942, NP-WSU, box 3, folder 3-9; Nowak radio address, August 10, 1942, NP-WSU, box 3, folder 3-10.

85. OSS/FNB report, "FOUR FREEDOMS RALLY," September 7, 1943, DB-WSU, box 5, folder 5-30.

86. Leaflet, *Opening of a Second Front Now Is Imperative*, National Committee, Russian-American Section, IWO, IWO-CU, box 13, folder 3.

87. FBI report, Polonia Society, IWO, August 7, 1942.

88. IWO "Win the War Statement" [1942], DB-WSU, box 5, folder 5-30; American-Russian Section IWO, Central Executive Committee report [1944], IWO-CU, box 25, folder 1; "Report on Work for Victory to the G.E.B. Plenary Meeting, November 6, 1942, by Max Bedacht, General Secretary," IWO-CU, box 2, folder 7; Resolutions for Action adopted by the IWO GEB, September 25–26, 1943, IWO-CU, box 2, folder 9.

89. Minutes, IWO GEB, plenary session meeting, February 8, 1942, IWO-CU, box 1, folder 9; Cpl. Gorelick to Middleton, and Sgt. Spivack to IWO, "Dear Brothers and Sisters." "Moral Lepers Like Hearst Peril Nation," *Národné noviny*, May 15, 1944, 5.

90. Matej Mráz, "Slovanský Kongres po srdcí všetkým len Hitleristom nie" [Slav Congress Heartily for Everything that Hitler Isn't], *Národné noviny*, May 6, 1942, 4; Ad, "70,000 members of the IWO," from ASC conference book, Detroit, April 1942, DB-WSU, box 5, folder 5-29.

91. "Slavs Indorse 4th Term—Plan National Congress," *Národné noviny*, June 7, 1944, 5. For prosecution of Socialist Workers Party members under the Smith Act, see Haverty-Stacke, *Trotskyists on Trial*.

92. "Communist-Line IWO Reorganizes to Emphasize Nationality." Earl Browder, *Teheran, Our Path in War and Peace* (New York: Workers Library, 1944).

93. "Communist-Line IWO Reorganizes to Emphasize Nationality"; OSS/FNB report, "Solidarity Rally" in New York sponsored by the Polish-American Section of the IWO, May 14, 1943, DB-WSU, box 5, folder 5-37; OSS/FNB report, "A Pro-Soviet Polish-American Rally" of the ASC at which Krzycki as well as IWO officials spoke in favor of a Polish-Soviet pact of friendship, March 3, 1944, DB-WSU, box 6, folder 6-24.

94. OSS/FNB report, "BUTTS 899," January 6, 1945, "Views and Actions of Leftwing IWO Leaders and Editors," "Vive Le Russe," DB-WSU, box 4, folder 4-29; OSS/FNB report, The Polish American Left, June 16, 1944, DB-WSU, box 2, folder 2-53.

95. Edward Falkowski, "What's Behind the Battle over Borders? The Truth about Polish Reactionaries," *Fraternal Outlook*, March 1944, 12–13, 30, IWO-CU, box 48. For defenses of Tito's partisans in Yugoslavia, see Lila Slocum, "Truth about Yugoslavia;

Americans of South Slavic Origins Combat Fifth Column," *Fraternal Outlook*, March 1944, 20–22, 29, ibid.; Peter Vukcevich, for the National Committee Serbian-American Section, IWO, and Nicholas Rajkovich, for the National Committee Croatian-American Section, IWO, to Spiros Skouras, President, 20th Century-Fox Film Corp., February 24, 1943, IWO-CU, box 13, folder 4; Ellen Davidson, organizer, Screen Office and Professional Employees Guild, to Leo Bacich, IWO, February 23, 1943, IWO-CU, box 13, folder 10. On conservative Poles' opposition to U.S. support for the Curzon boundary readjustment, see Robert Szymczak, "Uneasy Observers: The OSS Foreign Nationalities Branch and Perceptions of Polish Nationalism in the United States during World War II," *Polish American Studies* 56, no. 1 (Spring 1999): 7–73; Peter Irons, "'The Test Is Poland': Polish Americans and the Origins of the Cold War," *Polish American Studies* 30, no. 2 (Autumn 1973): 5–63. For Yugoslav Americans and the controversy between support for Tito or the Chetniks, see Enyeart, "Revolutionizing Cultural Pluralism."

96. Wendell Willkie, "We Must Work with Russia—Willkie," *New York Times Magazine*, January 17, 1943, box 43, Butler Library, Rare Books and Manuscripts Division, Max Nomad Collection, Columbia University [hereafter cited as MN-CU]; C. L. Sulzberger, "What the Russians Want—and Why; An Appraisal of Their Needs and Aims in the Light of the Nation's War Experiences," *New York Times Magazine*, June 10, 1945, 5, ibid. Slovak newspaper readers also learned that Secretary of State Edward Stettinius criticized Republican "defeatists" for carping on the terms of the Yalta agreement: Art Shields, "State Dept. Rebuffs Taft's Incitement on Poland," *Národné noviny*, April 11, 1945, 5.

97. "OSS/FNB Confidential," "Report #102, March 31, 1945," contains "excerpts from the report by Max Bedacht, . . . March 24–25, 1945," DB-WSU, box 4, folder 4-29; Report, "Our Ukrainian Society," IWO General Council meeting, March 16–17, 1946, IWO-NYU, folder 13.

98. Robert Szymczak, *From Popular Front to Communist Front: The American Slav Congress in War and Cold War, 1941–1951* (dissertation, Lancaster University, 2006); Szymczak, "Uneasy Observers." Debra Allen, "An Unacknowledged Consensus: Polish American Views about the Oder-Niesse Line during the Truman Administration," *Polish American Studies* 57, no. 1 (Spring 2000): 73–83; Confidential letter, J. Edgar Hoover to Frederick Lyon, chief, Division of Foreign Activity Correlation, Department of State, May 21, 1945, DB-WSU, box 4, folder 4-19.

99. Davidowitz, "History of the Jewish People's Fraternal Order," 4, citing Irving Freed, "A Road to Peace and Freedom," *Jewish Fraternalist*, December 1945, 11; Report, S. Cheifetz of Chicago to annual convention, JPFO, December 23, 1945, IWO-CU, box 27.1, folder 3.

100. Pamphlet, *Five Things You Can Do to Win the Peace*, Win the Peace Conference [1946], IWO-CU, box 46; "Declaration of Principles" of the Win the Peace Conference, April 6, 1946, resolutions on Latin America, Puerto Rico, the Philippines, Indonesia, India, and Africa, IWO-CU, box 22, folder 24.

101. George Pirinsky, *Slavic Americans in the Fight for Victory and Peace* (New York: American Slav Congress, 1946), 29–30, 44; Louis Adamic, "Conspiracy against Peace," *Slavic American*, Winter 1947, 5–6, 52; George Pirinsky, "What a New World War Would Mean and How Slavic Americans Can Help Prevent It," *Slavic American*, Spring–Summer 1948, 21–22; *Ľudový kalendár na rok 1947*.

102. FBI report on Stanley Nowak, March 5, 1951, DB-WSU, box 16, folder 16-36; Treasurer Peter Shipka, "Report of the Officers Presented to the General Council, IWO, February 3 and 4, 1951," IWO-NYU, folder 18; "The Issue in Indo-China," *Jewish Life*,

June 1954, 3, IWO-CU, box 53; FBI report, Nowak [1954] mentions a June 11, 1954, meeting at which the subject "Indo-China's fight for its independence" was addressed by Thomas Dombrowski, DB-WSU, box 7, folder 7-55.

103. Dayo Gore, *Radicalism at the Crossroads: African American Women Activists in the Cold War* (New York: New York University Press, 2011); Press release, Louise Patterson for Sojourners for Truth and Justice, and Hilda Freedman, Emma Lazarus Federation, to UNESCO, July 8, 1952, on racism and oppression against black women, LTP-EU, box 13, folder 2; Resolution on South Africa from the CAA to Conference of the Sojourners for Truth and Justice, March 23, 1952, LTP-EU, box 13, folder 4; Sojourners for Truth and Justice, Charlotta Bass and Louise Thompson Patterson, to Ray Alexander, Johannesburg, South Africa, and Bass to South African Delegation to the United Nations, both April 5, 1952, and Bertha Mkize, Durban, Natal, South Africa, to "Dear Friends" [Sojourners for Truth and Justice], April 20, 1952, ibid.; Flyer with petition, CAA, *Racism Threatens Us in South Africa as Here* [1952], LTP-EU, box 13, folder 37; Page "1950s" from book, *Salute to Paul Robeson, A Cultural Celebration of His 75th Birthday*, references his article in March 1954 *Freedom*, LTP-EU, box 11, folder 15; Paul Robeson, *The Negro People and the Soviet Union*, LTP-EU, box 11, folder 13.

104. "Sec. of Commerce Wallace Hits Those Talking of Soviet War," *Národné noviny*, June 13, 1945, 5; "Welles Says British Back Germany as Anti-Soviet Buffer," *Národné noviny*, August 1, 1945, 5, citing Sumner Welles's column in *New York Herald Tribune*, July 18, 1945; "Kartelisti chcú vyvolať vojnu proti Sovietskemu sväzu, hovorí orgán unie" [Monopolists Want to Wage a New War against the Soviets, Says Union Newspaper], *Národné noviny*, August 15, 1945, 1; "Churchill znova straší červeným súknom" [Churchill Warns of Red Menace] *Národné noviny*, September 12, 1945, 2. See *Národné noviny*, September 12, 1945, 2, for coverage of the Philadelphia memorial.

105. Minutes, General Council meeting, March 16–17, 1946, IWO-NYU, folder 13; Report by Bedacht to General Council and "Resolution on People's Peace Movement" passed at same meeting.

106. "From: Organization Circular for November 1947," Polonia Society, IWO-CU, box 26, folder 3; Call to 10th American Slav Congress of Michigan conference, May 27, 1951, NP-WSU, box 4, folder 4-2. FBI file on Stanley Nowak, May 1, 1952, including accounts of IWO and ASC peace activities in 1951 against rearming West Germany and against the Korean War, DB-WSU, box 7, folder 7-49; FBI report, March 5, 1951, on Nowak speaking at a meeting of the Polonia Society; American Slav Congress to President Truman, telegram, October 7, 1948, DB-WSU, box 1, folder 1-18.

107. "Nazis in Bavaria Regaining Position," *New York Times*, April 24, 1946, 3, MN-CU, box 17; Tania Long, "Munich University Hotbed of Nazism," *New York Times*, April 23, 1946, 8, ibid.; "Comeback of German Cartels—Why Soviets Hate Us," *New York Post*, September 2, 1948, 8, MN-CU, box 14; "Negotiate a German Settlement!" *Daily Worker*, editorial, July 19, 1948, MN-CU, box 15; "Can Russia's Army Be Beaten? A German Military Expert Answers; German Soldier 'Could Stop' Invader . . . Mobile Units Essential . . . Decisive Battle Is Still Fought on Soil," *U.S. News and World Report*, September 8, 1950, 24–26, MN-CU, box 43; "Open Air Mass Meeting, March 26, 1952, No Peace with Hitler's Heirs!" and pamphlet from the United Jewish People's Order, Toronto, *No Truck with Hitler's Heirs! Who Is the Adenauer Regime?* [1952], IWO-CU, box 43, folder 10.

108. Minutes, SWS national board meeting, March 23, 1947, IWO-CU, box 54; Organization letter, Polonia Society, October 1948, IWO-CU, box 26, folder 3; Sam Milgrom to "Dear Brother," May 13, 1947, and June 25, 1947, on conference of American

Council for a Democratic Greece, IWO-CU, box 4, folder 2; "Statement of National Executive Committee Jewish People Fraternal Order" [1947], IWO-CU, box 32, folder 66.

109. News release, "Hellenic American Brotherhood, IWO, Condemns Execution of Greek Patriots," May 7, 1948, IWO-NYU, folder 20.

110. HUAC report on ASC, 63, https://archive.org/details/reportonamerican00unit; "The Truman Doctrine," *Slavic American*, Summer 1948, 36, citing *New York Post* editorial, February 18, 1948.

111. Minutes, IWO General Council meeting, September 7–8, 1946, "Resolution on Quisling Immigration," IWO-NYU, folder 14.

112. Executive Secretary Sam Milgrom, "Report to General Council IWO, March 1, 1947," IWO-NYU, folder 17; "Jews? No! Nazis? Yes!" *The Patriot*, October 26, 1947, newsletter of JPFO Haym Solomon Lodge, Philadelphia, IWO-CU, box 32, folder 66.

113. Rachel Buff, "The Deportation Terror," *American Quarterly* 60, no. 3 (2008): 523–551; Flyer, *Should Miss Liberty Be Deported? The Case of Peter Harisiades* [1950], VM-NYPL, box 46; FBI report, IWO, Detroit division, November 20, 1953, cites *Glos Ludowy*, October 27, 1947, 12, "Podolski's Letter to the Executive Committee of the Polonia Society" on deportation of Polonia Society leader Henry Podolski, and *Romanul American*, July 19, 1947, newspaper of the Romanian-American Fraternal Society, IWO, denouncing the attempted deportation of Greek IWO leader Harisiades, DB-WSU, box 16, folder 16-38; "Jews? No! Nazis? Yes!"

114. HUAC report, ASC, 63, cites *Národná Volya*, January 14, 1949; "Slav Congress Scores Entry of Refugees; Says Law Only Allows 'Scum' to Enter," *Pittsburgh Press*, June 20, 1948; S. Cheifetz, secretary, Chicago JPFO, to Sam Milgrom, December 21, 1949, IWO-CU, box 5, folder 4.

115. Shipka, "Report of the Officers Presented to the General Council, IWO."

116. Davidowitz, "History of the Jewish People's Fraternal Order," citing Rubin Saltzman, "We Saw Them Build for Peace: IWO Vice-President Describes His Visit to the New Democracies of Europe," *Fraternal Outlook*, May 1948, 23; Frank Kofsky, *Harry S Truman and the War Scare of 1948: A Successful Campaign to Deceive the Nation* (New York: St. Martin's, 1995); Gabriel Kolko and Joyce Kolko, *The Limits of Power: The World and United States Foreign Policy, 1945–1954* (New York: Harper and Row, 1972). Flyer, *Truman's Fake Crisis*, issued by CP of New York County, box 1, folder 37, International Ladies Garment Workers Union Broadside Collection, 1907–1980, MSS 5780/109, Kheel Center for Labor-Management Documentation and Archives, Cornell University.

117. George Pirinsky, "The North Atlantic Pact—Defense against Aggression or Path to a New World War," *Slavic American*, Winter 1949, 6–7, 25; *The Struggle against the North Atlantic War Alliance*, State Educational Department, CP of California, May 1, 1949, CP-EU, box 7, folder 30.

118. Rockwell Kent in Stockholm to Editor-in-Chief, *Tass*, Moscow, March 18, 1950, Kent in Stockholm to Sam Milgrom, March 18, 1950, Kent to Milgrom, March 29, 1950, Kent to Milgrom, April 17, 1950, and Milgrom to Kent, June 20, 1950, IWO-CU, box 3, folder 10; Letter from Kent, "for use of International Workers Order" [1950], ibid. Invitation/ticket, "Welcome Home to I.W.O. President Rockwell Kent and J.P.F.O. President Albert Kahn on the occasion of their return from their peace mission in Paris Stockholm Moscow. April 12, 1950," IWO-CU, box 26, folder 10. Outline for speech by Dave Greene of the JPFO, Brooklyn, June 19, 1950, IWO-CU, box 4, folder 5. Polonia Society organizational bulletins, June and July 1950, IWO-CU, box 26, folder 5. Davidowitz, "History of the Jewish People's Fraternal Order," citing the IWO's resolution to "affirm the . . .

Stockholm Peace Pledge, calling for the outlawing of the atom bomb and the branding of any government that would first resort to its use as a war criminal, as our sentiment, and as voicing our aspiration for peace," *Fraternal Outlook*, June–July 1950.

119. Marian Mollin, *Radical Pacifism in Modern America: Egalitarianism and Protest* (Philadelphia: University of Pennsylvania Press, 2006); News release of letter, "From 'The Bulletin,' published by the Parents Association of P.S. 19, Manhattan, located at 344 E. 14th St.—issue of March 15, 1950," IWO-CU, box 40, folder 9. Letter from Edward Stephens, 337 E. 13th St., February 27, 1950.

CHAPTER 6

1. Arthur Sabin, *Red Scare in Court: New York versus the International Workers Order* (Philadelphia: University of Pennsylvania Press, 1993), 36, 51, 61; David Caute, *The Great Fear: The Anti-Communist Purge Under Truman and Eisenhower* (New York: Simon and Schuster, 1978); Ellen Schrecker, *Many Are the Crimes: McCarthyism in America* (Princeton, NJ: Princeton University Press, 1998); Alan Barth, *The Loyalty of Free Men* (New York: Viking Press, 1951); Robert Justin Goldstein, *American Blacklist: The Attorney General's List of Subversive Organizations* (Lawrence: University Press of Kansas, 2008). The Attorney General's List of Subversive Organizations, as published in *Federal Register* 13 on March 20, 1948, contained hundreds of organizations, many with Slavic interests and membership.

2. Rockwell Kent, Sam Milgrom, and Peter Shipka to "Brothers and Sisters" [December 1947], folder 6, International Workers Order Records, Robert F. Wagner Labor Archives, Tamiment Library, New York University [hereafter cited as IWO-NYU]; Minutes, Executive Committee meeting, December 8, 1947, "Action re: Clark's attack," box 1, folder 13, International Workers Order Records, 1915–2002, MSS 5276, Kheel Center for Labor-Management Documentation and Archives, Cornell University [hereafter cited as IWO-CU]. News release, "IWO Challenges Constitutionality of Attorney General Clark's Report; Plans Legal Action," December 5, 1947, IWO-NYU, folder 31.

3. FBI report, IWO, Detroit division, "Reaction to Subversive Listing," November 20, 1953, 18 and 19, *Romanul American*, January 3 and 10, 1948, and *Glos Ludowy*, June 30, 1948, box 16, folder 16-38, Don Binkowski Papers, Walter P. Reuther Library, Wayne State University [hereafter cited as DB-WSU]. Sam Milgrom to "Brother [Charles] Korenič" of the SWS, December 16, 1947, IWO-CU, box 5, folder 1. Similar letters went out to other ethnic lodge leaders. *Congressional Record*, remarks of Congressman Vito Marcantonio, December 17, 1947, IWO-CU, box 5, folder 2. For opposition to Marcantonio, see "They Couldn't Purge Vito," *Saturday Evening Post*, January 11, 1947, vol. 219, no. 28, 17; Louis Francis Budenz, "IWO—Red Bulwark: The Inside Story of an Outfit That Works Hand in Glove with the Communist Party and Which Now Faces a Crackdown That Is Long Overdue," March 1951, reprint, *American Legion Magazine*, box 3, International Workers Order Case Files, MSS 5940, Kheel Center for Labor-Management Documentation and Archives, Cornell University Library [hereafter cited as IWOCF-CU]. For a denunciation of the IWO's designation, New York Councilman Stanley Isaacs to Attorney General Tom Clark, January 6, 1948, IWO-NYU, folder 31.

4. N. Gish of Brooklyn to "Dear Brother Dave Greene," December 6, 1947, and Greene to Gish, December 8, 1947, IWO-CU, box 4, folder 4. Members resigned within days of issuance of the Attorney General's List. Greene sent letters to IWO members such as a trade union leader and a physician, both of the Bronx, urging them to reconsider: Greene to Nathan Reiser and Greene to Dr. Louis Roberts, both December 30, 1947, ibid.

5. Joseph Naretto of New Kensington, Pennsylvania, to "Dear Brother Secretary" of the Garibaldi Society, December 29, 1947, and Vito Magli to Naretto, n.d., IWO-CU, box 25, folder 5.

6. Letter and petition, M. Rosenblatt, corresponding secretary, Branch 2360, JPFO, to Attorney General Tom Clark, February 7, 1948, IWO-CU, box 17, folder 15.

7. "Notes and Materials for Speakers on Attorney General Clark's Report to the Loyalty Board," IWO-CU, box 17, folder 14; *The IWO Builds for Tomorrow. Leader's Guide for IWO Junior Leaders*, vol. 2, no. 2, March–April 1948, IWO-CU, box 5, folder 2; News release, "IWO Challenges Constitutionality of Attorney General Clark's Report; Plans Legal Action," December 27, 1947, references Henry Steele Commager, "Who Is Loyal to America?" *Harper's Magazine*, September 1947, IWO-NYU, folder 31.

8. Rubin Saltzman to "Dear Comrade," June 20, 1932, reel 234, delo 3037, Records of the Communist Party USA, Microfilm 21, 966, Library of Congress [hereafter cited as CPUSA-LC].

9. Rachel Ida Buff, *Against the Deportation Terror: The American Committee for the Protection of the Foreign Born and Immigrant Rights Advocacy, 1933–1982* (Philadelphia, PA: Temple University Press, 2018); Daniel Kanstroom, *Deportation Nation: Outsiders in American History* (Cambridge, MA: Harvard University Press, 2007).

10. Bill Gebert biography, April 15, 1932, DB-WSU, box 4, folder 4-14; FBI report, "Boleslaw K. Gebert, Bolshevik Agitator," July 25, 1919, DB-WSU, box 4, folder 4-22; FBI report on Gebert at Detroit, "Report made by J. S. Apelman. Detroit, Mich. July 10, 1919," and "Report made by J. S. Apelman. Detroit, Mich. July 8, 1919," affidavit, County of Wayne [Detroit, 1919] by a witness in the Gebert deportation hearing, ibid.; Memorandum on Gebert deportation proceedings, November 4, 1919, ibid.; Letter from Commissioner General of Immigration, October 13, 1919, and memorandum on B. K. Gebert attached to the deportation proceedings, DB-WSU, box 4, folder 4-23; FBI affidavit, Apelman, January 19, 1920, on Gebert, DB-WSU, box 4, folder 4-22; William Burns, FBI director, to Secretary of Labor, April 21, 1922, requesting the reopening of deportation proceedings against Gebert, DB-WSU, box 4, folder 4-23; "Brief by Alien" in Gebert's deportation proceeding [1931], ibid.; Hearing on deportation of Boleslaw Konstantin Gebert, November 18, 1931, Benton, Illinois, ibid.; Roger Baldwin of the ACLU to Daniel MacCormack, Commissioner General of Immigration, November 28, 1934, W. W. Brown, assistant to MacCormack, to Baldwin, January 17, 1935, David Bentall to Department of Labor, January 26, 1937, and J. R. Espinosa, Chief Supervisor of Special Inspections, Department of Justice, to "Mr. Brown" of the IS, October 20, 1941, ibid.; "Bon Voyage, Bill," *Fraternal Outlook* [1947], 18, DB-WSU, box 4, folder 4-14. Gebert's resignation letter, August 11, 1947, IWO-CU, box 5, folder 12. For Milgrom, see Sabin, *Red Scare in Court*, 280–281.

11. Louise Thompson to Sadie Doroshkin, June 19, 1934, Thompson to Max Bedacht, June 4, 1934, Thompson to C. B. Powell, Birmingham attorney, May 21, 1934, Thompson to Doroshkin, May 21, 1934, Powell to Thompson, May 22, 1934, Thompson to Joseph Brodsky, May 21, 1934, Doroshkin to Thompson, May 23, 1934, and Powell to Thompson, May 28, 1934, box 8, folder 8, Louise Thompson Patterson Papers, 1909–1999, MSS 869, Stuart A. Rose Manuscript, Archives, and Rare Book Library, Emory University [hereafter cited as LTP-EU]; Louise Thompson Patterson, interview by Linda Burnham, March 11 and 14, 1988, ibid.

12. Albert Fenely of Wendel, West Virginia, to "Dear Comrade Browder and all," May 5, 1936, CPUSA-LC, reel 205, delo 4034.

13. Joseph Brodsky, IWO General Counsel, report to IWO GEB, plenary session, September 10–11, 1938, 19–24, IWO-CU, box 1, folder 5; Max Bedacht report, "Reaction Threatens Our Order," to the IWO GEB, plenary session, September 10–11, 1938, 10, ibid. "International Workers Can't Issue Insurance. Mass. Commissioner Finds Purported Fraternal Order is Communistic," *Lewiston Evening Journal* [Maine], July 23, 1938, 4, Associated Press story.

14. Joseph Brodsky report to IWO GEB, plenary session, September 10–11, 1938, 19–24; Decision, Commonwealth of Massachusetts, Suffolk County, Supreme Judicial Court, *International Workers Order, Inc., v. Commissioner of Insurance of the Commonwealth, Findings, Ruling and Order*, March 6, 1939, IWO-CU, box 5, folder 2.

15. Brodsky report to IWO GEB. "Proposal for the Establishment of an Official Organ" [spring 1938], IWO-CU, box 2, folder 2.

16. "Dies Demands 'Alien' Groups Be Prosecuted. Note to Hull Claims Registration Law Violated," *Milwaukee Sentinel*, November 28, 1938, 3; FBI report, IWO, Detroit division, December 31, 1946, citing report of Special Sub-Committee on Un-American Activities, January 3, 1939, to House of Representatives, DB-WSU, box 16, folder 16-37.

17. FBI report, IWO, Detroit division, December 31, 1946, citing January 16, 1939, meeting in Detroit; Lodge 2501, La Progressiva, to Vito Marcantonio, telegram, January 24, 1939, box 47, Vito Marcantonio Papers, Manuscripts and Archives Division, The New York Public Library [hereafter cited as VM-NYPL]; Flyer, *Mass Meeting against the Dies Committee, for the New Deal*, in English and Italian, January 29, 1939, La Progressiva, endorsed by United Italian Associations of Harlem, ibid.; Letter on anti-Dies Committee rally in Harlem, sponsored by La Progressiva Lodge [January 1939], ibid.; Petition against the Dies HUAC, from Dante Alighieri Lodge 2579, Bronx [January 1939], ibid.

18. Peter Morell, "The Threat to Civil Liberties," *Fraternal Outlook*, November 1939, 3–5, 28, IWO-CU, box 48; "Koncentračné Tábory v Amerike? Výpad reakčných Kongresmanov proti 'Bill of Rights'" [Concentration Camps in America? Reactionary Congressman's Attack on the "Bill of Rights"], *Fraternal Outlook*, December 1939, 33, ibid. Paul Nadler, "Liberty Censored: Black Living Newspapers in the Federal Theatre Project," *African American Review* 29, no. 4 (Winter 1995): 615–622; Robert Davis, "Is Mr. Euripides a Communist? The Federal Theatre Project's 1938 Trojan Incident," *Comparative Drama* 44, no. 4 (Winter 2010): 457–476, 550.

19. Report of General Secretary to plenary session GEB, January 27, 1940, 16–17, IWO-CU, box 2, folder 4.

20. "Federal Judge Rules Seizure of Communist Party Files Illegal," *Daily Journal-World* [Lawrence, Kansas], May 3, 1940, 1.

21. "IWO National 'Stop Dies' Drive Gets Mass Support," *Daily Worker*, May 15, 1940, 5, CPUSA-LC, reel 318, delo 4243; Sabin, *Red Scare in Court*, 167.

22. "IWO Calls an Anti-Dies Rally in Brooklyn," *Daily Worker*, May 18, 1940, 5, CPUSA-LC, reel 318, delo 4243; Detroit Police Department, Office of Special Investigation Squad, report on IWO Lodge 747 meeting, March 10, 1940, DB-WSU, box 5, folder 5-30.

23. "Court Allows I.W.O. to Inspect Seized Files," *Daily Worker*, May 17, 1940, 5, CPUSA-LC, reel 318, delo 4243; Clare Hoffman, May 25, 1940, and Vito Marcantonio, May 28, 1940, both to Max Bedacht, IWO-CU, box 3, folder 12; Bedacht to Marcantonio, "Copy of following telegram sent to Martin Dies, Chairman, Investigating Un-American Activities" [May 1940], VM-NYPL, box 47.

24. FBI report, IWO, Detroit division, December 31, 1946, citing IWO circular letter, April 26, 1941.

25. Questionnaires, Morris Nusenow, the Bronx, April 29, 1941, Philip Kay, Atlantic City, May 27, 1941, Albert Strimling, Denver, April 16, 1941, and Helen Lane, Youngstown, Ohio, April 16, 1941, IWO-CU, box 18, folder 13.

26. "Letter from Elia Vitanoff, Fin. Sec. of Branch #985 in Madison, Ill. dated October 21, 1941, reporting an investigation of the FBI at his branch, reply to same from J. E. Middleton dated October 27, 1941, and reply from E. Vitanoff, dated October 30, 1941," IWO-CU, box 26, folder 10; "Miriam Hahn, Paterson, N.J., June 3, 1941. . . . Reply dated June 10, 1941, sgd: J. E. Middleton, denying any affiliations with political parties," ibid.

27. Vito Marcantonio speech, Proceedings, National Convention, IWO, July 2–7, 1944, 10–12, IWO-CU, box 3, folder 4.

28. Hearings, Senate Subcommittee on Immigration and Naturalization, George Pirinsky testimony, June 8, 1949, DB-WSU, box 2, folder 2-19; "Young Slavs in U.S. to be Wooed by Reds," *New York World-Telegram*, September 10, 1946, DB-WSU, box 1, folder 1-19; Archibald McLeish to "Dear Steve" [Steve Early?], April 22, 1942, and President Roosevelt to ASC, telegram, April 25, 1942, DB-WSU, box 1, folder 1-17; "The American Slav Congress Will Convene Saturday April 25th and Sunday April 26th," *Národné noviny*, April 22, 1942, 5, and "An Address by Paul McNutt, Chairman of the War Manpower Commission and Federal Security Administrator, at the American Slav Congress, April 26, 1942," *Národné noviny*, May 6, 1942, 5, ibid.

29. See chap. 5, note 82.

30. Mal Ring to "Dear Lester," October 28, 1941, IWO-CU, box 4, folder 1.

31. Middleton to Mitchell, and, Mitchell to Middleton.

32. "Miscellaneous correspondence," IWO-CU, box 26, folder 10; William Hull, executive assistant of the U.S. Civil Service Commission, to Joseph Brodsky, September 16, 1943, IWO-NYU, folder 6.

33. Marcantonio speech, Proceedings, National Convention, IWO. IWO to Marcantonio, telegram, February 4, 1943; Marcantonio to IWO, February 9, 1943, Dave Greene to Marcantonio, February 9, 1943, March 11, 1942, and Marcantonio to Greene, March 12, 1942, VM-NYPL, box 47.

34. "Flash! The IWO has filed suit . . ." from Rockwell Kent [1948], IWO-NYU, folder 6.

35. Petition, "$50,000 IWO Defense Fund, Defeat the Un-American Attack against the IWO. Protect the Integrity and Security of Your Fraternal Order," July 7, 1948, from Curtisville, Pennsylvania, Lodge 3006, IWO-CU, box 21, folder 38; Andy Hromiko of Tarentum, Pennsylvania, to "Dear Comrades," March 4, 1935, CPUSA-LC, reel 303, delo 3981; Spiridou Comanita of Youngstown, Ohio, to IWO, August 28, 1948, IWO-CU, box 17, folder 14; Dorothy Tripp, Endicott, New York, to Senator Irving Ives, February 21, 1948, IWO-CU, box 17, folder 15.

36. News release, "IWO Files Suit against Attorney General Clark; Challenges Constitutionality of 'Subversive' Lists," June 7, 1948, IWO-NYU, folder 31. Dave Greene "to all National Group Societies," August 22, 1947, quoting U.S. Civil Service Commission's 1943 ruling regarding IWO membership of federal government employees, IWO-CU, box 4, folder 3.

37. Pamphlet, *An Indictment: The People vs. Attorney General Tom Clark Before the Court of Public Opinion* [1947 or 1948], IWO-CU, box 48.

38. Ibid.

39. Ibid.

40. Sam Milgrom, "Americanism and Loyalty," *Jewish Fraternalist*, April 1948, 3–4, IWO-CU, box 46.

41. FBI report, IWO, Detroit division, November 20, 1953, cites *Michigan Edition—The Worker*, June 6, 1948, 9, and *Glos Ludowy*, June 19, 1948, DB-WSU, box 16, folder 16-38.

42. IWO news release, July 8, 1948, excerpt from speeches opposing placing IWO on Attorney General's List of Subversive Organizations, IWO-NYU, folder 31.

43. *An Indictment: The People vs. Attorney General Tom Clark*; Congressman Adolph Sabath to Rockwell Kent, August 12, 1948, Attorney General Tom Clark to Sabath, August 16, 1948, and Sabath to Kent, August 18, 1948, IWO-CU, box 3, folder 8. On the revocation of tax exemption, see Minutes, IWO Executive Committee meeting, June 14, 1948, IWO-CU, box 1, folder 14.

44. Memorandum, "Attorney General Clark's answer to IWO lawsuit" [1948], IWO-CU, box 3, folder 8. Minutes, IWO Executive Committee meeting, September 14, 1948, IWO-CU, box 1, folder 14.

45. Molly Tallentire to Rockwell Kent, September 30, 1948, IWO-CU, box 3, folder 8.

46. Peter Shipka, "Department of Justice Evades Justice," *Jewish Fraternalist*, November 1948, 3–4, IWO-CU, box 46.

47. Report from vice president of Washington, D.C., lodge, December 3, 1948, IWO-NYU, folder 29.

48. FBI report, IWO, Detroit division, November 20, 1953, citing *Glos Ludowy*, Section 2, English Section, 1, March 12, 1949; Representative John Wood to "Dear Colleagues," January 13, 1949, on Civil Rights Congress Freedom Crusade, VM-NYPL, box 47.

49. N. Chalpin of Philadelphia to Gedalia Sandler, March 10, 1947, and Sandler to Chalpin, March 26, 1947, IWO-CU, box 25, folder 9; Post Office Department to Seymour Goldman, November 30, 1948, "Interrogatories," IWO-CU, box 32, folder 31; Minutes, National Board, JPFO meeting, November 19, 1949, report by Lee Pressman on "the legal problems we have faced in the past few years," IWO-CU, box 27, folder 2.

50. Seymour Press of Hammond, Indiana, to Sylvia Rigel, January 10, 1950, IWO-CU, box 32, folder 24; Samuel Miller of Los Angeles to Pittsburgh, December 10, 1946, IWO-CU, box 25, folder 11; Routine Slovak correspondence, 1950, IWO-CU, box 26, folder 5. For other federal government employees quitting the IWO, see Benjamin Elian, the Bronx, to Frances Shifrin, March 24, 1947: "I'm sorry that I have to do this, as I have no alternative in this matter," Elian wrote (IWO-CU, box 32, folder 35); Manuel del Pozo, Cervantes Fraternal Society, Mutualista Obrera Puertorriqueña, Lodge 4765, to Dave Greene, September 26, 1949, on two members who quit because they were government employees, IWO-CU, box 26, folder 6.

51. Abraham Chapman to Lee Pressman, January 16, 1950, IWOCF-CU, box 1; Draft, *Fraternal Outlook* article, "Arthur L. Drayton Fights 'Loyalty' Suspension," ibid.

52. Sabin, *Red Scare in Court*, 290; Caute, *The Great Fear*, 168; Rosemary Feurer, *Radical Unionism in the Midwest, 1900–1950* (Urbana: University of Illinois Press, 2006); Shelton Stromquist, ed., *Labor's Cold War: Local Politics in a Global Context* (Urbana: University of Illinois Press, 2008); Schrecker, *Many Are the Crimes*, 67–70, 268, 336–340; Paul Robeson, *Here I Stand* (New York: Othello, 1958); Martin Duberman,

Paul Robeson (New York: Knopf, 1988); Jordan Goodman, *Paul Robeson: A Watched Man* (New York: Verso, 2013), 90–95, 104–114, 227–242; Tony Perucci, *Paul Robeson and the Cold War Performance Complex: Race, Madness, Activism* (Ann Arbor: University of Michigan Press, 2012), 33–38.

53. Luigi Ciarafoni of Shickashinny, Pennsylvania, to Vito Magli, July 20, 1949, C. Lippa to Ciarafoni, July 22, 1949, and Magli to Ciarafoni, August 1, 1949, IWO-CU, box 25, folder 5. Kiril Drobena, Omaha, to Daniel Kasustchik, June 4, 1950, and K. Ossip to Drobena, June 8, 1950, IWO-CU, box 25, folder 1.

54. Polonia Society lodge secretary, A. Stopera of Martins Ferry, Ohio, June 20, 1949, IWO-CU, box 26, folder 10; Peter Shipka to National Group Societies, July 27, 1949, IWO-CU, box 18, folder 14; Mario D'Inzillo and Vito Magli, "Notice to All Officers of the Garibaldi IWO Lodges," August 30, 1949, IWO-CU, box 10, folder 10; Sam Klezmer of Miami Beach to Rubin Saltzman, April 6, 1949, and Saltzman to Klezmer, April 14, 1949, IWO-CU, box 25, folder 10; Sol Rotenberg to Sam Milgrom, October 7, 1946, including newspaper article, "Raid Bares Club Honoring Tito; FBI Called In," from the *Philadelphia Record* [n.d.], on FBI raids of Yugoslav IWO lodges, IWO-CU, box 8, folder 11; Minutes, National Board, JPFO meeting, November 19, 1949, report by Lee Pressman; N. Suprun of Paulsboro, New Jersey, to Daniel Kasustchik, May 17, 1948, Kasustchik to Suprun, May 19, 1948, Suprun to Kasustchik, July 7, 1948, and Kasustchik to Suprun, July 26, 1948, IWO-CU, box 25, folder 1; Gustavo Caparoli of Arnold, Pennsylvania, August 23, 1950, and C. Lippa to Caparoli, August 28, 1950, IWO-CU, box 10, folder 10.

55. Fabio Ligi, financial secretary, Union, New York, to "Dear Secretary," May 26, 1947, IWO-CU, box 25, folder 5. An SWS member from Columbus, Ohio, wrote to Joseph Schiffel, SWS national leader, on October 30, 1950, that he was resigning because his son was in medical school and he didn't want him expelled: Schiffel letter, November 1, 1950, IWO-NYU, folder 42.

56. Michel Foucault, *Discipline and Punish: The Birth of the Prison* (New York: Vintage, 1979).

57. B. Felser of Scranton, Pennsylvania, to JPFO secretary, May 23, 1949, IWO-CU, box 25, folder 10; P. Krupsky, Russian Lodge 3001, Pittsburgh, to Daniel Kasustchik, November 7, 1949, and Kasustchik to Krupsky [1949], IWO-CU, box 25, folder 1; Margaret Wherry of Cleveland to Sam Milgrom, January 15, 1948, IWO-CU, box 8, folder 8.

58. Ligi to "Dear Secretary"; Sabin, *Red Scare in Court*, 55.

59. W. Sobol of Elbert, West Virginia, to Daniel Kasustchik [ca. June–July 1950], Kasustchik to W. Sobol, July 14, 1950, and Sobol to Kasustchik [ca. October 1950], IWO-CU, box 25, folder 1. For conditions in coal towns, see David Alan Corbin, *Life, Work, and Rebellion in the Coal Fields: The Southern West Virginia Miners, 1880–1922* (Urbana: University of Illinois Press, 1981); James Green, *The Devil Is Here in These Hills: West Virginia's Coal Miners and Their Battle for Freedom* (New York: Atlantic Monthly Press, 2015); Thomas Dublin, *When the Mines Closed: Stories of Struggles in Hard Times* (Ithaca, NY: Cornell University Press, 1998); Lon Savage, *Thunder in the Mountains: The West Virginia Mine War, 1920–1921* (Pittsburgh: University of Pittsburgh Press, 1990); John Gaventa, *Power and Powerlessness: Quiescence and Rebellion in an Appalachian Valley* (Urbana: University of Illinois Press, 1980); Victor Greene, *The Slavic Community on Strike: Immigrant Labor in Pennsylvania Anthracite* (Notre Dame, IN: Notre Dame University Press, 1968); Mildred Allen Beik, *The Miners of Windber* (University Park: Pennsylvania State University Press, 1996); Katherine Mayo, *Justice to All: The Story of the Pennsylvania State Police* (New York: G. P. Putnam's, 1916).

60. W. Sobol of Elbert, West Virginia, to Daniel Kasustchik [ca. June–July 1950], Kasustchik to W. Sobol, July 14, 1950, and Sobol to Kasustchik [ca. October 1950], IWO-CU, box 25, folder 1.

61. Ibid.

62. Translation of letter, Ludwik Paluch, secretary of Lodge 3575, Enterprise, West Virginia, IWO-CU, box 22, folder 1.

63. Letter from secretary to an ARFS lodge [place not specified, ca. late 1940s, early 1950s], IWO-CU, box 25, folder 1.

64. FBI report, IWO, Detroit division, November 20, 1953, includes report of February 18, 1951, meeting, Western Michigan Section, CP, Grand Rapids.

65. Daniel Kasustchik to Ya. Peters, N. Daneyko, and M. Burenko, Erie, Pennsylvania, September 20, 1950, IWO-CU, box 25, folder 1; S. Nowacki, assistant secretary of the Polonia Society, September 26, 1950, IWO-CU, box 26, folder 3; Ossip Blachnic, Erie, to Kasustchik, October 9, 1950, and Kasustchik to Blachnic October 11, 1950, IWO-CU, box 25, folder 1; Monthly letter, Garibaldi Society IWO, November 1950, IWO-CU, box 10, folder 10; "Anti-Red Law Effect Halted," *Milwaukee Journal*, October 27, 1950, 6.

66. B. Klein, secretary, JPFO Lodge 644, Atlantic Beach, Florida, to George Starr, September 14, 1950, and Starr to Klein, September 22, 1950, IWO-CU, box 32, folder 11. Klein's letter was accompanied by September 13, 1950, clippings from the *Florida Times-Union*, "Stab Wound, Fall Imperil Life of Red" and from a second, unidentified newspaper, "Trainor Still Reported on Critical List."

67. Letter "from Russian," "George" of Audubon, New Jersey, to the ARFS Central Committee, January 14, 1951, IWO-CU, box 25, folder 1.

68. Summary of correspondence in IWO office, Morris Dubin of the Bronx to Z. Aaronson, branch secretary, September 25, 1950, IWO-CU, box 25, folder 10; E. T. Besenyodi of Akron, Ohio, to IWO, May 17, 1948, IWO-CU, box 8, folder 8.

69. Solomon and Sarah Kleinberg, the Bronx, to Lee Pressman, April 13, 1949, IWO-CU, box 25, folder 10.

70. Buff, *Against the Deportation Terror*; Kanstroom, *Deportation Nation*; Michael Belknap, *Cold War Political Justice: The Smith Act, the Communist Party, and American Civil Liberties* (Westport, CT: Greenwood Press, 1977); Carole Boyce Davies, "Deportable Subjects: U.S. Immigration Laws and the Criminalizing of Communism," *South Atlantic Quarterly* 100, no. 4 (Fall 2001): 949–966; Barth, *The Loyalty of Free Men*; Goldstein, *American Blacklist*.

71. Press release, Sam Milgrom, on behalf of ACPFB, "Yugoslav-American Community Terrorized by Naturalization Officials," April 14, 1947, IWO-CU, box 4, folder 2; Press release, "IWO Urges Investigation of Immigration Office in Youngstown, Ohio," April 25, 1947, IWO-NYU, folder 31; FBI report on ASC made by Agent Douglas Williams, Indianapolis, January 26, 1944, contained in FBI file on the ASC. I thank FOIA and John Enyeart for providing this material.

72. United States Circuit Court of Appeals for the 1st Circuit—May 27, 1948, *Philip Stasiukevich v. Henry Nicolls*, District Director of Immigration and Naturalization [Massachusetts], IWOCF-CU, box 1.

73. Sarah Gualtieri, "Becoming 'White': Race, Religion and the Foundations of Syrian/Lebanese Ethnicity in the United States," *Journal of American Ethnic History* 20, no. 4 (Summer 2001): 29–58; Sarah Gualtieri, *Between Arab and White: Race and Ethnicity in the Early Syrian American Diaspora* (Berkeley: University of California Press,

2009); Matthew Frye Jacobson, *Whiteness of a Different Color: European Immigrants and the Alchemy of Race* (Cambridge, MA: Harvard University Press, 1998), 236–239.

74. Ada Shalan, Baltimore, to Daniel Kasustchik, February 19, 1948, Kasustchik to Shalan, March 6, 1948, Shalan to Kasustchik, May 12, 1948, and Kasustchik to Shalan, May 21, 1948, IWO-CU, box 25, folder 1.

75. SWS letter, Lodge 2130, Passaic, New Jersey, October 2, 1950, IWO-NYU, folder 42. Summary, case of Joseph Lipa and Bohumil Snyder, members of SWS called to INS hearing, Syracuse, New York, n.d., IWOCF-CU, box 1.

76. Carpatho-Russian member to "Michael" [Michael Logoyda], February 9, 1947, IWO-CU, box 25, folder 2.

77. Flyer, Trade Union Committee for Protection of Foreign Born, citing Nancy Seely, "'This Is Home and Here I Stay,' Vows Bronx Painter Facing Exile as Ex-Red," *New York Post*, June 5, 1952, IWO-CU, box 43, folder 7. Abner Green, "The Deportation Hysteria," *Jewish Fraternalist*, January 1950, 3–4, 16, IWO-CU, box 46; News releases, October 21 and November 1, 1949: rallies were listed in South Bend, Indiana; Steubenville, Youngstown, Warren, Akron, and Bellaire, Ohio; Masontown, Johnstown, New Kensington, Brownsville, and West Brownsville, Pennsylvania, IWO-CU, box 48. News release, "IWO Condemns Deportation Arrests in Detroit; Refutes Press Slanders," July 22, 1949, IWO-CU, box 48.

78. Interview with Stanley Nowak [Detroit, March 30, 1983]. Tapes 177 A–C. Oral History of the American Left Collection, 1940–2011, OH.002, Robert F. Wagner Labor Archives, Tamiment Library, New York University.

79. Pamphlet, *An American Family Faces Separation or Exile*, by the Stanley Nowak Defense Committee [April 1956], DB-WSU, box 7, folder 7-48.

80. Ibid. See, too, FBI report, Stanley Nowak Defense Committee [1953], citing defenses of Nowak in *Glos Ludowy*, January 17 and 31, 1953, DB-WSU, box 7, folder 7-49.

81. Stanley Nowak statement to HUAC, February 24, 1952, NP-WSU, box 5, folder 5-5. Goodman, *Paul Robeson*, 90–95, 104–114, 227–242; Perucci, *Paul Robeson and the Cold War Performance Complex*, 33–38.

82. Ernest Goodman of Goodman, Crockett, Eden, and Robb, to Victor Perlo of Flushing, New York, May 28, 1957, NP-WSU, box 9, folder 9-9; Buff, *Against the Deportation Terror*.

83. "Chicago, Ill. Sep. 24" to Sam Milgrom [ca. 1940s], telegram, regarding the white hate strike in Gary and the IWO's involvement in a campaign to integrate the Gary schools, IWO-CU, box 6, folder 12; "The Case of Katherine Hyndman—What Is True Americanism?" *The American Slav*, Winter 1949, 8. For more on Hyndman, see chap. 3, note 61.

84. See 1970 oral history with Hyndman conducted by Staughton Lynd, box 3, Oral History Project, Roosevelt University Archives; Susan Brown, "Katherine Hyndman: Region's Own Political Prisoner," *Northwest Times* [Gary, Indiana]), June 2, 2003.

85. Warrant for arrest of alien Samson Milgrom, May 9, 1950, IWOCF-CU, box 1; IWO news release, May 10, 1950, on attempted deportation of Milgrom, IWO-CU, box 48; Rockwell Kent to Milgrom, May 13, 1950, Kent to Molly Tallentire, May 13, 1950, Milgrom to Kent, May 26, 1950, Milgrom to Kent, June 20, 1950, and "Memorandum" against deportation drives, IWO-CU, box 3, folder 10; "Memorandum re: 'The Attacks on the Order,'" June 13, 1950, IWO-CU, box 10, folder 10; "IWO General Council Maps Defense of Order," *Fraternal Outlook*, June–July 1950, 4–7, IWO-CU, box 48.

86. Minutes, IWO Executive Committee, October 21, 1952, IWOCF-CU, box 3; "Committee for the Freedom of Sam Milgrom" to "Dear Friend," November 2, 1952,

with enclosed letter written by Milgrom from Ellis Island and second letter from Milgrom on Ellis Island to IWO members, IWO-CU, box 16, folder 11; Dave Greene to Peter Shipka, February 1953, IWO-CU, box 4, folder 6; Press release, "Rally Organized to Demand Milgrom's Release on Bail," February 4, 1953 [rally held February 24, 1953, New York], IWO-CU, box 16, folder 11; Speech to "Brothers and Sisters, Friends," February 24, 1953 [unclear by whom, on occasion of rally to demand release of Milgrom], ibid.; News release, Committee for the Freedom of Sam Milgrom, "Prominent Leaders Meet with Immigration Commissioner to Urge Release on Bail for Sam Milgrom," February 18, 1953, ibid. For the deportation of ASC executive secretary George Pirinsky, see "Arrest Slav Congress Aid as Red Alien," *Chicago Daily Tribune*, September 24, 1948; "Slav Congress Leader Is Seized on Charge of Communist Ties," *Washington Star*, September 25, 1948, DB-WSU, box 1, folder 1-18; George Pirinsky Defense Rally to President Truman, telegram, January 17, 1949, DB-WSU, box 1, folder 1-19; *Národné noviny*, July 13, 1949, 4; S. Nikolauk to Executive Committee of ARFS Lodge 3171, New Haven, Connecticut, September 13, 1949, IWO-CU, box 25, folder 1; Gerald Horne, *Red Seas: Ferdinand Smith and Radical Black Sailors in the United States and Jamaica* (New York: New York University Press, 2005), 203; George Pirinsky to Stanley Nowak, October 10, 1949, box 4, folder 4-16, Stanley and Margaret Collingwood Nowak Papers, Walter P. Reuther Library, Wayne State University [hereafter cited as NP-WSU]; "Statement of the American Slav Congress on the Arrest of George Pirinsky," October 23, 1950, NP-WSU, box 4, folder 4-2. Thanks to Rachel Buff for the *Chicago Tribune* article.

    87. Hannah Arendt, *The Origins of Totalitarianism* (New York: Harcourt, Brace and World, 1966), 296.

    88. Robeson, *Here I Stand*; Duberman, *Paul Robeson*; Goodman, *Paul Robeson*. Outline for speech by Dave Greene of the JPFO, Brooklyn, June 19, 1950, IWO-CU, box 4, folder 5. For Robeson's defense of the IWO, see News release, addresses by Robeson and Idaho Senator Glen Taylor, July 8, 1947, IWO-NYU, folder 31.

    89. Flyer, *Shall We Destroy the Statue of Liberty and Build Concentration Camps?* [Committee in Defense of Henry Podolski, ca. 1949], DB-WSU, box 8, folder 8-42; News release, "IWO Condemns Deportation Arrest of Henry Podolski," August 16, 1949, IWO-CU, box 48.

    90. Flyer, *Should Miss Liberty Be Deported? The Case of Peter Harisiades* [1950], VM-NYPL, box 46.

    91. "Appeal to Members of the Polonia Society, Let Us Defend Our Secretary," *Glos Ludowy*, September 10, 1949, 13, DB-WSU, box 16, folder 16-36; Green, "The Deportation Hysteria"; "Greek, Here Since 1916, Finally Deported as Red," *New York Herald Tribune*, November 13, 1952, IWOCF-CU, box 2; FBI report, IWO, Detroit division, November 20, 1953, cites *Glos Ludowy*, October 27, 1951, 12, "Podolski's letter to the Executive Committee of the Polonia Society."

    92. Deportation decision on Andrew Dmytryshyn, December 26, 1951, and memorandum to IWO from attorney Arthur Kinoy on Dmytryshyn decision [1951], IWOCF-CU, box 1; News releases, "Government Witnesses, Under Contract, Testify against a Man They Never Saw," August 8, 1950, "The Government Rests Its Case—On a Crew of Stoolpigeons" [1950], "Deporters on Merry-Go-Round," July 14, 1950, and "Sponsored by the U.S. Government: 'Mr. and Mrs. Informer,'" July 21, 1950, all by Fred Winter, IWO-CU, box 17, folder 14; "Appeal to Members of the Polonia Society, Let Us Defend Our Secretary."

    93. Sabin, *Red Scare in Court*, 48–49.

    94. Ibid., 54.

95. Ibid., 48–62.

96. Ibid., 48–62.

97. Complaint entered by Lee Pressman and Allan Rosenberg, February 15, 1949, IWO-CU, box 23, folder 1; "Haley Report for Purposes of Cross-Examination" [ca. 1950], IWO-CU, box 23, folder 6; Peter Shipka to Dave Greene, January 22, 1951, IWO-CU, box 23, folder 1.

98. "Haley Report for Purposes of Cross-Examination"; FBI report, IWO, Detroit division, November 20, 1953, 19, 54, 55, cites *Romanul American*, September 13, 1947, 1, article by George Vocila. A speaker at an IWO Russian section lodge in Muskegon, Michigan, made a similar point.

99. "Haley Report for Purposes of Cross-Examination;" Polonia Society, "From organization Bulletin for December, 1950," IWO-CU, box 26, folder 3.

100. Affidavit, Jacob Zeitlin, CPA, Newark, New Jersey, April 24, 1951, IWOCF-CU, box 3; "IWO General Council Maps Defense of Order." Sabin, *Red Scare in Court*, 79; Nelson Frank, "Their Books Balanced, But Politics Were in Red," *New York World-Telegram and Sun*, January 23, 1951, and "Among Reddest Red Nests," *New York World-Telegram and Sun*, January 20, 1951, IWOCF-CU, box 2. Louis Budenz, "IWO—Red Bulwark: The Inside Story of an Outfit That Works Hand in Glove with the Communist Party and Which Now Faces a Crackdown That Is Long Overdue," *American Legion Magazine*, March 1951, reprint, IWOCF-CU, box 3.

101. Sabin, *Red Scare in Court*, 70–75; "IWO General Council Maps Defense of Order."

102. SWS president to Brother Klimek, Binghamton, New York, October 5, 1950, IWO-CU, box 21, folder 8.

103. Ibid.

104. Sabin, *Red Scare in Court*, 77–78.

105. Memorandum, Peter Shipka to Raphael Weissman, January 9, 1951, IWO-CU, box 23, folder 1; Joseph Schiffel to Joseph Griger, February 6, 1951, IWO-CU, box 26, folder 5.

106. Peter Shipka to "Lodge Financial Secretaries," December 28, 1950, IWO-CU, box 5, folder 16; News release, "IWO Policyholders Form Protective Committee, Plan Albany Gathering and Visit to Gov. Dewey," December 28, 1950, IWO-CU, box 16, folder 13.

107. Louise Thompson Patterson, interview by Ruth and Bud Schultz, August 12, 1984, LTP-EU, box 27, folder 3.

108. "Resolutions, Adopted by Emergency Conference against the Liquidation of a People's Organization," February 10, 1951," IWO-CU, box 24.

109. Ibid.

110. Sabin, *Red Scare in Court*, 97–98, citing *New York Herald Tribune*, January 11, 1951, 3. "Medzinárodný Robotnícky Spolok nazvaný nástrojom Komunistov" [The International Workers Order called a tool of the Communists], *New Yorský denník*, January 10, 1951, 1; "Súd zakázal konvenciu Medzinárod. Robotníckeho Spolku v New Yorku" [Judge Forbids New York Convention of the International Workers Order], *New Yorský denník*, January 12, 1951, 1; "Šesť úradníkov Medzinárodného Spolku považovaní za Komunistov" [Six Officers of the International Workers Order Exposed as Communists], *New Yorský denník*, February 1, 1951, 1.

111. Budnez, "IWO—Red Bulwark."

112. "Resolutions, . . . Emergency Conference against the Liquidation of a People's Organization," February 10, 1951, IWO-CU, box 24; "Petition for Right to Hold Convention" [1951], IWOCF-CU, box 3; Dave Greene, "To Elected Delegates to the 8th

National Convention, To Lodge Officers and Active Builders of the IWO," February 20, 1951, IWO-NYU, folder 6. "Report of Peter Shipka, Secretary-Treasurer, to the General Council, IWO, February 3 and 4, 1951," IWO-NYU, folder 18.

113. Ad, IWO Policyholders Protective Committee, "An Open Letter to the N.Y. Superintendent of Insurance," *The Compass*, April 22, 1951, IWO-CU, box 23, folder 5; "Answer to Superintendent of Insurance Bohlinger, Adopted at Membership Meeting of the International Workers Order, March 7, 1951," IWO-CU, box 23, folder 4; Sabin, *Red Scare in Court*, 201. Alfred Bohlinger, Superintendent of Insurance, "To the Members of the International Workers Order Inc.," January 24, 1951, IWO-CU, box 23, folder 4.

114. Abraham Freeman to Alfred Bohlinger, February 22, 1951, and Nathan Witt of Witt and Cammer, lawyer and policyholder in the IWO, to Bohlinger, February 23, 1951, IWO-CU, box 23, folder 4. "An Open Letter to the N.Y. Superintendent of Insurance"; "Answer to Superintendent of Insurance Bohlinger"; D. Fedonik of Boston "to the Plenum of the IWO Committee," January 24, 1951, IWO-CU, box 25, folder 1.

115. Caute, *The Great Fear*, 137, cited in Sabin, *Red Scare in Court*, 111; Louis Goldblatt, secretary, Bridges-Robertson-Schmidt Defense Committee, to "Dear Sir and Brother," January 27, 1950, ILGWU-CU, MSS 5780/014, box 5, folder 4. For Powers's perjury, see News release, January 30, 1951, IWO-CU, box 23, folder 4.

116. "Digest of Testimony of Witnesses for the State," Powers testimony, 3–31; Sabin, *Red Scare in Court*, 122–128.

117. "Digest of Testimony of Witnesses for the State," Kornfeder testimony, 53–63; Sabin, *Red Scare in Court*, 139–140.

118. "Digest of Testimony of Witnesses for the State," Simon Weber testimony, 110, and Mathew Cvetic testimony, 150–186; Sabin, *Red Scare in Court*, 162.

119. Sabin, *Red Scare in Court*, 210, 213, 223–224, 229–230, 239–240, 274, 276.

120. Ibid., 243–244, 254.

121. Affidavit, John Hrusovsky, Irvington, New Jersey, April 24, 1951, IWOCF-CU, box 3.

122. Affidavit, Salvatore Spampinato, Los Angeles, April 23, 1951, ibid.

123. Affidavits, John Uhrin, Los Angeles, April 24, 1951, Charles Skulsky, Philadelphia, April 23, 1951, Dominica Alasina, Detroit, April 23, 1951, Jacob Balan, Highland Park, Michigan, April 23, 1951, Mary Granich, Philadelphia, April 23, 1951, Mary Stucka, Elizabeth, New Jersey, April 24, 1951, Michael Mišura, Philadelphia, April 24, 1951, and Miklos Petri, the Bronx, April 23, 1951, IWOCF-CU, box 3.

124. Letter from Donner and Kinoy, May 4, 1951, reminding recipients of the high court decision and adding that it was illegal to blacklist the IWO, IWO-NYU, folder 34; News release and letter, Garibaldi Society to all lodges, "Supreme Court Removed the IWO from the Subversive List," May 8, 1951, IWO-CU, box 10, folder 10; Donner and Kinoy to IWO, May 4, 1951, IWO-CU, box 23, folder 1; Monthly letter, C. Lippa to all Garibaldi Society lodges, June 1951, including "Digest of the Opinions of the Supreme Court Justices in the IWO Suit against the Attorney General's Subversive List," IWO-CU, box 10, folder 10. See Sabin, *Red Scare in Court*, 286, for the May 1951 *IWO News Bulletin* for news of the Supreme Court decision.

125. Sabin, *Red Scare in Court*, 284–290; Goldstein, *American Blacklist*.

126. Sabin, *Red Scare in Court*, 299–396.

127. Ibid., 306; "Alfred Bohlinger, Superintendent of Insurance, by William Karlin, senior Insurance Examiner," to Morris Greenbaum, CPA, March 25, 1952, and Eve Reidelman, secretary of Detroit JPFO, to Donner and Kinoy, December 21, 1951, IWOCF-CU, box 1.

128. Arthur Kinoy, preliminary notes on the NY State Appellate Court case, re: Liquidation of the IWO, to Sam Milgrom, Rubin Saltzman, Dave Greene, and Peter Shipka, July 8, 1952, IWOCF-CU, box 1; "Loyalty Question to Tenant Upheld," *New York Times*, March 9, 1954, 19, IWOCF-CU, box 3; Arthur Kinoy, *Rights on Trial* (Cambridge, MA: Harvard University Press, 1983), 39–96.

129. Petition for rehearing, filed by Philip McCook for IWO, September 11, 1952, IWOCF-CU, box 3; Memorandum to Supreme Court of NY State from Paul Williams and James Henry, special assistant attorneys general of NY State, September 16, 1952, ibid.

130. "Court of Appeals Opinion—I.W.O. v. Bohlinger, April 23, 1953," IWO-CU, box 23, folder 5; "Rozpustenie Medzinárod. Rob. Spolku" [Liquidation of the International Workers Order], *New Yorský denník*, April 25, 1953, 1. Pamphlet, *A Fraternal Organization Sentenced to Death! The Strange Case of the IWO Now Before the U.S. Supreme Court* [1953], IWO-CU, box 16, folder 13.

131. Joseph Petercsak, secretary, Lodge 1007, October 23, 1953, and Vera Gyurko, secretary, Lodge 1075, Hammond, Indiana, November 4, 1953, both to U.S. Supreme Court, IWOCF-CU, box 3.

132. News release, "Statement of the Policyholders Committee on U.S. Supreme Court Denial of Review of IWO Case," October 20, 1953, IWO-CU, box 16, folder 13; News release, "IWO Demands Re-Hearing of Supreme Court Denial to Hear Its Case" [1953], IWO-CU, box 23, folder 7; IWO lodges' petitions not to dissolve IWO, October 23 and November 4, 1953, IWOCF-CU, box 4; "Supreme Court Rejects Second Appeal of Order to Consider Appeal against Liquidation Order," *Morgen Freiheit*, December 5, 1953, 1, and "The Answer of the Members of the Order to the Dewey-Brownell Pogrom," *Morgen Freiheit*, editorial, December 9, 1953, 4, IWOCF-CU, box 2; Letter to all policyholders, November 18, 1953, IWO-CU, box 23, folder 3; Alfred Bohlinger to "All Policyholders and Certificate Holders of the International Workers Order," September 1, 1954, IWOCF-CU, box 2. Clipping, "Right to Belong to Fraternal Group Strangled by Gov't. Attack on IWO," *Daily Worker* [1953], IWOCF-CU, box 53.

133. William Karlin to "all Lodge officers of Lodges of IWO," December 15, 1953, IWO-CU, box 26, folder 14; Bohlinger to "All Policyholders and Certificate Holders of the International Workers Order"; Petition, "Assignment by Members of Cliffside Lodge No. 3118 of IWO to Arow Farm, Inc.," January 1955, and J. S. Landis to "Mr. Goldstein, re: IWO properties in New York area," May 8, 1956, IWO-CU, box 26, folder 11; Letter from Donner, Kinoy, and Perlin and Milton Friedman and Thomas Russel Jones, July 16, 1954, IWOCF-CU, box 3; Sam Pevzner to Arthur Kinoy, May 8, 1954 [actually 1955], IWOCF-CU, box 1. Michael Singer, "Camp Witchhunt Tries Intimidating Guests," *Daily Worker*, August 25, 1955, 3, IWO-CU, box 53.

134. "New Violation of Free Association," *Jewish Life*, March 1954, 30, IWO-CU, box 53.

135. "A Reply to 'Saint Bohlinger,'" *Morgen Freiheit*, February 4, 1954, 3, IWOCF-CU, box 2. On the following page, *Morgen Freiheit* printed a story about a member of the rival Socialist-led Workmen's Circle who opposed the IWO's liquidation.

136. Allan Rosenberg, counsel for IWO, to Attorney General Herbert Brownell, June 12, 1953, on why "the procedure" on subversive organizations is still unconstitutional, IWOCF-CU, box 2; Insurance Superintendent of New York to Arthur Kinoy, November 30, 1953, ibid.; Minutes, Executive Committee, IWO meeting, "Report on SACB," December 1, 1953, IWOCF-CU, box 3; Kinoy's appeal of denial of IWO request that Appeals Court order the NY Insurance Department to release funds so they could retain a lawyer for the SACB hearing, December 15, 1953, IWOCF-CU, box 2; SACB,

hearing for IWO, TS, December 16, 1953, IWOCF-CU, box 1; Order and report of the SACB, re: IWO, January 14, 1954, ibid.; Insurance Superintendent of New York to Kinoy; "Statement of the Former Officers of the Order Concerning the Order of the McCarran Board," *Morgen Freiheit*, January 16, 1954, 2, IWOCF-CU, box 2; Petition, Kinoy, to New York State Supreme Court to order the Insurance Department to release funds to pay the IWO's legal fees, February 3, 1954, IWOCF-CU, box 3; "A Court Throws Out Brownell's Order to the Late Order to Register," *Morgen Freiheit*, November 27 and 28, 1954, and Rockwell Kent's congratulation on a victory for democracy, IWOCF-CU, box 2; "IWO 'Subversive' Order Cancelled," *Jewish Life*, January 1955, 19, IWO-CU, box 53; Petercsak, and Gyurko, both to U.S. Supreme Court. Sabin, *Red Scare in Court*, 337–339.

CONCLUSION

1. Detroit Police report, August 26, 1948, box 2, folder 2-55, Don Binkowski Papers, Walter P. Reuther Library, Wayne State University [hereafter cited as DB-WSU]; Minutes, General Council meeting, September 7–8, 1946, folder 14, International Workers Order Records, Robert F. Wagner Labor Archives, Tamiment Library, New York University [hereafter cited as IWO-NYU]; George Starr, "To all Lodges in New Jersey, Philadelphia, Baltimore and Wash.," September 9, 1946, box 30, folder 7, International Workers Order Records, 1915–2002, MSS 5276, Kheel Center for Labor-Management Documentation and Archives, Cornell University [hereafter cited as IWO-CU].

2. Thomas Sugrue, "Crabgrass-Roots Politics: Race, Rights, and the Reaction against Liberalism in the Urban North, 1940–1964," *Journal of American History* 82, no. 2 (September 1995): 551–578; Thomas Sugrue, *The Origins of the Urban Crisis: Race and Inequality in Postwar Detroit* (Princeton, NJ: Princeton University Press, 1996).

3. Flyer, *Should Miss Liberty Be Deported? The Case of Peter Harisiades* [1950], box 46, Vito Marcantonio Papers, Manuscripts and Archives Division, The New York Public Library [hereafter cited as VM-NYPL]; Pamphlet, *A Fraternal Organization Sentenced to Death! The Strange Case of the IWO Now Before the U.S. Supreme Court* [1953], IWO-CU, box 16, folder 13.

4. FBI file, Detroit Polonia Society, 23, DB-WSU, box 5, folder 5-29; Detroit Police, Criminal Intelligence Bureau "red squad" surveillance, September 16, 1969, family-type picnic in Inkster, Michigan, DB-WSU, box 1, folder 1-11; Michigan State Police, Security Investigation Squad, complaint report, November 18, 1961, annual "Worker Bazaar" at Nowak Hall, Detroit, DB-WSU, box 7, folder 7-49; Michigan State Police, Security Investigation Squad, complaint report, Celebration, July 22, 1962, at Dom Polski, North Detroit, ibid.; Detroit Police, Criminal Intelligence Bureau report, February 16, 1966, Herbert Aptheker speaks against the Vietnam War, and flyer, *Eyewitness Report from Hanoi*, DB-WSU, box 2, folder 2-55; FBI report, October 31, 1964, Zygmunt Broniarek and Konrad Comorowski attend election rally and Halloween party for Coleman Young, DB-WSU, box 3, folder 3-8; Detroit Police, Intelligence Section report, "International Bazaar for Peace and Freedom," March 8, 1973, DB-WSU, box 2, folder 2-55; Detroit Police report, "The Communist Party in Detroit," October 21, 1936, includes mention of IWO hall, Muirland, and Fenkel Avenue, Detroit, ibid.

5. Erik McDuffie, *Sojourning for Freedom: Black Women, American Communism, and the Making of Black Left Feminism* (Durham, NC: Duke University Press, 2011); Dayo Gore, *Radicalism at the Crossroads: African American Women Activists in the Cold War* (New York: New York University Press, 2011).

6. *A Fraternal Organization Sentenced to Death!*

Index

Abraham Lincoln Brigade, 178–181
Abyssinia. *See* Ethiopia
Accidents, 20–23, 63, 64, 67, 74–75, 275n16
Adamic, Louis, 16, 129, 155, 161, 171, 206
Adi, Hakim, 98, 106–107
Aetna Life Insurance Company, 246
African Americans, 14, 35, 38, 43, 66, 82, 97, 102–104, 112–114, 118; colonialism and, 207; CPUSA and, 7, 65, 98–101, 109, 175; fascism and, 178, 181; insurance and, 3, 36, 45–46, 51, 102; police and, 60–61; Social Security and, 62; unions and, 79, 96
African National Congress, 113, 207
Agitational Propaganda Committee, CPUSA, 8
Ahmad, Jumal, 134–135
Al Moss Singers, 191
Alexander, June Granatir, 99
Alger, Horatio, 150
Alien Registration Act, 78, 186
All-American Anti-Imperialist League, 100
All Our Yesterdays, 15, 153
All-Slav Blood Donors' Parade, 196
Amalgamated Association of Iron, Steel and Tin Workers, 80–81
Amalgamated Clothing Workers of America, 80, 84
Amalgamation, 12, 29, 30, 36–41, 44, 101
Amalgamation Sub-Committee, Language Department, CPUSA, 39

Ambulances, 3, 180–182, 195, 199
American Civil Liberties Union, 78, 172, 221
American Committee for Protection of Foreign Born, 5, 236, 241
American Committee for the Defense of Ethiopia, 176
American Council for a Democratic Greece, 209
American Crusade against Lynching, 14, 97, 129, 262
American Federation of Labor, 79, 101, 221
American Labor Party, 159
American League Against War and Fascism, 183
American Legion, 164, 232
American Medical Association, 94; 298n125
American Negro Labor Congress, 100, 101
American Red Cross, 120, 191, 192, 195–197
American Russian Fraternal Society, IWO, 30, 199, 200, 232–234, 257
American Slav Congress, 4, 15, 84, 89, 171, 197–202, 223, 240–241; anti-militarism of, 209–210; civil rights and, 98, 111–112, 117, 122–123, 129, 135, 161; colonialism and, 16, 122, 129, 205–207; strikes and, 79, 86, 87
Americanization, 37, 38, 44, 47, 48, 54; ethnic pride and, 146–147, 154–156, 158; whiteness and, 99, 109
Amis, B. D., 60–61, 103

Amter, Israel, 107
Amusement parks, 140, 142, 172–173
Anarchism, 106, 168, 178–180, 324n28
Angelo Herndon, 151
Angelo Herndon Back in Atlanta, 151
Anticolonialism, 4, 15, 77, 120, 130, 167–168, 181, 184, 187–188, 190, 207, 328n61; American Slav Congress and, 122, 129–130, 205–207; CPUSA and, 100–101, 106–107, 130, 174–175; *Rovnosť ludu* and, 99–100
Anti-Communism, 8, 16, 92, 146, 163, 198, 215–218, 223–224, 232, 234–235; directed at civil-rights activists, 104, 113, 120, 125, 229, 231; HUAC and, 75–76, 87, 92, 219, 221–223, 229, 231, 240; liquidation trial and, 251–252
Antifascism, 167, 184, 189–190; civil rights and, 111, 117; Germany and, 170–172; Greece and, 209; Italy and, 43, 324n28; Spain and, 160, 172, 180–181; 327n46
Anti-militarism, 167–168, 187, 208–209, 226; Italy and, 43, 167, 176; Soviet Union and, 113, 160, 167, 207–209, 211–212
Anti-Nazi Federation of New York, 172–173, 323n17
Anti-Semitism, 11, 54, 113, 115, 117, 156
Anti-syndicalist laws, 78, 216
Apartheid, 100, 113–114, 207
Apelman, Joseph, 236–237
Aptheker, Herbert, 18, 263
Arabs, 1, 3, 10, 14, 46, 97, 102, 103
Arendt, Hannah, 241
Aria Singing Society, 236
Army, 17, 111, 116, 118, 199
Arow Farm, 158, 257
Art, 93–94, 119, 136, 150, 224
Artkino Films, 230
Asiatic Exclusion Laws, 121
Atlanta University, 152
Atlantic Charter, 4, 15, 122, 199, 205, 206
Attorney General's List of Subversive Organizations, 5, 17, 92, 213–215, 225–228, 231–232, 234; civil-rights activists and, 132, 163; INS and, 236; IWO liquidation and, 245, 255
Autoworkers, 6, 81, 86–88, 103

Bacich, Leo, 129
Bakhtin, Mikhail, 141
Bakunin, Mikhail, 22
Baldwin, Roger, 78

Baltimore Afro-American, 3, 45, 62, 118, 174
Bands, 14, 138, 141, 147, 150
Baron, Sam, 180
Barrett, James, 11, 79, 157
Barretta, Scott, 143
Baseball, 3, 14, 104, 131–132, 136, 138, 145, 147–148, 158, 251
Basketball, 4, 14, 136, 147–148, 158
Bates, Beth Tompkins, 109
Battle for Russia, 164
Battle of the Overpass, 87
Bedacht, Max, 33, 34, 48, 53, 61–62, 67, 218–219, 222; attitude toward capitalism, 55–58; fascism and, 170–171, 182, 220; civil rights and, 111, 129, 149; CPUSA and, 8, 21, 28, 32, 52, 64, 142, 221, 251; New Deal and, 70–72, 74–75; Soviet Union and, 166; supports CIO, 82–83, 92; supports Wagner-Murray-Dingell Bill, 93; World War II and, 42, 43, 187, 189, 195, 204
Belle Isle Park, Detroit, 158, 199
Benjamin, Herbert, 48, 189–191
Bentall, David, 78
Bethlehem Steel Company, 25, 38
Bilbo, Theodore G., 114–115, 159
Bill of Rights, 17, 44, 46, 115, 202, 215, 219–220, 227, 229, 262
Bill of Rights Day, 17, 215
Bimba, Anthony, 45, 144
Birth control, 49, 93, 298n121
Bittner, Van, 81
Bivouac, 151
Black Belt Thesis, 102–103
Black, Hugo, 255
Black Muslims, 3, 10, 14, 18, 46, 97, 103, 129, 134–135
Blood drives, 15, 120, 195–196, 223
Blues to Now—and Then Some!, 152
Boatini, Paul, 158
Bodnar, John, 99
Bohlinger, Alfred, 248, 250, 258, 263
Bonus Army, 59
Borich, Frank, 26–27
Boskey, Harry, 163
Bowling, 4, 138, 142, 149
Boxing, 136, 138, 147
Bridgeman, Reginald, 106–107
Bridges, Harry, 78, 251
Briggs, Cyril, 127
British Communist Party, 106
Broadway 1934, 147

Brodsky, Joseph R., 52, 104, 182, 191, 218, 224
Brooklyn Dodgers, 3, 131
Brotherhood Week, 119, 125, 156, 163
Browder, Earl, 6, 43, 68, 108, 176, 182, 217
Brown, John, 151
Brown v. Board of Education, 116
Budenz, Louis, 247, 249, 251
Buff, Rachel, 5, 78, 216, 240
Buhle, Paul, 9, 12
Bulgarian Workers' Mutual Benefit and Educational Society, 41
Bulgarians, 41–42
Bullitt, William, 166
The Bulls See Red, 149
Bulosan, Carlos, 78
Burrows Charles, 160

The Call, 31, 69, 180
Calypso, 120, 159
"Calypso Song of 'The Common Man'," 120, 159
Camp Kinderland, 119, 128, 136, 145, 158, 161
Camp Lakeland, 31, 128, 145, 160
Camp McGehee, Arkansas, 121
Camp Nitgedaiget, 136, 145
Camp Robin Hood, 163
Camp Wo-Chi-Ca, 146
Camp Wocolona, 145, 158
Candela, Luigi, 28, 43, 112, 126, 145, 176
Cape Verdeans, 45–46, 102
Capone, Al, 61
Carnegie Chamber Music Hall, 148
Carpatho-Russian Society, IWO, 83
Carpatho-Russians, 23, 83, 89, 156–157, 237
Carter, Dan, 104, 106, 107
Castledine, Jacqueline, 5
Caute, David, 234, 251
Cemeteries, 56, 197, 249, 256
Central Control Commission, CPUSA, 34
Cervantes Fraternal Society, IWO, 14, 46, 47, 91, 101–103, 148
Chamberlain, Neville, 184, 188
Chambers, Whittaker, 163
Chandra, Krishna, 241
Chapman, Abraham, 230
Chicago Cubs, 131
Chicago Defender, 45, 118, 148, 149
Chicago Tribune, 85–86
China, 130, 167, 169, 174–175, 209
Chinese, 36, 45, 121
Chomucky, Gizella, 179

Choruses, 4, 14, 119, 138, 141, 143–144, 149–150, 157
Churchill, Winston, 15, 122, 190, 199, 202, 204, 208
Cincinnati Reds, 131
Cinco de Mayo, 157
CIO News, 124
CIO Political Action Committee, 87, 92
Civil rights, 11, 13–14, 46, 97–98, 104, 110, 112, 115–117, 133, 253; American Slav Congress and, 123; anti-Communism and, 124–125, 135, 148, 229–231, 240, 252; CPUSA and, 68, 100–103; JPFO and, 96; supported by Polish Section, IWO, 60, 118–119, 229
Civil Rights Act, 10
Civil Rights Congress, 5, 35, 42, 115, 119, 124–125, 229, 231
Civilian and National Defense Exposition, 161–162, 191
Civilian defense, 46, 161–162, 191, 195
Clark, Tom, 7, 163, 213–216, 225–229, 231, 233, 235–236
Cleveland Indians, 132, 148
Cloward, Richard, 63
Club Calypso, Harlem, 159
Club Obrero Español, IWO, 160
Coal and Iron police, 26, 76
The Coal Digger, 76
Coal miners, 68, 140; Health and safety, 19–20, 51, 74–75, 293n72; strikes and, 23, 25, 35, 64–65, 76–79, 89–90, 141, 216, 217; unions and, 75–76, 78, 80; workers' compensation and, 51, 74–75
Codes of Fair Competition, NIRA, 67–69
Cold War, 16–18, 29, 205–207, 212, 234, 240, 244, 246, 251, 257; anticolonialism and, 168, 205–207; displaced persons and, 210; racism and, 113; Slavs and, 157, 160
Colón, Jesús, 102
Colonialism, 122, 130, 172, 187–189, 205, 207; American Slav Congress and, 129; CPUSA and, 99–101, 106, 174–175, 178
Colorado Fuel and Iron Company, 23
Columbus Day, 154
Commager, Henry Steele, 215
Committee for Democracy in Spain, 160
Committee in Defense of Henry Podolski, 242
Communist International, 5, 12, 25, 26, 69, 77, 98, 252
Communist Party Left Opposition, 34

Communist Party USA, 5–6, 8, 21, 230, 246, 249, 252; antifascism, 175, 177, 180; civil rights and, 61, 65, 98–100, 102–104, 108–110, 121–122, 130, 229; entertainment and, 140, 142, 144; New Deal and, 69–70; Social Security and, 59, 63–65, 75; unions and, 77–78, 83; work with fraternal societies, 9, 12, 24–29, 32–33, 37, 41, 43; World War II, 44, 47, 121–122, 183–186
Communist Political Association, 47
Company towns, 36, 66, 77, 79, 217, 232–233
The Compass, 250
Coney Island Stadium, Brooklyn, 141
Congress of Industrial Organizations, 2, 6, 35, 78, 90, 221; CPUSA and, 9, 231; IWO support for, 80–83, 87, 92; Memorial Day massacre, 85–87
Congressional Record, 120, 214
Connor, Eugene "Bull," 34, 217
Constitution, 115, 215, 222, 225, 227–229, 253
Continental Assurance Company of Illinois, 257
Coolidge, Calvin, 145
Cooperatives, 41
The Copper Miner, 66
Copper miners, 66
Council of African Affairs, 113–114, 178, 207, 261
Counter-Olympics, 147
Coward, Noel, 152
Cowie, Jefferson, 71
The Crisis, 230
Croatian American Civic Club, 236
Croatian Fraternal Union, 24–27, 81, 171, 236
Croatian Glee Club, Gary, Indiana, 236
Croatians, 24–27, 42, 81, 128–129, 171, 210, 236
Cruse, Harold, 133
Cuba, 99, 100, 212
Cubans, 46, 102, 188
Curzon Line, 203–204
Cvetic, Mathew, 251, 252
Czechoslovakia, 3, 4, 155, 164, 188, 203, 318n55
Czechs, 35, 39, 77

Dachau, 129
Dafora, Asadata, 152
Daily Forverts, 168
Daily Worker, 32, 34, 41, 45, 54, 126, 142, 144, 159, 166, 221; civil rights and, 50, 131;

foreign policy and, 176; IWO and, 50, 64, 81, 87, 138, 222, 246; New Deal and, 68; unions and, 81, 87, 92
Dainoff, Clara, 65–66, 289n36
Daladier, Édouard, 184, 188
D'Amato, Philip, 94
Danceland Auditorium, Detroit, 141–142
Dancing, 119, 140–142, 144, 148, 152, 154–156, 159–162, 174, 191, 218n55
Dante Alighieri Lodge, International Workers Order, 75
Darlan, François, 198
Davidowitz, Lucy, 29
Davis, Benjamin, 119, 159
Davis, John P., 178
Day nurseries, 49
De Valera, Eamon, 106
Debs, Eugene, 160
Declaration of Independence, 17, 46, 215, 242
Delco Worker, 68
Delray Communist Club, Michigan, 126
Democratic Party, 10, 12, 33, 37, 70, 117, 173, 217, 218, 221
Denning, Michael, 139, 159
Dental clinics, 1, 2, 40, 45, 49, 136
Deportations, 210, 216, 233; 236–245, 251–252, 255; Gebert, 77–78; Dainoff, 65–66; Hyndman, 117, 240–241; Milgrom, 216–217, 241; Nowak, 17, 238–241; Petrosky, 66; Yokinen, 127
Detroit Free Press, 146, 199, 200, 240
Dewey, Thomas, 248
Diallo, Abdoulay, 126
Diamond, Andrew, 10
Dickstein, Samuel, 124
Dies Bill, 216
Dies, Martin, 7, 56, 75, 87, 123, 124, 189, 216, 219–225
D'Inzillo, Mario, 118–119
Displaced Persons, 17, 209–211, 240–241
Dmytryshyn, Andrew, 211, 241, 244, 245, 252
Dobbs, Farrell, 179
Doby, Larry, 132
Don't You Want to Be Free?, 151–152
Doroshkin, Sadie, 81, 171
Douglass, Frederick, 101, 151, 180, 215
Douglass-Lincoln Society, IWO, 47, 101, 103, 119, 126, 134, 155, 161, 213
Dramatski Zbor "Nada," Chicago, 150
Drayton, Arthur, 230–231
Druggists, 49, 176

Du Bois, W.E.B., 10, 80
Du Sable Lodge, IWO, 35, 51, 81, 152
Dujka, Joe, 148
Dziennik Polski, 84

The Earth Moves, 147
Ebbets Field, 131, 148
Einstein, Albert, 182
Ellington, Duke, 159
Ellis Island, 241
Em-fuehrer Jones, 152
Emma Lazarus Division, 82, 113–114, 154–155, 207
Employee representation plans, 67
Engdahl, J. Louis, 106
England, Elizabeth, 151
English-language lodges, IWO, 14, 36, 38–39, 44–46, 48, 102
Esch, Elizabeth, 68, 109, 130
Estonians, 29
Ethiopia, 3, 15, 43, 167, 175–179, 181, 188, 189, 191, 324n28
Ethiopian World Federation, 178
Ethnic pride, 47, 102, 137–138, 146–148, 154–158, 161
Eureka Lodge, IWO, 34
Evictions, 2, 27, 64–67, 88
Eyerman, Ron, 143

Fair Employment Practices Committee, 3, 14, 111–117, 119
Fair Labor Standards Act, 70, 169
Falkowski, Ed, 88, 203–204
Famine in Ukraine, 168–169
Fascism, 3, 69–70, 89, 117, 167, 169, 210–211; in Germany, 170–174, 184, 189–190; in Greece, 209; in Italy, 175–178; in Japan, 174–175; in Spain, 178–181; in U.S., 67–68, 85, 91, 108, 115, 163, 198, 199, 214, 220, 226, 227, 234, 240, 241, 258, 262
Fast, Howard, 116
Federal Arts Project, 93–94
Federal Bureau of Investigation, 46, 49, 77, 130, 214, 222, 223, 227, 229–233, 251; Civil rights and, 115–117, 123–124, 126, 129, 161, 195; "Fifth Columnists" and, 16, 201; internal security index, 123–124, 309n82; IWO entertainments and, 15, 160–162; strikes and, 87; World War II, 190, 195, 196, 201, 236
Federal Mines Safety and Inspection Act, 75

Federation of Workers Choruses, 149–150
Ferrer, José, 50
Feurer, Rosemary, 9, 86
Fiesta Republicana, 160
"Fifth columnists," 16, 112, 199–202
Fijan, Carol, 153
Filipinos, 68, 121
Film, 50, 94, 111, 136, 138, 140, 144, 147, 152, 164, 230
Finland, 164
Finnish Bureau, CPUSA, 26
Finnish Progressive Hall, Harlem, New York, 127, 152
Finnish Workers' Clubs, 41
Finns, 26, 28, 41, 127, 152, 158, 186
Firestone, Harvey, 130
Five-year plan, 34, 55
Flamenco, 148, 160
Folk music, 143
Football, 136
Ford, Henry, 56, 143, 166, 189
Ford Hunger March, 41, 87
Ford, James, 38, 79, 103, 175–176
Ford Motor Company, 13, 41, 87
Ford "Service Department," 87
Foreign Nationalities Branch, OSS, 12, 137, 189, 202, 205
Forer, Morris, 116
The Forgotten Man, 151
Foster, William Z., 142, 159
Foucault, Michel, 232
Four Freedoms, 4, 12, 72, 98, 120, 122, 158, 199, 225
France, 15, 178, 180, 184–185, 187, 189–190, 242
Franco, Francisco, 3, 160, 167, 172, 178, 180, 181, 183
Frank, Waldo, 172
Frankensteen, Richard, 87
Franklin, Benjamin, 239
Franklin D. Roosevelt Hospital Fund, IWO, 256
Fraternal Orders Committee, 83
Fraternal Outlook, 78, 230, 245, 247; civil rights, 108–111, 128; HUAC, 219–221; Loyalist Spain, 183; Truman Doctrine, 211; universal health care, 93; World War II, 199, 203
Frazier-Lundeen Bill, 62
Frazier, Robeson Taj, 175
Freedom, 207

Freedom Crusade, 229
Freedom Road, 152
Freiheit Gesangs Verein, 143
Freiheit Mandolin Orchestra, 144
Friends of the Abraham Lincoln Brigade, 160
Friends of the Soviet Union, 143
Front Line Fighters Fund, IWO, 4, 15, 178, 191, 192, 194–197, 256
Furniture workers, 76, 80

Galperin, Isaac, 20, 21
Gandhi, Mohandas, 122
Gardos, Emil, 25, 37, 42–43, 49, 59, 105–106
Garibaldi Battalion, 179
Garibaldi Society, IWO, 42, 47; anti-Communism and, 215, 231–232, 247, 255; civil rights and, 112, 114, 118, 159; entertainments, 145; strikes and, 79; universal health care and, 94; "white chauvinism" and, 116, 125–126
Garland, Walter, 181
Garment workers, 22, 80
Garvey, Marcus, 100
Garveyites, 34–35, 100, 175–176
Gary Civil Liberties Committee, Indiana, 117
Gebert, Boleslaw K. (Bill), 42, 48, 205, 293n72; civil rights and, 108, 119; CPUSA work, 26–27, 32, 39, 77–78, 328n61; deportation attempts, 77–78, 216; unemployment insurance and, 68; unions and, 68, 77–78, 81
Gedicks, Al, 12, 28
Gellert, Hugo, 145
Gellman, Erik, 5, 98, 130
Gender, 3, 46, 82, 109, 143, 171, 207; anti-deportation campaigns, 238–239, 241; anti-eviction campaigns, 65–66; birth control, 49–50; civil rights and, 113–114; unions and, 35, 62, 65, 81, 141
General Motors Corporation, 90
German-American Committee for Spanish Relief, 182
German Bureau, CPUSA, 69
German Communist Party, 172
Germans, 38, 69, 76, 173
Germany, 17, 106, 167, 169–175, 178, 188, 201, 208, 227, 230
Geyer Bill, 110
Gilbert and Sullivan, 153
Girdler, Tom, 83–85
Gitlow, Ben, 141

Glos Ludowy, 196, 209, 212, 214, 227, 229, 242, 244
God's Trombones, 152
Gold, Ben, 173
Gold Coast, Africa, 106
Gold, Mike, 145
Goldman, Seymour, 229–230
Good Housekeeping, 145
Goodwin, Tom, 180
Gordon, June, 113, 114
Gore, Dayo, 5, 82, 130, 207, 263
Gramsci, Antonio, 139
Great Britain, 15, 44, 93, 106, 122, 178, 184–191, 202, 205–206, 208
Great Depression, 1–2, 12, 37–38, 52, 55–59, 61, 64, 73, 83, 240, 254; evictions and, 65; Soviet Union and, 166
Grecht, Rebecca, 80–81, 176–177
Greece, 206, 208–209, 244
Greek Catholic Union, 23
Greeks, 45, 46
Green, James, 9
Greenberg, Henry Clay, 247, 249–251, 253, 255–256
Greene, Dave, 21, 61, 92, 107, 161, 258
Greenfield Village, Michigan, 143
Greenhill, Jack, 47–48
Gropper, William, 94, 95, 219–220
Gross, Kali, 66
Guantanamo, 262
Guaranteed annual income, 13, 57, 63, 73–74
Guardian Life Insurance Company, 246
Guderian, Heinz, 208
Guthrie, Woody, 159
Gymnastics, 4, 14, 136, 147

Hahn, Steven, 100
Haiti, 99–100, 130, 207
Halder, Franz, 208
Haley, James, 244–245, 247, 253, 255
Haley Report, 244–245, 255
Hammersmark, Sam, 34
Harden, Reverend S. M., 51
Harisiades, Peter, 241–244
Harlem Community Center, 174–175
Harlem Division, CPUSA, 174
Harlem Labor Lyceum, 31
Harlem People's Art Group, 153
Harlem Renaissance, 159
Harlem Suitcase Theater, 14–15, 151–153
Harlem Workers' Center, 175–176

Harlem Workers School, 143
Harlem YWCA, 152
Harris, Lashawn, 65
Hate strikes, 88, 95–96, 117, 307n61
Hathaway, Clarence, 103, 182
Haym Solomon Lodge, Jewish Peoples Fraternal Order, 210
Haynes, John Earl, 5
Hays, Arthur Garfield, 172
Haywood, Harry, 127, 181
Health and Security for America, 94
Hearst, William Randolph, 16, 179, 201
Hellenic American Brotherhood, IWO, 209, 243–244
Herndon, Angelo, 14, 78, 105, 107, 108
Hill, Reverend Charles, 118, 125–126, 128, 158, 241
Hill, Rebecca, 151
Himmler, Heinrich, 227
Hirsch, Arnold, 10, 96, 118
Hiss, Alger, 163
Hitler, Adolf, 89–90, 111, 117, 122, 158, 178, 190–192, 195, 199–200, 258; alleged collaborators with, 17, 112, 114, 123, 179, 189, 190, 200–201, 208, 210, 211; leftist warnings about, 170–173; nonaggression pact and, 183, 185, 186, 188; Spain and, 160, 181
Ho Chi Minh, 207
Hobbs Bill, 219, 242
Hobbs, Sam, 219
Hoffman, Clare, 222
Hoover, Herbert, 2, 56, 57, 73, 130, 166
Hoover, J. Edgar, 7, 56, 123–124, 205, 309n82
Hoovervilles, 2, 57
Horne, Gerald, 80
Hospitals, 50, 156, 157, 241, 256, 298n121; charity hospitals, 49, 91; in Loyalist Spain, 180, 182; miners and, 75; Wagner-Murray-Dingell Bill and, 94
House Un-American Activities Committee, 8, 16, 163, 214, 237, 252; American Slav Congress and, 86; civil rights and, 120, 135, 231, 240; CIO and, 87, 92; Martin Dies and, 75–76, 124, 216, 219–223, 225
Housing conditions, 13, 51, 66, 88, 91, 124, 146, 252
Hromiko, Andy, 172, 225
Hughes, Langston, 14, 151–152, 159, 181
Hull, Cordell, 203
Hull, William, 224
Hungarian American Brotherhood, 101

Hungarian Bureau, CPUSA, 28, 29, 37, 42, 59
Hungarian Workers' Sick Benefit and Educational Federation, IWO, 9, 28, 29, 44–45, 105
Hungarians, 25, 35, 53; amalgamation and, 29, 39, 40; civil rights and, 87–88, 101, 105; CPUSA and, 28, 42; Unemployed Councils and, 59
Hungary, 203
Hyndman, Katherine, 117, 240–241

Ickes, Harold, 223
Ignatiev, Noel, 97
Imitations of Life, 152
Immigration and Naturalization Service, 78, 213, 216, 226, 233, 236–238, 245, 255
Independent Workmen's Circle, 12, 29
India, 15, 77, 101, 122, 147, 187–188, 190, 205–207, 328n61
Indian National Congress, 101, 122
Indonesia, 206
Industrial Workers of the World, 86, 101
Insurance, 1, 12, 21, 22, 37, 48–53, 70, 79; liquidation proceedings, 246–250; Massachusetts case against IWO, 217–218; racial discrimination and, 3, 36, 45, 46, 50–51, 103, 133–135, 152
Internal Revenue Service, 213, 228
Internal status markers, 138, 157
International Bazaar for Peace and Freedom, 263
International Brigades, 178, 180–181
International Fur and Leather Workers Union, 146, 173, 221
International Labor Defense, 85, 104–107, 142, 172, 221
International Ladies Garment Workers Union, 182
International Orchestra, 143
International Red Poets' Nite Dance Bacchanal, 159
International Union of Mine, Mill and Smelter Workers, 90
International Workers' Aid, 141
International Workers' Camp, Morristown, New Jersey, 141
International Workers' Home, Detroit, 140
Interracialism, 2, 3, 10, 11, 14, 18, 35, 45, 98, 105, 119–120, 133, 146, 159–163, 249; Civil Rights Congress and, 124–125; CPUSA and, 68, 101, 141–142, 163; in English-language

Interracialism (continued)
  IWO lodges, 38–39, 46, 102, 118; hospitals and, 50; sharecroppers and, 34, 76; unions, 61, 65, 76–78, 96, 101; "white chauvinism" and, 103, 160–161
Intersectionality, 57, 61, 68, 82, 88, 92, 96, 109, 113–114, 262
"Invasion Bonds," 199
Ireland, 106
Irish, 106
Irish Republican Army, 106
Irish Workers' Clubs, IWO, 106
Isolationism, 43–44, 185, 189, 191
Isserman, Maurice, 5, 184
Italian American Radio Club of Detroit, 94
Italian Anti-Fascist Committee, 179
Italian Bureau, CPUSA, 43, 145
Italian Communist Party, 172
Italians, 38, 50, 59; anti-fascism, 176–179; civil right and, 112, 114–116, 118; Communism and, 28, 42; HUAC and, 75, 219; "white chauvinism" and, 116, 125–126, 128
Italy, 169, 175, 177–179, 191
It's Funny as Hell, 147
IWO Band, 147
IWO Conference on Social Security, 62
IWO Dramatic Festival, 147
IWO Freedom Theatre, 15, 153
IWO Junior Band, 191
IWO Junior Branch, 180, 184, 215, 224
IWO League Against Fascism and Dictatorship, 185
IWO Medical Department, 49, 50, 176–177
IWO National Education Department, 45, 190
IWO National Film Division, 138, 164
IWO National Youth Day, 149
IWO News Bulletin, 255
IWO Policyholders Protective Committee, 18, 248, 250, 257, 263
IWO Sick Benefit Department, 20, 53
IWO Workers' Schools, 14, 45, 46, 256, 263
IWO Youth Section, 14, 44, 67, 104, 147, 197

Jacobson, Matthew Frye, 97, 195
Jacoby, Bob, 149–150
Japan, 167, 169, 174–175, 208
Japanese, 36, 38, 45, 68, 102, 120–121
Japanese American Committee for Democracy, 121
Jasper, James, 139, 141, 143
Jednota, 109, 196

Jefferson, Thomas, 17, 149, 215, 239, 244
Jenks, Marcus, 27–28
Jewish Children's Schools, 156, 157
Jewish Fraction, Communist Party Actions Committee, 29–30
Jewish Fraternalist, 95, 134, 205, 226
Jewish Life, 131, 206, 258
Jewish Peoples Committee for United Action Against Fascism and Anti-Semitism, 173
Jewish Peoples Fraternal Order, IWO, 48, 155, 214, 215, 230, 235, 236, 256; Civil rights and, 95–96, 113, 115, 118, 119, 161; Cold War, 205, 209, 210; CPUSA and, 32; ethnic pride and, 157; interracialism and, 158, 161; intersectionality and, 82; universal health care supported, 50; "white chauvinism" and, 128, 160; Workmen's Circle and, 7, 22, 29, 31; World War II, 192, 194–195
Jewish Peoples Schools, 173
Jews, 22, 28, 41, 44, 113, 115, 144, 158, 185–186, 210
Jim Crow. *See* Segregation
John Reed Branch, IWO, 34
John Reed Youth Club, Jersey City, 147
Johnson, Grace, 107
Johnson, James P., 152
Johnson, Manning, 251
Johnson, Paul, 119
Johnson, Timothy, 7
Joint Anti-Fascist Refugee Committee, 160
Jones, James Earl, 152
Jones, Robert Earl, 15, 152
Joseph R. Brodsky Welfare Fund, 19, 75, 235
JPFO Book Fund, 256
JPFO Fraternal Songsters, 157
Justice Department, 65, 118, 227–228, 233, 240–242, 244

Kahn, Albert, 212
Kanstroom, Daniel, 78, 216
Kapp putsch, 171
Karelia, 28
Karlin, William, 248, 256
Kasustchik, Daniel, 79, 170, 233, 234
Katz, Michael, 63
"Keep America Free," 155
Keep Up!, 153–154
Keeran, Roger, 6, 86
Keller, Paul, 149–150
Kelley, Robin, 7, 88, 103, 177
Kent, Rockwell, 155, 213, 225, 227, 228, 241,

249, 253; civil rights and, 132; during World War II, 198; passport denial, 8, 242; Stockholm Peace Conference, 212
Kimeldorf, Howard, 80
King Alexander of Yugoslavia, 171
Kinoy, Arthur, 256
Klehr, Harvey, 5
Kleinberg, Sarah, 235–236
Kleinberg, Solomon, 235–236
Knox, Frank, 198
Knudsen, William, 189
Koch, Ilse, 208
Koch, Jerome, 52, 70
Kofsky, Frank, 211
Končinský, František, 153
Konecky, Eugene, 131
Korea, 174
Korean War, 91, 211
Korematsu v. United States, 121
Korenič, Charles, 70, 77
Kornfeder, Joseph Zach, 252
Kosciuszko Day, 154
Kovess, Louis, 64
Krankenkasse Verein, 76
Krchmarek, Anthony, 195
Kristallnacht, 173
Krock, Arthur, 204
Kronstadt, 168
Kruse, Kevin, 10
Krzycki, Eugene, 160–161
Krzycki, Leo, 17, 84, 86, 98, 112, 159, 161, 271n52
Ku Klux Klan, 110, 122–125, 231, 240

La Follette, Robert M. Junior, 86
La Progressiva Lodge, IWO, 75
Labor Chautauquas, 141, 144
Labor Day, 80, 95, 154
Labor Defender, 85
Labor lyceums, 143
Labor Sports Union of America, 142
La Guardia, Fiorello, 131, 172
Landis, Kenesaw Mountain, 131
Landsmanshaftn, 22
Language Department, CPUSA, 24, 25, 27, 29, 37, 39, 64
Lassalle, Ferdinand, 22
Latvian Agitprop Bureau, CPUSA, 24
Latvians, 24, 44, 104, 150
Il Lavoratore, 145
League Against Imperialism, 106

League of Nations, 203
League of Struggle for Negro Rights, 104–105, 107, 127
Leibowitz, Samuel, 107
Lend-Lease, 43, 111, 186–187, 191
Lenin, Vladimir, 52, 141, 150
Leningrad Music Hall, 164
Let's Get Together, 15, 153
Levin, Emanuel, 108
Levine, Lawrence, 144, 154
Lewis, John L., 9, 80, 84, 87, 89–90
Liberia, 130
Liberty Singing Society, IWO, 158–159
Lidice, Czechoslovakia, 153
Limitations of Life, 152
Lincoln, Abraham, 149, 215, 222, 239, 244
The Lincoln Brigadiers, 148
Lincoln Players, Cleveland, 152
Lippmann, Walter, 204
Lipsitz, George, 64, 90
Liquidation, 8, 10, 17–18, 119, 138, 245–248, 250, 254–258; IWO members protest, 61, 133, 197, 250, 253–254, 258; private insurance companies and, 133, 134, 245, 257; Workmen's Circle protests, 346n135
Lithuanian Bureau, CPUSA, 41, 45
Lithuanian Working Women's Alliance of America, 143
Lithuanians, 24, 41, 45, 50, 62, 76, 127, 142, 143, 210–211
Litvinov, Maxim, 169, 178, 192
Longshoremen, 38, 80
Lord Beaverbrook, 199
Lord Halifax, 189
L'Ouverture, Toussaint, 207
Lovestone, Jay, 28, 143–144
Lovestonites, 103
Loyalty Board, 225, 228–230
Loyen, S. M., 127, 171
Ludlow Massacre, 23
Ľudový denník, 110, 155
Ľudový kalendár, 90, 206
Luis Olmo League, 148
Luna Park, Brooklyn, 172–173
L'Unita del Popolo, 232
Lynching, 2–3, 14, 97–99, 104–105, 107–112, 117, 129, 148, 149, 161, 187; dramatized, 151, 152, 155; *Fraternal Outlook* and, 108–109; Garibaldi Society against, 118–119; Slavic campaigns against, 97, 99, 108, 110, 119

MacArthur, Douglas, 59
Magli, Vito, 215
Majdanek, 113
Manchuria, 167, 188
Mandolin orchestras, 4, 14, 119, 143, 144, 150, 154
Mannerheim Line, 164, 186
Marcantonio, Vito: Attorney General's List of Subversive Organizations, 214; Civil rights and, 114–115, 118, 121, 123–125, 131–132, 159; CPUSA and, 227, 247, 249; FBI internal security index and, 17, 123–124, 309n82; HUAC and, 75, 219, 222; Loyalist Spain supported, 179, 182–183; Memorial Day massacre and, 85; New Deal and, 72, 75; WPA and, 71; World War II, 198
March on Washington movement, 111
Margaret Sanger Clinic, 49
Marine workers, 80, 91
Marines, 99, 130, 236
Marshall Plan, 209, 211, 245
Marx, Karl, 22, 52, 139, 141
Marxism, 7, 23, 139; CIO and, 83; IWO and, 20, 22, 32, 52, 57, 70, 102, 149, 255
Masculinity, 35, 57, 72, 151, 181
Massachusetts Department of Insurance, 182, 217–218
Maxwell, William, 5, 98
May Day, 140, 143
McCarran Act, 258
McCarran, Pat, 247
McCarran-Walter Act, 239–240, 242
McCarthy, Joseph, 86
McDuffie, Erik, 5, 98, 263
McGee, Willie, 108, 119, 161
McNutt, Paul, 223
McQueen, Butterfly, 152
Mead, James, 119
Medical Bureau and North American Committee to Aid Spanish Democracy, 182
Medical clinics, 1, 40, 45, 49–51, 57, 93–94
Memorial Day Massacre, 83–86
Mercer County Legislative Conference, New Jersey, 116
Metropolitan Interfaith and Interracial Coordinating Council, 131, 148
Metropolitan Life Insurance Company, 51
Mexicans, 3, 36, 38, 45, 100, 102, 157, 275n16
Mexico, 23, 94, 100, 212
Michels, Tony, 7, 9, 12, 28
Michigan Department of Insurance, 222

Middleton, John, 94, 116, 125, 198, 219, 224, 234
Mikołajczyk, Stanisław, 203
Milgrom, Sam, 155, 164, 213, 214; African American lodges and, 51; anti-racism and, 110, 115, 125, 128, 132, 148; Arabic lodges and, 46; deportation attempts, 216–217, 241; displaced persons and, 210; Wagner-Murray-Dingell Bill, 94–95
The Militant, 33
Miller, Benjamin, 104
Miller, James, 106
Miller, Karen, 10
Milwaukee Leader, 160
Minerich, Anthony, 76
Minor, Robert, 182
Minstrel shows, 160–161
Mircheff, Bocho, 41–42
Mitchell, Henry, 224
Mkize, Bertha, 113–114
Mollin, Marian, 212
Molly Maguires, 86
Monroe Doctrine, 99
Montreal New Theatre, 152
Mooney, Tom, 105
Moore, Pecola, 133–134
Moorer, James, 51, 158
Morawska, Ewa, 157
Morell, Peter, 219–220
Moreno, Peter, 148, 157
Morgen Freiheit, 31, 185, 238, 246, 252, 258
Morse, Wayne, 206
Moscow Conference, 202–203
Moscow purge trials, 169–170
Moscow University for Western Minorities, 41
Moseley, Bill, 177
Mount Sinai Hospital, Los Angeles, 157
Mount Sinai Hospital, New York, 241
Mumford, Lewis, 145
Mundt Bill, 242
Murray, James, 50, 93, 94
Murray, Philip, 2, 80, 82, 87
Mussolini, Benito, 43, 167, 172, 175–179, 181, 189, 225, 324n28
Mykytew, John, 118, 158, 160

Nadasen, Premilla, 64
Národné noviny, 93, 94, 120, 122, 124, 148, 201, 208
National Association for the Advancement of Colored People, 107, 109, 110, 132, 174, 230

National Association of Manufacturers, 82–83, 94
National Committee of the Unemployed, 61–62
National Emergency Civil Rights Mobilization, 132
National Federation of Postal Clerks, 230
National Hunger March, 58, 61
National Industrial Recovery Act, 67–70
National Labor Relations Act. *See* Wagner Act
National Labor Relations Board, 90
National Maritime Union, 158, 159
National Miners Union, 65–66, 68, 76, 77
National Negro Congress, 5, 110, 118, 172, 174, 178, 180, 182, 188
National Negro Labor for Victory Conference, 112
National Recovery Administration, 67–70
National Security Agency, 262
National Service Act, 43, 186
National Slovak Society, 22, 23, 93
National Sociological League, 121
National Textile Workers Union, 140, 142
National War Labor Board, 89
National Welfare Rights Organization, 64
Nation's Business, 169
The Native's Return, 171
Naturalization, 121, 228, 233, 236–238, 240
Negro Champion, 101
Negro History Week, 116, 119, 125, 133, 159, 163
Nelson, Edward, 102, 119, 126
Nelson, Steve, 77, 88, 179
Neutrality Acts, 182, 187, 191
Never Again!, 73, 93, 95
New Deal, 48, 53, 57, 139; IWO backs, 12, 13, 69–71, 75, 219; IWO opposes, 67–69, 166; NAM opposes, 169
New Jersey Independent Voters' League, 116
New Masses, 145
The New Order, 14, 67, 80, 82–83, 87, 136–137, 147, 148, 150
New School for Social Research, 172
New York City Board of Education, 197–198
New York City Central Committee, CPUSA, 49
New York Daily News, 114
New York Giants, 131
New York Herald Tribune, 204, 249
New York Medical Department, IWO, 49, 50, 176

New York Post, 208, 209, 238
New York State Department of Insurance, 6, 8, 11, 17, 120, 218, 244, 245, 247–251, 256–258
New York Sun, 177, 222
New York Times, 179, 204, 208
New York Urban League, 62
New York World-Telegram and Sun, 17, 92, 246
New Yorský denník, 109, 127
Newark Collective Theater, 151, 152
Nickoloff, Vera, 159
Nightingale, Florence, 181
Nixon, Richard, 86, 163, 255
Norris, Clarence, 105
Norris-LaGuardia Act, 91
North Atlantic Treaty Organization, 212
North Side Workers News, 172
Novy Mir, 83
Nowak, Margaret, 239
Nowak, Stanley, 47; civil rights and, 116–117, 119, 124, 240; deportation attempts, 17, 238–241; during World War II, 122, 158, 189–190, 200; internal security index, FBI, 271n52; union organizing, 88
Noxzema Company, 118
"The Numbskull Nine," 148

Odets, Clifford, 154
Oehler, Hugo, 34
Office of Strategic Services, 12, 47–48, 189, 199, 202–203, 205; IWO charges of fascism reported, 16; IWO cultural programs reported, 137–138, 153, 158–159, 164; IWO fiscal soundness noted, 49, 53–54; IWO social policies noted, 71, 87
Office of War Information, 195–196
Ohio Industrial Commission, 75
Olgin, Moissaye J., 31–32
Olympics, 147, 172
O'Neill, Eugene, 152
Orchestras, 4, 14, 138, 141, 149–150
Orr, Norman, 146
Oswiecim, 129
Our Plan for Plenty, 50, 57, 73–74
Owens, James, 67

Pacific Citizen, 121
Packinghouse workers, 81
Padmore, George, 106
Paine, Tom, 180

Palenchar, George, 74–75
Panama, 161, 206
The Paper, 107
Parker, Dorothy, 183
Partido Obrero de Unificación Marxista, 179–180
Passaic Central Labor Union, 25
Patrick Henry Lodge, IWO, 162
The Patriot, 210
Patriotism, 46, 107, 111, 180, 192–195, 197, 215, 238–239, 241, 242, 253–254; CIO and, 90; ethnic pride and, 15, 154–158, 194–195; JPFO and, 95, 157–158; Polonia Society and, 15, 194–195; right-wing, 85, 227
Patterson, Ellis, 221
Patterson, Haywood, 105
Patterson, Louise Thompson, 14, 36, 52, 61, 66, 77, 80, 102, 117, 125, 131, 149, 217, 221, 227, 248, 251; anticolonialism, 101, 113–114, 122, 171, 172–174, 176, 178, 187–188, 207; gender and, 35, 50, 62, 81–82, 113–114, 207; Harlem Suitcase Theater, 151–152; interracialism, 7, 34–35, 65, 76, 78, 103; Loyalist Spain and, 3, 172–173, 180–182
Patterson, Sam, 131
Patterson, William, 7, 35, 106–107, 112, 125
Pearl Harbor, 191, 196, 197, 213, 214, 236
Pennybacker, Susan, 106
Pentagon, 93, 168, 209, 211, 261
People's Parade Against Nazism, 172
People's Radio Foundation, 155, 318n56
Peters, Paul, 143, 151
Petrosky, Stella, 66
Philadelphia Daily News, 95
The Philippines, 99, 100, 188, 192, 206
Philpott, Thomas, 10
Pickens, William, 174
Picnics, 81, 133, 136, 142, 145, 163
Picolo, Josephine, 114–115
A Picture of Good Revolutions in History, 153
Piłsudski, Józef, 203
Ping-pong, 138
Pindar, Sir Lancelot, 120, 159
Pioneer Chorus, 143
Pirinsky, George, 122–123, 199, 206, 210, 212
Pittman, John, 121, 122
Piven, Frances Fox, 63
Podolski, Henry, 47, 60, 242, 244

Poland, 4, 47, 78, 183–184, 186, 203–205, 212, 216, 244
Poles: civil rights and, 119; displaced persons, 210; OSS and, 16, 48, 203; Social Security campaign by, 59–60, 68; "white chauvinism" and, 129; World War II, 186, 189, 195–197, 199, 203–204
Police, 57, 59, 162, 211, 221, 263; dramatized, 149, 153; Memorial Day Massacre, 83–86; as strikebreakers, 83–86, 90, 145, 217; Unemployed Councils and, 60–61
Polish Chamber of Labor, 60, 68
Polish Club, Detroit, 161
Polish government in exile, 42, 189, 202–203, 205
Polish Labor Democratic Club, Detroit, 130–131
Polish National Alliance, 23, 246
Polish People's Theater, 153
Polish Workers Solidarity Lodge, IWO, 190
Poll tax, 3, 97, 98, 104, 109–112, 117–119, 124, 148, 187
Polletta, Francesca, 143
Polo Grounds, 131–132, 148, 155
Polonia Society, IWO, 47, 48; American Slav Congress and, 112; civil rights and, 118–119, 229; Cold War, 208, 212–214, 242, 246; patriotism and, 15, 195; unions and, 87
Poole, DeWitt Clinton, 137
Popular Front, 12, 16, 33, 44, 54, 72, 85, 112, 149, 159, 195; and Roosevelt's policy shifts, 70; early embrace by IWO, 52, 59, 69, 173; interracialism and, 120
Portuguese, 45, 46, 52, 102
Postal workers, 17, 214, 229–230
Powell, Adam Clayton Jr., 116, 159
Powers, George, 104, 148, 170, 180, 251–252
Pressman, Lee, 225, 235–236
Price, Arthur, 125
Primus, Pearl, 159
Prisoners Relief Committee, Civil Rights Congress, 119
Progressive Party, 117, 125, 227, 228
Prudential Life Insurance Company, 246
Puerto Ricans, 3, 14, 45, 46, 101–102, 157–158
Puerto Rico, 100, 157, 206
Pullman porters, 80
Putnam, Robert, 163

Quislings, 198, 201, 209–210

Race riots, 3, 88, 100–101, 108, 112, 114, 117–118, 122–125, 158, 261–262
Racism, 80, 88, 92, 95–101, 104–118, 120–125, 127–128; armed forces, 111; insurance companies, 36, 50, 249; lynching, 108–111; police, 60–61; race riots, 112, 114, 117–118, 122–125; school strikes, 307n61; Scottsboro case, 104–108; unions, 96–97, 101
Radio, 94, 111, 122, 144, 149, 155, 181, 189–191, 195, 255, 318n56
Radischev Choir, 157
Radischev Russian Folk Dancers, 154–156, 161–162, 191, 318n55
Railroad workers, 38, 79, 91
Ramblers Sports Club, Clifton, New Jersey, 142
Randolph, A. Philip, 182
Rankin, John, 7, 115, 120, 132, 156, 159, 163, 225
Rebel Arts Bulletin, 151
Reconstruction Finance Corporation, 151
Recruit, 149
Red Army, 4, 15, 186, 190; American Slav Congress support for, 161; films of, 164, 187; IWO support for, 158, 192, 194, 195, 200
Red squads, 124–125, 221, 232, 262
Reid-Pharr, Robert, 181
Republic Steel Corporation, 83–84, 86
Republican Party, 90, 112, 130, 173, 200, 204, 218, 246, 250, 253
Reuther, Walter, 239
Revere, Paul, 85
Richmond Committee for the Defense of Ethiopia, 177
Right to Work Bill, 60
Risen from the Ranks, or From Office Boy to President, 150–151
River Rouge plant, Ford Motor Company, 13, 41, 87–88
Rivera, Diego, 150, 316n45
Roberts, Sam, 45
Robeson, Paul, 14, 107, 119, 128, 159–163, 191, 205, 227; anticolonialism, 114, 178, 207, 261; baseball integration and, 131; HUAC and, 120, 135, 231, 240; passport denial, 8, 242
Robinson, Jackie, 3, 147
Robotnícky kalendár, 110, 179
Rockefeller Center, 150
Rockefeller, John D., 150

Roediger, David, 10–11, 68, 79, 97, 98, 109, 130, 157
Rogge, O. John, 227
Romanians, 210, 214
Romano, Emanuel, 93–94
Romanul American, 214
Romero, Trini, 148
Roosevelt, Eleanor, 240
Roosevelt, Franklin, 43, 151, 155; civil rights and, 112, 119; Kristallnacht and, 173; Memorial Day Massacre and, 84; New Deal, 69, 70, 72, 73, 167, 225, 226; World War II, 4, 12, 16, 111, 122, 187, 188, 190, 199, 202–205, 223
Rosenberg, Ethel, 51
Rosenberg, Julius, 51
Rosenhaft, Eva, 106
Rovnosť ľudu, 39, 40, 68, 99–100
Russians, 76, 83, 105, 119, 169–170, 234
Russian War Relief, 15, 178
Rusyns. *See* Carpatho-Russians
Ruthenberg, Charles E., 28, 100
Rymer, Ernest, 131

Sabath, Adolph, 210, 228
Sabin, Arthur, 6, 232, 244, 247
Sacco and Vanzetti, 106
Saint Paul Workers Orchestra, 143
Salt of the Earth, 321n82
Saltzman, Benny, 238–239, 241
Saltzman, Rubin, 45, 46, 231, 253, 258; amalgamation and, 39; Camp Kinderland director, 145; civil rights activism, 118; Cold War and, 211; CPUSA and, 32, 145, 227, 251; fascism and, 173–174; HUAC and, 216; Workmen's Circle split, 31; World War II, 192, 194
Saltzman, Sadie, 238
Salvation Army, 59
Sanitariums, 1, 2, 40
Sans Souci Park, Nanticoke, Pennsylvania, 140
Schiffel, Joseph, 248
Schneiderman, William, 101
Schoenfeld, Bernard, 151
Schools, 137, 156, 172, 179; Cervantes Fraternal Society, 46; Harlem Workers School, 143; IWO, 14, 45, 154, 173, 256, 263; segregated, 117, 240; SWS, 143 Workmen's Circle, 31
Schubak, Frank, 20, 21

Scotch, 103
Scott, James, 141, 146
Scottsboro Boys, 14, 43, 104–108, 147, 148, 251
Second front, 4, 15, 158, 198–200
Section 7(a), NIRA, 67
Security Index, FBI, 17, 123–124, 309n82
Security with FDR, 72
Seeger, Pete, 153
Segregation, 14, 45, 78, 92, 97–101, 109–112, 116–118, 124–131; amusement parks, 142; armed forces, 111–112; housing, 3, 133–134
Seidel, Emil, 160
Selassie, Hailie, 178
Self, Robert, 10
Seminars in Negro History, 174–175
Senate Education and Labor Committee, 84
Sentner, Bill, 87, 231
Serbian American Federation, IWO, 119
Serbians, 24, 91, 119, 210
Shachtman, Max, 102–103
Shaffer, Nathan, 49, 105, 115
Sharecroppers, 7, 34, 65, 76, 108, 207
Shipka, Peter, 231, 241; Attorney General's List of Subversive Organizations and, 213, 228; civil rights and, 104; Cold War, 211; CPUSA and, 251; IWO recreation and, 137–138; liquidation and, 134, 138, 245–247; strikes and, 79; World War II, 195, 197
Shop papers, 66, 68, 172
Sinatra, Frank, 156
Slavic American, 209
Slavonia Club, Detroit, 162
Sleepy Lagoon Murder Case, 157
Slovak Catholic *Sokol*, 23
Slovak Radio Hour, SWS, 155
Slovak Gymnastic Union *Sokol*, 22
Slovak Hall, Philadelphia, 127, 208
Slovak Republic, 189
Slovák v Amerike, 99, 109
Slovak Workers Society, IWO, 9, 65, 217, 237; amalgamation and, 12, 39–40; American Slav Congress and, 112; Americanization and, 48; anticolonialism and, 206; civil rights and, 97, 99, 117–118; cultural programs, 143, 149, 153, 155; JRB Welfare Fund and, 19–20; liquidation and, 247, 248, 253; Loyalist Spain and, 179; opposes NRA, 68; Social Security and, 61; unions and, 91; "white chauvinism" and, 127; World War II and, 89, 188, 190, 195

Slovaks, 9, 12, 19–20, 22, 23, 25, 39, 77, 87, 104, 105, 164, 186
Slovenian National Benefit Union, 24
Slovenians, 16, 24, 25
Smith Act, 8, 179, 201, 216, 236, 246, 251, 253
Smith, Ferdinand, 158–160
Smith, Howard, 219
Smuts, Jan, 178
Soccer, 138
Social Security, 1, 2, 12, 13, 19, 70–73, 93, 252; Depression demonstrations for, 55, 57, 61, 62
Social Security Act, 22, 57, 61, 62, 70, 72
Socialist Educational Fund, 160
Socialist Party, 69, 76, 84, 111, 170, 221; CFU and, 24; Loyalist Spain and, 182; racism and, 160–161; Workmen's Circle and, 25, 30–33, 189
Socialist Workers Party, 33, 179, 201
Soft-ball, 138
Sojourner Truth Homes, 123
Sojourners for Truth and Justice, 82, 113–114, 207, 263
Soldier Field, Chicago, 199
Solidarity Lodge, IWO, 14, 43–44, 151–153, 174, 186–187
"The Soup Song," 67
South Africa, 100, 113–114, 130, 147, 178, 207
South Slav Singing Society, 143
South Slavic Bureau, CPUSA, 24, 26
South Slavic Women's Educational Club, 49–50
Southwest Africa, 178
Soviet-German Nonaggression Pact, 15, 44, 122, 164, 183–186, 188–190
Soviet Union, 21, 166–170, 179; Bedacht praises, 166; Cold War, 16, 113, 205–209, 211–212; Ethiopia and, 178; Five Year Plan, 55–56, 166; Loyalist Spain and, 178; nonaggression pact, 183–186, 188–189; World War II, 4, 15, 16, 89, 158, 159, 164–165, 183–186, 188–191, 198, 202–205, 245
Spain, 148, 155, 160, 167, 169, 172, 175, 178–183, 188–189, 327n46
Spain in Flames, 179
Spanish Refugee Relief Campaign, 183
Spampinato, Salvatore, 50, 254
The Spark, 56, 104, 136–137, 147
Stage for Action Players, 159
Stalin, Joseph, 16, 41, 42, 60, 89, 185–188, 199, 204, 235, 247

Stalingrad, 4, 120, 200
Starobin, Joseph, 73, 93, 95
Starr, George, 235
Stasiukevich, Philip, 236–237
State Department, 8, 131, 163, 191, 205, 210–211, 241
Statue of Liberty, 17, 76, 105, 240, 242
Steel and Metal Workers Industrial Union, 77
Steel Strike, 140, 154
Steel Workers Organizing Committee, 2, 81–84, 88
Steelworkers, 35, 59, 77, 80–82, 88, 100, 109, 140, 154, 240
Steffens, Lincoln, 56, 166
Stevenson, Charles, 43–44, 186–187
Stilwell, Joseph, 200
Stockholm Peace Conference, 212, 334–335n118
Storch, Randi, 65
Storrs, Landon, 8
Strikebreaking, 23, 25, 33, 67, 79–81, 83–87, 89–92, 101, 141, 145
Strikes, 25, 68, 70, 100, 141, 151, 154, 216; fraternal societies and, 23; gender and, 35; hate strikes, 95–96; IWO support for, 61, 64–65, 76–81, 83, 87–92, 159, 217; Memorial Day Massacre, 83–87; Socialist Workers Party and, 179; WPA and, 184; during World War II, 89–90, 95–96
Stuyvesant High School, New York, 179
Stuyvesant Town, 3, 134
Subversive Activities Control Board, 255, 258
Sugrue, Thomas, 10, 96, 117
Sulzberger, C. L., 204
Swidler, Ann, 139
Swimming, 127, 136, 138, 145
Sydenham Hospital, 50
The Sydenham Plan, 50
Syrians, 46
Szabo, Joseph, 101
Szymczak, Robert, 204

Taber, Max, 134
Taft-Hartley Act, 2, 90–92
Taft, Robert, 253
Taiwan, 174
Tallentire, Molly, 228
Tappes, Shelton, 118, 123
Taylor, Glen, 227
Teachers Union of the City of New York, 197
Teamsters, 38, 68, 80, 179

Teheran Conference, 16, 202
Tenerowicz, Rudolph, 123
Tennessee Valley Authority, 71
Tennis, 136, 147
Textile workers, 25, 76, 81, 88, 141
Theater, 4, 14–15, 136–140, 143, 145, 147, 149–154, 156
They Shall Not Die!, 151
"Third Period," 52
Thomas, Norman, 182
Thompson, Louise. *See* Patterson, Louise Thompson
Tiso, Jozef, 189
Tito, Josip Broz, 153, 155, 202
Tobacco workers, 91, 159
Tojo, Hideki, 121
Tom Mooney Lodge, IWO, 221
Tom Paine Lodge, JPFO, 157
Toohey, Pat, 151
Track and field, 138, 147
Trade Union Committee for Protection of Foreign Born, 238
Trade Union Unity League, 59, 77
Trauber, Jerry, 180
Treasury Department, 227–228
Trenton New Theatre, 152
Trenton Six, 107
Trinidad, 106, 120, 159
Trolley drivers, 95–97
Trotsky, Leon, 33
Trotskyists, 16, 33, 47, 170, 179–180
Trouble with the Angels, 151
Truman Doctrine, 208–209, 211
Truman, Harry, 91, 208–209, 211, 225, 241, 245
Turkey, 208–209
Tyomies, 41, 87

Új Előre, 101, 145
Ukraine, 168–169, 203–204
Ukraine in Flames, 164
Ukrainian-American Fraternal Union, IWO, 112, 204
Ukrainians, 54, 138, 143–144, 155; displaced persons, 210, 211; famine and, 168–169; interracialism, 3, 35, 102, 118, 119; strikebreaking, 15; unemployment insurance and, 59; unions and, 81; "white chauvinism," 127, 129; World War II, 33, 153, 158, 164, 186, 199, 203, 204
U.M.W. Bulletin, 141

Un-Americanism: Civil-rights activists labeled, 114, 120, 163, 231; left-wing defenses against, 17, 75–76, 92, 95, 215–216, 219, 222, 226, 241, 244; peace activists labeled, 212; rightists labeled, 95–96, 126, 179, 200, 215, 226, 227, 240; unions labeled, 86, 92, 219
Unemployed Councils, 59–61, 65, 66, 142
Unemployment, 1–2, 37, 40, 55, 57–61, 63–67, 78, 88, 105, 142
Unions. *See names of specific unions*
United Anti-Nazi Conference, 172
United Auto Workers, 86–88, 118, 123, 158, 239
United Electrical Workers, 9, 87, 90, 92, 231
United Film Productions, 94
United Italian Committees of Harlem, 219
United Mine Workers of America, 80, 89, 141, 217
United Nations (organization), 113, 206–207, 209, 226
United Nations (wartime alliance), 160, 199, 200
United Public Workers, 230
United States Chamber of Commerce, 169, 232
United States Civil Service Commission, 198, 223–224, 226
United States Steel Corporation, 83
United Toilers of America, 140
United Ukrainian Organizations of the United States, 168
United Ukrainian Toilers, 81
Universal health care, 2, 4, 13, 50, 57, 61, 70–74, 93–95, 99, 226, 263
Universal Negro Improvement Association, 34–35, 100, 176–177
University of Chicago, 181
Urban League, 62, 115
U.S. News and World Report, 208
Uus Illu, 29

Vail, Sol, 102
Vargas, Getúlio, 173
Veeck, Bill, 132
Venezuela, 93–94, 99
Victory for Freedom, 82–83
Vietnam, 4, 16, 18, 131, 206–207, 261, 263
Vilnis, 210
Vocila, George, 214
Voroshilov, Kliment, 159

Voting Rights Act, 10
Vrábel, Helen, 61, 65, 70, 188–190, 195–196, 289n36

Wagner Act, 53, 57, 70, 72, 78, 79, 83, 91, 169
Wagner-Capper-Van Nuys Anti-Lynching Bill, 110
Wagner-Murray-Dingell Bill, 13, 73, 93–95
Wagner, Robert, 93–94, 119
Waiting for Lefty, 151, 154
Walker, Thomas, 6, 34
Wallace, Henry, 120, 125, 227
Wallace-Johnson, I.T.A., 106–107
War Bonds, 191, 195, 197, 199, 223
War Department, 118, 195, 224
War Manpower Commission, 223
War Production Board, 89
Ward, Arnold, 106
Warsaw Ghetto Uprising, 155
Washington Conference on Social Insurance, 59–60
Washington, George, 195
Washington, Mary Helen, 61, 109
Weber, Simon, 252
Weiner, William, 43, 148, 173, 189
Weissman, Raphael, 247, 251, 253
Welles, Sumner, 208
Wells, Ida B., 181
Werber, Bill, 131–132
When Slavery was in Bloom in America, 151
"White chauvinism," 3, 11, 46, 98, 103, 109, 127–129, 140, 147, 160
White Russians, 170
Whiteness, 11, 96–99, 109–113, 115–118, 262; anti-Japanese animus and, 121; CPUSA and, 103, 127; Southeast Europeans' "inbetweenness," 66, 113, 115–118, 157; minstrel shows and, 160–161; unions and, 76, 79–80, 95, 96
Wilkins, Roy, 132
Willkie, Wendell, 204
Wilson, Frank, 152
Wilson, Woodrow, 100, 187
Win the Peace Conference, 205–206
Wolcott, Victoria, 142
Women's Congress Against War and Fascism, 171
Wood, John, 229
Workers' Bazaar, 18, 263
Workers (Communist) Party. *See* Communist Party USA

Workers' Cultural Federation, 140, 149
Workers' Dramatic Unions, 143
Workers International Relief, 142
Workers International Relief Mandolin Orchestra, 147
Workmen's Circle, 7, 9, 22, 25, 29–32, 69, 189, 346n135
Workmen's Circle Committee for Peace, 30
Workers' compensation laws, 2, 22, 51, 57, 74, 76
Works Progress Administration, 51, 71, 76, 184, 219
World War I, 59, 83, 90, 108, 187, 189, 328n61
World War II, 4, 13, 15–16, 120, 178; American Slav Congress and, 111–112, 117, 236; neutrality and, 122; no strike pledge and, 89; Polonia Society and, 42
Wrestling, 136, 147
Wright, Ada, 106
Wright, Alexander, 103, 177
Wright, Richard, 109
Wrigley, William, 131
Wyman, Mark, 26

Yalta Conference, 202, 204–205, 332n96
Yankee Stadium, 131
Yergan, Max, 174, 182
Yokinen, August, 127, 152
York, Pennsylvania, *Gazette & Daily*, 91
Young, Coleman, 263
Young Communist League, 36, 142, 151, 183–185
Young People's Socialist League, 161
Young Pioneers, 36, 41
Young Workers' Mandolin Orchestra, 143
Yugoslavia, 47, 171

Zimmer, Kenyon, 168
Zimmerman, Charles, 182
Zoot Suit Riots, 157
Zumoff, Jacob, 28, 98
Zuskár, John, 39
Związek Narodowy Polski. *See* Polish National Alliance
Zysman, Dale, 197–198, 223

Robert M. Zecker is Associate Professor in the Department of History at Saint Francis Xavier University. He is the author of *Race and America's Immigrant Press: How the Slovaks Were Taught to Think Like White People.*

www.ingramcontent.com/pod-product-compliance
Lightning Source LLC
Chambersburg PA
CBHW061253230426
43665CB00027B/2926